NOTES

ON THE

NEW TESTAMENT

EXPLANATORY AND PRACTICAL

BY

ALBERT BARNES

ENLARGED TYPE EDITION

EDITED BY

ROBERT FREW, D.D.

I CORINTHIANS

BAKER BOOK HOUSE
GRAND RAPIDS, MICHIGAN

Library of Congress Catalog Card Number: 50-7190

ISBN: 0-8010-0567-1

First Printing, May 1949
Second Printing, May 1950
Third Printing, December 1953
Fourth Printing, May 1957
Fifth Printing, January 1960
Sixth Printing, March 1962
Seventh Printing, July 1964
Eighth Printing, March 1967
Ninth Printing, January 1970
Tenth Printing, March 1972
Eleventh Printing, August 1973
Twelfth Printing, February 1975
Thirteenth Printing, November 1976
Fourteenth Printing, January 1977
Fifteenth Printing, February 1978
Sixteenth Printing, February 1979
Seventeenth Printing, May 1980
Eighteenth Printing, August 1981

PHOTOLITHOPRINTED BY CUSHING - MALLOY, INC.
ANN ARBOR, MICHIGAN, UNITED STATES OF AMERICA

INTRODUCTION.

§ 1. *The Situation of Corinth, and the Character of its Inhabitants.*

CORINTH was properly a small dynasty, or territory in Greece, bounded on the east by the gulf of Saron; on the south by the kingdom of Argos; on the west by Sicyon; and on the north by the kingdom of Megaris, and upper part of the isthmus and bay of Corinth, the latter of which is now called the Golfo de Lepanto, or the gulf of Lepanto. This tract, or region, not large in size, possessed a few rich plains, but was in general uneven, and the soil of an indifferent quality. The city of Corinth was the capital of this region. It stood near the middle of the isthmus, which in the narrowest part was about six miles wide, though somewhat wider where Corinth stood. Here was the natural *carrying place*, or portage from the Ionian sea on the west, to the Ægean on the east. Many efforts were made by the Greeks, and afterwards by the Romans, to effect a communication between the Ægean and Adriatic seas by cutting across this isthmus; and traces still remain of these attempts. Means were even contrived for transporting vessels across. This isthmus was also particularly important as it was the key of the Peloponnesus, and attempts were often made to fortify it. The city had two harbours,—Lechæum on the gulf of Corinth, or sea of Crissa on the west, to which it was joined by a double wall, twelve stadia, or about a mile and a half in length; and Cenchrea, or the sea of Saron on the east, distant about seventy stadia, or nearly nine miles. It was a situation therefore peculiarly favourable for commerce, and highly important in the defence of Greece.

The city is said to have been founded by Sisyphus, long before the siege of Troy, and was then called Ephyra. The time when it was founded is, however, unknown. The name *Corinth*, was supposed to have been given to it from Corinthus, who, by different authors, is said to have been the son of Jupiter, or of Marathon, or of Pelops, who is said to have rebuilt and adorned the city.

The city of Corinth was built at the foot of a high hill, on the top of which stood a citadel. This hill, which stood on the south of the city, was its defence in that quarter, as its sides were extremely steep. On the three other sides it was protected by strong and lofty ramparts. The circumference of the city proper was about forty stadia, or five miles. Its situation gave it great commercial advantages. As the whole of that region was mountainous and rather barren, and as the situation gave the city extraordinary commercial advantages, the inhabitants early turned their attention to commerce, and amassed great wealth. This fact was, to no inconsiderable extent, the foundation of the luxury, effeminacy, and vices for which the city afterwards became so much distinguished.

The merchandise of Italy, Sicily, and the western nations, was landed at Lechæum on the west; and that of the islands of the Ægean sea, of Asia Minor, and of the Phœnicians, and other oriental nations, at Cenchrea on the east. The city of Corinth thus became the mart of Asia and Europe; covered the sea with its ships, and formed a navy to protect its commerce. It was distinguished by building galleys and ships of a new and improved form; and its naval force procured it respect from other nations. Its population and its wealth was thus increased by the influx of foreigners. It became a city rather distinguished by its wealth, and naval force, and commerce, than by its military achievements, though it produced a few of the most valiant and distinguished leaders in the armies of Greece.

Its population was increased and its character somewhat formed from another circumstance. In the neighbourhood of the city the *Isthmian games* were celebrated, which attracted so much attention, and which drew so many strangers from distant parts of the world. To those games, the apostle Paul not infrequently refers, when recommending Christian energy and activity. See Note, 1 Cor. ix. 24, 26, 27; comp. Heb. xii. 1.

From these causes, the city of Corinth became eminent among all ancient cities for wealth, and luxury, and dissipation. It was the mart of the world. Wealth flowed into it from all quarters. Luxury, amusement, and dissipation, were the natural consequents, until it became the most gay and dissolute city of its times, —*the Paris of antiquity*.

There was another cause which contributed to its character of dissoluteness and corruption. I refer to its religion. The principal deity worshipped in the city was Venus; as Diana was the principal deity worshipped at Ephesus; Minerva at Athens, &c. Ancient cities were devoted usually to some particular god or goddess, and were supposed to be under their peculiar protection. See Note, Acts xiv. 13. Corinth was devoted, or dedicated thus to the goddess of love, or licentious passion; and the effect may be easily conceived. The temple of Venus was erected on the north side or slope of the Acrocorinthus, a mountain about half a mile in height on the south of the city, and from the summit of which a magnificent prospect opened on the north to Parnassus and Helicon, to the eastward the island of Ægina and the citadel of Athens, and to the west the rich and beautiful plains of Sicyon. This mountain was covered with temples and splendid houses; but was especially devoted to Venus, and was the place of her worship. Her shrine appeared above those of the other gods; and it was enjoined by law, that one thousand beautiful females should officiate as courtesans, or public prostitutes, before the altar of the goddess of love. In a time of public calamity and imminent danger, these women attended at the sacrifices, and walked with the other citizens singing sacred hymns. When Xerxes invaded Greece, recourse was had to their intercession to avert the impending calamity. They were supported chiefly by foreigners; and from the avails of their vice a copious revenue was derived to the city. Individuals, in order to ensure success in their undertakings, vowed to present to Venus a certain number of courtesans, which they obtained by sending to distant countries. Foreign merchants were attracted in this way to Corinth; and in a few days would be stripped of all their property. It thus became a proverb, "It is not for every one to go to Corinth,"—(οὐ παντὸς ἀνδρὸς εἰς Κόρινθον ἐστὶν ὁ πλους.) The effect of this on the morals of the city can be easily understood. It became the most gay, dissipated, corrupt, and ultimately the most effeminate and feeble portion of Greece. It is necessary to make these statements, because they go to show the exceeding grace of God in collecting a church in such a city, the power of the gospel in overcoming the strongest and most polluted passions of our nature; and because no small part of the irregularities which arose in the church at Corinth, and which gave the apostle occasion to write this epistle, were produced by this prevailing licentiousness of the people; and by the fact, that gross and licentious passions had received the countenance of law and the patronage of public opinion. See chap. v. vii. See article *Lais* in the Biographical Dictionaries.

Though Corinth was thus dissipated and licentious in its character, yet it was also distinguished for its refinement and learning. Every part of literature was cultivated there, so that before its destruction by the Romans, Cicero (pro lege Man. cap. v.) scrupled not to call it totius Græciæ lumen—the light of all Greece.

Corinth was, of course, exposed to all the changes and disasters which occurred to the other cities of Greece. After a variety of revolutions in its government, which it is not necessary here to repeat, it was taken by the Roman consul L. Mummius, 147 years before Christ. The riches which were found in the city were immense. During the conflagration, it is said that all the metals which were there were melted and run together, and formed that valuable compound which was so much celebrated as Corinthian brass. Others, however, with more probability, say that the Corinthian artists were accustomed to form a metal, by a mixture of brass with small quantities of gold and silver, which was so brilliant as to cause the extraordinary estimate in which this metal was held. Corinth, however, was again rebuilt. In the time of Julius Cesar, it was colonised by his order, and soon again resumed something of its former magnificence. By the Romans the whole of Greece was divided into two provinces, Macedonia and Achaia. Of the latter Corinth was the capital ; and this was its condition when it was visited by Paul. With its ancient splendour, it also soon relapsed into its former dissipation and licentiousness ; and when Paul visited it, it was perhaps as dissolute as at any former period of its history. The subsequent history of Corinth it is not necessary to trace. On the division of the Roman empire, it fell, of course, to the eastern empire, and when this was overthrown by the Turks, it came into their hands, and it remained under their dominion until the recent revolution in Greece. It still retains its ancient name ; but with nothing of its ancient grandeur. A single temple, itself dismantled, it is said, is all that remains, except the ruins, to mark the site of one of the most splendid cities of antiquity. For the authorities of these statements, see Travels of Anacharsis, vol. iii. pp. 369—388 ; Edin. Ency. art. Corinth ; Lemprière's Classical Dictionary, and Bayle's Dictionary, art. Corinth.

§ 2. *The Establishment of the Church at Corinth.*

THE apostle Paul first visited Corinth about A. D. 52. (Lardner.) See Acts xviii. 1. He was then on his way from Macedonia to Jerusalem. He had passed some time at Athens, where he had preached the gospel, but not with such success as to warrant him to remain, or to organize a church ; see Notes on Acts xvii. He was alone at Athens, having expected to have been joined there by Silas and Timothy, but in that he was disappointed ; Acts xvii. 15 ; comp. xviii. 5. He came to Corinth alone, but found Aquila and Priscilla there, who had lately come from Rome, and with them he waited the arrival of Silas and Timothy. When they arrived, Paul entered on the great work of preaching the gospel in that splendid and dissipated city, first to the Jews, and when it was rejected by them, then to the Greeks ; Acts xviii. 5, 6. His feelings when he engaged in this work, he has himself stated in 1 Cor. xvi. 2—5. (see Note on that place.) His embarrassments and discouragements were met by a gracious promise of the Lord that he would be with him, and would not leave him ; and that it was his purpose to collect a church there ; see Note on Acts xviii. 9, 10. In the city, Paul remained eighteen months, (Acts xviii. 11,) preaching without molestation, until he was opposed by the Jews under Sosthenes their leader, and brought before Gallio. When Gallio refused to hear the cause, and Paul was discharged, it is said, that he remained there yet "a good while," (Acts xviii. 18.) and then sailed into Syria.

Of the size of the church that was first organised there, and of the general character of the converts, we have no other knowledge than that which is con tained in the epistle. There is reason to think that Sosthenes, who was the principal agent of the Jews in arraigning Paul before Gallio, was converted, (see 1 Cor. i. 1.) and perhaps some other persons of distinction ; but it is evident that the church was chiefly composed of those who were in the more humble walks of life ; see Notes on 1 Cor. i. 26—29. It was a signal illustration of the grace of God, and the power of the gospel, that a church was organized in that city of gayety, fashion, luxury, and licentiousness ; and it shows that the gospel is adapted to meet and overcome all forms of wickedness, and to subdue all classes of people to itself. If a church was established in the gay and dissolute capital of Achaia, then there is not now a city on earth so gay and so profligate that the same gospel may not meet its corruptions, and subdue it to the cross of Christ. Paul subsequently visited Corinth about A. D. 58, or six years after the establishment of the church there. He passed the winter in Greece—doubtless in Corinth and its neighbourhood, on his journey from Macedonia to Jerusalem, the fifth time in which he visited the latter city. During this stay at Corinth he wrote the epistle to the Romans. See the introduction to the Epistle to the Romans.

§ 3. *The time and place of writing the first Epistle to the Corinthians.*

It has been uniformly supposed that this epistle was written at Ephesus. The circumstances which are mentioned incidently in the epistle itself, place this beyond a doubt. The epistle purports to have been written, not like that to the Romans, without having been at the place to which it was written, but *after* Paul had been at Corinth. "I, brethren, *when I came unto you*, came not with excellency of speech," &c. chap. ii. 1. It also purports to have been written when he was about to make another visit to that church ; chap. iv. 19, "But I will come to you shortly, if the Lord will." Chap. xvi. 5, "Now I will come to you when I pass through Macedonia, for I do pass through Macedonia." Now the history in the Acts of the Apostles informs us, that Paul did in fact visit Achaia, and doubtless Corinth twice ; see Acts xviii. 1, &c. ; xx. 1—3. The same history also informs us that it was from Ephesus that Paul went into Greece ; and as the epistle purports to have been written a short time before that journey, it follows, to be consistent with the history, that the epistle must have been written while he was at Ephesus. The narrative in the Acts also informs us, that Paul had passed two years in Ephesus before he set out on his second journey into Greece.

With this supposition, all the circumstances relating to the place where the apostle then was which are mentioned in this epistle agree. "If after the manner of men, I have fought with beasts at Ephesus, what advantageth it me, if the dead rise not?" chap. xv. 32. It is true, as Dr. Paley remarks, (*Horæ Paulinæ*,) that the apostle might say this wherever he was ; but it was much more natural, and much more to the purpose to say it, if he was at Ephesus at the time, and in the midst of those conflicts to which the expression relates. "The churches of Asia salute you," chap. xvi. 19. It is evident from this, that Paul was near those churches, and that he had intercourse with them. But Asia, throughout the Acts of the Apostles, and in the epistles of Paul, does not mean commonly the whole of Asia, nor the whole of Asia Minor, but a district in the interior of Asia Minor, of which Ephesus was the capital ; see Note, Acts ii. 9 ; vi. 9 ; xvi. 6 ; xx. 16. "Aquila and Priscilla salute you," chap. xvi. 19. Aquila and Priscilla were at Ephesus during the time in which I shall endeavour to show this epistle was written, Acts xviii. 26. It is evident, if this were so, that the epistle was written at Ephesus. "But I will tarry at Ephesus until Pentecost," chap. xvi. 8. This is almost an express declaration that he was at Ephesus when the epistle was written. "A great and effectual door is opened to me, and there are many adversaries," chap. xvi. 9. How well this agrees with the history, may be seen by comparing it with the account in Acts, when Paul was at Ephesus. Acts xix. 20, "So mightily grew the word of God and prevailed." That there were "many adversaries," may be seen from the account of the same period in Acts xix. 9, "But when divers were hardened, and believed not, but spake evil of that way before the multitude, he departed from them and separated the disciples," Comp. Acts xix. 23—41. From these circumstances, it is put beyond controversy, that the epistle was written from Ephesus. These circumstantial, and undesigned coincidences, between a letter written by Paul and an independent history by Luke, is one of those strong evidences so common in genuine writings, which go to show that neither is a forgery. An impostor in forging a history like that of the Acts, and then writing an epistle, would not have thought of these coincidences, or introduced them in the manner in which they occur here. It is perfectly manifest that the notes of the time, and place, and circumstances in the history, and in the epistle, were not introduced to correspond with each other, but have every appearance of genuineness and truth. See Paley's Horæ Paulinæ, on this epistle.

The circumstances which have been referred to in regard to the *place* where this epistle was written, serve also to fix the *date* of its composition. It is evident, from chap. xvi. 8, that Paul purposed to tarry at Ephesus until Pentecost. But this must have been written and sent away *before* the riot which was raised by Demetrius (Acts xix. 23—41), for immediately after that Paul left Ephesus and went to Macedonia, Acts xx. 1, 2. The reason why Paul purposed to remain in Ephesus until Pentecost, was, the success which he had met with in preaching the gospel, chap. xvi. 9. But after the riot excited by Demetrius, this hope was in a measure defeated, and he soon left the city. These circumstances serve to fix the time when this epistle was written to the interval which elapsed between what is recorded in Acts xix. 22, 23. This occurred about A. D. 56 or 57. Pearson and Mill place the date in the year 57 ; Lardner, in the spring of the year 56.

It has never been doubted that Paul was the author of this epistle. It bears his name ; has internal evidence of having been written by him, and is ascribed to him by the unanimous voice of antiquity. It has been made a question, however, whether this was the *first* letter which Paul wrote to them ; or whether he had previously written an epistle to them which is now lost. This inquiry has been caused by what Paul says in 1 Cor. v. 9, " I wrote unto you in an epistle," &c. Whether he there refers to another epistle, which he wrote to them before this, and which they had disregarded ; or whether to the previous chapters of this epistle ; or whether to a letter to some other church which they had been expected to read, has been made a question. This question will be considered in the Note on that verse.

§ 4. *The Occasion on which this Epistle was written.*

It is evident that this epistle was written in reply to one which had been addressed by the church at Corinth to Paul ; 1 Cor. vii. 1, " Now concerning the things whereof ye wrote unto me," &c. That letter had been sent to Paul while at Ephesus, by the hands of Stephanas, and Fortunatus, and Achaicus, who had come to consult with him respecting the state of the church at Corinth, 1 Cor. xvi. 17, 18. In addition to this, Paul had heard various reports of certain disorders which had been introduced into the church at Corinth, and which required his attention and correction. Those disorders, it seems, as was natural, had not been mentioned in the letter which they sent to him, but he had heard of them incidentally by some members of the family of Chloe, 1 Cor. i. 11. They pertained to the following subjects. (1.) The divisions which had arisen in the church by the popularity of a teacher who had excited great disturbance, (1 Cor. i. 12, 13.) Probably this teacher was a Jew by birth, and not improbably of the sect of the Sadducees (2 Cor. xi. 22), and his teaching might have been the occasion why in the epistle Paul entered so largely into the proof of the doctrine of the resurrection from the dead, 1 Cor. xv. (2.) The Corinthians, like all other Greeks, were greatly in danger of being deluded, and carried away by a subtile philosophy, and by a dazzling eloquence, and it is not improbable that the false teacher there had taken advantage of this, and made it the occasion of exciting parties, and of creating a prejudice against Paul, and of undervaluing his authority because he had made no pretensions to these endowments. It was of importance, therefore, for Paul to show the true nature and value of their philosophy, and the spirit which should prevail in receiving the gospel, chap. i. 18—31. ii. iii. (3.) Paul's authority had been called in question as an apostle, and not improbably by the false teacher, or teachers, that had caused the parties which had been originated there. It became necessary, therefore, for him to vindicate his authority, and show by what right he had acted in organizing the church, and in the directions which he had given for its discipline and purity. chap. iv. ix. (4.) A case of incest had occurred in the church which had not been made the subject of discipline, chap. v. This case was a flagrant violation of the gospel; and yet it is not improbable that it had been palliated, or vindicated by the false teachers; and it is certain that it excited no shame in the church itself. Such cases were not regarded by the dissolute Corinthians as criminal. In a city dedicated to Venus, the crimes of licentiousness had been openly indulged, and this was one of the sins to which they were particularly exposed. It became necessary, therefore, for Paul to exert his apostolic authority, and to remove the offender in this case from the communion of the church, and to make him an example of the severity of Christian discipline. (5.) The Corinthians had evinced a litigious spirit, a fondness for going to law, and for bringing their causes before heathen tribunals, to the great scandal of religion, instead of endeavouring to settle their difficulties among themselves. Of this the apostle had been informed, and this called also for his authoritative interposition, chap vi. 1—8. (6.) Erroneous views and practices had arisen, perhaps, under the influence of the false teachers, on the subject of temperance, chastity, &c. To the vices of intemperance, licentiousness, and gluttony, the Corinthian Christians from their former habits, and from the customs of their countrymen, were particularly exposed. Those vices had been judged harmless, and had been freely indulged in, and it is not improbable that the views of the apostle had been ridiculed as unnecessarily stern, and severe, and rigid. It became necessary, therefore, to correct their views, and to state the true nature of the Christian requirements, chap. vi. 8—20. (7.) The apostle having thus discussed those things of which he had incidentally heard, proceeds to notice particularly the things respecting which they had consulted him by letter. Those were, (*a*) *Marriage*, and the duties in regard to it in their circumstances, chap. vii. (*b*.) *The eating of things offered to idols*, chap. viii. In order to enforce his views of what he had said on the duty of abstaining from the use of certain food, if it was the occasion of giving offence, he shows them (chap. ix.) *that it was the great principle on which he had acted in his ministry;* that he was not imposing on them any thing which he did not observe himself; that though he had full authority as an apostle to insist on *a support* in preaching, yet for the sake of peace, and the prosperity of the church, he had voluntarily relinquished his *rights*, and endeavoured by all means to save some, chap. ix. By this example, he seeks to persuade them to a course of life as far as possible from a life of gluttony, and fornication, and self-indulgence, and to assure them that although they had been highly favoured, as the Jews had been also, yet like them, they might also fall, chap. x. 1—12. These principles he illustrates by a reference to their joining in feasts, and celebrations with idols, and the dangers to which they would subject themselves by so doing; and concludes that it would be *proper* in those circumstances wholly to abstain from partaking of the meat offered in sacrifice to idols if it were known to be such. This was to be done on the principle that no offence was to be given. And thus the *second* question referred to him was disposed of, chap. x. 13—33. In connection with this, and as an illustration of the principle on which he acted, and on which he wishes them to act, that of promoting mutual edification, and avoiding offence he refers (chap. xi.) to two other subjects, the one, the proper relation of the woman to the man, and the general duty of her being in subjection to him, (chap. xi. 1—16;) and the other, a far more important matter, the proper mode of celebrating the Lord's supper, chap. xi. 17—34. He had been led to speak of this, probably, by the discussion to which he had been invited on the subject of their *feasts*, and the discussion of *that* subject naturally led to the consideration of the much more important subject of their mode of celebrating the Lord's supper. That had been greatly abused to purposes of riot, and disorder, and abuse, which had grown directly out of their former views and habits in public festivals. Those views and habits they had transferred to the celebration of the eucharist. It became necessary, therefore, for the apostle to correct those views, to state the true design of the ordinance, to show the consequences of an improper mode of celebration, and to endeavour to reform them in their mode of observing it, chap. xi. 17—34. (*c*) Another subject which had probably been submitted to him in the letter was, the nature of spiritual gifts ; the design of the power of speaking with tongues, and the proper order to be observed in the church on this subject. These powers seem to have been imparted to the Corinthians in a remarkable degree ; and like most other things had been abused to the promotion of strife and ambition ; to pride in their possession, and to irregularity and disorder in their public assemblies. This whole subject the apostle discusses, (chap. xii. xiii. xiv.) He states the design of imparting this gift ; the use which should be made of it in the church, the necessity of due subordination in all the members and officers ; and in a chapter unequalled in beauty in any language, (chap. xiii.) shows the inferiority of the highest of these endowments to a kind, catholic spirit—to the prevalence of charity, and thus endeavours to allay all contentions and strifes for ascendancy, by the prevalence of the spirit of LOVE. In connection with this (chap. xiv.) he reproves the abuses which had arisen on *this* subject, as he had done on others, and seeks to repress all disorders. (8.) A very important subject, the apostle reserved to the close of the epistle—the resurrection of the dead. (chap. xv.) *Why* he chose to discuss it in this place, is not known. It is quite probable that he had not been *consulted* on this subject in the letter which had been sent to him. It is evident, however, that erroneous opinions had been entertained on the subject, and probably inculcated by the religious teachers at Corinth. The philosophic minds of the Greeks we know were much disposed to deride this doctrine (Acts xvii. 32), and in the Corinthian church it had been either called in question, or greatly perverted, chap. xv. 12. That the same body would be raised up had been denied, and the doctrine that came to be believed was, probably, simply that there would be a future state, and that the only resurrection was the resurrection of the soul from sin, and that this was past ; comp. 2 Tim. ii. 18. This subject the apostle had not before taken up, probably because he had not been consulted on it, and because it would find a more appropriate place *after* he had reproved their disorders, and answered their questions. After all those discussions, after examining all the opinions and practices that prevailed among them, it was proper *to place the great argument for the truth of the religion which they all professed on a permanent foundation, and to close the epistle by reminding them, and proving to them that the religion which they professed, and which they had so much abused, was from heaven.* The proof of this was the resurrection of the Saviour from the dead. It was indispensable to hold that in its obvious sense, and holding that, the truth of their own resurrection was demonstrated, and the error of those who denied it was apparent. (9). Having finished this demonstration, the apostle closes the epistle (chap. xvi.) with some miscellaneous directions and salutations.

§ 5. *Divisions of the Epistle.*

THE divisions of this epistle, as of the other books of the Bible, into chapters and verses, is arbitrary, and often not happily made. See the Introduction to the Notes on the Gospels. Various divisions of the epistle have been proposed in order to present a proper analysis to the mind. The division which is submitted here is one that arises from the previous statement of the scope and design of the epistle, and will furnish the basis of my analysis. According to this view, the body of this epistle may be divided into three parts, viz.—

I. The discussion of irregularities and abuses prevailing in the church at Corinth, of which the apostle had incidentally learned by report, chap. i.—vi.

II. The discussion of various subjects which had been submitted to him in a letter from the church, and of points which grew out of those inquiries, chap. vii.—xiv.

III. The discussion of the great doctrine of the resurrection of Christ—the foundation of the hope of man—and the demonstration arising from that, that the Christian religion is true, and the hopes of Christians well founded, chap. xv. (See the "Analysis" prefixed to the Notes.)

§ 6. *The Messengers by whom this Epistle was sent to the Church at Corinth, and its success.*

It is evident that Paul felt the deepest solicitude in regard to the state of things in the church at Corinth. Apparently as soon as he had heard of their irregularities and disorders through the members of the family of Chloe (chap. i. ii.) he had sent Timothy to them, if possible to repress the growing dissensions and irregularities; 1 Cor. iv. 17. In the mean time the church at Corinth wrote to him to ascertain his views on certain matters submitted to him (1 Cor. vii. 1), and the reception of this letter gave him occasion to enter at length into the subject of their disorders and difficulties. Yet he wrote the letter under the deepest solicitude about the manner of its reception, and its effect on the church, 2 Cor. ii. 4, "For out of much affliction and anguish of heart I wrote unto you with many tears," &c. Paul had another object in view which was dear to his heart, and which he was labouring with all diligence to promote, which was the collection which he proposed to take up for the poor and afflicted saints at Jerusalem; see Notes, Rom. xv. 25, 26. This object he wished to press at this time on the church at Corinth; 1 Cor. xvi. 1—4. In order, therefore, to ensure the success of his letter, and to facilitate the collection, he sent *Titus* with the letter to the church at Corinth, with instructions to have the collection ready, 2 Cor. vii. 7, 8, 13, 15. This collection, Titus was requested to finish; 2 Cor. viii. 6. With Titus, Paul sent another brother, perhaps a member of the church at Ephesus (2 Cor. xii. 8), a man whose praise, Paul says, was in all the churches, and who had been already designated by the churches to bear the contribution to Jerusalem, 2 Cor. viii. 18, 19. By turning to Acts xxi. 29, we find it incidentally mentioned that "Trophimus an Ephesian" was with Paul in Jerusalem, and undoubtedly this was the person here designated. This is one of the undesigned coincidences between Paul's epistle and the Acts of the Apostles, of which Dr. Paley has made so much use in his *Horæ Paulinæ* in proving the genuineness of these writings. Paul did not deem it necessary or prudent for him to go himself to Corinth, but chose to remain in Ephesus. The letter to Paul (1 Cor. vii. 1) had been brought to him by Stephanas, Fortunatus, and Achaicus (1 Cor. xvi. 17), and it is probable that they accompanied Titus and the other brother with him who bore Paul's reply to their inquiries.

The success of this letter was all that Paul could desire. It had the effect to repress their growing strifes, to restrain their disorders, to produce true repentance, and to remove the person who had been guilty of incest in the church. The whole church was deeply affected with his reproofs, and engaged in hearty zeal in the work of reform, 2 Cor. vii. 9—11. The authority of the apostle was recognised, and his epistle read with fear and trembling, 2 Cor. vii. 15. The act of discipline which he had required on the incestuous person was inflicted by the whole church, 2 Cor. ii. 6. The collection which he had desired (1 Cor. xvi. 1—4), and in regard to which he had boasted of their liberality to others, and expressed the utmost confidence that it would be liberal (2 Cor. ix. 2, 3), was taken up agreeably to his wishes, and their disposition on the subject was such as to furnish the highest satisfaction to his mind, 2 Cor. vii. 13, 14. Of the success of his letter, however, and of their disposition to take up the collection, Paul was not apprised until he had gone into Macedonia, where Titus came to him, and gave him information of the happy state of things in the church at Corinth, 2 Cor. vii. 4—7, 13. Never was a letter more effectual than this was, and never was authority in discipline exercised in a more happy and successful way.

General Character and Structure of the Epistle.

THE general style and character of this Epistle is the same as in the other writings of Paul. See Introduction to the Epistle to the Romans. It evinces the same strong and manly style of argument and language, the same structure of sentences, the same rapidity of conception, the same overpowering force of language and thought, and the same characteristics of temper and spirit in the author. The main difference between the style and manner of this epistle, and the other epistles of Paul, arises from the scope and design of the argument. In the epistle to the Romans, his object led him to pursue a close and connected train of argumentation. In this, a large portion of the epistle is occupied with *reproof*, and it gives occasion for calling into view at once the *authority* of an apostle, and the spirit and manner in which reproof is to be administered. The reader of this epistle cannot but be struck with the fact, that it was no part of Paul's character to show indulgence to sin; that he had no design to flatter; that he neither "cloaked nor concealed transgression;" that in the most open, firm, and manly manner possible, it was his purpose to rebuke them for their disorders, and to repress their growing irregularities. At the same time, however, there is full opportunity for the display of tenderness, kindness, love, charity, and for Christian instruction—an opportunity for pouring forth the deepest feelings of the human heart—an opportunity which Paul never allowed to escape unimproved. Amidst all the severity of reproof, there is the love of friendship; amidst the rebukes of an apostle, the entreaties and tears of a father. And we here contemplate Paul, not merely as the profound reasoner, not simply as a man of high intellectual endowments, but as evincing the feelings of the man, and the sympathies of the Christian.

Perhaps there is less difficulty in understanding this epistle than the epistle to the Romans. A few passages indeed have perplexed all commentators, and are to this day not understood. See chap. v. 9: xi. 10; xv. 29. But the general meaning of the epistle has been much less the subject of difference of interpretation. The reasons have probably been the following. (1.) The subjects here are more numerous, and the discussions more brief. There is, therefore, less difficulty in following the author than where the discussion is protracted, and the manner of his reasoning more complicated. (2.) The subjects themselves are far less abstruse and profound than those introduced into the epistle to the Romans. There is, therefore, less liability to misconception. (3.) The epistle has never been made the subject of theological warfare. No system of theology has been built on it, and no attempt made to press it into the service of abstract dogmas. It is mostly of a practical character, and there has been, therefore, less room for contention in regard to its meaning. (4.) No false and unfounded theories of philosophy have been attached to this epistle, as have been to the epistle to the Romans. Its simple sense, therefore, has been more obvious, and no small part of the difficulties in the interpretation of that epistle are wanting in this. (5.) The apostle's design has somewhat varied his style. There are fewer complicated sentences, and fewer parentheses, less that is abrupt and broken, and elliptical, less that is rapid, mighty, and overpowering in argument. We see the point of a reproof at once, but we are often greatly embarrassed in a complicated argument. The xvth chapter, however, for closeness and strength of argumentation, for beauty of diction, for tenderness of pathos, and for commanding and overpowering eloquence, is probably unsurpassed by any other part of the writings of Paul, and unequalled by any other composition. (6.) It may be added, that there is less in this epistle that opposes the native feelings of the human heart, and that humbles the pride of the human intellect, than in the epistle to the Romans. One great difficulty in interpreting that epistle has been that the doctrines relate to those high subjects that rebuke the pride of man, demand prostration before his Sovereign, require the submission of the understanding and the heart to God's high claims, and throw down every form of self-righteousness. While substantially the same features will be found in all the writings of Paul, yet his purpose in this epistle led him less to dwell on those topics than in the epistle to the Romans. The result is, that the *heart* more readily acquiesces in these doctrines and reproofs, and the general strain of this epistle; and as the *heart* of man has usually more agency in the interpretation of the Bible than the understanding, the obstacles in the way of a correct exposition of this epistle are proportionably fewer than in the epistle to the Romans.

The same spirit, however, which is requisite in understanding the epistle to the Romans, is demanded here. In all Paul's epistles, as in all the Bible, a spirit of candour, humility, prayer, and industry is required. The knowledge of God's truth is to be acquired only by toil, and candid investigation. The mind that is filled with prejudice is rarely enlightened. The proud, unhumbled spirit seldom receives benefit from reading the Bible, or any other book. He acquires the most complete, and the most profound knowledge of the doctrines of Paul, and of the Book of God in general, who comes to the work of interpretation with the most humble heart; and the deepest sense of his dependence on the aid of that Spirit by whom originally the Bible was inspired. For "the meek will he guide in judgment, and the meek will he teach his way," Ps. xxv. 9.

THE FIRST

EPISTLE TO THE CORINTHIANS.

CHAPTER I.

PAUL, called [a] *to be* an apostle of Jesus Christ through the will of God, and Sosthenes [b] *our* brother.

2 Unto the church of God which

a Rom. 1. 1.

b Mat. 12. 38.

CHAPTER I.

1. *Paul, called to be an apostle.* See Notes, Rom. i. 1. ¶ *Through the will of God.* Not by human appointment, or authority, but in accordance with the will of God, and his command. That *will* was made known to him by the special revelation granted to him at his conversion, and call to the apostleship; Acts ix. Paul often refers to the fact that he had received a direct commission from God, and that he did not act on his own authority; comp. Gal. i. 11, 12; 1 Cor. ix. 1—6; 2 Cor. xi. 22—33; xii. 1—12. There was a special reason why he commenced this epistle by referring to the fact that he was divinely called to the apostleship. It arose from the fact that his apostolic authority had been called in question by the false teachers at Corinth. That this was the case is apparent from the general strain of the epistle, from some particular expressions (2 Cor. x. 8—10); and from the fact that he is at so much pains throughout the two epistles to establish his divine commission. ¶ *And Sosthenes.* Sosthenes is mentioned in Acts xviii. 17, as "the chief ruler of the synagogue" at Corinth. He is there said to have been beaten by the Greeks before the judgment-seat of Gallio because he was a Jew, and because he had joined with the other Jews in arraigning Paul, and had thus produced disturbance in the city; see Note on this place. It is evident that at that time he was not a Christian. When he was converted, or why he left Corinth and was now with Paul at Ephesus, is unknown. Why Paul associated him with himself in writing this epistle is not known. It is evident that Sosthenes was not an apostle, nor is there any reason to think that he was inspired. Some circumstances are known to have existed respecting Paul's manner of writing to the churches, which may explain it. (1.) He was accustomed to employ an amanuensis or scribe in writing his epistles, and the amanuensis frequently expressed his concurrence or approbation in what the apostle had indicted; see Note, Rom. xvi. 22; comp. Col. iv. 18. "*The salutation* by the hand of Paul," 2 Thess. iii. 17; 1 Cor. xvi. 21. It is possible that Sosthenes might have been employed by Paul for this purpose. (2.) Paul not unfrequently associated others with himself in writing his letters to the churches, himself claiming authority as an apostle; and the others expressing their concurrence; 2 Cor. i. 1. Thus in Gal. i. 1, "all the brethren" which were with him, are mentioned as united with him in addressing the churches of Galatia; Phil. i. 1; Col. i. 1; 1 Thess. i. 1. (3.) Sosthenes was well known at Corinth. He had been the chief ruler of the synagogue there. His conversion would, therefore, excite a deep interest, and it is not improbable that he had been conspicuous as a preacher. All these circumstances would render it proper that Paul should associate him with himself in writing this letter. It would be bringing in the testimony of one well known as concurring with the views of the apostle, and tend much to conciliate those who were disaffected towards him.

is at Corinth, [a] to them [b] that are sanctified [c] in Christ Jesus, called [d] *to be* saints, with all that in every place call [e] upon the name of Jesus Christ our Lord, both theirs and ours:

a Acts 18. 1. b Jude 1. c John 17.19. d 2 Tim.1.9; 1 Pet.1.15. e 2 Tim.2.22.

2. *Unto the church of God which is at Corinth.* For an account of the time and manner in which the church was established in Corinth, see the Introduction, and Notes on Acts xviii. 1—17. The church is called "the church of God," because it has been founded by his agency, and was devoted to his service. It is worthy of remark, that although great disorders had been introduced into that church; though there were separations and erroneous doctrines; though there were some who gave evidence that they were not sincere Christians, yet the apostle had no hesitation in applying to them the name of a church of God. ¶ *To them that are sanctified.* To those who are made holy. This does not refer to the profession of holiness, but implies that they were *in fact* holy. The word means that they were *separated* from the mass of heathens around them, and devoted to God and his cause. Though the word used here (ἡγιασμένοις) has this idea of *separation* from the mass around them, yet it is separation on account of their being *in fact*, and not in profession merely, different from others, and truly devoted to God; see Note, Rom. i. 7. ¶ *In Christ Jesus.* That is, *by* (ἐν) the agency of Christ. It was by his authority, his power, and his Spirit, that they had been separated from the mass of heathens around them, and devoted to God; comp. John xvii. 19. ¶ *Called* to be *saints.* The word *saints* does not differ materially from the word *sanctified* in the former part of the verse. It means those who are *separated* from the world, and set apart to God as holy. The idea which Paul introduces here is, that they became such because they were *called* to be such. The idea in the former part of the verse is, that this was done "by Christ Jesus;" here he says that it was because they were *called* to this privilege. He doubtless means to say that it was not by any native tendency in themselves to holiness, but because God had called them to it. And this calling does not refer merely to an external invitation, but it was that which was made *effectual* in their case, or that on which the fact of their being saints could be predicated; comp. ver. 9; see 2 Tim. i. 9; "Who hath saved us, and called us with an holy calling, not according to our works, but according to his own purpose and grace," &c.; 1 Pet. i. 15; Note, Rom. i. 6, 7; viii. 28; Eph. iv. 1; 1 Tim. vi. 12; 1 Pet. ii. 9. ¶ *With all,* &c. This expression shows, (1.) That Paul had the same feelings of attachment to all Christians in every place; and (2.) That he expected that this epistle would be read, not only by the church at Corinth, but also by other churches. That this was the uniform intention of the apostle in regard to his epistles, is apparent from other places; comp. 1 Thess. v. 27; "I charge you by the Lord that this epistle be read unto all the holy brethren;" Col. iv. 16; "And when this epistle is read among you, cause that it be read also in the church of the Laodiceans." It is evident that Paul expected that his epistles would obtain circulation among the churches; and it was morally certain that they would be soon transcribed, and be extensively read.—The ardent feelings of Paul embraced all Christians in every nation. He knew nothing of the narrowness of exclusive attachment to *sect.* His heart was full of love, and he loved, as we should, all who bore the Christian name, and who evinced the Christian spirit. ¶ *Call upon the name of Jesus Christ.* To call upon *the name* of any person, in Scripture language, is to call on the person himself; comp. John iii. 18; Note, Acts iv. 12. The expression "*to call upon* the name" (ἐπικαλουμένοις), to invoke the name, implies worship, and prayer; and proves, (1.) That the Lord Jesus is an object of worship; and (2.) That

3 Grace [a] *be* unto you, and peace from God our Father, and *from* the Lord Jesus Christ.

4 I thank [b] my God always on your behalf, for the grace of God which is given you by Jesus Christ;

5 That in every thing ye are enriched by him, in all utterance, [c] and *in* all knowledge;

a 1 Pet.1.2. b Rom.1.8. c 2 Cor.8.7.

one characteristic of the early Christians, by which they were known and distinguished, was their calling upon the name of the Lord Jesus, or their offering worship to him. That it implies worship, see Note on Acts vii. 59; and that the early Christians called on Christ by prayer, and were distinguished by that, see the Note on Acts vii. 59, and compare Note, Acts i. 24, also Acts ii. 21; ix. 13; xxii. 16; 2 Tim. ii. 22. ¶ *Both theirs and ours.* The Lord of all—both Jews and Gentiles—of *all* who profess themselves Christians, of whatever country or name they might have originally been. Difference of nation or birth gives no pre-eminence in the kingdom of Christ, but all are on a level, having a common Lord and Saviour; comp. Eph. iv. 5.

3. *Grace be unto you,* &c.; see Note, Rom. i. 7.

4. *I thank my God,* &c. No small part of this epistle is occupied with reproofs for the disorders which had arisen in the church at Corinth. Before proceeding, however, to the specific statement of those disorders (ver. 10, seq.), the apostle *commends* them for the attainments which they had really made in divine knowledge, and thus shows that he was disposed to concede to them all that he could. It was no part of the disposition of Paul to withhold commendation where it was due. On the contrary, as he was disposed to be faithful in reproving the errors of Christians, he was no less disposed to commend them when it could be done; comp. Note, Rom. i. 8. A willingness to commend those who do well is as much in accordance with the gospel, as a disposition to reprove where it is deserved; and a minister, or a parent, may frequently do as decided good by judicious commendation as by reproof, and much more than by fault-finding and harsh crimination. ¶ *On your behalf.* In respect to you; that God has conferred these favours on you. ¶ *For the grace of God.* On account of the favours which God has bestowed on you through the Lord Jesus. Those favours are specified in the following verses. For the meaning of the word *grace,* see Note, Rom. i. 7.

5. *That in every thing.* In every respect, or in regard to all the favours conferred on any of his people. You have been distinguished by him in all those respects in which he blesses his own children. ¶ *Ye are enriched by him;* comp. Note, Rom. ii. 4. The meaning of this expression is, "you *abound* in these things; they are conferred abundantly upon you." By the use of this word, the apostle intends doubtless to denote *the fact* that these blessings had been conferred on them abundantly; and also that this was a *valuable endowment,* so as to be properly called *a treasure.* The mercies of God are not only conferred abundantly on his people, but they are a bestowment of inestimable value; comp. 2 Cor. vi. 10. ¶ *In all utterance.* With the power of speaking various languages (ἐν παντὶ λόγῳ). That this power was conferred on the church at Corinth, and that it was highly valued by them, is evident from chap. xiv; comp. 2 Cor. viii. 7. The power of speaking those languages the apostle regarded as a subject of thanksgiving, as it was a proof of the divine favour to them; see chap. xiv. 5, 22, 39. ¶ *And in all knowledge.* In the knowledge of divine truth. They had understood the doctrines which they had heard, and had intelligently embraced them. This was not true of *all* of them, but it was of the body of the church; and the hearty commendation and thanksgiving of the apostle for these favours, laid the foundation for the remarks which he

6 Even as the testimony of
Christ was confirmed in you.
7 So that ye come behind in
no gift; waiting [a] for the [1] coming
of our Lord Jesus Christ:
8 Who shall also confirm [b] you

[a] Tit.2.13. [1] *revelation.* [b] 1 Thess.3.13; 5.23,24.

had subsequently to make, and would tend to conciliate their minds, and dispose them to listen attentively, even to the language of reproof.

6. *Even as.* Καθώς. The force of this expression seems to be this, "The gospel of Christ was at first established among you by means of the miraculous endowments of the Holy Ghost. Those same endowments are still continued among you, and *now* furnish evidence of the divine favour, and of the truth of the gospel to you, *even as—i. e.* in the same measure as they did when the gospel was first preached." The power to speak with tongues, &c.; (chap. xiv.) would be a *continued miracle,* and would be a demonstration to them then of the truth of Christianity as it was at first. ¶ *The testimony of Christ.* The gospel. It is here called "the testimony of Christ," because it bore witness to Christ—to his divine nature, his miracles, his Messiahship, his character, his death, &c. The message of the gospel consists in bearing witness to Christ and his work; see chap. xv. 1—4; 2 Tim. i. 8. ¶ *Was confirmed.* Was established, or proved. It was proved to be divine, by the miraculous attestations of the Holy Spirit. It was confirmed, or made certain to their souls by the agency of the Holy Spirit, sealing it on their hearts. The word translated *confirmed* (ἐβεβαιώθη), is used in the sense of establishing, confirming, or demonstrating by miracles, &c.; in Mark xvi. 20; comp. Heb. xiii. 9; Phil. i. 7. ¶ *In you* (ἐν ὑμῖν). Among you as a people, or in your hearts. Perhaps the apostle intends to include both. The gospel had been established among them by the demonstrations of the agency of the Spirit in the gift of tongues, and had at the same time taken deep root in their hearts, and was exerting a practical influence on their lives.

7. *So that.* God has so abundantly endowed you with his favours. ¶ *Ye come behind* (ὑστερεῖσθαι). You are not wanting, or deficient. The word is usually applied to destitution, want, or poverty; and the declaration here is synonymous with what he had said, ver. 5, that they abounded in every thing. ¶ *In no gift.* In no favour, or gracious endowment. The word used here (χάρισμα), does not refer necessarily to extraordinary and miraculous endowments, but includes also *all* the kindnesses of God towards them in producing peace of mind, constancy, humility, &c. And the apostle meant evidently to say that they possessed, in rich abundance, all those endowments which were bestowed on Christians. ¶ *Waiting for.* Expecting, or looking for this coming with glad and anxious desire. This was, certainly, *one* of the endowments to which he referred, to wit, that they had grace given them earnestly to desire, and to wait for the second appearing of the Lord Jesus. An earnest wish to see him, and a confident expectation and firm belief that he will return, is an evidence of a high state of piety. It demands strong faith, and it will do much to elevate the feelings above the world, and to keep the mind in a state of peace. ¶ *The coming,* &c. Gr. The revelation—(τὴν ἀποκάλυψιν)—the manifestation of the Son of God. That is, waiting for his return to judge the world, and for his approbation of his people in that day. The earnest expectation of the Lord Jesus became one of the marks of early Christian piety. This return was promised by the Saviour to his anxious disciples, when he was about to leave them; John xiv. 3. The promise was renewed when he ascended to heaven; Acts i. 11. It became the settled hope and expectation of Christians that he would return; Tit. ii. 13; 2 Pet. iii 12; Heb. ix. 28. And with the earnest prayer that he would quickly come, John closes the volume of inspiration; Rev. xxii. 20, 21.

8. *Who shall also confirm you.* Wh

unto the end, *that ye may be* blameless in the day of our Lord Jesus Christ:

9 God *is* faithful, by whom ye were called unto the fellowship *a* of his Son Jesus Christ our Lord.

a 1 John 1.3.

shall establish you in the hopes of the gospel. He shall make you *firm* (βεβαιώσει) amidst all your trials, and all the efforts which may be made to shake your faith, and to remove you from that firm foundation on which you now rest. ¶ *Unto the end.* That is, to the coming of the Lord Jesus Christ. He would keep them to the end of life in the path of holiness, so that at the coming of the Lord Jesus they might be found blameless; comp. John xiii. 1. The sense is, that they should be kept, and should not be suffered to fall away and perish;—and this is one of the many places which express the strong confidence of Paul that those who are true Christians shall be preserved unto everlasting life; comp. Phil. i. 6. ¶ That ye may be *blameless.* The word rendered *blameless* (ἀνεγκλήτους) does not mean perfect, but properly denotes those against whom there is no charge of crime; who are unaccused, and against whom there is no ground of accusation. Here it does not mean that they were personally perfect, but that God would so keep them, and enable them to evince a Christian character, as to give evidence that they were his friends, and completely escape condemnation in the last day; see Notes on Rom. viii. 33, 34. There is no man who has not his faults; no Christian who is not conscious of imperfection; but it is the design of God so to keep his people, and so to justify and sanctify them through the Lord Jesus, that the church may be presented "a glorious church, without spot or wrinkle" (Eph. v. 37) in the day of judgment. ¶ *In the day,* &c. In the day when the Lord Jesus shall come to judge the world; and which will be called *his* day, because it will be the day in which *he* will be the great and conspicuous object, and which is especially appointed to glorify him; see 2 Thess. i. 10, "Who shall come to be glorified in his saints, and to be admired in all them that believe."

9. *God* is *faithful.* That is, God is true, and constant, and will adhere to his promises. He will not deceive. He will not promise, and then fail to perform; he will not commence any thing which he will not perfect and finish. The object of Paul in introducing the idea of the *faithfulness* of God here, is, to show the reason for believing that the Christians at Corinth would be kept unto everlasting life. The evidence that they will persevere depends on the fidelity of God; and the argument of the apostle is, that as they had been called *by him* into the fellowship of his Son, his faithfulness of character would render it certain that they would be kept to eternal life. The same idea he has presented in Phil. i. 6, "Being confident of this very thing that he which hath begun a good work in you, will also perform it until the day of Jesus Christ." ¶ *Ye were called.* The word "called" here does not refer merely to *an invitation* or an *offer of life,* but to the effectual influence which had been put forth; which had inclined them to embrace the gospel; Note, Rom. viii. 30; ix. 12; see Mark ii. 17; Luke v. 32; Gal. i. 6; v. 8, 13; Eph. i. 4; Col. iii. 15. In this sense the word often occurs in the Scriptures, and is designed to denote a power, or influence that goes forth *with* the external invitation, and that makes it effectual. That power is the agency of the Holy Spirit. ¶ *Unto the fellowship of his Son.* To participate with his Son Jesus Christ; to be *partakers* with him; see Notes, John xv. 1—8. Christians participate with Christ, (1.) In his feelings and views; Rom. viii. 9. (2.) In his trials and sufferings, being subjected to temptations and trials similar to his; 1 Pet. iv. 13, "But rejoice, inasmuch as ye are partakers of Christ's sufferings;" Col. i. 24; Phil. iii. 10. (3.) In his *heirship* to the inheritance and glory which awaits him; Rom. viii. 17, "And if children, then heirs, heirs of God and joint heirs with Christ;" I

10 Now I beseech you, brethren, by the name of our Lord Jesus Christ, [a] that ye all speak the same thing, and *that* there be

a John 17.19.

Pet. i. 4. (4.) In his triumph in the resurrection and future glory; Mat. xix. 28, "Ye which have followed me, in the regeneration when the Son of man shall sit on the throne of his glory, ye also shall sit upon twelve thrones, judging the twelve tribes of Israel;" John xiv. 19, "Because I live, ye shall live also;" Rev. iii. 21, "To him that overcometh will I grant to sit with me in my throne, even as I also overcame, and am set down with my Father in his throne."

[Immediately on our union to Christ, we have fellowship with him, in all the blessings of his purchase. This communion or fellowship *with* him is the necessary result of our union *to* him. On the saint's union to Christ, see supplementary Note on Rom. viii. 10. page 176.]

From all this, the argument of the apostle is, that as they *partake* with Christ in these high privileges, and hopes, and promises, they will be kept by a faithful God unto eternal life. God is faithful to his Son; and will be faithful to all who are united to him. The argument for the perseverance of the saints is, therefore, sure.

10. *Now I beseech you, brethren.* In this verse the apostle enters on the discussion respecting the irregularities and disorders in the church at Corinth, of which he had incidentally heard; see ver. 11. The first of which he had incidentally learned, was that which pertained to the divisions and strifes which had arisen in the church. The consideration of this subject occupies him to ver. 17; and as those divisions had been caused by the influence of philosophy, and the ambition for distinction, and the exhibition of popular eloquence among the Corinthian teachers, this fact gives occasion to him to discuss that subject at length (chap. i. 17—31; xi.); in which he shows that the gospel did not depend for its success on the reasonings of philosophy, or the persuasions of eloquence. This part of the subject he commences with the language of entreaty. "I beseech you, brethren"—the language of affectionate exhortation rather than of stern command. Addressing them as his brethren, as members of the same family with himself, he conjures them to take all proper measures to avoid the evils of schism and of strife. ¶ *By the name.* By the authority of his name; or from reverence for him as the common Lord of all. ¶ *Of our Lord Jesus Christ.* The reasons why Paul thus appeals to his name and authority here, may be the following. (1.) Christ should be regarded as the supreme head and leader of all his church. It was improper, therefore, that the church should be divided into portions, and its different parts enlisted under different banners. (2.) "The whole family in heaven and earth should be named" after him (Eph. iii. 15), and should *not* be named after inferior and subordinate teachers. The reference to "the venerable and endearing name of Christ here, stands beautifully and properly opposed to the various human names under which they were so ready to enlist themselves."—*Doddridge.* "There is scarce a word or expression that he [Paul] makes use of, but with relation and tendency to his present main purpose; as here, intending to abolish the names of leaders they had distinguished themselves by, he beseeches them by the name of Christ, a form that I do not remember he elsewhere uses."—*Locke.* (3.) The prime and leading thing which Christ had enjoined on his church was *union* and mutual love (John xiii. 34; xv. 17), and for this he had most earnestly prayed in his memorable prayer; John xvii. 21—23. It was well for Paul thus to appeal to the name of Christ—the sole head and Lord of his church, and the friend of union, and thus to rebuke the divisions and strifes which had arisen at Corinth. ¶ *That ye all speak the same thing.* "That ye hold the same doctrine."—*Locke.* This exhortation evidently refers to their holding and expressing the same reli-

no [1] divisions among you; but *that* ye be perfectly joined together in the same mind and in the same judgment.

11 For it hath been declared unto me of you, my brethren, by them *which are of the house* of Chloe, that there are contentions among you.

1 *schisms.*

---

gious sentiments, and is designed to rebuke that kind of contention and strife which is evinced where different opinions are held and expressed. To "speak the same thing" stands opposed to speaking different and conflicting things; or to controversy, and although *perfect* uniformity of opinion cannot be expected among men on the subject of religion any more than on other subjects, yet on the great and fundamental doctrines of Christianity, Christians may be agreed; on all points in which they differ they may evince a good spirit; and on all subjects they may *express* their sentiments in the language of the Bible, and thus "speak the same thing." ¶ *And* that *there be no divisions among you.* Greek, *σχίσματα, schisms.* No divisions into contending parties and sects. The church was to be regarded as one and indivisible, and not to be rent into different factions, and ranged under the banners of different leaders; comp. John ix. 16; 1 Cor. xi. 18; xii. 25. ¶ *But that ye be perfectly joined together* (ἦτε δὲ κατηρτισμένοι). The word here used and rendered "perfectly joined together," denotes properly to restore, mend, or repair that which is rent or disordered (Mat. iv. 21; Mark i. 19), to amend or correct that which is *morally* evil and erroneous (Gal. vi. 1), to render perfect or complete (Luke vi. 40), to fit or adapt any thing to its proper place so that it shall be complete in all its parts, and harmonious, (Heb. xi. 5); and thence to compose and settle controversies, to produce harmony and order. The apostle here evidently desires that they should be united in feeling; that every member of the church should occupy his appropriate place, as every member of a well proportioned body, or part of a machine has its appropriate place and use; see his wishes more fully expressed in chap. xii. 12—31. ¶ *In the same mind* (νοΐ); see Rom. xv. 5. This cannot mean that they were to be united in precisely the same shades of opinion, which is impossible—but that their minds were to be disposed towards each other with mutual good will, and that they should live in harmony. The word here rendered *mind,* denotes not merely the intellect itself, but that which is *in* the mind—the thoughts, counsels, plans; Rom. xi. 34; xiv. 5; 1 Cor. ii. 16; Col. ii. 18. *Bretschneider.* ¶ *And in the same judgment* (γνώμη). This word properly denotes science, or knowledge; opinion, or sentiment; and sometimes, as here, the purpose of the mind, or *will.* The sentiment of the whole is, that in their understandings and their volitions, they should be united and kindly disposed towards each other. Union of feeling is possible even where men differ much in their views of things. They may love each other much, even where they do not see alike. They may give each other credit for honesty and sincerity, and may be willing to suppose that others *may be right,* and *are honest* even where their own views differ. The foundation of Christian union is not so much laid in uniformity of intellectual perception as in right feelings of the heart. And the proper way to produce union in the church of God, is not to *begin* by attempting to equalize all *intellects* on the bed of Procrustes, but to produce supreme love to God, and elevated and pure Christian love to all who bear the image and the name of the Redeemer.

11. *For it hath been declared unto me.* Of the contentions existing in the church at Corinth, it is evident that they had not informed him in the letter which they had sent; see chap. vii. 1, comp. the Introduction. He had incidentally heard of their contentions. ¶ *My brethren.* A token of affectionate regard, evincing his love for them, and his deep interest in their welfare, even when he administered a needed rebuke. ¶ Of the house *of*

12 Now this I say, that every one of you saith, I am of Paul; and I of Apollos; [a] and I of Cephas; [b] and I of Christ.

a Acts 19.1. b John 1.42.

Chloe. Of the family of Chloe. It is most probable that Chloe was a member of the church at Corinth, some of whose family had been at Ephesus when Paul was, and had given him information of the state of things there. Who those members of her family were, is unknown. Grotius conjectures that they were Stephanas, Fortunatus, and Achaicus, mentioned in chap. xvi. 17, who brought the letter of the church at Corinth to Paul. But of this there is no certain evidence; perhaps not much probability. If the information had been obtained from them, it is probable that it would have been put in the letter which they bore. The probability is that Paul had received this information before they arrived.

12. *Now this I say.* This is what I mean; or, I give this as an instance of the contentions to which I refer. ¶ *That every one of you saith.* That you are divided into different factions, and ranged under different leaders. The word translated "that" (ὅτι) might be translated here, *because*, or *since*, as giving a reason for his affirming (ver. 11) that there were contentions there. "Now I say that there are contentions, *because* you are ranged under different leaders," &c.—*Calvin.* ¶ *I am of Paul.* It has been doubted whether Paul meant to affirm that the parties had actually taken the names which he here specifies, or whether he uses these names as illustrations, or suppositions, to show the absurdity of their ranging themselves under different leaders. Many of the ancient interpreters supposed that Paul was unwilling to specify the real names of the false teachers and leaders of the parties, and that he used these names simply by way of illustration. This opinion was grounded chiefly on what he says in chap. iv. 6, "And these things, brethren, I have *in a figure* transferred to myself and to Apollos for your sakes," &c. But in this place Paul is not referring so particularly to the factions or parties existing in the church, as he is to the necessity of modesty and humility; and in order to enforce this, he refers to himself and Apollos to show that even those most highly favoured should have a low estimate of their importance, since all *their* success depends on God; see chap. iii. 4—6. It can scarcely be doubted that Paul here meant to say that there were parties existing in the church at Corinth, who were called by the names of himself, of Apollos, of Cephas, and of Christ. This is the natural construction; and this was evidently the information which he had received by those who were of the family of Chloe. *Why* the parties were ranged under *these* leaders, however, can be only a matter of conjecture. Lightfoot suggests that the church at Corinth was composed partly of Jews and partly of Gentiles; see Acts xviii. The Gentile converts, he supposes, would range themselves under Paul and Apollos as their leaders; and the Jewish under Peter and Christ. Paul was the apostle to the Gentiles, and Peter particularly the apostle to the Jews (Gal. ii. 7); and this circumstance might give rise to the division. Apollos succeeded Paul in Achaia, and laboured successfully there; see Acts xviii. 27, 28. These two original parties might be again sub-divided. A part of those who adhered to Paul and Apollos might regard Saul with chief veneration, as being the founder of the church as the instrument of *their* conversion, as the chief apostle, as signally pure in his doctrine and manner; and a part might regard Apollos as the instrument of *their* conversion, and as being distinguished for eloquence. It is evident that the main reason why Apollos was regarded as the head of a faction was on account of his extraordinary eloquence, and it is probable that his followers might seek particularly to imitate him in the graces of popular elocution. ¶ *And I of Cephas,* Peter; comp. John i. 42. He was regarded particularly as the

13 Is Christ divided? was Paul crucified for you, or were ye baptized in the name of Paul?

apostle to the Jews; Gal. ii. 7. He had his own peculiarity of views in teaching, and it is probable that his teaching was not regarded as entirely harmonious with that of Paul; see Gal. ii. 11—17. Paul had everywhere among the Gentiles taught that it was not necessary to observe the ceremonial laws of Moses; and, it is probable, that Peter was regarded by the Jews as the advocate of the contrary doctrine. Whether Peter had been at Corinth is unknown. If not, they had heard of his name, and character; and those who had come from Judea had probably reported him as teaching a doctrine on the subject of the observance of Jewish ceremonies unlike that of Paul. ¶ *And I of Christ.* Why this sect professed to be the followers of Christ, is not certainly known. It probably arose from one of the two following causes. (1.) Either that they had been in Judea and had seen the Lord Jesus, and thus regarded themselves as particularly favoured and distinguished: or, (2.) More probably because they refused to call themselves by any inferior leader, and wished to regard Christ alone as their head, and possibly prided themselves on the belief that they were more conformed to him than the other sects.

13. *Is Christ divided?* Paul, in this verse, proceeds to show the impropriety of their divisions and strifes. His general argument is, that Christ alone ought to be regarded as their head and leader, and that his claims, arising from his crucifixion, and acknowledged by their baptism, were so pre-eminent that they could not be divided, and the honours due to him should not be rendered to any other. The apostle, therefore, asks, with strong emphasis, whether Christ was to be regarded as divided? Whether this single supreme head and leader of the church, had become the head of different contending factions? The strong absurdity of supposing that, showed the impropriety of their ranging themselves under different banners and leaders. ¶ *Was Paul crucified for you?* This question implies that the crucifixion of Christ had an influence in saving them which the sufferings of no other one *could* have, and that those sufferings were in fact the peculiarity which distinguished the work of Christ, and rendered it of so much value. The atonement was the grand, crowning work of the Lord Jesus. It was through this that *all* the Corinthian Christians had been renewed and pardoned. That work was so pre-eminent that it could not have been performed by another. And as they had *all* been saved by that alone; as they were alike dependent on his merits for salvation, it was improper that they should be rent into contending factions, and ranged under different leaders. If there is any thing that will recall Christians of different names and of contending sects from the heat of strife, it is the recollection of the fact that they have been purchased by the same blood, and that the same Saviour died to redeem them all. If this fact could be kept before their minds, it would put an end to angry strife everywhere in the church, and produce universal Christian love. ¶ *Or were ye baptized in the name of Paul.* Or, *into*, or *unto* the name of Paul; see Note, Mat. xxviii. 19. To be baptized *into*, or *unto* any one is to be devoted to him, to receive and acknowledge him as a teacher, professing to receive his rules, and to be governed by his authority.—*Locke.* Paul here solemnly reminds them that their *baptism* was an argument why they should not range themselves under different leaders. By that, they had been solemnly and entirely devoted to the service of the only Saviour. "Did I ever," was the implied language of Paul, "baptize in my own name? Did I ever pretend to organize a sect, announcing myself as a leader? Have not I always directed you to that Saviour into whose name and service you have been baptized?" It is remarkable here, that Paul refers to himself, and not to Apollos or Peter.

14 I thank God that I baptized none of you but Crispus [a] and Gaius; [b]

15 Lest any should say that I had baptized in mine own name.

16 And I baptized also the

a Acts 18.8. b Rom.16.23; 3 John 1,&c.

He does not insinuate that the claims of Apollos or Peter were to be disparaged, or their talents and influence to be undervalued, as a jealous rival would have done; but he numbers himself first, and alone, as having no claims to be regarded as a religious leader among them, or the founder of a sect. Even he, the founder of the church, and their spiritual father, had never desired or intended that they should call themselves by *his* name; and he thus showed the impropriety of their adopting the name of *any* man as the leader of a sect.

14. *I thank God,* &c. Why Paul did not himself baptize, see in ver. 17. To him it was now a subject of grateful reflection that he had *not* done it. He had not given any occasion for the suspicion that he had intended to set himself up as a leader of a sect or party. ¶ *But Crispus.* Crispus had been the chief ruler of the synagogue at Corinth; Acts xviii. 8. ¶ *And Gaius.* Gaius resided at Corinth, and at his house Paul resided when he wrote the epistle to the Romans; Rom. xvi. 23. It is also possible that the third epistle of John was directed to this man; see 3 John 1. And if so, then probably Diotrephes (3 John 9), who is mentioned as one who loved "to have the pre-eminence," had been one cause of the difficulties at Corinth. The other persons at Corinth had been probably baptized by Silas and Timothy.

15. *Lest any should say.* Lest any of those who had been baptized should pervert his design, and say that Paul had baptized them unto himself; or, lest any others should, with any appearance of truth, say that he had sought to make disciples to himself. The Ethiopic version renders this, "that ye should not say we were baptized in his name." Many of the ancient MSS. read this, "lest any should say that *ye were baptized* into my name." *Mill.*

16. *And I baptized also the household.* The family. Whether there were any infants in the family, does not appear. It is certain that the family was among the first converts to Christianity in Achaia, and that it had evinced great zeal in aiding those who were Christians; see chap. xvi. 15.—From the manner in which Paul mentions this, it is probable that Stephanas did not reside at Corinth when he was baptized, though he might have subsequently removed there. "I baptized none *of you* (ver. 14.)—*i. e.* none of those who permanently dwelt at Corinth, or who were members of the original church there, but Crispus and Gaius—but I baptized also the family of Stephanas, *now* of your number."—Or it may mean, "I baptized none of you *who are adult members of the church,* but Crispus and Gaius, though I also baptized the *family* of Stephanas." If this be the true interpretation, then it forms an argument to prove that Paul practised household baptism, or the baptism of the families of those who were themselves believers. Or the expression may simply indicate a *recollection* of the true circumstances of the case—a species of *correction* of the statement in ver. 14, "I recollect now also that I baptized the family of Stephanas." ¶ *Household* (οἶκον). The house; the family. The word comprises the whole family, including adults, domestics, slaves, and children. It includes, (1.) The *men* in a house, (Acts vii. 10; 1 Tim. iii. 4, 5, 12;) (2.) *Domestics,* (Acts x. 2; xi. 14; xvi. 15. 31; 1 Tim. iii. 4;) (3.) *The family* in general; Luke x. 5; xvi. 27. *Bretschneider.* It was the custom, doubtless, for the apostles to baptize the entire *household,* whatever might be the age, including domestics, slaves, and children. The head of a family gave up the entire *household* to God.

[That adult domestics and slaves were baptized without *personal* profession or other

household of Stephanas; [a] besides, I know not whether I baptized any other.

17 For Christ sent me not to baptize, but to preach the gospel: not with wisdom [b] of [1] words, lest the cross of Christ should be made of none effect.

a chap. 16.15,17.

b chap. 2.1,4,13. 1 or *speech*.

evidence of faith, is incredible. The word οικος indeed includes domestics as well as children, but while the latter must have been admitted on the profession of their parents, it is reasonable to suppose that the former would be received solely on their own.]

¶ *Of Stephanas.* Who Stephanas was, is not known. The Greek commentators say that he was the jailer of Philippi, who, after he had been baptized (Acts xvi. 33), removed with his family to Corinth. But of this there is no certain evidence. ¶ *Besides.* Besides these. ¶ *I know not,* &c. I do not know whether I baptized any others who are *now* members of that church. Paul would, doubtless, recollect that he had baptized others in other places, but he is speaking here particularly of Corinth. This is not to be urged as an argument against the *inspiration* of Paul, for (1.) It was not the design of inspiration to free the memory from defect in ordinary transactions, or in those things which were not to be received for the instruction of the church; (2.) The meaning of Paul may simply be, "I know not who of the original members of the church at Corinth may have removed, or who may have died; I know not who may have removed *to* Corinth from other places where I have preached and baptized, and consequently I cannot know whether I may not have baptized *some* others of your present number." It is evident, however, that if he had baptized any others, the number was small.

17. *For Christ sent me not to baptize.* That is, not to baptize as my main business. Baptism was not his principal employment, though he had a commission in common with others to administer the ordinance, and occasionally did it. The same thing was true of the Saviour, that he did not personally baptize, John iv. 2. It is probable that the business of baptism was intrusted to the ministers of the church of inferior talents, or to those who were connected with the churches permanently, and not to those who were engaged chiefly in travelling from place to place. The reasons of this may have been, (1.) That which Paul here suggests, that if the apostles had themselves baptized, it might have given occasion to strifes, and the formation of parties, as those who had been baptized by the apostles might claim some superiority over those who were not. (2.) It is probable that the rite of baptism was preceded or followed by a course of instruction adapted to it, and as the apostles were travelling from place to place, this could be better intrusted to those who were to be with them as their ordinary religious teachers. It was an advantage that those who imparted this instruction should also administer this ordinance. (3.) It is not improbable, as Doddridge supposes, that the administration of this ordinance was intrusted to inferiors, because it was commonly practised by immersion, and was attended with some trouble and inconvenience, while the time of the apostles might be more directly occupied in their main work. ¶ *But to preach the gospel.* As his main business; as the leading, grand purpose of his ministry. This is the grand object of all ministers. It is not to build up a sect or party; it is not to secure simply the *baptism* of people in this or that communion; it is to make known the glad tidings of salvation, and call men to repentance and to God. ¶ *Not with wisdom of words* (οὐκ ἐν σοφίᾳ λόγου) Not in wisdom of *speech.* Margin. The expression here is a Hebraism, or a form of speech common in the Hebrew writings, where a noun is used to express the meaning of an adjective, and means *not in wise words or discourse.* The *wisdom* here mentioned, refers, doubtless, to that which was

common among the Greeks, and which was so highly valued. It included the following things:—(1.) Their subtle and learned mode of disputation, or that which was practised in their schools of philosophy. (2.) A graceful and winning eloquence; the arts by which they sought to commend their sentiments, and to win others to their opinions. On this also the Greek rhetoricians greatly valued themselves, and this, probably, the false teachers endeavoured to imitate. (3.) That which is elegant and finished in literature, in style and composition. On this the Greeks greatly valued themselves, as the Jews did on miracles and wonders; comp. ver. 22. The apostle means to say, that the success of the gospel did not depend on these things; that he had not sought them; nor had he exhibited them in his preaching. His doctrine and his manner had not been such as to appear wise to the Greeks; and he had not depended on eloquence or philosophy for his success. Longinus (on the Sublime) enumerates Paul among men distinguished for eloquence; but it is probable that he was not distinguished for the graces of *manner* (comp. 2 Cor. x. 1. 10), so much as the strength and power of his reasoning.

Paul here introduces a *new* subject of discourse, which he pursues through this and the two following chapters—the effect of philosophy on the gospel, or the estimate which ought to be formed in regard to it. The *reasons* why he introduces this topic, and dwells upon it at such a length, are not perfectly apparent. They are supposed to have been the following. (1.) He had incidentally mentioned his own preaching, and his having been set apart particularly to that; verse 17. (2.) His authority, it is probable, had been called in question by the false teachers at Corinth. (3.) The ground of this, or the reason why they undervalued him, had been probably, that he had not evinced the eloquence of manner and the graces of oratory on which they so much valued themselves. (4.) They had depended for their success on captivating the Greeks by the charms of graceful rhetoric and the refinements of subtle argumentation. (5.) In every way, therefore, the deference paid to rhetoric and philosophy in the church, had tended to bring the pure gospel into disrepute; to produce faction; and to destroy the authority of the apostle. It was necessary, therefore, thoroughly to examine the subject, and to expose the real influence of the philosophy on which they placed so high a value. ¶ *Lest the cross of Christ.* The simple doctrine that Christ was crucified to make atonement for the sins of men. This was the peculiarity of the gospel; and on this doctrine the gospel depended for success in the world. ¶ *Should be made of none effect.* Should be rendered vain and ineffectual. That is, lest the success which might attend the preaching of the gospel should be attributed to the graces of eloquence, the charms of language, or the force of human argumentation, rather than to its true cause, the preaching of Christ crucified; or lest the *attempt* to recommend it by the charms of eloquence should divert the attention from the simple doctrines of the cross, and the preaching be really vain. The preaching of the gospel depends for its success on the simple power of its truths, borne by the Holy Spirit to the hearts of men; and not on the power of argumentation, and the charms of eloquence. To have adorned the gospel with the charms of Grecian rhetoric, would have obscured its wisdom and efficacy, just as the gilding of a diamond would destroy its brilliancy. True eloquence, and real learning and sound sense, are not to be regarded as valueless; but their use in preaching is to convey the truth with plainness; to fix the mind *on* the pure gospel; and to leave the conviction on the heart that this system is the power of God. The design of Paul here cannot be to condemn true eloquence and just reasoning, but to rebuke the vain parade, and the glittering ornaments, and dazzling rhetoric which were objects of so much esteem in Greece. A real belief of the gospel, a simple and natural statement of its sublime truths, will admit of, and prompt to, the most manly and noble kind of eloquence.

18 For the preaching of the cross is to them [a] that perish foolishness; but unto us which are saved it is the power [b] of God.

a 2 Cor.2.15. *b* Rom.1.16.

The highest powers of mind, and the most varied learning, may find ample scope for the illustration and the defence of the simple doctrines of the gospel of Christ. But it does not *depend* for its success on these, but on its pure and heavenly truths, borne to the mind by the agency of the Holy Spirit.

18. *For the preaching of the cross.* Greek, "the *word* (ὁ λόγος) of the cross;" *i. e.* the doctrine of the cross; or the doctrine which proclaims salvation only through the atonement which the Lord Jesus Christ made on the cross. This cannot mean that the statement that Christ died *as a martyr* on a cross, appears to be foolishness to men; because, if that was all, there would be nothing that would appear contemptible, or that would excite their opposition more than in the death of any other martyr. The statement that Polycarp, and Ignatius, and Paul, and Cranmer died as martyrs, does not appear to men to be foolishness, for it is a statement of an historical truth, and their death excites the high admiration of all men. And if, in the death of Jesus on the cross, there had been nothing more than a mere martyr's death, it would have been equally the object of admiration to all men. But the "preaching of he cross" must denote more than that; nd must mean, (1.) That Christ died as an atoning sacrifice for the sins of men, and that it was this which gave its peculiarity to his sufferings on the cross. (2.) That men can be reconciled to God, pardoned, and saved only by the merits and influence of this atoning sacrifice. ¶ *To them that perish* (τοις μεν απολλυμενοις). To those who are about to perish, or to those who have a character fitting them for destruction; *i. e.* to the wicked. The expression stands in contrast with those who are "saved," *i. e.* those who have seen the beauty of the cross of Christ, and who have fled to it for salvation. ¶ *Foolishness.* Folly. That is, it appears to them to be contemptibie and foolish, or unworthy of belief. To the great mass of the Jews, and to the heathen philosophers, and indeed, to the majority of the men of this world, it has ever appeared foolishness, for the following reasons. (1.) The humble origin of the Lord Jesus. They despise him that lived in Nazareth; that was poor; that had no home, and few friends, and no wealth, and little honour among his own countrymen. (2.) They despise him who was put to death, as an impostor, at the instigation of his own countrymen, in an ignominious manner on the cross—the usual punishment of slaves. (3.) They see not why there should be any particular efficacy in his death. They deem it incredible that he who could not save himself should be able to save them: and that glory should come from the ignominy of the cross. (4.) They are blind to the true beauty of his personal character; to the true dignity of his nature; to his power over the sick, the lame, the dying, and the dead; they see not the bearing of the work of atonement on the law and government of God; they believe not in his resurrection, and his present state of exalted glory. The world looks only at the fact, that the despised man of Nazareth was put to death on a cross, and smiles at the idea that such a death could have any important influence on the salvation of man.—It is worthy of remark, also, that to the ancient philosophers this doctrine would appear still more contemptible than it does to the men of these times. Every thing that came from Judea, they looked upon with contempt and scorn; and they would spurn above all things else the doctrine that they were to expect salvation only by the crucifixion of a Jew. Besides, the account of the crucifixion has now lost to us no small part of its reputation of ignominy. Even around the cross there is conceived to be no small amount of honour and glory. There is now a sacredness

19 For it is written, [a] I will destroy the wisdom of the wise, and will bring to nothing the understanding of the prudent

a Isa.29.14; Jer.8.9.

about it from religious associations; and a reverence which men in Christian lands can scarcely help feeling when they think of it. But to the ancients it was connected with every idea of ignominy. It was the punishment of slaves, impostors, and vagabonds; and had even a greater degree of disgrace attached to it than the gallows has with us. With them, therefore, the death on the cross was associated with the idea of all that is shameful and dishonourable; and to speak of salvation only by the sufferings and death of a crucified man, was fitted to excite in their bosoms only unmingled scorn. ¶ *But unto us which are saved.* This stands opposed to "them that perish." It refers, doubtless, to Christians, as being *saved* from the power and condemnation of sin; and as having a prospect of eternal salvation in the world to come. ¶ *It is the power of God.* See Note, Rom. i. 16. This may either mean that the gospel is called "the power of God," because it is the *medium* through which God exerts his power in the salvation of sinners; or, the gospel is adapted to the condition of man, and is efficacious in renewing him and sanctifying him. It is not an inert, inactive letter, but is so fitted to the understanding, the heart, the hopes, the fears of men, and all their great constitutional principles of action, that it actually overcomes their sin, and diffuses peace through the soul. This efficacy is not unfrequently attributed to the gospel. John xvii. 17; Heb. iv. 12; Jam. i. 18; 1 Pet. i. 22, 23.—When the gospel, however, or the preaching of the cross, is spoken of as effectual or powerful, it must be understood of all the agencies which are connected with it; and does not refer to simple, abstract propositions, but to the truth as it comes attended with the influences which God sends down to accompany it. It includes, therefore, the promised agency of the Holy Spirit, without which it would not be effectual. But the agency of the Spirit is designed to give efficacy to that which is *really adapted* to produce the effects, and not to act in an arbitrary manner. All the effects of the gospel on the soul—in regeneration, repentance, faith, sanctification;—in hope, love, joy, peace, patience, temperance, purity, and devotedness to God, are only such *as the gospel is fitted to produce.* It has a set of truths and promises just *adapted* to each of these effects; just fitted to the soul by him who knows it; and adapted to *produce* just these results. The Holy Spirit secures their influence on the mind; and is the grand living agent of accomplishing just what the truth of God is *fitted originally* to produce. Thus the preaching of the cross is "the power of God;" and every minister may present it with the assurance that he is presenting, not "a cunningly devised fable," but a system *really fitted* to save men; and yet, that its reception by the human mind depends on the promised presence of the Holy Spirit.

19. *For it is written.* This passage is quoted from Isa. xxix. 14. The Hebrew of the passage, as rendered in the English version is, "the wisdom of their wise *men* shall perish, and the understanding of their prudent *men* shall be hid." The version of the LXX. is, "I will destroy the wisdom of the wise, and the understanding of the prudent I will hide" (κρύψω), corresponding substantially with the quotation by Paul. The sense in the Hebrew is not materially different. The meaning of the passage as used by Isaiah is, that such was the iniquity and stupidity of "Ariel" (Isa. xxix. 1), that is, Jerusalem, that God would so execute his judgments as to confound their wise men, and overwhelm those who boasted of their understanding. Those in whom they had confided, and on whom they relied, should appear to be bereft of their wisdom; and they should be made conscious of their own want of coun-

20 Where [a] *is* the wise? where *is* the scribe? where *is* the disputer of this world? hath not God made foolish [b] the wisdom of this world?

a Isa.33.18. *b* Isa.44.25.

sel to meet and remove the impending calamities. The apostle does not affirm that this passage in Isaiah refers to the times of the gospel. The contrary is manifestly true. But it expresses a general principle of the divine administration—*that the coming forth of God is often such as to confound human prudence; in a manner which human wisdom would not have devised; and in such a way as to show that he is not dependent on the wisdom of man.* As such, the sentiment is applicable to the gospel; and expresses just the idea which the apostle wished to convey—that the wisdom of the wise should be confounded by the plan of God; and the schemes of human devising be set at naught. ¶ *I will destroy.* That is, I will abolish; or will not be dependent on it; or will show that my plans are not derived from the counsels of men. ¶ *The wisdom of the wise.* The professed wisdom of philosophers. ¶ *And will bring to nothing.* Will show it to be of no value in this matter. ¶ *The prudent.* The men professing understanding; the sages of the world. We may remark, (1.) That the plan of salvation was not the contrivance of human wisdom. (2.) It is *unlike* what men have themselves devised as systems of religion. It did not occur to the ancient philosophers; nor has it occurred to the modern. (3.) It may be expected to excite the opposition, the contempt, and the scorn of the wise men of this world; and the gospel makes its way usually, not with their friendship, but in the face of their opposition. (4.) Its success is such as to confound and perplex them. They despise it, and they see not its secret power; they witness its effects, but are unable to account for them. It has always been a question with philosophers why the gospel met with such success; and the various accounts which have been given of it by its enemies, show how much they have been embarrassed. The most elaborate part of Gibbon's "Decline and Fall of the Roman Empire," is contained in his attempt to state the causes of the early propagation of Christianity, in chap. xv. xvi.; and the obvious failure of the account shows how much the mind of the philosophic sceptic was embarrassed by the fact of the spread of Christianity. (5.) The reception of the gospel demands an humble mind; Mark x. 15. Men of good sense, of humble hearts, of childlike temper, embrace it; and they see its beauty, and are won by its loveliness, and controlled by its power. They give themselves to it; and find that it is fitted to save their souls. (6.) In this, Christianity is like all science. The discoveries in science are such as to confound the wise in their own conceits, and overthrow the opinions of the prudent, just as much as the gospel does, and thus show that both are from the same God—the God who delights to pour such a flood of truth on the mind as to overwhelm it in admiration of himself, and with the conviction of its own littleness. The profoundest theories in science, and the most subtle speculations of men of genius, in regard to the causes of things, are often overthrown by a few simple discoveries—and discoveries which are at first despised as much as the gospel is. The invention of the telescope by Galileo was to the theories of philosophers and astronomers, what the revelation of the gospel was to the systems of ancient learning, and the deductions of human wisdom. The one confounded the world as much as the other; and both were at first equally the object of opposition or contempt.

20. *Where* is *the wise?* Language similar to this occurs in Isa. xxxiii. 18, "Where is the scribe? where is the receiver? where is he that counted the towers?" Without designing to *quote* these words as having an original reference to the subject now under

21 For [a] after that, in the wisdom of God, the world by wisdom knew not God, it pleased God by the foolishness of

a Luke 10.21; Rom.1.20,22,28.

consideration, Paul uses them as any man does language where he finds words with which he or his readers are familiar, that will convey his meaning. A man familiar with the Bible, will naturally often make use of Scripture expressions in conveying his ideas. In Isaiah the passage refers to the deliverance of the people from the threatened invasion of Sennacherib. The 18th verse represents the people as meditating on the threatened terror of the invasion; and then in the language of exultation and thanksgiving at their deliverance, saying, "where is the wise man that laid the plan of destroying the nation? Where the Inspector General (see my Note on the passage in Isaiah), employed in arranging the forces? Where the receiver (marg. the *weigher*), the paymaster of the forces? Where the man that counted the towers of Jerusalem, and calculated on their speedy overthrow? All baffled and defeated; and their schemes have all come to naught." So the apostle uses the same language in regard to the boasted wisdom of the world in reference to salvation. It is all baffled, and is all shown to be of no value. ¶ *The wise* (σοφός). The sage. At first the Greek men of learning were called *wise men* (σοφοί), like the magicians of the East. They afterwards assumed a more *modest* appellation, and called themselves the *lovers of wisdom* (φιλοσοφοι), or *philosophers*. This was the name by which they were commonly known in Greece, in the time of Paul. ¶ *Where* is *the scribe?* (γραμματεύς). The scribe among the Jews was a learned man, originally employed in transcribing the law, but subsequently the term came to denote a learned man in general. Among the Greeks the word was used to denote a public notary; or a transcriber of the laws; or a secretary. It was a term, therefore, nearly synonymous with a man of learning; and the apostle evidently uses it in this sense in this place. Some have supposed that he referred to the Jewish men of learning here; but he probably had reference to the Greeks. ¶ *Where* is *the disputer of this world?* The acute and subtle sophist of this age. The word *disputer* (συζητητὴς), properly denotes one who *inquires* carefully into the causes and relations of things; one who is a subtle and abstruse investigator. It was applied to the ancient sophists and disputants in the Greek academies; and the apostle refers, doubtless, to them. The meaning is, that in all their professed investigations, in all their subtle and abstruse inquiries, they had failed of ascertaining the way in which man could be saved; and that God had devised a plan which had baffled all their wisdom, and in which their philosophy was disregarded. The term *world*, here (αἰῶνος), refers, probably, not to the world as a physical structure—though Grotius supposes that it does—but to that *age*—the disputer of that *age*, or generation—an age eminently wise and learned. ¶ *Hath not God made foolish*, &c. That is, has he not by the originality and superior efficacy of his plan of salvation, poured contempt on all the schemes of philosophers, and evinced their folly? Not only without the aid of those schemes of men, but in opposition to them, he has devised a plan for human salvation that evinces its efficacy and its wisdom in the conversion of sinners, and in destroying the power of wickedness. Paul here, possibly, had reference to the language in Isa. xliv. 25. God "turneth wise men backward, and maketh their knowledge foolish."

21. *For after that* (ἐπειδὴ). Since, or seeing that it is true that the world by wisdom knew not God. After all the experience of the world it was ascertained that men would never by their own wisdom come to the true knowledge of God, and it pleased him to devise another plan for salvation.

preaching to save them that believe.

22 For the Jews require a sign[a] and the Greeks seek after wisdom:

a Mat.12.38.&c.

¶ *In the wisdom of God.* This phrase is susceptible of two interpretations. (1.) The first makes it refer to "the wisdom of God" evinced in the works of creation—the demonstration of his existence and attributes found there, and, according to that, the apostle means to say, that the world by a survey of the works of God did not know him; or were, notwithstanding those works, in deep darkness. This interpretation is adopted by most commentators—by Lightfoot, Rosenmüller, Grotius, Calvin, &c. According to this interpretation, the word ἐν (*in*) is to be translated *by* or *through*. (2.) A second interpretation makes it refer to the wise arrangement or government of God, by which this was permitted. "For when, by the wise arrangement or government of God; after a full and fair trial of the native, unaided powers of man, it was ascertained that the true knowledge of God would not be arrived at by man, it pleased him," &c. This appears to be the correct interpretation, because it is the most obvious one, and because it suits the connection best. It is, according to this, a *reason* why God introduced a new method of saving men. This may be said to have been accomplished by a plan of God, which was *wise*, because, (1.) It was desirable that the powers of man should be *fully tried* before the new plan was introduced, in order to show that it was not dependent on human wisdom, that it was not originated by man, and that there was really need of such an interposition. (2.) Because *sufficient time* had been furnished to make the experiment. An opportunity had been given for four thousand years, and still it had failed. (3.) Because the experiment had been made in the most favourable circumstances. The human faculties had had time to ripen and expand; one generation had had an opportunity of profiting by the observation of its predecessor; and the most mighty minds had been brought to bear on the subject. If the sages of the east, and the profound philosophers of the west, had not been able to come to the true knowledge of God, it was in vain to hope that more profound minds could be brought to bear on it, or that more careful investigation would be bestowed on it. The experiment had been fairly made, and the result was before the world; see Notes on Rom. i. ¶ *The world.* The men of the world; particularly the philosophers of the world. ¶ *By wisdom.* By their own wisdom, or by the united investigations of the works of nature. ¶ *Knew not God.* Obtained not a true knowledge of him. Some denied his existence; some represented him under the false and abominable forms of idol worship; some ascribed to him horrid attributes; *all* showed that they had no true acquaintance with a God of purity, with a God who could pardon sin, or whose worship conduced to holiness of life; see Notes, Rom. i. ¶ *It pleased God.* God was disposed, or well pleased. The plan of salvation originated in his good pleasure, and was such as his wisdom approved. God *chose* this plan, so unlike all the plans of men. ¶ *By the foolishness of preaching.* Not "by foolish preaching," but by the preaching of the cross, which was regarded as foolish and absurd by the men of the world. The plan is wise, but it has been esteemed by the mass of men, and was particularly so esteemed by the Greek philosophers, to be egregiously foolish and ridiculous; see Note, ver. 18. ¶ *To save them that believe.* That believe in the Lord Jesus Christ; see Note, Mark xvi. 16. This was the peculiarity and essence of the plan of God, and this has appeared to the mass of men to be a plan devoid of wisdom and unworthy of God. The preaching of the cross which is thus esteemed foolishness, is made the means of saving them, because it sets forth God's only plan of mercy, and states the way in which lost sinners may become reconciled to God.

23 But we preach Christ crucified, unto the Jews a stumbling-block, [a] and unto the Greeks foolishness;

a Isa. 8.14; 1 Pet. 2.8.

22. *For the Jews require a sign.* A miracle, a prodigy, an evidence of divine interposition. This was the characteristic of the Jewish people. God had manifested himself to them by miracles and wonders in a remarkable manner in past times, and they greatly prided themselves on that fact, and always demanded it when any new messenger came to them, professing to be sent from God. This propensity they often evinced in their intercourse with the Lord Jesus; Mat. xii. 38; xvi. 1; Mark viii. 11; Luke xi. 16; xii. 54—56. Many MSS., instead of "sign" here in the singular, read *signs* in the plural; and Griesbach has introduced that reading into the text. The sense is nearly the same, and it means that it was a characteristic of the Jews to demand the constant exhibition of miracles and wonders; and it is also implied here, I think, by the reasoning of the apostle, that they believed that the communication of such signs to them as a people, would secure their salvation, and they therefore despised the simple preaching of a crucified Messiah. They expected a Messiah that should come with the exhibition of some stupendous signs and wonders from heaven (Mat. xii. 38, &c., as above); they looked for the displays of amazing power in his coming, and they anticipated that he would deliver them from their enemies by mere power; and they, therefore, were greatly offended (ver. 23), by the simple doctrine of a crucified Messiah. ¶ *And the Greeks,* &c. Perhaps this means the heathen in general, in opposition to the Jews; Note, Rom. i. 16. It was, however, peculiarly the characteristic of the Greek philosophers. They seek for schemes of philosophy and religion that shall depend on human wisdom, and they therefore despise the gospel.

23. *But we.* We who are Christian preachers make Christ crucified the grand subject of our instructions and our aims in contradistinction from the Jew and the Greek. *They* seek, the one miracles, the other wisdom, *we* glory only in the cross. ¶ *Christ crucified.* The word Christ, the anointed, is the same as the Hebrew name Messiah. The *emphasis* in this expression is on the word *crucified.* The Jews would make the Messiah whom they expected no less an object of glorifying than the apostles, but they spurned the doctrine that he was to be *crucified.* Yet in that the apostles boasted; proclaiming him crucified, or *having been crucified* as the only hope of man. This must mean more than that Christ was distinguished for moral worth, more than that he died as a martyr; because if that were all, no reason could be given why *the cross* should be made so prominent an object. It must mean that Christ was crucified for the sins of men, as an atoning sacrifice in the place of sinners. "We proclaim a crucified Messiah as the only redeemer of lost men." ¶ *To the Jews a stumbling-block.* The word *stumbling-block* (σκάνδαλον) means properly any thing in the way over which one may fall; then any thing that gives offence, or that causes one to fall into sin. Here it means that to the Jews, the doctrine that the Messiah was to be crucified gave great offence; excited, irritated, and exasperated them; that they could not endure the doctrine, and treated it with scorn. Comp. Note, Rom. ix. 33; 1 Pet. ii. 8. It is well known that to the Jews no doctrine was more offensive than this, that the Messiah was to be put to death, and that there was to be salvation in no other way. It was so in the times of the apostles, and it has been so since. They have, therefore, usually called the Lord Jesus, by way of derision, תלוי *Tolvi, the man that was hanged,* that is, on a cross; and Christians they have usually denominated, for the same reason, עבדי תלוי *Abdai Tolvi,—servants of the man that was hanged.* The reasons of this feeling are obvious. (1.) They had looked

24 But unto them which are called, both Jews and Greeks, Christ the [a] power of God, and the wisdom of God.

a ver. 18.

for a magnificent temporal prince; but the doctrine that their Messiah was crucified, dashed all their expectations. And they regarded it with contempt and scorn, just in proportion as their hopes had been elevated, and these high expectations cherished. (2.) They had the common feelings of all men, the native feelings of pride, and self-righteousness, by which they rejected the doctrine that we are dependent for salvation on one who was crucified. (3.) They regarded Jesus as one given over by God for an enormous attempt at imposition, as having been justly put to death; and the object of the curse of the Almighty. Isa. liii. 4, "We did esteem him stricken, *smitten* OF GOD." They endeavoured to convince themselves that he was the object of the divine dereliction and abhorrence; and they, therefore, rejected the doctrine of the cross with the deepest feelings of detestation. ¶ *To the Greeks.* To the Gentiles in general. So the Syriac, the Vulgate, the Arabic, and the Æthiopic versions all read it. The term *Greek* denotes all who were not Jews; thus the phrase, "the Jews and the Greeks" comprehended the whole human family, ver. 22. ¶ *Foolishness.* See Note on ver. 18. They regarded it as folly, (1.) Because they esteemed the whole account a fable, and an imposition; (2.) It did not accord with their own views of the way of elevating the condition of man; (3.) They saw no efficacy in the doctrine, no tendency in the statement that a man of humble birth was put to death in an ignominious manner in Judea, to make men better, or to receive pardon. (4.) They had the common feelings of unrenewed human nature; blind to the beauty of the character of Christ, and blind to the design of his death; and they therefore regarded the whole statement as folly. We may remark here, that the feelings of the Jews and of the Greeks on this subject, are the common feelings of men. Everywhere sinners have the same views of the cross; and everywhere the human heart, if left to itself, rejects it, as either a stumbling-block, or as folly. But the doctrine should be preached, though it is an offence, and though it appears to be folly. It is the only hope of man; and by the preaching of the cross alone can sinners be saved.

24. *But unto them which are called.* To all true Christians. Note, ver. 9. ¶ *Both Jews and Greeks.* Whether originally of Jewish or Gentile extraction, they have here a common, similar view of the crucified Saviour. ¶ *Christ the power of God.* Christ *appears* to them as the power of God; or it is through him that the power of salvation is communicated to them. Note, ver. 18. ¶ *And the wisdom of God.* The way in which God evinces *his* wisdom in the salvation of men. They see the plan to be *wise.* They see that it is adapted to the end. They see it to be fitted to procure pardon, and sanctification, and eternal life. It is God's wise plan for the salvation of men; and it is *seen* by those who are Christians, to be *adapted* to this end. They see that there is a beauty in his character; an excellency in his doctrines; and an efficacy in his atonement, to secure their salvation.—We may remark on this verse, (1.) That when men become Christians, their hearts are changed. The views of Christians are here represented as diametrically opposite to those of other men. To one class, Christ is a stumbling-block; to others, folly; to Christians he is full of beauty. But those views of the Christian, can be obtained only by a change of heart. And the change from regarding an object or being as *foolishness* to regarding it as full of beauty, must be a radical and a mighty change. (2.) All Christians have similar views of the Saviour. It matters not whether they were Jew or Greek; it matters not whether they were born in a northern or southern clime—"whether an Indian or an African sun has burned upon them;" whether they speak the same or different languages; whether they were born amidst the same or different

25 Because the foolishness of God is wiser than men; and the weakness of God is stronger than men.

---

denominations of Christians; whether in the same or different countries; or whether they are men in the same or different Christian communities, they have the same views of the Saviour. They see him to be the power and the wisdom of God. They are united in him, and therefore united to each other; and should regard themselves as belonging to the same family, and as bound to the same eternal home. (3.) There is *real efficacy* in the plan of salvation. It is a scheme of power. It is adapted to the end, and is admirably fitted to accomplish the great effects which God designs to accomplish. It is not a scheme intended to show its own imbecility, and the need of another and an independent agent to accomplish the work. All the effects which the Holy Ghost produces on the soul, are such, and *only* such, as the truth of the gospel is *adapted* to produce in the mind. The gospel is God's plan of putting forth *power* to save men. It seizes upon great elements in human nature; and is adapted to enlist them in the service of God. It is just *fitted* to man as a being capable of reasoning and susceptible of emotion; as a being who may be influenced by hope and fear; who may be excited and impelled to duty by conscience, and who may be roused from a state of lethargy and sin by the prospect of eternal life, and the apprehension of eternal death. *As such* it should always be preached —as a system *wise*, and *adapted* to the great end in view, as a system most powerful, and "mighty to the pulling down of strong holds."

25. *Because the foolishness of God.* That which God appoints, requires, commands, does, &c., which appears to men to be foolish. The passage is not to be understood as affirming that it is *really* foolish or unwise: but that it appears so to men.—Perhaps the apostle here refers to those parts of the divine administration where the wisdom of the plan is not seen; or where the reason of what God does is concealed. ¶ *Is wiser than men.* Is better adapted to accomplish important ends, and more certainly effectual than the schemes of human wisdom. This is especially true of the plan of salvation—a plan apparently foolish to the mass of men—yet indubitably accomplishing more for the renewing of men, and for their purity and happiness, than all the schemes of human contrivance. They have accomplished nothing towards men's salvation; this accomplishes every thing. They have always failed; this never fails. ¶ *The weakness of God.* There is really no weakness in God, any more than there is folly. This must mean, therefore, the things of his appointment which *appear* weak and insufficient to accomplish the end. Such are these facts—that God should seek to save the world by Jesus of Nazareth, who was supposed unable to save himself (Mat. xxvii. 40—43); and that he should expect to save men by the gospel, by its being preached by men who were without learning, eloquence, wealth, fame, or power. The instruments were feeble; and men judged that this was owing to the weakness or want of power in the God who appointed them. ¶ *Is stronger than men.* Is able to accomplish more than the utmost might of man. The feeblest agency that God puts forth—so feeble as to be esteemed weakness—is able to effect more than the utmost might of man. The apostle here refers particularly to the work of redemption; but it is true every where. We may remark, (1.) That God often effects his mightiest plans by that which seems to men to be weak and even foolish. The most mighty revolutions arise often from the slightest causes; his most vast operations are often connected with very feeble means. The revolution of empires; the mighty effects of the pestilence; the advancement in the sciences, and arts, and the operations of nature, are often brought about by means apparently as little fitted to accomplish the work as those which are employed in the plan of redemption. (2.) God is great. If his feeb-

26 For ye see your calling, brethren, how that not [a] many wise men
after the flesh, not many mighty
not many noble, *are called:*

a Zeph.3.12; John 7.48.

lest powers put forth, surpass the mightiest powers of man, how great must be his might. If the powers of man who rears works of art; who levels mountains and elevates vales; if the power which reared the pyramids, be as nothing when compared with the feeblest putting forth of divine power, how ighty must be his arm! How vast that strength which made, and which upholds the rolling worlds! How safe are his people in his hand! And how easy for him to crush all his foes in death!

26. *For ye see your calling.* You know the general character and condition of those who are Christians among you, that they have not been generally taken from the wise, the rich, and the learned, but from humble life. The design of the apostle here is, to show that the gospel did not depend for its success on human wisdom. His argument is, that *in fact* those who were blessed by it had not been of the elevated ranks of life mainly, but that God had shown his power by choosing those who were ignorant, and vicious, and abandoned, and by reforming and purifying their lives. The verb "ye see" (βλέπετε), is ambiguous, and may be either in the indicative mood, as our translators have rendered it, "ye do see; you are well apprised of it, and know it," or it may be in the imperative, "see; contemplate your condition;" but the sense is substantially the same. -*Your calling* (τὴν κλῆσιν) means 'those who are called" (ver. 9); as "the circumcision" means those who are circumcised. Rom. iii. 30. The ense is, "look upon the condition of those who are Christians." ¶ *Not many wise men.* Not many who are regarded as wise; or who are ranked with philosophers. This supposes that there were *some* of that description, though the mass of Christians were then, as now, from more humble ranks of life. That there were *some* of high rank and wealth at Corinth who became Christians, is well known. Crispus and Sosthenes, rulers of the synagogue there (Acts xviii, 8, 17; Comp. 1 Cor i. 1); Gaius, a rich, hospitable man (Rom. xvi. 23); and Erastus the chancellor of the city of Corinth (Rom xvi. 23), had been converted and were members of the church. Some have supposed (*Macknight*) that this should be rendered "not many mighty, wise. &c. *call you;* that is, God has not employed the wise and the learned *to call* you into his kingdom." But the sense in our translation is evidently the correct interpretation. It is the *obvious* sense; and it agrees with the design of the apostle, which was to show that God had not consulted the wisdom, and power, and wealth of men in the establishment of his church. So the Syriac and the Vulgate render it. ¶ *According to the flesh.* According to the maxims and principles of a sensual and worldly policy; according to the views of men when under the influence of those principles; *i. e.* who are unrenewed. The flesh here stands opposed to the spirit; the views of the men of this world in contradistinction from the wisdom that is from above. ¶ *Not many mighty.* Not many men of power; or men sustaining important *offices* in the state. Comp, Rev. vi. 15. The word may refer to those who wield power of any kind, whether derived from office, from rank, from wealth, &c. ¶ *Not many noble.* Not many of illustrious birth, or descended from illustrious families—εὐγενεῖς, *well-born.* In respect to each of these classes, the apostle does not say that there were *no* men of wealth, and power, and birth, but that the mass or body of Christians was not composed of such. They were made up of those who were in humble life. There were a few, indeed, of rank and property, as there are now; but then, as now, the great mass was composed of those who were from the lower conditions of society. The reason why God had chosen his people from that rank is stated in ver. 29.—The character of many of those who

27 But God [a] hath chosen the foolish things of the world, to confound the wise; and God hath chosen the weak things of the world, to confound the things which are mighty;

28 And base things of the world, and things which are de-

a Ps.8.2; Mat.11.25.

composed the church at Corinth before the conversion, is stated in chap. vi. 9—11, which see.

27. *But God hath chosen.* The fact of their being in the church at all was the result of his choice. It was owing entirely to his grace. ¶ *The foolish things.* The things esteemed foolish among men. The expression here refers to those who were destitute of learning, rank, wealth, and power, and who were esteemed as fools, and were despised by the rich and the great. ¶ *To confound.* To bring to shame; or that he might make them ashamed; *i. e.* humble them by showing them how little he regarded their wisdom; and how little their wisdom contributed to the success of his cause. By thus overlooking them, and bestowing his favours on the humble and the poor; by choosing his people from the ranks which they despised, and bestowing on them the exalted privilege of being called the sons of God, he had poured dishonour on the rich and the great, and overwhelmed them, and their schemes of wisdom, with shame. It is also true, that those who are regarded as fools by the wise men of the world are able often to confound those who boast of their wisdom; and that the arguments of plain men, though unlearned except in the school of Christ; of men of sound common sense under the influence of Christian principles, have a force which the learning and talent of the men of this world cannot gainsay or resist. They have *truth* on their side; and truth, though dressed in a humble garb, is more mighty than error, though clothed with the brilliancy of imagination, the pomp of declamation, and the cunning of sophistry. ¶ *And the weak things.* Those esteemed weak by the men of the world. ¶ *The mighty.* The great; the noble; the learned.

28. *And base things of the world.* Those things which by the world are esteemed ignoble. Literally, those which are not of noble, or illustrious birth (τὰ ἀγενῆ). ¶ *Things which are despised.* Those which the world regards as objects of contempt; comp. Mark ix. 12; Luke xviii. 19; Acts iv. 11. ¶ Yea. The introduction of this word by the translators does nothing to illustrate the sense, but rather enfeebles it. The language here is a striking instance of Paul's manner of expressing himself with great strength. He desires to convey in the strongest terms, the fact, that God had illustrated his plan by choosing the objects of least esteem among men. He is willing to admit *all* that could be said on this point. He says, therefore, that he had chosen the things of ignoble birth and rank—the base things of the world; but this did not fully express his meaning. He had chosen objects of contempt among men; but this was not strong enough to express his idea. He adds, therefore, that he had chosen those things which were absolutely *nothing*, which had no existence; which could not be supposed to influence him in his choice. ¶ *And things which are not* (τὰ μὴ ὄντα). That which is nothing; which is worthless; which has no existence; those things which were below contempt itself; and which, in the estimation of the world, were passed by as having no existence; as not having sufficient importance to be esteemed worthy even of the slight notice which is implied in contempt. For a man who despises a thing must at least notice it, and esteem it worth *some* attention. But the apostle here speaks of things *beneath* even that slight notice; as completely and totally disregarded, as having no existence. The language here is evidently that of hyperbole (comp. Note, John xxi. 25). It was a figure

spised, hath God chosen, *yea*, and things which are not, to bring to naught things that are;

29 That [a] no flesh should glory in his presence.

30 But of him are ye in [b]

a Rom.3.27.

b 2 Cor.5.17; Eph.1.3,10.

of speech common in the East, and not unusual in the sacred writings; comp. Isa. xl. 17.

> All nations before him are as nothing
> And they are counted to him less than nothing and vanity.

See also Rom. iv. 17, "God, who—calleth those things which be not, as though they were." This language was strongly expressive of the estimate which the Jews fixed on the Gentiles, as being a despised people, as being in fact *no* people; a people without laws, and organization, and religion, and privileges; see Hos. i. 10; ii. 23; Rom. ix. 25; 1 Pet. ii. 10. "When a man of rank among the Hindoos speaks of low-caste persons, of notorious profligates, or of those whom he despises, he calls them *alla-tha-varkal, i. e. those who are not.* The term does not refer to life or existence, but to a quality or disposition, and is applied to those who are vile and abominable in all things. "My son, my son, go not among them *who are not.*" "Alas! alas! those people are all *alla-tha-varkal.*" When wicked men prosper, it is said, "this is the time for those *who are not.*" "Have you heard that those *who are not* are now acting righteously?" Vulgar and indecent expressions are also called, "words that are not." To address men in the phrase *are not*, is provoking beyond measure."—*Roberts*, as quoted in Bush's Illustrations of Scripture. ¶ *To bring to naught.* To humble and subdue. To show them how vain and impotent they were. ¶ *Things that are.* Those who on account of their noble birth, high attainments, wealth, and rank, placed a high estimate on themselves and despised others.

29. *That no flesh.* That no men; no class of men. The word *flesh* is often thus used to denote men. Mat. xxiv. 22; Luke iii. 6; John xvii. 2; Acts ii. 17; 1 Pet. i. 24, &c. ¶ *Should glory.* Should boast; Rom. iii. 27. ¶ *In his presence.* Before him. That man should *really* have nothing of which to boast; but that the whole scheme should be adapted to humble and subdue him. On these verses we may observe, (1.) That it is to be expected that the great mass of Christian converts will be found among those who are of humble life—and it may be observed also, that true virtue and excellence; sincerity and amiableness; honesty and sincerity, are usually found there also. (2.) That while the mass of Christians are found there, there *are* also those of noble birth, and rank, and wealth, who become Christians. The aggregate of those who from elevated ranks and distinguished talents have become Christians, has not been small. It is sufficient to refer to such names as Pascal, and Bacon, and Boyle, and Newton, and Locke, and Hale, and Wilberforce, to show that religion can command the homage of the most illustrious genius and rank. (3.) The *reasons* why those of rank and wealth do not become Christians, are many and obvious. (*a*) They are beset with peculiar temptations. (*b*) They are usually satisfied *with* rank and wealth, and do not feel their need of a hope of heaven. (*c*) They are surrounded with objects which flatter their vanity, which minister to their pride, and which throw them into the circle of alluring and tempting pleasures. (*d*) They are drawn away from the means of grace and the places of prayer, by fashion, by business, by temptation. (*e*) There is something about the pride of learning and philosophy, which usually makes those who possess it unwilling to sit at the feet of Christ; to acknowledge their dependence on any power; and to confess that they are poor, and needy, and blind, and naked before God. (4.) The gospel is designed to produce humility, and to place all men on a

Christ Jesus, who of God is made unto us [a] wisdom, and righteousness, [b] sanctification,[c] and redemption:[d]

a Eph.1.17; Col.2.3. b Isa.45.24; Jer.23.5,6; Rom.4.25. c John 17.19. d Eph.1.7.

level in regard to salvation. There is no royal way to the favour of God. No monarch is saved because he is a monarch; no philosopher because he is a philosopher; no rich man because he is rich; no poor man because he is poor. All are placed on a level. All are to be saved in the same way. All are to become willing to give the entire glory to God. All are to acknowledge him as providing the plan, and as furnishing the grace that is needful for salvation. God's design is to bring down the pride of man, and to produce everywhere a willingness to acknowledge *him* as the fountain of blessings and the God of all.

30. *But of him.* That is, by his agency and power. It is not by philosophy; not from ourselves; but by his mercy. The apostle keeps it prominently in view, that it was not of their philosophy, wealth, or rank that they had been raised to these privileges, but of God as the author. ¶ *Are ye.* Ye are what you are by the mercy of God. 1 Cor. xv. 10. You owe your hopes to him. The emphasis in this verse is to be placed on this expression, " are ye." You are Christians, not by the agency of man, but by the agency of God.

[See the supplementary Note on Rom. viii. 10, page 176.]

¶ *In Christ Jesus.* Note, ver. 4. By the medium, or through the work of Christ, this mercy has been conferred on you. ¶ *Who of God.* From God (ἀπὸ Θεοῦ). Christ is given to us *by* God, or appointed *by* him to be our wisdom, &c. God originated the scheme, and God gave him for this end. ¶ *Wisdom.* That is, he is to us the source of wisdom; it is by him that we are made wise. This cannot mean that his wisdom becomes strictly and properly ours; that it is set over to us, and reckoned as our own, for that is not true. But it must mean simply, that Christians have become *truly wise* by the agency, the teaching, and the work of Christ. Philosophers had attempted to become wise by their own investigations and inquiries. But Christians had become wise by the work of Christ; that is, it had been by his instructions that they had been made acquainted with the true character of God; with his law; with their own condition; and with the great truth that there was a glorious immortality beyond the grave. None of these truths had been obtained by the investigations of philosophers, but by the instructions of Christ. In like manner it was that through him they had been made practically wise unto salvation. Comp. Col. ii. 3, " In whom are hid all the treasures of wisdom and knowledge." He is the great agent by whom we become truly wise. Christ is often represented as eminently wise, and as the source of all true wisdom to his people. Isa. xi. 1; Mat. xiii. 54; Luke ii. 40, 52; 1 Cor. i. 24; iii. 10. " Ye are wise in Christ." Many commentators have supposed that the beautiful description of wisdom, in Prov. viii. is applicable to the Messiah. Christ may be said to be made wisdom to us, or to communicate wisdom, (1.) Because he has in his own ministry instructed us in the true knowledge of God, and of those great truths which pertain to our salvation. (2.) Because he has by his word and spirit led us to see our true situation, and made us "wise unto salvation." He has turned us from the ways of folly, and inclined us to walk in the path of true wisdom. (3.) Because he is to his people now the source of wisdom. He enlightens their mind in the time of perplexity; guides them in the way of truth; and leads them in the path of real knowledge. It often happens that obscure and ignorant men, who have been taught in the school of Christ, have more true and real knowledge of that which concerns their welfare, and evince more real practical wisdom, than can be learned in all the schools of philosophy and learning on the earth. It is wise for a sinful and dying creature to prepare for eternity. But none but those who are instructed by the Son of God, become thus wise. ¶ *And righteousness.* By whom we become righteous in the sight of God. This declaration simply affirms that we become righteous through him, as it is affirmed that we become wise, sanctified, and redeemed through him. But neither of the expressions determine any thing as to the *mode* by which it is done. The leading idea of the apostle, which should never be lost sight of, is that the Greeks by their philosophy did *not* become truly wise, righteous, sanctified, and redeemed; but that this was accomplished through Jesus Christ. But *in what way* this was done, or by what process or mode, is not here stated; and it should be no more *assumed* from this text that we became *righteous* by the imputation of Christ's righteousness, than it should be that we became wise by the *imputation* of his wisdom, and sanctified by the imputation of his holiness. If this passage would prove one of these points, it would prove all. But as it is absurd to say that we became wise by the imputation of the personal wisdom of Christ, so this passage should not be brought to prove that we became righteous by the imputation of his righteousness. Whatever may be the truth of that doctrine, this passage does not prove it.

[The same objection is advanced by Whitby. "They who say that Christ is made our righteousness by his righteousness imputed to us, have the same reason to say also, that he is made our wisdom, by his wisdom imputed to us,"—to which Mr. Scott has replied, that "there might be some weight in this objection, if this were the only passage of Scripture, by which those who hold imputed righteousness prove their doctrine; if there were any other passages in the sacred oracles which even seem to countenance the notion of imputed wisdom, &c.; and if the nature of the case were not essentially different. Another may pay my debt, and allow me to receive the wages which he has earned, or the reward to which his services entitle him; thus his payment and his labour may be set down to my account, or imputed to me for my adequate advantage. But who can have wisdom, health or liberty, by imputation?"—*Scott's Commentary.* For a full discussion of the doctrine of imputation, see the supplementary Notes on Rom. i. 17; iv. 3; v. 12, 21; pages 31, 96, 114.]

By turning to other parts of the New Testament to learn in what way we are made righteous through Christ, or in what way he is made unto us righteousness; we learn that it is in two modes, (1.) Because it is by his merits alone that our sins are pardoned, and we are justified, and treated as righteous (see Note, Rom. iii. 26, 27); and (2.) Because by his influence, and work, and Spirit, and truth, we are made personally holy in the sight of God. The former is doubtless the thing intended here, as sanctification is specified after. The apostle here refers simply to the *fact*, without specifying the *mode* in which it is done. That is to be learned from other parts of the New Testament. Comp. Note, Rom. iv. 25. The doctrine of justification is, that God regards and treats those as righteous who believe on his Son, and who are pardoned on account of what he has done and suffered. The several steps in the process may be thus stated. (1.) The sinner is by nature exposed to the wrath of God. He is lost and ruined. He has no merit of his own. He has violated a holy law, and that law condemns him, and he has no power to make an atonement or reparation. He can never be pronounced a *just* man on his own merits. He can never *vindicate* his conduct, as a man can do in a court of justice where he is unjustly accused, and so be pronounced just. (2.) Jesus Christ has taken the sinner's place, and died in his stead. He has honoured a broken law; he has rendered it consistent for God to pardon. By his dreadful sufferings, endured in the sinner's place, God has shown his hatred of sin, and his willingness to forgive. His truth will be vindicated, and his law honoured, and his government secured, if now he shall pardon the offender when penitent. As he endured these sorrows for others, and not for himself, they can be *so* reckoned, and *are* so judged by God. All the *benefits* or *results* of that atonement, therefore, as it was made for others, can be applied to

31 That, according as it is written, [a] He that glorieth, let him glory in the Lord.

[a] Jer.9.23,24.

---

them, and all the advantage of such substitution in their place, can be made over to them, as really as when a man pays a note of hand for a friend; or when he pays for another a ransom. The price is reckoned *as* paid for them, and the *benefits* flow to the debtor and the captive. It is not reckoned that *they* paid it, for that is not true; but that it was done *for* them, and the benefit may be theirs, which *is* true. (3.) God has been pleased to promise that these benefits may be conferred on him who believes in the Saviour. The sinner is *united* by faith to the Lord Jesus, and is so adjudged, or reckoned. God *esteems* or judges him to be a believer according to the promise. And so believing, and so repenting, he deems it consistent to pardon and justify him who is so united to his Son by faith. He is justified, not by the *act* of faith; not by any merits of his own, but by the merits of Christ. He has no other ground, and no other hope. Thus he is *in fact* a pardoned and justified man; and God so reckons and judges. God's law is honoured, and the sinner is pardoned and saved; and it is now as consistent for God to treat him as a righteous man, as it would be if he had never sinned—since there is as high honour shown to the law of God, as there would have been had he been personally obedient, or had he personally suffered its penalty. And as, through the death of Christ, the same *results* are secured in upholding God's moral government as would be by his condemnation, it is *consistent* and *proper* for God to forgive him and treat him as a righteous man; and to do so accords with the infinite benevolence of his heart. ¶ *And sanctification.* By him we are sanctified or made holy. This does not mean, evidently, that his personal holiness is reckoned to us, but that by his work applied to our hearts, we become personally sanctified or holy. Comp. Eph. iv. 24. This is done by the agency of his Spirit applying *truth* to the mind (John xvii. 19), by the aid which he furnishes in trials, temptations, and conflicts, and by the influence of hope in sustaining, elevating and purifying the soul. All the *truth* that is employed to sanctify, was taught primarily by him; and all the *means* that may be used are the purchase of his death, and are under his direction; and the Spirit by whose agency Christians are sanctified, was sent into the world by him, and in answer to his prayers. John xiv. 16; xv. 26. ¶ *And redemption* (ἀπολύτρωσις). For the meaning of this word, see Note, Rom. iii. 24. Here it is evidently used in a larger sense than it is commonly in the New Testament. The things which are specified above, "justification and sanctification," are a part of the work of redemption. Probably the word is used here in a wide sense, as denoting the whole *group*, or class of influences by which we are brought at last to heaven; so that the apostle refers not only to his atonement, but to the work by which we are *in fact* redeemed from death, and made happy in heaven. Thus in Rom. viii. 23, the word is applied to the resurrection, "the *redemption* of the body." The sense is, "it is by Christ that we are redeemed; by him that an atonement is made; by him that we are pardoned; by him that we are delivered from the dominion of sin, and the power of our enemies; and by him that we shall be rescued from the grave, and raised up to everlasting life." Thus the whole work depends on him; and no part of it is to be ascribed to the philosophy, the talent, or the wisdom of men. He does not merely *aid* us; he does not complete that which is imperfect; he does not come in to do a part of the work, or to supply our defects; but it is *all* to be traced to him. See Col. ii. 10, "And ye are complete in him."

31. *As it is written.* This is evidently a quotation made from Jer. ix 23, 24. It is not made literally; but the apostle has *condensed* the sense of the prophet into a few words, and

CHAPTER II.

AND I, brethren, when I came to you, came not [a] with excellency of speech or of wisdom, declaring unto you the testimony of God.

[a] ver. 4, 13.

has retained essentially his idea. ¶ *He that glorieth.* He that boasts or exults. ¶ *In the Lord.* Not ascribing his salvation to human abilities, or learning, or rank, but entirely to God. And from this we see, (1.) That the design of the plan of salvation is to exalt God in view of the mind. (2.) That the design is to make us humble; and this is the design also of all his works no less than of the plan of salvation. All just views of the creation tend to produce true humility. (3.) It is an evidence of piety when we are thus disposed to exalt God, and to be humble. It shows that the heart is changed; and that we are truly disposed to honour him. (4.) We may rejoice in God. We have no strength, and no righteousness of which to boast; but we may rejoice in him. He is full of goodness and mercy. He is able to save us. He can redeem us out of the hand of all our enemies. And when we are conscious that we are poor, and feeble, and helpless; when oppressed with a sense of sin, we may rejoice in him as *our* God; and exult in him as *our* Saviour and Redeemer. True piety will delight to come and lay every thing at his feet; and whatever may be our rank, or talent, or learning, we shall rejoice to come with the temper of the humblest child of poverty, and sorrow, and want, and to say, "not unto us, not unto us, but unto thy name give glory for thy mercy, and for thy truth's sake," Ps. cxv. 1.

"Not to our names, thou only just and true,
Not to our worthless names is glory due;
Thy power and grace, thy truth and justice claim
Immortal honours to thy sovereign name."
Watts.

CHAPTER II.

THE design of this chapter is the same as the concluding part of chap. i. (ver. 17—31), to show that the gospel does not depend for its success on human wisdom, or the philosophy of men. This position the apostle further confirms, (1.) ver. 1—5, By a reference to his own example, as having been successful among them, and yet not endowed with the graces of elocution, or by a commanding address; yet (2.) Lest it should be thought that the gospel was real folly, and should be contemned, he shows in the remainder of the chapter (ver. 6—16), that it contained *true* wisdom; that it was a profound scheme—rejected, indeed, by the men of the world, but *seen* to be wise by those who were made acquainted with its real nature and value, ver. 5—16.

The first division of the chapter (ver. 1—5), is a continuation of the argument to show that the success of the gospel does not depend on human wisdom or philosophy. This he proves, (1.) By the fact that when he was among them, though his preaching was attended with success, yet he did not come with the attractions of human eloquence, ver. 1. (2.) This was in accordance with his purpose, not designing to attempt any thing like that, but having another object, ver. 2. (3.) In fact he had *not* evinced that, but the contrary, ver. 3, 4. (4.) His *design* was that their conversion should not *appear* to have been wrought by human wisdom or eloquence, but to have been manifestly the work of God, ver. 5.

1. *And I, brethren.* Keeping up the tender and affectionate style of address. ¶ *When I came unto you.* When I came at first to preach the gospel at Corinth. Acts xviii. 1, &c. ¶ *Came not with excellency of speech.* Came not with graceful and attractive eloquence. The apostle here evidently alludes to that nice and studied choice of language; to those gracefully formed sentences, and to that skill of arrangement in discourse and argument which was so much an object of regard with the Greek rhetoricians. It is probable that Paul

2 For I determined not to know any thing among you, save [a] Jesus Christ, and him crucified.

3 And I was with you in weakness, and in fear, and in much trembling.

[a] Gal.6.14.

was never much distinguished for these (comp. 2 Cor. x. 10), and it is certain he never made them an object of intense study and solicitude. Comp. ver. 4, 13. ¶ *Or of wisdom.* Of the wisdom of this world; of that kind of wisdom which was sought and cultivated in Greece. ¶ *The testimony of God.* The testimony or the witnessing which God has borne to the gospel of Christ by miracles, and by attending it everywhere with his presence and blessing. In ver. 6, the gospel is called "the testimony of Christ;" and here it may either mean the witness which the gospel bears to the true character and plans of God; or the witnessing which God had borne to the gospel by miracles, &c. The gospel contains the testimony of God in regard to his own character and plans; especially in regard to the great plan of redemption through Jesus Christ. Several MSS. instead of "testimony of God," here read "the mystery of God." This would accord well with the scope of the argument; but the present reading is probably the correct one. See *Mill.* The Syriac version has also *mystery.*

2. *For I determined.* I made a resolution. This was my fixed, deliberate purpose when I came there. It was not a matter of accident, or chance, that I made Christ my great and constant theme, but it was my deliberate purpose. It is to be recollected that Paul made this resolution, knowing the peculiar fondness of the Greeks for subtle disquisitions, and for graceful and finished elocution; that he formed it when his own mind, as we may judge from his writings, was strongly inclined by nature to an abstruse and metaphysical kind of discussion, which could not have failed to attract the attention of the acute and subtle reasoners of Greece; and that he made it when he must have been fully aware that the theme which he had chosen to dwell upon would be certain to excite derision and contempt. Yet he formed, and adhered to this resolution, though it might expose him to contempt; and though they might reject and despise his message. ¶ *Not to know.* The word *know* here (εἰδέναι) is used probably in the sense of *attend to, be engaged in,* or *regard.* I resolved not to give my time and attention while among you to the laws and traditions of the Jews; to your orators, philosophers, and poets; to the beauty of your architecture or statuary; to a contemplation of your customs and laws, but to *attend* to this only—making known the cross of Christ. The word (εἴδω) to know, is sometimes thus used. Paul says that he designed that this should be the only thing on which his mind should be fixed; the only object of his attention; the only object on which he there sought that knowledge should be diffused. Doddridge renders it "appear to know." ¶ *Any thing among you.* Any thing while I was with you. Or, any thing that may exist among you, and that may be objects of interest to you. I resolved to know nothing of it, whatever it might be. The former is, probably, the correct interpretation. ¶ *Save Jesus Christ.* Except Jesus Christ. This is the only thing of which I purposed to have any knowledge among you. ¶ *And him crucified.* Or, "*even* (καὶ) him that was crucified." He resolved not only to make the *Messiah* the grand object of his knowledge and attention there, but EVEN a *crucified* Messiah; to maintain the doctrine that the Messiah *was to be* crucified for the sins of the world; and that he who *had been* crucified was *in fact* the Messiah. See Note, chap. i. 23. We may remark here, (1.) That this should be the resolution of every minister of the gospel. This is *his* business. It is not to be a politician; not to engage in the strifes and controversies of men; it is not to be a

good farmer, or scholar merely; not to mingle with his people in festive circles and enjoyments; not to be a man of taste and philosophy, and distinguished mainly for refinement of manners; not to be a profound philosopher or metaphysician, but to make Christ crucified the grand object of his attention, and seek always and everywhere to make him known. (2.) He is not to be ashamed anywhere of the humbling doctrine that Christ was crucified. In this he is to glory. Though the world may ridicule; though philosophers may sneer; though the rich and the gay may deride it, yet this is to be the grand object of interest to him, and at no time, and *in no society* is he to be ashamed of it. (3.) It matters not what are the amusements of society around him; what fields of science, of gain, or ambition, are open before him, the minister of Christ is to know Christ and him crucified alone. If he cultivates science, it is to be that he may the more successfully explain and vindicate the gospel. If he becomes in any manner familiar with the works of art, and of taste, it is that he may more successfully show *to* those who cultivate them, the superior beauty and excellency of the cross. If he studies the plans and the employments of men, it is that he may more successfully meet them *in* those plans, and more successfully speak to them of the great plan of redemption. (4.) The preaching of the cross is the only kind of preaching that will be attended with success. That which has in it much respecting the divine mission, the dignity, the works, the doctrines, the person, and the atonement of Christ, will be successful. So it was in the time of the apostles; so it was in the Reformation; so it was in the Moravian missions; so it has been in all revivals of religion. There is a power about that kind of preaching which philosophy and human reason have not. "Christ is God's great ordinance" for the salvation of the world; and we meet the crimes and alleviate the woes of the world, just in proportion as we hold the cross up as appointed to overcome the one, and to pour the balm of consolation into the other.

3. *And I was with you.* Paul continued there at least a year and six months. Acts xviii. 11. ¶ *In weakness.* In conscious feebleness; diffident of my own powers, and not trusting to my own strength. ¶ *And in fear, and in much trembling.* Paul was sensible that he had many enemies to encounter (Acts xviii. 6.): and he was sensible of his own natural disadvantages as a public speaker, 2 Cor. x. 10. He knew too, how much the Greeks valued a manly and elegant species of oratory; and he, therefore, delivered his message with deep and anxious solicitude as to the success. It was at this time, and in view of these circumstances, that the Lord spoke to him by night in a vision, and said, "be not afraid, but speak, and hold not thy peace; for I am with thee, and no man shall set on thee to hurt thee; for I have much people in this city," Acts xviii. 9, 10. If Paul was conscious of weakness, well may other ministers be; and if Paul sometimes trembled in deep solicitude about the result of his message, well may other ministers tremble also. It was in such circumstances, and with such feelings, that the Lord met him to encourage him.—And it is when other ministers feel thus, that the promises of the gospel are inestimably precious. We may add, that it is *then,* and then only, that they are successful. Notwithstanding all Paul's fears, he was successful there. And it is commonly, perhaps always, when ministers go to their work conscious of their own weakness; burdened with the weight of their message; diffident of their own powers; and deeply solicitous about the result of their labours, that God sends down his Spirit, and converts sinners to God. The most successful ministers have been men who have evinced most of this feeling; and most of the revivals of religion have commenced, and continued, just as ministers have preached, conscious of their own feebleness, distrusting their own powers, and looking to God for aid and strength.

4. *And my speech.* The word *speech*

4 And my speech and my preaching *was* not with [1] enticing words
of [a] man's wisdom, but in demonstration [b] of the Spirit and of
power:
5 That your faith should not

1 or, *persuasible*. a 2 Pet.1.16.

b 1 Thess.1.5.

here—if it is to be distinguished from *preaching*—refers, perhaps, to his more private reasonings; his preaching to his public discourses. ¶ *Not with enticing words.* Not with the persuasive reasonings (πειθοῖς λόγοις) of the wisdom of men. Not with that kind of oratory that was adapted to captivate and charm; and which the Greeks so much esteemed. ¶ *But in demonstration.* In the showing (ἀποδείξει); or in the testimony or evidence which the Spirit produced. The meaning is, that the Spirit furnished the evidence of the divine origin of the religion which he preached, and that it did not depend for its proof on his own reasonings or eloquence. The proof, the demonstration which the Spirit furnished was, undoubtedly, the miracles which were wrought; the gift of tongues; and the remarkable conversions which attended the gospel.—The word *Spirit* here refers, doubtless, to the Holy Spirit; and Paul says that this Spirit had furnished demonstration of the divine origin and nature of the gospel. This had been by the gift of tongues (chap. i. 5—7. Comp. chap. xiv.), and by the effects of his agency in renewing and sanctifying the heart. ¶ *And of power,* That is, of the power of God (ver. 5); the divine power and efficacy which attended the preaching of the gospel there. Comp. 1 Thess. i. 5.—The *effect* of the gospel is the evidence to which the apostle appeals for its truth. That effect was seen, (1.) In the conversion of sinners to God of all classes, ages, and conditions, when all human means of reforming them was vain. (2.) In its giving them peace, joy, and happiness; and in its transforming their lives. (3.) In making them different men—in making the drunkard sober; the thief honest; the licentious pure; the profane reverent; the indolent industrious; the harsh and unkind, gentle and kind; and the wretched happy. (4.) In its diffusing a mild and pure influence over the laws and customs of society; and in promoting human happiness everywhere.—And in regard to this evidence to which the apostle appeals, we may observe, (1.) That is a kind of evidence which any one may examine, and which no one can deny. It does not need laboured, abstruse argumentation, but it is everywhere in society. Every man has witnessed the effects of the gospel in reforming the vicious, and no one can deny that it has this power. (2.) It is a mighty display of the power of God. There is no more striking exhibition of his power over mind than in a revival of religion. There is no where more manifest demonstration of his presence than when, in such a revival, the proud are humbled, the profane are awed, the blasphemer is silenced, and the profligate, the abandoned, and the moral—are converted unto God, and are led as lost sinners to the same cross, and find the same peace. (3.) The gospel has thus evidenced from age to age that it is from God. Every converted sinner furnishes such a demonstration; and every instance where it produces peace, hope, joy, shows that it is from heaven.

5. *That your faith.* That is, that your belief of the divine origin of the Christian religion. ¶ *Should not stand.* Greek, "should not *be*;" that is, should not rest upon this; or be sustained by this. God intended to furnish you a firm and solid demonstration that the religion which you embraced was from him; and this could not be if its preaching had been attended with the graces of eloquence, or the abstractions of refined metaphysical reasoning. It would then appear to rest on human wisdom. ¶ *In the power of God.* In the evidence of divine power accompanying the preaching of the gospel. The power of God would attend the exhibition of truth everywhere; and would be a

[1] stand in the wisdom of men, but
in the power of God.

1 be.

6 Howbeit we speak wisdom
among them [a] that are perfect:

a Phil.3.15.

demonstration that would be irresistible that the religion was not originated by man, but was from heaven. That power was seen in changing the heart; in overcoming the strong propensities of our nature to sin; in subduing the soul; and making the sinner a new creature in Christ Jesus. Every Christian has thus, in his own experience, furnished demonstration that the religion which he loves is from God, and not from man. *Man* could not subdue these sins; and man could not so entirely transform the soul. And although the unlearned Christian may not be able to investigate *all* the evidences of religion; although he cannot meet *all* the objections of cunning and subtle infidels, although he may be greatly perplexed and embarrassed by them, yet he may have the fullest proof that he loves God, that he is different from what he once was; and that all this has been accomplished by the religion of the cross. The blind man that was made to see by the Saviour (John x.), might have been wholly unable to tell *how* his eyes were opened, and unable to meet all the cavils of those who might doubt it, or all the subtle and cunning objections of physiologists, but of one thing he certainly could not doubt, that "whereas he was blind, he then saw;" John x. 25. A man may have no doubt that the sun shines, that the wind blows, that the tides rise, that the blood flows in his veins, that the flowers bloom, and that this could *not* be except it was from God, while he may have no power to explain these facts; and no power to meet the objections and cavils of those who might choose to embarrass him. So men may know that their hearts are changed; and it is on this ground that no small part of the Christian world, as in every thing else, depend for the most satisfactory evidence of their religion. On this ground humble and unlearned Christians have been often willing to go to the stake as martyrs—just as a humble and unlearned *patriot* is willing to die for his country. He *loves* it; and he is willing to die for it. A Christian *loves* his God and Saviour; and is willing to *die* for his sake.

6. *How be it.* But (δε). This commences the *second* head or argument in this chapter, in which Paul shows that if human wisdom *is* wanting in his preaching, it is not devoid of true, and solid, and even divine wisdom.—*Bloomfield.* ¶ *We speak wisdom.* We do not admit that we utter foolishness. We have spoken of the foolishness of preaching (chap. i. 21); and of the estimate in which it was held by the world (chap. i. 22—28); and of our own manner among you as not laying claim to human learning or eloquence; but we do not design to admit that we have been really speaking folly. We have been uttering that which is truly wise, but which is seen and understood to be such only by those who are qualified to judge—by those who may be denominated "perfect," that is, those who are fitted by God to understand it. By "wisdom" here, the apostle means that system of truth which he had explained and defended—the plan of salvation by the cross of Christ. ¶ *Among them that are perfect* (ἐν τοῖς τελείοις). This word "perfect" is here evidently applied to Christians, as it is in Phil. iii. 15, "Let us therefore as many as be perfect, be thus minded." And it is clearly used to denote those who were advanced in Christian knowledge; who were qualified to understand the subject; who had made progress in the knowledge of the mysteries of the gospel; and who thus saw its excellence. It does not mean here that they were *sinless,* for the argument of the apostle does not bear on that inquiry, but that they were qualified to understand the gospel in contradistinction from the gross, the sensual, and the carnally minded, who rejected it as foolishness. There is, perhaps, here an allusion to the heathen *mysteries,* where those who had been fully initiated were said to be *perfect*—fully instructed in those

yet not the wisdom of this world,
nor of the princes of this world
that come to [a] naught:
7 But we speak the wisdom
of God in a mystery, *even* the
hidden [b] *wisdom*, which God
ordained before the world unto
our glory:

a Ps.33.10.

b Eph.3.5,9.

rites and doctrines. And if so, then this passage means, that those only who have been fully instructed in the knowledge of the Christian religion, will be qualified to see its beauty and its wisdom. The gross and sensual do not see it, and those only who are enlightened by the Holy Spirit are qualified to appreciate its beauty and its excellency. ¶ *Not the wisdom of the world.* Not that which this world has originated or loved. ¶ *Nor of the princes of this world.* Perhaps intending chiefly here the rulers of the Jews; see ver. 8. They neither devised it, nor loved it, nor saw its wisdom; ver. 8. ¶ *That come to naught.* That is, whose plans fail; whose wisdom vanishes; and who themselves, with all their pomp and splendour, come to nothing in the grave; comp. Isa. xiv. All the plans of human wisdom shall fail; and this which is originated by God only shall stand.

7. *But we speak.* We who have preached the gospel. ¶ *The wisdom of God.* We teach or proclaim the wise plan of God for the salvation of men; we make known the divine wisdom in regard to the scheme of human redemption. This plan was of God, in opposition to other plans which were of men. ¶ *In a mystery,* even *the hidden* wisdom (ἐν μυστηρίῳ τὴν ἀποκεκρυμμένην). The words "even" and "wisdom" in this translation have been supplied by our translators; and the sense would be more perspicuous if they were omitted, and the translation should be literally made, "We proclaim the divine wisdom hidden in a mystery.' The apostle does not say that their *preaching* was mysterious, nor that their doctrine was unintelligible, but he refers to the fact that this wisdom had been *hidden in a mystery* from men until that time, but was *then* revealed by the gospel. In other words, he does not say that what they then declared was hidden in a mystery, but that they made known the divine wisdom which *had been* concealed from the minds of men. The word *mystery* with us is commonly used in the sense of that which is beyond comprehension; and it is often applied to such doctrines as exhibit difficulties which we are not able to explain. But this is not the sense in which it is commonly used in the Scriptures; see Note, Mat. xiii. 11; comp. Campbell on the Gospels, Diss. ix. part i. The word properly denotes that which is *concealed* or *hidden;* that which has not yet been made known; and is applied to those truths which until the revelation of Jesus Christ were *concealed* from men, which were either *hidden* under obscure types and shadows or prophecies, or which had been altogether unrevealed, and unknown to the world. The word stands opposed to that which is *revealed*, not to that which is in itself plain. The doctrines to which the word relates may be in themselves clear and simple, but they are hidden *in* mystery until they are revealed. From this radical idea in the word *mystery*, however, it came also to be applied not only to those doctrines which *had not* been made known, but to those also which were in themselves deep and difficult: to that which is enigmatical and obscure; 1 Cor. xiv. 2; 1 Tim. iii. 16. It is applied also to the secret designs and purposes of God; Rev. x. 7. The word is most commonly applied by Paul to the secret and long concealed design of God to make known his gospel to the Gentiles; to break down the wall between them and the Jews; and to spread the blessings of the true religion everywhere; Rom. xi. 25; xvi. 25; Eph. i. 9; iii. 9; vi. 19. Here, it evidently means the beauty and excellency of the person and plans of Jesus Christ, but which were IN FACT unknown to the princes of this world. It does not imply, of necessity, that they *could* not have understood them,

8 Which none of the princes of this world knew: for [a] had they known *it*, they would not have crucified the Lord of glory.

a Luke 23.34.

nor that they were unintelligible, but that, *in fact*, whatever was the cause, they were concealed from them. Paul says (ver. 8), that *had* they known his wisdom, they would not have crucified him—which implies at least that it was not in itself unintelligible; and he further says, that this mystery had been revealed to Christians by the Spirit of God, which proves that he does not here refer to that which is in itself unintelligible; ver. 10. "The apostle has here especially in view the all-wise counsel of God for the salvation of men by Jesus Christ, in the writings of the Old Testament only obscurely signified, and to the generality of men utterly unknown."—*Bloomfield.* ¶ *Which God ordained.* Which plan, so full of wisdom, God appointed in his own purpose before the foundation of the world; that is, it was a plan which from eternity he determined to execute. It was not a *new* device; it had not been got up to serve an occasion; but it was a plan laid deep in the eternal counsel of God, and on which he had his eye for ever fixed. This passage proves, that God had a plan, and that this plan was eternal. This is all that is involved in the doctrine of eternal decrees or purposes. And if God had a plan about this, there is the same reason to think that he had a plan in regard to all things. ¶ *Unto our glory.* In order that we might be honoured or glorified. This may refer either to the honour which was put upon Christians in this life, in being admitted to the privileges of the sons of God; or more probably to that "eternal weight of glory" which remains for them in heaven; 2 Cor. iv. 17. One design of that plan was to raise the redeemed to "glory, and honour, and immortality." It should greatly increase our gratitude to God, that it was a subject of eternal design; that he always has cherished this purpose; and that he has loved us with such love, and sought our happiness and salvation with such intensity, that in order to accomplish it, he was willing to give his own Son to die on a cross.

8. *Which none of the princes.* None of those rulers who were engaged in the crucifixion of the Messiah, referring both to the Jewish rulers, and the Roman governor. ¶ *Knew.* They did not perceive or appreciate the excellency of his character, the wisdom of his plan, the glory of his scheme of salvation. Their ignorance arose from not understanding the prophecies, and from an unwillingness to be convinced that Jesus of Nazareth had been truly sent by God. In Acts iii. 17, Peter says that it was through ignorance that the Jews had put him to death; see Note on this place. ¶ *For had they known* it. Had they fully understood his character, and seen the wisdom of his plan, and his work, they would not have put him to death; see Note on Acts iii. 17. Had they seen the hidden wisdom in that plan—had they understood the glory of his real character, the truth respecting his incarnation, and the fact that he was the long expected Messiah of their nation, they would not have put him to death. It is incredible that they would have crucified their Messiah, knowing and believing him to be such. They *might* have known it, but they were unwilling to examine the evidence. They expected a *different* Messiah, and were unwilling to admit the claims of Jesus of Nazareth. For *this* ignorance, however, there was no excuse. If they had not a full knowledge, it was their own fault. Jesus had performed miracles which were a complete attestation to his divine mission (John v. 36; x. 25); but they closed their eyes on those works, and were unwilling to be convinced.—God always gives to men sufficient demonstration of the truth, but they close their eyes, and are *unwilling* to believe. This is the sole reason why they are not converted to God and saved. ¶ *They would not have crucified.* It is perfectly manifest that the Jews would not have crucified their own Messiah, *knowing him to be*

9 But, as it is written, [a] Eye hath not seen, nor ear heard, neither have entered into the heart of man, the things which God

a Isa.64.4

such. He was the hope and expectation of their nation. All their desires were centered in him. And to him they looked for deliverance from all their foes. ¶ *The Lord of glory.* This expression is a Hebraism, and means "the glorious Lord;" or the "Messiah." Expressions like this, where a noun performs the office of an adjective, are common in the Hebrew language.—Grotius supposes that the expression is taken from that of "the King of glory," in Ps. xxiv. 7—9.

> Lift up your heads, O ye gates,
> Be ye lift up, ye everlasting doors,
> And the King of glory shall come in.
> Who is this King of glory?
> JEHOVAH, strong and mighty
> JEHOVAH, mighty in battle.
> Lift up your heads, O ye gates;
> Lift them up, ye everlasting doors;
> And the King of glory shall come in.
> Who is this King of glory?
> JEHOVAH of hosts, he is the King of glory.

God is called "the God of glory" in Acts vii. 2.—The fact that this appellation is given to JEHOVAH in the Old Testament, and to the Lord Jesus in the verse before us, is one of those incidental circumstances which show how the Lord Jesus was estimated by the apostles: and how familiarly they applied to him names and titles which belong only to God. The foundation of this appellation is laid in his exalted perfections; and in the honour and majesty which he had with the Father before the world was; John xvii. 1—5.

9. *But as it is written.* This passage is quoted from Isa. lxiv. 4. It is not quoted literally; but the sense only is given. The words are found in the apocryphal books of Elijah; and Origen and Jerome supposed that Paul quoted from those books. But it is evident that Paul had in his eye the passage in Isaiah; and intended to apply it to his present purpose. These words are often applied by commentators and others to the future life, and are supposed by them to be descriptive of the state of the blessed there. But against the supposition that they refer directly to the future state, there are insuperable objections. (1.) The first is, that the passage in Isaiah has no such reference. In that place it is designed clearly to describe the blessedness of those who were admitted to the divine favour; who had communion with God; and to whom God manifested himself as their friend. That blessedness is said to be superior to all that men elsewhere enjoy; to be such as could be found no where else but in God. See Isa. lxiv. 1, 4, 5, 8. It is used there, as Paul uses it, to denote the happiness which results from the communication of the divine favour to the soul. (2.) The object of the apostle is not to describe the future state of the redeemed. It is to prove that those who are Christians have true wisdom (ver. 6, 7); or that they have views of truth, and of the excellence of the plan of salvation which the world has not, and which those who crucified the Lord Jesus did not possess. The thing which he is describing here, is not merely the *happiness* of Christians, but their views of the *wisdom* of the plan of salvation. They have views of that which the eyes of other men have not seen; a view of wisdom, and fitness, and beauty which can be found in no other plan. It is true that this view is attended with a high degree of comfort; but the comfort is not the immediate thing in the eye of the apostle. (3.) The declaration in ver. 10, is conclusive proof that Paul does not refer to the happiness of heaven. He there says that God *has* revealed these things to Christians by his Spirit. But if *already* revealed, assuredly it does not refer to that which is *yet* to come. But although this does not refer *directly* to heaven, there may be an application of the passage to a future state in an *indirect* manner, which is not improper. If there are such manifestations of wisdom in the plan here; if Christians see so much of its beauty here on earth; and if their views so far surpass all that the world sees and enjoys, how much

hath prepared for them that love him.

10 But [a] God hath revealed *them* unto us by his Spirit: for the

a John 16.13.

greater and purer will be the manifestations of wisdom and goodness in the world of glory. ¶ *Eye hath not seen.* This is the same as saying, that no one had ever fully perceived and understood the value and beauty of those things which God has prepared for his people. All the world had been strangers to this until God made a revelation to his people by his Spirit. The blessedness which the apostle referred to had been unknown alike to the Jews and the Gentiles. ¶ *Nor ear heard.* We learn the existence and quality of objects by the external senses; and those senses are used to denote any acquisition of knowledge. To say that the eye had not seen, nor the ear heard, was, therefore, the same as saying that it was not known at all. All men had been ignorant of it. ¶ *Neither have entered into the heart of man.* No man has conceived it; or understood it. It is new; and is above all that man has seen, and felt, and known. ¶ *The things which God hath prepared.* The things which God "has held in reserve" *(Bloomfield);* that is, what God has appointed in the gospel for his people. The thing to which the apostle here refers particularly, is the wisdom which was revealed in the gospel; but he also intends, doubtless, to include *all* the provisions of mercy and happiness which the gospel makes known to the people of God. Those things relate to the pardon of sin; to the atonement, and to justification by faith; to the peace and joy which religion imparts; to the complete and final redemption from sin and death which the gospel is fitted to produce, and which it will ultimately effect. In all these respects, the blessings which the gospel confers, surpass the full comprehension of men; and are infinitely beyond all that man could know or experience without the religion of Christ. And if on earth the gospel confers such blessings on its friends, how much higher and purer shall be the joys which it shall bestow in heaven!

10. *But God hath revealed* them. That is, those elevated views and enjoyments to which men everywhere else had been strangers, and which have been under all other forms of religion unknown, have been communicated to us by the revelation of God. —This verse commences the *third* part of this chapter, in which the apostle shows *how* these truths, so full of wisdom had been communicated to Christians. It had not been by any native endowments of theirs; not by any strength of faculties, or powers. but solely by revelation from God, ¶ *Unto us.* That is, first to the apostles; secondly, to all Christians —to the church and the world *through* their inspired instructors; and third, to all Christians by the illuminating agency of the Spirit on their hearts. The connection shows that he did not mean to confine this declaration to the apostles merely, for his design was to show that *all* Christians had this knowledge of the true wisdom. It was true that this was revealed in an eminent manner to the apostles, and through their inspired preaching and writings; but it is also true, that the same truths are communicated by the agency of the same Spirit to all Christians; John xvi. 12—14. No truth is now communicated to Christians which was not revealed to and by the inspired writers; but the *same* truths are imparted by means of their writings, and by the illumination of the Spirit to all the true friends of God. ¶ *By his Spirit.* By the Holy Spirit, that was promised by the Saviour. John xiv. 26; xv. 26, 27; xvi. 7—14. This proves, (1.) That men by nature are not able to discover the deep things of God—the truths which are needful to salvation. (2.) That the apostles were inspired by the Holy Ghost; and if so, then the Scriptures are inspired. (3.) That all Christians are the subjects of the teaching of the Holy Spirit; that these truths are made known to them

Spirit searcheth all things, yea, the deep [a] things of God.

a Rom.11.33.

by his illumination; and that but for this, they would remain in the same darkness as other men. ¶ *For the Spirit.* The Holy Spirit, or the Spirit of God; see ver. 11. ¶ *Searcheth.* This word does not fully express the force of the original (ἐρευνᾷ). It means to search accurately, diligently, so as fully to understand; such profound research as to have thorough knowledge. So David uses the Hebrew word חקר in Ps. cxxxix. 1. So the word is used to denote a careful and accurate investigation of secret and obscure things, in 1 Pet. i. 11. Comp. John vii. 52; Rom. viii. 27; Rev. ii. 23, where it is used to denote that profound and accurate search by which the desires and feelings of the *heart* are known—implying the most profound knowledge of which we can have any conception; see Prov. xx. 27. Here it means, that the Holy Spirit has an intimate knowledge of all things. It is not to be supposed that he *searches,* or *inquires* as men do who are ignorant; but that he has an intimate and profound knowledge, such as is usually the *result* of a close and accurate search. The *result* is what the apostle means to state—the accurate, profound, and thorough knowledge, such as usually attends research. He does not state the *mode* in which it is obtained; but the fact. And he uses a word more emphatic than simple *knowledge,* because he designs to indicate that his knowledge is profound, entire, and thorough. ¶ *All things.* All subjects; all laws; all events; all beings. ¶ *The deep things of God.* He has a thorough knowledge of the hidden counsels or purposes of God; of all his plans and purposes. He sees all his designs. He sees all his councils; all his purposes in regard to the government of the universe, and the scheme of salvation. He knows all whom God designs to save; he sees all that they need; and he sees how the plan of God is fitted to their salvation.—This passage proves, (1.) That the Spirit is, in some respects, *distinct* from the Father, or from him who is here called God. Else how could he be said to *search* all things, even the deep purposes of God? To *search* implies *action, thought, personality.* An attribute of God cannot be said to *search.* How could it be said of the justice, the goodness, the power, or the wisdom of God that it *searches,* or *acts?* To search, is the action of an intelligent agent, and cannot be performed by an attribute. (2.) The Spirit is omniscient. He searches or clearly understands "all things"—the very definition of omniscience. He understands all the profound plans and counsels of God. And how can there be a higher demonstration of omniscience than to *know God?*—But if omniscient, the Holy Spirit is divine—for this is one of the incommunicable attributes of God; 1 Chron. xxviii. 9; Psal. cxxxix. 1; Jer. xvii. 10. (3.) He is not a distinct *being* from God. There is a *union* between him and God, such as may be compared to the union between a man and his soul, ver. 11. God is one; and though he subsists as Father, Son, and Spirit, yet he is one God, Deut. vi. 4.—This passage is, therefore, a very important, and a decisive one in regard to the personality and divinity of the Holy Spirit.

**11 For what [b] man knoweth
the things of a man, save the**

b Prov.14.10.

11. *For what man,* &c. The design of this is, to *illustrate* what he had just said by a reference to the way in which man acquires the knowledge of himself. The purpose is to show that the Spirit has an *exact* and *thorough* knowledge of the things of God; and this is done by the very striking thought that no man can know his own mind, his own plans and intentions, but himself—his own spirit. The essential idea is, that no man can know another; that his thoughts and designs can only be known by himself, or by his own spirit; and that unless he chooses to reveal them to others,

spirit of man which is in him? even so [a] the things of God knoweth no man, but the Spirit of God.

[a] Rom.11.33,34.

12 Now we have received, not [b] the spirit of the world, but the Spirit which is of God: that [c] we might know the things

[b] Rom.8.15. [c] 1 John 5.20.

they cannot ascertain them. So of God. No man can penetrate his designs; and unless he chooses to make them known by his Spirit, they must for ever remain inscrutable to human view. ¶ *The things of a man.* The "deep things"—the hidden counsels, thoughts, plans, intentions. ¶ *Save the spirit of man,* &c. Except his own mind; *i. e.* himself. No other man can fully know them. By the spirit of man here, Paul designs to denote the human soul—or the intellect of man. It is not to be supposed that he here intends to convey the idea that there is a perfect resemblance between the relation which the soul of man bears to the man, and the relation which the Holy Spirit bears to God. The illustration is to be taken in regard to the point immediately before him—which is, that no one could know and communicate the deep thoughts and plans of God except his Spirit—just as no one could penetrate into the intentions of a man, and fully know them, but himself. The passage proves, therefore, that there is a knowledge which the Spirit has of God, which no man, no angel can obtain, just as every man's spirit has a knowledge of his own plans which no other man can obtain; that the Spirit of God can *communicate* his plans and deep designs, just as a man can communicate his own intentions; and consequently, that while there is a *distinction* of some kind between the Spirit of God and God, as there is a distinction which makes it proper to say that a man has an intelligent soul, yet there is such a profound and intimate knowledge of God by the Spirit, that he must be equal with him; and such an intimate union, that he can be called "the Spirit of God," and be one with God, as the human soul can be called "the spirit of the man," and be one with him. In all respects we are not to suppose that there is a similarity. In these points there is.—It may be added that the *union,* the *oneness* of the Spirit of God with God, is no more absurd or inexplicable than the union of the spirit of man with the man; or the *oneness* of the complex person made up of body and soul, which we call *man.* When men have explained all the difficulties about *themselves*—in regard to their own bodies and spirits, it will be time to advance objections against the doctrines here stated in regard to God. ¶ *Even so.* To the same extent; in like manner. ¶ *The things of God.* His deep purposes and plans. ¶ *Knoweth no man.* Man cannot search into them—any more than one man can search the intentions of another.

12. *Now we have received.* We who are Christians; and especially we, the apostles. The following verse shows that he had himself and the other apostles chiefly in view; though it is true of all Christians that they have received, not the spirit of this world, but the spirit which is of God. ¶ *Not the spirit of this world.* Not the wisdom and knowledge which this world can give—not the learning and philosophy which were so much valued in Greece. The views of truth which we have, are not such as this world gives, but are such as are communicated by the Spirit of God. ¶ *But the Spirit which is of God.* We are under the teachings and influence of the Holy Spirit. ¶ *That we might know.* That we might fully understand and appreciate. The Spirit is given to us in order that we might fully understand the favours which God has conferred on us in the gospel. It was not only necessary that God should grant the blessings of redemption by the gift of his Son, but, such was the hardness and blindness of the human heart, it was needful that he should grant his Holy Spirit also, that men might be brought fully to see and appreciate the

that are freely given to us of God.

13 Which things also we speak, not *a* in the words which man's

a chap. 1. 17.

value of those favours. For men do not see them by nature; neither does any one see them who is not enlightened by the Holy Spirit of God. ¶ *The things that are freely given us.* That are conferred on us as a matter of grace or favour. He here refers to the blessings of redemption—the pardon of sin, justification, sanctification, the divine favour and protection, and the hope of eternal life.—These things we *know;* they are not matters of conjecture; but are surely and certainly confirmed to us by the Holy Spirit. It is possible for all Christians to know and be fully assured of the truth of those things, and of their interest in them.

13. *Which things we speak.* Which great, and glorious, and certain truths, we, the apostles, preach and explain. ¶ *Not in the words which man's wisdom teacheth.* Not such as human philosophy or eloquence would dictate. They do not have their origin in the devices of human wisdom, and they are not expressed in such words of dazzling and attractive rhetoric as would be employed by those who pride themselves on the wisdom of this world. ¶ *But which the Holy Ghost teacheth.* That is, in the words which the Holy Ghost imparts to us. Locke understands this as referring to the fact that the apostles used "the language and expressions" which the Holy Ghost had taught in the revelations of the Scriptures. But this is evidently giving a narrow view of the subject. The apostle is speaking of the whole course of instruction by which the deep things of God were made known to the Christian church; and all this was not made known in the very words which were already contained in the Old Testament. He evidently refers to the fact that the apostles were themselves under the direction of the Holy Spirit, in the words and doctrines which they imparted; and this passage is a full proof that they laid claim to divine inspiration. It is further observable that he says, that this was done in such "words" as the Holy Ghost taught, referring not to the doctrines or subjects merely, but to the manner of expressing them. It is evident here that he lays claim to an inspiration in regard to the words which he used, or to the manner of his stating the doctrines of revelation. Words are the signs of thoughts; and if God designed that his truth should be accurately expressed in human language, there must have been a supervision over the *words* used, that such should be employed, and such only, as should accurately express the sense which he intended to convey. ¶ *Comparing spiritual things with spiritual* (πνευματικοῖς πνευματικὰ συγκρίνοντες). This expression has been very variously interpreted; and is very difficult of explanation. Le Clerc renders it "speaking spiritual things to spiritual men." Most of the fathers rendered it "comparing the things which were written by the Spirit of the Old Testament with what is now revealed to us by the same Spirit, and confirming our doctrine by them." Calvin renders the word "*comparing*" by *fitting*, or adapting (*aptare*), and says that it means "that he adapted spiritual things to spiritual men, while he accommodated words to the thing; that is, he tempered that celestial wisdom of the Spirit with simple language, and which conveyed by itself the native energy of the Spirit." Thus, says he, he reproved the vanity of those who attempted to secure human applause by a turgid and subtle mode of argument. Grotius accords with the fathers, and renders it, "explaining those things which the prophets spake by the Spirit of God, by those things which Christ has made known to us by his Spirit." Macknight renders it, "explaining spiritual things in words taught by the Spirit." So Doddridge. — The word rendered "comparing" (συγκρίνοντες), means properly to collect, join, mingle, unite together; then to separate or distin-

wisdom teacheth, but which the Holy Ghost teacheth; comparing spiritual things with spiritual.

14 But the natural man receiveth [a] not the things of the Spirit of God; for they are foolishness

a Matt.13,11,&c; Rom.8.5,7.

guish parts of things and unite them into one; then to judge of the qualities of objects by carefully separating or distinguishing; then to *compare* for the purpose of judging, &c. As it means to compare one thing with another for the purpose of explaining its nature, it comes to signify to *interpret*, to *explain*; and in this sense it is often used by the LXX. as a translation of פתר *Phathar*, to open, unfold, explain. (See Gen. xl. 8, 16, 22; xli. 12, 15); also of פרש, to explain (Num. xv. 32); and of the Chaldee פרש, (Dan. v. 13, 17). See also Dan. ii. 4—7, 9, 16, 24, 26, 30, 36, 45; iv. 3, 4, 6, 16, 17; v. 7, 8, 13, 16, 18, 20; vii. 16, in all which places the noun σύγκρισις, is used in the same sense. In this sense the word is, doubtless, used here, and is to be interpreted in the sense of *explaining*, *unfolding*. There is no reason, either in the *word* here used, or in the *argument* of the apostle, why the sense of *comparing* should be retained. ¶ *Spiritual things* (πνευματικὰ). Things, doctrines, subjects that pertain to the teaching of the Spirit. It does not mean things *spiritual* in opposition to *fleshly*; or *intellectual* in opposition to things pertaining to *matter*; but spiritual as the things referred to were such as were wrought, and revealed by the Holy Spirit—his doctrines on the subject of religion under the new dispensation, and his influence on the heart. ¶ *With spiritual* (πνευματικοῖς). This is an adjective; and may be either masculine or neuter. It is evident, that some noun is understood. That may be either, (1.) ἀνθρώποις, *men*—and then it will mean "to spiritual men"—that is, to men who are enlightened or taught by the Spirit; and thus many commentators understand it; or, (2.) It may be λογοις, *words*—and then it may mean, either that the "spiritual things" were explained by "words" and illustrations drawn from the writings of the Old Testament, inspired by the Spirit—as most of the fathers, and many moderns understand it: or that the "things spiritual" were explained by words which the Holy Spirit *then* communicated, and which were adapted to the subject—simple, pure, elevated; not gross, not turgid, not distinguished for rhetoric, and not such as the Greeks sought, but such as became the Spirit of God communicating great, sublime, yet simple truths to men. It will then mean "explaining *doctrines* that pertain to the Spirit's teaching and influence in *words* that are taught by the same Spirit, and that are fitted to convey in the most intelligible manner those doctrines to men." Here the idea of the Holy Spirit's present agency is kept up throughout; the idea that *he* communicates the doctrine, and the mode of stating it to man.—The supposition that λογοις, *words*, is the word understood here, is favoured by the fact that it occurs in the previous part of this verse. And if this be the sense, it means that the words which were used by the apostles were pure, simple, unostentatious, and undistinguished by display—such as became *doctrines* taught by the Holy Spirit, when communicated in *words* suggested by the same Spirit.

14. *But the natural man* (ψυχικὸς δὲ ἄνθρωπος). The word *natural* here stands opposed evidently to *spiritual*. It denotes those who are governed and influenced by the natural instincts; the animal passions and desires, in opposition to those who are influenced by the Spirit of God. It refers to unregenerate men; but it has also not merely the idea of their being unregenerate, but that of their being influenced by the animal passions or desires. See Note on chap. xv. 44. The word *sensual* would correctly express the idea. The word is used by the Greek writers to denote that which man has in common with the brutes—to denote that they are under

unto him: neither can he know *them*, because they are spiritually discerned.

15 But he *a* that is spiritual [1] judgeth all things, yet he himself [2] is judged of no man.

a Prov.28.5.

1 or, *discerneth.* 2 or, *discerned.*

the influence of the senses, or the mere animal nature, in opposition to reason and conscience.—*Bretschneider*. See 1 Thess. v. 23. Here it denotes that they are under the influence of the senses, or the animal nature, in opposition to being influenced by the Spirit of God. Macknight and Doddridge render it "the animal man." Whitby understands by it the man who rejects revelation, the man who is under the influence of carnal wisdom. The word occurs but six times in the New Testament; 1 Cor. xv. 44, 44, 46; James iii. 15: Jude 19. In 1 Cor. xv. 44, 44, 46, it is rendered "natural," and is applied to the body as it exists before death, in contradistinction from that which shall exist after the resurrection—called a spiritual body. In James iii. 15, it is applied to wisdom, "This wisdom — is earthly, *sensual*, devilish." In Jude 19, it is applied to *sensual* persons, or those who are governed by the senses in opposition to those who are influenced by the Spirit: "These be they who separate themselves, *sensual*, having not the Spirit." The word here evidently denotes those who are under the influence of the senses; who are governed by the passions and the animal appetites, and natural desires; and who are uninfluenced by the Spirit of God. And it may be observed that this was the case with the great mass of the heathen world, even including the philosophers. ¶ *Receiveth not* (οὐ δέχεται), does not *embrace* or *comprehend* them. That is, he rejects them as folly; he does not perceive their beauty, or their wisdom; he despises them. He loves other things better. A man of intemperance does not receive or love the arguments for temperance; a man of licentiousness, the arguments for chastity; a liar, the arguments for truth. So a sensual or worldly man does not receive or love the arguments for religion. ¶ *The things of the Spirit of God.* The doctrines which are inspired by the Holy Spirit, and the things which pertain to his influence on the heart and life. The things of the Spirit of God here denote all the things which the Holy Spirit produces. ¶ *Neither can he know them.* Neither can he understand or comprehend them. Perhaps, also, the word *know* here implies also the idea of *loving*, or *approving* of them, as it often does in the Scripture. Thus to know the Lord often means to love him, to have a full, practical acquaintance with him. When the apostle says that the animal or sensual man cannot know those things, he may have reference to one of two things. Either, (1.) That those doctrines were not discoverable by human wisdom, or by any skill which the natural man may have, but were to be learned only by revelation. This is the main drift of his argument, and this sense is given by Locke and Whitby. Or, (2.) He may mean that the sensual, the unrenewed man cannot perceive their beauty and their force, even *after* they are revealed to man, unless the mind is enlightened and inclined by the Spirit of God. This is probably the sense of the passage. This is the simple affirmation of *a fact*—that while the man remains sensual and carnal, he cannot perceive the beauty of those doctrines. And this *is* a simple and well known fact. It is a truth—universal and lamentable—that the sensual man, the worldly man, the proud, haughty, and self-confident man; the man under the influence of his animal appetites—licentious, false, ambitious, and vain—*does not* perceive any beauty in Christianity. So the intemperate man perceives no beauty in the arguments for temperance; the adulterer, no beauty in the arguments for chastity; the liar, no beauty in the arguments for truth. It is a simple fact, that while he is intemperate, or licentious, or false, he *can* perceive no beauty in these doctrines. But this does not prove that he has no natural faculties for perceiving the force and beauty of these arguments; or that he *might* not apply his mind to their investigation, and be brought to embrace them; or that he *might* not abandon the love of intoxicating drinks, and sensuality, and falsehood, and be a man of temperance, purity, and truth. He has all the natural faculties which are requisite in the case; and all the inability is his *strong love* of intoxicating drinks, or impurity, or falsehood. So of the sensual sinner. While he thus remains in love with sin, he cannot perceive the beauty of the plan of salvation, or the excellency of the doctrines of religion. He needs just the *love* of these things, and the *hatred* of sin. He needs to cherish the influences of the Spirit; to *receive* what He has taught, and not to reject it through the love of sin; he needs to yield himself to their influences, and then their beauty will be seen. The passage here *proves* that *while* a man is thus sensual, the things of the Spirit will appear to him to be folly; it proves nothing about his ability, or his natural faculty, to see the excellency of these things, and to turn from his sin. It is the affirmation of a simple fact everywhere discernible, that the natural man *does* not perceive the beauty of these things; that while he remains in that state he *cannot;* and that if he is ever brought to perceive their beauty, it will be by the influence of the Holy Spirit. Such is his love of sin, that he never *will* be brought to see their beauty except by the agency of the Holy Spirit. "For wickedness perverts the judgment, and makes men err with respect to practical principles; so that no one can be wise and judicious who is not good." *Aristotle,* as quoted by Bloomfield. ¶ *They are spiritually discerned.* That is, they are perceived by the aid of the Holy Spirit enlightening the mind and influencing the heart.

[The expression ψυχικὸς ἄνθρωπος has given rise to much controversy. Frequent attempts have been made to explain it, merely of the animal or sensual man. If this be the true sense, the doctrine of human depravity, in as far at least as this text may be supposed to bear upon it, is greatly invalidated. The apostle would seem to affirm only, that individuals, addicted to the gross indulgences of sense, are incapable of discerning and appreciating spiritual things. Thus a large exception would be made in favour of all those who might be styled intellectual and moral persons, living above the inferior appetites, and directing their faculties to the candid investigation of truth. That the phrase, however, is to be explained of the natural or *unregenerate* man, whether distinguished for intellectual refinement, and external regard to morals, or degraded by animal indulgence, will appear evident from an examination of the passage. The word in dispute comes from ψυχη, which though it primarily signify the breath or animal life, is by no means confined to that sense, but sometimes embraces the mind or soul "as distinguished both from man's body and from his πνευμα, or spirit, breathed into him immediately by God".—*See Parkhurst's Greek Lexicon.* The etymology of the word does not necessarily require us, then, to translate it "sensual." The context therefore alone must determine the matter. Now the "natural man" is there opposed to the spiritual man, the ψυχικὸς to the πνευματικὸς, and if the latter be explained of "him who is enlightened by the Holy Spirit"—who is regenerate—the former must be explained of him who is *not* enlightened by that Spirit,—who is still in a state of nature; and will thus embrace a class far more numerous than the merely sensual part of mankind. Farther; the general scope of the passage demands this view. The Corinthians entertained an excessive fondness for human learning and wisdom. They loved philosophical disquisition and oratorical display, and may therefore have been impatient of the "unenticing words" of Paul. To correct their mistaken taste, the apostle asserts and proves the utter insufficiency of human wisdom, either to discover spiritual things, or to appreciate them when discovered. He exclaims "where is the *wise?*—where is the scribe? - where is the disputer of this world? —hath not God made foolish the wisdom of this world?" chap. i. 17, 31. Now it would be strange indeed, if in bringing his argument to a conclusion, he should simply assert, that *sensual* men were incapable of spiritual discernment. So lame and impotent a conclusion is not to be attributed to the apostle. The disputed phrase, therefore, must be understood of all unregenerate persons, however free from gross sin, or eminent in intellectual attainment. Indeed it is the *proud wisdom* of the world, and not its sensuality, that the apostle throughout has chiefly in view. Add to all this; that the simplicity of the gospel has *in reality* met with more bitter opposition and pointed scorn, from men of worldly wisdom,

16 For who [a] hath known the mind of the Lord, that he [1] may instruct him? But we have [b] the mind of Christ?

a Isa.40.13; Jer. 23.18. 1 shall. b John 17.8.

than from men of the sensual class. Of the former *especially* is it true that they have counted the gospel "foolishness" and contemptuously rejected its message.

Of this natural man it is affirmed that he *cannot* know the things of the Spirit of God. He *can* know them *speculatively*, and may enlarge on them with great accuracy and beauty, but he cannot know them so as to approve and receive. Allowing the incapacity to be moral, not natural or physical, that is to say, it arises from *disinclination or perversion of will:* still the spiritual perception *is* affected by the fall, and whether that be directly or indirectly through the will, matters not, *as far as the fact is concerned. It* remains the same. The mind of man when applied to spiritual subjects, has not now the same discernment it originally had, and as our author remarks, if ever it is brought to perceive their beauty, it must be by the agency of the Spirit. See the supplementary Note on Rom. viii. 7; page 174.]

15. *But he that is spiritual.* The man who is enlightened by the Holy Spirit in contradistinction from him who is under the influence of the *senses* only. ¶ *Judgeth.* Gr. *Discerneth.* (margin); the same word as in the previous verse. It means that the spiritual man has a discernment of those truths in regard to which the sensual man was blind and ignorant. ¶ *All things.* Not absolutely all things; or not that he is omniscient; but that he has a view of those things to which the apostle had reference—that is, to the things which are revealed to man by the Holy Spirit. ¶ *Yet he himself is judged.* Greek, as in the margin, "is discerned;" that is, his feelings, principles, views, hopes, fears, joys, cannot be fully understood and appreciated by any natural or sensual man. He does not comprehend the principles which actuate him; he does not enter into his joys; he does not sympathize with him in his feelings. This is a matter of simple truth and universal observation. The reason is added in the following verse,—that as the Christian is influenced by the Lord and as the natural man does not know him, so he cannot know him who is influenced by him; that is the Christian.

16. *For who hath known,* &c. This passage is quoted from Isa. xl. 13. The interrogative form is a strong mode of denying that *any* one has ever known the mind of the Lord. The argument of Paul is this, "No one can understand God. No one can fully comprehend his plans, his feelings, his views, his designs. No one by nature, under the influence of sense and passion, is either disposed to investigate his truths, or loves them when they are revealed. But the Christian is influenced by God. He has his Spirit. He has the mind of Christ; who had the mind of God. He sympathizes with Christ; he has his feelings, desires, purposes, and plans. And as no one can fully understand God by nature, so neither can he understand him who is influenced by God, and is like him; and it is not to be wondered at that he regards the Christian religion as folly, and the Christian as a fool. ¶ *The mind of Christ.* The views, feelings, and temper of Christ. We are influenced by his Spirit.

REMARKS.

1st. Ministers of the gospel should not be too anxious to be distinguished for excellency of speech or language, ver. 1. Their aim should be to speak the simple truth, in language pure and intelligible to all. Let it be remembered, that if there ever was any place where it would be proper to seek such graces of eloquence, it was Corinth. If in any city now, or in any refined and genteel society it would be proper, it would have been proper in Corinth. Let this thought rebuke those, who, when they preach to a gay and fashionable auditory, seek to fill their sermons with ornament rather than with solid thought; with the tinsel of rhetoric, rather than with pure language. Paul was *right* in his course; and was *wise.* True taste abhors meretricious ornaments as much as the gospel does. And the man who is called to preach in a rich and fashionable congregation, should remember, that he is stationed there not to please the ear, but to save the soul; that his object is not to display his talent or his eloquence, but to rescue his hearers from ruin. This purpose will make the mere ornaments of rhetoric appear small. It will give seriousness to his discourse; gravity to his diction; unction to his eloquence; heart to his arguments; and success to his ministry.

2d. The purpose of every minister should be like that of Paul, to preach Christ and him crucified only. See Note on ver. 2.

3d. If Paul trembled at Corinth in view of dangers and difficulties; if he was conscious of his own weakness and feebleness, then we should learn also to be humble. He is not much in danger of erring who imitates the example of this great apostle. And if he who had received a direct commission from the great Head of the church, and who was endowed with such mighty powers, was modest, unassuming, and diffident, then it becomes ministers of the gospel now, and all others to be humble also. We should not, indeed, be afraid of men; but we should be modest, humble, and lowly; much impressed, as if conscious of our mighty charge; and anxious to deliver just such a message as God will approve and bless.

> Would I describe a preacher, such as Paul,
> Were he on earth, would hear, approve, and own,
> Paul should himself direct me. I would trace
> His master-strokes, and draw from his design.
> I would express him simple, grave, sincere;
> In doctrine uncorrupt; in language plain;
> And plain in manner, decent, solemn, chaste,
> And natural in gesture: much impress'd
> Himself, as conscious of his awful charge;
> And anxious mainly that the flock he feeds
> May feel it too. Affectionate in look,
> And tender in address, as well becomes
> A messenger of grace to guilty men.
>
> *Task*, B. ii.

Our aim should be to commend our message to every man's conscience; and to do it with humility towards God, and deep solicitude; with boldness towards our fellow men—respectfully towards them—but still resolved to tell the truth, ver. 3.

4th. The faith of Christians does not stand in the wisdom of man. Every Christian has evidence in his own heart, in his experience, and in the transformation of his character, that none but God could have wrought the change on his soul. His hopes, his joys, his peace, his sanctification, his love of prayer, of the Bible, of Christians, of God, and of Christ, are all such as nothing could have produced but the mighty power of God. All these bear marks of their high origin. They are the work of God on the soul. And as the Christian is fully conscious that these are not the *native* feelings of his heart—that if left to himself he would never have had them; so he has the fullest demonstration that they are to be traced to a divine source. And can he be mistaken about their existence? Can a man doubt whether he *has* joy, and peace, and happiness? Is the infidel to tell him coolly that he must be mistaken in regard to the existence of these emotions, and that it is all delusion? Can a child doubt whether it loves a parent; a husband whether he loves his wife; a friend, a friend; a man, his country? And can he doubt whether this emotion produces joy? And can a man doubt whether he loves God? Whether he has different views from what he once had? Whether he has peace and joy in view of the character of God, and the hope of heaven? And by what right shall the infidel tell him that he is mistaken, and that all this is delusion? How can *he* enter into the soul, and pronounce the man who professes to have these feelings mistaken? What should we think of the man who should tell a wife that she did not love her husband; or a father that he did not love his children? How *can* he know this? And, in like manner, how *can* an infidel and a scoffer say to a Christian, that all his hopes and joys, his love and peace are delusion and fanaticism? The truth is, that the great mass of Christians are just as well satisfied of the truth of religion, as they are of their own existence; and that a Christian will die for his love to the Saviour, just as he will die for his wife, and children, and country. Martyrdom in the one case is on the same principle as martyrdom in the other. Martyrdom in either, is noble and honourable, and evinces the highest qualities and principles of the human mind.

5th. Christians are influenced by true wisdom, ver. 6. They are not fools; though they appear to be to their fellow men. They see a *real* beauty and wisdom in the plan of redemption which the world does not discern. It is not the wisdom of this world; but it is the wisdom which looks to eternity. Is a man a fool who acts with reference to the future? Is he a fool who believes that he shall live to all eternity, and who regards it as proper to make preparation for that eternity? Is he a fool who acts as if he were to die—to be judged—to enter on an unchanging destiny? Folly is manifested in closing the eyes on the reality of the condition; not in looking at it as it is. The man who is sick, and who strives to convince himself that he is well; the man whose affairs are in a state of bankruptcy, and who is unwilling to know it, is a fool. The man who is willing to know all about his situation, and to act accordingly, is a wise man. The one represents the conduct of a sinner, the other that of a Christian. A man who should see his child drowning, or his house on fire, or the pestilence breathing around him, and be unconcerned, or *dance* amidst such scenes, would be a fool or a madman. And is not the sinner who is gay and thoughtless over the grave and over *hell* equally foolish and mad? And if there be a God, a heaven, a Saviour, and a hell; if men are to die, and to be judged, is he not wise who acts *as if* it were so, and who lives accordingly? While Christians, therefore, may not be distinguished for the wisdom of this world—while many are destitute of learning, science, and eloquence, they *have* a wisdom which shall survive when all other is vanished away.

6th. All the wisdom of this world shall come to nought, ver. 6. What will be the value of political sagacity, when all governments shall come to an end but the divine government? What the value of eloquence, and graceful diction, when we stand at the judgment seat of Christ? What the value of science in this world, when all shall be revealed with the clearness of noonday? How low will appear *all* human attainments in that world, when the light of eternal day shall be shed over all the works of God? How little can human science do to advance the eternal interests of man? And how shall all fade away in the future world of glory—just as the feeble glimmering of the stars fades away before the light of the morning sun! How little, therefore, should we pride ourselves on the highest attainments of science, and the most elevated distinctions of learning and eloquence.

7th. God has a purpose in regard to the salvation of men, ver. 7. This scheme was ordained before the world. It was not a new device. It was not the offspring of chance, an accident, or an *after thought*. It was because God purposed it *from eternity*. God has a plan; and this plan contemplates the salvation of his people. And it greatly enhances the value of this benevolent plan in the eyes of his people, that it has been the object of *the eternal earnest desire and purpose of God*. How much a gift is enhanced in value from the fact that it has been long the purpose of a parent to bestow it; that he has toiled for it; that he has made arrangements for it; and that this has been the chief object of his efforts and his plan for years. So the favours of eternal redemption are bestowed on Christians as the fruit of the eternal purpose and desire of God. And how should our hearts rise in gratitude to him for his unspeakable gift!

8th. One great and prominent cause of sin is the fact that men are blind to the reality and beauty of spiritual objects. So it was with those who crucified the Lord, ver. 8. Had they seen his glory as it was, they would not have crucified him. And so it is now. When men blaspheme God, they see not his excellency: when they revile religion, they know not its real value; when they break the laws of God, they do not fully discern their purity and their importance. It is true they are wilfully ignorant, and their crime is often enhanced by this fact; but it is equally true that "they know not what they do." For such poor, blinded, deluded mortals, the Saviour prayed; and for such we should all pray. The man that curses God, has no just sense of what he is doing. The man who is profane, and a scoffer, and a liar, and an adulterer, has no just sense of the awful nature of his crime; and is an object of commiseration—while his *sin* should be *hated*—and is a proper subject of prayer.

9th. Men are often committing the most awful crimes when they are unconscious of it, ver. 8. What crime could compare with that of crucifying the only Son of God? And what crime could be attended with more dreadful consequences to its perpetrators? So of sinners now. They little know what they do; and they little know the consequences of their sins. A man may curse his Maker, and say it is in sport! But how will it be regarded in the day of judgment? A man may revile the Saviour! But how will it appear when he dies? It is a solemn thing to trifle with God and with his laws. A man is safer when he sports on a volcano, or when he makes a jest of the pestilence or the forked lightnings of heaven, than when he sports with religion and with God! In a world like this, men should be serious and fear God. A single deed, like that of the crucifixion of Christ, may be remembered, when all the circumstances of sport and mockery shall have passed away—remembered when the world shall be destroyed, and stars and suns shall rush to ruin.

10th. Christians have views of the beauties of religion, and have consolations arising from these views, which the world has not, ver. 9. They have different views of God, of Christ, of heaven, of eternity. They see a beauty in all these things, and a wisdom in the plan of salvation, which the men of the world do not see. The contemplations of this beauty and wisdom, and the evidence which they have that they are interested in all this, gives them a joy which the world does not possess. They see what the eye has not elsewhere seen; they enjoy what men elsewhere have not enjoyed; and they are elevated to privileges which men elsewhere do not possess. On earth they partake of happiness which the world never can give, and in heaven they shall partake of the fulness of that joy—of pleasures there which the eye had not before seen, nor the ear heard, nor the heart of man conceived. Who would not be a Christian?

11th. The Holy Ghost is in some sense distinct from the Father. This is implied in his action as an agent—in searching, knowing, &c. ver. 10, 11. An attribute; a quality, does not search and know.

12th. The Holy Spirit is divine. None can know God but one equal to himself. If the Spirit intimately knows the wisdom, the goodness, the omniscience, the eternity, the power of God, he must be divine. No created being can have this intelligence, ver. 10, 11.

13th. Christians are actuated by a different spirit from the men of this world, ver. 12. They are influenced by a regard to God and his glory. The men of the world are under the influence of pride, avarice, sensuality, ambition, and vain glory.

14th. The sinner does not perceive the beauty of the things of religion. To all this beauty he is blind. This is a sober and a most melancholy fact. Whatever may be the cause of it, the fact is undeniable and sad. It is so with the sensualist; with the men of avarice, pride, ambition, and licentiousness. The gospel is regarded as folly, and is despised and scorned by the men of this world. This is true in all places, among all people, and at all times. To this there are no exceptions in human nature; and over this we should sit down and weep.

15th. The *reason* of this is, that men love darkness. It is not that they are destitute of the natural faculties for

CHAPTER III.

AND I, brethren, could not speak unto you as [a] unto spiritual, but as unto carnal, *even* as unto babes [b] in Christ.

a chap. 2.14,15. *b* Heb.5.12,13; 1 Pet.2.2.

loving God, for they have as strong native powers as those who become Christians. It is because they *love sin*—and this simple fact, carried out into all its bearings, will account for all the difficulties in the way of the sinner's conversion. There is nothing else; and

16th. We see here the value of the influences of the Spirit. It is by this Spirit alone that the mind of the Christian is enlightened, sanctified, and comforted. It is by Him alone that he sees the beauty of the religion which he loves; it is by His influence alone that he differs from his fellow men. And no less important is it for the sinner. Without the influences of that Spirit his mind will always be in darkness, and his heart will always hate the gospel. How anxiously, therefore, should he cherish His influences! How careful should he be not to grieve Him away!

17th. There is a difference between Christians and other men. One is enlightened by the Holy Spirit, the other not; one sees a beauty in religion, to the other it is folly: the one has the mind of Christ, the other has the spirit of the world; the one discerns the excellency of the plan of salvation, to the other all is darkness and folly. How could beings differ more in their moral feelings and views than do Christians and the men of this world?

CHAPTER III.

THE design of this chapter is substantially the same as the former. It is to reprove the pride, the philosophy, the vain wisdom on which the Greeks so much rested; and to show that the gospel was not dependent on that for its success, and that that had been the occasion of no small part of the contentions and strifes which had arisen in the church at Corinth. The chapter is occupied mainly with an account of his own ministry with them; and seems designed to meet an objection which either *was* made, or *could have been* made by the Corinthians themselves, or by the false teacher that was among them. In chap. ii. 12—16, he had affirmed that Christians were in fact under the influence of the Spirit of God; that they were enlightened in a remarkable degree; that they understood all things pertaining to the Christian religion. To this, it either was, or could have been objected that Paul, when among them, had not instructed them fully in the more deep and abstruse points of the gospel; and that he had confined his instructions to the very rudiments of the Christian religion. Of this, probably the false teachers who had formed parties among them, had taken the advantage, and had pretended to carry the instruction to a much greater length, and to explain many things which Paul had left unexplained. Hence this division into parties. It became Paul, therefore, to state why he had confined his instructions to the rudiments of the gospel among them—and this occupies the first part of the chapter, v. 1—11. The *reason* was, that they were not prepared to receive higher instruction, but were carnal, and he could not address them as being prepared to enter fully into the more profound doctrines of the Christian religion. The *proof* that this was so, was found in the fact that they had been distracted with disputes and strifes, which demonstrated that they were not prepared for the higher doctrines of Christianity. He then *reproves* them for their contentions, on the ground that it was of little consequence by what instrumentality they had been brought to the knowledge of the gospel, and that there was no occasion for their strifes and sects. ALL success, whoever was the instrument, was to be traced to God (ver. 5—7), and the fact that one teacher or another had first instructed them, or that one was more eloquent than another, should not be the foundation for contending sects. God was the source of all blessings. Yet in order to show the real nature of his own work, in order to meet the whole of the objection, he goes on to state that he had done the most important part of the work in the church himself. He had laid the foundation; and all the others were but rearing the superstructure. And much as *his* instructions might appear to be elementary, and unimportant, yet it had been done with the same skill which an architect evinces who labours that the foundation may be well laid and firm, ver. 10, 11. The others who had succeeded him, whoever they were, were but builders upon this foundation. The foundation had been well laid, and they should be careful how they built on it, ver. 12—16. The mention of this fact—that he had laid the foundation, and that that foundation was Jesus Christ, and that they had been reared upon that as a church, leads him to the inference (ver. 16, 17), that they should be holy as the temple of God; and the conclusion from the whole is, (1.) That no man should deceive himself, of which there was so much danger (ver. 18—20); and, (2.) That no Christian should glory in men, for all things were theirs. It was no matter who had been their teacher on earth, all belonged to God; and they had a common interest in the most eminent teachers of religion, and they should rise above the petty rivalships of the world, and rejoice in the assurance that all things belonged to them, ver. 21—23.

1. *And I, brethren.* See chap. ii. 1. This is designed to meet an implied objection. He had said (chap. ii. 14—16) that Christians were able to understand all things. Yet, they would recollect that he had not addressed them as such, but had confined himself to the more elementary parts of religion when he came among them. He had not entered upon the abstruse and difficult points of theology—the points of speculation in which the subtle Greeks so much abounded and so much delighted. He now states the reason why he had not done it. The reason was one that was most humbling to their pride; but it was the true reason, and faithfulness demanded that it should be stated. It was, that they were *carnal*, and not qualified to understand the deep mysteries of the gospel; and the *proof* of this was unhappily at hand. It was too evident in their contentions and strifes, that they were under the influence of carnal feelings and views. ¶ *Could not speak unto you as unto spiritual.* "I could not regard you as spiritual—as qualified to enter into the full and higher truths of the gospel; I could not regard you as divested of the feelings which influence carnal men—the men of the world, and I addressed you accordingly. I could not discourse to you as to far-advanced and well-informed Christians. I taught you the *rudiments* only of the Christian religion." He refers here, doubtless, to his instructions when he founded the church at Corinth. See Note, chap. ii. 13—15. ¶ *But as unto carnal.* The word *carnal* here (σαρκινοῖς) is not the same which in chap. ii. 14, is translated *natural* (ψυχικός). *That* refers to one who is unrenewed, and who is wholly under the influence of his sensual or animal nature, and is no where applied to Christians. *This* is applied here to Christians—but to those who have much of the remains of corruption, and who are imperfectly acquainted with the nature of religion; babes in Christ. It denotes those who still evinced the feelings and views which pertain to the flesh, in these unhappy contentions, and strifes, and divisions. "The works of the flesh are hatred, variance, emulations, wrath, strife, seditions, envyings" (Gal. v. 20, 21); and these they had evinced in their divisions; and Paul knew that their danger lay in this direction, and he therefore addressed them according to their character. Paul applies the word to himself (Rom. vii. 14), "for I am carnal;" and here it denotes that they were as yet under the influence of the corrupt passions and desires which the flesh produces. ¶ *As unto babes in Christ.* As unto those recently born into his kingdom, and unable to understand the profounder doctrines of the Christian religion. It is a com-

2 I have fed you with milk, and
not with meat: for hitherto [a] ye
were not able *to bear it*, neither yet
now are ye able.
3 For ye are yet carnal: for
whereas [b] *there is* among you envying, and strife, and [1] divisions, are
ye not carnal, and walk [2] as men?
4 For while one saith, I [c] am of
Paul; and another, I *am* of Apollos; are ye not carnal?
5 Who then is Paul, and who *is*

a John 16.12. *b* James 3.16. 1 or, *factions*. 2 *according to man*. *c* chap.1.12.

mon figure to apply the term infants and children to those who are feeble in understanding, or unable, from any cause, to comprehend the more profound instructions of science or religion.

2. *I have fed you with milk.* Paul here continues the metaphor, which is derived from the custom of feeding infants with the lightest food. Milk here evidently denotes the more simple and elementary doctrines of Christianity—the doctrines of the new birth, of repentance, faith, &c. The same figure occurs in Heb. v. 11—14; and also in classical writers. See Wetstein. ¶ *And not with meat.* Meat here denotes the more sublime and mysterious doctrines of religion. ¶ *For hitherto.* Formerly, when I came among you, and laid the foundations of the church. ¶ *Not able* to bear it. You were not sufficiently advanced in Christian knowledge to comprehend the higher mysteries of the gospel. ¶ *Neither yet now*, &c. The reason why they were not then able he proceeds immediately to state.

3. *For ye are yet carnal.* Though you are Christians, and are the friends of God in the main, yet your divisions and strifes show that you are yet, in some degree, under the influence of the principles which govern the men of this world. Men who are governed solely by the principles of this world, evince a spirit of strife, emulation and contention; and just so far as you are engaged in strife, just so far do you show that you are governed by their principles and feelings. ¶ *For whereas.* In proof that you are carnal I appeal to your contentions and strifes. ¶ *Envying* (ζῆλος), zeal; used here in the sense of *envy*, as it is in James iii. 14, 16. It denotes, properly, any *fervour* of mind (from ζέω), and may be applied to any exciting and agitating passion. The envy here referred to, was that which arose from the superior advantages and endowments which some claimed or possessed over others. Envy everywhere is a fruitful cause of strife. Most contentions in the church are somehow usually connected with envy. ¶ *And strife.* Contention and dispute. ¶ *And divisions.* Dissensions and quarrels. The margin correctly renders it *factions*. The idea is, that they were split up into parties, and that those parties were embittered with mutual recriminations and reproaches, as they always are in a church. ¶ *And walk as men.* Marg. *according to man*. The word *walk* is used often in the Scriptures in the sense of *conduct* or *act*. You *conduct* as men, *i. e.* as men commonly do; you evince the same spirit that the great mass of men do. Instead of being filled with love; of being united and harmonious as the members of the same family ought to be, you are split up into factions as the men of the world are.

4. *For while one saith*, &c.; see Note, chap. i. 12.

5. *Who then is Paul*, &c.; see Notes, chap. i. 13. Why should a party be formed which should be named after Paul? What has he done or taught that should lead to this? What eminence has *he* that should induce any to call themselves by his name? He is on a level with the other apostles; and all are but ministers, or servants, and have no claim to the honour of giving names to sects and parties. God is the fountain of all your blessings, and whoever may have been the *instrument* by whom you have believed, it is improper to regard them as in any sense the fountain of your blessings, or to arrange yourselves under their name. ¶ *But ministers.* Our word *minister*, as now used, does not express the proper force of this word. We in applying it to preachers of the

Apollos, but ministers by whom ye believed, even [a] as the Lord gave to every man?

6 I have planted, Apollos watered; but God [b] gave the increase.

a Rom.12.3,6; 1 Pet.4.11.

b chap.15.10.

gospel do not usually advert to the original sense of the word, and the reasons why it was given to them. The original word (διάκονοι) denotes properly *servants* in contradistinction from *masters* (Mat. xx. 26; xxiii. 11; Mark ix. 35; x. 43); and denotes those of course who are in an inferior rank of life. They had not command, or authority, but were subject to the command of others. It is applied to the preachers of the gospel because they are employed in the *service* of God; because they go at his command, and are subject to his control and direction. They have not original authority, nor are they the source of influence or power. The idea here is, that they were the mere instruments or servants by whom God conveyed all blessings to the Corinthians; that they as ministers were on a level, were engaged in the same work, and that therefore, it was improper for them to form parties that should be called by their names. ¶ *By whom.* Through whom (δι' ὧν), by whose instrumentality. They were not the original source of faith, but were the mere servants of God in conveying to them the knowledge of that truth by which they were to be saved. ¶ *Even as the Lord gave to every man.* God is the original source of faith; and it is by his influence that any one is brought to believe; see Note, Rom. xii. 3, 6. There were diversities of gifts among the Corinthian Christians, as there are in all Christians. And it is here implied, (1.) That all that any one had was to be traced to God as its author; (2.) That he is a sovereign, and dispenses his favours to all as he pleases; (3.) That since *God* had conferred those favours, it was improper for the Corinthians to divide themselves into sects and call themselves by the name of their teachers, for *all* that they had was to be traced to God alone. This idea, that *all* the gifts and graces which Christians had, were to be traced to God alone, was one which the apostle Paul often insisted on; and if this idea had been kept before the minds and hearts of all Christians, it would have prevented no small part of the contentions in the church, and the formation of no small part of the sects in the Christian world.

6. *I have planted.* The apostle here compares the establishment of the church at Corinth to the planting of a vine, a tree, or of grain. The figure is taken from agriculture, and the meaning is obvious. Paul established the church. He was the first preacher in Corinth; and if any distinction was due to any one, it was rather to him than to the teachers who had laboured there subsequently; but he regarded himself as worthy of no such honour as to be the head of a party, for it was not himself, but God who had given the increase. ¶ *Apollos watered.* This figure is taken from the practice of watering a tender plant, or of watering a garden or field. This was necessary in a special manner in eastern countries. Their fields became parched and dry from their long droughts, and it was necessary to irrigate them by artificial means. The sense here is, that Paul had laboured in establishing the church at Corinth; but that subsequently Apollos had laboured to increase it, and to build it up. It is certain that Apollos did not go to Corinth until after Paul had left it; see Acts xviii. 18; comp. 27. ¶ *God gave the increase.* God caused the seed sown to take root and spring up; and God blessed the irrigation of the tender plants as they sprung up, and caused them to grow. This idea is still taken from the husbandman. It would be vain for the farmer to sow his seed unless God should give it life. There is no life in the seed, nor is there any inherent power in the earth to make it grow. God only, the giver of all life, can quicken the germ in the seed, and make it live. So it would be in vain for the farmer to water his plant unless God should

7 So then neither [a] is he that planteth any thing, neither he that watereth, but God that giveth the increase.

a John 15.5; 2 Cor.12.9—11.

8 Now he that planteth and he that watereth are one: and every man [b] shall receive his own reward according to his own labour.

b Ps.62.12; Rev.22.12.

bless it. There is no living principle in the water; no inherent power in the rains of heaven to make the plant grow. It is *adapted*, indeed, to this, and the seed would not germinate if it was not planted, nor grow if it was not watered; but the life is still from God. He arranged these means, and he gives life to the tender blade, and sustains it. And so it is with the word of life. It has no inherent power to produce effect by itself. The power is not in the naked word, nor in him that plants, nor in him that waters, nor in the heart where it is sown, but in God. But there is a *fitness* of the means to the end. The word is adapted to save the soul. The seed must be sown or it will not germinate. Truth must be sown in *the heart*, and the heart must be prepared for it—as the earth must be ploughed and made mellow, or it will not spring up. It must be cultivated with assiduous care, or it will produce nothing. But still it is all of God—as much so as the yellow harvest of the field, after all the toils of the husbandman is of God. And as the farmer who has just views, will take no praise to himself because his corn and his vine start up and grow after all his care, but will ascribe all to God's unceasing, beneficent agency; so will the minister of religion, and so will every Christian, after all their care, ascribe all to God.

7. *Any thing*. This is to be taken *comparatively*. They are nothing in comparison with God. Their agency is of no importance compared with his; see Note, chap. i. 28. It does not mean that their agency ought not to be performed; that it is not important, and indispensable in its place; but that the honour is due to God.—Their agency *is* indispensable. God *could* make seed or a tree grow if they were not planted in the earth. But he does not do it. The agency of the husbandman is indispensable in the ordinary operations of his providence. If he does not plant, God will not make the grain or the tree grow. God *blesses* his labours; he does not work a miracle. God attends *effort* with success; he does not interfere in a miraculous manner to accommodate the *indolence* of men. So in the matter of salvation. The efforts of ministers would be of no avail without God. They could do nothing in the salvation of the soul unless He should give the increase. But *their* labours are as indispensable and as necessary, as are those of the farmer in the production of a harvest. And as every farmer could say, "my labours are *nothing* without God, who alone can give the increase," so it is with every minister of the gospel.

8. *Are one* (ἕν εἰσιν). They are not the same person; but they are *one* in the following respects: (1.) They are *united* in reference to the same work. Though they are engaged in different things—for planting and watering are different kinds of work, yet it is one in regard to the end to be gained. The employments do not at all *clash*, but tend to the same end. It is not as if one planted, and the other was engaged in pulling up. (2.) Their work is *one*, because one is as necessary as the other. If the grain was not planted there would be no use in pouring water there; if not watered, there would be no use in planting. The work of one is as needful, therefore, as the other; and the one should not undervalue the labours of the other. (3.) They are *one* in regard to God. They are *both* engaged in performing one work; God is performing another. There are not three parties or portions of the work, but two. They two perform one part of the work; God *alone* performs the other. Theirs would be useless without him; he would not ordinarily perform his without their performing their part. They *could* not do his part if they would—as they cannot make a plant *grow;* he *could* perform their

9 For we are labourers together *a* with God: ye are God's [1] husbandry, *ye are* God's building. *b*

a 2 Cor.6.1. [1] or, *tillage*. *b* Heb.3.6; 1 Pet.2.5.

part—as *he* could plant and water without the farmer; but it is not in accordance with his arrangements to do it. ¶ *And every man.* The argument of the apostle here has reference only to ministers; but it is equally true of all men, that they shall receive their proper reward. ¶ *Shall receive.* In the day of judgment, when God decides the destiny of men. The decisions of that day will be simply determining what every moral agent *ought* to receive. ¶ *His own reward.* His fit, or proper (τον ἴδιον) reward; that which pertains to him, or which shall be a proper expression of the character and value of his labour.—The word *reward* (μισθὸν) denotes properly that which is given by contract for service rendered; an equivalent in value for services or for kindness; Note, Rom. iv. 4. In the Scriptures it denotes pay, wages, recompense given to day-labourers, to soldiers, &c. It is applied often, as here, to the retribution which God will make to men in the day of judgment; and is applied to the *favours* which he will then bestow on them, or to the *punishment* which he will inflict as the reward of their deeds. Instances of the former sense occur in Mat. v. 12; vi.; Luke vi. 23, 35; Rev. xi. 18; of the latter in 2 Pet. ii. 13, 15.—In regard to the righteous, it does not imply *merit*, or that they deserve heaven; but it means that God will render to them that which, according to the terms of his new covenant, he has promised, and which shall be a fit expression of his acceptance of their services. It is *proper*, according to these arrangements, that they should be blessed in heaven. It would *not* be proper that they should be cast down to hell.—Their original and their sole *title* to eternal life is the grace of God through Jesus Christ; the *measure*, or *amount* of the favours bestowed on them there, shall be according to the services which they render on earth. A parent may resolve to divide his estate among his sons, and their title to *any* thing may be derived from his mere favour, but he may determine that it shall be divided *according* to their expressions of attachment, and to their obedience to him.

9. *For we are labourers together with God* (Θεοῦ γάρ ἐσμεν συνεργοί). We are God's co-workers. A similar expression occurs in 2 Cor. vi. 1, "We then as workers together with him," &c. This passage is capable of two significations: *first*, as in our translation, that they were co-workers with God; engaged with him in his work, that he and they co-operated in the production of the effect; or that it was a *joint-work;* as we speak of a partnercy, or of joint-effort among men. So many interpreters have understood this. If this is the sense of the passage, then it means that as a farmer may be said to be a co-worker with God when he plants and tills his field, or does that without which God would not work in that case, or without which a harvest would not be produced, so the Christian minister co-operates with God in producing the same result. He is engaged in performing that which is indispensable to the end; and God also, by his Spirit, co-operates with the same design. If this be the idea, it gives a peculiar sacredness to the work of the ministry, and indeed to the work of the farmer and the vinedresser. There is no higher honour than for a man to be engaged in doing the same things which God does, and participating with him in accomplishing his glorious plans. But doubts have been suggested in regard to this interpretation. (1.) The Greek does not of necessity imply this. It is literally, not we are his co-partners, but we are his fellow-labourers, *i.e.* fellow-labourers in his employ, under his direction —as we say of servants of the same rank they are fellow-labourers of the same master, not meaning that the master was engaged in working *with*

10 According [a] to the grace of God which is given unto me, as a wise

a Rom.12.3.

---

them, but that *they* were fellow-labourers one with another in his employment. (2.) There is no expression that is parallel to this. There is none that speaks of God's operating *jointly* with his creatures in producing the *same* result. They may be engaged in regard to the same end; but the sphere of God's operations and of their operations is distinct. God does one thing; and they do another, though they may contribute to the same result. The sphere of God's operations in the growth of a tree is totally distinct from that of the man who plants it. The man who planted it has *no* agency in causing the juices to circulate; in expanding the bud or the leaf; that is, in the proper work of God.—In 3 John 8, Christians are indeed said to be "fellow-helpers to the truth" (συνεργοὶ τῇ ἀληθείᾳ); that is, they operate with the truth, and contribute by their labours and influence to that effect. In Mark also (xvi. 20), it is said that the apostles "went forth and preached everywhere, the Lord working with them" (τοῦ κυρίου συνεργοῦντος), where the phrase means that the Lord co-operated with them by miracles, &c. The Lord, by his own proper energy, and in his own sphere, contributed to the success of the work in which they were engaged. (3.) The main design and scope of this whole passage is to show that God is all—that the apostles are nothing; to represent the apostles not as joint-workers with God, but as working by themselves, and God as alone giving efficiency to all that was done. The idea is, that of depressing or humbling the apostles, and of exalting God; and this idea would not be consistent with the interpretation that they were *joint*-labourers with him. While, therefore, the Greek would bear the interpretation conveyed in our translation, the sense *may* perhaps be, that the apostles were joint-labourers with each other in God's service; that they were united in their work, and that God was all in all; that they were like servants employed *in* the service of a master, without saying that the master participated with them in their work. This idea is conveyed in the translation of Doddridge, "we are the fellow-labourers of God." So Rosenmüller. Calvin, however, Grotius, Whitby, and Bloomfield, coincide with our version in the interpretation. The Syriac renders it "We work with God." The Vulgate, "We are the aids of God." ¶ *Ye are God's husbandry* (γεώργιον); margin, *tillage*. This word occurs no where else in the New Testament. It properly denotes a *tilled* or *cultivated field;* and the idea is, that the church at Corinth was the field on which *God* had bestowed the labour of tillage, or culture, to produce fruit. The word is used by the LXX. in Gen. xxvi. 14, as the translation of עבדה, "For he had *possession* of flocks," &c.; in Jer. xli. 23, as the translation of צמד, *a yoke;* and in Prov. xxiv. 30; xxxi. 16, as the translation of שדה, *a field;* "I went by the *field* of the slothful," &c. The sense here is, that all their culture was of God; that as a church they were under his care; and that all that had been produced in them was to be traced to his cultivation. ¶ *God's building.* This is another metaphor. The object of Paul was to show that *all* that had been done for them had been really accomplished by God. For this purpose he first says that they were God's cultivated field; then he changes the figure; draws his illustration from architecture, and says, that they had been *built* by him as an architect rears a house. It does not rear itself; but it is reared by another. So he says of the Corinthians, "Ye are the building which God erects." The same figure is used in 2 Cor. vi. 16, and Eph. ii. 21; see also Heb. iii. 6; 1 Pet. ii. 5. The idea is, that God is the supreme agent in the founding and establishing of the church, in all its gifts and graces.

10. *According to the grace of God.* By the favour of God which is given to me. All that Paul had done had been by the mere favour of God. His appointment was from him; and all

master-builder, I have laid the foundation, and another buildeth thereon. But let every man take heed how he buildeth thereupon.

the skill which he had shown, and all the agency which he had employed, had been from him. The architectural figure is here continued with some striking additions and illustrations. By the "grace of God" here, Paul probably means his apostleship to the Gentiles, which had been conferred on him by the mere favour of God, and all the wisdom, and skill, and success which he had evinced in founding the church. ¶ *As a wise master-builder.* Gr. *Architect.* The word does not imply that Paul had any pre-eminence over his brethren, but that he had proceeded in his work as a skilful architect, who secures first a firm foundation. Every builder begins with the foundation; and Paul had proceeded in this manner in laying first a firm foundation on which the church could be reared. The word *wise* here means skilful, judicious; comp. Mat. vii. 24. ¶ *I have laid the foundation. What* this foundation was, he states in ver. 11. The meaning here is, that the church at Corinth had been at first established by Paul; see Acts xviii. 1, &c. ¶ *And another.* Other teachers. I have communicated to the church the first elements of Christian knowledge. Others *follow out* this instruction, and edify the church. The discussion here undergoes a slight change. In the former part of the chapter, *Christians* are compared to a building; here the *doctrines* which are taught in the church are compared to various parts of a building. *Grotius.* See similar instances of translation in Mat. xiii; Mark iv. John x. ¶ *But let every man,* &c. Every man who is a professed teacher. Let him be careful what instructions he shall give to a church that has been founded by apostolic hands, and that is established on the only true foundation. This is designed to guard against false instruction and the instructions of false teachers. Men should take heed what instruction they give to a church, (1.) Because of the fact that the church belongs to God, and they should be cautious what directions they give to it; (2.) Because it is important that Christians should not only be on the true foundation, but that they should be fully instructed in the nature of their religion, and the church should be permitted to rise in its true beauty and loveliness; (3.) Because of the evils which result from false instruction. Even when the foundation is firm, incalculable evils will result from the want of just and discriminating instruction. Error sanctifies no one. The effect of it even on the minds of true Christians is to mar their piety; to dim its lustre; and to darken their minds. No Christian can enjoy religion except under the full-orbed shining of the word of truth; and every man, therefore, who gives false instruction, is responsible for all the darkness he causes, and for all the want of comfort which true Christians under his teaching may experience. (4.) Every man must give an account of the nature of his instructions; and he should therefore "take heed to himself, and his doctrine" (1 Tim. iv. 16); and preach *such* doctrine as shall bear the test of the great day. And from this we learn, that it is important that the church should be built on the true foundation; and that it is scarcely less important that it should be built up in the knowledge of the truth. Vast evils are constantly occurring in the church for the want of proper instruction to young converts. Many seem to feel that provided the foundation be well laid, that is all that is needed. But the grand thing which is wanted at the present time, is, that those who *are* converted should, as soon as possible, be instructed FULLY in the nature of the religion which they have embraced. What would be thought of a farmer who should plant a tree, and never water or trim it: who should plant his seed, and never cultivate the corn as it springs up; who should sow his fields, and then think that all is well, and leave it to be overrun with weeds and thorns? Piety is often stunted, its early shootings blighted, its rapid growth checked,

11 For other foundation can no man lay than that is laid, [a] which is Jesus Christ.

12 Now if any man build upon this foundation gold, silver, precious stones, wood, hay, stubble;

a Isa.28.16; Mat.16.18; Eph.2.20; 2 Tim.2.19.

for the want of early culture in the church. And perhaps there is no one thing in which pastors more frequently fail than in regard to the culture which ought to be bestowed on those who are converted—especially in early life. Our Saviour's views on this were expressed in the admonition to Peter, "Feed my lambs," John xxi. 15.

11. *For other foundation.* It is *implied* by the course of the argument here, that *this* was the foundation which had been laid at Corinth, and on which the church there had been reared. And it is *affirmed* that no other foundation can be laid. A foundation is that on which a building is reared: the foundation of a church is the *doctrine* on which it is established; that is, the doctrines which its members hold—those truths which lie at the basis of their hopes, and by embracing which they have been converted to God. ¶ *Can no man lay.* That is, there *is* no other true foundation. ¶ *Which is Jesus Christ.* Christ is often called the foundation; the stone; the corner stone on which the church is reared; Isa. xxviii. 16; Mat. xxi. 42; Acts iv. 11; Eph. ii. 20; 2 Tim. ii. 19; 1 Pet. ii. 6. The meaning is, that no true church can be reared which does not embrace and hold the true doctrines respecting him —those which pertain to his incarnation, his divine nature, his instructions, his example, his atonement, his resurrection, and ascension. The reason why no true church can be established without embracing the truth as it is in Christ is, that it is by him only that men can be saved; and where *this* doctrine is wanting, all is wanting that enters into the essential idea of a church. The fundamental doctrines of the Christian religion must be embraced, or a church cannot exist; and where those doctrines are denied, no association of men can be recognised as a church of God. Nor can the foundation be modified or shaped so as to suit the wishes of men. It must be laid as it is in the Scriptures; and the superstructure must be reared on that alone.

12. *Now if any man.* If any teacher in the doctrines which he inculcates; or any private Christian in the hopes which he cherishes. The main discussion doubtless, has respect to the teachers of religion. Paul carries forward the metaphor in this and the following verses with respect to the building. He supposes that the *foundation* is laid; that it is a true foundation; that the essential doctrines in regard to the Messiah are the real basis on which the edifice is reared. But, he says, that even admitting that, it is a subject of vast importance to attend to the kind of structure which shall be reared on that; whether it shall be truly beautiful, and valuable in itself, and such as shall abide the trial of the last great day; or whether it be mean, worthless, erroneous, and such as shall at last be destroyed. There has been some difference of opinion in regard to the interpretation of this passage, arising from the question whether the apostle designed to represent *one* or *two* buildings. The former has been the more common interpretation, and the sense according to that is, "the true foundation is laid; but on that it is improper to place vile and worthless materials. It would be absurd to work them in with those which are valuable; it would be absurd to work in, in rearing a building, wood, and hay, and stubble, with gold, and silver, and precious stones; there would be a want of concinnity and beauty in this. So in the spiritual temple. There is an impropriety, an unfitness, in rearing the spiritual temple, to interweave truth with error; sound doctrine with false." See Calvin and Macknight. Grotius renders it, "Paul feigns to himself an edifice, partly regal, and partly rustic. He presents the image of a house whose walls are of marble, whose columns are made partly of gold and partly of

silver, whose beams are of wood, and whose roof thatched with straw." Others, among whom are Wetstein, Doddridge, Rosenmüller, suppose that he refers to *two* buildings that might be reared on this foundation—either one that should be magnificent and splendid; or one that should be a rustic cottage, or mean hovel, thatched with straw, and made of planks of wood. Doddridge paraphrases the passage, "*If any man build*, I say, *upon this foundation*, let him look to the materials and the nature of his work; whether he raise a stately and magnificent temple upon it, adorned as it were like the house of God at Jerusalem, with gold and silver, and large, beautiful, and costly stones; or a mean hovel, consisting of nothing better than planks of wood roughly put together, and thatched with hay and stubble. That is, let him look to it, whether he teach the substantial, vital truths of Christianity, and which it was intended to support and illustrate; or set himself to propagate vain subtilties and conceits on the one hand, or legal rites and Jewish traditions on the other; which although they do not entirely destroy the foundation, disgrace it, as a mean edifice would do a grand and extensive foundation laid with great pomp and solemnity." This probably expresses the correct sense of the passage. The foundation may be well laid; yet *on* this foundation an edifice may be reared that shall be truly magnificent, or one that shall be mean and worthless. So the true foundation of a church may be laid, or of individual conversion to God, in the true doctrine respecting Christ. That church or that individual *may be* built up and adorned with all the graces which truth is fitted to produce; or there may be false principles and teachings superadded; doctrines that shall delude and lead astray; or views and feelings cultivated *as* piety, and believed *to be* piety, which may be no part of true religion, but which are mere delusion and fanaticism. ¶ *Gold, silver.* On the meaning of these words it is not necessary to dwell; or o lay too much stress. Gold is the emblem of that which is valuable and precious, and may be the emblem of that truth and holiness which shall bear the trial of the great day. In relation to the figure which the apostle here uses, it may refer to the fact that columns or beams in an edifice might be gilded; or perhaps, as in the temple, that they might be solid gold, so as to bear the action of intense heat; or so that fire would not destroy them.—So the precious doctrines of truth, and all the feelings, views, opinions, habits, practices, which truth produces in an individual or a church, will bear the trial of the last great day. ¶ *Precious stones.* By the stones here referred to, are not meant *gems* which are esteemed of so much value for ornaments, but beautiful and valuable marbles. The word *precious* here (τιμίους) means those which are obtained at a *price*, which are costly and valuable; and is particularly applicable, therefore, to the costly marbles which were used in building. The figurative sense here does not differ materially from that conveyed by the silver and gold. By this edifice thus reared on the true foundation, we are to understand, (1.) The true doctrines which should be employed to build up a church—doctrines which would bear the test of the trial of the last day; and, (2.) Such views in regard to piety, and to duty; such feelings and principles of action, as should be approved, and seen to be genuine piety in the day of judgment. ¶ *Wood.* That might be easily burned. An edifice reared of wood instead of marble, or slight buildings, such as were often put for up for temporary purposes in the east—as cottages, places for watching their vineyards, &c.; see my Note, on Isa. i. 8. ¶ *Hay, stubble.* Used for thatching the building, or for a roof. Perhaps, also, grass was sometimes employed in some way to make the walls of the building. Such an edifice would burn readily; would be constantly exposed to take fire. By this is meant, (1.) Errors and false doctrines, such as will not be found to be true in the day of judgment, and as will then be swept away; (2.) Such practices and mistaken views of piety, as shall grow out of false doctrines and

13 Every man's work shall be made manifest: for the day shall declare it, because it shall [1] be revealed by fire; and the [a] fire shall try every man's work, of what sort it is.

[1] *is.*

[a] Zech.13.9; 2 Pet.1.7; 4.12.

errors.—The foundation may be firm. Those who are referred to may be building on the Lord Jesus, and may be true Christians. Yet there is much error among those who are not Christians. There are many things *mistaken* for piety which will yet be seen to be false. There is much enthusiasm, wildfire, fanaticism, bigotry; much affected humility; much that is supposed to be orthodoxy; much regard to forms and ceremonies; to "days, and months, and times, and years" (Gal. iv. 10); much over-heated zeal, and much precision, and solemn sanctimoniousness; much regard for external ordinances where the heart is wanting, that shall be found to be false, and that shall be swept away in the day of judgment.

13. *Every man's work shall be made manifest.* What every man has built on this foundation shall be seen. Whether he has held truth or error; whether he has had correct views of piety or false; whether what he has done has been what he *should* have done or not. ¶ *For the day.* The day of judgment. The great day which shall reveal the secrets of all hearts, and the truth in regard to what every man has done. The event will show what edifices on the true foundation are firmly, and what are weakly built. *Perhaps* the word *day* here may mean *time* in general, as we say, "time will show—" and as the Latin adage says, *dies docebit;* but it is more natural to refer it to the day of judgment. ¶ *Because it shall be revealed by fire.* The work, the edifice which shall be built on the true foundation shall be made known amidst the fire of the great day. The *fire* which is here referred to, is doubtless that which shall attend the consummation of all things—the close of the world. That the world shall be destroyed by fire, and that the solemnities of the judgment shall be ushered in by a universal conflagration, is fully and frequently revealed. See Isa. lxvi. 15; 2 Thess. i. 8; 2 Pet. iii. 7, 10, 11. The burning fires of that day, Paul says, shall reveal the character of every man's work, as fire sheds light on all around, and discloses the true nature of things. It may be observed, however, that many critics suppose this to refer to the fire of persecution, &c. *Macknight.* Whitby supposes that the apostle refers to the approaching destruction of Jerusalem. Others, as Grotius, Rosenmüller, &c. suppose that the reference is to *time* in general; it shall be declared ere long; it shall be seen whether those things which are built on the true foundation, are true by the test of time, &c. But the most natural interpretation is that which refers it to the day of judgment. ¶ *And the fire shall try every man's work.* It is the property of fire to test the qualities of objects. Thus, gold and silver, so far from being destroyed by fire, are purified from dross. Wood, hay, stubble, are consumed. The power of fire to try or test the nature of metals, or other objects, is often referred to in the Scripture. Comp. Isa. iv. 4; xxiv. 15; Mal. iii. 2; 1 Pet. i. 7. It is not to be supposed here that the material fire of the last day shall have any tendency to purify the soul, or to remove that which is unsound; but that the investigations and trials of the judgment shall remove all that is evil, as fire acts with reference to gold and silver. As they are not burned but purified; as they pass unhurt through the intense heat of the furnace, so shall all that is genuine pass through the trials of the last great day, of which trials the burning world shall be the antecedent and the emblem. That great day shall show what is genuine and what is not.

14. *If any man's work abide,* &c. If it shall appear that he hast taught the true doctrines of Christianity, and inculcated right practices and views of piety, and himself cherished right feelings: if the trial of the great day, when the real qualities of all objects shall be

14 If any man's work abide
which he hath built thereupon, he
shall receive a reward.
15 If any man's work shall be
burned, he shall suffer loss: but
he himself shall be saved; yet so [a]
as by fire.
16 Know ye not that ye [b] are
the temple of God, and *that* the
Spirit of God dwelleth in you?

a Zech. 3.2; Jude 23. *b* 2 Cor. 6.16.

---

known, shall show this. ¶ *He shall receive a reward.* According to the nature of his work. See Note on ver. 8. This refers, I suppose, to the proper rewards on the day of judgment, and not to the honours and the recompense which he may receive in this world. If *all* that he has taught and done shall be proved to have been genuine and pure, then his reward shall be in proportion.

15. *If any man's work shall be burned.* If it shall not be found to bear the test of the investigation of that day—as a cottage of wood, hay, and stubble would not bear the application of fire. If his doctrines have not been true; if he has had mistaken views of piety; if he has nourished feelings which *he* thought were those of religion; and inculcated practices which, however well meant, are not such as the gospel produces; if he has fallen into error of opinion, feeling, practice, however conscientious, yet he shall suffer loss. ¶ *He shall suffer loss.* (1.) He shall *not* be elevated to as high a rank and to as high happiness as he otherwise would. That which he supposed would be regarded as acceptable by the Judge, and rewarded accordingly, shall be stripped away, and shown to be unfounded and false; and in consequence, he shall not obtain those elevated rewards which he anticipated. This, compared with what he expected, may be regarded as a loss. (2.) He shall be injuriously affected by this for ever. It shall be a *detriment* to him to all eternity. The effects shall be felt in all his residence in heaven—not producing misery but attending him with the consciousness that he *might* have been raised to superior bliss in the eternal abode.—The phrase here literally means, "he shall be mulcted." The word is a law term, and means that he shall be fined, *i. e.* he shall suffer detriment. ¶ *But he himself shall be saved.* The apostle all along has supposed that the true foundation was laid (ver. 11), and if that is laid, and the edifice is reared upon that, the person who does it shall be safe. There may be much error, and many false views of religion, and much imperfection, still the man that is building on the true foundation shall be safe. His errors and imperfections shall be removed, and he may occupy a lower place in heaven, but he shall be safe. ¶ *Yet so as by fire* (ὡς διὰ πυρός). This passage has greatly perplexed commentators; but probably without any good reason. The apostle does not say that Christians will be doomed to the fires of purgatory; nor that they will pass through fire; nor that they will be exposed to pains and punishment at all; but he *simply carries out the figure* which he commenced, and says that they will be saved, *as if* the action of fire had been felt on the edifice on which he is speaking. That is, *as* fire would consume the wood, hay, and stubble, *so* on the great day every thing that is erroneous and imperfect in Christians shall be removed, and that which is true and genuine shall be preserved *as if* it had passed through fire. Their whole character and opinions shall be investigated; and that which is good shall be approved; and that which is false and erroneous be removed. The idea is not that of a man whose house is burnt over his head and who escapes through the flames, nor that of a man who is subjected to the pains and fires of purgatory; but that of a man who had been spending his time and strength to little purpose; who had built, indeed, on the true foundation, but who had reared so much on it which was unsound, and erroneous, and false, that he himself would be saved with great difficulty, and with the loss of much of that reward which he had

expected, *as if* the fire had passed over him and his works. The simple idea, therefore, is, that that which is genuine and valuable in his doctrines and works, shall be rewarded, and the man shall be saved: that which is not sound and genuine, shall be removed, and he shall suffer loss. Some of the fathers, indeed, admitted that this passage taught that all men would be subjected to the action of fire in the great conflagration with which the world shall close; that the wicked shall be consumed; and that the righteous are to suffer, some more and some less, according to their character. On passages like this, the Romish doctrine of purgatory is based. But we may observe, (1.) That this passage does not necessarily or naturally give any such idea. The interpretation stated above is the *natural* interpretation, and one which the passage will not only bear, but which it demands. (2.) *If* this passage *would* give any countenance to the absurd and unscriptural idea that the souls of the righteous at the day of judgment are to be re-united to their bodies, in order to be subjected to the action of intense heat, to be brought from the abodes of bliss and compelled to undergo the burning fires of the last conflagration, still it would give no countenance to the still more absurd and unscriptural opinion that those fires have been and are still burning; that all souls are to be subjected to them; and that they can be removed only by masses offered for the dead, and by the prayers of the living. The idea of danger and peril is, indeed, in this text; but the idea of personal salvation is retained and conveyed.

16. *Know ye not*, &c. The apostle here carries forward and completes the figure which he had commenced in regard to Christians. His illustrations had been drawn from architecture; and he here proceeds to say that Christians are that building (see ver. 9): that they were the sacred temple which God had reared; and that, therefore, they should be pure and holy. This is a practical application of what he had been before saying. ¶ *Ye are the temple of God.* This is to be understood of the *community* of Christians, or of the church, as being the place where God dwells on the earth. The idea is derived from the mode of speaking among the Jews, where they are said often in the Old Testament to be the temple and the habitation of God. And the allusion is probably to the fact that God dwelt by a visible symbol—*the Shechinah*—in the temple, and that his abode was there. As he dwelt there among the Jews; as he had there a temple—a dwelling place, so he dwells among Christians. *They* are his temple, the place of his abode. His residence is with them; and he is in their midst. This figure the apostle Paul several times uses, 1 Cor. vi. 19; 2 Cor. vi. 16; Eph. ii. 20—22. A great many passages have been quoted by Elsner and Wetstein, in which a virtuous mind is represented as the temple of God, and in which the obligation to preserve that inviolate and unpolluted is enforced. The figure is a beautiful one, and very impressive. A *temple* was an edifice erected to the service of God. The temple at Jerusalem was not only most magnificent, but was regarded as most sacred; (1.) From the fact that it was devoted to his service; and (2.) From the fact that it was the peculiar residence of JEHOVAH. Among the heathen also, temples were regarded as sacred. They were supposed to be *inhabited* by the divinity to whom they were dedicated. They were regarded as inviolable. Those who took refuge there were safe. It was a crime of the highest degree to violate a temple, or to tear a fugitive who had sought protection there from the altar. So the apostle says of the Christian community. They were regarded as *his temple*—God dwelt among them—and they should regard themselves as holy, and as consecrated to his service. And so it is regarded as a species of sacrilege to violate the temple, and to devote it to other uses, 1 Cor. vi. 19; see ver. 17. ¶ *And* that *the Spirit of God.* The Holy Spirit, the third person of the Trinity. This is conclusively proved by 1 Cor. vi. 19, where he is called "the Holy Ghost." ¶ *Dwelleth in*

17 If any man [1] defile the temple of God, him shall God destroy; for the temple of God is holy, which *temple* ye are.

1 or, *destroy*.

18 Let no man deceive himself. [a] If any man among you seemeth to be wise in this world, let him become a fool, that he may be wise.

a Prov.26.12.

you. As God dwelt formerly in the tabernacle, and afterwards in the temple, so his Spirit now dwells among Christians.—This cannot mean, (1.) That the Holy Spirit is *personally united* to Christians, so as to form a personal union; or, (2.) That there is to Christians any communication of his nature or personal qualities; or, (3.) That there is any union of *essence*, or *nature* with them, for God is present in all places, and can, *as* God, be no more present at one place than at another. The only sense in which he can be peculiarly present in any place is by his *influence*, or *agency*. And the idea is one which denotes agency, influence, favour, peculiar regard; and in that sense only can he be present with his church. The expression must mean, (1.) That the church is the seat of his operations, the field or abode on which he acts on earth; (2.) That his *influences* are there, producing the appropriate effects of his agency, love, joy, peace, long-suffering, &c.; (Gal. v. 22, 23); (3.) That he produces there consolations, that he sustains and guides his people; (4.) That they are regarded as dedicated or consecrated to him; (5.) That they are especially *dear* to him —that he loves them, and thus makes his abode with them. See Note, John xiv. 23.

["These words import the actual presence and inhabitation of the Spirit himself. The fact is plainly attested, but it is mysterious, and cannot be distinctly explained. In respect of his essence, he is as much present with unbelievers as with believers. His dwelling in the latter must therefore signify, that he manifests himself, in their souls, in a peculiar manner; that he exerts there his gracious power, and produces effects which other men do not experience—We may illustrate his presence with them, as distinguished from his presence with men in general, by supposing the vegetative power of the earth to produce, in the surrounding region, only common and worthless plants, but to throw out, in a select spot, all the riches and beauty of a cultivated garden."—*Dick's Theol. Vol. III.* p. 287.]

17. *If any man defile*, &c. Or, *destroy, corrupt* (φθείρει). The Greek word is the same in both parts of the sentence. "If any man *destroy* the temple of God, God shall *destroy* him." This is presented in the form of an adage or proverb. And the truth here stated is based on the fact that the temple of God was inviolable. That temple was holy; and if any man subsequently destroyed it, it might be presumed that God would destroy him. The figurative sense is, "If any man by his doctrines or precepts shall pursue such a course as *tends* to destroy the church, God shall severely punish him. ¶ *For the temple of God is holy.* The temple of God is to be regarded as sacred and inviolable. This was unquestionably the common opinion among the Jews respecting the temple at Jerusalem; and it was the common doctrine of the Gentiles respecting their temples. Sacred places were regarded as inviolable; and this general truth Paul applies to the Christian church in general.—Locke supposes that Paul had particular reference here to the false teachers in Corinth. But the expression, "if any man," is equally applicable to all other false teachers as to him. ¶ *Which* temple *ye are.* This proves that though Paul regarded them as lamentably corrupt in some respects, he still regarded them as a true church—as a part of the holy temple of God.

18. *Let no man deceive himself.* The apostle here proceeds to make a practical application of the truths which he had stated, and to urge on them humility, and to endeavour to repress the broils and contentions into which they had fallen. Let no man be puffed up with a vain conceit of his own wisdom, for this had been the real cause of all the evils which

19 For the wisdom of this world is foolishness with God: for it is

they had experienced. Grotius renders this, "See that you do not attribute too much to your wisdom and learning, by resting on it, and thus deceive your own selves." "All human philosophy," says Grotius, "that is repugnant to the gospel is but vain deceit."—Probably there were many among them who would despise this admonition as coming from Paul, but he exhorts them to take care that they did not deceive themselves. We are taught here, (1.) The danger of self-deception—a danger that besets all on the subject of religion. (2.) The fact that false philosophy is the most fruitful source of self-deception in the business of religion. So it was among the Corinthians; and so it has been in all ages since. ¶ *If any man among you.* Any teacher, whatever may be his rank or his confidence in his own abilities; or any private member of the church. ¶ *Seemeth to be wise.* Seems to himself; or is thought to be, has the credit, or reputation of being wise. The word *seems* (δοκεῖ) implies this idea—if any one seems, or is supposed to be a man of wisdom; if this is his reputation; and if he seeks that this should be his reputation among men. See instances of this construction in Bloomfield. ¶ *In this world.* In this *age*, or *world* (ἐν τῷ αἰῶνι τούτῳ). There is considerable variety in the interpretation of this passage among critics. It may be taken either with the preceding or the following words. Origen, Cyprian, Beza, Grotius, Hammond, and Locke, adopt the latter method, and understand it thus, "If any man among you thinks himself to be wise, let him not hesitate to be a fool in the opinion of this age in order that he may be truly wise."—But the interpretation conveyed in our translation, is probably the correct one. "If any man has the reputation of wisdom among the men of this generation, and prides himself on it," &c. If he is esteemed wise in the sense in which the men of this world are, as a philosopher, a man of science, learning, &c. ¶ *Let him become a fool.* (1.) Let him be willing to be regarded as a fool. (2.) Let him sincerely embrace this gospel, which will inevitably expose him to the charge of being a fool. (3.) Let all his earthly wisdom be esteemed in his own eyes as valueless and as folly in the great matters of salvation. ¶ *That he may be wise.* That he may have true wisdom—that which is of God.—It is implied here, (1.) That the wisdom of this world will not make a man truly wise. (2.) That a *reputation* for wisdom may contribute nothing to a man's true wisdom, but may stand in the way of it. (3.) That for such a man to embrace the gospel it is necessary that he should be willing to cast away dependence on his own wisdom, and come with the temper of a child to the Saviour. (4.) That to do this will expose him to the charge of folly, and the derision of those who are wise in their own conceit. (5.) That true wisdom is found only in that science which teaches men to live unto God, and to be prepared for death and for heaven—and that science is found only in the gospel.

19. *For the wisdom of this world.* That which is esteemed to be wisdom by the men of this world on the subject of religion. It does not mean that true wisdom is foolishness with him. It does not mean that science, and prudence, and law—that the knowledge of his works—that astronomy, and medicine, and chemistry, are regarded by him as folly, and as unworthy the attention of men. God is the friend of truth on all subjects; and he requires us to become acquainted with his works, and commends those who search them, Ps. xcii. 4; cxi. 2. But the apostle refers here to that which was esteemed to be wisdom among the ancients, and in which they so much prided themselves, their vain, self-confident, and false opinions on the subject of religion; and especially those opinions when they were opposed to the simple but sublime truths of revelation. See Note, chap. i. 20, 21. ¶ *Is foolishness with God.* Is esteemed by him

written, [a] He taketh the wise in their own craftiness.

20 And again, [b] The Lord knoweth the thoughts of the wise, that they are vain.

21 Therefore let [c] no man glory in men: for all things are yours;

22 Whether Paul, or Apollos, or Cephas, or the world, or life, or

a Job 5.13. b Ps.94.11. c Jer.9.23,24.

to be folly. Note, chap. i. 20.–24. ¶ *For it is written*, &c. Job v. 13. The word rendered "taketh" here denotes to clench with the fist, gripe, grasp. And the sense is, (1.) However crafty, or cunning, or skilful they may be; however self-confident, yet that they cannot deceive or impose upon God. He can thwart their plans, overthrow their schemes, defeat their counsels, and foil them in their enterprises, Job v. 12. (2.) He does it by their own cunning or craftiness. He allows them to involve themselves in difficulties or to entangle each other. He makes use of even their own craft and cunning to defeat their counsels. He allows the plans of one wise man to come in conflict with those of another, and thus to destroy one another. Honesty in religion, as in every thing else, is the best policy; and a man who pursues a course of conscientious integrity may expect the protection of God. But he who attempts to carry his purposes by craft and intrigue—who depends on skill and cunning instead of truth and honesty, will often find that he is the prey of his own cunning and duplicity.

20. *And again*, Ps. xciv. 11. ¶ *The Lord knoweth*. God searches the heart. The particular thing which it is here said that he knows, is, that the thoughts of man are vain. They have this quality; and this is that which the psalmist here says that God sees. The affirmation is not one respecting the *omniscience* of God, but with respect to what God sees of the nature of the thoughts of the wise. ¶ *The thoughts of the wise*. Their plans, purposes, designs. ¶ *That they are vain*. That they lack real wisdom; they are foolish; they shall not be accomplished as they expect; or be seen to have that wisdom which they now suppose they possess.

21 *Therefore*, &c. Paul here proceeds to apply the principles which he had stated above. Since all were ministers or servants of God; since God was the source of all good influences; since, whatever might be the pretensions to wisdom among men, it was all foolishness in the sight of God, the inference was clear, that no man should glory in man. They were all alike poor, frail, ignorant, erring, dependent beings. And hence, also, as *all* wisdom came from God, and as Christians partook *alike* of the benefits of the instruction of the most eminent apostles, they ought to regard this as belonging to them in common, and not to form parties with these names at the head. ¶ *Let no man glory in men;* see chap. i. 29; comp. Jer. ix. 23, 24. It was common among the Jews to range themselves under different leaders—as Hillel and Shammai; and for the Greeks, also, to boast themselves to be the followers of Pythagoras, Zeno, Plato, &c. The same thing began to be manifest in the Christian church; and Paul here rebukes and opposes it. ¶ *For all things are yours*. This is a *reason* why they should not range themselves in parties or factions under different leaders. Paul specifies what he means by "all things" in the following verses. The sense is, that since they had an interest in all that could go to promote their welfare; as they were *common* partakers of the benefits of the talents and labours of the apostles; and as they belonged to Christ, and all to God, it was improper to be split up into factions, *as if* they derived any *peculiar* benefit from one set of men, or one set of objects. In Paul, in Apollos, in life, death, &c. they had a *common* interest, and no one should boast that he had any special proprietorship in any of these things.

22. *Whether Paul, or Apollos*. The

death, or things present, or things to come; all are yours;

23 And ye [a] are Christ's; and Christ *is* God's.

a Rom.14.8.

sense of this is clear. Whatever advantages result from the piety, self-denials, and labours of Paul, Apollos, or any other preacher of the gospel, are *yours*—you have the benefit of them. One is as much entitled to the benefit as another; and all partake alike in the results of their ministration. You should therefore neither range yourselves into parties with their names given to the parties, nor suppose that one has any *peculiar* interest in Paul, or another in Apollos. Their labours belonged to the church in general. *They* had no partialities—no rivalship—no desire to make parties. They were united, and desirous of promoting the welfare of the *whole* church of God. The doctrine is, that ministers belong to the church, and should devote themselves to its welfare; and that the church enjoys, in common, the benefits of the learning, zeal, piety, eloquence, talents, example of the ministers of God. And it may be observed, that it is no small privilege thus to be permitted to regard *all* the labours of the most eminent servants of God as designed for our welfare; and for the humblest saint to feel that the labours of apostles, the self-denials and sufferings, the pains and dying agonies of martyrs, have been for *his* advantage. ¶ *Or Cephas.* Or Peter. John i. 42. ¶ *Or the world.* This word is doubtless used, in its common signification, to denote the things which God has made; the universe, the things which pertain to this life. And the meaning of the apostle probably is, that all things pertaining to this world which God has made—all the events which are occurring in his providence were so far *theirs*, that they would contribute to their advantage, and their enjoyment. This general idea may be thus expressed: (1.) The world was made by God their common Father, and they have an interest in it as *his* children, regarding it as the work of his hand, and seeing him present in all his works. Nothing contributes so much to the true *enjoyment* of the world—to comfort in surveying the heavens, the earth, the ocean, hills, vales, plants, flowers, streams, in partaking of the gifts of Providence, as this feeling, that *all* are the works of the Christian's Father, and that *they* may all partake of these favours as his children. (2.) The frame of the universe is sustained and upheld for their sake. The universe is kept by God; and one design of God in keeping it is to protect, preserve, and redeem his church and people. To this end he defends it by day and night; he orders all things; he keeps it from the storm and tempest; from flood and fire; and from annihilation. The sun, and moon, and stars—the times and seasons, are all thus ordered, that his church may be guarded, and brought to heaven. (3.) The course of providential events are ordered for their welfare also, Rom. viii. 28. The revolutions of kingdoms—the various persecutions and trials, even the rage and fury of wicked men, are all overruled, to the advancement of the cause of truth, and the welfare of the church. (4.) Christians have the promise of *as much* of this world as shall be needful for them; and in this sense "the world" is theirs. See Matt. vi. 33; Mark x. 29, 30; 1 Tim. iv. 8, "Godliness is profitable for all things, having promise of the life that now is, and of that which is to come." And such was the result of the long experience and observation of David, Ps. xxxvii. 25, "I have been young, and now am old; yet have I not seen the righteous forsaken, nor his seed begging bread." See Isa. xxxiii. 16. ¶ *Or life.* Life is theirs, because (1.) They *enjoy* life. It is *real* life to them, and not a vain show. They live for a *real* object, and not for vanity. Others live for parade and ambition—Christians live for the great purposes of life; and life to them has reality, as being a state preparatory to another and a higher world. Their life is not an endless circle of unmeaning ceremonies—of false and hollow pretensions to friendship—of a vain pursuit of happiness, which is never found, but is passed in a manner that is rational, and sober, and that truly deserves to be called *life*. (2.) The various events and occurrences of life shall all tend to promote their welfare, and advance their salvation. ¶ *Death*. They have an *interest*, or *property* even in death, usually regarded as a calamity and a curse. But it is theirs, (1.) Because they shall have *peace* and support in the dying hour. (2.) Because it has no terrors for them. It shall take away nothing which they are not willing to resign. (3.) Because it is the avenue which leads to their rest; and it is *theirs* just in the same sense in which we say that "this is *our* road" when we have been long absent, and are inquiring the way to our homes. (4.) Because they shall triumph over it. It is subdued by their Captain, and the grave has been subjected to a triumph by his rising from its chills and darkness. (5.) Because death is the means—the occasion of introducing them to their rest. It is the *advantageous circumstance* in their history, by which they are removed from a world of ills, and translated to a world of glory. It is to them a source of inexpressible *advantage*, as it translates them to a world of light and eternal felicity; and it may truly be called *theirs*. ¶ *Or things present, or things to come*. Events which are now happening, and all that can possibly occur to us, Note, Rom. viii. 38. All the calamities, trials, persecutions—all the prosperity, advantages, privileges of the present time, and all that shall yet take place, shall tend to promote our welfare and advance the interests of our souls, and promote our salvation. ¶ *All are yours*. All shall tend to promote your comfort and salvation.

23. *And ye are Christ's*. You belong to him; and should not, therefore, feel that you are devoted to any earthly leader, whether Paul, Apollos, or Peter. As you belong to Christ by redemption, and by solemn dedication to his service, so you should feel that you are his alone. You are his property—his people—his friends. You should regard yourselves as such, and feel that you all belong to the same family, and should not, therefore, be split up into contending factions and parties. ¶ *Christ is God's*. Christ is the mediator between God and man. He came to do the will of God. He was and is still devoted to the service of his Father. God has a proprietorship in all that he does, since Christ lived, and acted, and reigns to promote the glory of his Father. The argument here seems to be this, "You belong to Christ; and he to God. You are bound, therefore, not to devote yourselves to a *man*, whoever he may be, but to Christ, and to the service of that one true God, in whose service even Christ was employed. And as Christ sought to promote the glory of his Father, so should you in all things." This implies no inferiority of nature of Christ to God. It means only that he was employed in the service of his Father, and sought his glory—a doctrine every where taught in the New Testament. But this does not imply that he was inferior in his nature. A son may be employed in the service of his father, and may seek to advance his father's interests. But this does not prove that the son is inferior in nature to his father. It proves only that he is inferior in *some* respects—in office. So the Son of God consented to take an inferior office or rank; to become a mediator, to assume the form of a servant, and to be a man of sorrows; but this proves nothing in regard to his original rank or dignity. That is to be learned from the numerous passages which affirm that in nature he was equal with God. See Note, John i. 1.

REMARKS.

1st. Christians when first converted may be well compared to infants, ver. 1. They are in a new world. They just open their eyes on truth. They see new objects; and have new objects of attachment. They are feeble, weak, helpless. And though they often have high joy, and even great self-confidence, yet they are in themselves ignorant and weak, and in need of constant teaching. Christians should not only possess the spirit, but they should feel that they are *like* children. They are like them not only in their temper, but in their ignorance, and weakness, and helplessness.

2d. The instructions which are imparted to Christians should be adapted to their capacity, ver. 2. Skill and care should be exercised to adapt that instruction to the wants of tender consciences, and to those who are feeble in the faith. It would be no more absurd to furnish strong food to the new born babe than it is to present some of the higher doctrines of religion to the tender minds of converts. The *elements* of knowledge must be first learned; the tenderest and most delicate food must first nourish the body.—And perhaps in nothing is there more frequent error than in presenting the higher, and more difficult doctrines of Christianity to young converts, and *because* they have a difficulty in regard to them, or because they even reject them, pronouncing them destitute of piety. Is the infant destitute of life because it cannot digest the solid food which nourishes the man of fifty years? Paul adapted *his* instructions to the delicacy and feebleness of infantile piety; and those who are like Paul will feed with great care the lambs of the flock. All young converts should be placed under a course of instruction adapted to *their* condition, and should secure the careful attention of the pastors of the churches.

3d. Strife and contention in the church is proof that men are under the influence of carnal feelings. No matter what is the *cause* of the contention, the very fact of the existence of such strife is a proof of the existence of such feelings somewhere, ver. 3, 4. On what side soever the original fault of the contention may be, yet its existence in the church is always proof that *some*—if not all—of those who are engaged in it are under the influence of carnal feelings. Christ's kingdom is designed to be a kingdom of peace and love; and divisions and contentions are always attended with evils, and with injury to the spirit of true religion.

4th. We have here a rebuke to that spirit which has produced the existence of sects and parties, ver. 4. The practice of naming sects after certain men, we see, began early, and was as early rebuked by apostolic authority. Would not the same apostolic authority rebuke the spirit which now calls one division of the church after the name of Calvin, another after the name of Luther, another after the name of Arminius! Should not, and will not all these divisions yet be merged in the high and holy name of Christian? Our Saviour evidently supposed it possible that his church should be one (John xvii. 21—23); and Paul certainly supposed that the church at Corinth might be so united. So the early churches were; and is it *too much* to hope that some way may yet be discovered which shall break down the divisions into sects, and *unite* Christians both in feeling and in name in spreading the gospel of the Redeemer every where? Does not every Christian sincerely desire it? And may there not yet await the church *such* a union as shall concentrate all its energies in saving the world? How much effort, how much talent, how much wealth and learning are now wasted in contending with other denominations of the great Christian family! How much would this wasted—and worse than wasted wealth, and learning, and talent, and zeal do in diffusing the gospel around the world! Whose heart is not sickened at these contentions and strifes; and whose soul will not breathe forth a pure desire to Heaven that the time may soon come when all these contentions shall die away, and when the voice of strife shall be hushed; and when the united host of God's elect shall go forth to subdue the world to the gospel of the Saviour?

5th. The *proper* honour should be paid to the ministers of the gospel. ver. 5—7. They should not be put in the place of God; nor should their services, however important, prevent the supreme recognition of God in the conversion of souls. God is to be all and in all.—It is proper that the ministers of religion should be treated with respect (1 Thess. v. 12, 13); and ministers have a right to expect and to desire the affectionate regards of those who are blessed by their instrumentality. But Paul—eminent a a successful as he was—would do nothing that would diminish or obscure the singleness of view with which the agency of God should be regarded in the work of salvation. He regarded himself as nothing compared with God; and his highest desire was that God in all things might be honoured.

6th. God is the source of all good influence, and of all that is holy in the church. He only gives the increase. Whatever of humility, faith, love, joy, peace, or purity we may have, is all to be traced to him. No matter who plants, or who waters, *God* gives life to the seed; God rears the stalk; God expands the leaf; God opens the flower and gives it its fragrance; and God forms, preserves, and ripens the fruit. So in religion. No matter who the minister may be; no matter how faithful, learned, pious, or devoted, yet if any success attends his labours, it is *all* to be traced to God. This truth is never to be forgotten; nor should any talents, or zeal, however great, ever be allowed to dim or obscure its lustre in the minds of those who are converted.

7th. Ministers are on a level, ver. 8, 9. Whatever may be their qualifications or their success, yet they can claim no pre-eminence over one another. They are fellow labourers—engaged in *one* work, accomplishing the same object, though they may be in different parts of the same field. The man who plants is as necessary as he that waters; and both are inferior to God, and neither could do any thing without him.

8th. Christians should regard themselves as a holy people, ver. 9. They are the cultivation of God. All that they have is from him. His own agency has been employed in their conversion; his own Spirit operates to sanctify and save them. Whatever they have is to be traced to God; and they should remember that they are, therefore, consecrated to him.

9th. No other foundation can be laid in the church except that of Christ, ver. 10, 11. Unless a church is founded on the true doctrine respecting the Messiah, it is a false church, and should not be recognised as belonging to him. There can be no other foundation, either for an individual sinner, or for a church. How important then to inquire whether we are building our hopes for eternity on this tried foundation! How faithfully should we examine this subject lest our hopes should all be swept away in the storms of divine wrath! Matt. vii. 27, 28. How deep and awful will be the disappointment of those who suppose they have been building on the true foundation, and who find in the great day of judgment that all has been delusion!

10th. We are to be tried at the day of judgment, ver. 13, 14. All are to be arraigned, not only in regard to the *foundation* of our hopes for eternal life, but in regard to the superstructure,—the nature of our opinions and practices in religion. Every thing shall come into judgment.

11th. The trial will be such as to test our character. All the trials through which we are to pass are designed to do this. Affliction, temptation, sickness, death, are all intended to produce this result, and all have a tendency to this end. But, pre-eminently is this the case with regard to the trial at the great day of judgment. Amidst the light of the burning world, and the terrors of the judgment; under the blazing throne, and the eye of God, every man's character shall be seen, and a just judgment shall be pronounced.

12th. The trial shall remove all that is impure in Christians, ver. 14. They shall then see the truth; and in that world of truth, all that was erroneous in their opinions shall be corrected. They shall be in a world where fanaticism cannot be mistaken for the love of truth, and where enthu siasm cannot be substituted for zeal. All true and real piety shall there abide; all which is false and erroneous shall be removed.

13th. What a change will then take place in regard to Christians. *All* probably cherish *some* opinions which are unsound; all indulge in *some* things now supposed to be piety, which will not then bear the test. The great change will then take place from impurity to purity; from imperfection to perfection. The very passage from this world to heaven will secure this change; and what a vast revolution will it be thus to be ushered into a world where all shall be pure in sentiment; all perfect in love.

14th. Many Christians may be much disappointed in that day. Many who are now zealous for *doctrines*, and who pursue with vindictive spirit others who differ from them, shall then "suffer loss," and find that the *persecuted* had more real love of truth than the *persecutor*. Many who are now filled with zeal, and who denounce the comparatively leaden and tardy pace of others; many whose bosoms glow with rapturous feeling, and burn, as they suppose, with a seraph's love, shall find that *all* this was not piety—that animal feeling was mistaken for the love of God; and that a zeal for sect, or for the triumph of a party, was mistaken for love to the Saviour; and that the kindlings of an ardent imagination had been often substituted for the elevated emotions of pure and disinterested love.

15th. Christians, teachers, and people should examine themselves, and see what *is* the building which they are rearing on the true foundation. Even where the foundation of a building is laid broad and deep, it is of much importance whether a stately and magnificent palace shall be reared on it, suited to the nature of the foundation, or whether a mud-walled and a thatched cottage shall be all. Between the foundation and the edifice in the one case there is the beauty of proportion and fitness; in the other there is incongruity and unfitness. Who would lay such a deep and broad foundation as the basis on which to rear the hut of the savage or the mud cottage of the Hindoo? Thus in religion. The foundation to all who truly believe in the Lord Jesus is broad, deep, firm, magnificent. But the superstructure — the piety, the advancement in knowledge, the life, is often like the cottage that is reared on the firm basis—that every wind shakes, and that the fire would soon consume. As the *basis* of the Christian hope is firm, so should the superstructure be large, magnificent, and grand.

16th. Christians are to regard themselves as holy and pure, ver. 16, 17. They are the temple of the Lord —the dwelling place of the Spirit. A temple is sacred and inviolable. So should Christians regard themselves. They are dedicated to God. He dwells among them. And they should deem themselves holy and pure; and should preserve their minds from impure thoughts, from unholy purposes, from selfish and sensual desires. They should be in all respects such as will be the fit abode for the Holy Spirit of God. How pure should men be in whom the Holy Spirit dwells! How single should be their aims! How constant their self-denials! How single their desire to devote all to his service, and to live always to his glory! How heavenly should they be in their feelings; and how should pride, sensuality, vanity, ambition, covetousness, and the love of gayety, be banished from their bosoms! Assuredly in God's world there should be *one* place where he will delight to dwell—one place that shall remind of heaven, and that place should be the church which has been purchased with the purest blood of the universe.

17th. We see what is necessary if a man would become a Christian, ver. 18. He must be willing to be esteemed a fool; to be despised; to have his name cast out as evil; and to be regarded as even under delusion and deception. Whatever may be his rank, or his reputation for wisdom, and talent, and learning, he must be willing to be regarded as a fool by his former associates and companions; to cast off all reliance on his own wis-

CHAPTER IV.

LET a man so account of us, as of the ministers [a] of Christ, and stewards of the mysteries of God.

2 Moreover, it is required in

a 2 Cor.6.4.

dom; and to be associated with the poor, the persecuted, and the despised followers of Jesus. Christianity knows no distinctions of wealth, talent, learning. It points out no royal road to heaven. It describes but one way; and whatever contempt an effort to be saved may involve us in, it requires us to submit to that, and even to rejoice that our names are cast out as evil.

18th. This is a point on which men should be especially careful that they are not deceived, ver. 18. There is nothing on which they are more likely to be than this. It is not an easy thing for a proud man to humble himself; it is not easy for men who boast of their wisdom to be willing that their names should be cast out as evil. And there is great danger of a man's flattering himself that he is willing to be a Christian, who would *not* be willing to be esteemed a fool by the great and the gay men of this world. He still intends to be a Christian and be saved; and yet to keep up his reputation for wisdom and prudence. Hence every thing in religion which is not consistent with such a reputation for prudence and wisdom he rejects. Hence he takes sides with the world. As far as the world will admit that a man ought to attend to religion he will go. Where the world would pronounce any thing to be foolish, fanatical, or enthusiastic, he pauses. And his religion is not shaped by the New Testament, but by the opinions of the world.—Such a man should be cautious that he is not deceived. All *his* hopes of heaven are probably built on the sand.

19th. We should not overvalue the wisdom of this world, ver. 18, 19. It is folly in the sight of God. And we, therefore, should not over-estimate it, or desire it, or be influenced by it. True wisdom on any subject we should not despise; but we should especially value that which is connected with salvation.

20th. This admonition is of especial applicability to ministers of the gospel. They are in special danger on the subject; and it has been by *their* yielding themselves so much to the power of speculative philosophy, that parties have been formed in the church, and that the gospel has been so much corrupted.

21st. These considerations should lead us to live above contention, and the fondness of party. Sect and party in the church are not formed by the love of the pure and simple gospel, but by the love of some philosophical opinion, or by an admiration of the wisdom, talents, learning, eloquence, or success of some Christian teacher. Against this the apostle would guard us; and the considerations presented in this chapter should elevate us above all the causes of contention and the love of sect, and teach us to love as brothers all who love our Lord Jesus Christ.

22d. Christians have an interest in all things that can go to promote their happiness. Life and death, things present and things to come—all shall tend to advance their happiness, and promote their salvation; ver. 21—23.

23d. Christians have nothing to fear in death. Death is theirs, and shall be a blessing to them. Its sting is taken away; and it shall introduce them to heaven. What have they to fear? Why should they be alarmed? Why afraid to die? Why unwilling to depart and to be with Christ?

24th. Christians should regard themselves as devoted to the Saviour. They are his, and he has the highest conceivable claim on their time, their talents, their influence, and their wealth. To him, therefore, let us be devoted, and to him let us consecrate all that we have.

CHAPTER IV.

THIS chapter is a continuation of the subject discussed in those which go before, and of the argument which closes the last chapter. The proper division would have been at ver. 6.

stewards, [a] that a man be found faithful.

3 But with me it is a very small thing that I should be

a Luke 12.42; Tit.1.7; 1 Pet.4.10.

The design of the first six verses is to show the real estimate in which the apostles ought to be held as the ministers of religion. The remainder of the chapter (ver. 7—21) is occupied in setting forth further the claims of the apostles to their respect in contradistinction from the false teachers, and in reproving the spirit of vain boasting and confidence among the Corinthians. Paul (ver. 7) reproves their boasting by assuring them that they had no ground for it, since all that they possessed had been given to them by God. In ver. 8, he reproves the same spirit with cutting irony, as if they claimed to be eminently wise.—Still further to reprove them, he alludes to his own self-denials and sufferings, as contrasted with *their* ease, and safety, and enjoyment, ver. 9—14. He then shows that his labours and self-denials in their behalf, laid the foundation for his speaking to them with authority as a father, ver. 15, 16. And to show them that he claimed that authority over them as the founder of their church, and that he was not afraid to discharge his duty towards them, he informs them that he had sent Timothy to look into their affairs (ver. 17), and that himself would soon follow; and assures them that he had *power* to come to them with the severity of Christian discipline, and that it depended on *their* conduct whether he should come with a rod, or with the spirit of meekness and love, ver. 21.

1. *Let a man.* Let all; let this be the estimate formed of us by each one of you. ¶ *So account of us.* So think of us, the apostles. ¶ *As the ministers of Christ.* As the servants of Christ. Let them form a true estimate of us and our office—not as the head of a faction; not as designing to form parties, but as unitedly and entirely the servants of Christ; see chap. iii. 5. ¶ *And stewards.* Stewards were those who presided over the affairs of a family, and made provision for it, &c.; see Note, Luke xvi. 1. It was an office of much responsibility; and the apostle by using the term here seems to have designed to elevate those whom he seemed to have depreciated in chap. iii. 5. ¶ *Of the mysteries of God.* Of the gospel; Note, chap. ii. 7. The office of steward was to provide those things which were necessary for the use of a family. And so the office of a minister of the gospel, and a steward of its mysteries, is to dispense such instructions, guidance, counsel, &c., as may be requisite to build up the church of Christ; to make known those sublime truths which are contained in the gospel, but which had not been made known before the revelation of Jesus Christ, and which are, therefore, called *mysteries.* It is implied in this verse, (1.) That the office of a minister is one that is *subordinate* to Christ—they are his servants. (2.) That those in the office should not attempt to be the head of sect or party in the church. (3.) That the office is honourable as that of a steward is; and, (4.) That Christians should endeavour to form and cherish *just* ideas of ministers; to give them their *true* honour; but not to overrate their importance.

2. *Moreover,* &c. The fidelity required of stewards seems to be adverted to here, in order to show that the apostles acted from a higher principle than a desire to please man, or to be regarded as at the head of a party; and they ought so to esteem them as bound, like all stewards, to be faithful to the master whom they served. ¶ *It is required,* &c. It is expected of them; it is the *main* or *leading* thing in their office. Eminently in that office fidelity is required as an indispensable and cardinal virtue. Fidelity to the master, faithfulness to his trust, as THE virtue which by way of eminence is demanded there. In other offices other virtues may be particularly required. But here fidelity is demanded. This is required particularly because it is an office of trust; because the master's goods are at his disposal; because there is so much opportunity for the

judged of you, or of man's [1] judgment; yea, I judge not mine own self:

[1] *day.*

4 For I know nothing by myself; [a] yet am I not hereby jus-

[a] Ps.143.2.

steward to appropriate those goods to his own use, so that his master cannot detect it. There is a strong similarity between the office of a steward and that of a minister of the gospel. But it is not needful here to dwell on the resemblance. The idea of Paul seems to be, (1.) That a minister, like a steward, is devoted to his master's service, and should regard himself as such. (2.) That he should be faithful to that trust, and not abuse or violate it. (3.) That he should not be judged by his fellow-stewards, or fellow-servants, but that his main desire should be to meet with the approbation of his master. A minister should be faithful for obvious reasons. Because, (*a*) He is appointed by Jesus Christ; (*b*) Because he must answer to him; (*c*) Because the honour of Christ, and the welfare of his kingdom is entrusted to him; and (*d*) Because of the importance of the matter committed to his care; and the importance of fidelity can be measured only by the consequences of his labours to those souls in an eternal heaven or an eternal hell.

3. *But with me.* In my estimate; in regard to myself. That is, I esteem it a matter of no concern. Since I am responsible as a steward to my master only, it is a matter of small concern what *men* think of me, provided I have his approbation. Paul was not insensible to the good opinion of men. He did not despise their favour or court their contempt. But this was not the principal thing which he regarded; and we have here a noble elevation of purpose and of aim, which shows how direct was his design to serve and please the master who had appointed him to his office. ¶ *That I should be judged.* The word rendered *judged* here properly denotes to examine the qualities of any person or thing; and sometimes, as here, to express the *result* of such examination or judgment. Here it means to *blame* or *condemn.* ¶ *Of you.* By you. Dear as you are to me as a church and a people, yet my main desire is not to secure your esteem, or to avoid your censure, but to please my master, and secure his approbation. ¶ *Or of man's judgment.* Of *any* man's judgment. What he had just said, that he esteemed it to be a matter not worth regarding, whatever might be their opinion of him, might seem to look like arrogance, or appear as if he looked upon *them* with contempt. In order to avoid this construction of his language, he here says that it was not because he despised them, or regarded their opinion as of less value than that of others, but that he had the same feelings in regard to all men. Whatever might be their rank, character, talent, or learning, he regarded it as a matter of the least possible consequence what they thought of him. He was answerable not to them, but to his Master; and he could pursue an independent course whatever they might think of his conduct. This is designed also evidently to reprove them for seeking so much the praise of each other. The Greek here is "of man's *day*," where *day* is used, as it often is in Hebrew, to denote the day of trial; the day of judgment; and then simply judgment. Thus the word יום *day* is used in Job xxiv. 1; Ps. xxxvii. 13; Joel i. 15; ii. 1; iv. 19; Mal. iii. 19. ¶ *Yea, I judge not my own self.* I do not attempt to pronounce a judgment on myself. I am conscious of imperfection, and of being biased by self-love in my own favour. I do not feel that my judgment of myself would be strictly impartial, and in all respects to be trusted. Favourable as may be my opinion, yet I am sensible that I may be biased. This is designed to soften what he had just said about their judging him, and to show further the little value which is to be put on the judgment which man may form. "If I do not regard my own opinion of myself as of high value, I cannot be suspected of undervaluing you when I say that I do not much regard your opinion; and if I do not estimate highly my *own* opinion of

tified: but he that judgeth me is the Lord.

5 Therefore judge [a] nothing before the time, until the Lord come, who [b] both will bring to light the hidden things of darkness, and will make manifest the counsels of the hearts: and then

a Mat.7.1.

b Rom.2.16; Rev.20.2.

myself, then it is not to be expected that I should set a high value on the opinions of others."—God only is the infallible judge; and as we and our fellow-men are liable to be biased in our opinions, from envy, ignorance, or self-love, we should regard the judgment of the world as of little value.

4. *For I know nothing by myself.* There is evidently here an ellipsis to be supplied, and it is well supplied by Grotius, Rosenmüller, Calvin, &c. "I am not conscious of *evil*, or *unfaithfulness* to myself; that is, in my ministerial life." It is well remarked by Calvin, that Paul does not here refer to the whole of his life, but only to his apostleship. And the sense is, "I am conscious of integrity in this office. My own mind does not condemn me of ambition or unfaithfulness. Others may accuse me, but I am not conscious of that which should condemn me, or render me unworthy of this office." This appeal Paul elsewhere makes to the integrity and faithfulness of his ministry. So his speech before the elders of Ephesus at Miletus; Acts xx. 18, 19, 26, 27; comp. 2 Cor. vii. 2; xii. 17. It was the appeal which a holy and faithful man could make to the integrity of his public life, and such as every minister of the gospel *ought* to be able to make. ¶ *Yet am I not hereby justified.* I am not justified *because* I am not conscious of a failure in my duty. I know that God the judge may see imperfections where I see none. I know that I may be deceived; and therefore, I do not pronounce a judgment on myself as if it were infallible and final. It is not by the consciousness of integrity and faithfulness that I expect to be saved; and it does not follow that I claim to be free from all personal blame. I know that partiality to ourselves will often teach us to overlook many faults that others may discern in us. ¶ *He that judgeth me is the Lord.* By his judgment I am to abide; and by his judgment I am to receive my eternal sentence, and not by my own view of myself. He searcheth the hearts. He may see evil where I see none. I would not, therefore, be self-confident; but would, with humility, refer the whole case to him. Perhaps there is here a gentle and tender reproof of the Corinthians, who were so confident in their own integrity; and a gentle admonition to them to be more cautious, as it was *possible* that the Lord would detect faults in them where they perceived none.

5. *Therefore.* In view of the danger of being deceived in your judgment, and the impossibility of certainly knowing the failings of the heart. ¶ *Judge nothing.* Pass no decided opinion; see Note, Mat. vii. 1. The apostle here takes occasion to inculcate on them an important lesson—one of the leading lessons of Christianity—not to pass a harsh opinion on the conduct of any man, since there are so many things that go to make up his character which we cannot know; and so many secret failings and motives which are all concealed from us. ¶ *Until the Lord come.* The Lord Jesus at the day of judgment, when all secrets shall be revealed, and a true judgment shall be passed on all men. ¶ *Who both will bring to light;* see Note, Rom. ii. 16. ¶ *The hidden things of darkness.* The secret things of the heart which have been hidden as it were in darkness. The subsequent clause shows that this is the sense. He does not refer to the deeds of night, or those things which were wrought in the secret places of idolatry, but to the secret designs of the heart; and perhaps means gently to insinuate that there were many things about the character and feelings of his enemies which would not well bear the revelations of that day. ¶ *The counsels of the hearts.* The purposes, designs, and intentions of men. All their plans shall be made known in that day. And

shall every man have praise of God.

6 And these things, brethren, I have in a figure transferred to myself and *to* Apollos for your sakes; that ye might learn in us not to think *of men* above that which is written, that no one of you be puffed up for one against another.

---

it is a most fearful and alarming truth, that no man can conceal his purposes *beyond* the day of judgment. ¶ *And then shall every man have praise of God.* The word here rendered *praise* (ἔπαινος) denotes in this place *reward,* or that which is *due* to him; the just sentence which ought to be pronounced on his character. It does not mean as our translation would imply, that every man will then receive the divine approbation—which will not be true; but that every man shall receive what is due to his character, whether good or evil. So Bloomfield and Bretschneider explain it. Hesychius explains it by *judgment* (κρίσις). The word must be limited in its signification according to the subject or the connection. The passage teaches, (1.) That we should not be guilty of harsh judgment of others. (2.) The reason is, that we cannot know their feelings and motives. (3.) That all secret things will be brought forth in the great day, and nothing be concealed *beyond* that time. (4.) That every man shall receive justice there. He shall be treated as he ought to be. The destiny of no one will be decided by the opinions of men; but the doom of all will be fixed by God. How important is it, therefore, that we be prepared for that day; and how important to cherish such feelings, and form such plans, that they *may* be developed without involving us in shame and contempt!

6. *And these things.* The things which I have written respecting religious teachers (chap. ii. 5, 6, 22), and the impropriety of forming sects called after their names. ¶ *I have in a figure transferred to myself and Apollos.* The word here used (μετεσχημάτισα) denotes, properly, to put on another form or figure; *to change* (Phil. iii. 21, "who shall *change* our vile body"); to *transform* (2 Cor. xi. 13, "*transforming* themselves into the apostles of Christ"); and then to apply in the way of a figure of speech. This may mean that neither Paul, Apollos, or Peter, were set up among the Corinthians as heads of parties, but that Paul here made use of their names to show how improper it *would* be to make *them* the head of a party, and hence, how improper it was to make *any* religious teacher the head of a party; or Paul may mean to say that he had mentioned himself and Apollos *particularly,* to show the impropriety of what had been done; since, if it was improper to make *them* heads of parties, it was much more so to make inferior teachers the leaders of factions. Locke adopts the former interpretation. The latter is probably the true interpretation, for it is evident from chap. i. 12, 13, that there *were* parties in the church at Corinth that were called by the names of Paul, and Apollos, and Peter; and Paul's design here was to show the impropriety of this by mentioning *himself, Apollos,* and *Peter,* and thus by transferring the whole discussion from *inferior* teachers and leaders to show the impropriety of it. He might have argued against the impropriety of following other leaders. He might have mentioned their names. But this would have been invidious and indelicate. It would have excited *their* anger. He therefore says that he had transferred it all to himself and Apollos; and it *implied* that if it were improper to split themselves up into factions with *them* as leaders, much more was it improper to follow others; *i. e.* it was improper to form parties at all in the church. "I mention this of *ourselves;* out of delicacy I forbear to mention the names of others."—And this was one of the instances in which Paul showed great *tact* in accomplishing his object, and avoiding offence. ¶ *For your sakes.* To spare your feelings; or to show you in an inoffensive manner what I mean. And particularly by this that you may learn not to place an inordinate value on men. ¶ *That ye might*

7 For who [1] maketh thee to differ *from another?* and what[a] hast thou that thou didst not receive? Now if thou didst receive *it*, why dost thou glory, as if thou hadst not received *it?*

1 *distinguished thee.*

a James 1.17.

learn in us. Or *by* our example and views. ¶ *Not to think,* &c. Since you see the plan which we desire to take; since you see that we who have the rank of apostles, and have been so eminently favoured with endowments and success, do not wish to form parties, that you may also have the same views in regard to others. ¶ *Above that which is written.* Probably referring to what he had said in chap. iii. 5—9, 21; iv. 1. Or it *may* refer to the general strain ot Scripture requiring the children of God to be modest and humble. ¶ *That no one of you be puffed up.* That no one be proud or exalted in self-estimation above his neighbour. That no one be disposed to look upon others with contempt, and to seek to depress and humble them. They should regard themselves as brethren, and as all on a level. The *argument* here is, that if Paul and Apollos did not suppose that *they* had a right to put themselves at the head of parties, *much less* had any of them a right to do so. The *doctrine* is, (1.) That parties are improper in the church; (2.) That Christians should regard themselves as on a level; and, (3.) That no one Christian should regard others as beneath him, or as the object of contempt.

7. *For who maketh,* &c. This verse contains a *reason* for what Paul had ust said; and the reason is, that all that any of them possessed had been derived from God, and no endowments whatever, which they had, could be laid as the foundation for self-congratulation and boasting. The apostle here doubtless has in his eye the teachers ın the church of Corinth, and intends to show them that there was no occasion of pride or to assume pre-eminence. As all that they possessed had been given of God, it could not be the occasion of boasting or self-confidence. ¶ *To differ from another.* Who has *separated* you from another; or who has made you superior to others. This may refer to every thing in which one was superior to others, or distinguished from them. The apostle doubtless has reference to those attainments in piety, talents, or knowledge by which one teacher was more eminent than others. But the same question may be applied to native endowments of mind; to opportunities of education; to the arrangements by which one rises in the world; to health; to property; to piety; to eminence and usefulness in the church. It is God who makes one, in any of these respects, to differ from others; and it is especially true in regard to personal piety. Had not *God* interfered and made a difference, all would have remained alike under sin. The race would have together rejected his mercy; and it is only by his distinguishing love that *any* are brought to believe and be saved. ¶ *And what hast thou.* Either talent, piety, or learning. ¶ *That thou didst not receive.* From God. By whatever means you have obtained it, it has been the gift of God. ¶ *Why dost thou glory,* &c. Why dost thou boast as if it were the result of your own toil, skill or endeavour. This is not designed to discourage human exertion; but to discourage a spirit of vain-glory and boasting. A man who makes the most painful and faithful effort to obtain any thing good, will, if successful, trace his success to God. He will still feel that it is God who gave him the disposition, the time, the strength, the success. And he will be *grateful* that he was enabled to make the effort; not vain, or proud, or boastful, because that he was successful. This passage states a general doctrine, that the reason why one man differs from another is to be traced to God; and that this fact should repress all boasting and glorying, and produce true humility in the minds of Christians. It may be observed, however, that it is as true of intellectual rank, of health, of wealth, of food, of raiment, of liberty, of peace, as it is of

8 Now ye are full, now ye are rich, [a] ye have reigned as kings without us: and I would to God ye did reign, that we also might reign with you.

9 For I think, that God hath

a Rev.3.17.

religion, that *all* come from God; and as this fact which is so obvious and well known, does not repress the exertions of men to preserve their health and to obtain property, so it should not repress their exertions to obtain salvation. God governs the world on the same good principles every where; and the fact that he is the source of all blessings, should not operate to discourage, but should prompt to human effort. The hope of his aid and blessing is the only ground of encouragement in *any* undertaking.

8. *Now ye are full.* It is generally agreed that this is spoken in *irony*, and that it is an indignant sarcasm uttered against the false and self-confident teachers in Corinth. The design is to contrast them with the apostles; to show how self-confident and vain the false teachers were, and how laborious and self-denying the apostles were; and to show to them how little claim *they* had to authority in the church, and the *real* claim which the apostles had from their self-denials and labours. The whole passage is an instance of most pungent and cutting sarcasm and shows that there *may* be occasions when irony may be proper, though it should be rare. An instance of cutting irony occurs also in regard to the priests of Baal, in 1 Kings xviii. 27. The word translated "ye are full" (κεκορεσμένοι) occurs only here, and in Acts xxvii. 38, "And when they had eaten enough." It is usually applied to a feast, and denotes those who are satiated or satisfied. So here it means, "You think you have enough. You are satisfied with your conviction of your own knowledge, and do not feel your need of any thing more." ¶ *Ye are rich.* This is presenting the same idea in a different form. "You esteem yourselves to be rich in spiritual gifts, and graces, so that you do not feel the necessity of any more." ¶ *Ye have reigned as kings.* This is simply carrying forward the idea before stated; but in the form of a *climax.* The first metaphor is taken from persons *filled with food;* the second from those who are so *rich* that they do not feel their want of more; the third from those who are raised to a *throne*, the highest elevation, where there was nothing further to be reached or desired. And the phrase means, that they had been fully satisfied with their condition and attainments, with their knowledge and power, that they lived like rich men and princes—revelling, as it were, on spiritual enjoyments, and disdaining all foreign influence, and instruction, and control. ¶ *Without us.* Without our counsel and instruction. You have taken the whole management of matters on yourselves without any regard to our advice or authority. You did not feel your need of our aid; and you did not regard our authority. You supposed you could get along as well without us as with us. ¶ *And I would to God ye did reign.* Many interpreters have understood this as if Paul had really expressed a wish that they were literal princes, that they might afford protection to him in his persecution and troubles. Thus Grotius, Whitby, Locke, Rosenmüller, and Doddridge. But the more probable interpretation is, that Paul here drops the *irony*, and addresses them in a sober, earnest manner. It is the expression of a wish that they were as truly happy and blessed as they thought themselves to be. "I wish that you *were* so abundant in all spiritual improvements; I wish that you *had* made such advances that you could be represented as full, and as rich, and as princes, needing nothing, that when I came I might have nothing to do but to partake of your joy." So Calvin, Lightfoot, Bloomfield. It implies, (1.) A *wish* that they were truly happy and blessed; (2.) A doubt implied whether they *were* then so; and, (3.) A desire on the part of Paul to *partake* of their real and true joy, instead

set forth us the [1] apostles last, as it were appointed to death: for we [a] are made a [2] spectacle unto the world, and to angels, and to men.

10 We *are* fools for Christ's

1 or, *the last apostles.*
a Heb.10.33. 2 *theatre.*

of being compelled to come to them with the language of rebuke and admonition; see ver. 19, 21.

9. *For I think.* It seems to me. Grotius thinks that this is to be taken *ironically,* as if he had said, "It seems then that God has designed that we, the apostles, should be subject to contempt and suffering, and be made poor and persecuted, while you are admitted to high honours and privileges." But probably this is to be taken as a *serious* declaration of Paul, designed to show their actual condition and trials, while others were permitted to live in enjoyment Whatever might be *their* condition, Paul says that the condition of himself and his fellow-labourers was one of much contempt and suffering; and the inference seems to be, that they ought to doubt whether they were in a right state, or had any occasion for their self-congratulation, since they so little resembled those whom God had set forth. ¶ *Hath set forth.* Has *showed* us; or placed us in public view. ¶ *The apostles last.* Marg. or, *the last apostles* (τοὺς ἀποστόλους ἐσχάτους). Grotius supposes that this means in the lowest condition; the humblest state; a condition like that of beasts. So Tertullian renders it. And this interpretation is the correct one if the passage be ironical. But Paul may mean to refer to the custom of bringing forth those in the amphitheatre at the *conclusion* of the spectacles who were to fight with other men, and who had no chance of escape. These inhuman games abounded every where; and an allusion to them would be well understood, and is indeed often made by Paul; comp. 1 Cor. ix. 26; 1 Tim. vi. 12; 2 Tim. iv. 7; see Seneca Epis. chap. vii. This interpretation receives support from the words which are used here, "God hath exhibited," "spectacle," or *theatre,* which are all applicable to such an exhibition. Calvin, Locke, and others, however, suppose that Paul refers to the fact that he was the *last* of the apostles; but this interpretation does not suit the connection of the passage. ¶ *As it were* (ὡς). Intimating the *certainty* of death. ¶ *Appointed unto death* (ἐπιθανατίους). Devoted to death. The word occurs no where else in the New Testament. It denotes the certainty of death, or the fact of being destined to death; and implies that such were their continued conflicts, trials, persecutions, that it was morally certain that they would terminate *in* their death, and only *when* they died, as the last gladiators on the stage were destined to contend until they should die This is a very strong expression; and denotes the continuance, the constancy, and the intensity of their sufferings in the cause of Christ. ¶ *We are made a spectacle.* Marg. *theatre* (θέατρον). The theatre, or amphitheatre of the ancients was composed of an *arena,* or level floor, on which the combatants fought, and which was surrounded by circular seats rising above one another to a great height, and capable of containing many thousand spectators. Paul represents himself as on this arena or stage, contending with foes, and destined to death. Around him and above him are an immense host of men and angels, looking on at the conflict, and awaiting the issue. He is not alone or unobserved. He is made public; and the universe gazes on the struggle. Angels and men denote the universe, as gazing upon the conflicts and struggles of the apostles. It is a vain inquiry here, whether he means good or bad angels. The expression means that he was *public* in his trials, and that this was exhibited to the universe. The whole verse is designed to convey the idea that God had, for wise purposes, appointed them in the sight of the universe, to pains, and trials, and persecutions, and poverty, and want, which would terminate only in their death; see Heb. xii. 1, &c. What these trials were he specifies in the following verses.

sake, but ye *are* wise in Christ; we *are* weak, but ye *are* strong; ye *are* honourable, but we *are* despised.

10. We are *fools.* This is evidently ironical. "We are doubtless foolish men, but ye are wise in Christ. We, Paul, Apollos, and Barnabas, have no claims to the character of wise men—we are to be regarded as fools, unworthy of confidence, and unfit to instruct; but you are full of wisdom." ¶ *For Christ's sake* (διὰ Χριστόν.) On account of Christ; or in reference to his cause, or in regard to the doctrines of the Christian religion. ¶ *But ye* are *wise in Christ.* The phrase "*in* Christ," does not differ in signification materially from the one above; "for Christ's sake." This is wholly ironical, and is exceedingly pungent. "You, Corinthians, boast of your wisdom and prudence. You are to be esteemed very wise. You are unwilling to submit to be esteemed fools. You are proud of your attainments. We, in the mean time, who are apostles, and who have founded your church, are to be regarded as fools, and as unworthy of public confidence and esteem." The whole design of this irony is to show the folly of their boasted wisdom. That they only should be wise and prudent, and the apostles fools, was in the highest degree absurd; and this absurdity the apostle puts in a strong light by his irony. ¶ *We* are *weak.* We are timid and feeble, but you are daring, bold and fearless. This is irony. The very reverse was probably true. Paul was bold, daring, fearless in declaring the truth, whatever opposition it might encounter; and probably many of them were timid and time-serving, and endeavouring to avoid persecution, and to accommodate themselves to the prejudices and opinions of those who were wise in their own sight; the prejudices and opinions of the world. ¶ *Ye* are *honourable.* Deserving of honour and obtaining it. Still ironical. You are to be esteemed as worthy of praise. ¶ *We* are *despised* (ἄτιμοι). Not only actually contemned, but worthy to be so. This was irony also. And the design was to show them how foolish was their self-confidence and self-flattery, and their attempt to exalt themselves.

11. *Even unto this present hour.* Paul here drops the irony, and begins a serious recapitulation of his actual sufferings and trials. The phrase here used "unto this present hour" denotes that these things had been incessant through all their ministry. They were not merely at the commencement of their work, but they had continued and attended them everywhere. And even then they were experiencing the same thing. These privations and trials were still continued, and were to be regarded as a part of the apostolic condition. ¶ *We both hunger and thirst.* The apostles, like their master, were poor, and in travelling about from place to place, it often happened that they scarcely found entertainment of the plainest kind, or had money to purchase it. It is no dishonour to be poor, and especially if that poverty is produced by doing good to others. Paul might have been rich, but he chose to be poor for the sake of the gospel. To enjoy the luxury of doing good to others, we ought to be willing to be hungry and thirsty, and to be deprived of our ordinary enjoyments. ¶ *And are naked.* In travelling, our clothes become old and worn out, and we have no friends to replace them, and no money to purchase new. It is no discredit to be clad in mean raiment if that is produced by self-denying toils in behalf of others. There is no honour in gorgeous apparel; but there is real honour in voluntary poverty and want, when produced in the cause of benevolence. Paul was not ashamed to travel, to preach, and to appear before princes and kings, in a soiled and worn-out garment, for it was worn out in the service of his Master, and Divine Providence had arranged the circumstances of his life. But how many a minister now would be ashamed to appear in such clothing! How many professed Christians are ashamed

11 Even unto this present hour we both hunger and thirst, and are naked, [a] and are buffeted, and have no certain dwelling-place.

12 And labour, [b] working with our own hands: being reviled, [c] we bless; being persecuted, we suffer it:

13 Being defamed, we entreat:

a Rom.8.35. b Acts 20.34. c Matt.5.44; Acts 7.60.

to go to the house of God because they cannot dress well, or be in the fashion, or outshine their neighbours! If an apostle was willing to be meanly clad in delivering the message of God, then assuredly *we* should be willing to preach, or to worship him in such clothing as he provides. We may add here, what a sublime spectacle was here; and what a glorious triumph of the truth. Here was Paul with an impediment in his speech; with a personage small and mean rather than graceful; and in a mean and tattered dress; and often in chains, yet delivering truth before which kings trembled, and which produced every where a deep impression on the human mind. Such was the power of the gospel *then!* And such triumph did the truth then have over men. See Doddridge. ¶ *And are buffeted.* Struck with the hand; Note, Mat. xxvi. 67. Probably it is here used to denote harsh and injurious treatment in general; comp. 2 Cor. xii. 7. ¶ *And have no certain dwelling-place.* No fixed or permanent home. They wandered to distant lands; threw themselves on the hospitality of strangers, and even of the enemies of the gospel; when driven from one place they went to another; and thus they led a wandering, uncertain life, amidst strangers and foes. They who know what are the comforts of home; who are surrounded by beloved families; who have a peaceful and happy fire-side; and who enjoy the blessings of domestic tranquillity, may be able to appreciate the trials to which the apostles were subjected. All this was for the sake of the gospel; all to purchase the blessings which we so richly enjoy.

12. *And labour,* &c. This Paul often did. See Note, Acts xviii. 3; compare Acts xx. 34; 1 Thess. ii. 9. 2 Thess. iii. 8. ¶ *Being reviled.* That they were often reviled or reproached, their history every where shows. See the Acts of the Apostles. They were reviled or ridiculed by the Gentiles as Jews; and by all as Nazarenes, and as deluded followers of Jesus; as the victims of a foolish superstition and enthusiasm. ¶ *We bless.* We return good for evil. In this they followed the explicit direction of the Saviour; see Note, Matt v. 44. The *main* idea in these passages is, that they were reviled, were persecuted, &c. The other clauses, "we bless," "we suffer it," &c. seem to be thrown in *by the way* to show how they bore this ill treatment. As if he had said "we are reviled; and what is more, we bear it patiently, and return good for evil." At the same time that he was recounting his trials, he was, therefore, incidentally *instructing* them in the nature of the gospel, and showing how their sufferings were to be borne; and how to illustrate the excellency of the Christian doctrine. ¶ *Being persecuted.* Note, Matt. v. 11. ¶ *We suffer it.* We sustain it; we do not revenge it; we *abstain* from resenting or resisting it.

13. *Being defamed.* Greek, Blasphemed, *i. e.* spoken of and to, in a harsh, abusive, and reproachful manner. The original and proper meaning of the word is to speak in a reproachful manner of any one, whether of God or man. It is usually applied to God, but it may also be used of men. ¶ *We entreat.* Either God in their behalf, praying him to forgive them, or we entreat them to turn from their sins, and become converted to God. Probably the latter is the sense. They besought them to examine more candidly their claims instead of reviling them; and to save their souls by embracing the gospel instead of destroying them by rejecting it with contempt and scorn. ¶ *We are made.* We became; we are so regarded or esteemed. The word here does not imply that there was any positive agency in *making* them

we are made as the filth of the
earth, *and are* the off-scouring [a] of
all things unto this day.
14 I write not these things to

a Lam.3.45.

shame you, but as my beloved
sons [b] I warn *you*.
15 For though ye have ten thousand instructors in Christ, yet *have*

b 1 Thess.2.11.

such, but simply that they were in fact so regarded. ¶ *As the filth of the earth.* It would not be possible to employ stronger expressions to denote the contempt and scorn with which they were every where regarded. The word *filth* (περικαθάρματα) occurs nowhere else in the New Testament. It properly denotes filth, or that which is collected by sweeping a house, or that which is collected and cast away by purifying or cleansing any thing; hence any vile, worthless, and contemptible object. Among the Greeks the word was used to denote the victims which were offered to *expiate crimes*, and particularly men of ignoble rank, and of a worthless and wicked character, who were kept to be offered to the gods in a time of pestilence, to appease their anger, and to *purify* the nation. Bretschneider and Schleusner. Hence it was applied by them to men of the most vile, abject, and worthless character. But it is not certain that Paul had any reference to that sense of the word. The whole force of the expression may be met by the supposition that he uses it in the sense of that filth or dirt which is collected by the process of cleansing or scouring any thing, as being vile, contemptible, worthless. So the apostles were regarded. And by the use of the word *world* here, he meant to say that they were regarded as the most vile and worthless men which the *whole world* could furnish; not only the refuse of Judea, but of all the nations of the earth. As if he had said "more vile and worthless men could not be found on the face of the earth." ¶ And are *the off-scouring of all things.* This word (περίψημα) occurs no where else in the New Testament. It does not differ materially from the word rendered *filth.* It denotes that which is rubbed off by scouring or cleaning any thing; and hence any thing vile or worthless; or a vile and worthless man. This term was also applied to vile and worthless men who were sacrificed or thrown into the sea as an expiatory offering, as it were to purify the people. Suidas remarks that they said to such a man, "be then our περίψημα," our redemption, and then flung him into the sea as a sacrifice to Neptune. See Whitby, Calvin, Doddridge. ¶ *Unto this day.* Continually. We have been constantly so regarded. See ver. 11.

14. *To shame you.* It is not my design to put you to shame by showing you how little you suffer in comparison with us. This is not our design, though it may have this effect. I have no wish to make you ashamed, to appear to triumph over you or merely to taunt you. My design is higher and nobler than this. ¶ *But as my beloved sons.* As my dear children. I speak as a father to his children, and I say these things for your good. No father would desire to make his children ashamed. In his counsels, entreaties, and admonitions, he would have a higher object than that. ¶ *I warn* you. I do not say these things in a harsh manner, with a severe spirit of rebuke: but in order to *admonish* you, to suggest counsel, to instil wisdom into the mind. I say these things not to make you blush, but with the hope that they may be the means of your reformation, and of a more holy life. No man, no minister, ought to reprove another merely to overwhelm him with shame, but the object should always be to make a brother better; and the admonition should be so administered as to have this end, not sourly or morosely, but in a kind, tender, and affectionate manner.

15. *For though ye have ten thousand instructors.* Though you may have or though you should have. It matters not how many you have, yet it is still true that I only sustain the relation to you of spiritual father, and whatever respect it is proper for you to have

ye not many fathers; for in Christ Jesus I have begotten you through the gospel.

16 Wherefore, I beseech you, be ye followers of me.

17 For this cause have I sent unto you Timotheus, who is my beloved son and faithful in the Lord, who shall bring you into remembrance of my ways which be in Christ, as I teach everywhere in every church.

---

toward them, yet there is a peculiar right which I have to admonish you, and a peculiar deference which is due to me, from my early labours among you, and from the fact that you are my spiritual children. ¶ *Instructers.* Gr. Pedagogues, or those who conducted children to school, and who superintended their conduct out of school hours. Hence those who had the care of children, or teachers in general. It is then applied to instructers of any kind. ¶ *In Christ.* In the Christian system or doctrine. The authority which Paul claims here, is that which a *father* has in preference to such an instructer. ¶ *Not many fathers.* Spiritual fathers. That is, you have but one. You are to remember that however many teachers you have, yet that I alone am your spiritual father. ¶ *In Christ Jesus.* By the aid and authority of Christ. I have begotten you by preaching his gospel and by his assistance. ¶ *I have begotten you.* I was the instrument of your conversion. ¶ *Through the gospel.* By means of the gospel; by preaching it to you, that is, by the truth.

16. *Wherefore.* Since I am your spiritual father. ¶ *Be ye followers of me.* Imitate me; copy my example; listen to my admonitions. Probably Paul had particularly in his eye their tendency to form parties; and here admonishes them that *he* had no disposition to form sects, and entreats them in this to imitate his example. A minister should always so live as that he can, without pride or ostentation, point to his own example; and entreat his people to imitate him. He should have such a confidence in his own integrity; he should lead such a blameless life: and *he should be assured that his people have so much evidence of his integrity,* that he can point them to his own example, and entreat them to live like himself. And to do this, he should live a life of piety, and should furnish such evidence of a pure conversation, that his people may have reason to regard him as a holy man.

17. *For this cause.* In order to remind you of my doctrines and my manner of life. Since I am hindered from coming myself, I have sent a fellow labourer as my messenger, well acquainted with my views and feelings, that he might do what I would do if I were present. ¶ *Have I sent unto you Timotheus.* Timothy, the companion and fellow labourer of Paul. This was probably when Paul was at Ephesus. He sent Timothy and Erastus into Macedonia, probably with instructions to go to Corinth if convenient. Yet it was not quite certain that Timothy would come to them, for in chap. xvi. 10, he expresses a doubt whether he would. Paul was probably deeply engaged in Asia, and did not think it proper then for him to leave his field of labour. He probably supposed also, that Timothy, as his ambassador, would be able to settle the difficulties in Corinth as well as if he were himself present. ¶ *My beloved son.* In the gospel. See Acts xvi. 1—3; 1 Tim. i. 2. He supposed, therefore, that they would listen to him with great respect. ¶ *And faithful in the Lord.* A true Christian and a faithful servant of Christ; and who is, therefore, worthy of your confidence. ¶ *Of my ways.* My doctrine, my teaching, my mode of life. ¶ *Which be in Christ.* That is, my Christian life: my ministry; or my conduct as a Christian and a follower of the Saviour. ¶ *As I teach everywhere,* &c. This was designed probably to show them that he taught *them* no new or peculiar doctrines; he wished them simply to conform to the common rules of the churches,

18 Now some are puffed up, as though I would not come to you.

19 But I will come to you shortly, if [a] the Lord will; and will know, not the speech of them which are puffed up, but [b] the power.

20 For the kingdom [c] of God *is* not in word, but in power.

21 What will ye? shall [d] I come unto you with a rod, or in love, and *in* the spirit of meekness?

a James 4.15. *b* Gal.2.6. *c* Rom.14.17. *d* 2 Cor.13.10.

and to be like their Christian brethren every where. The Christian church is founded every where on the same doctrines; is bound to obey the same laws; and is fitted to produce and cherish the same spirit. The same spirit that was required in Ephesus or Antioch, was required at Corinth; the same spirit that was required at Corinth, at Ephesus, or at Antioch, is required now.

18. *Now some are puffed up.* They are puffed up with a vain confidence; they say that I would not dare to come; that I would be afraid to appear among them, to administer discipline, to rebuke them, or to supersede their authority. Probably he had been detained by the demand on his services in other places, and by various providential hinderances from going there, until they supposed that he stayed away from fear. And possibly he might apprehend that they would think he had sent Timothy because he was afraid to come himself. Their conduct was an instance of the haughtiness and arrogance which men will assume when they suppose they are in no danger of reproof or punishment.

19. *But I will come.* It is from no fear of them that I am kept away; and to convince them of this I will come to them speedily. ¶ *If the Lord will.* If the Lord permit; if by his providence he allows me to go. Paul regarded the entering on a journey as dependent on the will of God; and felt that God had all in his hand. No purpose should be formed without a reference to his will; no plan without feeling that he can easily frustrate it and disappoint us; see James iv. 15. ¶ *And will know.* I will examine; I will put to the test; I will fully understand. ¶ *Not the speech, &c.* Not their vain and empty boasting; not their confident assertions, and their self-complacent views. ¶ *But the power.* Their real power. I will put their power to the proof: I will see whether they are able to effect what they affirm; whether they have more real power than I have. I will enter fully into the work of discipline, and will ascertain whether they have such authority in the church, such a power of party and of combination, that they can resist me, and oppose my administration of the discipline which the church needs. "A passage," says Bloomfield, "which cannot, in nerve and vigour, or dignity and composed confidence, be easily paralleled, even in Demosthenes himself."

20. *For the kingdom of God.* The reign of God in the church (Note, Mat. iii. 2); meaning here, probably, the power or authority which was to be exercised in the government and discipline of the church. Or it may refer to the manner in which the church had been established. "It has not been set up by empty boasting; by pompous pretensions; by confident assertions. Such empty boasts would do little in the great work of founding, governing, and preserving the church; and unless men have some higher powers than this they are not qualified to be religious teachers and guides." ¶ *But in power.* (1.) In the miraculous power by which the church was established—the power of the Saviour and of the apostles in working miracles. (2.) In the power of the Holy Ghost in the gift of tongues, and in his influence on the heart in converting men; Note, chap. i. 18. (3.) In the continual power which is needful to protect, defend, and govern the church. Unless teachers showed that they had *such* power, they were not qualified for their office.

21. *What will ye.* It depends on yourselves how I shall come. If you lay aside your contentions and strifes;

if you administer discipline as you should; if you give yourselves heartily and entirely to the work of the Lord, I shall come, not to reprove or to punish, but as a father and a friend. But if you do not heed my exhortations or the labours of Timothy; if you still continue your contentions, and do not remove the occasions of offence, I shall come with severity and the language of rebuke. ¶ *With a rod.* To correct and punish. ¶ *In the spirit of meekness.* Comforting and commending instead of chastising. Paul intimates that this depended on themselves. They had the power, and it was their duty to administer discipline; but if they would not do it, the task would devolve on him as the founder and father of the church, and as intrusted with power by the Lord Jesus to administer the severity of Christian discipline, or to punish those who offended by bodily suffering; see chap. v. 5; chap. xi. 30. See also the case of Ananias and Sapphira (Acts v. 1, &c.), and of Elymas the sorcerer. (Acts xiii. 10, 11.)

REMARKS.

1st. We should endeavour to form a proper estimate of the Christian ministry; ver. 1. We should regard ministers as the servants of Jesus Christ, and honour them for their Master's sake; and esteem them also in proportion to their fidelity. They are entitled to respect as the ambassadors of the Son of God; but that respect also should be in proportion to their resemblance of him and their faithfulness in their work. They who love the ministers of Christ, who are like him, and who are faithful, love the Master that sent them; they who hate and despise them despise him; see Mat. x. 40—42.

2d. Ministers should be faithful; ver. 2. They are the stewards of Christ. They are appointed by him. They are responsible *to* him. They have a most important trust—more important than any other stewards, and they should live in such a manner as to receive the approbation of their master.

3d. It is of little consequence what the world thinks of us; ver. 3. A good name is on many accounts desirable; but it should not be the leading consideration; nor should we do any thing *merely* to obtain it. Desirable as is a fair reputation, yet the opinion of the world is not to be too highly valued; for, (1.) It often misjudges; (2.) It is prejudiced for or against us; (3.) It is not to decide our final destiny; (4.) To desire that simply, is a selfish and base passion.

4th. The esteem even *of friends* is not to be the leading object of life; ver. 2. This is valuable, but not so valuable as the approbation of God. Friends are partial, and even where they do not approve our course, if we are conscientious, we should be willing to bear with their disapprobation. A good conscience is every thing. The approbation even of friends cannot help us in the day of judgment.

5th. We should distrust ourselves; ver. 3, 4. We should not pronounce too confidently on our motives or our conduct. We may be deceived. There may be much even in our own motives that may elude our most careful inquiry. This should teach us humility, self-distrust, and charity. Knowing our *own* liableness to mis-judge ourselves, we should look with kindness on the faults and failings of others.

6th. We see here the nature of the future judgment; ver. 5. (1.) The hidden things of darkness will be brought out—all the secret crimes, and plans, and purposes of men will be developed. All that has been done in secret, in darkness, in the night, in palaces and in prisons, will be developed. What a development will take place in the great day when the secret crimes of a world shall be revealed; and when all that has now escaped the notice of men, and the punishment of courts, shall be brought out! (2.) Every man's secret thoughts shall be revealed: There will be no concealment then. All that we have devised or desired; all the thoughts that we have forgotten, shall there be brought out to noon-day. How will the sinner tremble when *all* his thoughts are made known! Suppose, unknown to him, some person had been writing down all that a man has *thought* for a day, a week, or a year, and should begin to *read* it to him. Who is there that would not hang his head with shame, and tremble at such a record? Yet at the day of judgment the thoughts of *the whole life* will be revealed. (3.) Every man shall be judged as he *ought* to be. God is impartial. The man that *ought* to be saved will be; the man that *ought not* will not be. How solemn will be the *impartial trial of the world!* Who can think of it but with alarm!

7th. We have no occasion for pride or vain-boasting; ver. 7. All that we have of beauty, health, wealth, honour, grace, has been given to us by God. For what he has given us we should be grateful; but it should not excite pride. It is, indeed, valuable *because* God gives it, and we should remember his mercies, but we should not boast. We have nothing to boast of. Had we our deserts, we should be driven away in his wrath, and made wretched. That any are out of hell is matter of thankfulness; that one possesses more than another proves that God is a sovereign, and not that we are more worthy than another, or that there is by nature any ground of preference which one has over another.

8th. Irony and sarcasm are sometimes lawful and proper; ver. 8—10. But it is not often as safe as it was in the hands of the apostle Paul. Few men can regulate the talent properly; few should allow themselves to indulge in it. It is *rarely* employed in the Bible; and it is rarely employed elsewhere where it does not do injury. The cause of truth can be usually sustained by sound argument; and that which cannot be thus defended is not worth defence. Deep wounds are often made by the severity of wit and irony; and an indulgence in this usually prevents a man from having a single friend.

9th. We see from this chapter what religion has cost; ver. 9—13. Paul states the sufferings that he and the other apostles endured in order to establish it. They were despised, and persecuted, and poor, and regarded as the refuse of the world. The Christian religion was founded on the blood of its author, and has been reared amidst the sighs and tears of its friends. All its early advocates were subjected to persecution and trial; and to engage in this work involved the certainty of being a martyr. We enjoy not a blessing which has not thus been purchased; and which has not come to us through the self-denials and toils of the best men that the earth has known. Persecution raged around all the early friends of the church; and it rose and spread while the fire of martyrdom spread, and while its friends were everywhere cast out as evil, and called to bleed in its defence.

10th. We have here an illustrious instance of the manner in which reproach, and contempt, and scorn should be borne; ver. 12, 13. The apostles imitated the example of their Master and followed his precepts. They prayed for their enemies, persecutors, and slanderers. There is nothing but religion that can produce this spirit; and this can do it always. The Saviour evinced it; his apostles evinced it; and all *should* evince it, who profess to be its friends.—We may remark, (1.) This is not produced by nature. It is the work of grace alone. (2.) It is the very spirit and genius of Christianity to produce it. (3.) Nothing but religion will enable a man to bear it, and will produce this temper and spirit. (4.) We have an instance here of what *all* Christians should evince. All should be in this like the apostles. All should be like the Saviour himself.

11th. We have an argument here for the truth of the Christian religion. The argument is founded on the fact that the apostles were willing to suffer so much in order to establish it.—They professed to have been eye-witnesses of what they affirmed. They had nothing to gain by spreading it if it was not true. They exposed themselves to persecution on this account, and became willing to die rather than deny its truth.—Take, for example, the case of the apostle Paul. (1.) He had every prospect of honour and of wealth in his own country. He had been liberally educated, and had the confidence of his countrymen. He might have risen to the highest station

CHAPTER V.

IT is reported commonly *that there is* fornication among you, and such fornication as is not so much as named among the Gentiles, that [a] one should have his father's wife.

a Deut.27.20.

of trust or influence. He had talents which would have raised him to distinction anywhere. (2.) He could not have been mistaken in regard to the events connected with his conversion; Acts ix. The scene, the voice, the light, the blindness, were all things which could not have been counterfeited. They were open and public. They did not occur "in a corner." (3.) He had no earthly motive to change his course. Christianity was despised when he embraced it; its friends were few and poor; and it had no prospect of spreading through the world. It conferred no wealth; bestowed no diadem; imparted no honours; gave no ease; conducted to no friendship of the great and the mighty. It subjected its friends to persecution, and tears, and trials, and death. What should *induce* such a man to make such a change? Why should Paul have embraced this, but from a conviction of its truth? How could he be convinced of that truth except by some argument that should be *so strong* as to overcome his hatred to it, make him willing to renounce all his prospects for it; to encounter all that the world could heap upon him, and even death itself, rather than deny it? But such a religion had a higher than any earthly origin, and must have been from God.

12th. We may expect to suffer reproach. It has been the common lot of all, from the time of the Master himself to the present. Jesus was reproached; the apostles were reproached; the martyrs were reproached, and we are not to be surprised that ministers and Christians are called to like trials now. It is enough "for the disciple that he be as his Master, and the servant as his Lord."

CHAPTER V.

THIS chapter is entirely occupied with a notice of an offence which existed in the church at Corinth, and with a statement of the measures which the apostle expected them to pursue in regard to it. Of the existence of this offence he had been informed, probably by "those of the house of Chloe," chap. i. 11, and there is reason to suppose that they had not even alluded to it in the letter which they had sent to him asking advice; see chap. vii. 1; comp. the Introduction. The apostle (ver. 1) reproves them for tolerating a species of licentiousness which was not tolerated even by the heathens; he reproves them (ver. 2) for being puffed up with pride even while this scandal existed in their church; he ordered them forthwith to purify the church by removing the incestuous person (ver. 4, 5); and exhorted them to preserve themselves from the influence which a single corrupt person might have, operating like leaven in a mass; (ver. 6, 7.) Then, lest they should mistake his meaning, and suppose that by commanding them not to keep company with licentious persons (ver. 9), he meant to say, that they should withdraw from all intercourse with the heathen who were known to be idolaters and corrupt, he says that that former command was not designed to forbid *all* intercourse with them, (ver. 9—12); but that he meant his injunction now to extend particularly to such as were professed members of the church; that they were not to cut off all intercourse with society at large because it was corrupt; that if any man professed to be a Christian and yet was guilty of such practices they were to disown him (ver. 11); that it was not his province, nor did he assume it, to judge the heathen world which was *without* the church (ver. 12); but that this was entirely consistent with the view that he had a right to exercise discipline *within* the church, on such as professed to be Christians; and that therefore, they were bound to put away that wicked person.

1. *It is reported.* Gr. It is heard. There is a rumour. That rumour had been brought to Paul, probably by the

2 And ye are puffed up, and have not rather mourned, [a] that he that hath done this deed might be taken away from among you.

a 2 Cor.7.7.

members of the family of Chloe, chap. i. 11. ¶ *Commonly* (Ὅλως). Every where. It is a matter of common fame. It is so public that it cannot be concealed; and so certain that it cannot be denied. This was an offence, he informs us, which even the heathen would not justify or tolerate; and, therefore, the report had spread not only in the churches, but even among the heathen, to the great scandal of religion.—When a report obtains *such* a circulation, it is certainly time to investigate it, and to correct the evil. ¶ That there is *fornication*. See Note, Acts xv. 20. The word is here used to denote incest; for the apostle immediately explains the nature of the offence. ¶ *And such fornication*, &c. An offence that is not tolerated or known among the heathen. This greatly aggravated the offence, that in a Christian church a crime should be tolerated among its members which even gross heathens would regard with abhorrence. That this offence was regarded with abhorrence by even the heathens has been abundantly proved by quotations from classic writers. See Wetstein, Bloomfield, and Whitby. Cicero says of the offence, expressly, that "it was an incredible and unheard of crime." Pro Cluen. 5. 6.—When Paul says that it was not "so much as named among the Gentiles," he doubtless uses the word (ὀνομάζεται) in the sense of *named with approbation, tolerated*, or *allowed*. The crime was known in a few instances, but chiefly of those who were princes and rulers; but it was no where regarded with approbation, but was always treated as abominable wickedness. All that the connection requires us to understand by the word "*named*" here is, that it was not tolerated or allowed; it was treated with abhorrence, and it was, therefore, more scandalous that it was allowed in a Christian church.—Whitby supposes that this offence that was tolerated in the church at Corinth gave rise to the scandals that were circulated among the heathen respecting the early Christians, that they allowed of licentious intercourse among the members of their churches. This reproach was circulated extensively among the heathen, and the primitive Christians were at much pains to refute it. ¶ *That one should have*. Probably as his wife; or it may mean simply that he had criminal intercourse with her. Perhaps some man had parted with his wife, on some account, and his son had married her, or maintained her for criminal intercourse. It is evident from 2 Cor. vii. 12, that the person who had suffered the wrong, as well as he who had done it, was still alive.—Whether this was marriage or concubinage, has been disputed by commentators, and it is not possible, perhaps, to determine. See the subject discussed in Bloomfield.

2. *And ye are puffed up*. Note, chap. iv. 18. You are filled with pride, and with a vain conceit of your own wisdom and purity, notwithstanding the existence of this enormous wickedness in your church. This does not mean that they were puffed up, or proud *on account* of the existence of this wickedness, but they were filled with pride *notwithstanding*, or in spite of it. They *ought* to have been a humbled people. They *should* have mourned; and should have given their first attention to the removal of the evil. But instead of this, they had given indulgence to proud feeling, and had become elated with a vain confidence in their spiritual purity. Men are always elated and proud when they have the least occasion for it. ¶ *And have not rather mourned*, &c. Have not rather been *so* afflicted and troubled as to take the proper means for removing the offence. The word *mourn* here is taken in that large sense. Ye have not been *so much* afflicted—so troubled with the existence of this wickedness, as to take the proper measures to remove the offender.—Acts of discipline in the

3 For I verily, as absent [a] in body, but present in spirit, have [1] judged already, as though I were present *concerning* him that hath so done this deed;

4 In the name [b] of our Lord

a Col.2.5. 1 or, *determined*. b 2 Cor.2.9,10.

church should always commence with *mourning* that there is occasion for it. It should not be *anger*, or pride, or revenge, or party feeling, which prompt to it. It should be deep *grief* that there is occasion for it; and tender compassion for the offender. ¶ *Might be taken away*. By excommunication. He should not, while he continues in this state, be allowed to remain in your communion.

3. *For I verily*. But I, whatever it may cost me; however you may esteem my interference; and whatever personal ill-will may be the result towards me, have adjudged this case to be so flagrant as to demand the exercise of discipline, and since the church to whom it belongs have neglected it, I use the authority of an apostle, and of a spiritual father, in directing it to take place. This was not a formal sentence of excommunication; but it was the declared opinion of an apostle that such a sentence *should* be passed, and an *injunction* on the church to exercise this act of discipline. ¶ *As absent in body*. Since I am not personally present with you, I express my opinion in this manner. I am absent in body from you, and cannot, therefore, take those steps in regard to it which I could were I present. ¶ *But present in spirit*. My heart is with you; my feelings are with you; I have a deep and tender interest in the case; and I judge *as if* I were personally present. Many suppose that Paul by this refers to a power which was given to the apostles, though at a distance, to discern the real circumstances of a case by the gift of the Spirit. Comp. Col. ii. 5; 2 Kings v. 26; vi. 12. (Whitby, Doddridge, &c.) But the phrase does not demand this interpretation. Paul meant, probably, that though he was absent, yet his mind and attention had been given to this subject; he felt as deeply as though he were present, and would act in the same way. He had, in some way, been fully apprized of all the circumstances of the case, and he felt it to be his duty to express his views on the subject. ¶ *Have judged already*. Margin, *Determined* (κέκρικα). I have made up my mind; have decided, and *do* decide. That is, he had determined what *ought* to be done in the case. It was a case in which the course which ought to be pursued was plain, and on this point his mind was settled. What that course should be he states immediately. ¶ *As though I were present*. As though I had a personal knowledge of the whole affair, and were with you to advise.—We may be certain that Paul had the fullest information as to this case; and that the circumstances were well known. Indeed, it was a case about *the facts* of which there could be no doubt. They were every where known (ver. 1), and there was no need, therefore, to attempt to establish them by formal proof.

4. *In the name*, &c. By the authority; or in the behalf; or acting by his commission or power. 2 Cor. ii 10. See Note, Acts iii. 6. This does not refer to Paul alone in declaring his opinion, but means that they were to be assembled in the name of the Lord Jesus, and that they were to proceed to exercise discipline by his authority. The idea is, that the authority to administer discipline is derived from the Lord Jesus Christ, and is to be exercised in his name, and to promote his honour. ¶ *When ye are gathered together*. Or, "You being assembled in the name of the Lord Jesus." This is to be connected with the previous words, and means, (1.) That they were to be assembled for the purpose of administering discipline; and (2.) That this was to be done in the name and by the authority of the Lord Jesus. ¶ *And my spirit*, ver. 3. As if I were with you; that is, with my declared opinion;

Jesus Christ, when ye are gathered together, and my spirit, with the power *a* of our Lord Jesus Christ,

5 To deliver *b* such an one unto Satan for the destruction of the flesh, that the *c* spirit may be saved in the day of the Lord Jesus.

a Mat.16.19; John 20.23. *b* 1 Tim.1.20. *c* chap.11.32.

knowing what I would advise, were I one of you; or, I being *virtually* present with you by having delivered my opinion. It cannot mean that Paul's soul would be really present with them, but that, knowing his views and feelings, and what he would do, and knowing his love for them, they could act as if he were there. This passage proves that discipline belongs to the church itself; and so deep was Paul's conviction of this, that even *he* would not administer it, without their concurrence and action. And if Paul would not do it, and in a case too where bodily pains were to be inflicted by miraculous agency, assuredly no other ministers have a right to assume the authority to administer discipline without the action and the concurrence of the church itself.

[The general doctrine of the New Testament is that the government of the church is invested, not in the people or church members at large, but in certain rulers or office-bearers, 1 Cor. xii. 28, Eph. iv. 11, 12; 1 Thess. v. 12, 13; Heb. xiii. 7; 1 Tim. v. 17. We find these elders or rulers existing in every church to which our attention is directed, while the people are continually exhorted to yield a willing submission to their authority. Now the passage under review must be explained in consistency with the analogy of truth, or the general scope of Scripture on the subject. It is unwise to build our conclusion on an insulated text. But, in reality, the language of the apostle, in this place, when fairly examined, gives no countenance to the idea that the judicial power of the church resides in the people. The case of the incestuous man was *judged by the apostle himself* previous to the transmission of his letter to the Corinthian church, which was therefore enjoined, not to adjudicate on the matter, but simply to give effect to the decision of Paul. "I verily *have judged already* concerning him who hath done this deed; in the name of our Lord Jesus Christ," &c. If it be still demanded why then were the people to assemble? the answer is obvious. It was necessary that the sentence should be published, where the crime had been committed, that the members of the church might concur in it, and withdraw from the society of the guilty person. The simple fact of the people being assembled, is no proof that they were judges.

Yet candour requires us to state that the words in the third verse, ἤδη κέκρικα (I have already judged) are supposed by some to intimate, not the delivering of an authoritative sentence, but the simple expression of an opinion in regard to what *ought* to be done. This, however, seems neither consistent with the scope of the passage, nor with just ideas of apostolical authority. The apostles had "the care of all the churches, with power to settle matters of faith and order, to determine controversies, and exercise the rod of discipline on all offenders, whether pastors or flock; 1 Cor. v. 3—6; 2 Cor. x. 8; xiii. 10."]

¶ *With the power*, &c. This phrase is to be connected with the following verse. "I have determined what ought to be done. The sentence which I have passed is this. You are to be assembled in the name and authority of Christ. I shall be virtually present. And you are to deliver such a one to Satan, *by the power of our Lord Jesus Christ.*" That is, it is to be done by you; and the *miraculous* power which will be evinced in the case will proceed from the Lord Jesus. The word *power* (δυνάμις), is used commonly in the New Testament to denote some miraculous and extraordinary power; and here evidently means that the Lord Jesus would put forth such a power in the infliction of pain and for the preservation of the purity of his church.

5. *To deliver.* This is the sentence which is to be executed. You are to deliver him to Satan, &c. ¶ *Unto Satan.* Beza, and the Latin fathers, suppose that this is only an expression of excommunication. They say, that in the Scriptures there are but two kingdoms recognised—the kingdom of God, or the church, and the kingdom of the world, which is regarded as under the control of Satan; and that to exclude a man from one is to subject him to the dominion of the other. There is some foundation for this

6 Your glorying [a] is not good. Know ye not that a little leaven [b] leaveneth the whole lump?

7 Purge out therefore the old leaven, that ye may be a new lump, as ye are unleavened. For

a James 4.16. *b* Luke 13.21.

opinion; and there can be no doubt that *excommunication* is here intended, and that, *by* excommunication, the offender was in some sense placed under the control of Satan. It is further evident that it is here supposed that by being thus placed under him the offender would be subject to corporal inflictions by the agency of Satan, which are here called the "destruction of the flesh." Satan is elsewhere referred to as the author of bodily diseases. Thus in the case of Job, Job ii. 7. A similar instance is mentioned in 1 Tim. i. 20, where Paul says he had delivered Hymeneus and Alexander to "Satan, that they might learn not to blaspheme." It may be observed here that though this was to be done by the concurrence of the church, as having a right to administer discipline, yet it was directed by apostolic authority; and there is no evidence that this was the usual form of excommunication, nor ought it now to be used. There was evidently *miraculous* power evinced in this case, and that power has long since ceased in the church. ¶ *For the destruction of the flesh.* We may observe here, (1.) That this does not mean that the man was *to die* under the infliction of the censure, for the object was to recover him; and it is evident that, whatever he suffered as the consequence of this, he survived it, and Paul again instructed the Corinthians to admit him to their fellowship, 2 Cor. ii. 7. (2.) It was designed to punish him for licentiousness of life—often called in the Scriptures one of the sins, or works of the flesh (Gal. v. 19), and the design was that the punishment should follow *in the line of the offence*, or be a just retribution—as punishment often does. Many have supposed that by the "destruction of the flesh" Paul meant only the destruction of his fleshly appetites or carnal affections; and that he supposed that this would be effected by the act of excommunication. But it is very evident from the Scriptures that the apostles were imbued with the power of inflicting diseases or bodily calamities for crimes. See Acts xiii. 11; 1 Cor. xi. 30. What this bodily malady was, we have no means of knowing. It is evident that it was not of very long duration, since when the apostle exhorts them (2 Cor. ii. 7) again to receive him, there is no mention made of his suffering then under it.—This was an extraordinary and miraculous power. It was designed for the government of the church in its infancy, when every thing was fitted to show the direct agency of God; and it ceased, doubtless, with the apostles. The church now has no such power. It cannot now work miracles; and all its discipline now is to be *moral* discipline, designed not to inflict bodily pain and penalties, but to work a moral reformation in the offender. ¶ *That the spirit may be saved.* That his soul might be saved; that he might be corrected, humbled, and reformed by these sufferings, and recalled to the paths of piety and virtue. This expresses the true design of the discipline of the church, and it ought *never* to be inflicted but with a direct intention to benefit the offender, and to save the soul. Even when he is cut off and disowned, the design should not be vengeance, or punishment merely, but it should be to recover him and save him from ruin. ¶ *In the day of the Lord Jesus.* The day of judgment when the Lord Jesus shall come, and shall collect his people to himself.

6. *Your glorying.* Your boasting; or confidence in your present condition, as if you were eminent in purity and piety. ¶ *Is not good.* Is not well, proper, right. Boasting is never good; but it is especially wrong when, as here, there is an existing evil that is likely to corrupt the whole church. When men are disposed to boast, they should at once make the inquiry whether there is not some sin indulged in,

even Christ [a] our passover is [1] sacrificed for us:

8 Therefore let us keep [2] the feast, [b] not with old leaven, nei-

a Isa.53.7; 1 Pet.1.19; Rev.5.6,12. 1 or, *slain*. 2 or, *holy day*. *b* Ex.13.6.

on account of which they should be humbled and subdued. If all individual Christians, and all Christian churches, and all men of every rank and condition, would look at things as they are, they would never find occasion for boasting. It is only when we are blind to the realities of the case, and overlook our faults, that we are disposed to boast. The reason why this was improper in Corinth, Paul states—that any sin would tend to corrupt the whole church, and that therefore they ought not to boast until that was removed. ¶ *A little leaven,* &c. A small quantity of leaven or yeast will pervade the entire mass of flour, or dough, and diffuse itself through it all. This is evidently a proverbial saying. It occurs also in Gal. v. 9. Comp. Note, Matt. xiii. 33. A similar figure occurs also in the Greek classic writers.—By *leaven* the Hebrews metaphorically understood whatever had the power of *corrupting,* whether doctrine, or example, or any thing else. See Note, Matt. xvi. 6. The sense here is plain. A single sin indulged in, or allowed in the church, would act like leaven—it would pervade and corrupt the whole church, unless it was removed. On this ground, and for this reason, discipline should be administered, and the corrupt member should be removed.

7. *Purge out therefore,* &c. Put away; free yourselves from. ¶ *The old leaven.* The apostle here takes occasion, from the mention of *leaven,* to exhort the Corinthians to put away vice and sin. The figure is derived from the custom of the Jews in putting away leaven at the celebration of the passover. By the *old* leaven he means vice and sin; and also here the person who had committed the sin in their church. As the Jews, at the celebration of the passover, gave all diligence in removing leaven from their houses—searching every part of their dwellings with candles, that they might remove every particle of leavened bread from their habitations—so the apostle exhorts them to use all diligence to search out and remove all sin. ¶ *That ye may be a new lump.* That you may be like a new mass of flour, or dough, before the leaven is put into it. That you may be pure, and free from the corrupting principle. ¶ *As ye are unleavened.* That is, as ye are bound by your Christian profession to be unleavened, or to be pure. Your very *profession* implies this, and you ought, therefore, to remove all impurity, and to become holy. Let there be no impurity, and no mixture inconsistent with that holiness which the gospel teaches and requires. The apostle here does not refer merely to the case of the incestuous person, but he takes occasion to exhort them to put away *all* sin. Not only to remove this occasion of offence, but to remove *all* impurity, that they might become entirely and only holy. The doctrine is, that Christians are by their profession holy, and that therefore they ought to give all diligence to remove every thing that is impure. ¶ *For even Christ,* &c. As the Jews, when their paschal lamb was slain, gave great diligence to put away all leaven from their dwellings, so we Christians, since *our* passover is slain, ought to give the like diligence to remove all that is impure and corrupting from our hearts.—There can be no doubt here that the paschal lamb was a type of the Messiah; and as little that the leaven was understood to be emblematic of impurity and sin, and that their being required to put it away was intended to be an emblematic action designed to denote that all sin was to be removed and forsaken. ¶ *Our passover.* Our *paschal lamb,* for so the word πάσχα usually signifies. The sense is, "We Christians have a paschal lamb; and that lamb is the Messiah. And as the Jews, when *their* paschal lamb was slain, were required to put away all leaven from their dwellings, so *we,* when *our* paschal lamb is slain, should put away all sin from our hearts and

ther with the [a] leaven of malice and wickedness, but with the unleavened *bread* of sincerity and truth.

a Mat.16.6,12.

from our churches." This passage proves that Paul meant to teach that Christ had *taken the place* of the paschal lamb—that that lamb was designed to adumbrate or typify him—and that consequently when *he* was offered, the paschal offering was designed to cease. Christ is often in the Scriptures compared to a *lamb*. See Isa. liii. 7; John i. 29; 1 Pet. i. 19; Rev. v. 6, 12. ¶ *Is sacrificed for us.* Margin, Or *slain* (ἐτύθη). The word θύω may mean simply to slay or kill; but it is also used often in the sense of making a sacrifice as an expiation for sin; Acts xiv. 13, 18; 1 Cor. x. 20; comp. Gen. xxxi. 54; xlv. 1; Ex. iii. 18; v. 3, 8, 17; viii. 8, 25—29; xiii. 15; xx. 24; 2 Chron. xv. 26, where it is used as the translation of the word צבח, to sacrifice. It is used as the translation of this word no less than ninety-eight times in the Old Testament, and perhaps always in the sense of a *sacrifice*, or bloody offering. It is also used as the translation of the Hebrew word טבח, and שחט, to slay, to kill, &c. in Ex. xii. 21; 1 Kings xi. 19; xxv. 11; 2 Chron. xxix. 22, &c.; in all in eleven places in the Old Testament. It is used in a similar sense in the New Testament, in Matt. xxii. 4; Luke xv. 23, 27, 30; John x. 10; Acts x. 13; xi. 7. It occurs no where else in the New Testament than in the places which have been specified.—The true sense of the word here is, therefore, to be found in the doctrine respecting the passover. That that was intended to be a sacrifice for sin is proved by the nature of the offering, and by the account which is every where given of it in the Old Testament. The paschal lamb was slain as a sacrifice. It was slain in the temple; its blood was poured out as an offering; it was sprinkled and offered by the priests in the same way as other sacrifices; see Ex. xxiii. 18; xxxiv. 25; 2 Chron. xxx. 15, 16. And if so, then this passage means that Christ was offered *as a sacrifice for sin*—in accordance with the numerous passages of the New Testament, which speak of his death in this manner (see Note, Rom. iii. 25); and that his offering was designed to take the place of the paschal sacrifice, under the ancient economy. ¶ *For us.* For us who are Christians. He died in our stead; and as the Jews, when celebrating *their* paschal feast, put away all leaven, so *we*, as Christians, should put away all evil from our hearts, since that sacrifice has now been made once for all.

8. *Let us keep the feast.* Margin, *Holy day* (ἑορτάζωμεν). This is language drawn from the paschal feast, and is used by Paul frequently to carry out and apply his illustration. It does not mean literally the paschal supper here—for that had ceased to be observed by Christians—nor the Lord's supper particularly; but the sense is "As the Jews when they celebrated the paschal supper, on the slaying and sacrifice of the paschal lamb, put away all leaven—as emblematic of sin—so let us, in the slaying of *our* sacrifice, and in all the duties, institutions and events consequent thereon, put away all wickedness from our hearts as individuals, and from our societies and churches. Let us engage in the service of God by putting away all evil." ¶ *Not with the old leaven.* Not under the influence, or in the indulgence of the feelings of corrupt and unrenewed human nature.—The word *leaven* is very expressive of that former or *old* condition, and denotes the corrupt and corrupting passions of our nature before it is renewed. ¶ *The leaven of malice.* Of unkindness and evil—which would *diffuse* itself, and pervade the mass of Christians. The word *malice* (κακίας) denotes *evil* in general. ¶ *And wickedness.* Sin; evil. There is a *particular* reference here to the case of the incestuous person. Paul means that *all* wickedness should be put away from those who had been saved by the sacrifice of their *Passover*, Christ; and, therefore, this sin in a special manner.

9 I wrote unto you in an epistle
[a] not to company with fornicators:

10 Yet not altogether with the
fornicators of this world, or

a Eph.5.11; 2 Thess.3.14.

¶ *But with the unleavened* bread, &c. That is, with sincerity and truth. Let us be sincere, and true, and faithful; as the Jews partook of bread unleavened, which was emblematic of purity, so let us *be* sincere and true. It is implied here that this could not be done unless they would put away the incestuous person.—No Christians can have, or give evidence of sincerity, who are not willing to put away all sin.

9. *I wrote unto you.* I have written (ἔγραψα). This word may either refer to this epistle, or to some former epistle. It simply denotes that he *had* written to them, but whether in the former part of this, or in some former epistle which is now lost, cannot be determined by the use of this word. ¶ *In an epistle* (ἐν τῇ ἐπιστολῇ). There has been considerable diversity of opinion in regard to this expression. A large number of commentators as Chrysostom, Theodoret, Oecumenius, most of the Latin commentators, and nearly all the Dutch commentators – suppose that this refers to the same epistle, and that the apostle means to say that in the former part of this epistle (ver. 2) he had given them this direction. And in support of this interpretation they say that τῇ here is used for ταυτῇ, and appeal to the kindred passages in Rom. xvi. 2; Col. iv. 6; 1 Thess. v. 27; 2 Thess. iii. 3, 4. Many others—as Grotius, Doddridge, Rosenmüller, &c.—suppose it to refer to some other epistle which is now lost, and which had been sent to them before their messengers had reached him. This epistle might have been very brief, and might have contained little more than this direction. That this is the correct opinion, may appear from the following considerations, viz: (1.) It is the *natural* and *obvious* interpretation—one that would strike the great mass of men. It is just such an expression as Paul *would* have used on the supposition that he *had* written a previous epistle. (2.) It is the very expression which he uses in 2 Cor. vii. 8, where he is referring to this epistle as one which he had sent to them. (3.) It is not true that Paul had in any former part of this epistle given this direction. He had commanded them to remove an incestuous person, and such a command might seem to imply that they ought not to keep company with such a person; but it was not a general command *not* to have intercourse with them. (4.) It is altogether probable that Paul would write more letters than we have preserved. We have but fourteen of his remaining. Yet he laboured many years; founded many churches; and had frequent occasion to write to them. (5.) We know that a number of books have been lost which were either inspired or which were regarded as of authority by inspired men. Thus the books of Jasher, of Iddo the seer, &c., are referred to in the Old Testament, and there is no improbability that similar instances may have occurred in regard to the writers of the New Testament. (6.) In ver. 11, he expressly makes a distinction between the epistle which he was then writing and the former one. "But now," *i. e.* in this epistle, "I have written (ἔγραψα) to you," &c. an expression which he would not use if ver. 9, referred to the *same* epistle. These considerations seem to me to be unanswerable, and to prove that Paul had sent another epistle to *them* in which he had given this direction. (7.) This opinion accords with that of a very large number of commentators. As an instance, Calvin says, "The epistle of which he here speaks, is not now extant. Nor is it to be doubted that many others have perished; but it is sufficient that these survive to us which the Lord saw to be needful." If it be objected that this may affect the doctrine of the inspiration of the New Testament, since it is not to be supposed that God would suffer the

with the covetous, or extortioners, or with idolaters; for then must ye needs go out of the world.

---

writings of inspired men to be lost, we may reply, (*a*) That there is no evidence that these writings were inspired. Paul often makes a distinction in regard to his own words and doctrines, as inspired or uninspired (see chap. vii.); and the same thing may have occurred in his writings. (*b*) This does not affect the inspiration of the books which remain, even on the supposition that those which were lost were inspired. It does not prove that these are not from God. If a man loses a guinea it does not prove that those which he has *not* lost are counterfeit or worthless. (*c*) If inspired, they may have answered the purpose which was designed by their inspiration—and then have been suffered to be lost—as *all* inspired *books* will be destroyed at the end of the world. (*d*) It is to be remembered that a large part of the *discourses* of the inspired apostles, and even the Saviour himself (John xxi. 25), have been lost. And why should it be deemed any more wonderful that inspired *books* should be lost than inspired *oral teaching?* Why more wonderful that a brief letter of Paul should be destroyed than that numerous discourses of him "who spake as never man spake," should be lost to the world? (*e*) We should be thankful for the books that remain, and we may be assured that all the truth that is needful for our salvation has been preserved and is in our hands. That *any* inspired books have been preserved amidst the efforts which have been made to destroy them *all*, is more a matter of wonder than that a few have been lost, and should rather lead us to gratitude that we have them than to grief that a few, probably relating to local and comparatively unimportant matters, have been destroyed. ¶ *Not to company*, &c. Not to associate with; see Eph. v. 11; 2 Thess. iii. 14. This, it seems, was a *general* direction on the subject. It referred to *all* who had this character. But the direction which he *now* (ver. 11) proceeds to give, relates to a different matter—the proper degree of intercourse with those who were *in the church.*

10. *Yet not altogether*, &c. In my direction not "to company" with them, I did not mean that you should refuse *all* kinds of intercourse with them; that you should not treat them with civility, or be engaged with them in any of the transactions of life, or in the ordinary intercourse of society between man and man, for this would be impossible—but that you should not *so* associate with them as to be esteemed to belong to them, or so as to be corrupted by their example. You are not to make them companions and friends. ¶ *With the fornicators.* Most heathen were of this description, and particularly at Corinth. See the Introduction to this epistle. ¶ *Of this world.* Of those who are out of the church; or who are not professed Christians. ¶ *Or with the covetous.* The avaricious; those greedy of gain. Probably his direction in the former epistle had been that they should avoid them. ¶ *Or extortioners.* Rapacious persons; greedy of gain, and oppressing the poor, the needy, and the fatherless, to obtain money. ¶ *Or an idolater.* All the Corinthians before the gospel was preached there worshipped idols. ¶ *Then must ye needs*, &c. It would be necessary to leave the world. The world is full of such persons. You meet them every where. You cannot avoid them in the ordinary transactions of life, unless you either destroy yourselves, or withdraw wholly from society. This passage shows, (1.) That that society was *full* of the licentious and the covetous, of idolaters and extortioners. (Comp. Notes, Rom. i.) (2.) That it is not right either to take our own lives to avoid them, or to withdraw from society and become monks; and therefore, that the whole monastic system is contrary to Christianity; and, (3.) That it is needful we should have *some* intercourse with the men of the world; and to have dealings with them as

11 But now I have written unto you not to keep company, if [a] any man that is called a brother be a fornicator, or covetous, or an

a Rom.16.17; 2 John 10.

neighbours, and as members of the community. *How far* we are to have intercourse with them is not settled here. The general principles may be, (1.) That it is only so far as is necessary for the purposes of good society, or to show kindness to them as neighbours and as members of the community. (2.) We are to deal *justly* with them in all our transactions. (3.) We may be connected with them in regard to the things which *we have in common*—as public improvements, the business of education, &c. (4.) We are to endeavour to do them good, and for *that* purpose we are not to shun their society. But, (5.) We are not to make them our companions; or to associate with them *in* their wickedness, or *as* idolaters, or covetous, or licentious; we are not to be known as partakers with them in these things. And for the same reason we are not to associate with the gay *in* their gayety; with the proud *in* their pride; with the fashionable *in* their regard to fashion; with the friends of the theatre, the ball-room, or the splendid party, *in* their attachment to these amusements. In all these things we are to be separate; and are to be connected with them only in those things which we may have *in common* with them; and which are not inconsistent with the holy rules of the Christian religion. (6.) We are not *so* to associate with them as to be corrupted by their example; or so as to be led *by* that example to neglect prayer and the sanctuary, and the deeds of charity, and the effort to do good to the souls of men. We are to make it a great point that our *piety* is not to suffer by that intercourse; and we are never to do any thing, or conform to any custom, or to have any such intercourse with them as to *lessen* our growth in grace; divert our attention from the humble duties of religion; or mar our Christian enjoyment.

11. *But now.* In this epistle. This shows that he had written a former letter. ¶ *I have written to you.* Above. I have *designed* to give this injunction that you are to be entirely separated from one who is a professor of religion and who is guilty of these things. ¶ *Not to keep company.* To be wholly separated and withdrawn from such a person. Not to associate with him in any manner. ¶ *If any man that is called a brother.* Any professing Christian; any member of the church. ¶ *Be a fornicator,* &c. Like him who is mentioned, ver. 1. ¶ *Or an idolater.* This must mean those persons who while they professed Christianity still attended the idol feasts, and worshipped there. Perhaps a *few* such may have been found who had adopted the Christian profession hypocritically. ¶ *Or a railer.* A reproachful man; a man of coarse, harsh, and bitter words: a man whose characteristic it was to *abuse* others; to vilify their character, and wound their feelings. It is needless to say how much this is contrary to the spirit of Christianity, and to the example of the Master, "who when he was reviled, reviled not again." ¶ *Or a drunkard.* Perhaps there might have been some then in the church, as there are now, who were addicted to this vice. It has been the source of incalculable evils to the church; and the apostle, therefore, solemnly enjoins on Christians to have no fellowship with a man who is intemperate. ¶ *With such an one no not to eat.* To have no intercourse or fellowship with him of any kind; not to do any thing that would seem to acknowledge him as a brother; with such an one not even to eat at the same table. A similar course is enjoined by John; 2 John 10, 11. This refers to the intercourse of common life, and not particularly to the communion. The true Christian was wholly to disown such a person, and not to do any thing that would seem to imply that he regarded him as a Christian brother. It will be seen here that the rule was much more strict in regard to one who professed to be a Christian than to those who

idolator, or a railer, or a drunkard, or an extortioner; with such an one no not to eat.

12 For what have I to do to judge them also that are without? [a] do not ye judge them that are within?

[a] Mark 4.11.

were known and acknowledged heathens. The reasons may have been, (1.) The necessity of keeping the church pure, and of not doing any thing that would seem to imply that Christians were the patrons and friends of the intemperate and the wicked. (2.) In respect to the heathen, there could be no danger of its being supposed that Christians regarded them as brethren, or showed to them any more than the ordinary civilities of life; but in regard to those who professed to be Christians, but who were drunkards, or licentious, if a man was on terms of intimacy with them, it would seem as if he acknowledged them as brethren and recognised them as Christians. (3.) This entire separation and withdrawing from *all* communion was necessary in these times to save the church from scandal, and from the injurious reports which were circulated. The heathen accused Christians of all manner of crime and abominations. These reports were greatly injurious to the church. But it was evident that currency and plausibility would be given to them if it was known that Christians were on terms of intimacy and good fellowship with heathens and intemperate persons. Hence it became necessary to withdraw *wholly* from them; to withhold even the ordinary courtesies of life; and to draw a line of total and entire separation. Whether this rule in its utmost strictness is demanded now, since the nature of Christianity is known, and since religion cannot be in *so much* danger from such reports, may be made a question. I am inclined to the opinion that the ordinary civilities of life may be shown to such persons; though certainly nothing that would seem to *recognise* them as Christians. But as neighbours and relatives; as those who may be in distress and want, we are assuredly not forbidden to show towards them the offices of kindness and compassion. Whitby and some others, however, understand this of the communion of the Lord's supper, and of that only.

12. *For what have I to do*, &c. I have no authority over them; and can exercise no jurisdiction over them. All my rules, therefore, must have reference only to those who are within the church. ¶ *To judge.* To pass sentence upon; to condemn; or to punish. As a Christian apostle I have no jurisdiction over them. ¶ *Them also that are without.* Without the pale of the Christian church; heathens; men of the world; those who did not profess to be Christians. ¶ *Do not ye judge*, &c. Is not your jurisdiction as Christians confined to those who are *within* the church, and professed members of it? *Ought* you not to exercise discipline there, and inflict punishment on its unworthy members? Do you not in fact thus exercise discipline, and separate from your society unworthy persons—and ought it not to be done in this instance, and in reference to the offender in your church?

13. *But them*, &c. They who are unconnected with the church are under the direct and peculiar government of God. They are indeed sinners, and they deserve punishment for their crimes. But it is not *ours* to pronounce sentence upon them, or to inflict punishment. God will do that. *Our* province is in regard to the church. We are to judge these; and these alone. All others we are to leave entirely in the hands of God. ¶ *Therefore.* Gr. *And* (καὶ). "Since it is yours to judge the members of your own society, do you exercise discipline on the offender and put him away." ¶ *Put away from among yourselves.* Excommunicate him; expel him from your society. This is the utmost power which the church has; and this the church is bound to exercise on all those who have openly offended against the laws of Jesus Christ.

13 But **them that are without God judgeth. Therefore put away** [a] **from among yourselves that wicked person.**

a Mat.18.17.

REMARKS.

1st. A public rumour with regard to the existence of an offence in the church should lead to discipline. This is due to the church itself that it may be pure and uninjured; to the cause, that religion may not suffer by the offence; and to the individual, that he may have justice done him, and his character vindicated if he is unjustly accused; or that if guilty he may be reclaimed and reformed.—Offences should not be *allowed* to grow until they become scandalous; but when they *do*, every consideration demands that the matter should be investigated; ver. 1.

2d. Men are often filled with pride when they have least occasion for it; ver. 2. This is the case with individuals—who are often elated when their hearts are full of sin—when they are indulging in iniquity; and it is true of churches also, that they are most proud when the reins of discipline are relaxed, and their members are cold in the service of God, or when they are even living so as to bring scandal and disgrace on the gospel.

3d. We see in what way the Christian church should proceed in administering discipline; ver. 2. It should not be with harshness, bitterness, revenge, or persecution. It should be with *mourning* that there is necessity for it; with *tenderness* toward the offender; with *deep grief* that the cause of religion has been injured; and with *such grief* at the existence of the offence as to lead them to prompt and decided measures to remove it.

4th. The exercise of discipline belongs to the church itself; ver. 4. The church at Corinth was to be assembled with reference to this offence, and was to remove the offender. Even Paul, an apostle, and the spiritual father of the church, did not claim the authority to remove an offender except *through* the church. The church was to take up the case; to act on it; to pass the sentence; to excommunicate the man. There could scarcely be a stronger proof that the power of discipline is *in* the church, and is not to be exercised by any independent individual, or body of men, foreign to the church, or claiming an independent right of discipline. If *Paul* would not presume to exercise such discipline independently of the church, assuredly no minister, and no body of ministers have any such right now. Either by themselves in a collective congregational capacity, or through their representatives in a body of elders, or in a committee appointed by them; every church is *itself* to originate and execute all the acts of Christian discipline over its members. [See the Supplementary note on ver. 4].

5th. We see the *object* of Christian discipline; ver. 5. It is not revenge, hatred, malice, or the mere exercise of power that is to lead to it; it is *the good of the individual* that is to be pursued and sought. While the church endeavours to remain pure, its aim and object should be mainly to correct and reform the offender, that his spirit may be saved. When discipline is undertaken from any other motive than this; when it is pursued from private pique, or rivalship, or ambition, or the love of power; when it seeks to overthrow the influence or standing of another, it is wrong. The salvation of the offender and the glory of God should prompt to all the measures which should be taken in the case.

6th. We see the danger of indulging in *any* sin—both in reference to ourselves as individuals, or to the church; ver. 6. The smallest sin indulged in will spread pollution through the whole body, as a little leaven will effect the largest mass.

7th. Christians should be pure; ver. 7, 8. Their Saviour—their paschal lamb, was pure; and he died that they might be pure. He gave himself that his people might be holy; and by all the purity of his character; by all the labours and self-denials of his life; by all his sufferings and groans in our behalf, are we called on to be holy.

8th. We are here presented with directions in regard to our intercourse with those who are not members of the church; ver. 10. There is nothing that is more difficult to be understood than the duty of Christians respecting such intercourse. Christians often feel that they are in danger from it, and are disposed to withdraw almost entirely from the world. And they ask with deep solicitude often, what course they are to pursue? Where shall the line be drawn? How far shall they go? And where shall they deem the intercourse with the world unlawful or dangerous?—A few remarks here as rules may aid us in answering these questions.

(I.) Christians are not *wholly* to withdraw from intercourse with the people of this world. This was the error of the monastic system, and this error has been the occasion of innumerable corruptions and abominations in the papal church.—They are not to do this because,

(*a*) It is impossible. They must needs then, says Paul, go out of the world.

(*b*) Because religion is not to be regarded as dissocial, and gloomy, and unkind.

(*c*) Because they have many interests in common with those who are unconnected with the church, and they are not to abandon them. The interests of justice, and liberty, and science, and morals, and public improvements, and education, are all interests in which they share in common with others.

(*d*) Many of their best friends—a father, a mother, a son, a daughter, may be out of the church, and religion does not *sever* those ties, but binds them more tenderly and closely.

(*e*) Christians are inevitably connected in commercial dealings with those who are not members of the church; and to cease to have *any* connection with them would be to destroy their own business, and to throw themselves out of employment, and to break up society.

(*f*) It would prevent the possibility of doing much good either to the bodies or the souls of men. The poor, the needy, and the afflicted are, many of them, out of the church, and they have a claim on the friends of Christ, and on their active beneficence.

(*g*) It would break up and destroy the church altogether. Its numbers are to be increased and replenished from age to age by the efforts of Christians; and this demands that Christians should have *some* intercourse with the men of the world whom they hope to benefit.

(*h*) An effort to withdraw wholly from the world injures religion. It conveys the impression that religion is morose, severe, misanthropic; and all *such* impressions do immense injury to the cause of God and truth.

(II.) The *principles* on which Christians should regulate their intercourse with the world, are these:

(*a*) They are not to be conformed to the world; they are not to do any thing that shall countenance the views, feelings, principles of the world *as such*, or as distinguished from religion. They are not to do any thing that would show that they *approve* of the peculiar fashions, amusements, opinions of the people of the world; or to leave the impression that *they* belong to the world.

(*b*) They are to do justice and righteousness to every man, whatever may be his rank, character, or views. They are not to do any thing that will be calculated to give an unfavourable view of the religion which they profess to the men of the world.

(*c*) They are to discharge with fidelity all the duties of a father, husband, son, brother, friend, benefactor, or recipient of favours, towards those who are out of the church; or with whom they may be connected.

(*d*) They are to do good to all men—to the poor, the afflicted, the needy, the widow, the fatherless.

(*e*) They are to endeavour so to live and act—so to converse, and so to form their plans as to promote the salvation of all others. They are to seek their spiritual welfare; and to endeavour by example, and by conversation; by exhortation and by all the means in

CHAPTER VI.

DARE any of you, having a matter against another, go to law before the unjust, and not before the saints?

2 Do ye not know that the saints

their power to bring them to the knowledge of Christ. For this purpose they are kept on the earth instead of being removed to heaven; and to this object they should devote their lives.

9th. We see from this chapter who are *not* to be regarded as Christians, whatever may be their professions; ver. 11. A man who is, (1.) a fornicator: or, (2.) COVETOUS; or, (3.) an idolater; or, (4.) a *railer;* or, (5.) a drunkard; or, (6.) an *extortioner*, is not to be owned as a Christian brother. Paul has placed the covetous man, and the railer, and extortioners, in most undesirable company. They are ranked with fornicators and drunkards. And yet how many such persons there are in the Christian church—and many, too, who would regard it as a special insult to be ranked with a drunkard or an adulterer. But in the eye of God both are alike unfit for his kingdom, and are to be regarded as having no claims to the character of Christians.

10th. God will judge the world, ver. 12, 13. The world that is *without* the church—the mass of men that make no profession of piety, must give an account to God. They are travelling to his bar; and judgment in regard to them is taken into God's own hands, and he will pronounce their doom. It is a solemn thing *to be judged* by a holy God; and they who have no evidence that they are Christians, should tremble at the prospect of being soon arraigned at his bar.

CHAPTER VI.

THE main design of this chapter is to reprove the Corinthians for the practice of going to law before heathen courts, or magistrates, instead of settling their differences among themselves. It seems that after their conversion they were still in the habit of carrying their causes before heathen tribunals, and this the apostle regarded as contrary to the genius and spirit of the Christian religion, and as tending to expose religion to contempt in the eyes of the men of the world. He, therefore, (ver. 1—7,) reproves this practice, and shows them that their differences should be settled among themselves. It seems also that the spirit of litigation and of covetousness had led them in some instances to practice fraud and oppression of each other, and he, therefore, takes occasion (ver. 8—11) to show that this was wholly inconsistent with the hope of heaven and the nature of Christianity.

It would seem, also, that some at Corinth had not only indulged in these and kindred vices, but had actually defended them. This was done by plausible, but sophistical arguments, drawn from the strong passions of men; from the fact that the body was made for eating and drinking, &c. To these arguments the apostle replies in the close of the chapter, (ver. 12—20,) and especially considers the sin of fornication, to which they were particularly exposed in Corinth, and shows the heinousness of it, and its entire repugnance to the pure gospel of Christ.

1. *Dare any of you.* The *reasons* why the apostle introduced this subject here may have been, (1.) That he had mentioned the subject of *judging* (chap. v. 13), and that naturally suggested the topic which is here introduced; and, (2.) This might have been a prevailing evil in the church of Corinth, and demanded correction. The word *dare* here implies that it was inconsistent with religion, and improper. "*Can* you do it; is it proper or right; or do you presume so far to violate all the principles of Christianity as to do it." ¶ *Having a matter.* A subject of litigation; or a suit. There may be differences between men in regard to property and right, in which there shall be no blame on either side. They may both be desirous of having it equitably and amicably adjusted. It is not a *difference* between men that is in itself wrong, but it is the spirit with which the difference is adhered to, and the unwillingness to have justice done that is so often wrong. ¶ *Against*

[a] shall judge the world? and if the world shall be judged by you, are ye unworthy to judge the smallest matters?

a Dan.7.22; Mat.19.28: Jude 14,15; Rev.20.4.

another. Another member of the church. A Christian brother. The apostle here directs his reproof against the *plaintiff*, as having the choice of the tribunal before which he would bring the cause. ¶ *Before the unjust.* The heathen tribunals; for the word *unjust* here evidently stands opposed to the saints. The apostle does not mean that they were always unjust in their decisions, or that equity could in no case be hoped from them, but that they were classed in that division of the world which was different from the saints, and is synonymous with *unbelievers,* as opposed to believers. ¶ *And not before the saints.* Before Christians. Can you not settle your differences among yourselves as Christians, by leaving the cause to your brethren, as arbitrators, instead of going before heathen magistrates? The Jews would not allow any of their causes to be brought before the Gentile courts. Their rule was this, "He that tries a cause before the judges of the Gentiles, and before their tribunals, although their judgments are as the judgments of the Israelites, so this is an ungodly man," &c. Maimon, Hilch, Sanhedrim, chap. xxvi. § 7. They even looked on such an action as as bad as profaning the name of God.

2. *Do ye not know,* &c. The object of this verse is evidently to show that Christians were qualified to determine controversies which might arise among themselves. This the apostle shows by reminding them that they shall be engaged in determining matters of much more moment than those which could arise among the members of a church on earth; and that if qualified for that, they must be regarded as qualified to express a judgment on the questions which might arise among their brethren in the churches. ¶ *The saints. Christians,* for the word is evidently used in the same sense as in ver. 1. The apostle says that they knew this, or that this was so well established a doctrine that none could doubt it. It was to be admitted on al. hands. ¶ *Shall judge the world.* A great variety of interpretations has been given to this passage. Grotius supposes it means that they shall be *first* judged by Christ, and then act as *assessors* to him in the judgment, or join with him in condemning the wicked; and he appeals to Mat. xix. 28; Luke xxii. 30, where Christ says that they which have followed him should "sit on thrones judging the twelve tribes of Israel." See Note on Mat. xix. 28. Whitby supposes that it means that Christians are to judge or condemn the world by their example, or that there shall be Christian magistrates, according to the prophecy of Isaiah (xlix. 23), and Daniel (vii. 18). Rosenmüller supposes it means that Christians are to judge the errors and sins of men pertaining to religion, as in chap. ii. 13, 16; and that they ought to be able, therefore, to judge the smaller matters pertaining to this life. Bloomfield, and the Greek fathers, and commentators, suppose that this means, that the saints will furnish matter to *condemn* the world; that is, by their lives and example they shall be the occasion of the greater condemnation of the world. But to this there are obvious objections. (1.) It is an unusual meaning of the word *judge.* (2.) It does not meet the case before us. The apostle is evidently saying that Christians will occupy so high and important a station in the work of judging the world that they ought to be regarded as qualified to exercise judgment on the things pertaining to this life; but the fact that their holy lives shall be the occasion of the deeper condemnation of the world does not seem to furnish any plain reason for this.—To the opinion, also, of Whitby, Lightfoot, Vitringa, &c. that it refers to the fact that Christians would be magistrates, and governors, &c. according to the predictions of Isaiah and Daniel, there are obvious objections. (1.) The judgment to

3 Know ye not that we shall judge angels? how much more things that pertain to this life?

which Paul in this verse refers is different from that pertaining to things of this life (ver. 3), but the judgment which Christian magistrates would exercise, as such, would relate to them. (2.) It is not easy to see in this interpretation how, or in what sense, the saints shall judge the angels, ver. 3. The common interpretation, that of Grotius, Beza, Calvin, Doddridge, &c. is that it refers to the future judgment, and that Christians will in that day be employed in some manner in judging the world. That this is the true interpretation, is apparent for the following reasons. (1.) It is the *obvious* interpretation—that which will strike the great mass of men, and is likely, therefore, to be the true one. (2.) It accords with the account in Mat. xix. 28, and Luke xxii. 30. (3.) It is the only one which gives a fair interpretation to the declaration that the saints should judge angels in ver. 3. If asked *in what way* this is to be done, it may be answered, that it may be meant simply that Christians shall be exalted to the right hand of the Judge, and shall encompass his throne; that they shall assent to, and approve of his judgment, that they shall be elevated to a post of honour and favour, AS IF they were associated with him in the judgment. They shall then be regarded as his friends, and express their approbation, and that *with a deep sense of its justice*, of the condemnation of the wicked. Perhaps the idea is, not that they shall *pronounce* sentence, which will be done by the Lord Jesus, but that they shall then be qualified to see the justice of the condemnation which shall be passed on the wicked; they shall have a clear and distinct view of the case; they shall even see the propriety of their everlasting punishment, and shall not only approve it, but be qualified to enter into the subject, and to pronounce upon it intelligently. And the argument of the apostle is, that if they would be qualified to pronounce on the eternal doom of men and angels; if they had such views of justice and right, and such integrity as to form an opinion and express it in regard to the everlasting destiny of an immense host of immortal beings, assuredly they ought to be qualified to express their sense of the smaller transactions in this life, and pronounce an opinion between man and man. ¶ *Are ye unworthy.* Are you disqualified. ¶ *The smallest matters.* Matters of least consequence—matters of little moment, scarcely worth naming compared with the great and important realities of eternity. The "smallest matters" here mean, the causes, suits, and litigations relating to property, &c.

3. *Shall judge angels.* All the angels that shall be judged, good or bad. Probably the reference is to fallen angels, as there is no account that holy angels will then undergo a trial. The sense is, "Christians will be qualified to see the justice of even the sentence which is pronounced on fallen angels. They will be able so to embrace and comprehend the nature of law, and the interests of justice, as to see the propriety of their condemnation. And if they can so far enter into these important and eternal relations, assuredly they ought to be regarded as qualified to discern the nature of justice *among men*, and to settle the unimportant differences which may arise in the church." Or, perhaps, this may mean that the saints shall in the future world be raised to a rank in some respects more elevated than even the angels in heaven. (Prof. Stuart.) In what respects they will be thus elevated, if this is the true interpretation, can be only a matter of conjecture. It may be supposed that it will be because they have been favoured by being interested in the plan of salvation—a plan that has done so much to honour God; and that *to have been* thus saved by the *immediate* and *painful* intervention of the Son of God, will be a higher honour than all the privileges which beings *can* enjoy who are innocent themselves.

4 If then ye have judgments of things pertaining to this life, set them to judge who are least esteemed in the church.

5 I speak to your shame. Is it so, that there is not a wise man among you? no, not one that shall be able to judge between his brethren?

---

4. *Ye have judgments.* Causes; controversies; suits. ¶ *Things pertaining to this life.* Property, &c. ¶ *Set them to judge,* &c. The verb translated set (καθίζετε) may be either in the imperative mood, as in our translation, and then it will imply a command; or it may be regarded as in the indicative, and to be rendered interrogatively, "Do ye set or appoint them to judge who are of little repute for their wisdom and equity?" *i. e.* heathen magistrates. The latter is probably the correct rendering, as according to the former no good reason can be given why Paul should command them to select as judges those who had little repute for wisdom in the church. Had he designed this as a command, he would doubtless have directed them to choose their most aged, wise and experienced men, instead of those "least esteemed." It is manifest, therefore, that this is to be read as a question: "Since you are abundantly qualified yourselves to settle your own differences, do you employ the heathen magistrates, in whom the church can have little confidence for their integrity and justice?" It is designed, therefore, as a severe reproof for what they had been accustomed to do; and an implied injunction that they should do it no more. ¶ *Who are least esteemed* (ἐξουθενημένους). Who are *contemned,* or regarded as of no value or worth; in whose judgment and integrity you can have little or no confidence. According to the interpretation given above of the previous part of the verse this refers to the heathen magistrates—to men in whose virtue, piety and qualifications for just judgment Christians could have little confidence; and whose judgment *must* be regarded as in fact of very little value, and as very little likely to be correct. That the heathen magistrates were in general very corrupt there can be no doubt. Many of them were men of abandoned character, of dissipated lives, men who were easily bribed, and men, therefore, in whose judgment Christians could repose little confidence. Paul reproves the Corinthians for going before them with their disputes when they could better settle them themselves. Others, however, who regard this whole passage as an *instruction* to Christians to appoint those to determine their controversies who were least esteemed, suppose that this refers to the *lowest orders* of judges among the Hebrews; to those who were least esteemed, or who were almost despised; and that Paul directs them to select *even* them in preference to the heathen magistrates. See Lightfoot. But the objection to this is obvious and insuperable. Paul would not have recommended this class of men to decide their causes, but would have recommended the selection of the most wise and virtuous among them. This is proved by ver. 5, where, in directing them to settle their matters among themselves, he asks whether there is not a "*wise* man" among them, clearly proving that he wished their difficulties adjusted, not by the most obscure and the least respected members of the church, but by the most wise and intelligent members. ¶ *In the church.* By the church. That is, the heathen magistrates evince such a character as not to be worthy of the confidence of the church in settling matters of controversy.

5. *I speak to your shame.* I declare that which is a reproach to you, that your matters of dispute are carried before heathen tribunals. ¶ *Is it so,* &c. Can it be that in the Christian church—the church collected in refined and enlightened Corinth—there is not a single member so wise, intelligent and prudent that his brethren may have confidence in him, and refer their causes to him? Can this be the case in a church that boasts so much of its wisdom, and that prides itself so

6 But brother goeth to law with brother, and that before the unbelievers.

7 Now therefore there is utterly a fault among you, because ye go to law one with another. Why do

much in the number and qualifications of its intelligent members?

6. *But brother*, &c. One Christian goes to law with another. This is designed as a reproof. This was wrong, (1.) Because they ought rather to take wrong and suffer themselves to be injured (ver. 7); (2.) Because they might have chosen some persons to settle the matter by arbitration without a formal trial; and, (3.) Because the civil constitution would have allowed them to have settled all their differences without a law-suit. Josephus says that the Romans (who were now masters of Corinth) permitted the Jews in foreign countries to decide private affairs, where nothing capital was in question, among themselves. And Dr. Lardner observes, that the Christians might have availed themselves of this permission to have settled *their* disputes in the same manner. Credibility, vol. i. p. 165.

7. *There is utterly a fault.* There is *altogether* a fault; or you are entirely wrong in this thing. ¶ *That ye go to law*, &c. That is, in the sense under discussion, or before heathen magistrates. This was the point under discussion, and the interpretation should be limited to this. Whatever may be the propriety or impropriety of going to law before Christian magistrates, yet the point which the apostle refers to was that of going to law before heathens. The passage, therefore, should not be interpreted as referring to *all* litigation, but only of that which was the subject of discussion. The apostle says that that was wholly wrong; that they ought by no means to go with their causes against their fellow Christians before heathen magistrates; that *whoever* had the right side of the question, and *whatever* might be the decision, *the thing itself* was unchristian and wrong; and that rather than dishonour religion by a trial or suit of this kind they ought to be willing to *take* wrong, and to suffer any personal and private injustice. The argument is, that greater evil would be done to the cause of Christ by the fact of Christians appearing before a heathen tribunal with their disputes than could result to either party from the injury done by the other.—And this is probably *always* the case; so that although the apostle refers here to heathen tribunals the same reasoning, on the principle, would apply to Christians carrying their causes into the courts at all. ¶ *Why do ye not rather take wrong?* Why do ye not suffer yourself to be injured rather than to dishonour the cause of religion by your litigations? They *should* do this, (1.) Because religion requires its friends to be willing to suffer wrong patiently; Prov. xx. 22; Mat. v. 39, 40; Rom. xii. 17, 19; 1 Thess. v. 15. (2.) Because great injury results to the cause of religion from such trials. The private wrong which an individual would suffer, in perhaps all cases, would be a less evil on the whole than the *public* injury which is done to the cause of piety by the litigations and strifes of Christian brethren before a civil court. (3.) The differences among Christians could be adjusted among themselves, by a reference to their brethren. In ninety-nine cases of a hundred, the decision would be more likely to be just and satisfactory to all parties from an amicable reference, than from the decisions of a civil court. In *the very few* cases where it would be otherwise, it would be better for the individual to suffer, than for the cause of religion to suffer. Christians *ought* to love the cause of their Master more than their own individual interest. They ought to be more afraid that the cause of Jesus Christ would be injured than that they should be a few pounds poorer from the conduct of others, or than that they should individually suffer in their character from the injustice of others. ¶ To *be defrauded?* Receive injury; or suffer a loss of property. Grotius thinks that the word "take wrong" refers to personal insult; and

ye not rather take [a] wrong? why do ye not rather *suffer yourselves to* be defrauded? [b]

8 Nay, ye do wrong, and defraud, and that *your* brethren.

9 Know ye not that the unrighte-

a Prov.20.22; Mat.5.39,40; Rom.12.17,19; 1 Thess.5.15.

b 1Thess.iv.6.

the word "defrauded" refers to injury in property. Together, they are probably designed to refer to all kinds of injury and injustice. And the apostle means to say, that they had better submit to any kind of injustice than carry the cause against a Christian brother before a heathen tribunal. The doctrine here taught is that Christians ought by no means to go to law with each other before a heathen tribunal; that they ought to be willing to suffer any injury from a Christian brother rather than do it. And by *implication* the same thing is taught in regard to the duty of all Christians, *that they ought to suffer any injury to their persons and property rather than dishonour religion by litigations before civil magistrates.* It may be asked then whether law suits are never proper; or whether courts of justice are *never* to be resorted to by Christians to secure their rights? To this question we may reply, that the discussion of Paul relates only to Christians, when both parties are Christians, and that it is designed to prohibit such an appeal to courts by them. If *ever* lawful for Christians to depart from this rule, or for Christians to appear before a civil tribunal, it is conceived that it can be only in circumstances like the following. (1.) Where two or more Christians may have a difference, and where they know not what *is* right, and what the law is in a case. In such instances there may be a reference to a civil court to determine it—to have what is called *an amicable suit,* to ascertain from the proper authority what the law is, and what is justice in the case. (2.) When there are causes of difference between Christians and the men of the world. As the men of the world do not acknowledge the propriety of submitting the matter to the church, it may be proper for a Christian to carry the matter before a civil tribunal. Evidently, there is no other way, in such cases, of settling a cause; and this mode may be resorted to not with a spirit of revenge, but with a spirit of love and kindness. Courts are instituted for the settlement of the rights of *citizens,* and men by becoming Christians do not alienate their rights as citizens. Even these cases, however, might commonly be adjusted by a reference to impartial men, better than by the slow, and expensive, and tedious, and often irritating process of carrying a cause through the courts. (3.) Where a Christian is *injured* in his person, character, or property, he has a right to seek redress. Courts are instituted for the protection and defence of the innocent and the peaceable against the fraudulent, the wicked, and the violent. And a Christian owes it to his country, to his family, and to himself, that the man who has injured him should receive the proper punishment. The peace and welfare of the community demand it. If a man murders my wife or child, I owe it to the laws and to my country, to justice and to God, to endeavour to have the law enforced. So if a man robs my property, or injures my character, I may owe it to *others* as well as to myself that the law in such a case should be executed, and the rights of others also be secured. But in all these cases, a Christian should engage in such prosecutions not with a desire of revenge, not with the love of litigation, but with the love of justice, and of God, and with a mild, tender, candid and forgiving temper, with a real desire that the opponent may be benefited, and that all *his* rights also should be secured; comp. Notes on Rom. xiii.

8. *Nay, ye do wrong,* &c. Instead of enduring wrong patiently and cheerfully, they were themselves guilty of injustice and fraud. ¶ *And that* your *brethren.* Your fellow Christians.

ous shall not inherit the kingdom of God? Be not deceived; neither [a] fornicators, nor idolaters, nor adulterers, nor effeminate, nor abusers of themselves with mankind,

a Gal.5.19—21; Eph.5.4,5; Heb.12.14; 13.4; Rev.22. 15.

As if they had injured those of their own family—those to whom they ought to be attached by most tender ties. The offence in such cases is aggravated, not because it is in itself any worse to injure a Christian than another man, but because it shows a deeper depravity, when a man overcomes all the ties of kindness and love, and injures those who are near to him, than it does where no such ties exist. It is for this reason that parricide, infanticide, &c. are regarded everywhere as crimes of peculiar atrocity, because a child or a parent must have sundered all the tenderest cords of virtue before it could be done.

9. *Know ye not*, &c. The apostle introduces the declaration in this verse to show the *evil* of their course, and especially of the injustice which they did one to another, and their attempt to enforce and maintain the evil by an appeal to the heathen tribunals. He assures them, therefore, that the unjust could not be saved. ¶ *The unrighteous.* The unjust (ἄδικοι)—such as he had just mentioned—they who did *injustice* to others, and attempted to do it under the sanction of the courts. ¶ *Shall not inherit.*—Shall not possess; shall not enter into. The kingdom of heaven is often represented as an *inheritance;* Mat. xix. 29; xxv. 34; Mark x. 17; Luke x. 25; xviii. 18; 1 Cor. xv. 50; Eph. i. 11, 14; v. 5. ¶ *The kingdom of God.* Cannot be saved; cannot enter into heaven; see Note, Mat. iii. 2. This *may* refer either to the kingdom of God in heaven; or to the church on earth—most probably the former. But the sense is the same essentially, whichever is meant. The man who is not fit to enter into the one is not fit to enter into the other. The man who is fit to enter the kingdom of God on earth, shall also enter into that in heaven. ¶ *Be not deceived.* A most important direction to be given to all. It implies, (1.) That they were *in danger* of being deceived. (*a*) Their own *hearts* might have deceived them. (*b*) They might be deceived by their false opinions on these subjects. (*c*) They might be in danger of being deceived by their *leaders*, who perhaps held the opinion that some of the persons who practised these things could be saved. (2.) It implies, that there was *no necessity* of their being deceived. They might know the truth. They might easily understand these matters. It *might* be plain to them that those who indulged in these things could not be saved. (3.) It implies that it was of high *importance* that they should *not* be deceived. For, (*a*) The soul is of infinite value. (*b*) To lose heaven—to be *disappointed* in regard to that, will be a tremendous loss. (*c*) To inherit hell and its woes will be a tremendous curse. O how anxious should all be that they be not deceived, and that while they *hope* for life they do not sink down to everlasting death! ¶ *Neither fornicators;* see Gal. v. 19—21; Eph. v. 4, 5; Heb. xii. 14; xiii. 4. Note, Rom. i. 29. ¶ *Nor effeminate* (μαλακοὶ). This word occurs in Mat. xi. 8, and Luke vii. 25, where it is applied to clothing, and translated "*soft* raiment;" that is, the light, thin garments worn by the rich and great. It occurs no where else in the New Testament except here. Applied to morals, as it is here, it denotes those who give themselves up to a soft, luxurious, and indolent way of living; who make self-indulgence the grand object of life; who can endure no hardship, and practise no self-denial in the cause of duty and of God. The word is applied in the classic writers to the Cinædi, the Pathics, or Catamites; those who are given up to wantonness and sensual pleasures, or who are kept to be prostituted to others. Diog. Laer. vii. 5, 4. Xenoph. Mem. iii. 7. 1. Ovid Fast. iv. 342. The connection here seems to demand such an interpreta-

10 Nor thieves, nor covetous, nor drunkards, nor revilers, nor extortioners, shall inherit the kingdom of God.

11 And such [a] were some of you; but ye are washed, [b] but ye are sanctified, [c] but ye are justified [d] in the name of the Lord Jesus, and by the Spirit of our God.

12 All things are lawful unto me

a Eph.2.1,2; 5.8; Col.3.7; Tit.3.3—6. b Heb.10.22. c Heb.2.11. d Rom.8.30.

tion, as it occurs in the description of vices of the same class—sensual and corrupt indulgences.—It is well known that this vice was common among the Greeks—and particularly prevailed at Corinth. ¶ *Abusers of themselves with mankind* (ἀρσενοκοῖται). Pæderastæ or Sodomites. Those who indulged in a vice that was common among all the heathen; see Notes, Rom. i. 27.

10. *Nor covetous;* see Note, chap. v. 10. It is remarkable that the apostle always ranks *the covetous* with the most abandoned classes of men. ¶ *Nor revilers.* The same word which in chap. v. 11, is rendered *railer;* see Note on that place. ¶ *Nor extortioners;* Note, chap. v. 11. ¶ *Shall inherit.* Shall enter; shall be saved, ver. 9.

11. *And such.* Such drunkards, lascivious, and covetous persons. This shows, (1.) The exceeding grace of God that could recover even *such* persons from sins so debasing and degrading. (2.) It shows that we are not to despair of reclaiming the most abandoned and wretched men. (3.) It is well for Christians to look back on what they once were. It will produce (*a*) humility, (*b*) gratitude, (*c*) a deep sense of the sovereign mercy of God, (*d*) an earnest desire that others may be recovered and saved in like manner; comp. Eph. ii. 1, 2; v. 8; Col. iii. 7; Tit. iii. 3, 6.—The *design* of this is to remind them of what they were, and to show them that they were now under obligation to lead better lives—by all the mercy which God had shown in recovering them from sins so degrading, and from a condition so dreadful. ¶ *But ye are washed;* Heb. x. 22. Washing is an emblem of purifying. They had been made pure by the Spirit of God. They had been, indeed, baptized, and their baptism was an emblem of purifying, but the thing here particularly referred to is not baptism, but it is something that had been done by the Spirit of God, and must refer to his agency on the heart in cleansing them from these pollutions. Paul here uses *three* words, *washed, sanctified, justified,* to denote the various agencies of the Holy Spirit by which they had been recovered from sin. The first, that of *washing,* I understand of that work of the Spirit by which the process of purifying was *commenced* in the soul, and which was especially signified in baptism—the work of regeneration or conversion to God. By the agency of the Spirit the defilement of these pollutions had been washed away or removed— as filth is removed by ablution.—The agency of the Holy Ghost in regeneration is elsewhere represented by washing, Tit. iii. 5, "The washing of regeneration." comp. Heb. x. 22. ¶ *Ye are sanctified.* This denotes the progressive and advancing process of purifying which succeeds regeneration in the Christian. Regeneration is the commencement of it—its close is the perfect purity of the Christian in heaven; see Note, John xvii. 17. It does not mean that they were *perfect*—for the reasoning of the apostle shows that this was far from being the case with the Corinthians; but that the work was advancing, and that they were in fact under a process of sanctification. ¶ *But ye are justified.* Your sins are pardoned, and you are accepted as righteous, and will be treated as such on account of the merits of the Lord Jesus Christ; see Note, Rom. i. 17; iii. 25, 26; iv. 3. The apostle does not say that this was *last* in the order of *time,* but simply says that this was done to them. Men are justified *when* they believe, and when the work of sanctification commences in the soul. ¶ *In the name of the Lord Jesus.* That is, by the Lord Jesus; by his authority, appointment, influence;

but all things are not [1] expedient: all things are lawful for me, but I will not be brought under the power [a] of any.

1 or, *profitable*.

a chap.9.27.

Note, Acts iii. 6. All this had been accomplished *through* the Lord Jesus; that is, in his name remission of sins had been proclaimed to them (Luke xxiv. 47); and by his merits all these favours had been conferred on them. ¶ *And by the Spirit of our God*. The Holy Spirit. All this had been accomplished by *his* agency on the heart. —This verse brings in the whole subject of redemption, and states in a most emphatic manner the various stages by which a sinner is saved, and by this single passage, a man may obtain all the essential knowledge of the plan of salvation. All is *condensed* here in few words. (1.) He is by nature a miserable and polluted sinner —without merit, and without hope. (2.) He is renewed by the Holy Ghost, and washed by baptism. (3.) He is justified, pardoned, and accepted as righteous, through the merits of the Lord Jesus alone. (4.) He is made holy—becomes sanctified—and more and more like God, and fit for heaven. (5.) All this is done by the agency of the Holy Ghost. (6.) The *obligation* thence results that he should lead a holy life, and forsake sin in every form.

12. *All things are lawful unto me*. The apostle here evidently makes a transition to another subject from that which he had been discussing—a consideration of the propriety of using certain things which had been esteemed lawful. The expression, "all things are lawful," is to be understood as used by those who palliated certain indulgences, or who vindicated the vices here referred to, and Paul designs to reply to them. His reply follows. He had been reproving them for their vices, and had specified several. It is not to be supposed that they would indulge in them without some show of defence; and the declaration here has much the appearance of a proverb, or a common saying—that all things were lawful; that is, "God has formed all things for our use, and there can be no evil if we use them." By the phrase "all things" here, perhaps, may be meant *many* things; or things in general; or there is nothing in itself unlawful. That there were many vicious persons who held this sentiment there can be no doubt; and though it cannot be supposed that there were any in the Christian church who would openly advocate it, yet the design of Paul was to *cut up* the plea altogether *wherever it might be urged*, and to show that it was false and unfounded. The particular things which Paul here refers to, are those which have been called *adiaphoristic*, or indifferent; *i. e.*, pertaining to certain meats and drinks, &c. With this Paul connects also the subject of fornication—the subject particularly under discussion. *This* was defended as "lawful," by many Greeks, and was practised at Corinth; and was the vice to which the Corinthian Christians were particularly exposed. Paul designed to meet *all* that could be said on this subject; and to show them that these indulgences could *not* be proper for Christians, and could not in *any* way be defended.—We are not to understand Paul as admitting that fornication is in any case lawful; but he designs to show that the practice cannot possibly be defended in any way, or by any of the arguments which had been or could be used. For this purpose, he observes, (1.) That *admitting* that all things were lawful, there were many things which ought not to be indulged; (2.) That *admitting* that they were lawful, yet a man ought not to be under the power of any improper indulgence, and should abandon any habit when it had the mastery. (3.) That fornication was positively wrong, and against the very nature and essence of Christianity, ver. 13—20. ¶ *Are not expedient*. This is the first answer to the objection. Even should we admit that the practices under discussion are lawful, yet there are many things which are not expedient; that is, which do not *profit*, for so the word (συμφέρει) properly signifies; they are injurious

13 Meats [a] for the belly, and the
belly for meats: but God shall
destroy both it and them. Now
the body *is* not for [b] fornication.

a Matt.15.17,20; Rom.14.17.

b 1 Thess.4.3,7.

and hurtful. They might injure the body; produce scandal; lead others to offend or to sin. Such was the case with regard to the use of certain meats, and even with regard to the use of wine. Paul's rule on this subject is stated in 1 Cor. viii. 13. That if these things did injury to others, he would abandon them for ever; even though they were in themselves lawful; see Note on chap. viii. and on Rom. xiv. 14—23. There are many customs which, perhaps, cannot be strictly proved to be unlawful or sinful, which yet do injury in some way if indulged in; and which as their indulgence can do no good, should be abandoned. Any thing that does evil—however small—and no good, should be abandoned at once. ¶ *All things are lawful.* Admitting this; or even on the supposition that all things are in themselves right. ¶ *But I will not be brought under the power.* I will not be subdued by it; I will not become the *slave* of it. ¶ *Of any.* Of any custom, or habit, no matter what it is. This was Paul's rule; the rule of an independent mind. The principle was, that even admitting that certain things were in themselves right, yet his grand purpose was *not to be the slave of habit*, not to be subdued by any practice that might corrupt his mind, fetter his energies, or destroy his freedom as a man and as a Christian. We may observe, (1.) That this is a good rule to act on. It was Paul's rule (1 Cor. ix. 27), and it will do as well for us as for him. (2.) It is the true rule of an independent and noble mind. It requires a high order of virtue; and is the only way in which a man may be useful and active. (3.) It may be applied to *many things* now. Many a Christian and Christian minister *is a slave;* and is completely under the *power* of some habit that destroys his usefulness and happiness. He is the SLAVE of indolence, or carelessness, or of some VILE HABIT—as the use of tobacco, or of wine. He has not independence enough to break the cords that bind him; and the consequence is, that life is passed in indolence, or in self-indulgence, and time, and strength, and property are wasted, and religion blighted, and souls ruined. (4.) The man that has not courage and firmness enough to act on this rule should doubt his piety. If he is a voluntary slave to some idle and mischievous habit, how can he be a Christian! If he does not love his Saviour and the souls of men enough to break off from such habits which he knows are doing injury, how is he fit to be a minister of the self-denying Redeemer?

13. *Meats for the belly*, &c. This has every appearance of being an adage or proverb. Its meaning is plain. "God has made us with appetites for food; and he has made food adapted to such appetites, and it is right, therefore, to indulge in luxurious living." The word *belly* here (κοιλία) denotes the *stomach;* and the argument is, that as God had created the natural appetite for food, and had created food, it was right to indulge in eating and drinking to any extent which the appetite demanded. The word *meats* here (βρώματα) does not denote animal food particularly, or flesh, but *any kind* of food. This was the sense of the English word formerly. Matt. iii. 4; vi. 25; ix. 10; x. 10; xiv. 9, &c. ¶ *But God shall destroy.* This is the reply of Paul to the argument. This reply is, that as both are so soon to be destroyed, they were unworthy of the care which was bestowed on them, and that attention should be directed to better things. It is unworthy the immortal mind to spend its time and thought in making provision for the body which is soon to perish. And especially a man should be willing to abandon indulgences in these things when they tended to injure the mind, and to destroy the soul. It is unworthy a mind that is to live for ever, thus to be anxious about that which is so soon to be destroyed in the grave. We may observe here, (1.)

but for the Lord, [a] and the Lord [b] for the body.

14 And God [c] hath both raised up the Lord, and will also raise up us by his own power.

15 Know ye not that your bodies

a Rom.12.1 b Eph.5 23. c Rom.6.5,8.

This *is* the great rule of the mass of the world. The pampering of the appetites is the great purpose for which they live, and the only purpose. (2.) It is folly. The body will soon be in the grave; the soul in eternity. How low and grovelling is the passion which leads the immortal mind always to anxiety about what the body shall eat and drink! (3.) Men should act from higher motives. They should be thankful for *appetites* for food; and that God *provides* for the wants of the body; and should eat to obtain strength to serve him, and to discharge the duties of life. Man often degrades himself below—far below—the brutes in this thing. *They* never pamper their appetites, or *create artificial* appetites. Man, in death, sinks to the same level; and all the record of his life is, that "he lived to eat and drink, and died as the brute dieth." How low is human nature fallen! How sunken is the condition of man! ¶ *Now the body* is *not,* &c. "But (δὲ) the body is not designed for licentiousness, but to be devoted to the Lord." The remainder of this chapter is occupied with an argument against indulgence in licentiousness—a crime to which the Corinthians were particularly exposed. See the Introduction to this epistle. It cannot be supposed that any members of the church would indulge in this vice, or would vindicate it; but it was certain, (1.) That it was *the* sin to which they were particularly exposed; (2.) That they were in the midst of a people who *did* both practise and vindicate it; comp. Rev. ii. 14, 15. Hence the apostle furnished them with *arguments* against it, as well to *guard* them from temptation, as to enable them to meet those who did defend it, and also to settle the morality of the question on an immovable foundation. The *first* argument is here stated, that the body of man was designed by its Maker to be devoted to him, and should be consecrated to the purposes of a pure and holy life. We are, therefore, bound to devote our animal as well as our rational powers to the service of the Lord alone. ¶ *And the Lord for the body.* "The Lord is in an important sense for the body, that is, he acts, and plans, and provides for it. He sustains and keeps it; and he is making provision for its immortal purity and happiness in heaven. It is not right, therefore, to take the body, which is nourished by the kind and constant agency of a holy God, and to devote it to purposes of pollution." That there is a reference in this phrase to the resurrection, is apparent from the following verse. And as God will exert his mighty power in raising up the body, and will make it glorious, it ought not to be prostituted to purposes of licentiousness.

14. *And God hath both raised up,* &c. This is the *second* argument against indulgences in this sin. It is this. "We are united to Christ. God has raised him from the dead, and made his body glorified. Our bodies will be like his (comp. Phil. iii. 21); and since our body is to be raised up by the power of God; since it is to be perfectly pure and holy, and since this is to be done by his agency, it is wrong that it should be devoted to purposes of pollution and lust." It is unworthy (1.) Of our *connection* with that pure Saviour who has been raised from the dead—the image of our resurrection from the death and defilements of sin (comp. Notes, Rom. vi. 1—12); and (2.) Unworthy of the hope that our bodies shall be raised up to perfect and immortal purity in the heavens. No argument could be stronger. A deep sense of our union with a pure and risen Saviour, and a lively hope of immortal purity, would do more than all other things to restrain from licentious indulgences.

15, 16. *Know ye not,* &c. This is the *third* argument against licentiousness. It is, that we as Christians are united to Christ (comp. Notes, John

are the members [a] of Christ? shall I then take the members of Christ, and make *them* the members of an harlot? God forbid!

16 What! know ye not that he which is joined to an harlot is one body? for two, [b] saith he, shall be one flesh.

17 But he that is joined unto the Lord is one [c] spirit.

18 Flee [d] fornication. Every sin that a man doeth is without

a Eph.5.30. b Gen.2.24; Matt.19.5. c John 17.21—23; Eph.4.4. d Pro.6.25—32; 7.24—27.

xv. 1, &c.); and that it is abominable to take the members of Christ and subject them to pollution and sin. Christ was pure—wholly pure. We are professedly united to him. We are bound therefore to be pure, as he was. Shall that which is a part, as it were, of the pure and holy Saviour, be prostituted to impure and unholy embraces? ¶ *God forbid!* Note, Rom. iii. 4. This expresses the deep abhorrence of the apostle at the thought. It needed not *argument* to show it. The whole world revolted at the idea; and language could scarcely express the abomination of the very thought. ¶ *Know ye not*, &c. This is designed to confirm and strengthen what he had just said. ¶ *He which is joined.* Who is *attached* to; or who is connected with. ¶ *Is one body.* That is, is to be regarded as one; is closely and intimately united. Similar expressions occur in classic writers. See Grotius and Bloomfield. ¶ *For two, saith he*, &c. This Paul *illustrates* by a reference to the formation of the marriage connection in Gen. ii. 14. He cannot be understood as affirming that that passage had original reference to illicit connections; but he uses it for purposes of illustration. God had declared that the man and his wife became one; in a similar sense in unlawful connections the parties became one.

17. *But he that is joined to the Lord.* The true Christian, united by faith to the Lord Jesus; see John xv. 1, seq. ¶ *Is one spirit.* That is, in a sense similar to that in which a man and his wife are one body. It is not to be taken literally; but the sense is, that there is a close and intimate union; they are united in feeling, spirit, intention, disposition. The argument is beautiful. It is, "As the union of souls is more important than that of bodies; as that union is more lasting, dear, and enduring than any union of body with body can be, and as our union with him is with a Spirit pure and holy, it is improper that we should *sunder* that tie, and break that sacred bond, by being joined to a harlot. The union with Christ is more intimate, entire, and pure than that can be between a man and woman; and *that* union should be regarded as sacred and inviolable." O, if all Christians felt and regarded this as they should, how would they shrink from the connections which they often form on earth! Comp. Eph. iv. 4.

18. *Flee fornication.* A solemn command of God—as explicit as any that thundered from mount Sinai. None can disregard it with impunity—none can violate it without being exposed to the awful vengeance of the Almighty. There is force and emphasis in the word *flee* (φεύγατε). Man should *escape* from it; he should not stay to *reason* about it; to debate the matter; or even to *contend* with his propensities, and to try the strength of his virtue. There are some sins which a man can *resist;* some about which he can reason without danger of pollution. But this is a sin where a man is *safe* only when he flies; free from pollution only when he refuses to entertain a thought of it; secure when he seeks a victory by flight, and a conquest by retreat. Let a man turn away from it without reflection on it and he is safe. Let him think, and reason, and he may be ruined. "The very passage of an impure thought through the mind leaves pollution behind it." An argument on the subject often leaves pollution; a description ruins; and even the presentation of motives *against* it may often fix the mind with dangerous inclination on the crime. There is no way of avoid-

the body; but he that committeth fornication sinneth against his own body.
19 What! know ye not that your [a] body is the temple of the Holy Ghost *which is* in you which ye have of God, and ye are not [b] your own?
20 For ye are bought [c] with a price: therefore glorify [d] God in your body, and in your spirit which are God's.

a 2 Cor.6.16. *b* Rom.14.7,8. *c* Acts 20.28; 1 Pet.1.18,19; Rev.5.9. *d* 1 Pet.2.9.

ing the pollution but in the manner prescribed by Paul; there is no man safe who will not follow his direction. How many a young man would be saved from poverty, want, disease, curses, tears, and hell, could these TWO WORDS be made to blaze before him like the writing before the astonished eyes of Belshazzar (Dan. v.), and could they terrify him from even the *momentary* contemplation of the crime. ¶ *Every sin,* &c. This is to be taken *comparatively*. Sins in general; the common sins which men commit do not *immediately* and directly affect the *body,* or waste its energies, and destroy life. Such is the case with falsehood, theft, malice, dishonesty, pride, ambition, &c. They do *not* immediately and directly impair the constitution and waste its energies. ¶ *Is without the body.* Does not immediately and directly affect the body. The more immediate effect is on the mind; but the sin under consideration produces an immediate and direct effect on the body itself. ¶ *Sinneth against his own body.* This is the *fourth* argument against indulgence in this vice; and it is more striking and forcible. The sense is, "It wastes the bodily energies; produces feebleness, weakness, and disease; it impairs the strength, enervates the man, and shortens life." Were it proper, this might be *proved* to the satisfaction of every man by an examination of the effects of licentious indulgence. Those who wish to see the effects stated, may find them in Dr. Rush on the Diseases of the Mind. Perhaps no single sin has done so much to produce the most painful and dreadful diseases, to weaken the constitution, and to shorten life as this. Other vices, as gluttony and drunkenness, do this also, and all sin has *some* effect in destroying the body, but it is true of this sin in an eminent degree.

19. *What! know ye not,* &c. This is the *fifth* argument against this sin. The Holy Ghost dwells in us; our bodies are his temples; and they should not be defiled and polluted by sin; Note, chap. iii. 16, 17. As this Spirit is *in* us, and as it is *given* us by God, we ought not to dishonour the gift and the giver by pollution and vice. ¶ *And ye are not your own.* This is the *sixth* argument which Paul uses. We are purchased; we belong to God; we are his by redemption; by a precious price paid; and we are bound, therefore, to devote ourselves, body, soul, and spirit, as he directs, to the glory of his name, not to the gratification of the flesh; see Note, Rom. xiv. 7, 8.

20. *For ye are bought.* Ye Christians are *purchased;* and by right of purchase should therefore be employed as he directs. This doctrine is often taught in the New Testament, and the argument is often urged that, therefore, Christians should be devoted to God; see chap. vii. 23; 1 Pet. i. 18, 19; ii. 9; 2 Pet. ii. 1; Rev. v. 9; see Note on Acts xx. 28. ¶ *With a price* (τίμῆ). A *price* is that which is *paid* for an article, and which, in the view of the seller, is a fair compensation, or a valuable consideration why he should part with it; that is, the price paid is as valuable to him as the thing itself would be. It may not be the same thing either in quality or quantity, but it is that which to him is a sufficient consideration why he should part with his property. When an article is bought for a valuable consideration, it becomes wholly the property of the purchaser. He may keep it, direct it, dispose of it. Nothing else is to be allowed to control it

without his consent.—The language here is figurative. It does not mean that there was strictly a *commercial* transaction in the redemption of the church, a literal *quid pro quo*, for the thing spoken of pertains to moral government, and not to commerce. It means, (1.) That Christians have been redeemed, or recovered to God; (2.) That this has been done by a *valuable consideration*, or that which, in his view, was a full equivalent for the sufferings that they would have endured if they had suffered the penalty of the law; (3.) That this valuable consideration was the blood of Jesus, as an atoning sacrifice, an offering, a ransom, which *would accomplish the same great ends in maintaining the truth and honour of God, and the majesty of his law, as the eternal condemnatian of the sinner would have done;* and which, therefore, may be called, *figuratively*, the price which was paid. For if the same ends of justice could be accomplished by his atonement which *would* have been by the death of the sinner himself, then it was consistent for God to pardon him. (4.) Nothing else could or would have done this. There was no *price* which the sinner could pay, no atonement which *he* could make; and consequently, if Christ had not died, the sinner would have been the slave of sin, and the servant of the devil for ever. (5.) As the Christian is thus purchased, ransomed, redeemed, he is bound to devote himself to God only, and to keep his commands, and to flee from a licentious life. ¶ *Glorify God.* Honour God; live to him; see Note, Matt. v. 16; John xii. 28; xvii. 1. ¶ *In your body*, &c. Let your entire person be subservient to the glory of God. Live to him; let your life tend to his honour. No stronger arguments could be adduced for purity of life, and they are such as all Christians must feel.

REMARKS.

1st. We see from this chapter (ver. 1—8.) the evils of law-suits, and of contentions among Christians. Every law-suit between Christians is the means of greater or less dishonour to the cause of religion. The contention and strife; the time lost and the money wasted; the hard feelings engendered, and bitter speeches caused; the ruffled temper, and the lasting animosities that are produced, always injure the cause of religion, and often injure it for years. Probably no law-suit was ever engaged in by a Christian that did not do *some* injury to the cause of Christ. Perhaps *no* law-suit was ever conducted between Christians that ever did any good to the cause of Christ.

2d. A contentious spirit, a fondness for the agitation, the excitement, and the strife of courts, is inconsistent with the spirit of the gospel. Religion is retiring, peaceful, calm. It seeks the peace of all, and it never rejoices in contentions.

3d. Christians should do nothing that will tend to injure the cause of religion in the eye of the world, ver. 7, 8. How much better is it that I should lose a few pounds, than that my Saviour should lose his honour! How much better that my purse should be empty of glittering dust, even by the injustice of others, than that a single gem should be taken from his diadem! And how much better even that I should lose all, than that *my* hand should be reached out to pluck away one jewel, by my misconduct, from his crown! Can silver, can gold, can diamonds be compared in value to the honour of Christ and of his cause?

4th. Christians should *seldom* go to law, even with others; never, if they can avoid it. Every other means should be tried first; and the law should be resorted to only when all else fails. How few law-suits there would be if man had no bad passions! How seldom is the law applied to from the simple love of justice; how seldom from pure benevolence; how seldom for the glory of God! In nearly *all* cases that occur between men, a friendly reference to others would settle all the difficulty; always if there were a right spirit between the parties. Comparatively *few* suits at law will be approved of, when men come to die; and the man who has had the least to do with the law, will have the least, usually, to regret when he enters the eternal world.

5th. Christians should be honest—strictly honest—always honest, ver. 8. They should do justice to all; they should defraud none. Few things occur that do more to disgrace religion than the suspicions of *fraud*, and overreaching, and deception, that often rest on professors of religion. How can a man be a Christian, and not be an honest man? Every man who is not strictly honest and honourable in his dealings, should be regarded, whatever may be his pretensions, as an enemy of Christ and his cause.

6th. The unholy cannot be saved, ver. 9, 10. So God has determined; and this purpose cannot be evaded or escaped. It is fixed; and men may think of it as they please, still it is true that there are large classes of men who, if they continue such, cannot inherit the kingdom of God. The fornicator, the idolater, the drunkard, and the covetous, cannot enter heaven. So the Judge of all has said, and who can unsay it? So he has decreed, and who can change his fixed decree? And so it should be. What a place would heaven be if the drunkard, and the adulterer, and the idolater were there! How impure and unholy would it be! How would it destroy all our hopes, dim all our prospects, mar all our joys, if we were told that they should sit down with the just in heaven! Is it not one of our fondest hopes that heaven will be pure, and that *all* its inhabitants shall be holy? And *can* God admit to his eternal embrace, and treat as his eternal friend, the man who is unholy; whose life is stained with abomination; who loves to corrupt others; and whose happiness is found in the sorrows, and the wretchedness, and vices of others? No; religion is pure, and heaven is pure; and whatever men may think, of one thing they may be assured, that the fornicator, and the drunkard, and the reviler shall not inherit the kingdom of God.

7th. If none of these *can* be saved as they are, what a host are travelling down to hell! How large a part of every community is made up of such persons! How vast is the number of drunkards that are known! How vast the host of extortioners, and of covetous men, and revilers of all that is good! How many curse their God and their fellow men! How difficult to turn the corner of a street without hearing an oath! How necessary to guard against the frauds and deceptions of others! How many men and women are known to be impure in their lives! In all communities how much does this sin abound! and how many shall be revealed at the great day as impure, who are now unsuspected! how many disclosed to the universe as all covered with pollution, who now boast even of purity, and who are received into the society of the virtuous and the lovely! Verily, the broad road to hell is thronged! And verily, the earth is pouring into hell a most dense and wretched population, and rolling down a tide of sin and misery that shall fill it with groans and gnashing of teeth for ever.

8th. It is well for Christians to reflect on their former course of life, as contrasted with their present mercies, ver. 11. Such were they, and such they would still have been but for the mercy of God. Such as is the victim of uncleanness and pollution, such as is the profane man and the reviler, such we should have been but for the mercy of God. That alone has saved us, and that only can keep us. How should we praise God for his mercy, and how are we bound to love and serve him for his amazing compassion in raising us from our deep pollution, and saving us from hell?

9th. Christians should be pure; ver. 11—19. They should be above suspicion. They should avoid the appearance of evil. No Christian can be *too* pure; none can feel too much the obligation to be holy. By every sacred and tender consideration God urges it on us; and by a reference to our own happiness as well as to his own glory, he calls on us to be holy in our lives.

10th. May we remember that we are not our own; ver. 20. We belong to God. We have been ransomed by sacred blood. By a reference to the

CHAPTER VII.

NOW concerning the things whereof ye wrote unto me: *It is* good for a man not to touch a woman.

2 Nevertheless, *to avoid* fornica-

value of that blood; by all its preciousness and worth; by all the sighs, and tears, and groans that bought us; by the agonies of the cross, and the bitter pains of the death of God's own Son, we are bound to live to God, and to him alone. When we are tempted to sin, let us think of the cross. When Satan spreads out his allurements, let us recall the remembrance of the sufferings of Calvary, and remember that all these sorrows were endured that *we* might be pure. O how would sin appear were we *beneath* the cross, and did we feel the warm blood from the Saviour's open veins trickle upon us! Who would *dare* indulge in sin there? Who *could* do otherwise than devote himself, body, and soul, and spirit, unto God?

CHAPTER VII.

THIS chapter commences the *second* part or division of this epistle, or, *the discussion of those points which had been submitted to the apostle in a letter from the church at Corinth, for his instruction and advice.* See the Introduction to the epistle. The letter in which they proposed the questions which are here discussed, has been lost. It is manifest that, if we now had it, it would throw some light on the *answers* which Paul has given to their inquiries in this chapter. The *first* question which is discussed (ver. 1—9) is, whether it were lawful and proper to enter into the marriage relation. How this question had arisen, it is not now possible to determine with certainty. It is probable, however, that it arose from disputes between those of Jewish extraction, who held not only the lawfulness but the importance of the marriage relation, according to the doctrines of the Old Testament, and certain followers or friends of some Greek philosophers, who might have been the advocates of celibacy. But *why* they advocated that doctrine is unknown. It is known, however, that many even of the Greek philosophers, among whom were Lycurgus, Thales, Antiphanes, and Socrates (see Grotius), thought that, considering "the untractable tempers of women, and how troublesome and fraught with danger was the education of children," it was the part of wisdom not to enter into the marriage relation. From them may have been derived the doctrine of celibacy in the Christian church; a doctrine that has been the cause of so much corruption in the monastic system, and in the celibacy of the clergy among the papists. The Jews, however, everywhere defended the propriety and duty of marriage. They regarded it as an ordinance of God. And to this day they hold that a man who has arrived to the age of twenty years, and who has not entered into this relation, unless prevented by natural defects, or by profound study of the law, sins against God. Between these two classes, of those in the church who had been introduced there from these two classes, the question would be agitated whether marriage was lawful and advisable.

Another question which, it seems, had arisen among them was, whether it was proper to continue *in* the married state in the existing condition of the church, as exposed to trials and persecutions; or whether it was proper for those who had become converted, to continue their relations in life with those who were unconverted. This the apostle discusses in ver. 10—24. Probably many supposed that it was unlawful to live with those who were not Christians; and they thence inferred that the relation which subsisted *before* conversion should be dissolved. And this doctrine they carried to the relation between master and servant, as well as between husband and wife. The general doctrine which Paul states in answer to this is, that the wife was not to depart from her husband (ver. 10); but if she did, she was not at liberty to marry again, since her former marriage was still binding; ver. 11. He added that a believing man, or Christian, should not put away his

tion, let every man have his own wife, and let every woman have her own husband.

3 Let the[a] husband render unto the wife due benevolence: and likewise also the wife unto the husband

a Ex.21.10; 1 Pet.3.7.

unbelieving wife (ver. 12), and that the relation *should* continue, notwithstanding a difference of religion; and that *if* a separation ensued, it should be in a peaceful manner, and the parties were not at liberty to marry again; ver. 13—17. So, also, in regard to the relation of master and slave. It was not to be violently sundered. The relations of life were not to be broken up by Christianity; but every man was to remain in that rank of life in which he was when he was converted, unless it could be changed in a peaceful and lawful manner; ver. 18—24.

A *third* subject submitted to him was, whether it was advisable, in existing circumstances, that the unmarried virgins who were members of the church should enter into the marriage relation; ver. 25—40. This the apostle answers in the remainder of the chapter. The *sum* of his advice on that question is, that it would be *lawful* for them to marry, but that it was not then advisable; and that, at all events, they should so act as to remember that life was short, and so as not be too much engrossed with the affairs of this life, but should live for eternity. He said that though it was *lawful*, yet, (1.) In their present distress it might be unadvisable; ver. 26. (2.) That marriage tended to an increase of care and anxiety, and it might not be proper *then* to enter into that relation; ver. 32—35. (3.) That they should live to God; ver. 29—31. (4.) That a man should not be oppressive and harsh towards his daughter, or towards one under his care; but that, if it would be severe in him to *forbid* such a marriage, he should allow it; ver. 36. And, (5.) That on the whole it was advisable, under existing circumstances, *not* to enter into the marriage relation; ver. 38—40.

1. *Now, concerning*, &c. In reply to your inquiries. The first, it seems, was in regard to the propriety of marriage; that is, whether it was lawful and expedient. ¶ *It is good.* It is well. It is fit, convenient, or, it is suited to the present circumstances, or, the thing itself is well and expedient in certain circumstances. The apostle did not mean that marriage was unlawful, for he says (Heb. xiii. 4) that "marriage is honourable in all." But he here admits, with one of the parties in Corinth, that it was well, and proper in some circumstances, not to enter into the marriage relation; see ver. 7, 8, 26, 28, 31, 32.

¶ *Not to touch a woman.* Not to be connected with her by marriage. Xenophon (Cyro. b. 1) uses the same word (ἅπτω, *to touch*) to denote marriage; comp. Gen. xx. 4, 6; xxvi. 11; Prov. vi. 29.

2. *Nevertheless.* But (δὲ). Though this is to be admitted as proper where it can be done, when a man has entire control of himself and his passions, and though in present circumstances it would be expedient, yet it may be proper also to enter into the marriage connection. ¶ To avoid *fornication.* Gr. On account of (διὰ) fornication. The word fornication is used here in the large sense of licentiousness in general. For the sake of the purity of society, and to avoid the evils of sensual indulgence, and the corruptions and crimes which attend an illicit intercourse, it is proper that the married state should be entered. To this vice they were particularly exposed in Corinth. See the Introduction. Paul would keep the church from scandal. How much evil, how much deep pollution, how many abominable crimes would have been avoided, which have since grown out of the monastic system, and the celibacy of the clergy among the papists, if Paul's advice had been followed by all professed Christians! Paul says that marriage is honourable, and that the relations of domestic life should be formed to avoid the evils which would otherwise result. The world is the witness of the evils which flow from the neglect of his advice. Every community where

4 The wife hath not power of
her own body, but the husband:
and likewise also the husband hath
not power of his own body, but
the wife.
5 Defraud ye not one another,
except *it be* [a] with consent for a
time, that ye may give yourselves
to fasting and prayer; and come
together again, that [b] Satan tempt
you not for your incontinency.
6 But I speak this by per-

a Joel 2.16. *b* 1 Thess.3.5.

---

the marriage tie has been lax and feeble, or where it has been disregarded or dishonoured, has been full of pollution, and it ever will be. Society is pure and virtuous, just as marriage is deemed honourable, and as its vows are adhered to and preserved. ¶ *Let every man*, &c. Let the marriage vow be honoured by all. ¶ *Have his own wife.* And one wife to whom he shall be faithful. Polygamy is unlawful under the gospel; and divorce is unlawful. Let every man and woman, therefore, honour the institution of God, and avoid the evils of illicit indulgence.

3. *Let the husband*, &c. "Let them not imagine that there is any virtue in living separate from each other, as if they were in a state of celibacy."—*Doddridge.* They are bound to each other; in every way they are to evince kindness, and to seek to promote the happiness and purity of each other. There is a great deal of *delicacy* used here by Paul, and his expression is removed as far as possible from the *grossness* of heathen writers. His meaning is plain; but instead of using a *word* to express it which would be indelicate and offensive, he uses one which is not indelicate in the slightest degree. The word which he uses (εὔνοιαν, *benevolence*) denotes kindness, good-will, affection of mind. And by the use of the word "due" (ὀφειλομένην), he reminds them of the sacredness of their vow, and of the fact that in person, property, and in every respect, they belong to each other. It was *necessary* to give this direction, for the contrary might have been regarded as proper by many who would have supposed there was special virtue and merit in living separate from each other;—as facts have shown that many *have* imbibed such an idea:—and it was not possible to give the rule with more *delicacy* than Paul has done. Many MSS., however, instead of "due benevolence," read ὀφειλὴν, *a debt*, or *that which is owed;* and this reading has been adopted by Griesbach in the text. Homer, with a delicacy not unlike the apostle Paul, uses the word φιλότητα, *friendship*, to express the same idea.

4. *The wife hath not power*, &c. By the marriage covenant that power, in this respect, is transferred to the husband. ¶ *And likewise, also, the husband.* The equal rights of husband and wife, in the Scriptures, are everywhere maintained. They are to regard themselves as united in most intimate union, and in most tender ties.

5. *Defraud ye not*, &c. Of the right mentioned above. Withdraw not from the society of each other. ¶ *Except it be with consent.* With a mutual understanding, that you may engage in the extraordinary duties of religion; comp. Ex. xix. 15. ¶ *And come together again*, &c. Even by mutual consent, the apostle would not have this separation to be perpetual; since it would expose them to many of the evils which the marriage relation was designed to avoid. ¶ *That Satan*, &c. That Satan take not advantage of you, and throw you into temptation, and fill you with thoughts and passions which the marriage compact was designed to remedy.

6. *But I speak this by permission*, &c. It is not quite certain whether the word "this" (τοῦτο), in this verse, refers to what precedes, or to what follows. On this commentators are divided. The more natural and obvious interpretation would be to refer it to the preceding statement. I am inclined to think that the more natural construction is the true one. and that Paul refers to what he had said in ver. 5. Most recent commentators,

mission, *and* not of commandment.

7 For I would that all men were even as I myself. But

as Macknight and Rosenmüller, however, suppose it refers to what follows, and appeal to similar places in Joel i. 2: Ps. xlix. 2; 1 Cor. x. 23. Calvin supposes it refers to what was said in ver. 1. ¶ *By permission* (συγγνώμην). This word means *indulgence*, or *permission*, and stands opposed to that which is expressly enjoined; comp. ver. 25. "I am *allowed* to say this; I have no express command on the subject; I give it as my opinion; I do not speak it directly under the influence of divine inspiration;" see ver. 10, 25, 40. Paul here does not claim to be under inspiration in these directions which he specifies. But this is no argument against his inspiration in general, but rather the contrary. For, (1.) It shows that he was an honest man, and was disposed to state the exact truth. An impostor, pretending to inspiration, would have claimed to have been *always* inspired. Who ever heard of a *pretender* to divine inspiration admitting that in *any thing* he was not under divine guidance? Did Mahomet ever do this? Do impostors now ever do it? (2.) It shows that in other cases, where no exception is made, he *claimed* to be inspired. These few exceptions, which he expressly makes, prove that in everywhere else he claimed to be under the influence of inspiration. (3.) We are to suppose, therefore, that in all his writings where he makes no express exceptions, (and the exceptions are *very few* in number,) Paul claimed to be inspired. Macknight, however, and some others, understand this as mere *advice*, as an inspired man, though not as a command. ¶ *Not of commandment.* Not by express instruction from the Lord; see ver. 25. I do not claim in this to be under the influence of inspiration; and my counsel here may be regarded, or not, as you may be able to receive it.

7. *For I would*, &c. I would prefer. ¶ *That all men*, &c. That Paul was unmarried is evident from 1 Cor. ix. 5. But he does not refer to this fact here. When he wishes that all men were like himself, he evidently does not intend that he would prefer that all should be unmarried, for this would be against the divine institution, and against his own precepts elsewhere. But he would be glad if all men had control over their passions and propensities as he had; had the gift of continence, and could abstain from marriage when circumstances of trial, &c., would make it proper. We may add, that when Paul wishes to exhort to any thing that is difficult, he usually adduces *his own example* to show that *it may be done;* an example which it would be well for all ministers to be able to follow. ¶ *But every man hath his proper gift.* Every man has his own peculiar talent, or excellence. One man excels in one thing, and another in another. One may not have this particular virtue, but he may be distinguished for another virtue quite as valuable. The *doctrine* here is, therefore, that we are not to judge of others by ourselves, or measure their virtue by ours. We may excel in some one thing, they in another. And because they have not *our* peculiar virtue, or capability, we are not to condemn or denounce them; comp. Mat. xix. 11, 12. ¶ *Of God.* Bestowed by God either in the original endowments and faculties of body or mind, or by his grace. In either case it is the gift of God. The virtue of continence is his gift as well as any other; and Paul had reason, as any other man must have, to be thankful that God had conferred it on him. So if a man is naturally amiable, kind, gentle, large-hearted, tender, and affectionate, he should regard it as the gift of God, and be thankful that he has not to contend with the evils of a morose, proud, haughty, and severe temper. It is true, however, that all these virtues may be greatly strengthened by discipline, and that religion gives vigour and comeliness to them all. Paul's virtue in this was strengthened by his resolution; by his manner of life; by his frequent fastings and trials, and *by the abundant employment* which God gave him in the apostleship. And it is true still,

[a] every man hath his proper gift
of God, one after this manner, and
another after that.

8 I say therefore to the unmarried and widows, It is good for
them if they abide even as I.

9 But if they cannot contain, let
[b] them marry: for it is better to
marry than to burn.

10 And unto the married I command, *yet* not I, but the Lord, Let [c]
not the wife depart from *her* husband:

a Mat 19.11,12. *b* 1 Tim.5.14. *c* Mal.2.14-16; Mat.19.6-9.

that if a man is desirous to overcome the lusts of the flesh, industry, and hardship, and trial, and self-denial will enable him, by the grace of God, to do it. *Idleness* is the cause of no small part of the corrupt desires of men; and God kept Paul from these, (1.) By giving him enough *to do;* and, (2.) By giving him enough *to suffer.*

8. *It is good for them.* It may be advisable, in the present circumstances of persecution and distress, not to be encumbered with the cares and anxieties of a family; see ver. 26, 32—34. The word *unmarried* (ἀγάμοις) may refer either to those who had never been married, or to widowers. It here means simply those who were at that time unmarried, and his reasoning applies to both classes. ¶ *And to widows.* The apostle specifies these, though he had not specified *widowers* particularly. The reason of this distinction seems to be, that he considers more particularly the case of those females who had never been married, in the close of the chapter, ver. 25. ¶ *That they abide.* That they remain, in the present circumstances, unmarried; see ver. 26.

9. *But if they cannot contain.* If they have not the gift of continence; if they cannot be secure against temptation; if they have not strength of virtue enough to preserve them from the danger of sin, and of bringing reproach and scandal on the church. ¶ *It is better.* It is to be preferred. ¶ *Than to burn.* The passion here referred to is often compared to a fire; see Virg. Æn. iv. 68. It is better to marry, even with all the inconveniences attending the marriage life in a time of distress and persecution in the church (ver. 26), than to be the prey of raging, consuming, and exciting passions.

10. *And unto the married.* This verse commences the *second* subject of inquiry; to wit, whether it was proper, in the existing state of things, for those who *were* married to continue this relation, or whether they ought to separate. The *reasons* why any may have supposed that it was best to separate, may have been, (1.) That their troubles and persecutions might be such that they might judge it best that families should be broken up; and, (2.) Probably many supposed that it was unlawful for a Christian wife or husband to be connected at all with a heathen and an idolater. ¶ *I command,* yet *not I, but the Lord.* Not I so much as the Lord. This injunction is not to be understood as *advice* merely, but as a solemn, divine command, from which you are not at liberty to depart. Paul here professes to utter the language of inspiration, and demands obedience. The express command of "the Lord" to which he refers, is probably the precept recorded in Mat. v. 32, and xix. 3—10. These precepts of Christ asserted that the marriage tie was sacred and inviolable. ¶ *Let not the wife depart,* &c. Let her not prove faithless to her marriage vows; let her not, on any pretence, desert her husband. Though she is a Christian, and he is not, yet let her not seek, on that account, to be separate from him.—The law of Moses did not permit a wife to divorce herself from her husband, though it was sometimes done (comp. Mat. x. 12); but the Greek and Roman laws allowed it.—*Grotius.* But Paul here refers to a formal and legal separation before the magistrates, and not to a voluntary separation, without intending to be formally divorced. The reasons for this opinion are, (1.) That such divorces were known and practised among both Jews and heathens. (2.) It was important

11 But and if she depart, let her remain unmarried, or be reconciled to *her* husband: and let not the husband put away *his* wife.

12 But to the rest speak I, not [a] the Lord: If any brother hath a wife that believeth not, and she be pleased to dwell with him, let him not put her away.

13 And the woman which hath

a Ezra 10.11, &c.

to settle the question whether they were to be allowed in the Christian church. (3.) The claim would be set up, probably, that it might be done. (4.) The question whether a *voluntary separation* might not be proper, where one party was a Christian, and the other not, he discusses in the following verses, ver. 12—17. Here, therefore, he solemnly repeats the law of Christ, that *divorce*, under the Christian economy, was not to be in the power either of the husband or wife.

11. *But and if she depart.* If she have withdrawn by a rash and foolish act; if she has attempted to dissolve the marriage vow, she is to remain unmarried, or be reconciled. She is not at liberty to marry another. This may refer, I suppose, to instances where wives, ignorant of the rule of Christ, and supposing that they had a right to separate themselves from their husbands, had rashly left them, and had supposed that the marriage contract was dissolved. Paul tells them that this was impossible; and that *if* they had so separated from their husbands, the pure laws of Christianity did not recognise this right, and they must either be reconciled to their husbands, or remain alone. The marriage tie was so sacred that it could not be dissolved by the will of either party. ¶ *Let her remain unmarried.* That is, let her not marry another. ¶ *Or be reconciled to her husband.* Let this be done, if possible. If it cannot be, let her remain unmarried. It was a *duty* to be reconciled if it was possible. If not, she should not violate her vows to her husband so far as to marry another. It is evident that this rule is still binding, and that no one who has separated from her husband, whatever be the cause, unless there be a regular divorce, according to the law of Christ (Mat. v. 32), can be at liberty to marry again. ¶ *And let not the husband;* see Note, Mat. v. 32. This right, granted under the Jewish law, and practised among all the heathen, was to be taken away wholly under the gospel. The marriage tie was to be regarded as sacred; and the tyranny of man over woman was to cease.

12. *But to the rest.* "I have spoken in regard to the duties of the unmarried, and the question whether it is right and advisable that they should marry, ver. 1—9. I have also uttered the command of the Lord in regard to those who are married, and the question whether separation and divorce were proper. Now in regard to *the rest of the persons and cases* referred to, I will deliver my opinion." *The rest*, or remainder, here referred to, relates particularly to the cases in which one party was a Christian and the other not. In the previous verses he had delivered the solemn, explicit law of Christ, that *divorce* was to take place on neither side, and in no instance, except agreeably to the law of Christ; Mat. v. 32. That was settled by divine authority. In the subsequent verses he discusses a different question; whether a *voluntary separation* was not advisable and proper when the one party was a Christian and the other not. The word *rest* refers to these instances, and the questions which would arise under this inquiry. ¶ *Not the Lord;* Note, ver. 6. "I do not claim, in this advice, to be under the influence of inspiration; I have no express command on the subject from the Lord; but I deliver my opinion as a servant of the Lord (ver. 40), and as having a right to offer advice, even when I have no express command from God, to a church which I have founded, and which has consulted me on the sub-

a husband that believeth not, and if he be pleased to dwell with her, let her not leave him.

14 For the unbelieving husband is sanctified by the wife, and the unbelieving wife is sanctified by the husband; else were your children unclean; but now[a] are they holy.

[a] Mal.2.15,16.

ject." This was a case in which both he and they were to follow the principles of Christian prudence and propriety, when there was no express commandment. Many such cases may occur. But few, perhaps none, can occur, in which some Christian principle shall not be found, that will be sufficient to direct the anxious inquirer after truth and duty. ¶ *If any brother.* Any Christian. ¶ *That believeth not.* That is not a Christian; that is a heathen. ¶ *And if she be pleased.* If it seems best to her; if she consents; approves of living together still. There might be many cases where the wife or the husband, that was not a Christian, would be so opposed to Christianity, and so violent in their opposition, that they would not be willing to live with a Christian. When this was the case, the Christian husband or wife could not prevent the separation. When this was *not* the case, they were not to seek a separation themselves. ¶ *To dwell with him.* To remain in connection with him as his wife, though they differed on the subject of religion. ¶ *Let him not put her away.* Though she is a heathen, though opposed to his religion, yet the marriage vow is sacred and inviolable. It is not to be sundered by any change which can take place in the opinions of either party. It is evident that if a man were at liberty to dissolve the marriage tie, or to discard his wife when his own opinions were changed on the subject of religion, that it would at once destroy all the sacredness of the marriage union, and render it a nullity. Even, therefore, when there is a difference of opinion on the vital subject of religion, the tie is not dissolved; but the only effect of religion should be, to make the converted husband or wife more tender, kind, affectionate, and faithful than they were before; and all the more so as their partners are without the hopes of the gospel, and as they may be won to love the Saviour, ver. 16.

13. *Let her not leave him.* A change of phraseology from the last verse, to suit the circumstances. The wife had not power to *put away* the husband, and expel him from his own home; but she might think it her duty to be separated from him. The apostle counsels her not to do this; and this advice should still be followed. She should still love her husband and seek his welfare; she should be still a kind, affectionate, and faithful wife; and all the more so that she may show him the excellence of religion, and win him to love it. She should even bear much, and bear it long; nor should she leave him unless her life is rendered miserable, or in danger; or unless he wholly neglects to make provision for her, and leaves her to suffering, to want, and to tears. In such a case no precept of religion forbids her to return to her father's house, or to seek a place of safety and of comfort. But even then it is not to be a separation on account of a difference of religious sentiment, but for brutal treatment. Even then the marriage tie is not dissolved, and neither party are at liberty to marry again.

14. *For the unbelieving husband.* The husband that is not a Christian; who still remains a heathen, or an impenitent man. The apostle here states *reasons* why a separation should not take place when there was a difference of religion between the husband and the wife. The first is, that the unbelieving husband is sanctified by the believing wife. And the *object* of this statement seems to be, to meet an objection which might exist in the mind, and which might, perhaps, be urged by some. "Shall I not be *polluted* by such a connection? Shall I not be defiled, in the eye of God, by living in a close union with a heathen, a sinner, an enemy of God, and an opposer of the gospel?" This objec-

tion was natural, and is, doubtless, often felt. To this the apostle replies, "No; the contrary may be true. The connection produces a species of sanctification, or diffuses a kind of holiness over the unbelieving party by the believing party, so far as to render their children holy, and therefore it is improper to seek for a separation." ¶ *Is sanctified* (ἡγίασται). There has been a great variety of opinions in regard to the sense of this word. It does not comport with my design to state these opinions. The usual meaning of the word is, to make holy; to set apart to a sacred use; to consecrate, &c; see Note, John xvii. 17. But the expression cannot mean here, (1.) That the unbelieving husband would become holy, or be a Christian, *by the mere fact* of a connection *with* a Christian, for this would be to do violence to the words, and would be contrary to facts every where; nor, (2.) That the unbelieving husband *had been* sanctified by the Christian wife (Whitby), for this would not be *true* in all cases; nor, (3.) That the unbelieving husband would gradually become more favourably inclined to Christianity, by observing its effects on the wife (according to Semler); for, though this might be true, yet the apostle was speaking of something *then*, and which rendered their children at that time holy; nor, (4.) That the unbelieving husband *might* more easily be sanctified, or become a Christian, by being connected with a Christian wife (according to Rosenmüller and Schleusner), because he is speaking of something in the connection which made the children holy; and because the word ἁγιάζω is not used in this sense elsewhere. But it is a good rule of interpretation, that the words which are used in any place are to be limited in their signification by the connection; and all that we are required to understand here is, that the unbelieving husband was sanctified *in regard to the subject under discussion;* that is, in regard to the question whether it was proper for them to live together, or whether they should be separated or not. And the sense may be, "They are by the marriage tie one flesh. They are indissolubly united by the ordinance of God. As they are one by his appointment, as they have received his sanction to the marriage union, and as one of them is holy, so the other is to be regarded as sanctified, or made *so* holy by the divine sanction to the union, that it is proper for them to live together in the marriage relation." And in proof of this, Paul says if it were *not* so, if the connection was to be regarded as impure and abominable, then their children were to be esteemed as illegitimate and unclean. But now they were *not* so regarded, and *could* not so be; and hence it followed that they might lawfully continue together. So Calvin, Beza, and Doddridge interpret the expression. ¶ *Else were your children unclean* (ἀκάθαρτα). Impure; the opposite of what is meant by holy. Here observe, (1.) That this is a reason why the parents, one of whom was a Christian and the other not, should not be separated; and, (2.) The reason is founded on the fact, that *if* they were separated, the offspring of such a union must be regarded as illegitimate, or unholy; and, (3.) It *must* be improper to separate in such a way, and for such a reason, because even *they* did not believe, and could not believe, that their children were defiled, and polluted, and subject to the shame and disgrace attending illegitimate children. This passage has often been interpreted, and is often adduced to prove that children are "federally holy," and that they are entitled to the privilege of baptism on the ground of the faith of one of the parents. But against this interpretation there are insuperable objections. (1.) The phrase "federally holy" is unintelligible, and conveys no idea to the great mass of men. It occurs no where in the Scriptures, and what can be meant by it? (2.) It does not accord with the scope and design of the argument. There is not one word about baptism here; not one allusion to it; nor does the argument in the remotest degree bear upon it. The question was not whether children should be baptized, but it was whether there should be a separation between man and wife, where the one was a Christian and the other not. Paul states, that *if* such a separation should take place, it would *imply* that the marriage was improper; and *of course* the children must be regarded as unclean. But how would the supposition that they were federally holy, and the proper subjects of baptism, bear on this? Would it not be equally true that it was proper to baptize the children whether the parents were separated or not? Is it not a doctrine among Pedobaptists every where, that the children are entitled to baptism on the faith of *either* of the parents, and that that doctrine is not affected by the question here agitated by Paul? Whether it was proper for them to live together or not, was it not equally true that the child of *a* believing parent was to be baptized? But, (3.) The supposition that this means that the children would be regarded as *illegitimate* if such a separation should take place, is one that accords with the whole scope and design of the argument. "When one party is a Christian and the other not, shall there be a separation?" This was the question. "No," says Paul; "if there *be* such a separation, it must be because the marriage *is improper;* because it would be wrong to live together in such circumstances." What would follow from this? Why, that all the children that have been born since the one party became a Christian, must be regarded as having been born while a connection existed that was improper, and unchristian, and unlawful, and of course they must be regarded as illegitimate. But, says he, you do not *believe* this yourselves. It follows, therefore, that the connection, even according to your own views, is proper. (4.) This accords with the meaning of the word *unclean* (ἀκάθαρτα). It properly denotes that which is impure, defiled, idolatrous, unclean (*a*) In a Levitical sense; Lev. v. 2. (*b*) In a moral sense. Acts x. 28; 2 Cor. vi. 17; Eph. v. 5. The word will appropriately express the sense of illegitimacy; and the argument, I think, evidently requires this. It may be summed up in a few words. "Your separation would be a proclamation to all that you regard the *marriage* as invalid and improper. From this it would follow that the offspring of such a marriage would be illegitimate. But *you* are not prepared to admit this; you do not believe it. Your children you esteem to be legitimate, and they are so. The marriage tie, therefore, should be regarded as binding, and separation unnecessary and improper." See, however, Doddridge and Bloomfield for a different view of this subject.—I believe infant baptism to be proper and right, and an inestimable privilege to parents and to children. But a good cause should not be made to rest on feeble supports, nor on forced and unnatural interpretations of the Scriptures. And such I regard the usual interpretation placed on this passage. ¶ *But now are they holy.* Holy in the same sense as the unbelieving husband is *sanctified* by the believing wife; for different forms of the same word are usual. That is, they are legitimate. They are not to be branded and treated as bastards, as they would be by your separation. *You* regard them as having been born in lawful wedlock, and they *are* so; and they should be treated as such by their parents, and not be exposed to shame and disgrace by your separation.

The Note of Dr. Doddridge, to which the author has candidly referred his readers, is here subjoined: "On the maturest and most impartial consideration of this text, I must judge it to refer to infant baptism. Nothing can be more apparent, than that the word "holy" signifies persons who might be admitted to partake of the distinguishing rites of God's people; comp. Exod. xix. 6; De. vii. 6; xiv. 2; xxvi. 19; xxxiii. 3; Ezra ix. 2, with Isa. xxxv. 8; lii. 1; Acts x. 28. And as for the interpretation which so many of our brethren the Baptists have contended for, that *holy* signifies *legitimate*, and *unclean, illegitimate* (not to urge that this seems an unscriptural sense of the word,) nothing can be more evident than that the argument will by no means bear it; for it would be proving a thing by itself *idem peridem* to argue, that the converse of the parents was lawful because the children were not bastards, whereas all

15 But if the unbelieving depart, let him depart. A brother or a sister is not under bondage in such *cases:* but God hath called [a] us [1] to peace.

16 For what knowest thou, O

a Rom.12.18; 14.19; Heb.12.14. 1 *in.*

who thought the converse of the parents unlawful, must think that the children were illegitimate."

The sense of the passage seems to be this: Christians are not to separate from their unconverted partners, although the Jews were commanded to put away their strange or heathen wives; because the unbelieving party is so far sanctified by the believing party, that the marriage connection is quite *lawful for Christians. There is nothing in the Christian religion that forbids it.* Otherwise, argues the Apostle, your children would be unclean, just as the offspring of unequal and forbidden marriages among the Jews, was unclean, and therefore denied the privilege of circumcision; whereas your infants, as appears from their right to baptism, acknowledged in all the churches, are holy, just as the Jewish children who had a right to circumcision were holy, not *internally* but externally and legally, in consequence of their covenant relation to God. Or briefly thus.—Do not separate. The marriage is quite lawful for Christians, otherwise your children could not be reckoned holy, in the sense of having a right to the seal of the covenant, *i. e.* baptism. The argument for infant baptism is indeed incidental, but not the less strong on that account. And to say there is no allusion whatever to that subject is a mere begging of the question.

To evade this conclusion in favour of infant baptism, the Baptists have strenuously contended, that the proper sense of "holy" is legitimate or lawfully born. But, 1. The word in the original (*ἁγιος*) does not in a single instance bear this sense. The question is not what sense *may* possibly be attached to the term, but what *is* its real meaning. It is on the other hand, very frequently used in the sense assigned to it by Doddridge and others. 2. According to this view (viz. of legitimacy), the apostle is made gravely to tell the Corinthians, that the marriage, in the supposed case, was lawful in a *civil sense*, a thing which they could not possibly doubt, and which must have been *equally true if both parties had been unbelieving.* It is incredible that the Corinthians should wish or need to be informed on any such point? But if we call to mind what has been noticed above, concerning the command, binding the Jews to dissolve their unequal marriages, and to treat the offspring of them as unclean (Ezra x. 3.), we can easily imagine the Corinthians anxious to ascertain whether the Christian religion had retained any such injuction. No, says the apostle, you see your children are holy, as the children of equal or allowed marriage among the Jews were. Therefore you need have no scruples on the point; you require not to separate. Any obscurity that rests on the passage arises from inattention to the Jewish laws, and to the senses in which the Jews used the words "unclean" and "holy." In primitive times these terms, applied to children, would be readily understood, without any explanation such as is needed now. 3. As Doddridge in the above Note has acutely remarked, the supposition that the apostle proves the lawfulness of the marriage in a civil sense, from the legitimacy of the children, makes him argue in a circle. The thing to be proven, and the proof, are in reality one and the same. If the Corinthians knew that their children were legitimate, how could they think of applying to Paul on a subject so simple as the legality of of their marriages. It is as if they had said, "We know that our children are legitimate. Inform us if our marriages are legal!"

15. *But if the unbelieving depart.* If they choose to leave you. ¶ *Let him depart.* You cannot prevent it, and you are to submit to it patiently, and bear it as a Christian. ¶ *A brother or a sister is not under bondage,* &c. Many have supposed that this means that they would be at liberty to marry again when the unbelieving wife or husband had gone away; as Calvin, Grotius, Rosenmüller, &c. But this is contrary to the strain of the argument of the apostle. The sense of the expression "is not bound," &c. is, that *if* they forcibly depart, the one that is left is not bound by the marriage tie to make provision for the one that departed; to do acts that might be prejudicial to religion by a violent effort to compel the departing husband or wife to live with the one that is forsaken; but is at liberty to live separate, and should regard it as proper so to do. ¶ *God hath called us to peace.* Religion is peaceful. It would prevent contentions and broils. This is to be a grand principle. If it cannot be obtained by living together, there should be a peaceful separation; and *where* such a separation has taken place, the one

wife, whether thou shalt save [a] *thy* husband? or how [1] knowest thou, O man, whether thou shalt save *thy* wife?

a 1Pet.3.1,2. 1 *what.*

which has departed should be suffered to remain separate in peace. God has called us to live in peace with all if we can. This is the general principle of religion on which we are always to act. In our relation to our partners in life, as well as in all other relations and circumstances, this is to guide us. Calvin supposes that this declaration pertains to the former part of this verse; and that Paul means to say, that if the unbelieving depart, he is to be suffered to do so peaceably rather than to have contention and strife, for God has called us to a life of peace.

16. *For what knowest thou,* &c. The apostle here assigns a *reason* why the believing party should not separate from the other needlessly, or why he should not desire to be separated. The reason is, the possibility, or the probability, that the unbelieving party might be converted by the example and entreaties of the other. ¶ *Whether then,* &c. How do you know *but* this may be done? Is there not a possibility, nay a probability of it, and is not this a sufficient reason for continuing together? ¶ *Save thy husband.* Gain him over to the Christian faith; be the means of his conversion and salvation; comp. Rom. xi. 26.—We learn from this verse, (1.) That there is a possibility that an unbelieving partner in life may be converted by the example of the other (2.) That this should be an object of intense interest to the Christian husband or wife, because (*a*) It will promote the happiness of the other; (*b*) It will promote their usefulness; (*c*) It will be the means of blessing their family, for parents should be *united* on the subject of religion, and in their example and influence in training up their sons and daughters; and (*d*) Because the salvation of a beloved husband or wife should be an object of intense interest, (3.) This object is of so much importance that the Christian should be willing to submit to much, to bear much, and to bear long, in order that it may be accomplished. Paul said that it was desirable even to live with a heathen partner to do it; and so also it is desirable to bear much, very much, with even an unkind and fretful temper, with an unfaithful and even an intemperate husband, or with a perverse and peevish wife, if there is a prospect that they may be converted. (4.) This same direction is elsewhere given; 1 Pet. iii. 1, 2. (5.) It is often done. It is not hopeless. Many a wife has thus been the means of saving a husband; many a husband has been the means of the salvation of the wife.—In regard to the *means* by which this is to be hoped for, we may observe that it is not by a harsh, fretful, complaining temper; it is to be by kindness, and tenderness, and love. It is to be by an exemplification of the excellency of religion by example; by patience when provoked, meekness when injured, love when despised, forbearance when words of harshness and irritation are used, and by showing *how* a Christian *can* live, and what is the true nature of religion; by kind and affectionate conversation when alone, when the heart is tender, when calamities visit the family, and when the thoughts are drawn along by the events of Providence towards death. Not by harshness or severity of manner, is the result to be hoped for, but by tender entreaty, and mildness of life, and by prayer. Pre-eminently this is to be used. When a husband will not hear, God can hear; when he is angry, morose, or unkind, God is gentle, tender, and kind; and when a husband or a wife turn away from the voice of gentle entreaty. God's ear is open, and God is ready to hear and to bless. Let one thing guide the life. We are never to cease to set a Christian example; never to cease to live as a Christian should live; never to cease to pray fervently to the God of grace, that the partner

17 But as God hath distributed to every man, as [a] the Lord hath called every one, so let him walk. And [b] so ordain I in all churches.

18 Is any man called being circumcised? let him not become uncircumcised. Is any called in uncircumcision? [c] let him not be circumcised.

19 Circumcision [d] is nothing,

a ver.20,24. b chap.4.17; 2 Cor.11.28. c Acts 15.1,&c.; Gal.5.2,&c.; d Gal.5.6; 6.15.

of our lives may be brought under the full influence of Christian truth, and meet us in the enjoyments of heaven.

17. *But as God hath distributed*, &c. As God hath *divided* (ἐμέρισεν); *i. e.* given, imparted to any one. As God has given grace to every one. The words εἰ μὴ denote simply *but* in the beginning of this verse. The apostle here introduces a new subject; or an inquiry varying somewhat from that preceding, though of the same general nature. He had discussed the question whether a husband and wife ought to be separated on account of a difference in religion. He now says that the general principle there stated ought to rule everywhere; that men who become Christians ought not to seek to change their condition or calling in life, but to remain in that situation in which they were when they became Christians, and show the excellence of their religion IN that particular calling. The *object* of Paul, therefore, is to preserve order, industry, faithfulness in the relations of life, and to show that Christianity does not design to break up the relations of social and domestic intercourse. This discussion continues to ver. 24. The phrase "as God hath distributed" refers to the *condition* in which men are placed in life, whether as rich or poor, in a state of freedom or servitude, of learning or ignorance, &c. And it implies that *God* appoints the lot of men, and orders the circumstances of their condition; that religion is not designed to interfere *directly* with this; and that men should seek to show the real excellence of religion in the particular sphere in which they may have been placed by divine providence *before* they became converted. ¶ *As the Lord hath called every one.* That is, in the condition or circumstances in which any one is when he is called by the Lord to be a Christian. ¶ *So let him walk. In* that sphere of life; in that calling (ver. 20); in that particular relation in which he was, let him remain, unless he can consistently change it for the better, and THERE let him illustrate the true beauty and excellence of religion. This was designed to counteract the notion that the fact of embracing a new religion dissolved the relations of life which existed before. This idea probably prevailed extensively among the Jews. Paul's object is to show that the gospel, instead of dissolving those relations, only strengthened them, and enabled those who were converted the better to discharge the duties which grow out of them. ¶ *And so ordain I*, &c. This is no peculiar rule for you Corinthians. It is the universal rule which I everywhere inculcated. It is not improbable that there was occasion to insist everywhere on this rule, and to repress disorders which might have been attempted by some who might suppose that Christianity dissolved the former obligations of life.

18. *Is any man called?* Does any one become a Christian? Note, chap. i. 26. ¶ *Being circumcised.* Being a native-born Jew, or having become a Jewish proselyte, and having submitted to the initiatory rite of the Jewish religion. ¶ *Let him not become uncircumcised.* This could not be literally done. But the apostle refers here to certain efforts which were made to remove the marks of circumcision which were often attempted by those who were ashamed of having been circumcised. The practice is often alluded to by Jewish writers, and is described by them; comp. 1 Mac. i. 15. It is not decorous or proper here to show how this was done. The process is described in Cels. de Med. vii. 25; see Grotius and Bloomfield

and uncircumcision is nothing, but
the keeping [a] of the commandments of God.

a John 15.14; 1 John 2.3.

20 Let every man abide [b] in the
same calling wherein he was called.
21 Art thou called *being* a ser-

b Prov.27.8.

¶ *Is any called in uncircumcision?* A Gentile, or one who had not been circumcised. ¶ *Let him not be circumcised.* The Jewish rites are not binding, and are not to be enjoined on those who have been converted from the Gentiles; see Notes, Rom. ii. 27—30.

19. *Circumcision is nothing,* &c. It is of no consequence in itself. It is not that which God requires now. And the mere external rite can be of no consequence one way or the other. The heart is all; and that is what God demands; see Note, Rom. ii. 29. ¶ *But the keeping of the commandments of God.* Is something, *is* the main thing, *is* every thing; and this can be done whether a man is circumcised or not.

20. *Let every man abide.* Let him remain or continue. ¶ *In the same calling.* The same occupation, profession, rank of life. We use the word *calling* in the same sense to denote the occupation or profession of a man. Probably the original idea which led men to designate a profession as a *calling* was the belief that *God* called every man to the profession and rank which he occupies; that is, that it is by his *arrangement,* or *providence,* that he occupies that rank rather than another. In this way every man has a *call* to the profession in which he is engaged as really as ministers of the gospel; and every man should have as clear evidence that *God* has *called* him to the sphere of life in which he moves as ministers of the gospel should have that God has called *them* to their appropriate profession. This declaration of Paul, that every one is to remain in the same occupation or rank in which he was when he was converted, is to be taken in a general and not in an unqualified sense. It does not design to teach that a man is in *no* situation to seek a *change* in his profession when he becomes pious. But it is intended to show that religion was the friend of order; that it did not disregard or disarrange the relations of social life; that it was fitted to produce *contentment* even in an humble walk, and to prevent repinings at the lot of those who were more favoured or happy. That it did not design to prevent *all* change is apparent from the next verse, and from the nature of the case. *Some* of the circumstances in which a change of condition, or of calling, may be proper when a man is converted, are the following. (1.) When a man is a *slave,* and he can obtain his freedom, ver. 21. (2.) When a man is pursuing a *wicked* calling or course of life when he was converted, even if it is lucrative, he should abandon it as speedily as possible. Thus if a man is engaged, as John Newton was, in the slave-trade, he should at once abandon it. If he is engaged in the manufacture or sale of ardent spirits, he should at once forsake the business, even at great personal sacrifice, and engage in a lawful and honourable employment; see Note, Acts xix. 19. No considerations can justify a continuance in a course of life like this after a man is converted. No consideration can make a business which is "evil, and only evil, and that continually," proper or right. (3.) Where a man can increase his usefulness by choosing a new profession. Thus the usefulness of many a man is greatly promoted by his leaving an agricultural, or mechanical employment; or by his leaving the bar, or the mercantile profession, and becoming a minister of the gospel. In such situations, religion not only *permits* a man to change his profession, but it *demands* it; nor will God smile upon him, or bless him, unless the change is made. An opportunity to become more useful imposes an obligation to change the course of life. And no man is permitted to *waste* his life and talents in a mere scheme of money-making, or

vant? care [a] not for it: but if thou mayest be made free, use *it* rather.

22 For he that is called in the Lord, *being* a servant, is [b] the

a Heb.13.5.

b John 8.36; Rom.6.18,22.

in self-indulgence, when by changing his calling he can do more for the salvation of the world.

21. *Being a servant* (δοῦλος). A slave. Slaves abounded in Greece, and in every part of the heathen world. Athens, *e. g.*, had, in her best days, twenty thousand freemen, and four hundred thousand slaves. See the condition of the heathen world on this subject illustrated at length, and in a very learned maner, by Rev. B. B. Edwards, in the Bib. Repository for Oct. 1835, pp. 411—436. It was a very important subject to inquire what *ought* to be done in such instances. Many slaves who had been converted might argue that the institution of slavery was contrary to the rights of man; that it destroyed their equality with other men; that it was cruel, and oppressive, and unjust in the highest degree; and that therefore they ought not to submit to it, but that they should burst their bonds, and assert their rights as freemen. In order to prevent restlessness, uneasiness, and insubordination; in order to preserve the peace of society, and to prevent religion from being regarded as disorganizing and disorderly, Paul here states the principle on which the slave was to act. And by referring to this case, which was the strongest which could occur, he designed doubtless to inculcate the duty of order, and contentment in general in all the other relations in which men might be when they were converted. ¶ *Care not for it.* Let it not be a subject of deep anxiety and distress; do not deem it to be disgraceful; let it not affect your spirits; but be content in the lot of life where God has placed you. If you can in a proper way obtain your freedom, do it; if not let it not be a subject of painful reflection. In the sphere of life where God by his providence has placed you, strive to evince the Christian spirit, and show that you are able to bear the sorrows and endure the toils of your humble lot with submission to the will of God, and so as to advance *in* that relation the interest of the true religion. *In* that calling do your duty, and evince always the spirit of a Christian. This duty is often enjoined on those who were servants, or slaves; Eph. vi. 5; Col. iii. 22; 1 Tim. vi. 1; Tit. ii. 9; 1 Pet. ii. 18. This duty of the slave, however, does not make the oppression of the master right or just, any more than the duty of one who is persecuted or reviled to be patient and meek makes the conduct of the persecutor or reviler just or right; nor does it prove that the master has a *right* to hold the slave as *property*, which can never be right in the sight of God; but it requires simply that the slave should evince, even in the midst of degradation and injury, the spirit of a Christian, just as it is required of a man who is injured in any way, to bear it as becomes a follower of the Lord Jesus. Nor does this passage prove that a slave ought not to *desire* freedom if it can be obtained, for this is supposed in the subsequent clause. Every human being has a right to desire to be free, and to seek liberty. But it should be done in accordance with the rules of the gospel; so as not to dishonour the religion of Christ, and so as not to injure the true happiness of others, or overturn the foundations of society. ¶ *But if thou mayest be free.* If thou *canst* (δύνασαι), if it is in your power to become free. That is, if your master or the laws set you free; or if you can purchase your freedom; or if the laws can be changed in a regular manner. If freedom *can* be obtained in *any* manner that is not *sinful*. In many cases a Christian master might set his slaves free; in others, perhaps, the laws might do it; in some, perhaps, the freedom of the slave might be purchased by a Christian friend. In all these instances it would be proper to embrace the opportunity of becoming free. The

Lord's [1] freeman; likewise also he that is called, *being* free, is [a] Christ's servant.

23 Ye are bought [b] with a price; be not ye the servants of men.

1 *made free*. a Ps.116.16; 1 Pet.2.16.

b chap.6.20; 1 Pet.1.18,19.

apostle does not speak of insurrection, and the whole scope of the passage is *against* an attempt on their part to obtain freedom by force and violence. He manifestly teaches them to remain in their condition, to bear it patiently and submissively, and *in* that relation to bear their hard lot with a Christian spirit, unless their freedom could be obtained without *violence* and *bloodshed.* And the same duty is still binding. Evil as slavery is, and always evil, and only evil, yet the Christian religion requires patience, gentleness, forbearance; not violence, war, insurrection, and bloodshed. Christianity would teach *masters* to be kind, tender, and gentle; to liberate their slaves, and to change the laws so that it may be done; to be *just* towards those whom they have held in bondage. It would *not* teach the slave to rise on his master, and imbrue his hands in his blood; to break up the relations of society by violence; or to dishonour his religion by the indulgence of the feelings of revenge and by murder. ¶ *Use* it *rather*. Avail yourselves of the privilege if you can, and be a freeman. There are disadvantages attending the condition of a slave, and if you can escape from them in a proper manner, it is your privilege and your duty to do it.

22. *For he that is called in the Lord.* He that is called *by* the Lord; he that becomes a Christian. ¶ Being *a servant.* A slave when he is converted. ¶ *Is the Lord's freeman.* Marg. *Made free* (ἀπελεύθερος). Is manumitted, made free, endowed with liberty by the Lord. This is designed evidently to comfort the heart of the slave, and to make him contented with his condition; and it is a most delicate, happy, and tender argument. The sense is this. "You are blessed with freedom from the bondage of sin by the Lord. You were formerly a slave to sin, but now you are liberated. *That* bondage was far more grievous, and far more to be lamented than the bondage of the body. But from that long, grievous, and oppressive servitude you are now free. Your condition, even though you are a slave, is far better than it was before; nay, *you* are now the true freeman, the freeman of the Lord. Your spirit is free; while those who are not slaves, and perhaps your own masters, are even now under a more severe and odious bondage than yours. You should rejoice, therefore, in deliverance from the greater evil, and be glad that in the eye of God you are regarded as *his* freeman, and endowed by him with more valuable freedom than it would be to be delivered from the bondage under which you are now placed. Freedom from sin is the highest blessing that can be conferred on men; and if *that* is yours, you should little regard your external circumstances in this life. You will soon be admitted to the eternal liberty of the saints in glory, and will forget all your toils and privations in this world." ¶ *Is Christ's servant.* Is the *slave* (δοῦλος) of Christ; is bound to obey law, and to submit himself, as you are, to the authority of another. This too is designed to promote *contentment* with his lot, by the consideration that *all* are bound to obey law; that there is no such thing as absolute independence; and that, since law *is* to be obeyed, it is not degradation and ignominy to submit to those which God has imposed on us by his providence in an humble sphere of life. Whether a freeman or a slave, we are bound to yield obedience to law, and everywhere must obey the laws of God. It is not, therefore, degradation to submit to *his* laws in a state of servitude, though these laws come to us through an earthly master. In this respect, the slave and the freeman are on a level, as *both* are required to submit to the laws of Christ; and, even if freedom could be obtained, there is no

24 Brethren, let[a] every man, wherein he is called, therein abide with God.

25 Now concerning virgins I have no commandment [b] of the Lord ; yet I give my judgment, as one that hath obtained mercy of the Lord to be faithful [c]

a ver.17,20.

b ver.6,10,40. c 1 Tim 1.12.

such thing as absolute independence. This is a very beautiful, delicate and happy argument; and perhaps no consideration could be urged that would be more adapted to produce contentment.

23. *Ye are bought with a price.* Though you are slaves to men, yet you have been purchased for God by the blood of his Son ; Note, chap. vi. 20. You are, therefore, in his sight of inestimable worth, and are bound to be his. ¶ *Be not ye the servants of men.* That is, "Do not *regard yourselves* as the slaves OF MEN. Even in your humble relation of life, even as servants under the laws of the land, regard yourselves as the servants of God, as obeying and serving him *even in this relation*, since *all* those who are bought with a price—all Christians, whether bond or free—are in fact the servant (slaves, δοῦλοι) of God, ver. 22. *In* this relation, therefore, esteem yourselves as the servants of God, as bound by his laws, as subject to him, and as really serving him, while you yield all proper obedience to your master." Rosenmüller, Grotius, and some others, however, think that this refers to Christians in general; and that the apostle means to caution them against subjecting themselves to needless rites and customs which the false teachers would impose on them. Others have supposed (as Doddridge) that it means that they should not sell themselves into slavery; but assuredly a caution of this kind was not needful. The view given above I regard as the interpretation demanded by the connection. And in this view it would promote contentment, and would even prevent their taking any improper measures to disturb the relations of social life, by the high and solemn consideration that even *in* that relation they were in common with all Christians, the true and real servants of God. They belonged to God, and they should serve *him.* In all things which their masters commanded, that were in accordance with the will of God, and that could be done with a quiet conscience, they were to regard themselves as serving God; if at any time they were commanded to do that which God had forbidden, they were to remember that they were the servants OF GOD, and that he was to be obeyed rather than man.

24. *Brethren,* &c.; see Note, v. 20.

25. *Now concerning virgins.* This commences the *third* subject on which the opinion of Paul seems to have been asked by the church at Corinth —whether it was proper that those who had unmarried daughters, or wards, should give them in marriage. The reason why this question was proposed may have been, that many in the church at Corinth were the advocates of celibacy, and this, perhaps, on two grounds. (1.) Some may have supposed that in the existing state of things—the persecutions and trials to which Christians were exposed – it would be advisable that a man who had unmarried daughters, or wards, should keep them from the additional cares and trials to which they would be exposed with a family; and, (2.) Some may have already been the advocates for celibacy, and have maintained that that state was more favourable to piety, and was altogether to be preferred. It is known that that opinion had an early prevalence, and gave rise to the establishment of *nunneries* in the papal church; an opinion that has everywhere been attended with licentiousness and corruption. It is not improbable that there may have been advocates for this opinion even in the church of Corinth; and it was well, therefore, that the authority of an apostle should be employed to sanction and to honour the marriage union. ¶ *I have no commandment,* &c. No positive, express revelation; see Notes

26 I suppose therefore that this
is good for the present [1] distress;
I say, that [a] *it is* good for a man so
to be.
27 Art thou bound unto a wife?
seek not to be loosed. Art thou
loosed from a wife? seek not a wife
28 But and if thou marry, thou
hast not sinned; and if a virgin
marry, she hath not sinned. Never-

1 or, *necessity*. *a* ver.1,8.

b Heb.13.4.

---

on ver. 6, 10. ¶ *Yet I give my judgment.* I give my opinion, or advice; see Note, ver. 6. ¶ *As one that hath obtained mercy of the Lord.* As a Christian; one who has been pardoned, whose mind has been enlightened, and who has been endued with the grace of God. ¶ *To be faithful.* Faithful to my God. As one who would not give advice for any selfish, or mercenary, or worldly consideration; as one known to act from a desire to honour God, and to seek the best interests of the church, even though there is no explicit command. The advice of *such* a man—a devoted, faithful, self-denying, experienced Christian—is entitled to respectful deference, even where there is no claim to inspiration. Religion qualifies to give advice; and the advice of a man who has no selfish ends to gratify, and who is known to seek supremely the glory of God, should not be disregarded or slighted. Paul had a special claim to give this advice, because he was the founder of the church at Corinth.

26. *I suppose.* I think; I give the following advice. ¶ *For the present distress.* In the present state of trial. The word *distress* (ἀνάγκην, *necessity*) denotes calamity, persecution, trial, &c.; see Luke xxi. 23. The word rendered *present* (ἐνεστῶσαν) denotes that which *urges on*, or that which at that time presses on, or afflicts. Here it is implied, (1.) That at that time they were subject to trials so severe as to render the advice which he was about to give proper; and, (2.) That he by no means meant that this should be a *permanent arrangement* in the church, and of course it cannot be urged as an argument for the monastic system. What the *urgent distress* of this time was, is not certainly known. If the epistle was written about A. D. 59 (see the Introduction), it was in the time of Nero; and probably he had already begun to oppress and persecute Christians. At all events, it is evident that the Christians at Corinth were subject to some trials which rendered the cares of the marriage life undesirable. ¶ It is *good for a man so to be.* The emphasis here is on the word *so* (οὕτως); that is, it is best for a man to conduct *in the following manner;* the word *so* referring to the advice which follows. "I advise that he conduct in the following manner, to wit." Most commentators suppose that it means *as he is; i. e.*, unmarried; but the interpretation proposed above best suits the connection. The advice given is in the following verses.

27. *Art thou bound unto a wife?* Art thou already married? Marriage is often thus represented as a *tie*, a *bond*, &c.; see Note, Rom. vii. 2. ¶ *Seek not to be loosed.* Seek not a *dissolution* (λύσιν) of the connection, either by divorce or by a separation from each other; see Notes on ver. 10—17. ¶ *Art thou loosed from a wife?* Art thou unmarried? It should have been rendered *free from* a wife; or art thou single? It does not imply of necessity that the person had been married, though it *may* have that meaning, and signify those who had been separated from a wife by her death. There is no necessity of supposing that Paul refers to persons who had divorced their wives. So Grotius, Schleusner, Doddridge, &c.

28. *Thou hast not sinned.* There is no express command of God on this subject. The counsel which I give is mere advice, and it may be observed or not as you shall judge best. Marriage is honourable and lawful; and though there may be circumstances where it is *advisable* not to enter into this relation, yet there is no law which prohibits it. The same advice

theless such shall have trouble in the flesh: but I spare you.
29 But this I say, brethren, the time [a] *is* short: it remaineth that both they that have wives be as though they had none;

[a] 1 Pet.4.7; 2 Pet.3.8,9.

would be proper now, if it were a time of persecution; or if a man is poor, and cannot support a family; or if he has already a dependent mother and sisters to be supported by him, it would be well to follow the advice of Paul. So also when the cares of a family would take up a man's time and efforts; when *but* for this he might give himself to a missionary life, the voice of wisdom may be in accordance with that of Paul; that a man may be free from these cares, and may give himself with more undivided interest and more successful toil to the salvation of man. ¶ *Such shall have trouble in the flesh.* They shall have anxiety, care, solicitude, trials. Days of persecution are coming on, and you may be led to the stake, and in those fiery trials your families may be torn asunder, and a part be put to death. Or you may be poor, and oppressed, and driven from your homes, and made wanderers and exiles, for the sake of your religion. ¶ *But I spare you.* I will not dwell on the melancholy theme. I will not pain your hearts by describing the woes that shall ensue. I will not do any thing to deter you from acting as you deem right. If you choose to marry, it is lawful; and I will not imbitter your joys and harrow up your feelings by the description of your future difficulties and trials. The word *flesh* here denotes outward circumstances in contradistinction from the mind. They might have peace of mind, for religion would furnish that; but they would be exposed to poverty, persecution, and calamity.

29. *But this I say.* Whether you are married or not, or in whatever condition of life you may be, I would remind you that life hastens to a close, and that its grand business is to be prepared to die. It matters little in what condition or rank of life we are, if we are ready to depart to another and a better world. ¶ *The time is short.* The time is *contracted, drawn into a narrow space* (συνεσταλμένος). The word which is here used is commonly applied to the act of *furling* a sail, *i. e.*, reducing it into a narrow compass; and is then applied to any thing that is reduced within narrow limits. Perhaps there was a reference here to the fact that the time was *contracted,* or made short, by their impending persecutions and trials. But it is always equally true that time is short. It will soon glide away, and come to a close. The idea of the apostle here is, that the plans of life should all be formed in view of this truth, THAT TIME IS SHORT. No plan should be adopted which does not contemplate this; no engagement of life made when it will not be appropriate to think of it; no connection entered into when the thought "time is short," would be an unwelcome intruder; see 1 Pet. iv. 7; 2 Pet. iii. 8, 9. ¶ *It remaineth* (τὸ λοιπόν). The remainder is; or this is a consequence from this consideration of the shortness of time. ¶ *Both they that have wives,* &c. This does not mean that they are to treat them with unkindness or neglect, or fail in the duties of love and fidelity. It is to be taken in a general sense, that they were to live above the world; that they were not to be unduly attached to them that they were to be ready to part with them; and that they should not suffer attachment to them to interfere with any duty which they owed to God. They were in a world of trial; and they were exposed to persecution; and as Christians they were bound to live entirely to God, and they ought not, therefore, to allow attachment to earthly friends to alienate their affections from God, or to interfere with their Christian duty. In one word, they ought to be *just as faithful to God,* and *just as pious,* in every respect, as if they had no wife and no earthly friend. Such a consecration to God is difficult, but not impossible. Our earthly attachments and cares

30 And they that weep, as though they wept not; and they that rejoice, as though they rejoiced not; and they that buy, as though they possessed not;
31 And they that use this world,

draw away our affections from God, but they need not do it. Instead of being the occasion of *alienating* our affections from God, they should be, and they might be, the means of binding us more firmly and entirely to him and to his cause. But alas, how many professing Christians live *for* their wives and children only, and not *for* God *in* these relations! how many suffer these earthly objects of attachment to alienate their minds from the ways and commandments of God, rather than make them the occasion of uniting them more tenderly to him and his cause!

30. *And they that weep.* They who are afflicted. ¶ *As though they wept not.* Restraining and moderating their grief by the hope of the life to come. *The general idea in all these expressions is, that in whatever situation Christians are, they should be dead to the world, and not improperly affected by passing events.* It is impossible for human nature *not* to feel when persecuted, maligned, slandered, or when near earthly friends are taken away. But religion will calm the troubled spirit; pour oil on the agitated waves; light up a smile in the midst of tears; cause the beams of a calm and lovely morning to rise on the anxious heart; silence the commotions of the agitated soul, and produce joy even in the midst of sorrow. Religion will keep us from immoderate grief, and sustain the soul even when in distress nature forces us to shed the tear of mourning. Christ sweat great drops of blood, and Christians often weep; but the heart may be calm, peaceful, elevated, confident in God in the darkest night and the severest tempest of calamity. ¶ *And they that rejoice.* They that are happy; they that are prospered; that have beloved families around them; that are blessed with success, with honour, with esteem, with health. They that have occasion of rejoicing and gratitude. ¶ *As though they rejoiced not.* Not rejoicing with excessive or immoderate joy. Not with riot or unholy mirth. Not satisfied *with* these things; though they may rejoice *in* them. Not forgetting that they must soon be left; but keeping the mind in a calm, serious, settled, thoughtful state, in view of the fact that all these things must soon come to an end. O how would this thought silence the voice of unseemly mirth; How would it produce calmness, serenity, heavenly joy, where is now often unhallowed riot; and true peace, where now there is only forced and boisterous revelry! ¶ *As though they possessed not.* It is right to buy and to obtain property. But it should be held with the conviction that it is by an uncertain tenure, and must soon be left. Men may give a deed that shall secure from their fellow men; but no man can give a title that shall not be taken away by death. Our lands and houses, our stocks and bonds and mortgages, our goods and chattels, shall soon pass into other hands. Other men will plough our fields, reap our harvests, work in our shops, stand at our counters, sit down at our firesides, eat on our tables, lie upon our beds. Others will occupy our places in society, have our offices, sit in our seats in the sanctuary. Others will take possession of our gold, and appropriate it to their own use; and *we* shall have no more interest in it, and no more control over it, than our neighbour has now, and no power to eject the man that has taken possession of our houses and our lands. Secure therefore as our titles are, safe as are our investments, yet how soon shall we lose *all* interest in them by death; and how ought this consideration to induce us to live above the world, and to secure a treasure in that world where no thief approaches, and no moth corrupts.

31. *And they that use this world* That make a necessary and proper use of it to furnish raiment, food.

as not abusing *it:* for the fashion
[a] of this world passeth away.
32 But I would have you with
out carefulness. He that is unmarried [b] careth for the things
that [1] belong to the Lord, how he
may please the Lord:
33 But he that is married careth

a Ps.39.6;James4.14;1Pet.4.7;1John2.17.

b 1Tim.5.5. 1 *of the Lord*, as ver.34.

clothing, medicine, protection, &c. It is right so to *use* the world, for it was made for these purposes. The word *using* here refers to the lawful use of it (χρώμενοι). ¶ *As not abusing it.* (καταχρώμενοι). The preposition κατα, in composition here has the sense of *too much, too freely*, and is taken not merely in an intensive sense, but to denote evil, the *abuse* of the world. It means that we are not to use it *to excess;* we are not to make it a mere matter of indulgences, or to make that the main object and purpose of our living. We are not to give our appetites to indulgence; our bodies to riot; our days and nights to feasting and revelry. ¶ *For the fashion of this world* (τὸ σχῆμα.) The form, the appearance. In 1 John ii. 17, it is said that "the world passeth away and the lust thereof." The word "fashion" here is probably taken from the shifting scenes of the drama; where, when the scene changes, the imposing and splendid pageantry passes off. The form, the fashion of the world is like a splendid, gilded pageant. It is unreal and illusive. It continues but a little time; and soon the scene changes, and the fashion that allured and enticed us now passes away, and *we* pass to other scenes. ¶ *Passeth away* (παράγει). Passes off like the splendid, gaudy, shifting scenes of the stage. What a striking description of the changing, unstable, and unreal pageantry of this world! Now it is gay, splendid, gorgeous, lovely; to-morrow it is gone, and is succeeded by new actors and new scenes. Now all is busy with one set of actors; to-morrow a new company appears, and again they are succeeded by another, and all are engaged in scenes that are equally changing, vain, gorgeous, and delusive. A simliar idea is presented in the well known and beautiful description of the great British dramatist:—

"All the world's a stage,
And all the men and women merely players.
They have their exits and their entrances,
And one man in his time plays many parts."

If such be the character of the scenes in which we are engaged, how little should we fix our affections on them, and how anxious should we be to be prepared for the *real* and *unchanging* scenes of another world!

32. *But I would have you.* I would advise you to such a course of life as should leave you without carefulness My advice is regulated by that wish, and that wish guides me in giving it. ¶ *Without carefulness* (ἀμερίμνους). Without anxiety, solicitude, care; without such a necessary attention to the things of this life as to take off your thoughts and affections from heavenly objects; see Notes on Mat. vi. 25—31. ¶ *Careth for the things that belong to the Lord.* Marg. "The things of the Lord;" the things of religion. His attention is not distracted by the cares of this life; his time is not engrossed, and his affections alienated by an attendance on the concerns of a family, and especially by solicitude for them in times of trial and persecution. He can give his *main* attention to the things of religion. He is at leisure to give his chief thoughts and anxieties to the advancement of the Redeemer's kingdom. Paul's own example showed that this was the course which *he* preferred; and showed also that in some instances it was lawful and proper for a man to remain unmarried, and to give himself entirely to the work of the Lord. But the divine commandment (Gen i. 28), and the commendation everywhere bestowed upon marriage in the Scriptures, as well as the nature of the case, show that it was not designed that celibacy should be general.

33. *Careth for the things of the world.* Is under a necessity of giving

for the things that are of the world, how he may please *his* wife.

34 There is difference *also* between a wife and a virgin. The unmarried woman careth for the things of the Lord, that she may be holy both in body and in spirit:

---

attention to the things of the world; or cannot give his undivided attention and interest to the things of religion. This would be especially true in times of persecution. ¶ *How he may please* his *wife.* How he may gratify her; how he may accommodate himself to her temper and wishes, to make her happy. The apostle here plainly intimates that there would be *danger* that the man would be *so* anxious to gratify his wife, as to interfere with his direct religious duties. This may be done in many ways. (1.) The *affections* may be taken off from the Lord, and bestowed upon the wife. *She* may become the object of even improper attachment, and may take the place of God in the affections. (2.) The *time* may be taken up in devotion to her, which should be given to secret prayer, and to the duties of religion. (3.) She may demand his *society* and *attention* when he ought to be engaged in doing good to others, and endeavouring to advance the kingdom of Christ. (4.) She may be gay and fashionable, and may lead him into improper expenses, into a style of living that may be unsuitable for a Christian, and into society where his piety will be injured, and his devotion to God lessened; or, (5.) She may have erroneous opinions on the doctrines and duties of religion; and a desire to please her may lead him insensibly to modify his views, and to adopt more lax opinions, and to pursue a more lax course of life in his religious duties. Many a husband has thus been injured by a gay, thoughtless, and imprudent wife; and though that wife *may be* a Christian, yet her course may be such as shall greatly retard his growth in grace, and mar the beauty of his piety.

34. *Between a wife and a virgin,* Between a woman that is married and one that is unmarried. The apostle says that a similar difference between the condition of her that is married and her that is unmarried takes place, which had been observed between the married and the unmarried *man.* The Greek word here (μεμέρισται) may mean, *is divided,* and be rendered, "the wife and the virgin are *divided* in the same manner;" *i. e.* there is the same difference in their case as exists between the married and the unmarried man. ¶ *The unmarried women,* &c. Has more advantages for attending to the things of religion; has fewer temptations to neglect her proper duty to God ¶ *Both in body and in spirit.* Entirely holy; that she may be entirely devoted to God. Perhaps in her case the apostle mentions the "body," which he had not done in the case of the man, because her temptation would be principally in regard to that —the danger of endeavouring to decorate and adorn her person to please her husband. ¶ *How she may please* her *husband.* The apostle here intends, undoubtedly, to intimate that there were dangers to personal piety in the married life, which would not occur in a state of celibacy; and that the unmarried female would have greater opportunities for devotion and usefulness than if married. And he intimates that the married female would be in danger of losing her zeal and marring her piety, by attention to her husband, and by a constant effort to please him. Some of the ways in which this might be done are the following. (1.) As in the former case (ver. 33), her *affections* might be transferred from God to the partner of her life. (2.) Her *time* will be occupied by an attention to him and to his will; and there would be danger that that attention would be allowed to interfere with her hours of secret retirement and communion with God. (3.) Her time will be necessarily broken in upon by the cares of a family, and she should therefore guard with peculiar vigilance, that

but she that is married [a] careth for the things of the world, how she may please *her* husband.

35 And this I speak for your own profit; not that I may cast a snare upon you, but for that

a Luke 10.40-42.

---

she may *redeem* time for secret communion with God. (4.) The time which she before gave to benevolent objects, may now be given to please her husband. Before her marriage she may have been distinguished for zeal, and for active efforts in every plan of doing good; subsequently, she may lay aside this zeal, and withdraw from these plans, and be as little distinguished as others. (5.) Her piety may be greatly injured by false notions of what should be done to please her husband. If he is a worldly and fashionable man, she may seek to please him by "gold, and pearls, and costly array." Instead of cultivating the ornament of "a meek and quiet spirit," her main wish may be to decorate her person, and render herself attractive by the adorning of her *person* rather than of her *mind*. (6.) If he is opposed to religion, or if he has lax opinions on the subject, or if he is sceptical and worldly, she will be in danger of relaxing in *her* views in regard to the strictness of Christianity, and of becoming conformed to his. She will insensibly become *less* strict in regard to the Sabbath, the Bible, the prayer meeting, the Sabbath-school, the plans of Christian benevolence, the *doctrines* of the gospel. (7.) To please him, she will be found in the gay circle,—perhaps in the assembly room, or even the theatre, or amidst companies of gayety and amusement, and will forget that she is professedly devoted only to God. And, (8.) She is in danger, as the result of all this, of forsaking her old religious friends, the companions of purer, brighter days, the humble and devoted friends of Jesus; and of seeking society among the gay, the rich, the proud, the worldly. Her piety thus is injured; she becomes worldly and vain, and less and less like Christ; until heaven, perhaps, in mercy smites her idol, and he dies, and leaves her again to the blessedness of single-hearted devotion to God. O! how many a Christian female has thus been injured by an unhappy marriage with a gay and worldly man! How often has the church occasion to mourn over piety that is dimmed, benevolence that is quenched, zeal that is extinguished by devotion to a gay and worldly husband! How often does humble piety weep over such a scene! How often does the cause of sacred charity sigh! How often is the Redeemer wounded in the house of his friends! And O how often does it become NECESSARY for God to interpose, and to remove by death the object of the affection of his wandering child, and to clothe her in the habiliments of mourning, and to bathe her cheeks in tears, that "by the sadness of the countenance her heart may be made better." Who can tell how many a widow is made such from this cause; who can tell how much religion is injured by thus stealing away the affections from God?

35. *For your own profit.* That you may avail yourselves of all your advantages and privileges, and pursue such a course as shall tend most to advance your personal piety and salvation. ¶ *Not that I may cast a snare upon you.* The word rendered *snare* (βρόχον) means a cord, a rope, a bond; and the sense is, that Paul would not *bind* them by any rule which God had not made; or that he would not restrain them from that which is lawful, and which the welfare of society usually requires. Paul means, that his object in his advice was their welfare; it was not by any means to bind, fetter, or restrain them from any course which would be for their real happiness, but to promote their real and permanent advantage. The idea which is here presented by the word *snare*, is usually conveyed by the use of the word *yoke* (Mat. xi. 29; Acts xv. 10; Gal. v. 1), and sometimes by the word *burden*; Mat. xxiii. 4; Acts xv. 28. ¶ *But*

which is comely, and that ye may attend upon the Lord without distraction.

36 But if any man think that he behaveth himself uncomely toward his virgin, if she pass the flower of *her* age, and need so require, let him do what he will he sinneth not: let them marry.

37 Nevertheless he that standeth steadfast in his heart, having no necessity, but hath power over his

---

for that which is comely (εὔσχημον). Decorous, fit, proper, noble. For that which is best *fitted* to your present condition, and which, on the whole, will be best, and most for your own advantage. There would be a fitness and propriety in their pursuing the course which he recommended. ¶ *That ye may attend on the Lord.* That you may engage in religious duties and serve God. ¶ *Without distraction.* Without being drawn away (ἀπερισπάστως); without care, interruption, and anxiety. That you may be free to engage with undivided interest in the service of the Lord.

36. *That he behaveth himself uncomely.* Acts an unbecoming part, imposes an unnecessary, painful, and improper constraint, crosses her inclinations which are in themselves proper. ¶ *Toward his virgin.* His daughter, or his ward, or any unmarried female committed to his care. ¶ *If she pass the flower of* her *age.* If she pass the marriageable age and remains unmarried. It is well known that in the east it was regarded as peculiarly dishonourable to remain unmarried; and the authority of a father, therefore, might be the means of involving his daughter in shame and disgrace. When this would be the case, it would be wrong to prohibit her marriage. ¶ *And need so require.* And she ought to be allowed to marry. If it will promote her happiness, and if she would be unhappy, and regarded as dishonoured, if she remained in a state of celibacy. ¶ *Let him do what he will.* He has the *authority* in the case, for in the east the *authority* resided with the father. He may either give her in marriage or not, as he pleases. But in this case it is advisable that she should marry ¶ *He sinneth not.* He errs not; he will do nothing positively wrong in the case. Marriage is lawful, and in this case it is advisable, and he may consent to it, for the reasons above stated, without error or impropriety.

37. *Nevertheless.* But. The apostle in this verse states *some* instances where it would *not* be proper to give a daughter in marriage; and the verse is a kind of summing up of all that he had said on the subject. ¶ *That standeth steadfast in his heart,* &c. Most commentators have understood this of the father of the virgin, and suppose that it refers to his purpose of keeping her from the marriage connection. The phrase to stand steadfast, is opposed to a disposition that is vacillating, unsettled, &c., and denotes a man who has command of himself, who adheres to his purpose, a man who has *hitherto* adhered to his purpose, and to whose happiness and reputation it is important that he should be known as one who is not vacillating, or easily moved. ¶ *Having no necessity.* Where there is nothing in *her* disposition or inclination that would make marriage necessary, or when there is no *engagement* or *obligation* that would be violated if she did not marry. ¶ *But hath power over his own will.* Hath power to do as he pleases; is not bound in the case by another. When there is no *engagement,* or *contract,* made in childhood, or promise made in early life that would bind him. Often daughters were espoused, or promised when they were very young, and in such a case a man would be bound to adhere to his engagement; and much as he might *desire* the reverse, and her celibacy, yet he would not have power over his own will, or be at liberty to withhold her. ¶ *And hath so decreed in his heart.* Has so *judged,* determined, resolved. ¶ *That he will keep his virgin.* His daughter, or ward, in an unmarried state. He has *power* and *authority* to do it, and if he does it he will not sin. ¶ *Doeth well.* In

own will, and hath so decreed in his heart that he will keep his virgin, doeth well.

38 So then, [a] he that giveth *her* in marriage doeth well; but he that giveth *her* not in marriage doeth better.

39 The wife [b] is bound by the law as long as her husband liveth: but if her husband be dead, she is

a ver.28. *b* Rom.7.2.

either of these cases, he does well. If he has a daughter, and chooses to retain her in an unmarried state, he does well or right.

38. *Doeth well.* Does right; violates no law in it, and is not to be blamed for it. ¶ *Doeth better.* Does that which is on the whole to be preferred, if it can be done. He more certainly, in the present circumstances, consults her happiness by withholding her from the marriage connection than he could by allowing her to enter it.

39. *The wife is bound,* &c.; see Notes, Rom. vii. 2. ¶ *Only in the Lord.* That is, only to one who is a Christian; with a proper sense of her obligations to Christ, and so as to promote his glory. The apostle supposed that could not be done if she were allowed to marry a heathen, or one of a different religion. The same sentiment he advances in 2 Cor. vi. 14, and it was his intention, undoubtedly, to affirm that it was proper for a widow to marry no one who was not a Christian. The reasons at that time would be obvious. (1.) They could have no sympathy and fellow-feeling on the most important of all subjects, if the one was a Christian and the other a heathen; see 2 Cor. vi. 14, 15, &c. (2.) If she should marry a heathen, would it not be showing that she had not as deep a conviction of the importance and truth of her religion as she ought to have? If Christians were required to be "separate," to be "a peculiar people," not "to be conformed to the world," how could these precepts be obeyed if the society of a heathen was voluntarily chosen, and if she became united to him for life? (3.) She would in this way greatly hinder her usefulness; put herself in the control of one who had no respect for her religion, and who would demand her time and attention, and thus interfere with her attendance on the public and private duties of religion, and the offices of Christian charity. (4.) She would thus greatly endanger her piety. There would be danger from the opposition, the taunts, the sneers of the enemy of Christ; from the secret influence of living with a man who had no respect for God; from his introducing her into society that was irreligious, and that would tend to mar the beauty of her piety, and to draw her away from simple-hearted devotion to Jesus Christ. And do not these *reasons* apply to similar cases now? And if so, is not the law still binding? Do not such unions now, as really as they did then, place the Christian where there is no mutual sympathy on the subject dearest to the Christian heart? Do they not show that she who forms such a union has not as deep a sense of the importance of piety, and of the pure and holy nature of her religion as she ought to have? Do they not take time from God and from charity; break up plans of usefulness, and lead away from the society of Christians, and from the duties of religion? Do they not expose often to ridicule, to reproach, to persecution, to contempt, and to pain? Do they not often lead into society, by a desire to please the partner in life, where there is no religion, where God is excluded, where the name of Christ is never heard, and where the piety is marred, and the beauty of simple Christian piety is dimmed? *And if so,* are not such marriages contrary to the law of Christ? I confess, that this verse, to my view, proves that all such marriages are a violation of the New Testament; and if they are, they should not on *any* plea be entered into; and it will be found, in perhaps nearly *all* instances, that they are disastrous to the piety of the married Christian, and the occasion of ultimate regret, and the cause of a loss of comfort, peace, and usefulness in the married life.

at liberty to be married to whom she will; only [a] in the Lord.

40 But she is happier if she so abide, after [b] my judgment: and I think [c] also that I have the Spirit of God.

a 2 Cor.6.14. b ver.25. c 2 Pet.3.15,16.

40. *If she so abide.* If she remain a widow even if she could be married to a Christian. ¶ *After my judgment.* In my opinion; ver. 25. ¶ *And I think also that I have the Spirit of God.* Macknight and others suppose that this phrase implies entire certainty; and that Paul means to affirm that in this he was clear that he was under the influence of inspiration. He appeals for the use of the term (δωκῶ) to Mark x. 32; Luke viii. 18; 1 Cor. iv. 9; viii. 2; xi. 16; Heb. iv. 1, &c. But the word does not usually express absolute certainty. It implies a doubt; though there may be a strong persuasion or conviction; or the best judgment which the mind can form in the case; see Mat. vi. 7; xxvi. 53; Mark vi. 49; Luke viii. 18; x. 36; xii. 51; xiii. 24; xxii. 24; Acts xvii. 18; xxv. 27; 1 Cor. xvi. 12, 22, &c. It implies here a belief that Paul was under the influence of the infallible Spirit, and that his advice was such as accorded with the will of God. Perhaps he alludes to the fact that the teachers at Corinth deemed themselves to be under the influence of inspiration, and Paul said that he judged also of himself that he was divinely guided and directed in what he said.—*Calvin.* And as Paul in this could not be mistaken; as his *impression* that he was under the influence of that Spirit was, in fact, a *claim* to divine inspiration, so this advice should be regarded as of divine authority, and as binding on all. This interpretation is further demanded by the circumstances of the case. It was necessary that he should assert divine authority to counteract the teaching of the false instructors in Corinth; and that he should interpose that authority in prescribing rules for the government of the church there, in view of the *peculiar* temptations to which they were exposed.

REMARKS.

We learn from this chapter,

1st. The sacredness of the marriage union; and the nature of the feelings with which it should be entered; ver. 1—13. On a most delicate subject Paul has shown a seriousness and delicacy of expression which can be found in no other writings, and which demonstrate how pure his own mind was, and how much it was filled with the fear of God. In all things his aim is to promote purity, and to keep from the Christian church the innumerable evils which everywhere abounded in the pagan world. The marriage connection should be formed in the fear of God. In all that union, the parties should seek the salvation of the soul; and so live as not to dishonour the religion which they profess.

2d. The duty of labouring earnestly for the conversion of the party in the marriage connection that may be a stranger to piety; ver. 16. This object should lie very near the heart; and it should be sought by all the means possible. By a pure and holy life; by exemplifying the nature of the gospel; by tenderness of conversation and of entreaty; and by fidelity in all the duties of life, we should seek the conversion and salvation of our partners in the marriage connection. Even if both are Christians, this great object should be one of constant solicitude—to advance the piety and promote the usefulness of the partner in life.

3d. The duty of contentment in the sphere of life in which we are placed; ver. 18, &c. It is no disgrace to be poor, for Jesus chose to be poor. It is no *disgrace,* though it is a calamity, to be a slave. It is no disgrace to be in an humble rank of life. It is disgraceful only to be a sinner, and to murmur and repine at our allotment. God orders the circumstances of our life; and they are well ordered when under the direction of his hand. The great object should be to do right in the relation which we sustain in life. If poor, to be industrious, submissive, resigned, virtuous; if rich, to be grateful, benevolent, kind. If a slave or a servant, to be faithful, kind, and obedient; using liberty, if it can be lawfully obtained; resigned, and calm, and gentle, if by the providence of God such must continue to be the lot in life.

4th. The duty of preserving the order and regularity of society; ver. 20—23. The design of the gospel is not to produce insubordination or irregularity. It would not break up society; does not dissolve the bonds of social life; but it cements and sanctifies the ties which connect us with those around us. It is designed to promote human happiness; and that is promoted, not by resolving society into its original elements; not by severing the marriage tie, as atheists would do; not by teaching children to disregard and despise their parents, or the common courtesies of life, but by teaching them to maintain inviolate all these relations. Religion promotes the interests of society; it does not, like infidelity, dissolve them. It advances the cause of social virtue; it does not, like atheism, retard and annihilate it. Every Christian becomes a better parent, a more affectionate child, a kinder friend, a more tender husband or wife, a more kind neighbour, a better member of the community.

5th. Change in a man's calling should not be made from a slight cause. A Christian should not make it unless his former calling were wrong, or unless he can by it extend his own usefulness. But when that can be done, he *should* do it, and do it without delay. If the course is wrong, it should be forthwith abandoned. No consideration can make it right to continue it for a day or an hour: no matter what may be the sacrifice of property, it should be done. If a man is engaged in the slave-trade, or in smuggling goods, or in piracy, or highway robbery, or in the manufacture and sale of poison, it should be at once and for ever abandoned. And in like manner, if a young man who is converted can increase his usefulness by changing his plan of life, it should be done as soon as practicable. If by becoming a minister of the gospel he can be a more useful man, every consideration demands that he should leave *any* other profession, however lucrative or pleasant, and submit to the self-denials, the cares, the trials, and the toils which attend a life devoted to Christ in the ministry in Christian or pagan lands. Though it should be attended with poverty, want, tears, toil, or shame, yet the single question is, "Can I be more useful to my Master there than in my present vocation?" If he *can* be, that is an indication of the will of God which he cannot disregard with impunity.

6th. We should live above this world; ver. 29, 30. We should partake of all our pleasures, and endure all our sufferings, with the deep feeling that we have here no continuing city and no abiding place. Soon all our earthly pleasures will fade away; soon all our earthly sorrows will be ended. A conviction of the shortness of life will tend much to regulate our desires for earthly comforts, and will keep us from being improperly attached to them; and it will diminish our sorrows by the prospect that they will soon end.

7th. We should not be immoderately affected with grief; ver. 30. It will all soon end, in regard to Christians. Whether our tears arise from the consciousness of our sins or the sins of others; whether from persecution or contempt of the world; or whether from the loss of health, property, or friends, we should bear it all patiently, for it will soon end; a few days, and all will be over; and the *last* tear shall fall on our cheeks, and the *last* sigh be heaved from our bosom.

8th. We should not be immoderate in our joy, ver. 30. Our highest earthly joys will soon cease. Mirth, and the sound of the harp and the viol, the loud laugh and the song will soon close. What a change should this thought make in a world of gayety, and mirth, and song! It should not make men gloomy and morose; but it should make them serious, calm, thoughtful. O, did all feel that death was near, that the solemn realities of eternity were approaching, what a change *would* it make in a gay and thoughtless world! How would it close the theatre and the ball-room; how would it silence the jest, the

CHAPTER VIII.

NOW as touching things offered [a] unto idols, we know that we all have knowledge. [b] Knowledge [c] puffeth up, but charity [d] edifieth.

a Acts 15.10,19. b Rom.14.14,22. c Isa.47.10. d chap xiii.

jeer, and the loud laugh; and how would it diffuse seriousness and calmness over a now gay and thoughtless world! "Laughter is mad," says Solomon; and in a world of sin, and sorrow, and death, assuredly seriousness and calm contemplation are demanded by every consideration.

9th. What an effect would the thought that "time is short," and that "the fashion of this world passeth away," have on the lovers of wealth! It would, (1.) Teach them that property is of little value. (2.) That the possession of it can constitute no distinction beyond the grave: the rich man is just as soon reduced to dust, and is just as offensive in his splendid mausoleum, as the poor beggar. (3.) A man feeling this, would be led (or *should* be) to make a good use of his property on earth. See Note, Luke xvi. 1—9. (4.) He would be led to seek a better inheritance, an interest in the treasures that no moth corrupts, and that never fade away. Note, Matt. vi. 20. This single thought, that the fashion of this world is soon to pass away—an idea which no man can doubt or deny—if allowed to take firm hold of the mind, would change the entire aspect of the world.

10th. We should endeavour so to live in all things as that our minds should not be oppressed with undue anxiety and care, ver. 32. In all our arrangements and plans, and in all the relations of life, our grand object should be to have the mind free for the duties and privileges of religion. We should seek not to be encumbered with care; not to be borne down with anxiety; not to be unduly attached to the things of this life.

11th. We should enter into the relations of life so as not to interfere with our personal piety or usefulness, but so as to promote both, ver. 32—35. All our arrangements should be so formed as that we may discharge our religious duties, and promote our usefulness to our fellow men. But, alas, how many enter into the marriage relation with unchristian companions, whose active zeal is for ever quenched by such a connection! How many form commercial connections or partnerships in business with those who are not Christians, where the result is to diminish their zeal for God, and to render their whole lives useless to the church! And how much do the cares of life, in all its relations, interfere with simple-hearted piety, and with the faithful discharge of the duties which we owe to God and to a dying world! May God of his mercy enable us so to live in all the relations of life as that our usefulness shall not be retarded but augmented; and so to live that we can see without one sigh of regret the "fashion of this world pass away;" our property or our friends removed; or even the magnificence of the entire world, with all its palaces, and temples, and "cloud-capped towers," passing away amidst the fires that shall attend the consummation of all things!

CHAPTER VIII.

In this chapter another subject is discussed, which had been proposed by the church at Corinth for the decision of the apostle: *Whether it was right for Christians to partake of the meat that had been offered in sacrifice to idols?* On this question there would be doubtless a difference of opinion among the Corinthian Christians. When those sacrifices were made to heathen gods, a part of the animal was given to the priest that officiated, a part was consumed on the altar, and a part (probably the principal part) was the property of him who offered it. This part was either eaten by him at home, as food which had been in some sense consecrated or blessed by having been offered to an idol; or it was partaken of at a feast in honour of the idol; or it was in some instances exposed for sale in the market in the same way as other meat. Whether, therefore, it would be right to partake of that food, either when invited to the house of a heathen friend, or when it was exposed for sale in the market, was a question which could not but present itself to a conscientious Christian. The *objection* to partaking of it would be, that to partake of it either in the temples or at the feasts of their heathen neighbours, would be to lend their countenance to idolatry. On the other hand, there were many who supposed that it was always lawful, and that the scruples of their brethren were needless. Some of their arguments Paul has alluded to in the course of the chapter: they were, that an idol was nothing in the world; that there was but one God, and that every one must know this; and that, therefore, there was no danger that any worshipper of the true God could be led into the absurdities of idolatry, ver. 4—6. To this the apostle replies, that though there *might* be this knowledge, yet, (1.) Knowledge sometimes puffed up, and made us proud, and that we should be careful lest it should lead us astray by our vain self-confidence, ver. 1, 2, 7. (2.) That *all* had not that knowledge (ver. 7); and that they even then, notwithstanding all the light which had been shed around them by Christianity, and notwithstanding the absurdity of idolatry, still regarded an idol as a real existence, as a god, and worshipped it as such; and that it would be highly improper to countenance in any way that idea. He left the inference, therefore, that it was not proper, *from this argument*, to partake of the sacrifices to idols.

A second argument in favour of partaking of that food is alluded to in ver. 8, to wit, that it must be in itself a matter of indifference; that it could make no difference before God, where all depended on *moral* purity and holiness of heart, whether a man had eaten *meat* or not; that we were really no better or worse for it; and that, therefore, it was proper to partake of that food. To this Paul replies, (1.) That though this was true, as an abstract proposition, yet it might be the occasion of leading others into sin, ver. 9. (2.) That the effect on a weak brother would be to lead him to suppose that an idol *was* something, and to confirm him in his supposition that an idol should have some regard, and be worshipped in the temple, ver. 10. (3.) That the consequence might be, that a Christian of little information and experience might be drawn away and perish, ver. 11. (4.) That this would be to sin against Christ, if a feeble Christian should be thus destroyed, ver. 12. And, (5.) That as for himself, if indulgence in meat was in any way the occasion of making another sin, he would eat no meat as long as the world stood (ver. 13); since to abstain from *meat* was a far less evil than the injury or destruction of an immortal soul.

1. *Now as touching.* In regard to; in answer to your inquiry whether it is right or not to partake of those things. ¶ *Things offered unto idols.* Sacrifices unto idols. Meat that had been offered in sacrifice, and then either exposed to sale in the market, or served up at the feasts held in honour of idols, at their temples, or at the houses of their devotees. The priests, who were entitled to a part of the meat that was offered in sacrifice, would expose it to sale in the market; and it was a custom with the Gentiles to make feasts in honour of the idol gods on the meat that was offered in sacrifice; see ver. 10, of this chapter, and chap. x. 20, 21. Some Christians would hold that there could be no harm in partaking of this meat any more than any other meat, since an idol was nothing; and others would have many scruples in regard to it, since it would seem to countenance idol worship. The request made of Paul was, that he should settle some *general principle* which they might all safely follow. ¶ *We know.* We admit; we cannot dispute; it is so plain a case that no one can be ignorant on this point. Probably these are the words of the Corinthians, and perhaps they were contained in the letter which was sent to Paul. They would affirm that they were not ignorant in regard to the nature of idols; they were well assured that they were

nothing at all; and hence they seemed to *infer* that it might be right and proper to partake of this food any-where and every where, even in the idol temples themselves; see ver. 10. To this Paul replies in the course of the chapter, and particularly in ver. 7. ¶ *That we all have knowledge.* That is, on this subject; we are acquainted with the true nature of idols, and of idol worship; we *all* esteem an idol to be nothing, and cannot be in danger of being led into idolatry, or into any improper views in regard to this subject by participating of the food and feasts connected with idol worship This is the statement and argument of the Corinthians. To this Paul makes *two* answers. (1.) In a *parenthesis* in ver. 1—3, to wit, that it was not safe to rely on mere *knowledge* in such a case, since the effect of mere knowledge was often to puff men up and to make them proud, but that they ought to act rather from "charity," or love; and, (2.) That though the mass of them might have this knowledge, yet that *all* did not possess it, and they might be injured, ver. 7. Having stated this argument of the Corinthians, that all had knowledge, in ver. 1, Paul then in a parenthesis states the usual effect of knowledge, and shows that it is not a safe guide, ver. 1—3. In ver. 4, he *resumes* the statement (commenced in ver. 1) of the Corinthians, but which, in a mode quite frequent in his writings, he had broken off by his parenthesis on the subject of knowledge; and in ver. 4—6, he states the argument more at length; concedes that there was to them but one God, and that the majority of them must know that; but states in ver. 7, that *all* had not this knowledge, and that those who *had* knowledge ought to act so as not to injure those who had not. ¶ *Knowledge puffeth up.* This is the beginning of the parenthesis. It is the reply of Paul to the statement of the Corinthians, that all had knowledge. The sense is, "Admitting that you all have knowledge; that you know what is the nature of an idol, and of idol worship; yet mere *knowledge* in this case is not a safe guide; its effect *may* be to puff up, to fill with pride and self-sufficiency, and to lead you astray. *Charity*, or love, as well as knowledge, should be allowed to come in as a guide in such cases, and will be a safer guide than mere knowledge." There had been some remarkable proofs of the impropriety of relying on mere *knowledge* as a guide in religious matters among the Corinthians, and it was well for Paul to remind them of it. These pretenders to uncommon wisdom had given rise to their factions, disputes, and parties, (see chap. i. ii. iii.); and Paul now reminds them that it was not safe to rely on such a guide. And it is no more safe now than it was then. Mere *knowledge*, or science, when the *heart* is not right, fills with pride; swells a man with vain self-confidence and reliance in his own powers, and very often leads him entirely astray. Knowledge combined with right feelings, with pure principles, with a heart filled with love to God and men, may be trusted: but not mere intellectual attainments; mere abstract science; the mere cultivation of the intellect. Unless the *heart* is cultivated *with* that, the effect of knowledge is to make a man a pedant; and to fill him with vain ideas of his own importance; and thus to lead him into error and to sin. ¶ *But charity edifieth.* Love (ἡ ἀγάπη); so the word means; and so it would be well to translate it. Our word *charity* we now apply almost exclusively to alms-giving, or to the favourable opinion which we entertain of others when they seem to be in error or fault. The word in the Scripture means simply *love.* See Notes on chap. xiii. The sense here is, "Knowledge is not a safe guide, and should not be trusted. *Love* to each other and to God, true Christian affection, will be a safer guide than mere knowledge. Your conclusion on this question should not be formed from mere abstract *knowledge;* but you should ask what LOVE to others—to the peace, purity, happiness, and salvation of your brethren—would demand. If *love* to them would prompt to this course, and permit you

2 And if [a] any man think that he knoweth any thing, he knoweth nothing yet as he ought to know.

3 But if any man love God, the same is known [b] of him.

4 As concerning therefore the

a Rom.11.25; Gal.6.3; 1 Tim.6 3.4.

b Nah.1.7; 2 Tim.2.19.

to partake of this food, it should be done; if not, if it would injure them, whatever mere *knowledge* would dictate, it should *not* be done." The doctrine is, that love to God and to each other is a better guide in determining what to do than mere knowledge. And it is so. It will prompt us to seek the welfare of others, and to avoid what would injure them. It will make us tender, affectionate, and kind; and will better tell us *what* to do, and *how* to do it in the best way, than all the abstract knowledge that is conceivable. The man who is influenced by love, ever pure and ever glowing, is not in much danger of going astray, or of doing injury to the cause of God. The man who relies on his knowledge is heady, high-minded, obstinate, contentious, vexatious, perverse, opinionated; and most of the difficulties in the church arise from such men. Love makes no difficulty, but heals and allays all: mere knowledge heals or allays none, but is often the occasion of most bitter strife and contention. Paul was wise in recommending that the question should be settled by *love;* and it would be wise if all Christians would follow his instructions.

2. *And if any think,* &c. The connection and the scope of this passage require us to understand this as designed to condemn that vain conceit of knowledge, or self-confidence, which would lead us to despise others, or to disregard their interests. "If any one is conceited of his knowledge, is so vain, and proud, and self-confident, that he is led to despise others, and to disregard their true interests, he has not yet learned the very first elements of true knowledge as he ought to learn them. True knowledge will make us humble, modest, and kind to others. It will not puff us up, and it will not lead us to overlook the real happiness of others." See Rom. xi. 25. ¶ *Any thing.* Any matter pertaining to science, morals, philosophy, or religion. This is a general maxim pertaining to all *pretenders* to knowledge. ¶ *He knoweth nothing yet,* &c. He has not known what is most necessary to be known on the subject; nor has he known the true use and design of knowledge, which is to edify and promote the happiness of others. If a man has not *so* learned any thing as to make it contribute to the happiness of others, it is a proof that he has never learned the true design of the first elements of knowledge. Paul's design is to induce them to seek the welfare of their brethren. Knowledge, rightly applied, will promote the happiness of all. And it is true now as it was then, that if a man is a *miser* in knowledge as in wealth; if he lives to accumulate, never to impart; if he is filled with a vain conceit of his wisdom, and seeks not to benefit others by enlightening their ignorance, and guiding them in the way of truth, he has never learned the true use of science, any more than the man has of wealth who always hoards, never gives. It is valueless unless it is diffused, as the light of heaven would be valueless unless diffused all over the world, and the waters would be valueless if always preserved in lakes and reservoirs, and never diffused over hills and vales to refresh the earth.

3. *But if any man love God.* If any man is truly attached to God; if he seeks to serve him, and to promote his glory. The sense seems to be this. "There is no true and real knowledge which is not connected with love to God. This will prompt a man also to love his brethren, and will lead him to promote their happiness. A man's course, therefore, is not to be regulated by mere knowledge, but the grand principle is love to God and love to man. Love edifies; love promotes happiness; love will prompt to what is right; and love will secure the approbation of God." Thus explained, this difficult verse accords

eating of those things that are
offered in sacrifice unto idols, we
know that an idol [a] *is* nothing in
the world, and that *there is* none
other [b] God but one.
5 For though there be that are

a Isa.41.24.

b Deut.4.39; Isa.44.8,24.

---

with the whole scope of the parenthesis, which is to show that a man should not be guided in his intercourse with others by mere knowledge, however great that may be; but that a safer and better principle was *love, charity* (ἀγάπη), whether exercised towards God or man. Under the guidance of this, man would be in little danger of error, Under the direction of mere *knowledge* he would never be sure of a safe guide; see chap. xiii. ¶ *The same is known of him.* The words "is known" (ἔγνωσται) I suppose to be taken here in the sense of "is approved by God; is loved by him; meets with his favour," &c. In this sense the word *known* is often used in the Scriptures. Note, Matt. vii. 23. The sense is, "If any man acts under the influence of sacred charity, or love to God, and consequent love to man, he will meet with the approbation of God. He will seek his glory, and the good of his brethren; he will be likely to do right; and God will approve of his intentions and desires, and will regard him as his child. Little distinguished, therefore, as he may be for human knowledge, for that science which puffs up with vain self-confidence, yet he will have a more truly elevated rank, and will meet with the approbation and praise of God. This is of more value than mere knowledge, and this love is a far safer guide than any mere intellectual attainments." So the world would have found it to be if they had acted on it; and so Christians would always find it.

4. *As concerning therefore,* &c. The parenthesis closes with ver. 3. The apostle now proceeds to the real question in debate, and *repeats* in this verse the question, and the admission that all had knowledge. The *admission* that all had knowledge proceeds through ver. 4, 5, and 6; and in ver. 7 he gives the answer to it. In ver. 4—6 *every thing* is admitted by Paul which they asked in regard to the real extent of their knowledge on this subject; and in ver. 7 he shows that even on the ground of this admission, the conclusion would not follow that it was right to partake of the food offered in sacrifice in the temple of an idol. ¶ *The eating of those things,* &c Whether it is right to eat them. Here the question is varied somewhat from what it was in ver. 1, but substantially the same inquiry is stated. The question was, whether it was right for Christians to eat the meat of animals that had been slain in sacrifice to idols. ¶ *We know,* ver. 1. We Corinthians know; and Paul seems fully to admit that they had all the knowledge which they claimed, ver. 7. But his object was to show that even *admitting* that, it would not follow that it would be right to partake of that meat. It is well to bear in mind that the *object* of their statement in regard to knowledge was, to show that there could be no impropriety in partaking of the food. This argument the apostle answers in ver. 7. ¶ *That an idol is nothing.* Is not the true God; is not a proper object of worship. We are not so stupid as to suppose that the block of wood, or the carved image, or the chiseled marble is a real intelligence, and is conscious and capable of receiving worship, or benefiting its votaries. We fully admit, and know, that the whole thing is delusive; and there can be no danger that, by partaking of the food offered in sacrifice to them, we should ever be brought to a belief of the stupendous falsehood that they *are* true objects of worship, or to deny the true God. There is no doubt that the more intelligent heathen had this knowledge; and doubtless nearly all Christians possessed it, though a few who had been educated in the grosser views of heathenism might still have regarded the idol with a superstitious reverence. For whatever might have been the knowledge of statesmen and

[a] called gods, whether in heaven or in earth, (as there be gods many and lords many,)

a John 10.34,35.

6 But as to us [b] *there is but* one God, the Father, of whom *are* all things, and we in [1] him; and one

b Mal.2.10; Eph.4.6. 1 or, *for*.

philosophers on the subject, it was still doubtless true that the great mass of the heathen world *did* regard the dumb idols as the proper objects of worship, and supposed that they were inhabited by invisible spirits—the gods. For purposes of state, and policy, and imposition, the lawgivers and priests of the pagan world were careful to cherish this delusion; see ver. 7. ¶ *Is nothing.* Is delusive; is imaginary. There may have been a reference here to the name of an idol among the Hebrews. They called idols אלילים (*Elilim*), or in the singular אליל (*Elil*), vain, null, nothing-worth, nothingness, vanity, weakness, &c.; indicating their vanity and powerlessness; Lev. xxvi. 1; 1 Chron. xvi. 26; Isa. ii. 8; x. 10; xix. 11, 13, 20; xxxi. 7; Ps. xc. 5; Ezek. xxx. 13; Hab. ii. 18; Zech. xi. 17, &c. ¶ *In the world.* It is nothing at all; it has no power over the world; no real existence anywhere. There *are* no such gods as the heathens pretend to worship. There is but *one* God; and that fact is known to us all. The phrase "in the world" seems to be added by way of emphasis, to show the *utter* nothingness of idols; to explain in the most emphatic manner the belief that they had no real existence. ¶ *And that* there is *none other God but one.* This was a great cardinal truth of religion; see Note, Mark xii. 29; comp. Deut. vi. 4, 5. To keep this great truth in mind was the grand object of the Jewish economy; and this was so plain, and important, that the Corinthians supposed that it must be admitted by all. Even though they should partake of the meat that was offered in sacrifice to idols, yet they supposed it was not possible that any of them could forget the great cardinal truth that there was but one God.

5. *That are called gods.* Gods so called. The heathens everywhere worshipped multitudes, and gave to them the name of gods. ¶ *Whether in heaven.* Residing in heaven, as a part of the gods were supposed to do. Perhaps, there may be allusion here to the sun, moon, and stars; but I rather suppose that reference is made to the celestial deities, or to those who were supposed to *reside* in heaven, though they were supposed occasionally to visit the earth, as Jupiter, Juno, Mercury, &c. ¶ *Or in earth.* Upon the earth; or that reigned particularly over the earth, or sea, as Ceres, Neptune, &c. The ancient heathens worshipped some gods that were supposed to dwell in heaven; others that were supposed to reside on earth; and others that presided over the inferior regions, as Pluto, &c. ¶ *As there be gods many* (ὥσπερ), &c. As there are, in fact, many which are so called or regarded. It is a fact that the heathens worship many whom they esteem to be gods, or whom they regard as such. This cannot be an admission of Paul that they were truly gods, and ought to be worshipped; but it is a declaration that they *esteemed* them to be such, or that a *large number* of imaginary beings were thus adored. The emphasis should be placed on the word *many;* and the design of the parenthesis is, to show that the number of these that were worshipped was not a few, but was immense; and that they were *in fact* worshipped as gods, and allowed to have the influence over their minds and lives which they *would* have if they were real; that is, that the *effect* of this popular belief was to produce just as much fear, alarm, superstition, and corruption, as though these imaginary gods had a real existence. So that though the more intelligent of the heathen put no confidence in them, yet the effect on the great mass was the same as if they had had a real existence, and exerted over them a real control. ¶ *And lords many* (κύριοι πολλοί). Those who had

Lord Jesus Christ, by whom [a] *are* all things, and we by him.

7 Howbeit *there is* not in every man that knowledge: for some

a John 1.3; Heb.1.2.

a *rule* over them; to whom they submitted themselves; and whose laws they obeyed. This name *lord* was often given to their idol gods. Thus among the nations of Canaan their idols was called בעל (*Baal*, or *lord*), the tutelary god of the Phenicians and Syrians; Judg. viii. 33; ix. 4, 46. It is used here with reference to the *idols*, and means that the laws which they were supposed to give in regard to their worship had *control* over the minds of their worshippers.

6. *But to us.* Christians. We acknowledge but one God, Whatever the heathen worship, we know that there is but one God; and he alone has a right to rule over us. ¶ *One God, the Father.* Whom we acknowledge as the Father of all; Author of all things; and who sustains to all his works the relation of a father. The word "Father" here is not used as applicable to the first person of the Trinity, as distinguished from the second, but is applied to God *as* God; not as the Father in contradistinction from the Son, but to the divine nature as such, without reference to that distinction—the Father as distinguished from his offspring, the works that owe their origin to him. This is manifest, (1.) Because the apostle does not use the correlative term "Son" when he comes to speak of the "one Lord Jesus Christ;" and (2.) Because the scope of the passage requires it. The apostle speaks of *God*, of the divine nature, the one infinitely holy Being, as sustaining the relation of Father *to his creatures.* He produced them, He provides for them. He protects them, as a father does his children. He regards their welfare; pities them in their sorrows; sustains them in trial; shows himself to be their friend. The name *Father* is thus given frequently to God, as applicable to the one God, the divine Being; Ps. ciii. 13; Jer. xxxi. 9; Mal. i. 6; ii. 10; Matt. vi. 9; Luke xi. 2, &c. In other places it is applied to the first person of the Trinity as distinguished from the second; and in these instances the correlative *Son* is used, Luke x. 22; xxii. 42; John i. 18; iii. 35; v. 19—23, 26, 30, 36; Heb. i. 5; 2 Pet. i. 17, &c. ¶ *Of whom* (ἐξ οὗ). From whom as a fountain and source; by whose counsel, plan, and purpose. He is the great source of all; and all depend on him. It was by his purpose and power that all things were formed, and *to* all he sustains the relation of a Father. The *agent* in producing all things, however, was the Son, Col. i. 16; Note, John i. 3. ¶ Are *all things.* These words evidently refer to the whole work of creation, as deriving their origin from God, Gen. i. 1. Every thing has thus been formed in accordance with his plan; and all things now depend on him as their Father. ¶ *And we.* We Christians. We are what we are by him. We owe our existence to him; and by him we have been regenerated and saved. It is owing to his counsel, purpose, agency, that we have an existence; and owing to him that we have the hope of eternal life. The leading idea here is, probably, that to God Christians owe their hopes and happiness. ¶ *In him* (εἰς αὐτόν); or rather *unto* him: that is, we are formed *for* him, and should live to his glory. We have been made what we are, as Christians, that we may promote his honour and glory. ¶ *And one Lord,* &c. One Lord in contradistinction from the "*many* lords" whom the heathens worshipped. The word *Lord* here is used in the sense of *proprietor*, ruler, governor, or king; and the idea is, that Christians acknowledge subjection to *him alone,* and not to *many* sovereigns, as the heathens did. Jesus Christ is the Ruler and Lord of his people. They acknowledge their allegiance to him as their supreme Lawgiver and King. They do not acknowledge subjection to *many* rulers, whether imaginary gods or men; but receive their laws from him alone. The word "Lord" here does not imply of necessity any

inferiority to God; since it is a term which is frequently applied to God himself. The idea in the passage is, that from God, the Father of all, we derive our existence, and all that we have; and that we acknowledge *immediate* and *direct* subjection to the Lord Jesus as our Lawgiver and Sovereign. From him Christians receive their laws, and to him they submit their lives. And this idea is so far from supposing *inferiority* in the Lord Jesus to God, that it rather supposes equality; since a right to give laws to men, to rule their consciences, to direct their religious opinions and their lives, can appropriately appertain only to one who has equality with God. ¶ *By whom,* &c. (δι' οὗ). By whose *agency;* or through whom, as the agent. The word "*by*" (δι') stands in contradistinction from "*of*" (ἐξ) in the former part of the verse; and obviously means, that, though "all things" derived their existence *from* God as the fountain and author, yet it was "*by*" the agency of the Lord Jesus. This doctrine, that the Son of God was the great agent in the creation of the world, is elsewhere abundantly taught in the Scriptures; see Note, John i. 3. ¶ Are *all things.* The universe; for so the phrase τὰ πάντα properly means. No words could better express the idea of the universe than these; and the declaration is therefore explicit that the Lord Jesus created all things. Some explain this of the "new creation;" as if Paul had said that *all things* pertaining to our salvation were from him. But the objections to this interpretation are obvious. (1.) It is not the natural signification. (2.) The phrase "all things" naturally denotes the universe. (3.) The scope of the passage requires us so to understand it. Paul is not speaking of the new creature; but he is speaking of the question whether there is more than one God, one Creator, one Ruler over the wide universe. The heathen said there was; Christians affirmed that there was not. The scope, therefore, of the passage requires us to understand this of the vast material universe; and the obvious declaration here is, that the Lord Jesus was the Creator of all. ¶ *And we.* We Christians (1 Pet. i. 21); or, we as men; we have derived our existence "*by*" (δι') or *through* him. The expression will apply either to our original creation, or to our hopes of heaven, as being *by* him; and is equally true respecting both. Probably the idea is, that *all* that we have, as men and as Christians, our lives and our hopes, are *through* him and by his agency. ¶ *By him* (δι' αὐτοῦ). By his agency. Paul had said, in respect to God the Father of all, that we were *unto* (εἰς) him; he here says that in regard to the Lord Jesus, we are *by* (δι') him, or by his agency. The sense is, "God is the author, the former of the plan; the source of being and of hope; and we are to live *to* him: but Jesus is the *agent* by whom all these things are made, and through whom they are conferred on us." Arians and Socinians have made use of this passage to prove that the Son was inferior to God; and the argument is, that the *name* God is not given to Jesus, but another name implying inferiority; and that the design of Paul was to make a *distinction* between God and the Lord Jesus. It is not the design of these Notes to examine opinions in theology; but in reply to this argument we may observe, briefly, (1.) That those who hold to the divinity of the Lord Jesus do not deny that there is a *distinction* between him and the Father: they fully admit and maintain it, both in regard to his eternal existence (*i. e.* that there is an eternal distinction of persons in the Godhead) and in regard to his office as mediator. (2.) The term "Lord," given here, does not of necessity suppose that he is inferior to God. (3.) The *design* of the passage supposes that there was equality in some respects. God the Father and the Lord Jesus sustain relations to men that in some sense correspond to the "many gods" and the "many lords" that the heathen adored; but they were equal in nature. (4.) The work of creation is expressly in this passage ascribed to the Lord Jesus. But the work of creation can-with conscience of the idol unto this hour, eat *it* as a thing offered unto an idol; and their conscience being weak is defiled.

8 But meat [a] commendeth us not to God: for neither if we eat, [1] are we the better; neither if we eat not, [2] are we the worse.

a Rom.14.17.

1 or, *have we the more.* 2 or, *have we the less.*

not be performed by a creature. There can be no delegated *God,* and no delegated *omnipotence,* or delegated infinite wisdom and omnipresence. The work of creation implies divinity; or it is impossible to prove that there *is* a God: and if the Lord Jesus made "ALL THINGS," he must be God.

7. *Howbeit.* But. In the previous verses Paul had stated the argument of the Corinthians—that they *all* knew that an idol was nothing; that they worshipped but one God; and that there could be no danger of their falling into idolatry, even should they partake of the meat offered in sacrifice to idols. Here he replies, that though this might be *generally* true, yet it was not universally; for that some were ignorant on this subject, and supposed that an idol had a real existence, and that to partake of that meat would be to confirm them in their superstition. The *inference* therefore is, that on their account they should abstain; see ver. 11—13. ¶ There is *not,* &c. There are some who are weak and ignorant; who have still remains of heathen opinions and superstitious feelings. ¶ *That knowledge.* That there is but one God; and that an idol is nothing. ¶ *For some with conscience of the idol.* From conscientious regard *to* the idol; believing that an idol god has a real existence; and that his favour should be sought, and his wrath be deprecated. It is not to be supposed that converted men would regard idols as the *only* God; but they might suppose that they were *intermediate* beings, good or bad angels, and that it was proper to seek their favour or avert their wrath. We are to bear in mind that the heathen were exceedingly ignorant; and that their former notions and superstitious feelings about the gods whom their fathers worshipped, and whom they had adored, would not soon leave them, even on their conversion to Christianity. This is just one instance, like thousands, in which former erroneous opinions, prejudices, or superstitious views may influence those who are truly converted to God, and greatly mar and disfigure the beauty and symmetry of their religious character. ¶ *Eat* it *as a thing,* &c. As offered to an idol who was entitled to adoration; or as having a right to their homage. They supposed that some invisible spirit was present with the idol; and that his favour should be sought, or his wrath averted by sacrifice. ¶ *And their conscience being weak.* Being unenlightened on this subject; and being too weak to withstand the temptation in such a case. Not having a conscience sufficiently clear and strong to enable them to resist the temptation; to overcome all their former prejudices and superstitious feelings; and to act in an independent manner, as if an idol were nothing. Or their conscience was morbidly sensitive and delicate on this subject: they might be disposed to do right, and yet not have sufficient knowledge to convince them that an idol was nothing, and that they ought not to regard it. ¶ *Is defiled.* Polluted; contaminated. By thus countenancing idolatry he is led into sin, and contracts guilt that will give him pain when his conscience becomes more enlightened; ver. 11, 13. From superstitious reverence of the idol, he might think that he was doing right; but the effect would be to lead him to a conformity to idol worship that would defile his conscience, pollute his mind, and ultimately produce the deep and painful conviction of guilt. The general reply, therefore, of Paul to the first argument in favour of partaking of the meat offered in sacrifice to idols is, that *all* Christians have not full knowledge on the subject; and that to partake of that might lead them into the sin of idolatry, and corrupt and destroy their souls.

8. *But meat commendeth us not to*

9 But take heed lest by any means this [1] liberty [a] of yours become a stumbling-block to them that are weak.

1 or, *power*. *a* Rom.14.13,20; Gal.5.13.

10 For if any man see thee which hast knowledge sit at meat in the idol's temple, shall not the conscience of him which is weak

God. This is to be regarded as the view presented by the Corinthian Christians, or by the advocates for partaking of the meat offered in sacrifice to idols. The sense is, "Religion is of a deeper and more spiritual nature than a mere regard to circumstances like these. God looks at the heart. He regards the motives, the thoughts, the moral actions of men. The mere circumstance of eating *meat*, or abstaining from it, cannot make a man better or worse in the sight of a holy God. The acceptable worship of God is not placed in such things. It is more spiritual; more deep; more important. And *therefore*," the inference is, "it cannot be a matter of much importance whether a man eats the meat offered in sacrifice to idols, or abstains." To this argument the apostle replies (ver. 9—13), that, although this might be true in itself, yet it might be the occasion of leading others into sin, and it would *then* become a matter of *great importance* in the sight of God, and should be in the sight of all true Christians. The word "commendeth" (παρίστησι) means properly to introduce to the favour of any one, as a king or ruler; and here means to *recommend* to the favour of God. God does not regard this as a matter of importance. He does not make his favour *depend* on unimportant circumstances like this. ¶ *Neither if we eat*. If we partake of the meat offered to idols. ¶ *Are we the better*. Margin, *Have we the more*. Gr. Do we abound (περισσεύομεν); that is, in moral worth or excellence of character; see Note, Rev. xiv. 17. ¶ *Are we the worse*. Margin, *Have we the less*. Greek, Do we lack or want (ὑστερούμεθα); that is, in moral worth or excellence.

9. *But take heed*. This is the reply of Paul to the argument of the Corinthians in ver. 8. "Though all that you say should be admitted to be true, as it must be; though a man *is* neither morally better nor worse for partaking of meat or abstaining from it; yet the grand principle to be observed is, so to act as not to injure your brethren. Though you may be no better or worse for eating or not eating, yet if your conduct shall injure others, and lead them into sin, *that* is a sufficient guide to determine you what to do in the case. You should abstain entirely. It is of far more importance that your brother should *not* be led into sin, than it is that you should partake of meat which you acknowledge (ver. 8) is in itself of no importance." ¶ *Lest by any means* (μή πως). You should be careful that by no conduct of yours your brother be led into sin. This is a general principle that is to regulate Christian conduct in all matters that are in themselves indifferent. ¶ *This liberty of yours*. This which you *claim* as a right; this power which you have, and the exercise of which is in itself lawful. The *liberty* or power (ἐξουσία) here referred to was that of partaking of the meat that was offered in sacrifice to idols; ver. 8. A man may have a *right* abstractly to do a thing, but it may not be prudent or wise to exercise it. ¶ *Become a stumbling-block*. An occasion of sin; Note, Mat. v. 29; also Note, Rom. xiv. 13. See that it be not the occasion of leading others to sin, and to abandon their Christian profession; ver. 10. ¶ *To them that are weak*. To those professing Christians who are not fully informed or instructed in regard to the true nature of idolatry, and who still may have a superstitious regard for the gods whom their fathers worshipped.

10. *For if any man*. Any Christian brother who is ignorant, or any one who might otherwise become a Christian. ¶ *Which hast knowledge*. Who are fully informed in regard to the real nature of idol worship. You will be looked up to as an example. You will be presumed to be partaking of this feast in honour of the idol. You will thus encourage him, and he will

be [1] emboldened to eat those things
which are offered to idols;
11 And through thy knowledge

1 *edified.*

shall the weak brother perish, for
whom Christ died?
12 But [a] when ye sin so against

a Mat.25.40,45.

partake of it with a conscientious regard to the idol. ¶ *Sit at meat.* Sitting down to an entertainment in the temple of the idol. Feasts were often celebrated, as they are now among the heathen, in honour of idols. Those entertainments were either in the temple of the idol, or at the house of him who gave it. ¶ *Shall not the conscience of him which is weak.* Of the man who is not fully informed, or who still regards the idol with superstitious feelings; see ver. 7. ¶ *Be emboldened.* Margin, *Edified* (οἰκοδομηθήσεται). Confirmed; established. So the word *edify* is commonly used in the New Testament; Acts ix. 31. Rom. xiv. 19; Eph. iv. 12; 1 Thess. v. 11. The sense here is, "Before this he had a superstitious regard for idols. He had the remains of his former feelings and opinions. But he was not *established* in the belief that an idol was any thing; and his superstitious feelings were fast giving way to the better Christian doctrine that they were nothing. But *now,* by your example, he will be fully *confirmed* in the belief that an idol *is* to be regarded with respect and homage. He will see you in the very temple, partaking of a feast in honour of the idol; and he will infer not only that it is right, but that it is a matter of conscience with you, and will follow your example."

11. *And through thy knowledge.* Because you *knew* that an idol was nothing, and that there could be really no danger of falling into idolatry from partaking of these entertainments. You will thus be the means of deceiving and destroying him. The *argument* of the apostle here is, that if *this* was to be the result, the duty of those who *had* this knowledge was plain. ¶ *Shall the weak brother.* The uninformed and ignorant Christian. That it means a real Christian there can be no doubt. For (1.) It is the *usual* term by which Christians are designated—the endearing name of *brother;* and (2.) The scope of the passage requires it so to be understood; see Note, Rom. xiv. 20. ¶ *Perish.* Be destroyed; ruined; lost; Note, John x. 28. So the word ἀπολεῖται properly and usually signifies. The sense is, that the *tendency* of this course would be to lead the weak brother into sin, to apostacy, and to ruin. But this does not prove that any who were truly converted should apostatize and be lost; for (1.) There may be a *tendency* to a thing, and yet that thing may never happen. It may be arrested, and the event not occur. (2.) The *warning* designed to prevent it may be effectual, and be the means of saving. A man in a canoe floating down the Niagara river may have a *tendency* to go over the falls; but he may be hailed from the shore, and the hailing may be effectual, and he may be saved. The call to him was *designed* to save him, and actually had that effect. So it may be in the warnings to Christians. (3.) The apostle does not say that any true Christian would be lost. He puts a question; and affirms that if *one* thing was done, *another might* follow. But this is not affirming that any one *would* be lost. So I might say that *if* the man *continued* to float on towards the falls of Niagara, he would be destroyed. If one thing was done, the other would be a consequence. But this would be very different from a statement that a man *had actually* gone over the falls, and been lost. (4.) It is elsewhere abundantly proved that no one who has been truly converted will apostatize and be destroyed; see Notes, John x. 28; comp. Note, Rom. viii. 29, 30. ¶ *For whom Christ died.* This is urged as an argument why we should not do any thing that would tend to destroy the souls of men. And no stronger argument could be used. The argument is, that we should not do any thing that would tend to frustrate the work of Christ, that would render the shedding of his blood vain. The *possibility* of doing this is urged; and that

the brethren, and wound their weak conscience, ye sin against Christ.

13 Wherefore, if meat make my brother to offend, I will eat no flesh while the world standeth, lest [a] I make my brother to offend.

[a] chap.9.22.

bare possibility should deter us from a course of conduct that might have this tendency. It is an appeal drawn from the deep and tender love, the sufferings, and the dying groans of the Son of God. If *he* endured so much to *save* the soul, assuredly we should not pursue a course that would tend to *destroy* it. If he *denied* himself so much to *redeem,* we should not, assuredly, be so fond of self-gratification as to be unwilling to abandon any thing that would tend to *destroy.*

12. *But when ye sin so against the brethren.* This is designed further to show the evil of causing others to sin; and hence the evil which might arise from partaking of the meat offered to idols. The word *sin* here is to be taken in the sense of *injuring, offending, leading into sin.* You violate the law which requires you to love your brethren, and to seek their welfare, and thus you sin against them. Sin is properly against God; but there may be a course of injury pursued against men, or doing them injustice or wrong, and this is *sin* against them. Christians are bound to do right towards all. ¶ *And wound their weak conscience.* The word *wound* here (τύπτοντες, *smiting, beating*) is taken in the sense of *injure.* Their consciences are ill-informed. They have not the knowledge which you have. And by your conduct they are led farther into error, and believe that the idol *is* something, and is to be honoured. They are thus led into sin, and their conscience is more and more perverted, and oppressed more and more with a sense of guilt. ¶ *Ye sin against Christ.* Because (1.) Christ has commanded you to love them, and seek their good, and not to lead them into sin, and (2.) Because they are so intimately united to Christ (Notes, John xv. 1, &c.) that to offend them is to offend him; to injure the members is to injure the head; to destroy their souls is to pain his heart and to injure his cause; Note, Mat. x. 40; comp. Luke x. 16.

13. *Wherefore.* As the conclusion of the whole matter. ¶ *If meat,* &c. Paul here proposes his own views and feelings, or tells them how he would act in order to show them how they should act in these circumstances. ¶ *Make my brother to offend.* Lead him into sin; or shall be the cause of leading him into error and guilt. It does not mean, if the eating of meat should *enrage* or *irritate* another; but if it is the occasion of his being led into transgression. How this might be done is stated in ver. 10. ¶ *I will eat no flesh,* &c. My eating meat is a matter of comparative unimportance. I can dispense with it. It is of much less importance to me than happiness, a good conscience, and salvation are to my brother. And the law of love therefore to him requires me to deny myself rather than to be the occasion of leading him into sin. This is a noble resolution; and marks a great, disinterested, and magnanimous spirit. It is a spirit that seeks the good of all; that can deny itself; that is supremely anxious for the glory of God and the salvation of man, and that can make personal comfort and gratification subservient to the good of others. It was the principle on which Paul always acted; and is the very spirit of the self-denying Son of God. ¶ *While the world standeth.* Greek, For ever. The phrase 'I will *never* eat meat' would express the idea. ¶ *Lest I make,* &c. Rather than lead him into sin, by my indulging in eating the meat offered in sacrifice to idols.

REMARKS.

This chapter is very important, as it settles some *principles* in regard to the conduct of Christians; and shows how they should act in reference to things that are *indifferent;* or which in themselves can be considered as neither right nor wrong; and in reference to those things which may be considered in themselves as *right* and *lawful*, but whose indulgence might injure others. And from the chapter we learn,—

1st. That Christians, though they are truly converted, yet may have many erroneous views and feelings in reference to many things, ver. 6. This was true of those converted from ancient heathenism, and it is true of those who are *now* converted from heathenism, and of all young converts. Former opinions, and prejudices, and even superstitions, abide long in the mind, and cast a long and withering influence over the regions of Christian piety. The morning dawn is at first very obscure. The change from night to daybreak is at first scarcely perceptible. And so it may be in conversion. The views which a heathen entertained from his childhood could not at once be removed. The influence of corrupt opinions and feelings, which a sinner has long indulged, may *travel over* in his conversion, and may long endanger his piety and destroy his peace. Corrupt and infidel thoughts, associations of pollution, cannot be destroyed at once; and we are not to expect from a child in the Christian life, the full vigour, and the elevated principle, and the strength to resist temptation, which we expect of the man matured in the service of the Lord Jesus. This should lead us to *charity* in regard to the imperfections and failings of young converts; to a willingness to aid and counsel them; to *carefulness* not to lead them into sin; and it should lead us *not* to expect the same amount of piety, zeal, and purity in converts from degraded heathens, which we expect in Christian lands, and where converts have been trained up under all the advantages of Sabbath-schools and Bible-classes.

2d. Our opinions should be formed, and our treatment of others regulated, not by abstract *knowledge*, but by love, ver. 1. A man is usually much more likely to act *right* who is influenced by charity and love, than one who is guided by simple knowledge, or by self-confidence. One is humble, kind, tender towards the frailties of others, sensible himself of infirmity, and is *disposed* to do right; the other may be vain, harsh, censorious, unkind, and severe. Knowledge is useful; but for the practical purposes of life, in an erring and fallen world, love is more useful; and while the one often leads astray, the other seldom errs. Whatever *knowledge* we may have, we should make it a point from which we are never to depart, that our opinions of others, and our treatment of them, should be formed under the influence of love.

3d. We should not be self-confident of our wisdom, ver. 2. Religion produces humility. Mere knowledge may fill the heart with pride and vanity. True knowledge is not inconsistent with humility; but it must be joined with a *heart* that is right. The men that have been most eminent in knowledge have also been distinguished for humility; but the *heart* was right; and they saw the folly of depending on mere knowledge.

4th. There is but one God, ver. 4—6. This great truth lies at the foundation of all true religion; and yet is so simple that it may be known by all Christians, however humble, and is to be *presumed* to be known by all. But though simple, it is a great and glorious truth. To keep this before the minds of men was one great purpose of all God's revelations; and to communicate it to men is now the grand object of all missionary enterprises. The world is full of idols and idolaters; but the knowledge of this simple truth would change the moral aspect of the entire globe. To spread this truth should be the great aim and purpose of all true Christians; and when this truth *is* spread, the idols of the heathen will fall to the dust.

5th. Christians acknowledge one and only one Lord, ver. 6. He rules over them. His laws bind them. He controls them. He has a right to them. He can dispose of them as he pleases. They are not their own; but are bound to live entirely to him, and for the promotion of his cause.

6th. It becomes Christians to exercise continual care, lest their conduct, even in things which are in themselves lawful, should be the occasion of leading others into sin, ver. 9. Christians very often pursue a course of conduct which may not be in itself unlawful, but which may lead others who have not their intelligence, or strength of principle, into error. One man may be safe where another man is in danger. One man may be able to resist temptations which would entirely overcome another. A course of life may, perhaps, be safe for a man of years and of mature judgment, which would be ruinous to a young man. And the grand principle here should be, not to do that, even though it may be lawful itself, which would be the occasion of leading others into sin.

7th. We see here the importance and the power of example, ver. 10, 11. Nothing is of more value than a correct Christian example. And this applies particularly to those who are in the more elevated ranks of life, who occupy stations of importance, who are at the head of families, colleges, and schools. The ignorant will be likely to follow the example of the learned; the poor of the rich; those in humble life will imitate the manners of the great. Even in things, therefore, which may not be in themselves unlawful in these circumstances, they should set an example of self-denial, of plainness, of abstinence, for the sake of those beneath them. They should so live that it would be safe and right for all to imitate their example. Christ, though he was rich, yet so lived that *all* may safely imitate him; though he was honoured of God, and exalted to the highest office as the Redeemer of the world, yet he lived so that all in every rank may follow him; though he had all power, and was worshipped by angels, yet so lived that he might teach the most humble and lowly *how* to live; and so lived that it is safe and proper for all to live as he did. So should every monarch, and prince, and rich man; every noble, and every learned man; every man of honour and office; every master of a family, and every man of age and wisdom, live that all others may learn of them *how* to live, and that they may safely walk in their footsteps.

8th. We have here a noble instance of the principles on which Paul was willing to act, ver. 13. He was willing to deny himself of any gratification, if his conduct was likely to be the occasion of leading others into sin. Even from that which was in itself lawful he would abstain for ever, if by indulgence he would be the occasion of another's falling into transgression. But how rare is this virtue! How seldom is it practised! How few Christians and Christian ministers are there who deny themselves any gratification in things in themselves right, lest they should induce others to sin! And yet this is the grand principle of Christianity; and this should influence and guide all the professed friends and followers of Christ. This *principle* might be applied to many things in which many Christians now freely indulge; and *if* applied, would produce great and important changes in society. (1.) Entertainments and feasts which, perhaps, you may be able to *afford* (that is, *afford* in the supposition that what you have is *yours*, and not the Lord's) may lead many of those who cannot afford it to imitate you, and to involve themselves in debt, in extravagance, in ruin. (2.) You might *possibly* be safe at a festival, at a public dinner, or in a large party; but your *example* would encourage others where they would *not* be safe; and yet, how could you reply should they say that you were there, and that they were encouraged by you? (3.) On the supposition that the use of wine and other fermented liquors may be in themselves lawful, and that you *might* be safe in using them, yet *others* may be led by your example to an improper use of them, or contract a taste for stimulating drinks that may end in their ruin. Would it be right for *you* to continue the use of wine in such circumstances? Would Paul have done it? Would he not have adopted the noble principle in this chapter, that he would not touch it while the

CHAPTER IX.

AM I not an apostle? am I not free? have I not [a] seen Jesus Christ our Lord? are not ye my work [b] in the Lord?

a Acts 9.3,17. b chap.4.15.

world stands, if it led him to sin? (4.) You might be safe in a party of amusement, in the circle of the gay, and in scenes of merriment and mirth. I say you *might* be, though the supposition is scarcely *possible* that Christian piety is ever safe in such scenes, and though it is certain that Paul or the Saviour would not have been found there. But how will it be for the young, and for those of less strength of Christian virtue? Will they be safe there? Will they be able to guard against these allurements as you could? Will they not be led into the love of gayety, vanity, and folly? And what would Paul have done in such cases? What would Jesus Christ have done? What should Christians now do? This single principle, if fairly applied, would go far to change the aspect of the Christian world. If all Christians had Paul's delicate sensibilities, and Paul's strength of Christian virtue, and Paul's willingness to deny himself to benefit others, the aspect of the Christian world would soon change. How many practices now freely indulged in would be abandoned! And how soon would every Christian be seen to set such an example that all others could safely follow it!

CHAPTER IX.

The apostle had in chap. viii. 13, mentioned his willingness to deny himself if he might be the means of benefitting others. On this principle he had acted; and on this he purposed to act. The mention of this principle of action seems to have led him to a further illustration of it in his own case, and *in* the illustration to meet an objection that had been urged against him at Corinth; and the scope of this chapter seems to have been not only to give an *illustration* of this principle (see chap. ix. 27), but to show that this principle on which he acted would account for his conduct when with them, and would meet all the objections which had been made against his apostleship. These objections seem to have been, (1.) That he had not seen Jesus Christ; and therefore *could* not be an apostle; ver. 1. (2.) That he did not live like the other apostles, that he was unmarried, was a solitary man, and a wanderer, and was unlike the other apostles in his mode of life, not indulging as apostles *might* do in the ordinary comforts of life; ver. 4, 5. (3.) That he and Barnabas were compelled to labour for their support, and were *conscious*, therefore, that they had no pretensions to the apostolic office; ver. 6. And (4.) That the fact that he was unsupplied; that he did not apply to Christians for his maintenance; that he did not urge this as a *right*, showed that he was conscious that he had no claims to the apostolic character and rank.

To all this he replies in this chapter, and the main drift and design of his reply is, to show that he acted on the principle suggested in chap. viii. 13, that of denying himself; and consequently, that though he had a *right* to maintenance, yet that the fact that he did not *urge* that right was no proof that he was not sent from God, but was rather a proof of his being actuated by the high and holy principles which *ought* to influence those who were called to this office. In urging this reply, he shows,—

(1.) That he *had* seen Jesus Christ, and had this qualification for the office of an apostle; ver. 1.

(2.) That he had the power like others to partake of the common enjoyments of life, and that his *not* doing it was no proof that he was not an apostle; ver. 4.

(3.) That he was not prohibited from entering the domestic relations as others had done, but had the right to enjoy the same privileges if he chose; and that his *not* doing it was no proof that he was not an apostle, but was an instance of his denying himself for the good of others; ver. 5.

(4.) That he was not under a *necessity* of labouring with his own hands.

but that he might have required support as others did; that his labouring was only another instance of his readiness to deny himself to promote the welfare of others; ver. 6.

This sentiment he illustrates through the remainder of the chapter by showing that he had a *right* to support in the work of the apostleship, and that his not insisting on it was an instance of his being willing to deny himself that he might do good to others; that he did not *urge* this right because to do that might injure the cause (ver. 12, 15); and that whether he received support or not, he was bound to preach the gospel. In this he shows (*a*) (ver. 7—10, 13) That *God* gave him the *right* to support if he chose to exercise it; (*b*) That it was *equitable* that he should be supported (ver. 11); (*c*) That the Lord had ordained this as a general law, that they which preached the gospel should live by it (ver. 14); (*d*) That he had not chosen to avail himself of it because it might do injury (ver. 12, 15); (*e*) That necessity was laid upon him at all events to preach the gospel (ver. 16); (*f*) That if he did this without an earthly reward, he would be rewarded in heaven in a distinguished manner (ver. 17, 18); (*g*) That he had made it the grand principle of his life, not to make money, but to save souls, and that he had sought this by a course of continued self-denial (ver. 19—22); (*h*) That all this was done for the sake of the gospel (ver. 23); and (*i*) That he had a grand and glorious object in view, which required him, after the manner of the Athletae, to keep his body under, to practise self-denial, to be temperate, to forego many comforts of which he might otherwise have partaken, and that the grandeur and glory of this object was enough to justify all his self denial, and to make all his sacrifices pleasant; ver. 24—27.

Thus the whole chapter is an *incidental* discussion of the subject of his apostleship, in *illustration* of the sentiment advanced in chap. viii. 13, that he was willing to practise self-denial for the good of others; and is one of the most elevated, heavenly, and beautiful discussions in the New Testament, and contains one of the most ennobling descriptions of the virtue of self-denial, and of the principles which should actuate the Christian ministry, any where to be found. All classic writings would be searched in vain, and all records of profane history, for an instance of such pure and elevated principle as is presented in this chapter.

1. *Am I not an apostle?* This was the point to be settled; and it is probable that some at Corinth had denied that he *could* be an apostle, since it was requisite, in order to that, to have seen the Lord Jesus: and since it was supposed that Paul had *not* been a witness of his life, doctrines, and death. ¶ *Am I not free?* Am I not a free man; have I not the liberty which all Christians possess, and especially which all the apostles possess? The *liberty* referred to here is doubtless the privilege or right of abstaining from labour; of enjoying as others did the domestic relations of life; and of a support as a public minister and apostle. Probably some had objected to his claims of apostleship that he had not used this right, and that he was conscious that he had no claim to it. By this mode of interrogation, he strongly *implies* that he *was* a freeman, and that he had this right. ¶ *Have I not seen Jesus Christ our Lord?* Here it is implied, and seems to be admitted by Paul, that in order to be an *apostle* it was necessary to have seen the Saviour. This is often declared expressly; see Note on Acts i. 21, 22. The *reason* of this was, that the apostles were appointed to be WITNESSES of the life, doctrines, death, and resurrection of the Lord Jesus, and that in their *being witnesses* consisted the PECULIARITY of the apostolic office. That this was the case is abundantly manifest from Mat. xxviii. 18, 19; Luke xxiv. 48 Acts i. 21, 22; ii. 32; x. 39—41. Hence it was essential, in order that any one should be such a witness, and an apostle, that he should have *seen* the Lord Jesus. In the case of Paul, therefore, who was called to this office *after* the death and resurrection of the

2 If I be not an apostle unto others, yet doubtless I am to you; for the seal of mine apostleship are ye in the Lord.

Saviour, and who had not therefore had an opportunity of seeing and hearing him when living, this was provided for by the fact that the Lord Jesus showed himself to him *after* his death and ascension, in order that he might have this qualification for the apostolic office, Acts ix. 3—5, 17. To the fact of his having been thus in a miraculous manner *qualified* for the apostolic office, Paul frequently appeals, and always with the same view that it was *necessary* to have *seen* the Lord Jesus to qualify one for this office, Acts xxii. 14, 15; xxvi. 16; 1 Cor. xv. 8. It follows from this, therefore, that no one was an *apostle* in the strict and proper sense who had not *seen* the Lord Jesus. And it follows, also, that the apostles could have no successors in that which constituted the PECULIARITY of their office; and that the office must have commenced and ended with them. ¶ *Are not ye my work in the Lord?* Have you not been converted by my labours, or under my ministry; and are you not a proof that the Lord, when I have been *claiming* to be an apostle, has owned me *as an apostle,* and blessed me in this work? God would not give his sanction to an impostor, and a false pretender; and as Paul had laboured there *as* an apostle, this was an argument that he had been truly commissioned of God. A minister *may* appeal to the blessing of God on his labours in proof that he is sent of Him. And one of the best of all arguments that a man is sent from God exists where multitudes of souls are converted from sin, and turned to holiness, by his labours. What better credentials than this can a man need that he is in the employ of God? What more consoling to his own mind? What more satisfactory to the world?

2. *If I be not an apostle unto others.* "If I have not given evidence to others of my apostolic mission; of my being sent by the Lord Jesus, yet I have to you. Assuredly you, among whom I have laboured so long and so successfully, should not doubt that I am sent from the Lord. You have been well acquainted with me; you have witnessed my endowments, you have seen my success, and you have had abundant evidence that I have been sent on this great work. It is therefore strange in you to doubt my apostolic commission; and it is unkind in you so to construe my declining to accept your contributions and aid for my support, as if I were conscious that I was not entitled to that." ¶ *For the seal of mine apostleship.* Your conversion is the demonstration that I am an apostle. Paul uses strong language. He does not mean to say that their conversion furnished *some* evidence that he was an apostle; but that it was absolute proof, and irrefragable demonstration, that he was an apostle. A *seal* is that which is affixed to a deed, or other instrument, to make it firm, secure, and indisputable. It is the proof or demonstration of the validity of the conveyance, or of the writing; Notes, John iii. 33; vi. 27. The sense here is, therefore, that the conversion of the Corinthians was a certain demonstration that he was an apostle, and should be so regarded by them, and treated by them. It was such a proof, (1.) Because Paul *claimed* to be an apostle while among them, and God blessed and owned this claim; (2.) Their conversion could not have been accomplished by man. It was the work of God. It was the evidence then which God gave to Paul and to them, that he was with him, and had sent him. (3.) They knew him, had seen him, heard him, were acquainted with his doctrines and manner of life, and could bear testimony to what he was, and what he taught. We may remark, that the conversion of sinners is the best evidence to a minister that he is sent of God. The divine blessing on his labours should cheer his heart, and lead him to believe that God has sent and that he approves him. And every minister should so live and labour, should so deny himself, that he may be able *to appeal* to the people among

3 Mine answer to them that do examine me is this;
4 Have we not power to eat and to drink?

5 Have we not power to lead about a sister, a [1] wife, as well as other apostles, and *as* the brethren of the Lord, and Cephas?

1 or, *woman.*

whom he labours that he is a minister of the Lord Jesus.

3. *Mine answer.* Gr. Ἡ ἐμὴ ἀπολογία. My *apology;* my defence. The same word occurs in Acts xxii. 1; xxv. 16; 2 Cor. vii. 11; Phil. i. 7, 17; 2 Tim. iv. 16; 1 Pet. iii. 15; see Note, Acts xxii. 1. Here it means his answer, or defence against those who sat in judgment on his claims to be an apostle. ¶ *To them that do examine me.* To those who *inquire* of me; or who *censure* and condemn me as not having any claims to the apostolic office. The word used here (ἀνακρίνω) is properly a *forensic* term, and is usually applied to judges in courts; to those who sit in judgment, and investigate and decide in litigated cases brought before them; Luke xxiii. 14; Acts iv. 9; xii. 19; xxiv. 8. The apostle here may possibly allude to the *arrogance* and pride of those who presumed to sit as judges on *his* qualification for the apostolic office. It is not meant that this answer *had* been given by Paul before this, but that this was the defence which he had to offer. ¶ *Is this.* This which follows; the statements which are made in the following verses. In these statements (ver. 4, 5, 6, &c.) he seems to have designed to take up their objections to his apostolic claims one by one, and to show that they were of no force.

4. *Have we not power* (ἐξουσίαν). Have we not the *right.* The word *power* here is evidently used in the sense of *right* (comp. John i. 12, *margin);* and the apostle means to say that though they had not exercised this *right* by *demanding* a maintenance, yet it was not because they were conscious that they had no such right, but because they chose to forego it for wise and important purposes. ¶ *To eat and to drink.* To be maintained at the expense of those among whom we labour. Have we not a right to demand that they shall yield us a proper support? By the interrogative form of the statement, Paul intends more strongly to *affirm* that they *had* such a right. The interrogative mode is often adopted to express the strongest affirmation. The *objection* here urged seems to have been this, "You, Paul and Barnabas, labour with your own hands. Acts xviii. 3. Other religious teachers lay claim to maintenance, and are supported without personal labour. This is the case with pagan and Jewish priests, and with Christian teachers among us. You must be *conscious,* therefore, that you are not apostles, and that you have no claim or right to support." To this the *answer* of Paul is, "We admit that we labour with our own hands. But your inference does not follow. It is not because we have not a *right* to such support, and it is not because we are *conscious* that we have no such claim, but it is for a higher purpose. It is because it will do good if we should not urge this right, and enforce this claim." That they *had* such a right, Paul proves at length in the subsequent part of the chapter.

5. *Have we not power?* Have we not a right? The objection *here* seems to have been, that Paul and Barnabas were unmarried, or at least that they travelled without wives. The objectors urged that others had wives, and that they took them with them, and expected provision to be made for them as well as for themselves. They therefore showed that they felt that they had a *claim* to support for their families, and that they were conscious that they were sent of God. But Paul and Barnabas had no families. And the objectors inferred that they were *conscious* that they had no claim to the apostleship, and no right to support. To this Paul replies as before, that they had a *right* to do as others did, but they chose *not* to do it for other rea-

sons than that they were conscious that they *had* no such right. ¶ *To lead about.* To have in attendance with us; to conduct from place to place; and to have them maintained at the expense of the churches amongst which we labour. ¶ *A sister, a wife.* Marg. " or *woman.*" This phrase has much perplexed commentators. But the simple meaning seems to be, " A wife who should be a Christian, and regarded as sustaining the relation of a Christian sister." Probably Paul meant to advert to the fact that the wives of the apostles *were* and *should be* Christians; and that it was a matter of course, that if an apostle led about a wife she would be a Christian; or that he would marry no other; comp. 1 Cor. iii. 11. ¶ *As well as other apostles.* It is evident from this that the apostles generally were married. The phrase used here is (οἱ λοιποὶ ἀπόστολοι (*the remaining apostles,* or the other apostles). And if *they* were married, it is right and proper for ministers to marry now, whatever the papist may say to the contrary. It is safer to follow the example of the apostles than the opinions of the papal church. The *reasons* why the apostles had wives with them on their journeys may have been various. They may have been either to give instruction and counsel to those of their own sex to whom the apostles could not have access, or to minister to the wants of their husbands as they travelled. It is to be remembered that they travelled among heathens; they had no acquaintance and no friends there; they therefore took with them their female friends and wives to minister to them, and sustain them in sickness, trial, &c. Paul says that he and Barnabas had a *right* to do this; but they had not used this right because they chose rather to make the gospel without charge (ver. 18), and that thus they judged they could do more good. It follows from this, (1.) That it is right for ministers to marry, and that the papal doctrine of the celibacy of the clergy is contrary to apostolic example. (2.) It is *right* for missionaries to marry, and to take their wives with them to heathen lands. The apostles were missionaries, and spent their lives in heathen nations as missionaries do now, and there *may be* as good reasons for missionaries marrying now as there were then. (3.) Yet there are men, like Paul, who can do more good without being married. There *are* circumstances, like his, where it is not advisable that they should marry, and there can be no donbt that Paul regarded the unmarried state for a missionary as preferable and advisable. Probably the same is to be said of most missionaries at the present day, that they could do more good if unmarried, than they can if burdened with the cares of families. ¶ *And as the brethren of the Lord.* The brothers of the Lord Jesus,—James and Joses, and Simon and Judas, Mat. xiii. 55. It seems from this, that although at first they did not believe in him (John vii. 5), and had regarded him as disgraced (Mark iii. 21), yet that they had subsequently become converted, and were employed as ministers and evangelists. It is evident also from this statement that they were married, and were attended with their wives in their travels. ¶ *And Cephas.* Peter; Note, John i. 42. This proves, (1.) as well as the declaration in Mat. viii. 14, that Peter *had been* married. (2.) That he had a wife after he became an apostle, and while engaged in the work of the ministry. (3.) That his wife accompanied him in his travels. (4.) That it is right and proper for ministers and missionaries to be married now. Is it not strange that the *pretended* successor of Peter, the pope of Rome, should forbid marriage when Peter himself was married? Is it not a proof how little the papacy regards the Bible, and the example and authority of those from whom it pretends to derive its power? And is it not strange that this doctrine of the celibacy of the clergy, which has been the source of abomination, impurity, and licentiousness every where, should have been sustained and countenanced at all by the Christian world? And is it not strange that this, with all the other corrupt doctrines of the papacy,

6 Or I only and Barnabas, have not we [a] power to forbear working?

7 Who goeth a warfare [b] any time at his own charges? who planteth [c] a vineyard, and eateth

a 2 Thess.3.8,9. *b* 1 Tim.1.18. *c* Deut.20.6; Pr.27.18.

should be attempted to be imposed on the enlightened people of the United States, or of Great Britain, as a part of the religion of Christ?

6. *Or I only and Barnabas.* Paul and Barnabas had wrought together as tent-makers at Corinth; Acts xviii. 3. From this fact it had been inferred that they *knew* that they had no claim to a support. ¶ *Power to forbear working.* To abstain from labour, and to receive support as others do. The question implies a strong affirmation that they *had* such power. The sense is, 'Why should *I* and Barnabas be regarded as having no right to support? Have we been less faithful than others? Have we done less? Have we given fewer evidences that we are sent by the Lord, or that God approves us in our work? Have we been less successful? Why then should *we* be singled out; and why should it be supposed that *we* are obliged to labour for our support? *Is there no other conceivable reason* why we should support ourselves than a consciousness that we have no right to support from the people with whom we labour?" It is evident from ver. 12, that Barnabas as well as Paul relinquished his right to a support, and laboured to maintain himself. And it is manifest from the whole passage, that there was some peculiar "spleen" (*Doddridge*) against these two ministers of the gospel. What it was we know not. It might have arisen from the enmity and opposition of Judaizing teachers, who were offended at their zeal and success among the Gentiles, and who could find no other cause of complaint against them than that they chose to support themselves, and not live in idleness, or to tax the church for their support. That must have been a bad cause which was sustained by such an argument.

7. *Who goeth a warfare,* &c. Paul now proceeds to illustrate the RIGHT which he knew ministers had to a support (ver. 7—14), and then to show the REASON why he had not availed himself of that right; ver. 15—23. The *right* he illustrates from the nature of the case (ver. 7. 11); from the authority of Scripture (ver. 8—10); from the example of the priests under the Jewish law (ver. 13); and from the authority of Jesus Christ; ver. 14. In this verse (7th) the right is enforced by the nature of the case, and by three illustrations. The first is, the right of a soldier or warrior to his wages. The Christian ministry is compared to a warfare, and the Christian minister to a soldier; comp. 1 Tim. i. 18. The soldier had a right to receive pay from him who employed him. He did not go at his own expense. This was a matter of common equity; and on this principle all acted who enlisted as soldiers. So Paul says it is but equitable also that the soldier of the Lord Jesus should be sustained, and should not be required to support himself. And why, we may ask, should he be, any more than the man who devotes his strength, and time, and talents to the defence of his country? The work of the ministry is as arduous, and as self-denying, and perhaps as dangerous, as the work of a soldier; and common justice, therefore, demands that he who devotes his youth, and health and life to it, for the benefit of others should have a competent support Why should not he receive a competent support who seeks to *save* men, as well as he who lives to *destroy* them? Why not he who endeavours to recover them to God, and make them pure and happy, as well as he who lives to destroy life, and pour out human blood, and to fill the air with the shrieks of new-made widows and orphans? Or why not he who seeks, though in another mode, to defend the great interests of his country, and to maintain the interests of justice, truth, and mercy, for the benefit of mankind, as well as he

not of the fruit thereof? or who feedeth [a] a flock, and eateth not of the milk of the flock?

8 Say I these things as a man? or saith not the law the same also?

a 1 Pet.5.2.

who is willing in the tented field to spend his time, or exhaust his health and life in protecting the rights of the nation? ¶ *At his own charges.* His own expense. On the meaning of the word "charges" (ὀψωνίοις) see Note, Luke iii. 14; comp. Rom. vi. 23; 2 Cor. xi. 8. The word does not occur elsewhere in the New Testament. ¶ *Who planteth a vineyard,* &c. This is the *second* illustration from the nature of the case, to show that ministers of the gospel have a right to support. The argument is this: 'It is reasonable that those who labour should have a fair compensation. A man who plants a vineyard does not expect to labour for nothing; he expects support from that labour, and looks for it *from* the vineyard. The vineyard owes its beauty, growth, and productiveness to him. It is reasonable, therefore, that *from* that vineyard he should receive a support, as a compensation for his toil. So *we* labour for your welfare. You derive advantage from our toil. We spend our time, and strength, and talent for your benefit; and it is reasonable that we should be supported while we thus labour for your good." The church of God is often compared to *a vineyard;* and this adds to the beauty of this illustration; see Isa. v. 1—4; Notes, Luke xx. 9—16. ¶ *Who feedeth a flock,* &c. This is the *third* illustration drawn from the nature of the case, to show that ministers have a right to support. The word "feedeth" (ποιμαίνει) denotes not only to *feed,* but to guard, protect, defend, as a shepherd does his flock; see Notes, John xxi. 15—17. "The wages of the shepherds in the East do not consist of ready money, but in a part of the milk of the flocks which they tend. Thus Spon says of the shepherds in modern Greece, "These shepherds are poor Albanians, who feed the cattle, and live in huts built of rushes: they have a tenth part of the milk and of the lambs which is their whole wages: the cattle belong to the Turks." The shepherds in Ethiopia, also, according to Alvarez, have no pay except the milk and butter which they obtain from the cows, and on which they and their families subsist."—*Rosenmüller.* The church is often compared to a flock; see Note, John x. 1, &c. The argument here is this: "A shepherd spends his days and nights in guarding his folds. He leads his flock to green pastures, he conducts them to still waters (comp. Ps. xxiii. 2); he defends them from enemies; he guards the young, the sick, the feeble, &c. He spends his time in protecting it and providing for it. He expects support, when in the wilderness or in the pastures, mainly from the milk which the flock should furnish. He labours for their comfort; and it is proper that he should derive a maintenance from them, and he has a right to it. So the minister of the gospel watches for the good of souls. He devotes his time, strength, learning, talents, to their welfare. He instructs, guides, directs, defends; he endeavours to guard them against their spiritual enemies, and to lead them in the path of comfort and peace. He lives to instruct the ignorant; to warn and secure those who are in danger; to guide the perplexed; to reclaim the wandering; to comfort the afflicted; to bind up the broken in heart; to attend on the sick; to be an example and an instructor to the young; and to be a counsellor and a pattern to all. As he labours for their good, it is no more than equal and right that they should minister to his temporal wants, and compensate him for his efforts to promote their happiness and salvation. And can any man say that this is NOT right and just?

8. *Say I these things as a man?* Do I speak this on my own authority, or without the sanction of God? Is not this, which appears to be so rea-

9 For it is written [a] in the law of Moses, Thou shalt not muzzle the mouth of the ox that treadeth out the corn. Doth God take care for oxen?
10 Or saith he *it* altogether

[a] Deut.25.4; 1 Tim.5.18.

sonable and equitable, also supported by the authority of God? ¶ *Or saith not the law the same also?* The law of Moses, to which the *Jewish* part of the church at Corinth—which probably had mainly urged these objections —professed to bow with deference. Paul was accustomed, especially in arguing with the Jews, to derive his proofs from the Old Testament. In the previous verse he had shown that it was *equitable* that ministers of the gospel should be supported. In this and the following verses he shows that the same *principle* was recognised and acted on under the Jewish dispensation. He does not mean to say, by this example of the ox treading out the corn, that the law as given by Moses referred to the Christian ministry; but that the *principle* there was settled that the labourer should have a support, and that a suitable provision should not be withheld even from an ox; and if God so regarded the welfare of a brute when labouring, it was much more reasonable to suppose that he would require a suitable provision to be made for the ministers of religion.

9. *For it is written;* Deut. xxv. 4. ¶ *In the law of Moses;* see Note, Luke xxiv. 44. ¶ *Thou shalt not muzzle the mouth,* &c. To muzzle means, "to bind the mouth; to fasten the mouth to prevent eating or biting."—*Webster.* This was done either by passing straps around the mouth, or by placing, as is now sometimes done, a small *basket* over the mouth, fastened by straps to the horns of the animal, so as to prevent its eating, but not to impede its breathing freely. This was an instance of the humanity of the laws of Moses. The idea is, that the ox should not be prevented from eating when it was in the midst of food; and that as it laboured for its owner, it was *entitled* to support; and there was a propriety that it should be permitted to partake of the grain which it was threshing. ¶ *That treadeth,* &c. This was one of the common modes of threshing in the east, as it is with us; see Note and illustration on Mat. iii. 12. ¶ *The corn.* The *grain,* of any kind; wheat, rye, barley, &c. Maize, to which we apply the word *corn,* was then unknown; see Note, Mat. xii. 1. ¶ *Doth God take care for oxen?* Doth God take care for oxen ONLY? Or is not this rather *a principle* which shows God's care for *all* that labour, and the humanity and equity of his laws? And if he is so solicitous about the welfare of brutes as to frame an express law in their behalf, is it not to be presumed that the same *principle* of humanity and equity will run through all his dealings and requirements? The apostle does not mean to deny that God does take care for oxen, for the very law was proof that he did; but he means to ask whether it is to be supposed that God would regard the comfort of oxen and not of men also? whether we are not to suppose that the same principle would apply also to those who labour in the service of God? He uses this passage, therefore, not as originally having reference to men, or to ministers of the gospel, which cannot be; but as establishing a general *principle* in regard to the equity and humanity of the divine laws; and as thus showing that the *spirit* of the law of God would lead to the conclusion that God intended that the labourer everywhere should have a competent support.

10. *Or saith he it altogether for our sakes?* The word "altogether" (πάντως) cannot mean that this was the *sole* and *only* design of the law, to teach that ministers of the gospel were entitled to support; for, (1.) This would be directly contrary to the law itself, which had *some* direct and undoubted reference to oxen; (2.) The scope of the argument here does not require this interpretation, since the whole object will be met by

for our sakes? For our sakes, no doubt, *this* is written; that he [a] that ploweth should plow in hope; and that he that thresheth in hope should be partaker of his hope?

11 If [b] we have sown unto you spiritual things, *is it* a great

a 2 Tim.2.6. b Rom. 15.27.

supposing that this settled a *principle* of humanity and equity in the divine law, according to which it was *proper* that ministers should have a support; and, (3.) The word "altogether" (πάντως) does not of necessity require this interpretation. It may be rendered *chiefly, mainly, principally,* or *doubtless;* Luke iv. 23, "Ye will *surely* (πάντως, certainly, surely, doubtless) say unto me this proverb," &c.; Acts xviii. 21, "I must *by all means* (πάντως, certainly, surely) keep this feast; Acts xxi. 22, "The multitude *must needs* (πάντως, will certainly, surely, inevitably) come together," &c.; Acts xxviii. 4, "*No doubt* (πάντως) this man is a murderer," &c. The word here, therefore, means that the *principle* stated in the law about the oxen was so broad and humane, that it might *certainly, surely, particularly* be regarded as applicable to the case under consideration. An important and material argument might be drawn from it; an argument from the less to the greater. The precept enjoined justice, equity, humanity; and that was *more* applicable to the case of the ministers of the gospel than to the case of oxen. ¶ *For our sakes,* &c. To show that the laws and requirements of God are humane, kind, and equitable: not that Moses had Paul or any other minister in his eye, but the *principle* was one that applied particularly to this case. ¶ *That he that ploweth,* &c. The Greek in this place would be more literally and more properly rendered, "For (ὅτι) he that ploweth OUGHT (ὀφείλει) to plow in hope;" *i. e.* in hope of reaping a harvest, or of obtaining success in his labours: and the sense is, "The man who cultivates the earth, in order that he may be excited to industry and diligence, *ought* to have a reasonable prospect that he shall himself be permitted to enjoy the fruit of his labours. This *is* the case with those who *do* plow: and if this should be the case with those who cultivate the earth, it is *as* certainly reasonable that those who labour in God's husbandry, and who devote their strength to his service, should be encouraged with a reasonable prospect of success and support." ¶ *And that he that thresheth,* &c. This sentence, in the Greek, is very elliptical and obscure; but the sense is, evidently, "He that thresheth *ought* to partake of his hope;" *i. e.* of the fruits of his hope, or of the result of his labour. It is fair and right that he should enjoy the fruits of his toil. So in God's husbandry; it is right and proper that they who toil for the advancement of his cause should be supported and rewarded." The same sentiment is expressed in 2 Tim. ii. 6, "The husbandman that laboureth must be first partaker of the fruits."

11. *If we have sown unto you spiritual things.* If we have been the means of imparting to you the gospel, and bestowing upon you its high hopes and privileges; see Note, Rom. xv. 27. The figure of *sowing,* to denote the preaching of the gospel, is not unfrequently employed in the Scriptures; see John iv. 37, and the parable of the sower, Mat. xiii. 3, &c. ¶ Is it *a great thing,* &c.; Note, Rom. xv. 27. Is it to be regarded as unequal, unjust, or burdensome? Is it to be supposed that we are receiving that for which we have not rendered a valuable consideration? The sense is, "We impart blessings of more value than we receive. We receive a supply of our temporal wants. We impart to you, under the divine blessing, the gospel, with all its hopes and consolations. We make you acquainted with God; with the plan of salvation; with the hope of heaven. We instruct your children; we guide you

thing if we shall reap your carnal things?

12 If others be partakers of *this* power over you, *are* not we

in the path of comfort and peace; we raise you from the degradations of idolatry and of sin; and we open before you the hope of the resurrection of the just, and of all the bliss of heaven: and to do this, we give ourselves to toil and peril by land and by sea. And can it be made a matter of question whether all these high and exalted hopes are of as much value to dying man as the small amount which shall be needful to minister to the wants of those who are the means of imparting these blessings?" Paul says this, therefore, from the reasonableness of the case. The propriety of support *might* be further urged, (1.) Because without it the ministry would be comparatively useless. Ministers, like physicians, lawyers, and farmers, should be allowed to attend mainly to the great business of their lives, and to their appropriate work. No physician, no farmer, no mechanic, could accomplish much, if his attention was constantly turned off from his appropriate business to engage in something else. And how can the minister of the gospel, if his time is nearly all taken up in labouring to provide for the wants of his family? (2.) The great mass of ministers spend their early days, and many of them all their property, in preparing to preach the gospel to others. And as the mechanic who has spent his early years in learning a trade, and the physician and lawyer in preparing for their profession, receive support *in* that calling, why should not the minister of the gospel? (3.) Men in other things cheerfully *pay* those who labour for them. They compensate the schoolmaster, the physician, the lawyer, the merchant, the mechanic; and they do it cheerfully, because they suppose they receive a valuable consideration for their money. But is it not so with regard to ministers of the gospel? Is not a man's family as *certainly* benefited by the labours of a faithful clergyman and pastor, as by the skill of a physician or a lawyer, or by the service of the schoolmaster? Are not the affairs of the soul and of eternity as important to a man's family as those of time and the welfare of the body? So the music-master and the dancing master are paid, and paid cheerfully and liberally; and yet can there be any comparison between the value of their services and those of the minister of the gospel? (4.) It might be added, that society is benefited in a *pecuniary* way by the service of a faithful minister to a far greater extent than the amount of compensation which he receives. One drunkard, reformed under his labours, may earn and save to his family and to society as much as the whole salary of the pastor. The promotion of order, peace, sobriety, industry, education, and regularity in business, and honesty in contracting and in paying debts, saves much more to the community at large than the cost of the support of the gospel. In regard to this, any man may make the comparison at his leisure, between those places where the ministry is established, and where temperance, industry, and sober habits prevail, and those places where there is *no* ministry, and where gambling, idleness, and dissipation abound. It is always a matter of *economy* to a people, in the end, to support schoolmasters and ministers as they ought to be supported. ¶ *Reap your carnal things.* Partake of those things which relate to the present life; the support of the body, *i. e.* food and raiment.

12. *If others.* Other teachers living with you. There can be no doubt that the teachers in Corinth urged this right, and received a support. ¶ *Be partakers of* this *power.* Of this right to a support and maintenance. ¶ Are *not we rather.* We the apostles; we who have laboured for your conversion; who have founded your church; who have been the first, and the most laborious in instructing you, and imparting to you spiritual blessings? Have not we a better claim than they? ¶ *Nevertheless we have not used this power.* We have not urged this claim; we have chosen to forego this

rather? Nevertheless [a] we have not used this power; but suffer all things, lest we should hinder the gospel of Christ.

13 Do ye not know, that they which minister about holy things [1] live *of the things* of the temple? and they [b] which wait

a 2 Cor.11.7—9; 12.14.

1 or, *feed*. b Num.18.8,&c.; Deut.18.1.

right, and to labour for our own support. The *reason* why they had done this, he states in the subsequent part of the chapter; see 2 Cor. xi. 7—9; xii. 14; comp. Acts xviii. 3; xx. 34, 35. ¶ *But suffer all things.* Endure all privations and hardships; we subject ourselves to poverty, want, hunger, thirst, nakedness, rather than urge a *claim* on you, and thus leave the suspicion that we are actuated by mercenary motives. The word used here (στέγομεν suffer) means properly *to cover*, to keep off, as rain, &c., and then to *contain*, to *sustain, tolerate, endure.* Here it means to bear, or endure all hardships; comp. Notes, chap. iv. 11—13. ¶ *Lest we should hinder the gospel of Christ.* Paul here states the reason why he had not urged a claim to support in preaching the gospel. It was not because he was not entitled to a full support, but it was that by denying himself of this right he could do good, and avoid some evil consequences which would have resulted if he had strenuously urged it. His conduct therefore in this was just one illustration of the principle on which he said (ch. viii. 13) he would always act; a readiness to deny himself of things lawful, if by that he could promote the welfare of others. The *reasons* why his urging this claim might have hindered the gospel may have been many. (1.) It might have exposed him and the ministry generally to the charge of being mercenary. (2.) It would have prevented his presenting in bold relief the fact that he was bound to preach the gospel at all events, and that he was actuated in it by a simple conviction of its truth. (3.) It might have alienated many minds who might otherwise have been led to embrace it. (4.) It would have prevented the exercise of self-denial in him, and the benefits which resulted from that self-denial, &c., ver. 17, 18, 23, 27.

13. *Do ye not know*, &c. In this verse Paul illustrates the doctrine that the ministers of religion were entitled to a support from the fact that those who were appointed to offer sacrifice receive a maintenance in their work. ¶ *They which minister about holy things.* Probably the *Levites.* Their office was to render assistance to the priests, to keep guard around the tabernacle, and subsequently around the temple. It was also their duty to see that the temple was kept clean, and to prepare supplies for the sanctuary, such as oil, wine, incense, &c. They had the care of the revenues, and after the time of David were required to sing in the temple, and to play upon instruments. Num. iii. 1—36; iv. 1, 30, 35, 42; viii. 5—22; 1 Chron. xxiii. 3—5, 24, 27; xxiv. 20—31. ¶ *Live* of the things *of the temple.* Marg., *Feed; i. e.*, are supported in their work by the offerings of the people, and by the provisions which were made for the temple service; see Num. xviii. 24—32. ¶ *And they which wait at the altar.* Probably the *priests* who were employed in offering sacrifice. ¶ *Are partakers with the altar.* That is, a part of the animal offered in sacrifice is burned as an offering to God, and a part becomes the property of the priest for his support; and thus the altar and the priest become joint participators of the sacrifice. From these offerings the priest derived their maintenance; see Num. xviii. 8—19; Deut. xviii. 1, &c. The argument of the apostle here is this: "As the ministers of religion under the Jewish dispensation were entitled to support by the authority and the law of God, that fact settles a general principle which is applicable also to the gospel, that he intends that the ministers of religion should derive their support *in* their work. If it was reasonable then, it is reasonable now. If God com-

at the altar are partakers with the altar?

14 Even so hath the Lord *a* ordained, that they *b* which preach the gospel should live of the gospel.

15 But I *c* have used none of

a Luke 10.7. *b* Gal.6.6. *c* Acts 20.33; 2 Thess.3.8.

manded it then, it is to be presumed that he intends to require it now.

14. *Even so.* In the same manner, and for the same reasons. ¶ *Hath the Lord ordained.* Hath the Lord appointed, commanded, *arranged* that it should be so (διέταξε). The word here means that he has made this a law, or has required it. The word "Lord" here doubtless refers to the Lord Jesus, who has sent forth his ministers to labour in the great harvest of the world. ¶ *That they which preach the gospel.* They who are sent forth by him; who devote their lives to this work; who are called and employed by him in this service. This refers, therefore, not only to the apostles, but to all who are duly called to this work, and who are his ambassadors. ¶ *Should live of the gospel.* Should be supported and maintained *in* this work. Paul here probably refers to the appointment of the Lord Jesus, when he sent forth his disciples to preach, Mat. x. 10; Luke x. 8; comp. Gal. vi. 6. The man may be said to "live in the gospel" who is supported while he preaches it, or who derives his maintenance *in* that work. Here we may observe, (1.) That the command is that they shall *live* (ζῆν) of the gospel. It is not that they should grow rich, or lay up treasures, or speculate in it, or become merchants, farmers, teachers, or bookmakers for a living; but it is that they should have such a maintenance as to constitute a livelihood. They should be made comfortable; not rich. They should receive so much as to keep their minds from being harassed with cares, and their families from want; not so much as to lead them to forget their dependence on God, or on the people. Probably the true rule is, that they should be able to live as the *mass* of the people among whom they labour live; that they should be able to receive and entertain the poor, and be willing to do it; and so that the rich also may not despise them, or turn away from their dwelling. (2.) This is a *command* of the Lord Jesus; and if it is a *command*, it should be obeyed as much as any other law of the Redeemer. And if this is a command, then the minister is *entitled* to a support; and then also a people are not at liberty to withhold it. Further, there are as strong reasons why they should support him, as there are why they should pay a schoolmaster, a lawyer, a physician, or a day-labourer. The minister usually toils as hard as others; expends as much in preparing for his work; and does *as much* good. And there is even a higher claim in this case. God has given an *express* command in this case; he has not in the others. (3.) The salary of a minister should not be regarded as a *gift* merely, any more than the pay of a congress-man, a physician, or a lawyer. He has a claim to it; and God has commanded that it should be paid. It is, moreover, a matter of stipulation and of compact, by which a people agree to compensate him for his services. And yet, is there any thing in the shape of *debt* where there is so much looseness as in regard to this subject? Are men usually as conscientious in this as they are in paying a physician or a merchant? Are not ministers often in distress for that which has been promised them, and which they have a right to expect? And is not their usefulness, and the happiness of the people, and the honour of religion intimately connected with obeying the rule of the Lord Jesus in this respect?

15. *But I have used none of these things.* I have not urged and enforced this right. I have chosen to support myself by the labour of my own hands. This had been objected to him as a reason why he could not be an apostle. He here shows that *that* was not the reason why he had not urged this claim; but that it was because in this way he could do most to honour the gospel and save the souls

these things: neither have I written these things, that it should be so done unto me: for [a] *it were* better for me to die than that any man should make my glorying void.

16 For though I preach the gospel, I have nothing to glory of: for [b] necessity is laid upon me; yea, woe is unto me if I preach not the gospel.

a 2 Cor.11.10.

b Jer.50.17; 20.9.

of men; comp. Acts xx. 33; 2 Thess. iii. 8. The sense is, "Though my right to a support is established, in common with others, both by reason, the nature of the case, the examples in the law, and the command of the Lord Jesus, yet there are reasons why I have not chosen to avail myself of this right, and why I have not urged these claims." ¶ *Neither have I written these things,* &c. "I have not presented this argument now in order to induce you to provide for me. I do not intend now to ask or receive a support from you. I urge it to show that I *feel* that I have a right to it; that my conduct is not an argument that I am conscious I am not an apostle; and that I *might* urge it were there not strong reasons which determine me not to do it. I neither ask you to send me now a support, nor, if I visit you again, do I expect you will contribute to my maintenance." ¶ *For it were better for me to die,* &c. There are advantages growing out of my not urging this claim which are of more importance to me than life. Rather than forego these advantages, it would be better for me—it would be a thing which I would prefer—to pine in poverty and want; to be exposed to peril, and cold, and storms, until life should close. I esteem my "glorying," the advantages of my course, to be of more value than life itself. ¶ *Than that any man should make my glorying void.* His glorying, or boasting, or *joying,* as it may be more properly rendered (τὸ καύχημά μου; comp. Phil. i. 26; Heb. iii. 6), was, (1.) That he had preached the gospel without expense to anybody, and had thus prevented the charge of avarice (ver. 18); and (2.) That he had been able to keep his body under, and pursue a course of self-denial that would result in his happiness and glory in heaven, ver. 23—27. "Any man" would have made that "void," if he had supported Paul; had prevented the necessity of his labour, and had thus exposed him to the charge of having preached the gospel for the sake of gain.

16. *For though I preach the gospel,* &c. This, with the two following verses, is a very difficult passage, and has been very variously understood by interpreters. The general scope and purpose of the passage is to show what was the ground of his "glorying," or of his hope of "reward" in preaching the gospel. In ver. 15. he had intimated that he had cause of "glorying," and that that cause was one which he was determined no one should take away. In this passage (ver. 16—18.) he states what that was. He says, it was not simply that he preached; for there was a necessity laid on him, and he could not help it: his call was such, the command was such, that his life would be miserable if he did not do it. *But* all idea of "glorying," or of "reward," must be connected with some *voluntary* service—something which would show the inclination, disposition, desire of the soul. And as that in his case could not be well shown where a "necessity" was laid on him, it could be shown only in his submitting *voluntarily* to trials; in denying himself; in being willing to forego comforts which he *might* lawfully enjoy; and in thus furnishing a full and complete test of his readiness to do any thing to promote the gospel. The essential idea here is, therefore, that there was such a *necessity* laid on him in his call to preach the gospel, that his compliance with that call could not be regarded as appropriately connected with reward; and that in his case the circumstance which showed that reward would be proper, was, his denying himself, and making the gospel without

charge. This would show that *his heart was in the thing;* that he was was not urged on by necessity; that he loved the work; and that it would be consistent for the Lord to reward him for his self-denials and toils in his service. ¶ *I have nothing to glory of.* The force of this would be better seen by a more literal translation. "It is not to me glorying;" *i. e.* this is not the cause of my glorying, or rejoicing (οὐκ ἔστι μοι καύχημα). In ver. 15 he had said that he *had* a cause of glorying, or of joy (καύχημα). He here says that *that* joy or glorying did not consist in the simple fact that he *preached* the gospel; for necessity was laid on him; there was some *other* cause and source of his joy or glorying than that simple fact; ver. 18. Others preached the gospel also: in common with them, it might be a source of joy to him that he preached the gospel; but it was not the source of his *peculiar* joy, for *he* had been called into the apostleship in such a manner as to render it inevitable that he should preach the gospel. *His* glorying was of another kind. ¶ *For necessity is laid upon me.* My preaching is in a manner inevitable, and cannot therefore be regarded as that in which I peculiarly glory. I was called into the ministry in a miraculous manner; I was addressed personally by the Lord Jesus; I was arrested when I was a persecutor; I was commanded to go and preach; I had a direct commission from heaven. There was no room for hesitancy or debate on the subject (Gal. i. 16), and I gave myself at once and entirely to the work; Acts ix. 6. I have been urged to this by a direct call from heaven; and to yield obedience to this call cannot be regarded as evincing such an inclination to give myself to this work as if the call had been in the usual mode, and with less decided manifestations. We are not to suppose that Paul was *compelled* to preach, or that he was not voluntary in his work, or that he did not prefer it to any other employment: but he speaks in a popular sense, as saying that he "could not help it;" or that the evidence of his call was irresistible, and left no room for hesitation. He was free; but there was not the slightest room for debate on the subject. The evidence of his call was so strong that he could not but yield. Probably none now have evidences of their call to the ministry *as* strong as this. But there are many, very many, who feel that a kind of *necessity* is laid on them to preach. Their consciences urge them to it. They would be miserable in any other employment. The course of Providence has shut them up to it. Like Saul of Tarsus, they may have been persecutors, or revilers, or "injurious," or blasphemers (1 Tim. i. 13); or they may, like him, have commenced a career of ambition; or they may have been engaged in some scheme of money-making or of pleasure; and in an hour when they little expected it, they have been arrested by the truth of God, and their attention directed to the gospel ministry. Many a minister has, before entering the ministry, formed many other purposes of life; but the providence of God barred his way, hemmed in his goings, and constrained him to become an ambassador of the cross. ¶ *Yea, woe is unto me,* &c. I should be miserable and wretched if I did not preach. My preaching, therefore, in itself considered, cannot be a subject of glorying. I am shut up to it. I am urged to it in every way. I should be wretched were I not to do it, and were I to seek any other calling. My conscience would reproach me. My judgment would condemn me. My heart would pain me. I should have no comfort in any other calling; and God would frown upon me. Learn hence, (1. That Paul had been converted. Once he had no love for the ministry, but persecuted the Saviour. With the feelings which he *then* had, he would have been wretched *in* the ministry; with those which he *now* had, he would have been wretched *out* of it. His heart, therefore, had been wholly changed. (2.) All ministers who are duly called to the work can say the same thing. They would be wretched in any other calling. Their conscience would reproach them. They would have no interest in the plans of the world; in the schemes of wealth, and

17 For if I do this thing willingly, I have a reward: but if against my will, a dispensation [a] *of the gospel* is committed unto me.

a Col.1.25.

---

pleasure, and fame. Their heart is in *this* work, and in this alone. In this, though amidst circumstances of poverty, persecution, nakedness, cold, peril, sickness, they have comfort. In any other calling, though surrounded by affluence, friends, wealth, honours, pleasures, gayety, fashion, they would be miserable. (3.) A man whose heart is not in the ministry, and who would be *as* happy in any other calling, is not fit to be an ambassador of Jesus Christ. Unless his *heart* is there, and he *prefers* that to any other calling, he should never think of preaching the gospel. (4.) Men who *leave* the ministry, and voluntarily devote themselves to some other calling when they might preach, never had the proper spirit of an ambassador of Jesus. If for the sake of ease or gain; if to avoid the cares and anxieties of the life of a pastor; if to make money, or secure money when made; if to cultivate a farm, to teach a school, to write a book, to live upon an estate, or to *enjoy life,* they lay aside the ministry, it is proof that they never had a call to the work. So did not Paul; and so did not Paul's Master and ours. They loved the work, and they left it not till death. Neither for ease, honour, nor wealth; neither to avoid care, toil, pain, or poverty, did they cease in their work, until the one could say, "I have fought a good fight, *I have finished my course,* I have kept the faith" (2 Tim. iv. 7; and the other, "I have finished the work which thou gavest me to do;" John xvii. 4. (5.) We see the reason why men are sometimes *miserable* in other callings. They *should* have entered the ministry. God called them to it; and they became hopefully pious. But they chose the law, or the practice of medicine, or chose to be farmers, merchants, teachers, professors, or statesmen. And God withers their piety, blights their happiness, follows them with the reproaches of conscience, makes them sad, melancholy, wretched. They do no good; and they have no comfort in life. Every man should do the will of God, and then every man would be happy.

17. *For if I do this thing willingly.* If I preach so as to show that my heart is in it; that I am not compelled. If I pursue such a course as to show that I prefer it to all other employments. If Paul took a compensation for his services, he could not well do this; if he did not, he showed that his heart was in it, and that he preferred the work to all others. Even though he had been in a manner *compelled* to engage in that work, yet he *so* acted *in* the work as to show that it had his hearty preference. This was done by his submitting to voluntary self-denials and sacrifices in order to spread the Saviour's name. ¶ *I have a reward.* I shall meet with the approbation of my Lord, and shall obtain the reward in the world to come, which is promised to those who engage heartily, and laboriously, and successfully in turning sinners to God; Prov. xi. 30; Dan. xii. 3; Mat. xiii. 43; xxv. 21—23; James v. 20. ¶ *But if against my will* (ἄκων). If under a necessity (ver. 16); if by the command of another (*Grotius*); if I do it by the fear of punishment, or by any strong necessity which is laid on me. ¶ *A dispensation* of the gospel *is committed unto me.* I am intrusted with (πεπίστευμαι) this dispensation, office, economy (οἰκονομίαν) of the gospel. It has been laid upon me; I have been called to it; I *must* engage in this work; and if I do it from mere compulsion or in such a way that my will shall not acquiesce in it, and concur with it, I shall have no distinguished reward. The work *must* be done; I *must* preach the gospel; and it becomes me so to do it as to show that my heart and will entirely concur; that it is not a matter of compulsion, but of choice. This he proposed to do by so denying himself, and so foregoing comforts which he might lawfully enjoy, and so subjecting himself to perils and toils in preaching the gospel, as to show that his heart was *in* the work, and that he truly loved it

18 What is my reward then? *Verily* that, when I preach the gospel, I may make the gospel of Christ without charge; that I abuse not my power in the gospel.

19 For though I be free from all *men*, yet have I made myself

18. *What is my reward then?* What is the source of my reward? or what is there in my conduct that will show that I am entitled to reward? What is there that will demonstrate that my heart is in the work of the ministry; that I am free and voluntary, and that I am not urged by mere necessity? Though I have been called by miracle, and though necessity is laid upon me, so that I cannot *but* preach the gospel, yet how shall I so do it as to make it proper for God to reward me as a voluntary agent? Paul immediately states the circumstance that showed that he was entitled to the reward, and that was, that he denied himself, and was willing to forego his lawful enjoyments, and even his rights, that he might make the gospel without charge. ¶ *I may make the gospel of Christ without charge.* Without expense to those who hear it. I will support myself by my own labour, and will thus show that I am not urged to preaching by mere "necessity," but that I love it. Observe here, (1.) That Paul did not give up a support because he was not entitled to it. (2.) He does not say that it would be well or advisable for others to do it. (3.) It is right, and well for a man, if he chooses, and can do it, to make the gospel without charge, and to support himself. (4.) All that *this* case proves is, that it would be proper only where a "necessity" was laid on a man, as it was on Paul; when he could not otherwise show that his heart was in the work, and that he was voluntary and loved it. (5.) This passage cannot be urged *by a people* to prove that ministers ought not to have a support. Paul says they have a *right* to it. A man may forego a right if he pleases. He may *choose* not to urge it; but no one can demand of him that he should not urge it; much less have they a *right* to demand that he should give up *his* rights. (6.) It is best in general that those who hear the gospel should contribute to its support. It is not only equal and right, but it is best for them. We generally set very little value on that which costs us nothing; and the very way to make the gospel contemptible is, to have it preached by those who are supported by the state, or by their own labour in some other department: or by men who neither by their talents, their learning, nor their industry have any claim to a support. All ministers are not like Paul. They have neither been called as he was; nor have they his talent, his zeal, or his eloquence. Paul's example then should not be urged as an authority for a people to withhold from their pastor what is his due; nor, because Paul *chose* to forego his rights, should people now *demand* that a minister should devote his time, and health, and life to their welfare for naught. ¶ *That I abuse not my power in the gospel.* Paul had a right to a support. This power he might urge. But to urge it in his circumstances would be a hinderance of the gospel. And to do that would be to abuse his power, or to pervert it to purposes for which it was never designed.

19. *For though I be free.* I am a freeman. I am under obligation to none. I am not bound to give them my labours, and at the same time to toil for my own support. I have claims like others, and could urge them; and no man could demand that I should give myself to a life of servitude, and comply with their prejudices and wishes, as if I were *a slave*, in order to their conversion; comp. ver. 1; Notes, chap. vi. 12. ¶ *From all* men (ἐκ πάντων). This may either refer to all *persons* or to all *things*. The word *men* is not in the original. The connection, however, seems to fix the signification to *persons*. "I am a freeman. And although I have conducted like a slave, yet it has been done voluntarily." ¶ *I have made myself the servant of all.* Greek, "I

servant [a] unto all, that I might gain the more.

20 And unto the Jews [b] I became as a Jew, that I might gain the Jews; to them that are under the law, as under the law, that I might gain them that are under the law;

a Rom.1.14; Gal.5.13. *b* Acts 16.3; 21. 23—26.

have *enslaved myself* (ἐμαυτὸν ἐδούλωσα) unto all." That is, (1.) I *labour* for them, or in their service, and to promote their welfare. (2.) I do it, as the slave does, without reward or hire. I am not paid for it, but submit to the toil, and do it without receiving pay. (3.) Like the slave who wishes to gratify his master, or who is compelled from the necessity of the case, I comply with the prejudices, habits, customs, and opinions of others as far as I can with a good conscience. The *slave* is subject to the master's will. That will must be obeyed. The whims, prejudices, caprices of the master must be submitted to, even if they are *mere* caprice, and wholly unreasonable. So Paul says that he had voluntarily put himself into this condition, a condition making it necessary for him to suit himself to the opinions, prejudices, caprices, and feelings of all men, so far as he could do it with a good conscience, in order that he might save them. We are not to understand nere that Paul embraced any opinions which were false in order to do this, or that he submitted to any thing which is morally wrong. But he complied with their customs, and habits, and feelings, as far as it could lawfully be done. He did not needlessly offend them, or run counter to their prejudices. ¶ *That I might gain the more.* That I might gain more to Christ; that I might be the means of saving more souls. What a noble instance of self-denial and true greatness is here! How worthy of religion! How elevated the conduct! How magnanimous, and how benevolent! No man would do this who had not a greatness of intellect that would rise above narrow prejudices; and who had not a nobleness of heart that would seek at personal sacrifice the happiness of all men. It is said that not a few early Christians, in illustration of this principle of conduct, actually sold themselves into slavery in order that they might have access to and benefit slaves, an act to which nothing would prompt a man but the religion of the cross; comp. Note, Rom. i. 14.

20. *And unto the Jews.* In this verse, and the two following, Paul states more at length the conduct which he had exhibited, and to which he refers in ver. 19. He had shown this conduct to all classes of men. He had preached much to his own countrymen, and had evinced these principles there. ¶ *I became as a Jew.* I complied with their rites, customs, prejudices, as far as I could with a good conscience. I did not needlessly offend them. I did not attack and oppose their views, when there was no danger that my conduct should be mistaken. For a full illustration of Paul's conduct in this respect, and the principles which influenced him, see Notes on Acts xvi. 3; xviii. 18; xxi. 21 –27; xxiii. 1—6. ¶ *To those that are under the law.* This I understand as another form of saying that he conformed to the rites, customs, and even prejudices of the Jews. The phrase "under the law" means undoubtedly the law of Moses; and probably he here refers particularly to those Jews who lived in the land of Judea, as being more *immediately* and *entirely* under the law of Moses, than those who lived among the Gentiles. ¶ *As under the law.* That is, I conformed to their rites and customs as far as I could do it. I did not violate them unnecessarily. I did not disregard them for the purpose of offending them; nor refuse to observe them when it could be done with a good conscience. There can be no doubt that Paul, when he was in Judea, submitted himself to the laws, and lived in conformity with them. ¶ *That I might gain.* That I might obtain their confidence and affection. That I might not outrage their feelings, excite their prejudices, and provoke them to anger; and that I might thus have access to their

21 To them that are without law, as without law, (being not [a] without law to God, but under the law to Christ,) that I might gain them that are without law.
22 To the weak [b] became I as

a chap.7.22. *b* Rom.15.1; 2Cor.11.29.

minds, and be the means of converting them to the Christian faith.

21. *To them that are without law* To the Gentiles, who have not the law of Moses; see Note, Rom. ii. 12, 14. ¶ *As without law.* Not practising the peculiar rites and ceremonies enjoined in the law of Moses. Not insisting on them, or urging them: but showing that the *obligation* to those rites had been done away; and that they were not binding, though when among the Jews I might still continue to observe them; see Notes, Acts xv.; and the argument of Paul in Gal. ii. 11—18. I neglected the ceremonial precepts of the Mosaic law, when I was with those who had not *heard* of the law of Moses, or those who did not observe them, because I knew that the binding obligation of these ceremonial precepts had ceased. I did not, therefore, *press* them upon the Gentiles, nor did I superstitiously and publicly practise them. In all this, Paul has reference only to those things which he regarded as in themselves *indifferent*, and not a matter of conscience; and his purpose was not needlessly to excite the prejudice or the opposition of the world. Nothing is ever gained by *provoking* opposition for the mere sake of opposition. Nothing tends more to hinder the gospel than that. In all things of *conscience* and *truth* a man should be firm, and should lose his life rather than abandon either; in all things of indifference, of mere custom, of prejudice, he should yield, and accomodate himself to the modes of thinking among men, and adapt himself to their views, feelings, and habits of life, that he may win them to Christ. ¶ *Being not without law to God.* Not regarding myself as being *absolutely* without law, or as being freed from obligation to obey God. Even in all this, I endeavoured so to live as that it might be seen that I felt myself bound by law to God. I was not a despiser, and contemner, and neglector of *law as such*, but only regarded myself as not bound by the peculiar ceremonial law of Moses. This is an instance of Paul's conscientiousness. He would not leave room to have it supposed for a moment that he disregarded all law. He was bound to God by law; and in the conduct to which he was referring he felt that he was obeying *him*. He was bound by higher law than those ceremonial observances which were now to be done away. This passage would destroy all the refuges of the Antinomians. Whatever privileges the gospel has introduced, it has not set us free from the restraints and obligations of law. That is binding still; and no man is at liberty to disregard the moral law of God. Christ came to magnify, strengthen, and to honour the law, not to destroy it. ¶ *But under the law to Christ.* Bound by the law enjoined by Christ; under the law of affectionate gratitude and duty to him. I obeyed his commands; followed his instructions; sought his honour; yielded to his will. In this he would violate none of the rules of the moral law. And he here intimates, that his grand object was to yield obedience to the law of the Saviour, and that this was the governing purpose of his life. And this *would* guide a man right. In doing this, he would never violate any of the precepts of the moral law, for Christ obeyed them, and enjoined their observance. He would never feel that he was without law to God, for Christ obeyed God, and enjoined it on all. He would never feel that religion came to set him free from law, or to authorize licentiousness; for its grand purpose and aim is to make men holy, and to bind them every where to the observance of the pure law of the Redeemer.

[Believers are "delivered from the law" as a covenant of works. They do not seek to us

weak, that I might gain the weak; I [a] am made all things to all *men*, that [b] I might by all means save some.

23 And this I do for the gospel's sake, that I might be partaker thereof with *you*.

a chap.10.33. *b* Rom.11.14.

justified by it, neither can it condemn them. Still the authority of Christ binds them to regard it as a rule of life, or directory of conduct. Thus they are "not without law to God, being under the law to Christ" See the Supplementary Notes on Rom. vii.]

22. *To the weak*; see Note, Rom. xv. 1. To those weak in faith; scrupulous in regard to certain observances; whose consciences were tender and unenlightened, and who would be offended even by things which might be in themselves lawful. He did not lacerate their feelings, and run counter to their prejudices, for the mere sake of doing it. ¶ *Became I as weak.* I did not shock them. I complied with their customs. I conformed to them in my dress, habits, manner of life, and even in the services of religion. I abstained from food which *they* deemed it their duty to abstain from; and where, if I had partaken of it, I should have offended them. Paul did not do this to gratify himself, or them, but to do them good. And Paul's example should teach us not to make it the main business of life to gratify ourselves: and it should teach us not to lacerate the feelings of others; not to excite their prejudices needlessly; not to offend them where it will do no good. If truth offends men, we cannot help it. But in matters of ceremony, and dress, and habits, and customs, and forms, we should be willing to conform to them, as far as can be done, and for the sole purpose of saving their souls. ¶ *I am made all things to all* men. I *become* all things; that is, I accommodate myself to them in all things, so far as can be done with a good conscience. ¶ *That I might by all means* (πάντως). That I might use every possible endeavour that some at least might be saved. It is implied here that the opposition to the gospel was everywhere great; that men were reluctant to embrace it; that the great mass were going to ruin, and that Paul was willing to make the highest possible exertions, to deny himself, and practise every innocent art, that he might save *a few at least* out of the innumerable multitudes that were going to death and hell. It follows from this, (1.) That men are in danger of ruin. (2.) We should make an effort to save men. We should deny ourselves, and give ourselves to toil and privation, that we may save some at least from ruin. (3.) The doctrine of universal salvation is not true. If it were, what use or propriety would there have been in these efforts of Paul? If *all* were to be saved, why should he deny himself, and labour, and toil, to save "SOME?" Why should a man make a constant effort to save *a few at least*, if he well knew that *all* were to be saved? Assuredly Paul did not *know* or believe that all men would be saved; but if the doctrine is true, he would have been quite as likely to have known it as its modern advocates and defenders.

23. *For the gospel's sake.* That it may be advanced, and may be successful. ¶ *That I might be partaker thereof with* you. You hope to be saved. You regard yourselves as Christians; and I wish to give evidence also that *I* am a Christian, and that I shall be admitted to heaven to partake of the happiness of the redeemed. This he did, by so denying himself as to give evidence that he was truly actuated by Christian principles.

24. *Know ye not*, &c. In the remainder of this chapter, Paul illustrates the general sentiment on which he had been dwelling—the duty of practising self-denial for the salvation of others—by a reference to the well known games which were celebrated near Corinth. Throughout the chapter, his object had been to show that in declining to receive a support for preaching, he had done it, not because he was conscious that he had no claim

24 Know ye not that they which run in a race run all, but one receiveth a prize? So run, [a] that ye may obtain.

a Phil.2 16; 3.14; 1Tim.6.12; 2Tim.2.5.

to it, but because by doing it he could better advance the salvation of men, the furtherance of the gospel, and in his peculiar case (ver. 16, 17) could obtain better evidence, and furnish to others better evidence that he was actuated by a sincere desire to honour God in the gospel. He had denied himself. He had voluntarily submitted to great privations. He had had a great object in view in doing it. And he now says, that in the well known athletic games at Corinth, the same thing was done by the *racers* (ver. 24), and by *wrestlers*, or *boxers;* ver. 25. If *they* had done it, for objects so comparatively unimportant as the attainment of an *earthly* garland, assuredly it was proper for him to do it to obtain a crown which should never fade away. This is one of the most beautiful, appropriate, vigorous, and bold illustrations that can anywhere be found; and is a striking instance of the force with which the most vigorous and self-denying efforts of Christians can be vindicated, and can be *urged* by a reference to the conduct of men in the affairs of this life. By the phrase "know ye not," Paul intimates that those games to which he alludes were well known to them, and that they must be familiar with their design, and with the manner in which they were conducted. The games to which the apostle alludes were celebrated with extraordinary pomp and splendour, every fourth year, on the isthmus which joined the Peloponnesus to the main land, and on a part of which the city of Corinth stood. There were in Greece four species of games,—the Pythian, or Delphic; the Isthmian, or Corinthian; the Nemean, and the Olympic. On these occasions persons were assembled from all parts of Greece, and the time during which they continued was devoted to extraordinary festivity and amusement. The Isthmian or Corinthian games were celebrated in the narrow part of the Isthmus of Corinth, to the north of the city, and were doubtless the games to which the apostle more particularly alluded, though the games in each of the places were substantially of the same nature, and the same illustration would in the main apply to all. The Nemean games were celebrated at *Nemœa*, a town of Argolis, and were instituted by the Argives in honour of Archemorus, who died by the bite of a serpent, but were renewed by Hercules. They consisted of horse and foot races, of boxing, leaping, running, &c. The conqueror was at first rewarded with a crown of olive, afterwards of green parsley. They were celebrated every third, or, according to others, every fifth year. The *Pythian* games were celebrated every four years at Delphi, in Phocis, at the foot of mount Parnassus, where was the seat of the celebrated Delphic oracle. These games were of the same character substantially as those celebrated in other places, and attracted persons not only from other parts of Greece, but from distant countries; see Travels of Anacharsis, vol. ii. pp. 375—418. The *Olympic* games were celebrated in Olympia, a town of Elis, on the southern bank of the Alphias river, on the western part of the Peloponnesus. They were on many accounts the most celebrated of any in Greece. They were said to have been instituted by Hercules, who planted a grove called *Altis*, which he dedicated to Jupiter. They were attended not only from all parts of Greece, but from the most distant countries. These were celebrated every fourth year; and hence, in Grecian chronology, a period of four years was called an Olympiad; see Anacharsis, vol. iii. 434, seq. It thus happened that in one or more of these places there were games celebrated every year, to which no small part of the inhabitants of Greece were attracted. Though the apostle probably had *particular* reference to the *Isthmian* games celebrated in the vicinity of Corinth, yet his illustration is applicable to them all; for in all the exercises were nearly the same. They consisted chiefly in leaping, running, throwing the discus or quoit, boxing, wrestling, and were expressed in the following line :—

'Αλμά, ποδωκείην, δίσκον, ἄκοντα, πάλην,

leaping, running, throwing the quoit, darting, wrestling. Connected with these were also, sometimes, other exercises, as races of chariots, horses, &c. The apostle refers to but *two* of these exercises in his illustration. ¶ *They which run.* This was one of the principal exercises at the games. Fleetness or swiftness was regarded as an extraordinary virtue; and great pains were taken in order to excel in this. Indeed they regarded it so highly that those who prepared themselves for it thought it worth while to use means to burn their spleen, because it was believed to be a hinderance to them, and to retard them in the race. Rob. Cal. Homer tells us that swiftness was one of the most excellent endowments with which a man can be blessed.

"No greater honour e'er has been attain'd,
Than what strong hands or nimble feet have
gain'd."

One reason why this was deemed so valuable an attainment among the Greeks, was, that it fitted men eminently for war as it was then conducted. It enabled them to make a sudden and unexpected onset, or a rapid retreat. Hence the character which Homer constantly gives of Achilles is, that he was swift of foot. And thus David, in his poetical lamentations over Saul and Jonathan, takes special notice of this qualification of theirs, as fitting them for war.

"They were swifter than eagles,
Stronger than lions." 2 Sam. i. 23.

For these races they prepared themselves by a long course of previous discipline and exercise; and nothing was left undone that might contribute to secure the victory. ¶ *In a race* (ἐν σταδίῳ). In the *stadium.* The *stadium,* or running ground, or place in which the boxers contended, and where races were run. At Olympia the stadium was a causeway 604 feet in length, and of proportionable width. Herod. lib. 2. c. 149. It was surrounded by a terrace, and by the seats of the judges of the games. At one end was fixed the boundary or goal to which they ran. ¶ *Run all.* All run who have entered the lists. Usually there were many racers who contended for the prize. ¶ *But one receiveth the prize.* The victor, and he alone. The prize which was conferred was a wreath of olive at the Olympic games; a wreath of apple at Delphi; of pine at the Isthmian; and of parsley at the Nemean games.—*Addison.* Whatever the prize was, it was conferred on the successful champion on the last day of the games, and with great solemnity, pomp, congratulation, and rejoicing. "Every one thronged to see and congratulate them; their relations, friends, and countrymen, shedding tears of tenderness and joy, lifted them on their shoulders to show them to the crowd, and held them up to the applauses of the whole assembly, who strewed handfuls of flowers over them." Anachar. iii. 448. Nay, at their return home, they rode in a triumphal chariot; the walls of the city were broken down to give them entrance; and in many cities a subsistence was given them out of the public treasury, and they were exempted from taxes. Cicero says that a victory at the Olympic games was not much less honourable than a triumph at Rome see Anachar. iii. 469, and Rob. Cal. art. *Race.* When Paul says that the one receives the prize, he does not mean to say that there will be the same small proportion among those who shall enter into heaven, and among Christians. But his idea is, that as *they* make an effort to obtain the prize, so should we; as many who strive for it then lose it, it is possible that we may; and that therefore we should strive for the crown, and make an effort for it, *as if* but one out of many could obtain it. This, he says, was the course which he pursued; and it shows, in a most striking manner, the fact that an effort *may* be made, and *should* be made to enter into heaven. ¶ *So run, that ye may*

25 And every man that striveth for the mastery is temperate in all things. Now they *do it* to obtain a corruptible crown; but we an incorruptible.[a]

a 2 Tim.4.8; James 1.12; 1 Pet.5.4; Rev.2.10; 3.11.

---

obtain. So run in the Christian race, that you may obtain the prize of glory, the crown incorruptible. So live; so deny yourselves; so make constant exertion, that you may not fail of that prize, the crown of glory, which awaits the righteous in heaven; comp. Heb. xii. 1. Christians may do this when (1.) They give themselves wholly to God, and make this the grand business of life; (2.) "When they lay aside every weight" (Heb. xii. 1); and renounce all sin and all improper attachments; (3.) When they do not allow themselves to be *diverted* from the object, but keep the goal constantly in view; (4.) When they do not flag, or grow weary in their course; (5.) When they deny themselves; and (6.) When they keep their eye fully fixed on Christ (Heb. xii. 2) as their example and their strength, and on heaven as the end of their race, and on the crown of glory as their reward.

25. *And every man that striveth for the mastery* (ὁ ἀγωνιζόμενος). That *agonizes;* that is, that is engaged in the exercise of *wrestling, boxing,* or pitching the bar or quoit; comp. Note, Luke xiii. 24. The sense is, every one who endeavours to obtain a victory in these athletic exercises. ¶ *Is temperate in all things.* The word which is rendered "is temperate" (ἐγκρατεύεται) denotes *abstinence* from all that would excite, stimulate, and ultimately enfeeble; from wine, from exciting and luxurious living, and from licentious indulgences. It means that they did all they could to make the body vigorous, active, and supple. They pursued a course of entire temperate living; comp. Acts xxiv. 25; 1 Cor. vii. 9; Gal. v. 23; 2 Pet. i. 6. It relates not only to indulgences unlawful in themselves, but to abstinence from many things that were regarded as *lawful,* but which were believed to render the body weak and effeminate. The phrase "in all things" means that this course of temperance or abstinence was not confined to one thing, or to one class of things, but to every kind of food and drink, and every indulgence that had a tendency to render the body weak and effeminate. The preparations which those who propose to contend in these games made is well known; and is often referred to by the classic writers. Epictetus, as quoted by Grotius (in loco), thus speaks of these preparations. "Do you wish to gain the prize at the Olympic games? consider the requisite preparations and the consequence. You must observe a strict regimen; must live on food which is unpleasant; must abstain from all delicacies; must exercise yourself at the prescribed times in heat and in cold; you must drink nothing cool (ψυχρὸν); must take no wine as usual; you must put yourself under a *pugilist,* as you would under a physician, and afterwards enter the lists." Epict. chap. xxxv. Horace has described the preparations necessary in the same way.

Qui studet optatam cursu contingere metam
Multa tulit fecitque puer; sudavit, et alsit,
Abstinuit venere et Baccho.

De Arte Poet. 412.

A youth who hopes the Olympic prize to gain,
All arts must try, and every toil sustain;
The extremes of heat and cold must often prove,
And shun the weakening joys of wine and love.

Francis.

¶ *To obtain a corruptible crown.* A garland, diadem, or civic wreath, that must soon fade away. The garland bestowed on the victor was made of olive, pine, apple, laurel, or parsley. That would soon lose its beauty and fade; of course, it could be of little value. Yet we see how eagerly they sought it; how much self-denial those who entered the lists would practice to obtain it; how long they would deny themselves of the common pleasures of life that they might be successful. So much *temperance* would heathens practise to obtain a fading wreath of laurel, pine, or parsley

Learn hence, (1.) The duty of denying ourselves to obtain a far more valuable reward, the incorruptible crown of heaven. (2.) The duty of all Christians who strive for that crown to be temperate in all things. If the heathens practised temperance to obtain a fading laurel, should not we to obtain one that never fades? (3.) How much *their* conduct puts to shame the conduct of many professing Christians and Christian ministers. *They* set such a value on a civic wreath of pine or laurel, that they were willing to deny themselves, and practise the most rigid abstinence. *They* knew that indulgence in WINE and in luxurious living unfitted them for the struggle and for victory; *they* knew that it enfeebled their powers, and weakened their frame; and, like men intent on an object dear to them, they abstained wholly from these things, and embraced the principles of *total abstinence.* Yet how many professed Christians, and Christian ministers, though striving for the crown that fadeth not away, indulge in wine, and in the filthy, offensive, and disgusting use of tobacco; and in luxurious living, and in habits of indolence and sloth! How many there are that WILL not give up these habits, though they know that they are enfeebling, injurious, offensive, and destructive to religious comfort and usefulness. Can a man be truly in earnest in his professed religion; can he be a sincere Christian, who is not willing to abandon any thing and every thing that will tend to impair the vigour of his mind, and weaken his body, and make him a stumbling-block to others? (4.) The value of *temperance* is here presented in a very striking and impressive view. When even the heathens wished to accomplish any thing that demanded skill, strength, power, vigour of body, they saw the necessity of being temperate, and they were so. And this *proves* what all experiment has proved, that if men wish to *accomplish* much, they must be temperate. It *proves* that men can do *more* without intoxicating drink than they can with it. The example of these Grecian *Athletae*—their wrestlers, boxers, and racers, is *against* all the farmers, and mechanics, and seamen, and day-labourers, and *gentlemen,* and *clergymen,* and *lawyers,* who plead that stimulating drink is necessary to enable them to bear cold and heat, and toil and exposure. A little *experience* from men like the Grecian wrestlers, who had something that they wished to do, is much better than a great deal of philosophy and sophistical reasoning from men who *wish* to drink, and to find some argument for drinking that shall be a *salvo* to their consciences. Perhaps the world has furnished no stronger argument in favour of *total abstinence* than the example of the Grecian *Athletae.* It is certain that their example, the example of men who wished to accomplish much by bodily vigour and health, is an effectual and irrefragable argument against all those who plead that stimulating drinks are desirable or necessary in order to increase the vigour of the bodily frame. ¶ *But we.* We Christians. ¶ *An incorruptible.* An incorruptible, an unfading crown. The blessings of heaven that shall be bestowed on the righteous are often represented under the image of a crown or diadem; a crown that is unfading, and eternal; 2 Tim. iv. 8; James i. 12; 1 Pet. v. 4. Rev. ii. 10; iii. 11; iv. 4. The doctrine here taught is, the necessity of making an effort to secure eternal life. The apostle never thought of entering heaven by indolence, or by inactivity. He urged, by every possible argument, the necessity of making an exertion to secure the rewards of the just. His *reasons* for this effort are many. Let a few be pondered. (1.) The work of salvation is difficult. The thousand obstacles arising, the love of sin, and the opposition of Satan and of the world, are in the way. (2.) The *danger* of losing the crown of glory is great. Every moment exposes it to hazard, for at any moment we may die. (3.) The danger is not only great, but it is *dreadful.* If any thing should arouse man, it should be the apprehension of eternal damnation and everlasting wrath. (4.) Men in this life, in the games of Greece, in the

26 I therefore so run, not as uncertainly; so fight I, not as one that beateth the air:
27 But I [a] keep under my body, and bring *it* into subjection; lest that by any means, when I have preached to others, I myself should be a cast-away.

a Rom.8.13.

career of ambition, in the pursuit of pleasure and wealth, make immense efforts to obtain the fading and perishing object of their desires. Why should not a man be willing to make *as great* efforts at least to secure eternal glory? (5.) The value of the interest at stake. Eternal happiness is before those who will embrace the offers of life. If a man should be influenced by any thing to make an effort, should it not be by the prospect of eternal glory? What *should* influence him if this should not?

26. *I therefore so run.* In the Christian race; in my effort to obtain the prize, the crown of immortality. I exert myself to the utmost, that I may not fail of securing the crown. ¶ *Not as uncertainly* (οὐκ ἀδήλως). This word occurs no where else in the New Testament. It usually means, in the classic writers, *obscurely.* Here it means that he did not run as not knowing to what object he aimed. "I do not run at hap-hazard; I do not exert myself for naught; I know at what I aim, and I keep my eye fixed on the object; I have the goal and the crown in view." Probably also the apostle intended to convey this idea, "I so live and act that I am *sure* of obtaining the crown. I make it a great and grand point of my life *so* to live that there may be no room for doubt or hesitancy about this matter. I believe it *may* be obtained; and that by a proper course there may be a constant certainty of securing it; and I so LIVE." O how happy and blessed would it be if all Christians thus lived! How much doubt, and hesitancy, and despondency would it remove from many a Christian's mind! And yet it is morally certain that if every Christian were to be only *as* anxious and careful as were the ancient Grecian wrestlers and racers in the games, they would have the undoubted assurance of gaining the prize. Doddridge and Macknight, however, render this "as not out of view;" or as not distinguished; meaning that the apostle was not *unseen,* but that he regarded himself as constantly in the view of the judge, the Lord Jesus Christ. I prefer the other interpretation, however, as best according with the connection and with the proper meaning of the word. ¶ *So fight I* (οὕτω πυκτεύω). This word is applied to the *boxers,* or the pugilists, in the Grecian games. The exercise of boxing, or *fighting* with the fist, was a part of the entertainment with which the *enlightened* nations of Greece delighted to amuse themselves. ¶ *Not as one that beateth the air.* The *phrase* here is taken from the habits of the pugilists or boxers, who were accustomed, before entering the lists, to exercise their limbs with the gauntlet, in order to acquire greater skill and dexterity. There was also, before the real contest commenced, a *play* with their fists and weapons, by way of show or bravado, which was called σκιᾶμαχία, a mock-battle, or a fighting the air. The phrase also is applicable to a *missing the aim,* when a blow was struck in a real struggle, and when the adversary would elude the blow, so that it would be spent in the empty air. This last is the idea which Paul means to present. He did not miss his aim; he did not exert himself and spend his strength for naught. Every blow that he struck *told;* and he did not waste his energies on that which would produce no result. He did not strive with rash, ill-advised, or uncertain blows; but all his efforts were directed, with good account, to the grand purpose of subjugating his enemy—sin, and the corrupt desires of the flesh—and bringing every thing into captivity to God. Much may be learned from this. Many an effort of Christians is merely beating the air. The energy is expended for naught. There is a want of wisdom, or skill, or perseverance;

there is a failure of plan; or there is a mistake in regard to what *is* to be done, and what should be done. There is often among Christians very little *aim* or object; there is no *plan;* and the efforts are wasted, scattered, inefficient efforts; so that, at the close of life, many a man may say that he has spent his ministry or his Christian course mainly, or entirely, *in beating the air.* Besides, many a one sets up a man of straw, and fights that. He *fancies* error and heresy in others, and opposes that. He becomes a *heresy-hunter;* or he opposes some irregularity in religion that, if left alone, would die of itself; or he fixes all his attention on some minor evil, and devotes his life to the destruction of that alone. When death comes, he may have never struck a blow at one of the *real* and dangerous enemies of the gospel; and the simple record on the tombstone of many a minister and many a private Christian might be, "Here lies one who spent his life in beating the air."

27. *But I keep under my body* (ὑπωπιάζω). This word occurs in the New Testament only here and in Luke xviii. 5, "Lest by her continual coming she *weary* me." The word is derived probably from ὑπώπιον, the part of the face *under the eye* (*Passow*), and means properly, to strike under the eye, either with the fist or the cestus, so as to render the part livid, or as we say, black and blue; or as is vulgarly termed, to give any one a black eye. The word is derived, of course, from the athletic exercises of the Greeks. It then comes to mean, *to treat any one with harshness, severity,* or *cruelty;* and thence also, so to treat any evil inclinations or dispositions; or to subject one's-self to mortification or self-denial, or to a severe and rigid discipline, that all the corrupt passions might be removed. The word here means, that Paul made use of all possible means to subdue his corrupt and carnal inclinations; to show that he was not under the dominion of evil passions, but was wholly under the dominion of the gospel. ¶ *And bring it into subjection.* (δουλαγωγῶ). This word properly means, to reduce to servitude or slavery; and probably was usually applied to the act of subduing an enemy, and leading him captive from the field of battle; as the captives in war were regarded as slaves It then means, effectually and totally to subdue, to conquer, to reduce to bondage and subjection. Paul means by it, the purpose to obtain a complete *victory* over his corrupt passions and propensities, and a design to gain the mastery over all his natural and evil inclinations. ¶ *Lest that by any means;* Note, ver. 22. Paul designed to make every possible effort to be saved. He did not *mean* to be lost, but he *meant* to be saved. He felt that there was danger of being deceived and lost; and he *meant* by some means to have evidence of piety that would abide the trial of the day of judgment. ¶ *When I have preached to others.* Doddridge renders this, "lest after having served as a herald to others, I should myself be disapproved;" and supposes that there was allusion in this to the Grecian *herald,* whose business it was to proclaim the conditions of the games, to display the prizes, &c. In this interpretation, also, Macknight, Rosenmüller, Koppe, and most of the modern interpreters agree. They suppose, therefore, that the allusion to the games is carried through all this description. But there is this difficulty in this interpretation, that it represents the apostle as *both* a herald and a contender in the games, and thus leads to an inextricable confusion of metaphor. Probably, therefore, this is to be taken in the usual sense of the word *preaching* in the New Testament; and the apostle here is to be understood as *dropping* the metaphor, and speaking in the usual manner. He had preached to others, to many others. He had proclaimed the gospel far and near He had preached to many thousands, and had been the means of the conversion of thousands. The contest, the agony, the struggle in which he had been engaged, was that of preaching the gospel in the most effectual manner. And yet he felt that there was a *possibility* that even after all this he might be lost.

[The apostle's language seems not to imply any doubt in regard to his own final perseverance, a matter concerning which in numerous other places he expresses the most decided assurance; but points rather to the *means* by which that perseverance was secured, and without which it could not possibly be attained. "Whom God predestinates he calls, whom he calls he justifies, and whom he justifies he glorifies." Not a link in this golden chain can be broken. But God fulfils his purpose not *without* exertion and self-denial but *by means* of these. And the means are involved in the decree, as well as the end. Paul therefore, "ran, and fought, and kept his body under," *that* in the end he might not be disapproved. *It is certain*, that all who neglect the diligent use of means, under whatever doctrinal notions they may shield themselves, shall, in the day of trial, be rejected, as base and counterfeit metal. If Paul himself neglected these, *even he* should be "cast away!"]

¶ *I myself should be a cast-away.* This word (ἀδόκιμος) is taken from *bad metals*, and properly denotes those which will not bear the *test* that is applied to them; that are found to be base and worthless, and are therefore rejected and cast away. The apostle had subjected himself to trials. He had given himself to self-denial and toil; to persecution and want; to perils, and cold, and nakedness, and hunger. He had done this, among other things, to give his religion a fair trial, to see whether it would bear all these tests; as metal is cast into the fire to see whether it is genuine, or is base and worthless. In doing this, he had endeavoured to subdue his corrupt propensities, and bring everything into captivity to the Redeemer, that it might be found that he was a sincere, and humble, and devoted Christian. Many have supposed that the word "cast-away" here refers to those who had entered the lists, and had contended, and who had then been examined as to the manner in which they had conducted the contest, and had been found to have departed from the rules of the games, and who were then rejected. But this interpretation is too artificial and unnatural. The simple idea of Paul is, that he was afraid that he should be disapproved, rejected, cast off; that it would appear, after all, that he had no religion, and would then be cast away as unfit to enter into heaven.

From the many remarks which might be made from this interesting chapter, we may select the following:

1st. We see the great anxiety which Paul had to save souls. This was his grand purpose; and for this he was willing to deny himself and to bear any trial.

2d. We should be kind to others; we should not needlessly offend them; we should conform to them, as far as it can be done consistently with Christian integrity.

3d. We should make an effort to be saved. O, if men made such exertions to obtain a corruptible crown, how much greater should we make to obtain one that fadeth not away!

4th. Ministers, like others, are in danger of losing their souls. If *Paul* felt this danger, who is there among the ministers of the cross who should not feel it? If Paul was not safe, who is? [See the Supplementary Note on ver. 27.]

5th. The fact that a man has preached to many is no certain evidence that he will be saved, ver. 27. Paul had preached to thousands, and yet he felt that after all this there was a possibility that he might be lost.

6th. The fact that a man has been very successful in the ministry is no certain evidence that he will be saved. God converts men; and he may sometimes do it by the instrumentality of those who themselves are deceived, or are deceivers. They may preach much truth; and God may bless that truth, and make *it* the means of saving the soul. There is no conclusive evidence that a man is a Christian simply because he is a successful and laborious preacher, any more than there is that a man is a Christian because he is a good farmer, and because God sends down the rain and the sunshine on his fields. Paul felt that even *his* success was no certain evidence that he would be saved. And if Paul felt thus, who should *not* feel that after the most distinguished success, he may himself be at last a cast-away?

7th. It will be a solemn and awful

CHAPTER X.

MOREOVER, brethren, I would not that ye should be ignorant, how that all our fathers were under [a] the cloud, and [b] all passed through the sea;

a Ex.13.21,22; Num.9.18-22. b Ex.14.19-22,29.

thing for a minister of the gospel, and a *successful* minister, to go down to hell. What more fearful doom can be conceived, than after having led others in the way to life; after having described to them the glories of heaven; after having conducted them to the "sweet fields beyond the swelling flood" of death, he should find himself shut out, rejected, and cast down to hell! What more terrible can be imagined in the world of perdition than the doom of one who was once a minister of God, and once esteemed as a light in the church and a guide of souls, now sentenced to inextinguishable fires, while multitudes saved by him shall have gone to heaven! How fearful is the condition and how solemn the vocation of a minister of the gospel!

8th. Ministers should be solicitous about their personal piety. Paul, one might suppose, might have rested contented with the remarkable manner of his conversion. He might have supposed that that put the matter beyond all possible doubt. But he did no such thing. He felt that it was necessary to have evidence day by day that he was *then* a Christian. Of all men, Paul was perhaps *least* disposed to live on past experience, and to trust to such experience. Of all men, he had perhaps most reason to trust to such experience; and yet how seldom does he refer to it, how little does he regard it! The great question with him was, "Am I *now* a Christian? am I living as a Christian should *now?* am I evincing to others, am I giving to myself daily, constant, growing evidence that I am actuated by the pure principles of the gospel, and that that gospel is the object of my highest preference, and my holiest and constant desire?" O how holy would be the ministry, if all should endeavour every day to live and act for Christ and for souls with as much steadiness and fidelity as did the apostle Paul

CHAPTER X.

IN regard to the design of this chapter commentators have not been agreed. Some have supposed that there is no connection with the preceding, but that this is a digression. The ancient Greek expositors generally, and some of the moderns, as Grotius, supposed that the connection was this: Paul had in the previous chapter described himself as mortifying his flesh, and keeping his body under, that he might gain the prize. In this chapter they suppose that his object is to exhort the Corinthians to do the same; and that in order to do this, he admonishes them not to be lulled into security by the idea of the many spiritual gifts which had been conferred upon them. This admonition he enforces by the example of the Jews, who had been highly favoured also, but who had nevertheless been led into idolatry. This is also the view of Doddridge, Calvin, and others. Macknight regards the chapter as an independent discussion of the three questions, which he supposes had been submitted to Paul: (1.) Whether they might innocently go with their friends into the heathen temples, and partake of the feasts which were there made in honour of the idol. (2.) Whether they might buy and eat meat sold in the markets which had been sacrificed to idols. (3.) Whether, when invited to the houses of the heathens, they might partake of the meat sacrificed to idols, and which was set before them as a common meal.—I regard this chapter as having a very close connection with chap. viii. In the close of chap. viii. (ver. 13), Paul had stated, when examining the question whether it was right to eat meat offered in sacrifice to idols, that the grand principle on which *he* acted, and on which *they* should act, was that of *self-denial.* To illustrate this he employs the ninth chapter, by showing how *he* acted on it in reference to a maintenance; showing that it was this principle that led him to decline a support to which he was really entitled. Having illustrated that, he *returns* in this chapter to the subject which he was discussing in chap. viii.; and the design of this chapter is further to explain and enforce the sentiments advanced there, and to settle some other inquiries pertaining to the same general subject. The *first* point, therefore, on which he insists is, *the danger of relapsing into idolatry*—a danger which would arise should they be in the habit of frequenting the temples of idols, and of partaking of the meats offered in sacrifice; ver. 1—24. Against this he had cautioned them in general, in chap. viii. 7, 9—12. This danger he now sets forth by a variety of illustrations. He first shows them that the Jews had been highly favoured, had been solemnly consecrated to Moses and to God, and had been under the divine protection and guidance (ver. 1—4); yet that this had not kept them from the displeasure of God when they sinned; ver. 5. He shows that notwithstanding their privileges, they had indulged in inordinate desires (ver. 6); that they had become idolaters (ver. 7); that they had been guilty of licentiousness (ver. 8); that they had tempted their leader and guide (ver. 9); that they had murmured (ver. 10); and that, as a consequence of this, many of them had been destroyed. In view of all this, Paul cautions the Corinthians not to be self-confident, or to feel secure; and not to throw themselves in the way of temptation by partaking of the feasts of idolatry; ver. 12—14. This danger he further illustrates (ver. 15, 24) by showing that if they partook of those sacrifices, they in fact became identified with the worshippers of idols. This he proved by showing that in the Christian communion, those who partook of the Lord's supper were identified with Christians (ver. 16, 17); that in the Jewish sacrifices the same thing occurred, and that those who partook of them were regarded as Jews, and as worshippers of the same God with them (ver. 18); and that the same thing must occur, in the nature of the case, by partaking of the sacrifices offered to idols. They were *really* partaking of that which had been offered to *devils;* and against any such participation Paul would solemnly admonish them; ver. 19—22. Going on the supposition, therefore, that there was nothing wrong in itself in partaking of the meat that had been thus killed in sacrifice, yet Paul says (ver. 23), that it was not expedient thus to expose themselves to danger; and that the grand principle should be to seek the comfort and edification of others; ver. 24. Paul thus strongly and decisively admonishes them *not* to enter the temples of idols to partake of those feasts; not to unite with idolaters in their celebration; not to endanger their piety by these temptations.

There were, however, two other questions on the subject which it was important to decide, and which had probably been submitted to him in the letter which they had sent for counsel and advice. The first was, whether it was right to purchase and eat the meat which had been sacrificed, and which was exposed indiscriminately with other meat in the market; ver. 25. To this Paul replies, that as no evil could result from this, as it could not be alleged that they purchased it *as* meat sacrificed to idols, and as all that the earth contained belonged to the Lord, it was not wrong to purchase and to use it. Yet if even this was pointed out to them as having been sacrificed to idols, he then cautioned them to abstain from it; ver. 28. The other question was, whether it was right for them to accept the invitation of a heathen, and to partake of meat then that had been offered in sacrifice; ver. 27. To this a similar answer was returned. The general principle was, that no questions were to be asked in regard to what was set before them; but if the food was expressly pointed out as having been offered in sacrifice, then to partake of it would be regarded as a public recognition of the idol; ver. 28—30. Paul then concludes the discussion by stating the noble rule that is to guide in all this: that every thing is to be done to the glory of God (ver. 31); and that the great effort of the Christian should be so to act in all things as to honour his religion, as not to lead others into sin; ver. 32, 33.

1. *Moreover, brethren.* But, or now (δὲ). This verse, with the following illustrations (ver. 1—4), is properly connected in Paul's argument with the statements which he had made in chap. viii. 8, &c., and is designed to show the danger which would result from their partaking of the feasts that were celebrated in honour of idols. It is not improbable, as Mr. Locke supposes, that the Corinthians might have urged that they were constantly solicited by their heathen friends to attend those feasts; that in their circumstances it was scarcely possible to avoid it; that there could be no danger of their relapsing into idolatry; and their doing so could not be offensive to God, since they were known to be Christians; since they had been baptized, and purified from sin; since they were devoted to his service; since they knew that an idol was nothing in the world; and since they had been so highly favoured, as the people of God, with so many extraordinary endowments, and were so strongly guarded against the possibility of becoming idolaters. To meet these considerations, Paul refers them to the example of the ancient Jews. They also were the people of God. They had been solemnly dedicated to Moses and to God. They had been peculiarly favoured with spiritual food from heaven, and with drink miraculously poured from the rock. Yet notwithstanding this, they had forgotten God, had become idolaters, and had been destroyed. By their example, therefore, Paul would warn the Corinthians against a similar danger. ¶ *I would not that ye should be ignorant.* A large part of the church at Corinth were Gentiles. It could hardly be supposed that they were well informed respecting the ancient history of the Jews. Probably they had read these things in the Old Testament; but they might not have them distinctly in their recollection. Paul brings them distinctly before their minds, as an illustration and an admonition. The sense is, "I would not have you unmindful or forgetful of these things; I would have you recollect this case, and suffer their example to influence your conduct. I would not have you suppose that even a solemn consecration to God and the possession of distinguished tokens of divine favour are a security against the danger of sin, and even apostasy; since the example of the favoured Jews shows that even in such circumstances there is danger." ¶ *How that all our fathers.* That is, the fathers of the Jewish community; the fathers of us who are Jews. Paul speaks here as being himself a Jew, and refers to his own ancestors as such. The word "all" here seems to be introduced to give emphasis to the fact that even those who were destroyed (ver. 5) also had this privilege. It could not be pretended that *they* had not been devoted to God, since *all* of them had been thus consecrated professedly to his service. The entire Jewish community which Moses led forth from Egypt had thus been devoted to him. ¶ *Were under the cloud.* The cloud—the *Shechinah*—the visible symbol of the divine presence and protection that attended them out of Egypt. This went before them by day as a cloud to guide them, and by night it became a pillar of fire to give them light; Ex. xiii. 21, 22. In the dangers of the Jews, when closely pressed by the Egyptians, it went *behind* them, and became dark to the Egyptians, but light to the Israelites, thus constituting a defence; Ex. xiv. 20. In the wilderness, when travelling through the burning desert, it seems to have been expanded over the camp as a covering, and a defence from the intense rays of a burning sun; Num. x. 34, "And the cloud of JEHOVAH was upon them by day;" Num. xiv. 14, "Thy cloud standeth over them." To this fact the apostle refers here. It was a symbol of the divine favour and protection; comp.

2 And were all baptized unto Moses in the cloud and in the sea;

3 And did all eat the same spiritual meat; [a]

[a] Ex.16.15,35; Neh.9.15,20; Ps.78,24,25.

Isa. iv. 5. It was a guide, a shelter, and a defence. The Jewish Rabbins say that "the cloud *encompassed* the camp of the Israelites as a wall encompasses a city, nor could the enemy come near them." Pirke Eleazer, chap. 44, as quoted by Gill. The probability is, that the cloud extended over the whole camp of Israel, and that to those at a distance it appeared as *a pillar*. ¶ *And all passed through the sea.* The Red sea, under the guidance of Moses, and by the miraculous interposition of God; Ex. xiv. 21, 22. This was also a proof of the divine protection and favour, and is so adduced by the apostle. His object is to *accumulate* the evidences of the divine favour to them, and to show that they had as many securities against apostasy as the Corinthians had, on which they so much relied.

2. *And were all baptized.* In regard to the meaning of the word *baptized*, see Note on Mat. iii. 6. We are not to suppose that the rite of baptism, as we understand it, was formally administered by Moses, or by any other person, to the Jews, for there is not the least evidence that any such rite was then known, and the very circumstances here referred to forbid such an interpretation. They were baptized "in the cloud" and "in the sea," and this cannot be understood as a religious rite administered by the hand of man. It is to be remembered that the word *baptism* has two senses—the one referring to the application of water as a religious rite, in whatever mode it is done; and the other the sense of *dedicating, consecrating, initiating into*, or bringing under obligation to. And it is evidently in this latter sense that the word is used here, as denoting that they were *devoted* to Moses as a leader, they were brought under his laws, they became bound to obey him, they were placed under his protection and guidance by the miraculous interposition of God. This was done by the fact that their passing through the sea, and under the cloud, in this manner, brought them under the authority and direction of Moses as a leader, and was a public recognition of their being his followers, and being bound to obey his laws. ¶ *Unto Moses* (εἰς). This is the same preposition which is used in the form of baptism prescribed in Mat. xxviii. 19. See Note on that place. It means that they were thus devoted or dedicated to Moses; they received and acknowledged him as their ruler and guide; they professed subjection to his laws, and were brought under his authority. They were thus *initiated into* his religion, and thus recognised his divine mission, and bound themselves to obey his injunctions.—*Bloomfield.* ¶ *In the cloud.* This cannot be proved to mean that they were enveloped and, as it were, *immersed* in the cloud, for there is no evidence that the cloud thus enveloped them, or that they were immersed in it as a person is in water. The whole account in the Old Testament leads us to suppose that the cloud either passed before them as a pillar, or that it had the same form in the rear of their camp, or that it was suspended over them, and was thus the symbol of the divine protection. It would be altogether improbable that the dark cloud would *pervade* the camp. It would thus embarrass their movements, and there is not the slightest intimation in the Old Testament that it did. Nor is there any probability in the supposition of Dr. Gill and others, that the cloud, as it passed from the rear to the front of the camp, "let down a plentiful rain upon them, whereby they were in such a condition as if they had been all over dipped in water." For, (1.) There is not the slightest intimation of this in the Old Testament (2.) The supposition is contrary to the very design of the cloud. It was not a natural cloud, but was a symbol of the divine presence and protection. It was

not to give rain on the Israelites, or on the land, but it was to guide, and to be an emblem of the care of God. (3.) It is doing violence to the Scriptures to introduce suppositions in this manner without the slightest authority. It is further to be observed, that this supposition does by no means give any aid to the cause of the Baptist after all. In what conceivable sense were they, even on this supposition, *immersed?* Is it *immersion in water* when one is exposed to a shower of rain? We speak of being *sprinkled* or *drenched* by rain, but is it not a violation of all propriety of language to say that a man is *immersed* in a shower? If the supposition, therefore, is to be admitted, that rain fell from the cloud as it passed over the Jews, and that this is meant here by "baptism unto Moses," then it would follow that *sprinkling* would be the mode referred to, since this is the only form that has resemblance to a falling shower. But the supposition is not necessary. Nor is it needful to suppose that water was applied to them at all. The thing itself is improbable; and the whole case is met by the simple supposition that the apostle means that they were initiated in this way into the religion of Moses, recognised his divine mission, and under the cloud became his followers and subject to his laws. And if this interpretation is correct, then it follows that the word *baptize* does not of necessity mean to *immerse.* ¶ *And in the sea.* This is another expression that goes to determine the sense of the word *baptize.* The sea referred to here is the Red sea, and the event was the passage through that sea. The fact in the case was, that the Lord caused a strong east wind to blow all night, and made the sea dry land, and the waters were divided (Ex. xiv. 21), and the waters were a wall unto them on the right hand and on the left, Ex. xiv. 22. From this whole narrative it is evident that they passed through the sea without being *immersed* in it. The waters were driven into high adjacent walls for the very purpose that they might pass between them dry and safe. There is the fullest proof that they were not submerged in the water. Dr. Gill supposes that the water stood up above their heads, and that "they seemed to be immersed in it." This might be true; but this is to give up the idea that the word baptize means always to immerse in water, since it is a fact, according to this supposition, that they were *not* thus immersed, but only seemed to be. And all that can be meant, therefore, is, that they were in this manner initiated into the religion of Moses, convinced of his divine mission, and brought under subjection to him as their leader, lawgiver, and guide. This passage is a very important one to prove that the word baptism does not necessarily mean entire immersion in water. It is perfectly clear that neither the cloud nor the waters touched them. "They went through the midst of the sea on *dry* ground." It remains only to be asked whether, if immersion was the only mode of baptism known in the New Testament, the apostle Paul would have used the word not only so as not necessarily to imply that, but as *necessarily* to mean something else?

2. *And did all eat the same spiritual meat.* That is, *manna.* Ex. xvi. 15, 35; Neh. ix. 15, 20. The word *meat* here is used in the old English sense of the word, to denote *food* in general. They lived on *manna.* The word *spiritual* here is evidently used to denote that which was given by the Spirit, or by God; that which was the result of his miraculous gift, and which was not produced in the ordinary way, and which was not the gross food on which men are usually supported. It had an excellency and value from the fact that it was the immediate gift of God, and is thus called "angel's food." Ps. lxxviii. 25. It is called by Josephus "divine and extraordinary food." Ant. iii. 1. In the language of the Scriptures, that which is distinguished for excellence, which is the immediate gift of God, which is unlike that which is gross and of earthly origin, is called *spiritual,* to denote its purity, value, and excellence. Comp. Rom. vii. 14; 1 Cor. iii. 1; xv. 44, 46; Eph. i. 3

4 And did all drink the same spiritual drink; [a] for they drank of that spiritual Rock that [1] followed them: and that Rock was Christ.

[a] Ex.17.6; Num.20.11.

[1] or, *went with.*

The idea of Paul here is, that *all* the Israelites were nourished and supported in this remarkable manner by food given directly by God; that they all had thus the evidence of the divine protection and favour, and were all under his care.

4. *And did all drink the same spiritual drink.* The idea here is essentially the same as in the previous verse, that they had been highly favoured of God, and enjoyed tokens of the divine care and guardianship. That was manifested in the miraculous supply of water in the desert, thus showing that they were under the divine protection, and were objects of the divine favour. There can be no doubt that by "spiritual drink" here, the apostle refers to the water that was made to gush from the rock that was smitten by Moses. Ex. xvii. 6; Num. xx. 11. Why this is called "spiritual" has been a subject on which there has been much difference of opinion. It cannot be because there was any thing peculiar in the nature of the water, for it was evidently real water, fitted to allay their thirst. There is no evidence, as many have supposed, that there was a reference in this to the drink used in the Lord's supper. But it must mean that it was bestowed in a miraculous and supernatural manner; and the word "spiritual" must be used in the sense of supernatural, or that which is immediately given by God. Spiritual blessings thus stand opposed to natural and temporal blessings, and the former denote those which are immediately given by God as an evidence of the divine favour. That the Jews used the word "spiritual" in this manner is evident from the writings of the Rabbins. Thus they called the manna "spiritual food" (Yade Mose in Shemor Rabba, fol. 109. 3); and their sacrifices they called "spiritual bread" (Tzeror Hammor, fol. 93. 2).—*Gill.* The drink, therefore, here referred to was that bestowed in a supernatural manner and as a proof of the divine favour. ¶ *For they drank of that spiritual Rock.* Of the waters which flowed from that Rock. The Rock here is called "spiritual," not from any thing peculiar in the nature of the rock, but because it was the source to them of supernatural mercies, and became thus the emblem and demonstration of the divine favour, and of spiritual mercies conferred upon them by God. ¶ *That followed them.* Margin. *Went with* (ἀκολουθούσης). This evidently cannot mean that the rock itself literally followed them, any more than that they literally drank the rock, for one is as expressly affirmed, if it be taken literally, as the other. But as when it is said they "drank of the rock," it must mean that they drank of the *water* that flowed from the rock; so when it is said that the "rock followed" or accompanied them, it must mean that the *water* that flowed from the rock accompanied them. This figure of speech is common everywhere. Thus the Saviour said (1 Cor. xi. 25), "This cup is the new testament," that is, the *wine* in this cup represents my blood, &c.; and Paul says (1 Cor. xi. 25, 27), "whosoever shall drink this *cup* of the Lord unworthily," that is, the *wine* in the cup, &c., and "as often as ye drink this cup," &c., that is, the wine contained in the cup. It would be absurd to suppose that the rock that was smitten by Moses literally followed them in the wilderness; and there is not the slightest evidence in the Old Testament that it did. Water was twice brought out of a rock to supply the wants of the children of Israel. Once at mount Horeb, as recorded in Ex. xvii. 6, in the wilderness of Sin, in the first year of their departure from Egypt. The second time water was brought from a rock about the time of the death of Miriam at Kadesh, and probably in the fortieth year of their departure from Egypt, Num. xx. 1. It was to the former of these occasions that the apostle evidently refers. In regard

to this we may observe, (1.) That there must have been furnished a large quantity of water to have supplied the wants of more than two millions of people. (2.) It is expressly stated Deut. ix. 21), that "the brook (הנחל, stream, torrent, or river, see Num. xxxiv. 5; Josh. xv. 4, 47; 1 Kings viii. 65; 2 Kings xxiv. 7) descended out of the mount," and was evidently a stream of considerable size. (3.) Mount Horeb was higher than the adjacent country, and the water that thus gushed from the rock, instead of collecting into a pool and becoming stagnant, would flow off in the direction of the sea. (4.) The sea to which it would naturally flow would be the Red sea, in the direction of the Eastern or Elanitic branch of that sea. (5.) The Israelites would doubtless, in their journeyings, be influenced by the natural direction of the water, or would not wander far from it, as it was daily needful for the supply of their wants. (6.) At the end of thirty-seven years we find the Israelites at Ezion-geber, a sea-port on the eastern branch of the Red sea, where the waters probably flowed into the sea; Num. xxxiii. 36. In the fortieth year of their departure from Egypt, they left this place to go into Canaan by the country of Edom, and were immediately in distress again by the want of water. It is thus *probable* that the water from the rock continued to flow, and that it constituted a stream, or river; that it was near their camp all the time till they came to Ezion-geber; and that thus, together with the daily supply of manna, it was a proof of the protection of God, and an emblem of their dependence. If it be said that there is *now* no such stream to be found there, it is to be observed that it is represented as miraculous, and that it would be just as reasonable to look for the daily descent of manna there in quantities sufficient to supply more than two millions of men, as to expect to find the gushing and running river of water. The only question is, whether God *can* work a miracle, and whether there is evidence that he has done it. This is not the place to examine that question. But the evidence is as strong that he wrought this miracle as that he gave the manna, and neither of them is inconsistent with the power, the wisdom, or the benevolence of God. ¶ *And that Rock was Christ.* This cannot be intended to be understood *literally*, for it was not literally true. The rock from which the water flowed was evidently an ordinary rock, a part of mount Horeb; and all that this can mean is, that that rock, with the stream of water thus gushing from it, was a *representation* of the Messiah. The word *was* is thus often used to denote similarity or representation, and is not to be taken literally. Thus, in the institution of the Lord's supper, the Saviour says of the bread, "This *is* my body," that is, it *represents* my body. Thus also of the cup, "This cup *is* the new testament in my blood," that is, it represents my blood, 1 Cor. xi. 24, 25. Thus the gushing fountain of water might be regarded as a representation of the Messiah, and of the blessings which result from him. The apostle does not say that the Israelites knew that this was designed to be a representation of the Messiah, and of the blessings which flow from him, though there is nothing improbable in the supposition that they so understood and regarded it, since all their institutions were probably regarded as typical. But he evidently *does* mean to say that the rock was a vivid and affecting representation of the Messiah; that the Jews *did* partake of the mercies that flow from him; and that even in the desert they were under his care, and had in fact among them a vivid representation of him in some sense corresponding with the emblematic representation of the same favours which the Corinthian and other Christians had in the Lord's supper. This representation of the Messiah, *perhaps*, was understood by Paul to consist in the following things: (1.) Christians, like the children of Israel, are passing through the world as pilgrims, and to them that world is a wilderness—a desert. (2.) They need continued supplies, as the Israelites did, in their

5 But with many of them God was not well pleased; for they were overthrown [a] in the wilderness.

6 Now these things were [1] our examples, to the intent we should not lust after evil things, as they [b] also lusted.

7 Neither be ye idolaters, as *were* some of them; as it is writ-

a Num.14.29-35; 26.64,65; Heb.3.17; Jude 5.

1 *the figures.* b Num.11.4,33,34.

journey. The world, like that wilderness, does not meet their necessities, or supply their wants. (3.) That rock was a striking representation of the fulness of the Messiah, of the abundant grace which he imparts to his people. (4.) It was an illustration of their continued and constant dependence on him for the daily supply of their wants. It should be observed that many expositors understand this literally. Bloomfield translates it, "and they were supplied with drink from the spiritual Rock which followed them, even Christ." So Rosenmüller, Calvin, Glass, &c. In defence of this interpretation, it is said, that the Messiah is often called "a rock" in the Scriptures; that the Jews believe that the "angel of JEHOVAH" who who attended them (Ex. iii. 2, and other places) was the Messiah; and that the design of the apostle was, to show that this *attending Rock*, the Messiah, was the source of all their blessings, and particularly of the water that gushed from the rock. But the interpretation suggested above seems to me to be most natural. The *design* of the apostle is apparent. It is to show to the Corinthians, who relied so much on their privileges, and felt themselves so secure, that the Jews *had the very same privileges*—had the highest tokens of the divine favour and protection, were under the guidance and grace of God, and were partakers constantly of that which adumbrated or typified the Messiah, in a manner as real, and in a form as much fitted to keep up the remembrance of their dependence, as even the bread and wine in the Lord's supper.

5. *But with many of them*, &c. That is, with their conduct. They rebelled and sinned, and were destroyed. The design of the apostle here is, to remind them that although they enjoyed so many privileges, yet they were destroyed; and thus to admonish the Corinthians that *their* privileges did not constitute an absolute security from danger, and that *they* should be cautious against the indulgence of sin. The phrase rendered here "with many" (ἐν τοῖς πλείοσιν) should have been rendered "with most of them," literally "with *the* many; and it means that with the greater part of them God was not well pleased; that is, he was pleased with but few of them. ¶ *Was not well pleased.* Was offended with their ingratitude and rebellion. ¶ *For they were overthrown*, &c. That is, by the pestilence, by wars, or died by natural and usual diseases, so that they did not reach the land of Canaan. But two men of that generation, Caleb and Joshua, were permitted to enter the land of promise; Num. xiv. 29, 30.

6. *Now these things.* The judgments inflicted on them by God for their sins. ¶ *Were our examples.* Greek, *Types* (τύποι). Margin, *Figures.* They were not *designed* to be types of us, but they are to be held up as furnishing an admonition to us, or a warning that we do not sin in the same way. The same God directs our affairs that ordered theirs; and if we sin as they did, we also must expect to be punished, and excluded from the favour of God, and from heaven. ¶ *Lust after evil things.* Desire those things which are forbidden, and which would be injurious. They lusted after flesh, and God granted them their desires, and the consequence was a plague, and the destruction of multitudes; Ex. xi. 4, 31—34. So Paul infers that the Corinthian Christians should not lust after, or desire the meat offered in sacrifice to idols, lest it should lead them also to sin and ruin.

7. *Neither be ye idolaters.* This caution is evidently given in view of the danger to which they would be exposed if they partook of the feasts that were celebrated in honour of idols in their temples. The particular idol-

ten, [a] The people sat down to
eat and drink, and rose up to
play.
8 Neither let us commit fornication, as some [b] of them committed,
and fell in one day three and twenty
thousand.
9 Neither let us tempt Christ,

a Ex.32.6. b Num.25.1—9. c Ex.17.2,7.

atry which is referred to here is, the worship of the golden calf that was made by Aaron; Ex. xxxii. 1—5. ¶ *As it is written;* Ex. xxxii. 6. ¶ *The people sat down to eat and to drink.* To worship the golden calf. They partook of a feast in honour of that idol. I have already observed that it was common to keep a feast in honour of an idol, and that the food which was eaten on such an occasion was mainly the meat which had been offered in sacrifice to it. This instance was particularly to the apostle's purpose, as he was cautioning the Corinthians against the danger of participating in the feasts celebrated in the heathen temples. ¶ *And rose up to play* (παίζειν). The Hebrew word used in Ex. xxxii. 7 (לצחק) means to laugh, to sport, to jest, to mock, to insult (Gen. xxi. 9); and then to engage in dances accompanied with music, in honour of an idol. This was often practised, as the worship of idols was celebrated with songs and dances. This is particularly affirmed of this instance of idol worship (Ex. xxxii. 19); and this was common among ancient idolaters; and this mode of worship was even adopted by David before the ark of the Lord; 2 Sam. vi. 5; 1 Chron. xiii. 8; xv. 29. All that the word "to play" here necessarily implies is, that of choral songs and dances, accompanied with revelry in honour of the idol. It was, however, the fact that such worship was usually accompanied with much licentiousness; but that is not necessarily implied in the use of the word. Most of the oriental dances were grossly indecent and licentious, and the word here *may* be designed to include such indelicacy and licentiousness.

8. *Neither let us commit fornication,* &c. The case referred to here was that of the licentious intercourse with the daughters of Moab, referred to in Num. xxv. 1—9. ¶ *And fell in one day.* Were slain for their sin by the plague that prevailed. ¶ *Three and twenty thousand.* The Hebrew text in Num. xxv. 9, is twenty-four thousand. In order to reconcile these statements, it may be observed that perhaps twenty-three thousand fell directly by the plague, and one thousand were slain by Phinehas and his companions (*Grotius*); or it may be that the number was between twenty-three and twenty-four thousand, and it might be expressed in round numbers by either.—*Macknight.* At all events, Paul has not exceeded the truth. There were *at least* twenty-three thousand that fell, though there might have been more. The *probable* supposition is, that the three and twenty thousand fell immediately by the hand of God in the plague, and the other thousand by the judges; and as Paul's design was particularly to mention the proofs of the immediate divine displeasure, he refers only to those who fell by that, in illustration of his subject.—There was a particular reason for this caution in respect to licentiousness. (1.) It was *common* among all idolaters; and Paul in cautioning them against idolatry, would naturally warn them of this danger. (2.) It was common at Corinth. It was the prevalent vice there. To *Corinthianize* was a term synonymous among the ancients with licentiousness. (3.) So common was this at Corinth, that, as we have seen (see the Introduction), not less than a thousand prostitutes were supported in a single temple there; and the city was visited by vast multitudes of foreigners, among other reasons on account of its facilities for this sin. Christians, therefore, were in a peculiar manner exposed to it; and hence the anxiety of the apostle to warn them against it.

9. *Neither let us tempt Christ,* &c. The word *tempt,* when applied to man, means to present motives or induce-

as some of them also tempted, and were destroyed of serpents. [a]

10 Neither murmur ye, as some of them also murmured, [b] and were destroyed of the destroyer. [c]

11 Now all these things hap-

a Num.21.6. *b* Num.14.2, 29. *c* 2 Sam.24.16.

ments to sin: when used with reference to God, it means to try his patience, to provoke his anger, or to act in such a way as to see how much he will bear, and how long he will endure the wickedness and perverseness of men. The Israelites tempted him, or *tried his patience and forbearance*, by rebellion, murmuring, impatience, and dissatisfaction with his dealings. In what way the Corinthians were in danger of tempting Christ is not known, and can only be conjectured. It may be that the apostle cautions them against exposing themselves to temptation in the idol temples—placing themselves, as it were, under the unhappy influence of idolatry, and thus needlessly *trying* the strength of their religion, and making an experiment on the grace of Christ, as if he were bound to keep them even in the midst of dangers into which they needlessly ran. They would have the promise of grace to keep them only when they were in the way of their duty, and using all proper precautions. To go beyond this, to place themselves in needless danger, to *presume* on the grace of Christ to keep them in all circumstances, would be to *tempt* him, and provoke him to leave them; see Note on Mat. iv. 7. ¶ *As some of them also tempted.* There is evidently here a word to be understood, and it may be either "Christ" or "God." The construction would naturally require the former; but it is not certain that the apostle meant to say that the Israelites tempted *Christ.* The main idea is that of *temptation*, whether it be of Christ or of God; and the purpose of the apostle is to caution them against the danger of tempting Christ, from the fact that the Israelites were guilty of the sin of tempting their leader and protector, and thus exposing themselves to his anger. It cannot be denied, however, that the more natural construction of this place is that which supposes that the word "Christ" is understood here rather than "God." In order to relieve this interpretation from the difficulty that the Israelites could not be said with any propriety to have tempted "*Christ*," since he had not then come in the flesh, two remarks may be made. First, by the "angel of the covenant," and the "angel of his presence" (Ex. xxiii. 20, 23; xxxii. 36; xxxiii. 2; Num. xx. 16; Isa. lxiii. 9; Heb. xi. 26), that went with them, and delivered them from Egypt, there is reason to think the sacred writers understood the Messiah to be intended; and that he who subsequently became incarnate was he whom they tempted. And secondly, We are to bear in mind that the term *Christ* has acquired with us a signification somewhat different from that which it originally had in the New Testament. *We* use it as *a proper name,* applied to Jesus of Nazareth. But it is to be remembered that it is the mere Greek word for the Hebrew "Anointed," or the "Messiah;" and by retaining this signification of the word here, no small part of the difficulty will be avoided; and the expression then will mean simply that the Israelites "tempted *the Messiah;*" and the idea will be that he who conducted them, and against whom they sinned, and whom they tempted, was *the Messiah,* who afterwards became incarnate; an idea that is in accordance with the ancient ideas of the Jews respecting this personage, and which is not forbidden, certainly, in any part of the Bible. ¶ *And were destroyed of serpents.* Fiery serpents; see Num. xxi. 6.

10. *Neither murmur ye.* Do not repine at the allotments of Providence, or complain of his dealings. ¶ *As some of them also murmured;* Num. xiv. 2. The ground of their murmuring was, that they had been disappointed; that they had been brought out of a land of plenty into a wilderness of want; and that instead of being conducted at once to the land of promise, they were left to perish in the desert. They therefore complained of their leaders,

pened unto them for [1] ensamples: and they are written for our admonition, upon whom the ends of the world are come.

12 Wherefore [a] let him that thinketh he standeth take heed lest he fall.

13 There hath no temptation

1 or, *types*.

a Prov.28.14; Rom.11.20.

and proposed to return again into Egypt. ¶ *And were destroyed of the destroyer.* That is, they were doomed to die in the wilderness without seeing the land of Canaan; Ex. xiv. 29. The "destroyer" here is understood by many to mean *the angel of death,* so often referred to in the Old Testament, and usually called by the Jews *Sammael.* The work of death, however, is attributed to an angel in Ex. xii. 23; comp. Heb. xi. 28. It was customary for the Hebrews to regard most human events as under the direction of angels. In Heb. ii. 14, he is described as he "that had the power of death;" comp. the book of Wisdom xviii. 22, 25. The simple idea here, however, is, that they *died* for their sin, and were not permitted to enter the promised land.

11. *For ensamples.* Greek, *Types* (τύποι). The same word which is used in ver. 6. This verse is a repetition of the admonition contained in that verse, in order to impress it more deeply on the memory; see Note on verse 6. The sense is, not that these things took place simply and solely *to be* examples, or admonitions, but that their occurrence illustrated great principles of human nature and of the divine government; they showed the weakness of men, and their liability to fall into sin, and their need of the divine protection, and they might thus be used for the admonition of succeeding generations. ¶ *They are written for our admonition.* They are recorded in the writings of Moses, in order that we and all others might be admonished not to confide in our own strength. The admonition did not pertain merely to the Corinthians, but had an equal applicability to Christians in all ages of the world. ¶ *Upon whom the ends of the world are come.* This expression is equivalent to that which so often occurs in the Scriptures, as, "the last time," "the latter day," &c.; see it fully explained in Notes on Acts ii. 17. It means the last dispensation; or, that period and mode of the divine administration under which the affairs of the world would be wound up. There would be no mode of administration *beyond* that of the gospel. But it by no means denotes necessarily that the continuance of this period called "the last times," and "the ends of the world" would be brief, or that the apostle believed that the world would soon come to an end. It might be the *last* period, and yet be longer than any one previous period, or than all the previous periods put together. There may be a last dynasty in an empire, and yet it may be longer than any previous dynasty, or than all the previous dynasties put together. The apostle Paul was at special pains in 2 Thess. ii. to show, that by affirming that the last time had come, he did not mean that the world would soon come to an end.

12. *Wherefore.* As the result of all these admonitions. Let this be the effect of all that we learn from the unhappy self-confidence of the Jews, to admonish us not to put reliance on our own strength. ¶ *That thinketh he standeth.* That supposes himself to be firm in the love of God, and in the knowledge of his truth; that regards himself as secure, and that will be therefore disposed to rely on his own strength. ¶ *Take heed lest he fall.* Into sin, idolatry, or any other form of iniquity. We learn here, (1.) That a confidence in our own security is no evidence that we are safe. (2.) Such a confidence may be one of the strongest evidences that we are in danger. Those are most safe who feel that they are weak and feeble, and who feel their need of divine aid and strength. They will then rely on the true source of strength; and they will be secure. (3.) All professed Christians should be admonished. All are in danger of falling into sin, and of dishonouring

taken you but [1] such as is common to man: but God *is* faithful, who [a] will not suffer you to be tempted above that ye are able; [b]

1 or, *moderate*.

a Dan.3.17; 2Pet.2.9. b James 5.11.

their profession; and the exhortation cannot be too often or too urgently pressed, that they should take heed lest they fall into sin. The leading and special idea of the apostle here should not be forgotten or disregarded. It is, that Christians *in their favoured moments*, when they are permitted to approach near to God, and when the joys of salvation fill their hearts, should exercise peculiar caution. For (*a*) Then the adversary will be peculiarly desirous to draw away their thoughts from God, and to lead them into sin, as *their* fall would most signally dishonour religion; (*b*) Then they will be less likely to be on their guard, and more likely to feel themselves strong, and not to need caution and solicitude. Accordingly, it often happens that Christians, after they have been peculiarly favoured with the tokens of the divine favour, soon relapse into their former state, or fall into some sin that grieves the hearts of their brethren, or wounds the cause of religion. So it is in revivals; so it is in individuals. Churches that are thus favoured are filled with joy, and love, and peace. Yet they become self-confident and elated; they lose their humility and their sense of their dependence; they cease to be watchful and prayerful, supposing that all is safe; and the result often is, that a season of revival is succeeded by a time of coldness and declension. And thus, too, it is with individuals. Just the opposite effect is produced from what should be, and from what need be. Christians should *then* be peculiarly on their guard; and if they then availed themselves of their elevated advantages, churches *might* be favoured with continued revivals and ever-growing piety; and individuals *might* be filled with joy, and peace, and holiness, and ever-expanding and increasing love.

13. *There hath no temptation taken you.* What temptation the apostle refers to here is not quite certain. It is probable, however, that he refers to such as would, in their circumstances, have a tendency to induce them to forsake their allegiance to their Lord, and to lead them into idolatry and sin. These might be either open persecutions, or afflictions on account of their religion; or they might be the various allurements which were spread around them from the prevalence of idolatry. They might be the open attacks of their enemies, or the sneers and the derision of the gay and the great. The design of the apostle evidently is, to show them that, if they were faithful, they had nothing to fear from any such forms of temptation, but that God was able to bring them through them all. The sentiment in the verse is a very important one, since the general principle here stated is as applicable to Christians now as it was to the Corinthians. ¶ *Taken you.* Seized upon you, or assailed you. As when an enemy *grasps* us, and attempts to hold us fast. ¶ *But such as is common to man* (εἰ μὴ ἀνθρώπινος). Such as is *human*. Margin, *Moderate.* The sense is evident. It means such as human nature is liable to, and has been often subjected to; such as the human powers, under the divine aid may be able to resist and repel. The temptations which they had been subjected to were not such as would be fitted to angelic powers, and such as would require angelic strength to resist; but they were such as human nature had been often subjected to, and such as man had often contended with successfully. There is, therefore, here a recognition of the doctrine that man has natural ability to resist all the temptations to which he is subject; and that consequently, if he yields, he is answerable for it. The *design* of the apostle is to comfort the Corinthians, and to keep their minds from despondency. He had portrayed their danger; he had shown them how others had fallen; and they

might be led to suppose that in such circumstances they could not be secure. He therefore tells them that they might still be safe, for their temptations were such as human nature had often been subject to, and God was able to keep them from falling. ¶ *But God is faithful.* This was the only source of security; and this was enough. If they looked only to themselves, they would fall. If they depended on the faithfulness of God, they would be secure. The sense is, not that God would keep them without any effort of their own; not that he would secure them if they plunged into temptation; but that if they used the proper means, if they resisted temptation, and sought his aid, and depended on his promises, then he would be faithful. This is everywhere implied in the Scriptures; and to depend on the faithfulness of God, otherwise than in the proper use of means and in avoiding the places of temptation, is to *tempt him*, and provoke him to wrath; see Notes on Mat. iv. ¶ *Who will not suffer you to be tempted,* &c. This is a general promise, just as applicable to all Christians as it was to the Corinthians. It implies, (1.) That all the circumstances, causes, and agents that lead to temptation are under the control of God. Every man that tempts another; every fallen spirit that is engaged in this; every book, picture, place of amusement; every charm of music, and of song; every piece of indecent statuary; and every plan of business, of gain or ambition, are all under the control of God. He can check them; he can control them; he can paralyze their influence; he can destroy them; comp. Mat. vi. 13. (2.) When men are *tempted,* it is because God *suffers* or permits it. He does not himself tempt men (James i. 13); he does not infuse evil thoughts into the mind; he does not *create* an object of temptation to place in our way, but he suffers it to be placed there by others. When we are tempted, therefore, we are to remember that it is because he *suffers* or *permits* it; not because he *does* it. His agency is that of sufferance, not of creation. We are to remember, too, that there is some good reason why it is thus permitted; and that it *may* be turned in some way to his glory, and to our advancement in virtue. (3.) There is a certain extent to which we are *able* to resist temptation. There is a *limit* to our power. There is a point beyond which we are not *able* to resist it. We have not the strength of angels. (4.) That limit will, in all cases, be beyond the point to which we are tempted. If not, there would be no sin in falling, any more than there is sin in the oak when it is prostrated before the tempest. (5.) If men fall into sin, under the power of temptation, they only are to blame. They have strength to resist all the temptations that assail them, and God has given the assurance that no temptation shall occur which they shall not be able, by his aid, to resist. In all instances, therefore, where men fall into sin; in all the yielding to passion, to allurement, and to vice, man is to blame, and must be responsible to God. And this is especially true of Christians, who, whatever may be said of others, cannot plead that there was not power sufficient to meet the temptation, or to turn aside its power. ¶ *But will with the temptation,* &c. He will, at the same time that he suffers the trial or temptation to befall us, make a way of deliverance; he will save us from being entirely overcome by it. ¶ *That ye may be able to bear* it. Or that you may be able to bear up under it, or endure it. God knows what his people are *able* to endure, and as he has entire control of all that can affect them, he will adapt all trials to their strength, and will enable them to bear all that is appointed to them. This is a general promise, and is as applicable to other Christians as it was to the Corinthians. It was to them a positive promise, and to all in the same circumstances it may be regarded as such now. It may be used, therefore, (1.) As a ground of *encouragement* to those who are in temptation and trial. God knows what they are able to endure; and he will sustain them in their temptations. It matters not how severe the trial;

but will with the temptation also make a way to escape, that ye may be able to bear *it*.

14 Wherefore, my dearly beloved, [a] flee from idolatry.

a 1John 5.21.

15 I speak as to wise men; judge ye what I say.

16 The cup of blessing which we bless, is it not the communion of the blood of Christ? the bread

---

or how long it may be continued; or how much they may feel their own feebleness; yet He who has appointed the trial is abundantly able to uphold them. They may, therefore, repose their all upon him, and trust to his sustaining grace. (2.) It may be used as an *argument*, that none who are true Christians, and who are thus tried, shall ever fall away, and be lost. The promise is positive and certain, that a way shall be made for their escape, and they shall be able to bear it. God is faithful to them; and though he *might* suffer them to be tempted beyond what they are able to bear, yet he will not, but will secure an egress from all their trials. With this promise in view, how can it be believed that any true Christians who are tempted will be suffered to fall away and perish? If they do, it must be from one of the following causes; either because God is *not* faithful; or because he *will* suffer them to be tempted above what they are able to bear; or because he will *not* make a way for their escape. As no Christian can believe either of these, it follows that they who are converted shall be kept unto salvation.

14. *Wherefore.* In view of the dangers and temptations that beset you; in view of your own feebleness, and the perils to which you would be exposed in the idol temples, &c. ¶ *Flee from idolatry.* Escape from the service of idols; from the feasts celebrated in honour of them; from the temples where they are worshipped. This was one of the dangers to which they were peculiarly exposed; and Paul therefore exhorts them to escape from every thing that would have a tendency to lead them into this sin. He had told them, indeed, that God was faithful; and yet he did not expect God would keep them without any effort of their own. He therefore exhorts them to flee from all approaches to it, and from all the customs which would have a tendency to lead them into idolatrous practices. He returns, therefore, in this verse, to the particular subject discussed in chap. viii—the propriety of partaking of the feasts in honour of idols; and shows the danger which would follow such a practice. That danger he sets forth in view of the admonitions contained in this chapter, from ver. 1 to ver. 12. The remainder of the chapter is occupied with a discussion of the question stated in chap. viii., whether it was right for them to partake of the meat which was used in the feasts of idolaters.

15. *I speak as to wise men*, &c. I speak to men qualified to understand the subject; and present *reasons* which will commend themselves to you. The reasons referred to are those which occupy the remainder of the chapter.

16. *The cup of blessing which we bless.* The *design* of this verse and the following verses seems to be, to prove that Christians, by partaking of the Lord's supper, are solemnly set apart to the service of the Lord Jesus; that they acknowledge *him* as their Lord, and dedicate themselves to him, and that as they could not and ought not to be devoted to idols and to the Lord Jesus at the same time, so they ought not to participate in the feasts in honour of idols, or in the celebrations in which idolaters would be engaged; see ver. 21. He states, therefore, (1.) That Christians are *united* and dedicated to Christ in the communion; ver. 16, 17. (2.) That this was true of the Israelites, that they were one people, devoted by the service of the altar to the same God; ver. 18. (3.) That though an idol was nothing, yet the heathen actually sacrificed to devils, and Christians ought not to partake with them; ver.

which we break, is it not the communion of the body of Christ?

17 For we, *being* many are one bread, *and* one body; for

19—21. The phrase "cup of blessing" evidently refers to the wine used in the celebration of the Lord's supper. It is called "the cup of blessing" because over it Christians praise or bless God for his mercy in providing redemption. It is not because it is the means of conveying a blessing to the souls of those who partake of it—though that is true—but because thanksgiving, blessing, and praise were rendered to God in the celebration, for the benefits of redemption; see Note, Mat. xxvi. 26. Or it may mean, in accordance with a well known Hebraism, *the blessed cup;* the cup that is blessed. This is the more literal interpretation; and it is adopted by Calvin, Beza, Doddridge, and others. ¶ *Which we bless.* Grotius, Macknight, Vatablus, Bloomfield, and many of the Fathers suppose that this means, "over which we bless God;" or, "for which we bless God." But this is to do violence to the passage. The more obvious signification is, that there is a sense in which it may be said that the cup is blessed, and that by prayer and praise it is set apart and rendered in some sense sacred to the purposes of religion. It cannot mean that the cup has undergone any physical change, or that the wine is any thing but wine; but that it has been solemnly set apart to the service of religion, and by prayer and praise designated to be used for the purpose of commemorating the Saviour's love. That may be said to be blessed which is set apart to a sacred use (Gen. ii. 3; Ex. xx. 11); and in this sense the cup may be said to be blessed; see Luke ix. 16, "And he took the five loaves and the two fishes, and looking up to heaven, he blessed THEM," &c; comp. Gen. xiv. 9; xxvii. 23, 33, 41; xxviii. 1; Lev. ix. 22, 23; 2 Sam. vi. 18; 1 Kings viii. 41. ¶ *Is it not the communion of the blood of Christ?* Is it not the emblem by which the blood of Christ is exhibited, and the means by which our union through that blood is exhibited? Is it not the means by which we express our attachment to him as Christians; showing our union to him and to each other; and showing that we partake in common of the benefits of his blood? The main idea is, that by partaking of this cup they showed that they were united to him and to each other; and that they should regard themselves as set apart to him. We have communion with one (κοινωνία,) that which is in *common*, that which pertains to all, that which evinces fellowship) when we partake together; when all have an equal right, and all share alike; when the same benefits or the same obligations are extended to all. And the sense here is, that Christians *partake alike* in the benefits of the blood of Christ; they share the same blessings; and they *express* this together, and in common, when they partake of the communion. ¶ *The bread,* &c. In the commnnion. It shows, since we all partake of it, that we share alike in the benefits which are imparted by means of the broken body of the Redeemer. In like manner it is implied that if Christians should partake with idolaters in the feasts offered in honour of idols, that they would be regarded as *partaking* with them in the services of idols, or as united to them, and therefore such participation was improper.

17. *For we.* We Christians. ¶ Being *many.* Gr. *The many* (οἱ πολλοί). This idea is not, as our translation would seem to indicate, that Christians were numerous, but that *all* (for οἱ πολλοί is here evidently used in the sense of παντες, *all*) were united, and constituted one society. ¶ *Are one bread.* One loaf; one cake. That is, we are united, or are one. There is evident allusion here to the fact that the loaf or cake was composed of many separate grains of wheat, or portions of flour united in one; or, that as one loaf was broken and partaken by all, it was implied that they were all one. We are all one society; united as one, and for the same object. Our partaking of

we are all partakers of that one bread.

18 Behold Israel after [a] the flesh: [b] are not they which eat of the sacrifices partakers of the altar?

19 What say I then? that the idol [c] is any thing? or that which is offered in sacrifice to idols is any thing

20 But *I say*, that the things

a Rom.4.1,12. *b* chap.9.13. *c* chap.8.4.

the same bread is an emblem of the fact that we are one. In almost all nations the act of eating together has been regarded as a symbol of unity or friendship. ¶ And *one body*. One society; united together. ¶ *For we are all partakers*, &c. And we thus show publicly that we are united, and belong to the same great family. The argument is, that if we partake of the feasts in honour of idols with their worshippers, we shall thus show that we are a part of their society.

18. *Behold Israel*. Look at the Jews. The design here is to illustrate the sentiment which he was establishing, by a reference to the fact that among the Jews those who partook of the same sacrifices were regarded as being one people, and as worshipping one God. So, if they partook of the sacrifices offered to idols, they would be regarded also as being fellow-worshippers of idols with them. ¶ *After the flesh;* see Rom. iv. 1. The phrase "after the flesh" is designed to denote the Jews who were not converted to Christianity; the natural descendants of Israel, or Jacob. ¶ *Are not they which eat of the sacrifices*. A portion of the sacrifices offered to God was eaten by the offerer, and another portion by the priests. Some portions of the animal, as the fat, were burnt; and the remainder, unless it was a holocaust, or whole burnt-offering, was then the property of the priests who had officiated, or of the persons who had brought it; Ex. xxix. 13, 22; Lev. iii. 4, 10, 15; iv. 9; vii. 3, 4; viii. 26. The right shoulder and the breast was the part which was assigned to the priests; the remainder belonged to the offerer. ¶ *Partakers of the altar*. Worshippers of the same God. They are united in their worship, and are so regarded. And in like manner, if you partake of the sacrifices offered to idols, and join with their worshippers in their temples, you will be justly regarded as *united* with them in their worship, and partaking with them in their abominations.

19. *What say I then?* This is in the present tense; τί οὖν φημι, what *do* I say? What is my meaning? What follows from this? Do I mean to say that an idol is anything; that it has a real existence? Does my reasoning lead to that conclusion; and am I to be understood as affirming that an idol is of itself of any consequence? It must be recollected that the Corinthian Christians are introduced by Paul (chap. viii. 4) as saying that they knew that an idol was nothing in the world. Paul did not *directly* contradict that; but his reasoning had led him to the necessity of calling the propriety of their attending on the feasts of idols in question; and he introduces the matter now by asking these questions, thus leading the mind *to* it rather than directly affirming it at once. "Am I in this reasoning to be understood as affirming that an idol is any thing, or that the meat there offered differs from other meat? No; you know, says Paul, that this is not my meaning. I admit that an idol in itself is nothing; but I do *not* admit, therefore, that it is right for you to attend in their temples; for though the *idol* itself—the block of wood or stone—is nothing, yet the offerings are really made to devils; and I would not have you engage in such a service;" ver. 20, 21. ¶ *That the idol is any thing?* That the block of wood or stone is a real living object of worship, to be dreaded or loved? See Note, chap. viii. 4. ¶ *Or that which is offered in sacrifice to idols is any thing?* Or that the meat which is offered *differs* from that which is not offered; that the mere act of offering it changes its qualities? I do not admit or suppose this.

which the Gentiles sacrifice, they sacrifice to devils, [a] and not to God: and I would not that ye should have fellowship with devils.

a Lev.17.7; Deut.32.17; Ps.106.37.

20. *But.* The negative here is omitted, but is understood. The ellipsis of a negative after an interrogative sentence is common in the classical writers as well as in the Scriptures. *Bloomfield.* The sense is, "No; I do not say *this*, but I say that there are reasons why you should not partake of those sacrifices; and one of those reasons is, that they have been really offered to devils." ¶ *They sacrifice to devils* (δαιμονίοις, *demons*). The heathens used the word *demon* either in a good or a bad sense. They applied it commonly to spirits that were supposed to be inferior to the supreme God; genii; attending spirits; or, as they called them, divinities, or gods. A part were in their view good, and a part evil. Socrates supposed that such a *demon* or genius attended him, who suggested good thoughts to him, and who was his protector. As these beings were good and well disposed, it was not supposed to be necessary to offer any sacrifices in order to appease them. But a large portion of those genii were supposed to be evil and wicked, and hence the necessity of attempting to appease their wrath by sacrifices and bloody offerings. It was therefore true, as the apostle says, that the sacrifices of the heathen were made, usually at least, to devils or to evil spirits. Many of these spirits were supposed to be the souls of departed men, who were entitled to worship after death, having been enrolled among the gods. The word "demons," among the Jews, was employed only to designate evil beings. It is not implied in their writings to good angels or to blessed spirits, but to evil angels, to idols, to false gods. Thus in the LXX. the word is used to translate אלילים, *Elilim, idols* (Ps. xcv. 5; Isa. lxv. 10); and שד, *Shaid*, as in Deut. xxxii. 17, in a passage which Paul has here almost literally used, "They sacrificed unto devils, not to God." No where in the Septuagint is it used in a good sense. In the New Testament the word is uniformly used also to denote *evil spirits*, and those usually which had taken possession of men in the time of the Saviour; Mat. vii. 22; ix. 33, 34; x. 8; xi. 18; Mark i. 34, 39, et alii. See also Campbell on the Gospels, Pre. Diss. vi. part i. § 14—16. The precise force of the original is not, however, conveyed by our translation. It is not true that the heathens sacrificed to *devils*, in the common and popular sense of that word, meaning thereby the apostate angel and the spirits under his direction; for the heathens were as ignorant of their existence as they were of the true God; and it is not *true* that they *designed* to worship such beings. But it is true, (1.) That they did not worship the supreme and the true God. They were not acquainted with his existence; and they did not profess to adore him. (2.) They worshipped *demons;* beings that they regarded as inferior to the true God; created spirits, or the spirits of men that had been enrolled among the number of the gods. (3.) It was true that many of these beings were supposed to be malign and evil in their nature, and that their worship was designed to deprecate their wrath. So that, although an idol was nothing in itself, the gold or wood of which it was made was inanimate, and incapable of aiding or injuring them; and although there *were* no real beings such as the heathens supposed —no *genii* or inferior gods; yet they *designed* to offer sacrifice to such beings, and to deprecate their wrath. To join them in this, therefore, would be to express the belief that there were such beings, and that they ought to be worshipped, and that their wrath should be deprecated. ¶ *I would not that ye should have fellowship with devils.* I would not that you should have communion with demons. I would not have you express a belief of their existence; or join in worship to them; or par-

21 Ye cannot drink the cup of
the Lord, and the cup [a] of devils:
ye cannot be partakers of the
Lord's table, and of the table of
devils.
22 Do we [b] provoke the Lord

[a] Deut.32.38.

[b] Deut.32.21; Job 9.4; Ezek.22.14.

---

take of the spirit by which they are supposed to be actuated—a spirit that would be promoted by attendance on their worship. I would not have you, therefore, join in a mode of worship where such beings are acknowledged. You are solemnly dedicated to Christ; and the homage due to him should not be divided with homage offered to devils, or to imaginary beings.

21. *Ye cannot drink the cup of the Lord,* &c. This does not mean that they had no physical ability to do this, or that it was a natural impossibility; for they certainly had *power* to do it. But it must mean that they could not *consistently* do it. It was not fit, proper, decent. They were solemnly bound to serve and obey Christ: they had devoted themselves to him: and they could not, consistently with these obligations, join in the worship of demons. This is a striking instance in which the word *cannot* is used to denote not natural but moral inability. ¶ *And the cup of devils.* Demons; ver. 20. In the feasts in honour of the gods, wine was poured out as a libation, or drank by the worshippers; see Virg. Æn. viii. 273. The custom of drinking *toasts* at feasts and celebrations arose from this practice of pouring out wine, or drinking in honour of the heathen gods; and is a practice that partakes still of the nature of heathenism. It was one of the abominations of heathenism to suppose that their gods would be pleased with the intoxicating draught. Such a pouring out of a libation was usually accompanied with a *prayer* to the idol god, that he would accept the offering; that he would be propitious; and that he would grant the desire of the worshipper. From that custom the habit of expressing a sentiment, or proposing a toast, uttered in drinking wine, has been derived. The toast or sentiment which now usually accompanies the drinking of a glass in this manner, if it mean anything, is now also *a prayer:* but to whom? to the god of wine? to a heathen deity? Can it be supposed that it is a prayer offered to the true God; the God of purity? Has Jehovah directed that *prayer* should be offered to him in such a manner? Can it be acceptable to him? Either the sentiment is unmeaning, or it is a prayer offered to a heathen god, or it is mockery of JEHOVAH; and in either case it is improper and wicked. And it may as truly be said now of Christians as in the time of Paul. "Ye cannot consistently drink the cup of the Lord at the communion table, and the cup where a PRAYER is offered to a false god, or to the dead, or to the air; or when, if it means any thing, it is a mockery of JEHOVAH." Now can a Christian with any more consistency or propriety join in such celebrations, and in such unmeaning or profane libations, than he could go into the temple of an idol, and partake of the idolatrous celebrations there? ¶ *And of the table of devils.* Demons. It is not needful to the force of this that we should suppose that the word means necessarily evil spirits. They were not God; and to worship them was idolatry. The apostle means that Christians could not consistently join in the worship that was offered to them, or in the feasts celebrated in honour of them.

22. *Do we provoke the Lord to jealousy?* That is, shall we, by joining in the worship of idols, *provoke* or *irritate* God, or excite him to anger? This is evidently the meaning of the word παραζηλοῦμεν, rendered "provoke to jealousy." The word קנא, usually rendered by this word by the LXX., has this sense in Deut. xxxii. 21; 1 Kings xiv. 22; Ezra viii. 3; Ps. lxxviii. 58. There is a reference here, doubtless, to the truth recorded in Ex. xx. 5, that God "is a jealous God," and that he regards the worship of idols as a direct

to jealousy? are we stronger than he?

23 All *a* things are lawful for me, but all things are not expedient: all things are lawful for me, but all things edify not.

24 Let *b* no man seek his own, but every man another's *wealth*.

a chap.6.12.

b Phil.2.4,21

affront to himself. The sentiment of Paul is, that to join in the worship of idols, or in the observance of their feasts, would be to participate in that which had ever been regarded by God with peculiar abhorrence, and which more than any thing else tended to provoke his wrath. We may observe, that any course of life that tends to alienate the affections from God, and to fix them on other beings or objects, is a sin of the same kind as that referred to here. Any inordinate love of friends, of property, of honour, has substantially the same idolatrous nature, and will tend to provoke him to anger. And it may be asked of Christians now, whether they will by such inordinate attachments provoke the Lord to wrath? whether they will thus excite his displeasure, and expose themselves to his indignation? Very often Christians *do* thus provoke him. They become unduly attached to a friend, or to wealth, and God in anger takes away that friend by death, or that property by the flames: or they conform to the world, and mingle in its scenes of fashion and gayety, and forget God; and in displeasure he visits them with judgments, humbles them, and recalls them to himself. ¶ *Are we stronger than he?* This is given as a reason why we should not provoke his displeasure. We cannot contend successfully with him; and it is therefore madness and folly to contend with God, or to expose ourselves to the effects of his indignation.

23. *All things are lawful for me.* See Note, chap. vi. 12. This is a repetition of what he had said before; and it is here applied to the subject of eating the meat that had been offered to idols. The sense is, "Though it may be admitted that it was strictly *lawful* to partake of that meat, yet there were strong reasons why it was inexpedient; and those reasons ougnt to have the binding force of law." ¶ *All things edify not.* All things do not tend to build up the church, and to advance the interests of religion; and when they do *not* have this effect, they are not expedient, and are improper. Paul acted for the welfare of the church. His object was to save souls. Any thing that would promote that object was proper; any thing which would hinder it, though in itself it might not be strictly unlawful, was in his view improper. This is a simple rule, and might be easily applied by all. If a man has his heart on the conversion of men and the salvation of the world, it will go far to regulate his conduct in reference to many things concerning which there may be no exact and positive law. It will do much to regulate his dress; his style of living; his expenses; his entertainments; his mode of intercourse with the world. He may not be able to fix his finger on any positive law, and to say that this or that article of dress is improper; that this or that piece of furniture is absolutely forbidden; or that this or that manner of life is contrary to any explicit law of Jehovah; but he *may* see that it will interfere with his great and main purpose, *to do good on the widest scale possible;* and THEREFORE to him it will be inexpedient and improper. Such a grand leading purpose is a much better guide to direct a man's life than would be exact positive statutes to regulate every thing, even if such minute statutes were possible.

24. *Let no man seek his own.* This should be properly interpreted of the matter under discussion, though the direction assumes the form of a general principle. Originally it meant, "Let no man, in regard to the question about partaking of the meat offered in sacrifice to idols, consult his own pleasure, happiness, or convenience; but let him, as the leading rule on the subject, ask what will be for the welfare of others. Let him not

25 Whatsoever [a] is sold in the shambles, *that* eat, asking no question for conscience' sake.

26 For [b] the earth *is* the Lord's and the fulness thereof.

27 If any of them that believe

a 1 Tim.4.4.

b Deut.10.14; Ps.24.1; 50.12.

gratify his own taste and inclinations, regardless of their feelings, comfort, and salvation; but let him in these things have a primary reference to their welfare." He may dispense with these things without danger or injury; he cannot indulge in them without endangering the happiness or purity of others. His duty therefore requires him to abstain. The injunction, however, has a general form, and is applicable to all Christians, and to all cases *of a similar kind.* It does not mean that a man is not in any instance to regard his own welfare, happiness, or salvation; it does not mean that a man owes no duty to himself or family; or that he should neglect all these to advance the welfare of others: but the precept means, that *in cases like that under consideration,* when there is no positive law, and when a man's example would have a great influence, he should be guided in his conduct, not by a reference to his own ease, comfort or gratification, but by a reference to the purity and salvation of others. And the observance of this simple rule would make a prodigious change in the church and the world. ¶ *But every man another's* wealth. The word *wealth* is not in the Greek. Literally, "that which is of another;" the word τὸ referring to any thing and every thing that pertains to his comfort, usefulness, happiness, or salvation.—The sentiment of the whole is, *when a man is bound and directed by no positive law, his grand rule should be the comfort and salvation of others.* This is a simple rule; it might be easily applied; and this would be a sort of balance-wheel in the various actions and plans of the world. If every man would adopt this rule, he could not be in much danger of going wrong; he would be certain that he would not live in vain.

25. *Whatsoever is sold in the shambles.* In the market. The meat of animals offered in sacrifice would be exposed there to sale as well as other meat. The apostle says that it might be purchased, since the mere fact that it had been offered in sacrifice could not change its quality, or render it unfit for use. They were to abstain from attending on the feasts of the idols in the temple, from partaking of meat that had been offered them, and from celebrations observed expressly in honour of idols; but lest they should become too scrupulous, the apostle tells them that if the meat was offered indiscriminately in the market with other meat, they were not to hesitate to purchase it, or eat it. ¶ *Asking no question for conscience' sake.* Not hesitating or doubting, as if it might *possibly* have been offered in sacrifice. Not being scrupulous, as if it were *possible* that the conscience should be defiled. This is a good rule still, and may be applied to a great many things. But, (1.) That which is purchased should be in itself lawful and right. It would not be proper for a man to use ardent spirits or any other intoxicating drinks because they were offered for sale, any more than it would be to commit suicide because men offered pistols, and bowie-knives, and halters to sell. (2.) There are many things now concerning which similar questions may be asked; as, *e. g.* is it right to use the productions of slave-labour, the sugar, cotton, &c., that are the price of blood? Is it right to use that which is known to be made on the Sabbath; or that which it is known a man has made by a life of dishonesty and crime? The consciences of many persons are tender on all such questions; and the questions are not of easy solution. Some rules may perhaps be suggested arising from the case before us. (*a*) If the article is exposed indiscriminately with others in the market, if it be in itself lawful, if there is no ready mark of distinction, then the apostle would direct us not to hesitate. (*b*) If the use and purchase of the article would go directly and knowingly to countenance

not bid you *to a feast*, and ye be disposed to go; whatsoever [a] is set before you, eat, asking no question for conscience' sake.

28 But if any man say unto you, This is offered in sacrifice unto idols, eat not, [b] for his sake that showed it, and for conscience' sake:

a Luke 10.7.

b chap.8.10,12.

the existence of slavery, to encourage a breach of the Sabbath, or to the continuance of a course of dishonest living, then it would seem equally clear that it is not right to purchase or to use it. If a man abhors slavery, and Sabbath-breaking, and dishonesty, then how can he knowingly partake of that which goes to patronise and extend these abominations? (*c*) If the article is expressly pointed out to him as an article that has been made in this manner, and his partaking of it will be *construed* into a participation of the crime, then he ought to abstain; see ver. 28. No man is at liberty to patronise slavery, Sabbath-breaking, dishonesty, or licentiousness, in any form. Every man *can* live without doing it; and where it can be done it should be done. And perhaps there will be no other way of breaking up many of the crimes and cruelties of the earth than for good men to act conscientiously, and to refuse to partake of the avails of sin, and of gain that results from oppression and fraud.

26. *For the earth* is *the Lord's*. This is quoted from Ps. xxiv. 1. The same sentiment is also found in Ps. l. 11, and in Deut. x. 14. It is here urged as a reason why it is right to partake of the meat offered in the market. It all belongs to the Lord. It does not *really* belong to the idol, even though it has been offered to it. It may, therefore, be partaken of as his gift, and should be received with gratitude. ¶ *And the fulness thereof.* All that the earth produces belongs to him. *He* causes it to grow; and he has given it to be food for man; and though it may have been devoted to an idol, yet its nature is not changed. It is still the gift of God; still the production of his hand; still the fruit of his goodness and love.

27. *If any of them that believe not.* That are not Christians; that are still heathens. ¶ *Bid you* to a feast. Evidently not a feast in the temple of an idol, but at his own house. If he *ask* you to partake of his hospitality. ¶ *And ye be disposed to go.* Greek, "And you will to go." It is evidently implied here that it would be not improper to go. The Saviour accepted such invitations to dine with the Pharisees (see Note, Luke xi. 37); and Christianity is not designed to abolish the courtesies of social life; or to break the bonds of intercourse; or to make men misanthropes or hermits. It allows and cultivates, under proper Christian restraints, the intercourse in society which will promote the comfort of men, and especially that which may extend the usefulness of Christians. It does not require, therefore, that we should withdraw from social life, or regard as improper the courtesies of society; see Note on chap. v. 10. ¶ *Whatever is set before you*, &c. Whether it has been offered in sacrifice or not; for so the connection requires us to understand it. ¶ *Eat.* This should be interpreted strictly. The apostle says "*eat*," not "*drink*;" and the principle will not authorize us to *drink* whatever is set before us, asking no questions for conscience' sake; for while it was a matter of indifference in regard to eating, whether the meat had been sacrificed to idols or not, it is *not* a matter of indifference whether a man may drink intoxicating liquor. *That* is a point on which the *conscience* should have much to do; and on which its honest decisions, and the will of the Lord, should be faithfully and honestly regarded.

28. *But if any man.* If any fellow guest; any scrupulous fellow Christian who may be present. That the word "any" (τις) refers to a fellow guest seems evident; for it is not probable that the host would point out any part of the food on his own table, of the lawfulness of eating which he would suppose there was any doubt

for [a] the earth *is* the Lord's, and the fulness thereof:

29 Conscience, I say, not thine own, but of the other: for why is my liberty judged of another *man's* conscience?

30 For if I by [1] grace be a partaker, why am I evil spoken of for that for which I give thanks? [b]

31 Whether [c] therefore ye eat or drink, or whatsoever ye do, do all to the glory of God.

a ver.26. 1 or, *thanksgiving*. b Rom.14.6. c Col.3.17; 1 Pet.4.11.

Yet there might be present some scrupulous fellow Christian who would have strong doubts of the propriety of partaking of the food, and who would indicate it to the other guests. ¶ *For his sake that showed it.* Do not offend him; do not lead him into sin; do not pain and wound his feelings. ¶ *And for conscience' sake.* Eat not, out of respect to the conscientious scruples of him that told thee that it had been offered to idols. The word *conscience* refers to the conscience of the informer (ver. 29); still *he* should make it a matter of conscience not to wound his weak brethren, or lead them into sin. ¶ *For the earth is the Lord's,* &c.; see ver. 26. These words are wanting in many MSS. (see Mill's Gr. Tes.), and in the Vulgate, Syriac, Coptic, and Arabic versions; and are omitted by Griesbach. Grotius says that they should be omitted. There might easily have been a mistake in transcribing them from ver. 26. The authority of the MSS., however, is in favour of retaining them; and they are quoted by the Greek fathers and commentators. If they are to be retained, they are to be interpreted, probably, in this sense; "There is no *necessity* that you should partake of this food. All things belong to God; and he has made ample provision for your wants without subjecting you to the necessity of eating this. Since this is the case, it is best to regard the scruples of those who have doubts of the propriety of eating *this* food, and to abstain."

29. *Conscience, I say, not thine own.* I know that you may have no scruples on the subject. I do not mean that with you this need be a matter of conscience. I do not put it on that ground, as if an idol were any thing, or as if it were in itself wrong, or as if the quality of the meat so offered had been changed; but I put it on the ground of not wounding the feelings of those who are scrupulous, or of leading them into sin. ¶ *For why is my liberty,* &c. There is much difficulty in this clause; for as it now stands, it seems to be entirely contradictory to what the apostle had been saying. He had been urging them to *have* respect to other men's consciences, and in some sense to give up their liberty *to* their opinions and feelings. Macknight and some others understand it as an objection: "Perhaps you will say, But why is my liberty to be ruled by another man's conscience?" Doddridge supposes that this and ver. 30 come in as a kind of parenthesis, to prevent their extending his former caution beyond what he designed. "I speak only of acts obvious to human observation for as to what immediately lies between God and my own soul, why is my liberty to be judged, arraigned, condemned at the bar of another man's conscience?" But it is probable that this is not an objection. The sense may be thus expressed: "I am free; I have *liberty* to partake of that food, if I please; there is no *law* against it, and it is not morally wrong: but if I do, when it is pointed out to me as having been sacrificed to idols, my liberty—the right which I exercise—will be *misconstrued, misjudged, condemned* (for so the word κρίνεται seems to be used here) by others. The weak and scrupulous believer will censure, judge, condemn me as regardless of what is proper, and as disposed to fall in with the customs of idolaters; and will suppose that I cannot have a good conscience. Under these circumstances, why should I act so as to expose myself to this censure and condemnation? It is better for me to abstain, and not to use this liberty in the case, but to deny myself for the sake of others."

30. *For if I by grace be a partaker*

Or rather, "If I *partake* by grace; if by the grace and mercy of God, I have a *right* to partake of this; yet why should I so conduct as to expose myself to the reproaches and evil surmises of others? Why should I lay myself open to be blamed on the subject of eating, when there are so many bounties of Providence for which I may be thankful, and which I may partake of without doing injury, or exposing myself in any manner to be blamed?" ¶ *Why am I evil spoken of.* Why should I pursue such a course as to expose myself to blame or censure? ¶ *For that for which I give thanks.* For my food. The phrase "for which I give thanks" seems to be a periphrasis for *food,* or for that of which he partook to nourish life. It is implied that he always gave thanks for his food; and that this was with him such a universal custom, that the phrase "for which I give thanks" might be used as convenient and appropriate phraseology to denote his ordinary food. The idea in the verse, then, is this: "By the favour of God, I have a *right* to partake of this food. But if I did, I should be evil spoken of, and do injury. And it is unnecessary. God has made ample provision elsewhere for my support, for which I may be thankful. I will not therefore expose myself to calumny and reproach, or be the occasion of injury to others by partaking of the food offered in sacrifice to idols."

31. *Whether therefore ye eat or drink.* This direction should be strictly and properly applied to the case in hand; that is, to the question about eating and drinking the things that had been offered in sacrifice to idols. Still, however, it contains a general direction that is applicable to eating and drinking at all times; and the phrase "whatsoever ye do" is evidently designed by the apostle to make the direction universal. ¶ *Or whatsoever ye do.* In all the actions and plans of life; whatever be your schemes, your desires, your doings, let all be done to the glory of God. ¶ *Do all to the glory of God.* The phrase "the glory of God" is equivalent to the *honour* of God; and the direction is, that we should *so* act in all things as to *honour* him as our Lawgiver, our Creator, our Redeemer; and so as to lead others by our example to praise him and to embrace his gospel. A child acts so as to honour a father when he always cherishes reverential and proper thoughts of him; when he is thankful for his favours; when he keeps his laws; when he endeavours to advance his plans and his interests; and when he so acts as to lead all around him to cherish elevated opinions of the character of a father. He *dishonours* him when he has no respect to his authority; when he breaks his laws; when he leads others to treat him with disrespect. In like manner. we live to the glory of God when we honour him in all the relations which he sustains to us; when we keep his laws; when we partake of his favours with thankfulness, and with a deep sense of our dependence; when we pray unto him; and when we so live as to lead those around us to cherish elevated conceptions of his goodness, and mercy, and holiness. Whatever plan or purpose will tend to advance his kingdom, and to make him better known and loved, will be to his glory. We may observe in regard to this, (1.) That the rule is *universal.* It extends to every thing. If in so small matters as eating and drinking we should seek to honour God, assuredly we should in all other things. (2.) It is designed that this should be the constant rule of conduct, and that we should be often reminded of it. The acts of eating and drinking must be performed often; and the command is attached to that which *must* often occur, that we may be often reminded of it, and that we may be kept from forgetting it. (3.) It is intended that we should honour God in our families and among our friends. We eat with them; we share together the bounties of Providence; and God designs that we should honour him when we partake of his mercies, and that thus our daily enjoyments should be sanctified by a constant effort to glorify him. (4.) We should devote the strength which we derive from the bounties of his hand to his honour and in his ser-

32 Give [a] none offence, neither to the Jews, nor to the [1] Gentiles, nor to the church of God:

33 Even as I please all *men* in all *things*, not seeking mine own profit, but the *profit* of many, that they may be saved.

a Rom.14.13; 2 Cor.6.3.

1 *Greeks*.

vice. He gives us food; he makes it nourishing; he invigorates our frame; and that strength should *not* be devoted to purposes of sin, and profligacy, and corruption. It is an act of high dishonour to God, when HE gives us strength, that WE should at once devote that strength to pollution and to sin. (5.) This rule is designed to be one of the chief directors of our lives. It is to guide all our conduct, and to constitute a *test* by which to try our actions. Whatever can be done to advance the honour of God is right; whatever cannot be done with that end is wrong. Whatever plan a man can form that will have this end is a good plan; whatever cannot be made to have this tendency, and that cannot be commenced, continued, and ended with a distinct and definite desire to promote his honour, is wrong, and should be forthwith abandoned. (6.) What a change would it make in the world if this rule were every where followed! How differently would even professing Christians live! How many of their plans would they be constrained at once to abandon! And what a mighty revolution would it at once make on earth should all the actions of men begin to be performed to promote the glory of God! (7.) It may be added that sentiments like that of the apostle were found among the Jews, and even among heathens. Thus Maimonides, as cited by Grotius, says, "Let every thing be in the name of Heaven," *i. e.* in the name of God. Capellus cites several of the rabbinical writers who say that all actions, even eating and drinking, should be done *in the name of God.* See the *Critici Sacri.* Even the heathen writers have something that resembles this. Thus Arrian (Ep. i. 19) says, "Looking unto God in all things small and great.' Epictetus, too, on being asked how any one may eat so as to please God, answered, "By eating justly, temperately, and thankfully."

32. *Give none offence.* Be inoffensive; that is, do not act so as to lead others into sin; see Note, Rom. xiv. 13. ¶ *Neither to the Jews,* &c. To no one, though they are the foes of God or strangers to him. To the Jews be inoffensive, because they think that the least approach to idol worship is to be abhorred. Do not *so* act as to lead them to think that you connive at or approve idol worship, and so as to prejudice them the more against the Christian religion, and lead them more and more to oppose it. In other words, do not attend the feasts in honour of idols. ¶ *Nor to the Gentiles.* Gr. *Greeks.* To the pagans who are unconverted. They are attached to idol worship. They seek every way to justify themselves in it. Do not countenance them in it, and thus lead them into the sin of idolatry. ¶ *Nor to the church of God.* To Christians. Many of them are weak. They may not be as fully instructed as you are. Your example would lead them into sin. Abstain, therefore, from things which, though they are in themselves strictly *lawful*, may yet be the occasion of leading others into sin, and endangering their salvation.

33. *Even as I,* &c. Paul here proposes his own example as their guide. The example which he refers to is that which he had exhibited as described in this and the preceding chapters. *His* main object had been to please all men; *i. e.* not to alarm their prejudices, or needlessly to excite their opposition (see Note on chap. ix. 19—23), while he made known to them the truth, and sought their salvation.—It is well when a minister can without ostentation appeal to his own example, and urge others to a life of self-denial and holiness, by his own manner of living, and by what he

CHAPTER XI.

BE ye followers [a] of me, even as
I also *am* of Christ.
2 Now I praise you, brethren,
that [b] ye remember me in all things,
and keep [c] the ordinances, [1] as I
delivered *them* to you.
3 But I would have you know,

a Eph.5.1; 1 Thess.1.6. b chap.4.17. c Luke 1.6. 1 traditions.

is himself in his daily walk and conversation.

CHAPTER XI.

THE first verse in this chapter properly belongs to the preceding, and is the conclusion of the discussion which the apostle had been carrying on in that and the previous chapters. It has been improperly separated from that chapter, and in reading should be read in connection with it. The remainder of the chapter is properly divided into two parts: I. A discussion respecting the impropriety of a woman's praying or prophesying with her head uncovered (ver. 2—16); and, II. A reproof of their irregularities in the observance of the Lord's supper, ver. 17—36.

I. In regard to the first, it seems probable that some of the women who, on pretence of being inspired, had prayed or prophesied in the Corinthian church, had cast off their veils after the manner of the heathen priestesses. This indecent and improper custom the apostle reproves. He observes, therefore, that the pre-eminence belongs to man over the woman, even as pre-eminence belonged to Christ over the man; that it was a dishonour to Christ when a man prayed or prophesied with his head covered, and in like manner it was regarded every where as dishonourable and improper for a woman to lay aside the appropriate symbol of her sex, and the emblem of subordination, and to be uncovered in the presence of the man (ver. 3—5;) that if a woman was not veiled, if she laid aside the appropriate emblem of her sex and of her subordinate condition, she might as well part with her hair, which all knew would be dishonourable and improper (ver. 6); that the woman had been created for a subordinate station, and should observe it (ver. 7—9); that she should have power on her head because of the angels (ver. 10); and yet, lest this should *depress* her, and seem to convey the idea of her utter inferiority and unimportance, he adds, that in the plan of salvation they are in many respects on an equality with the man, that the same plan was adapted to both, that the same blessings are appointed for both sexes, and the same high hopes are held out to both (ver. 11, 12); and that nature on this subject was a good instructor, and showed that it was uncomely for a woman to pray with her head uncovered, that her hair had been given her for an ornament and for beauty, and that, as it would be *as* improper for her to remove her veil as to cut off her hair, nature itself required that this symbol of her subordination should be laid aside in public, ver. 13—16.

II. Next, as to the irregularities in the observance of the Lord's supper, the apostle observes (ver. 17), that he could not commend them for what he was about to say. There had been and there were irregularities among them, which it was his duty to reprove. In ver. 18—22, he states what those irregularities were. He then (ver. 23—26) states the true nature and design of the Lord's supper, as it was very evident that they had not understood it, but supposed it was a common feast, such as they had been accustomed to observe in honour of idols. In ver. 27—29, he states the consequences of observing this ordinance in an improper manner, and the proper way of approaching it; and in ver. 30—32, observes that their improper mode of observing it was the cause of the punishment which many of them had experienced. He then concludes by directing them to celebrate the Lord's supper *together;* to eat at home when they were hungry; and not to abuse the Lord's supper by making it an occasion of feasting; and assures them that the other matters of irregularity he would set in order when he should come among them.

that the head [a] of every man is Christ; [b] and the head of the woman *is* the man; [c] and the head of Christ *is* God.

a Eph.5.23. b Gen.3.16; 1 Pet.3.1,5,6. c John 14.28; chap.15.27,28.

1. *Be ye followers of me.* Imitate my example in the matter now under discussion. As I deny myself; as I seek to give no offence to any one; as I endeavour not to alarm the prejudices of others, but in all things to seek their salvation, so do you. This verse belongs to the previous chapter, and should not have been separated from it. It is the close of the discussion there. ¶ *Even as I also* am *of Christ.* I make Christ my example. He is my model in all things; and if you follow him, and follow me as far as *I* follow him, you will not err. This is the only safe example; and if we follow this, we can never go astray.

2. *Now I praise you, brethren.* Paul always chose to commend Christians when it could be done, and never seemed to suppose that such praise would be injurious to them. Note, chap. i. 4, 5. On this occasion he was the more ready to praise them as far as it could be done, because there were some things in regard to them in which he would have occasion to reprove them. ¶ *That ye remember me in all things.* That you are disposed to regard my authority and seek my direction in all matters pertaining to the good order of the church. There can be little doubt that they had consulted him in their letter (chap. vii. 1) about the proper manner in which a woman ought to demean herself if she was called upon, under the influence of divine inspiration, to utter any thing in public. The question seems to have been, whether, since she was inspired, it was proper for her to retain the marks of her inferiority of rank, and remain covered; or whether the fact of her inspiration did not release her from that obligation, anr make it proper that she should lay aside her veil, and appear as public speakers did among men. To this the apostle refers, probably, in the phrase "all things," that even in matters of this kind, pertaining to the good order of the church, they were disposed to regard his authority. ¶ *And keep the ordinances.* Margin, *Traditions* (τὰς παραδόσεις). The word does not refer to any thing that had been delivered down from a former generation, or from former times, as the word *tradition* now usually signifies; but it means that which had been *delivered to them* (παραδίδωμι); *i. e. by the apostles.* The apostles had *delivered* to them certain doctrines, or rules, respecting the good order and the government of the church; and they had in general observed them, and were disposed still to do it. For this disposition to regard his authority, and to keep what he had enjoined, he commends them. He proceeds to specify what would be proper in regard to the particular subject on which they had made inquiry.

3. *But I would have you know.* "I invite your attention particularly to the following considerations, in order to form a correct opinion on this subject." Paul does not *at once* answer the inquiry, and determine what ought to be done; but he invites their attention to a series of remarks on the subject, which led *them* to draw the conclusion which he wished to establish. The phrase here is designed to call the attention to the subject, like that used so often in the New Testament, "he that hath ears to hear, let him hear." ¶ *That the head,* &c. The word *head,* in the Scriptures, is designed often to denote *master, ruler, chief.* The word ראש is often thus used in the Old Testament; see Num. xvii. 3; xxv. 15; Deut. xxviii. 13, 44; Judg. x. 18; xi. 8, 11; 1 Sam. xv. 17; 2 Sam. xxii. 44. In the New Testament the word is used in the sense of Lord, ruler, chief, in Eph. i. 22; iv. 15; v. 23; Col. ii. 10. Here it means that Christ is the ruler, director, or Lord of the Christian man. This truth was to be regarded in all their feelings and arrangements, and was never to be forgotten. Every Christian should recollect the relation in which he stands to him, as one that is fitted to produce the strictest

4 Every man praying or prophesying, having *his* head covered, dishonoureth his head.

5 But every woman [a] that prayeth or prophesieth with *her* head uncovered, dishonoureth her head: for that is even all one as if she were shaven.

[a] Acts 21.9.

---

decorum, and a steady sense of subordination. ¶ *Of every man.* Every Christian. All acknowledge Christ as their Ruler and Master. They are subject to him; and in all proper ways recognise their subordination to him. ¶ *And the head of the woman* is *the man.* The sense is, she is subordinate to him; and in all circumstances—in her demeanour, her dress, her conversation, in public and in the family circle—should recognise her subordination to him. The particular thing here referred to is, that if the woman is inspired, and speaks or prays in public, she should by no means lay aside the usual and proper symbols of her subordination. The danger was, that those who were under the influence of inspiration would regard themselves as freed from the necessity of recognising that, and would lay aside the *veil,* the usual and appropriate symbol of their occupying a rank inferior to the man. This was often done in the temples of the heathen deities by the priestesses, and it would appear also that it had been done by Christian females in the churches. ¶ *And the head of Christ* is *God.* Christ, as Mediator, has consented to assume a subordinate rank, and to recognise God the Father as superior in office. Hence he was obedient in all things as a Son; he submitted to the arrangement required in redemption; he always recognised his subordinate rank as Mediator, and always regarded God as the supreme Ruler, even in the matter of redemption. The sense is, that Christ, throughout his entire work, regarded himself as occupying a subordinate station to the Father; and that it was proper from his example to recognise the propriety of rank and station every where.

4. *Every man praying or prophesying.* The word *prophesying* here means, evidently, *teaching;* or publicly speaking to the people on the subject of religion; see Note on Acts ii. 17. See also the subject considered more at length in the Notes on chap. xiv. Whether these persons who are here said to prophesy were all inspired, or claimed to be inspired, may admit of a question. The simple idea here is, that they spoke in the public assemblies, and professed to be the expounders of the divine will. ¶ *Having* his *head covered.* With a veil, or turban, or cap, or whatever else is worn on the head. To remove the hat, the turban, or the covering of the head, is a mark of respect for a superior when in his presence. ¶ *Dishonoureth his head.* Does dishonour to Christ as his head (ver. 2): that is, he does not, in his presence and in his service, observe the usual and proper custom by which a subordinate station is recognised, and which indicates respect for a superior. In the presence of a prince or a nobleman, it would be considered as a mark of disrespect should the head be covered. So in the presence of Christ, in whose name he ministers, it is a mark of disrespect if the head is covered. This illustration is drawn from the customs of all times and countries by which respect for a superior is indicated by removing the covering from the head. This is *one* reason why a man should not cover his head in public worship. Another is given in ver. 7. Other interpretations of the passage may be seen in Bloomfield's Critical Digest.

5. *But every woman that prayeth or prophesieth.* In the Old Testament prophetesses are not unfrequently mentioned. Thus Miriam is mentioned (Ex. xv. 20); Deborah (Judg. iv. 4); Huldah (2 Kings xxii. 14); Noadiah (Neh. vi. 14). So also in the New Testament Anna is mentioned as a prophetess; Luke ii. 36. That there were females in the early Christian church who corresponded to those known among the Jews in

some measure as endowed with the inspiration of the Holy Spirit, cannot be doubted. What was their precise office, and what was the nature of the public services in which they were engaged, is not however known. That they prayed is clear; and that they publicly expounded the will of God is apparent also; see Note on Acts ii. 17. As the presumption is, however, that they were inspired, their example is no warrant now for females to take part in the public services of worship, unless they also give evidence that they are under the influence of inspiration, and the more especially as the apostle Paul has expressly forbidden their becoming public teachers; 1 Tim. ii. 12. If it is now pled, from this example, that women should speak and pray in public, yet it should be just so far only *as this example goes*, and it should be *only* when they have the qualifications that the early *prophetesses* had in the Christian church. If there are any such; if any are directly inspired by God, there then will be an evident propriety that they should publicly proclaim his will, and not till then. It may be further observed, however, that the fact that Paul here mentions the custom of women praying or speaking publicly in the church, does not prove that it was right or proper. His immediate object now was not to consider whether the practice was itself right, but to condemn the manner of its performance as a violation of all the proper rules of modesty and of subordination. On another occasion, in this very epistle, he fully condemns the practice in any form, and enjoins silence on the female members of the church in public; chap. xiv. 34. ¶ *With* her *head uncovered.* That is, with the veil removed which she usually wore. It would seem from this that the women removed their veils, and wore their hair dishevelled, when they pretended to be under the influence of divine inspiration. This was the case with the heathen priestesses; and in so doing, the Christian women imitated them. On this account, if on no other, Paul declares the impropriety of this conduct. It was, besides, a custom among ancient females, and one that was strictly enjoined by the traditional laws of the Jews, that a woman should not appear in public unless she were veiled. See this proved by Lightfoot *in loco.* ¶ *Dishonoureth her head.* Shows a want of proper respect to man,—to her husband, to her father, to the sex in general. The veil is a token of modesty and of subordination. It is regarded among Jews, and everywhere, as an emblem of her sense of inferiority of rank and station. It is the customary mark of her sex, and that by which she evinces her modesty and sense of subordination. To remove that, is to remove the appropriate mark of such subordination, and is a public act by which she thus shows dishonour to the man. And as it is proper that the grades and ranks of life should be recognised in a suitable manner, so it is improper that, even on pretence of religion, and of being engaged in the service of God, these marks should be laid aside. ¶ *For that is even all one as if she were shaven.* As if her long hair, which nature teaches her she should wear for a veil (ver. 15, *margin,*) should be cut off. Long hair is, by the custom of the times, and of nearly all countries, a mark of the sex, an ornament of the female, and judged to be beautiful and comely. To remove that is to appear, in this respect, like the other sex, and to lay aside the badge of her own. This, says Paul, all would judge to be improper. You yourselves would not allow it. And yet to lay aside the veil—the appropriate badge of the sex, and of her sense of subordination—would be an act of the same kind. It would indicate the same feeling, the same forgetfulness of the proper sense of subordination; and if that is laid aside, ALL the usual indications of modesty and subordination might be removed also. Not even under religious pretences, therefore, are the usual marks of sex, and of propriety of place and rank, to be laid aside. Due respect is to be shown, in dress, and speech, and deportment, to those whom God has placed above us; and

6 For if the woman be not covered, let her also be shorn: [a] but if it be a shame for a woman to be shorn or shaven, let her be covered.

7 For a man indeed ought not to cover *his* head, forasmuch as he is the image [b] and glory of God: but the woman is the glory of the man.

a Num.5.18; Deut.21.12.

b Gen.5.1.

neither in language, in attire, nor in habit are we to depart from what all judge to be proprieties of life, or from what God has judged and ordained to be the proper indications of the regular gradations in society.

6. *For if the woman be not covered.* If her head be not covered with a veil. ¶ *Let her also be shorn.* Let her long hair be cut off. Let her lay aside all the usual and proper indications of her sex and rank in life. If it is done in one respect, it may with the same propriety be done in all, see Note above. ¶ *But if it be a shame,* &c. If custom, nature, and habit; if the common and usual feelings and views among men would pronounce this to be a shame, the other would be pronounced to be a shame also by the same custom and common sense of men. ¶ *Let her be covered.* With a veil. Let her wear the customary attire indicative of modesty and a sense of subordination. Let her not lay this aside even on any pretence of religion.

7. *For a man indeed ought not to cover* his *head.* That is, with a veil; or in public worship; when he approaches God, or when in His name he addresses his fellow men. It is not fit and proper that he should be covered. The reason why it is not proper, the apostle immediately states. ¶ *Forasmuch as he is the image and glory of God.* The phrase "the image of God" refers to the fact that man was made in the likeness of his Maker (Gen. i. 27); and proves that, though fallen, there is a sense in which he is still the image of God. It is not because man is holy or pure, and thus resembles his Creator; but it evidently is because he was invested by his Maker with authority and dominion; he was superior to all other creatures; Gen. i. 28. This is still retained; and this the apostle evidently refers to in the passage before us, and this he says should be recognised and regarded. If he wore a veil or turban, it would be a mark of servitude or inferiority. It was therefore improper that he should appear in this manner; but he should be so clad as not to obscure or hide the great truth that he was the direct representative of God on the earth, and had a superiority to all other creatures. ¶ *And glory of God.* The word *glory* in the classic writers means, (1.) Opinion, sentiment, &c.; (2.) Fame, reputation. Here it means, as it often does, splendour, brightness, or that which stands forth to *represent* God, or by which the glory of God is known. Man was created first; he had dominion given him; by him, therefore, the divine authority and wisdom first shone forth; and this fact should be recognised in the due subordination of rank, and even in the apparel and attire which shall be worn. The impression of his rank and superiority should be everywhere retained. ¶ *But the woman is the glory of the man.* The honour, the ornament, &c. She was made *for* him; she was made after he was; she was taken from him, and was "bone of his bone, and flesh of his flesh.' All her comeliness, loveliness, and purity are therefore an expression of his honour and dignity, since all that comeliness and loveliness were made of him and for him. This, therefore, ought to be acknowledged by a suitable manner of attire; and in his presence this sense of her inferiority of rank and subordination should be acknowledged by the customary use of the veil. She should appear with the symbol of modesty and subjection, which are implied by the head being covered. This sense is distinctly expressed in the following verse.

8 For[a] the man is not of the woman; but the woman of the man;
9 Neither was the man created for the woman, but the woman for the man.
10 For this cause ought the

a Gen.2.18,22,23.

8. *For the man is not of the woman.* The man was not formed *from* the woman. ¶ *But the woman of the man.* From his side; Gen. ii. 18. 22, 23.

9 *Neither was the man created for the woman,* &c. This is a simple statement of what is expressed in Genesis. The woman was made for the comfort and happiness of the man. Not to be a slave, but a help-meet; not to be the minister of his pleasures, but to be his aid and comforter in life; not to be regarded as of inferior nature and rank, but to be his friend, to divide his sorrows, and to multiply and extend his joys; yet still to be in a station subordinate to him. He is to be the head: the ruler; the presider in the family circle; and she was created to aid him in his duties, to comfort him in his afflictions, to partake with him of his pleasures. Her rank is therefore honourable, though it is subordinate. It is, in some respects, the more honourable because it is subordinate; and as her happiness is dependent on him, she has the higher claim to his protection and his tender care. The whole of Paul's idea here is, that her situation and rank as subordinate should be recognised by her at all times, and that in his presence it was proper that she should wear the usual symbol of modesty and subordination, the veil.

10. *For this cause,* &c. There is scarcely any passage in the Scriptures which has more exercised the ingenuity of commentators than this verse. The various attempts which have been made to explain it may be seen in Pool, Rosenmüller, Bloomfield, &c. After all the explanations which have been given of it, I confess, I do not understand it. It is not difficult to see what the connection requires us to suppose in the explanation. The obvious interpretation would be, that a woman should have a veil on her head because of the angels who were supposed to be present, observing them in their public worship; and it is generally agreed that the word *power* (ἐξουσίαν) denotes a veil, or a covering for the head. But the word *power* does not occur in this sense in any classic writer. Bretschneider understands it of a veil, as being a defence or guard to the face, lest it should be seen by others. Some have supposed that it was the name of a female ornament that was worn on the head, formed of braids of hair set with jewels. Most commentators agree that it means a *veil,* though some think (see Bloomfield) that it is called *power* to denote the veil which was worn by married women, which indicated the superiority of the married woman to the maiden. But it is sufficient to say in reply to this, that the apostle is not referring to married women in contradistinction from those who are unmarried, but is showing that *all* women who prophecy or pray in public should be veiled. There can, perhaps, be no doubt that the word "power" has reference to a veil, or to a covering for the head; but why it is called *power* I confess I do not understand; and most of the comments on the word are, in my view, egregious trifling. ¶ *Because of the angels.* Some have explained this of good angels, who were supposed to be present in their assemblies (see Doddridge); others refer it to evil angels; and others to messengers or spies who, it has been supposed, were present in their public assemblies, and who would report greatly to the disadvantage of the Christian assemblies if the women were seen to be unveiled. I do not know what it means; and I regard it as one of the very few passages in the Bible whose meaning as yet is wholly inexplicable. The most natural interpretation seems to me to be this: "A woman in the public assemblies, and in speaking in the presence of men, should wear a veil—

woman to have power [1] on *her* head, because of the angels.

11 Nevertheless, neither is the man without the woman, neither

1 i. e. *a covering, in sign that she is under the honour of her husband*, Gen.24.65.

the usual symbol of modesty and subordination—because the angels of God are witnesses of your public worship (Heb. i. 13), and because they know and appreciate the propriety of subordination and order in public assemblies." According to this, it would mean that the simple reason would be that the angels were witnesses of their worship; and that they were the friends of propriety, due subordination, and order; and that they ought to observe these in all assemblies convened for the worship of God.—I do not know that this sense has been proposed by any commentator; but it is one which strikes me as the most obvious and natural, and consistent with the context. The following remarks respecting the ladies of Persia may throw some light on this subject:—"The head-dress of the women is simple; their hair is drawn behind the head, and divided into several tresses: the beauty of this head-dress consists in the thickness and length of these tresses, which should fall even down to the heels, in default of which, they lengthen them with tresses of silk. The ends of these tresses they decorate with pearls and jewels, or ornaments of gold or silver. The head is covered, *under* the veil or kerchief (*course chef*), only by the end of a small *bandeau*, shaped into a triangle; this *bandeau*, which is of various colours, is thin and light. The *bandalette* is embroidered by the needle, or covered with jewellery, according to the quality of the wearer. This is, in my opinion, the ancient *tiara*, or *diadem*, of the queens of Persia: only married women wear it; and it is the mark by which it is known that they are under subjection (*c'est là la marque à laquelle on reconnoit qu'elles sont sous* PUISSANCE—*power*). The girls have little *caps*, instead of this kerchief or tiara; they wear no veil at home, but let two tresses of their hair fall under their cheeks. The caps of girls of superior rank are tied with a row of pearls. Girls are not shut up in Persia till they attain the age of six or seven years; before that age they go out of the seraglio, sometimes with their father, so that they may then be seen. I have seen some wonderfully pretty. They show the neck and bosom; and more beautiful cannot be seen."—*Chardin*. "The wearing of a veil by a married woman was a token of her being under power. The Hebrew name of the veil signifies dependence. Great importance was attached to this part of the dress in the East. All the women of Persia are pleasantly apparelled. When they are abroad in the streets, all, both rich and poor, are covered with a great veil, or sheet of very fine white cloth, of which one half, like a forehead cloth, comes down to the eyes, and, going over the head, reaches down to the heels; and the other half muffles up the face below the eyes, and being fastened with a pin to the left side of the head, falls down to their very shoes, even covering their hands, with which they hold that cloth by the two sides, so that, except the eyes, they are covered all over with it. Within doors they have their faces and breasts uncovered; but the Armenian women in their houses have always one half of their faces covered with a cloth, that goes athwart their noses, and hangs over their chin and breasts, except the maids of that nation, who, within doors, cover only the chin until they are married." *Thevenot*.

11. *Nevertheless*. Lest the man should assume to himself too much superiority, and lest he should regard the woman as made solely for his pleasure, and should treat her as in all respects inferior, and withhold the respect that is due to her. The design of this verse and the following is to show, that the man and woman are united in the most tender interests; that the one cannot live comfortably

the woman without the man in the Lord.

12 For as the woman *is* of the man, even so *is* the man also by the woman: but all [a] things of God.

13 Judge in yourselves: is it comely that a woman pray unto God uncovered?

14 Doth not even nature itself teach you, that if a man have long hair, it is a shame unto him?

a Rom.11.36.

without the other; that one is necessary to the happiness of the other; and that though the woman was formed from the man, yet it is also to be remembered that the man is descended from the woman. She should therefore be treated with proper respect, tenderness, and regard. ¶ *Neither is the man without the woman*, &c. The man and the woman were formed for union and society. They are not in any respect independent of each other. One is necessary to the comfort of the other; and this fact should be recognised in all their intercourse. ¶ *In the Lord.* By the arrangements or direction of the Lord. It is the appointment and command of the Lord that they should be mutual helps, and should each regard and promote the welfare of the other.

12. *As the woman* is *of the man.* In the original creation, she was formed from the man. ¶ *So* is *the man also by the woman.* Is born of the woman, or descended from her. The sexes are dependent on each other, and should therefore cultivate an indissoluble union. ¶ *But all things of God.* All things were created and arranged by him. This expression seems designed to suppress any spirit of complaint or dissatisfaction with this arrangement; to make the woman contented in her subordinate station, and to make the man humble by the consideration that it is all owing to the appointment of God. The woman should therefore be contented, and the man should not assume any improper superiority, since the whole arrangement and appointment is of God.

13. *Judge in yourselves.* Or, "Judge among yourselves." I appeal to you. I appeal to your natural sense of what is proper and right. Paul had used various arguments to show them the impropriety of their females speaking unveiled in public. He now appeals to their natural sense of what was decent and right, according to established and acknowledged customs and habits. ¶ *Is it comely*, &c. Is it decent, or becoming? The Grecian women, except their priestesses, were accustomed to appear in public with a veil.—*Doddridge.* Paul alludes to that established and proper habit, and asks whether it does not accord with their own views of propriety that women in Christian assemblies should also wear the same symbol of modesty.

14. *Doth not even nature itself.* The word *nature* (φύσις) denotes evidently that sense of propriety which all men have, and which is expressed in any prevailing or universal custom. That which is universal we say is according to nature. It is such as is demanded by the natural sense of fitness among men. Thus we may say that nature demands that the sexes should wear different kinds of dress; that nature demands that the female should be modest and retiring; that nature demands that the toils of the chase, of the field, of war—the duties of office, of government, and of professional life, should be discharged by men. Such are in general the customs the world over; and if any reason is asked for numerous habits that exist in society, no better answer can be given than that *nature*, as arranged by God, has demanded it. The word in this place, therefore, does not mean the constitution of the sexes, as Locke, Whitby, and Pierce maintain; nor reason and experience, as Macknight supposes; nor simple use and custom, as Grotius, Rosenmüller, and most recent expositors suppose; but it refers to a deep internal sense of what is proper and right; a sense which is expressed extensively in all nations, showing what that sense is. No *reason* can be given, in the nature of

15 But if a woman have long hair it is a glory to her: for *her* hair is given her for a [1] covering.

1 or, *veil*.

16 But [a] if any man seem to be contentious, we have no such custom, neither the churches of God.

a 1 Tim.6.4.

things, why the woman should wear long hair and the man not; but the custom prevails extensively everywhere, and nature, in all nations, has prompted to the same course. "Use is second nature;" but the usage in this case is not arbitrary, but is founded in an anterior universal sense of what is proper and right. A few, and only a few, have regarded it as comely for a man to wear his hair long. Aristotle tells us, indeed (Rhet. i.—see Rosenmüller), that among the Lacedemonians, freemen wore their hair long. In the time of Homer, also, the Greeks were called by him καρηκομόωντες Ἀχαῖοι, long-haired Greeks; and some of the Asiatic nations adopted the same custom. But the general habit among men has been different. Among the Hebrews, it was regarded as disgraceful to a man to wear his hair long, except he had a vow as a Nazarite, Num. vi. 1—5; Judg. xiii. 5; xvi. 17; 1 Sam. i. 11. Occasionally, for affectation or singularity, the hair was suffered to grow, as was the case with Absalom (2 Sam. xiv. 26); but the traditional law of the Jews on the subject was strict. The same *rule* existed among the Greeks; and it was regarded as disgraceful to wear long hair in the time of Ælian; Hist. lib. ix. c. 14. Eustath. on Hom. ii. v. ¶ *It is a shame unto him.* It is improper and disgraceful. It is doing that which almost universal custom has said appropriately belongs to the female sex.

15. *It is a glory unto her.* It is an ornament, and adorning. The same instinctive promptings of nature which make it proper for a man to wear short hair, make it proper that the woman should suffer hers to grow long. ¶ *For a covering.* Marg. *Veil.* It is given to her as a sort of natural veil, and to indicate the propriety of her wearing a veil. It answered the purposes of a veil when it was suffered to grow long, and to spread over the shoulders and over parts of the face, before the arts of dress were invented or needed. There may also be an allusion here to the fact that the hair of women naturally grows longer than that of men. See Rosenmüller. The value which eastern females put on their long hair may be learned from the fact that when Ptolemy Euergetes, king of Egypt, was about to march against Seleucus Callinicus, his queen Berenice vowed, as the most precious sacrifice which she could make, to cut off and consecrate her hair if he returned in safety. "The eastern ladies," says Harmer, "are remarkable for the length and the great number of the tresses of their hair. The men there, on the contrary, wear very little hair on their heads." Lady M. W. Montague thus speaks concerning the hair of the women: "Their hair hangs at full length behind, divided into tresses, braided with pearl or riband, which is always in great quantity. I never saw in my life so many fine heads of hair. In one lady's I have counted one hundred and ten of these tresses, all natural; but it must be owned that every kind of beauty is more common here than with us." The men there, on the contrary, shave all the hair off their heads, excepting one lock; and those that wear hair are thought effeminate. Both these particulars are mentioned by Chardin, who says they are agreeable to the custom of the East: "the men are shaved; the women nourish their hair with great fondness, which they lengthen, by tresses and tufts of silk, down to the heels. The young men who wear their hair in the East are looked upon as effeminate and infamous."

16. *But if any man seem to be contentious.* The sense of this passage is probably this: "If any man, any teacher, or others, *is disposed* to be strenuous about this, or to make it a matter of difficulty; if he is disposed

17 Now in this that I declare *unto you* I praise *you* not, that ye come together not for the better, but for the worse.

18 For first of all, when ye come together in the church, I hear [a] that there be divisions [1] among you; and I partly believe it.

a chap. 1. 11, 12.

1 or, *schisms*.

to call in question my reasoning, and to dispute my premises and the considerations which I have advanced, and to maintain still that it is proper for women to appear unveiled in public, I would add that in Judea we have no such custom, neither does it prevail among any of the churches. This, therefore, would be a sufficient reason why it should not be done in Corinth, even if the abstract reasoning should not convince them of the impropriety. It would be singular; would be contrary to the usual custom; would offend the prejudices of many and should, therefore, be avoided." ¶ *We have no such custom.* We the apostles in the churches which we have elsewhere founded; or we have no such custom in Judea. The sense is, that it is contrary to custom there for women to appear in public unveiled. This custom, the apostle argues, ought to be allowed to have some influence on the church of Corinth, even though they should not be convinced by his reasoning. ¶ *Neither the churches of God.* The churches elsewhere. It is customary there for the woman to appear veiled. If at Corinth this custom is not observed, it will be a departure from what has elsewhere been regarded as proper; and will offend these churches. Even, therefore, if the *reasoning* is not sufficient to silence all cavils and doubts, yet the propriety of uniformity in the habits of the churches, the fear of giving offence should lead you to discountenance and disapprove the custom of your females appearing in public without their veil.

17. *Now in this that I declare.* In this that I am about to state to you; to wit, your conduct in regard to the Lord's supper. Why this subject is introduced here is not very apparent. The connection may be this. In the subjects immediately preceding he had seen much to commend, and he was desirous of commending them as far as it could be done. In ver. 2 of this chapter he commends them *in general* for their regard to the ordinances which he had appointed when he was with them. But while he thus commended them, he takes occasion to observe that there was *one* subject on which he could not employ the language of approval or praise. Of their irregularities in regard to the Lord's supper he had probably heard by rumour, and as the subject was of great importance, and their irregularities gross and deplorable, he takes occasion to state to them again more fully the nature of that ordinance, and to reprove them for the manner in which they had celebrated it. ¶ *That ye come together.* You assemble for public worship. ¶ *Not for the better, but for the worse.* Your meetings, and your observance of the ordinances of the gospel, do not promote your edification, your piety, spirituality, and harmony; but tend to division, alienation, and disorder. You *should* assemble to worship God, and promote harmony, love, and piety; the actual effect of your assembling is just the reverse. In what way this was done he states in the following verses. These evil consequences were chiefly two,—first, divisions and contentions; and, secondly, the abuse and profanation of the Lord's supper.

18. *For first of all.* That is, I mention as the first thing to be reproved. ¶ *When ye come together in the church.* When you come together in a religious assembly; when you convene for public worship. The word *church* here does not mean, as it frequently does with us, a *building*. No instance of such a use of the word occurs in the New Testament; but it means when they came together as a Christian assembly; when they convened for the worship of God. These divisions took place *then;* and from some cause which

19 For there must [a] be also [1] heresies among you, that [b] they

a Mat.18.7; 2 Pet.2.1,2. 1 or, sects. b Luke 2.35.

it seems *then* operated to produce alienations and strifes. ¶ *I hear.* I have learned through some members of the family of Chloe; chap. i. 11. ¶ *That there be divisions among you.* Greek, as in the margin, *Schisms.* The word properly means *a rent,* such as is made in cloth (Mat. ix. 16; Mark ii. 21), and then a division, a split, a faction among men; John vii. 43; ix. 16; x. 19. It does not mean here that they had proceeded so far as to form separate churches, but that there was discord and division in the church itself; see Notes on chap. i. 10, 11. ¶ *And I partly believe it.* I credit a part of the reports; I have reason to think, that, though the evil may have been exaggerated, yet that it is true at least in part. I believe that there *are* dissensions in the church that should be reproved.

19. *For there must be.* It is necessary (δεῖ); it is to be expected; there are reasons why there should be. What these reasons are he states in the close of the verse; comp. Mat. xviii. 7; 2 Pet. ii. 1, 2. The meaning is, not that divisions are inseparable from the nature of the Christian religion, not that it is the design and wish of the Author of Christianity that they should exist, and not that they are physically impossible, for then they could not be the subject of blame; but that such is human nature, such are the corrupt passions of men, the propensity to ambition and strifes, that they are to be expected, and they serve the purpose of showing who are, and who are not, the true friends of God. ¶ *Heresies.* Margin, *Sects.* Gr. Αἱρέσεις; see Note, Acts xxiv. 14. The words *heresy* and *heresies* occur only in these places, and in Gal. v. 20; 2 Pet. ii. 1. The Greek word occurs also in Acts v. 17 (translated *sect*); xv. 5; xxiv. 5; xxvi. 5; xxviii. 22, in all which places it denotes, and is translated, *sect.* We now attach to the word usually the idea of a fundamental error in religion, or some *doctrine* the holding of which will exclude from salvation. But there is no evidence that the word is used in this signification in the New Testament. The only place where it can be supposed to be so used, unless this is one, is in Gal. v. 20, where, however, the word *contentions* or *divisions,* would be quite as much in accordance with the connection. That the word here does not denote error in doctrine, but schism, division, or *sects,* as it is translated in the margin, is evident from two considerations. (1.) It is the proper philological meaning of the word, and its established and common signification in the Bible. (2.) It is the sense which the connection here demands. The apostle had made no reference to error of doctrine, but is discoursing solely of *irregularity in conduct;* and the first thing which he mentions, is, that there were schisms, divisions, strifes. The idea that the word here refers to *doctrines* would by no means suit the connection, and would indeed make nonsense. It would then read, "I hear that there are divisions or parties among you, and this I cannot commend you for. For it must be expected that there would be *fundamental errors of doctrine* in the church.," But *Paul* did not reason in this manner. The sense is, "There are divisions among you. It is to be expected: there are causes for it; and it cannot be avoided that there should be, in the present state of human nature, divisions and sects formed in the church; and this is to be expected in order that those who are true Christians should be separated from those who are not." The *foundation* of this necessity is not in the Christian religion itself, for that is pure, and contemplates and requires union; but the existence of sects, and denominations, and contentions may be traced to the following causes. (1.) The love of power and popularity. Religion may be made the means of power; and they who have the control of the consciences of men, and of their religious feelings and opinions, can control them altogether. (2.) Showing more respect to a religious teacher than to Christ: see Notes on chap. i. 12. (3.) The

which are approved may be made manifest among you.

20 When ye come together therefore into one place, [1] *this* is not to eat the Lord's supper.

[1] or, *ye cannot eat.*

multiplication of tests, and the enlargement of creeds and confessions of faith. The consequence is, that every new doctrine that is incorporated into a creed gives occasion for those to separate who cannot accord with it. (4.) The passions of men—their pride, and ambition, and bigotry, and unenlightened zeal. Christ evidently meant that his church should be one; and that all who were his true followers should be admitted to her communion, and acknowledged everywhere as his own friends. And the time may yet come when this union shall be restored to his long distracted church, and that while there may be an honest difference of opinion maintained and allowed, still the bonds of Christian love shall secure union of *heart* in all who love the Lord Jesus, and union of *effort* in the grand enterprise in which ALL can unite—that of making war upon sin, and securing the conversion of the whole world to God. ¶ *That they which are approved.* That they who are approved of God, or who are his true friends, and who are disposed to abide by his laws. ¶ *May be made manifest.* May be known; recognised; seen. The effect of divisions and separations would be to show who were the friends of order, and peace, and truth. It seems to have been assumed by Paul, that they who made divisions *could* not be regarded as the friends of order and truth; or that their course could not be approved by God. The effect of these divisions would be to show who they were. So in all divisions, and all splitting into factions, where the great truths of Christianity are held, and where the corruption of the mass does not require separation, such divisions show who are the restless, ambitious, and dissatisfied spirits; who they are that are *indisposed* to follow the things that make for peace, and the laws of Christ enjoining union; and who they are who are gentle and peaceful, and disposed to pursue the way of truth, and love, and order, without contentions and strifes. This is the effect of schisms in the church; and the whole strain of the argument of Paul is to reprove and condemn such schisms, and to hold up the authors of them to reproof and condemnation; see Rom. xvi. 17, "Mark them which cause divisions, and AVOID THEM."

20. *When ye come together therefore,* &c. When you are assembled as a church; comp. Heb. x. 25, and Note on Acts ii. 1. Christians were constantly in the habit of *assembling* for public worship. It is probable that at this early period all the Christians in Corinth were accustomed to meet in the same place. The apostle here particularly refers to their assembling to observe the ordinance of the Lord's supper. At that early period it is probable that this was done on every Lord's day. ¶ This *is not,* &c. Margin, "Ye cannot eat.' The meaning of this expression seems to be this. "Though you come together professedly to worship God, and to partake of the Lord's supper, yet this cannot be the *real design* which you have in view. It *cannot be* that such practices as are allowed among you can be a part of the celebration of that supper, or consistent with it. Your greediness (ver. 21); your intemperance (ver. 21); your partaking of the food separately and not in common, *cannot* be a celebration of the Lord's supper. Whatever, therefore, you may profess to be engaged in, yet really and truly you are *not* celebrating the Lord's supper." ¶ *The Lord's supper.* That which the Lord Jesus instituted to commemorate his death. It is called "the Lord's," because it is his appointment, and is in honour of him; it is called "supper" (δεῖπνον), because the word denotes the evening repast; it was instituted in the evening; and it is evidently most proper that it should be observed in the after part of the day. With most churches the time is improperly changed to the morning—

21 For in eating, every one taketh before *other* his own supper: and one is hungry and [a] another is drunken.

a 2 Pet.2.13; Jude 12.

a custom which has no sanction in the New Testament; and which is a departure from the very idea of a supper.

21. *For in eating.* When you eat, having professedly come together to observe this ordinance. In order to understand this, it seems necessary to suppose that they had in some way made the Lord's supper either connected with a common feast, or that they regarded it as a mere common festival to be observed in a way similar to the festivals among the Greeks. Many have supposed that this was done by making the observance of the supper follow a festival, or what were afterwards called *love feasts* ('Αγαπαι —*Agapae*). Many have supposed that that custom was derived from the fact that the Saviour instituted the supper *after* a festival, a feast in which he had been engaged with his disciples, and that thence the early Christians derived the custom of observing such a festival, or common meal, before they celebrated the Lord's supper. But it may be observed, that the passover was not a mere preliminary festival, or feast. It had no resemblance to the so called love feasts. It was itself a religious ordinance; a direct appointment of God; and was never regarded as designed to be *preliminary* to the observance of the Lord's supper, but was always understood as designed to be *superseded* by that. Besides, I know not that there is the slightest evidence, as has been often supposed, that the observance of the Lord's supper was *preceded*, in the times of the apostles, by such a festival as a love feast. There is no evidence in the passage before us; nor is any adduced from any other part of the New Testament. To my mind it seems altogether improbable that the disorders in Corinth would assume this form—that they would *first* observe a common feast, and *then* the Lord's supper in the regular manner. The statement before us leads to the belief that *all* was irregular and improper; that they had entirely mistaken the nature of the ordinance, and had converted it into an occasion of ordinary festivity, and even intemperance; that they had come to regard it as a feast in honour of the Saviour on some such principles as they observed feasts in honour of idols, and that they observed it in some such manner; and that all that was supposed to make it *unlike* those festivals was, that it was in honour of Jesus rather than an idol, and was to be observed with some reference to his authority and name. ¶ *Every one taketh before* other *his own supper.* That is, each one is regardless of the wants of the others; instead of making even a meal in common, and when all could partake together, each one ate by himself, and ate that which he had himself brought. They had not only erred, therefore, by misunderstanding altogether the nature of the Lord's supper, and by supposing that it was a common festival like those which they had been accustomed to celebrate; but they had also entirely departed from the idea that it was a festival to be partaken of in common, and at a common table. It had become a scene where every man ate by himself; and where the very idea that there was any thing like a *common* celebration, or a celebration *together*, was abandoned. There is allusion here, doubtless, to what was a custom among the Greeks, that when a festival was celebrated, or a feast made, it was common for each person to provide, and carry a part of the things necessary for the entertainment. These were usually placed in common, and were partaken of alike by all the company. Thus Xenophon (Mem. lib. iii. cap. xiv.) says of Socrates, that he was much offended with the Athenians for their conduct at their common suppers, where some prepared for themselves in a delicate and sumptuous manner, while others were poorly provided for. Socrates endeavoured, he adds, to shame them out of this indecent custom by offering his provisions to all the company. ¶ *And one is hungry.* It

22 What! have ye not houses to eat and to drink in? or despise ye the church of God, and shame them that [1] have not? What shall I say to you? shall I praise you in this? I praise *you* not.

1 *are poor.*

deprived of food. It is all monopolized by others. ¶ *And another is drunken.* The word here used (μεθύω) means properly to become inebriated, or intoxicated; and there is no reason for understanding it here in any other sense. There can be no doubt that the apostle meant to say, that they ate and drank to excess; and that their professed celebration of the Lord's supper became a mere revel. It may seem remarkable that such scenes should ever have occurred in a Christian church, or that there could have been such an entire perversion of the nature and design of the Lord's supper. But we are to remember the following things: (1.) These persons had recently been heathens, and were grossly ignorant of the nature of true religion when the gospel was first preached among them. (2.) They had been accustomed to such revels in honour of idols under their former modes of worship, and it is the less surprising that they transferred their views to Christianity. (3.) When they had once so far misunderstood the nature of Christianity as to suppose the Lord's supper to be like the feasts which they had formerly celebrated, all the rest followed as a matter of course. The festival would be observed in the same manner as the festivals in honour of idolaters; and similar scenes of gluttony and intemperance would naturally follow. (4.) We are to bear in mind, also, that they do not seem to have been favoured with pious, wise, and prudent teachers. There were false teachers; and there were those who prided themselves on their wisdom, and who were self-confident, and who doubtless endeavoured to model the Christian institutions according to their own views; and they thus brought them, as far as they could, to a conformity with pagan customs and idolatrous rites. We may remark here, (1.) We are not to expect perfection at once among a people recently converted from paganism. (2.) We see how prone men are to abuse even the most holy rites of religion, and hence how corrupt is human nature. (3.) We see that even Christians, recently converted, need constant guidance and superintendence; and that if left to themselves they soon, like others, fall into gross and scandalous offences.

22. *What!* This whole verse is designed to convey the language of severe rebuke for their having so grossly perverted the design of the Lord's supper. ¶ *Have ye not houses,* &c. Do you not know that the church of God is not designed to be a place of feasting and revelry: nor even a place where to partake of your ordinary meals? Can it be, that you will come to the places of public worship, and make them the scenes of feasting and riot? Even on the supposition that there had been no disorder; no revelry; no intemperance; yet on every account it was grossly irregular and disorderly to make the place of public worship a place for a festival entertainment. ¶ *Or despise ye the church of God.* The phrase "church of God" Grotius understands of the place. But the word *church* (ἐκκλησία) is believed not to be used in that sense in the New Testament; and it is not necessary to suppose it here. The sense is, that their conduct was such as if they had held in contempt the whole church of God, in all places, with all their views of the sacredness and purity of the Lord's supper. ¶ *And shame them that have not.* Margin, *Are poor.* Something must here be understood in order to make out the sense. Probably it meant something like *possessions, property, conveniences, accommodations.* The connection would make it most natural to understand "houses to eat and drink in;" and the sense then would be, "Do you thus expose to public shame those who have no accommodations at home; who are destitute and poor? You thus reflect publicly

23 For [a] I have received of the Lord that which also I delivered

a chap.15.3.

upon their poverty and want, while you bring your own provisions and fare sumptuously, and while those who are thus unable to provide for themselves are thus seen to be poor and needy." It is hard enough, the idea is, to be poor, and to be destitute of a home. But it greatly aggravates the matter to be *publicly treated* in that manner; to be exposed publicly to the contempt which such a situation implies. Their treatment of the poor in this manner would be a public exposing them to shame; and the apostle regarded this as particularly dishonourable, and especially in a Christian church, where all were professedly on an equality. ¶ *What shall I say to you?* &c. How shall I sufficiently express my surprise at this, and my disapprobation at this course? It cannot be possible that this is right. It is not possible to conceal surprise and amazement that this custom exists, and is tolerated in a Christian church.

23. *For*, &c. In order most effectually to check the evils which existed, and to bring them to a proper mode of observing the Lord's supper, the apostle proceeds to state distinctly and particularly its design. They had mistaken its nature. They supposed it might be a common festival. They had made it the occasion of great disorder. He therefore adverts to the solemn circumstances in which it was instituted; the particular object which it had in view—the commemoration of the death of the Redeemer, and the purpose which it was designed to subserve, which was not that of a festival, but to keep before the church and the world a constant remembrance of the Lord Jesus until he should again return, ver. 26. By this means the apostle evidently hoped to recall them from their irregularities, and to bring them to a just mode of celebrating this holy ordinance. He did not, therefore, denounce them even for their irregularity and gross disorder: he did not use harsh, violent, vituperative language, but he expected to reform the evil by a mild and tender statement of the truth, and by an appeal to their consciences as the followers of the Lord Jesus. ¶ *I have received of the Lord.* This cannot refer to tradition, or mean that it had been communicated to him through the medium of the other apostles; but the whole spirit and scope of the passage seems to mean that he had derived the knowledge of the institution of the Lord's supper *directly* from the Lord himself. This might have been when on the road to Damascus, though that does not seem probable, or it may have been among the numerous revelations which at various times had been made to him; comp. 2 Cor. xii. 7. The *reason* why he here says that he had received it directly from the Lord is, doubtless, that he might show them that it was of divine authority. "The institution to which I refer is what I myself received an account of *from personal and direct communication with the Lord Jesus himself, who appointed it.* It is not, therefore, of human authority. It is not of my devising, but is of divine warrant, and is holy in its nature, and is to be observed in the exact manner prescribed by the Lord himself." ¶ *That which also I delivered*, &c. Paul founded the church at Corinth; and of course he first instituted the observance of the Lord's supper there. ¶ *The* same *night in which he was betrayed.* By Judas; see Mat. xxvi. 23—25, 48—50. Paul seems to have mentioned the fact that it was on the very night on which he was betrayed, in order to throw around it the idea of greater solemnity. He wished evidently to bring before their minds the deeply affecting circumstances of his death; and thus to show them the utter impropriety of their celebrating the ordinance with riot and disorder. The idea is, that in order to celebrate it in a proper manner, it was needful *to throw themselves as much as possible into the very circumstances in which it was instituted;* and one of these circumstances most fitted to affect the mind deeply was the fact that he was

unto you, That the Lord Jesus, [a] the *same* night in which he was betrayed, took bread:

24 And when he had given thanks, he brake *it*, and said, Take, eat; this is my body, which is broken for you: this do in [1] remembrance of me.

25 After the same manner also *he took* the cup, when he had sup-

a Mat.26.26.

1 or, *for a*.

betrayed by a professed friend and follower. It is also a circumstance the memory of which is eminently fitted to prepare the mind for a proper celebration of the ordinance now. ¶ *Took bread.* Evidently the bread which was used at the celebration of the paschal supper. He took the bread which happened to be before him—such as was commonly used. It was not *a wafer* such as the papists now use; but was the ordinary bread which was eaten on such occasions; see Note on Mat. xxvi. 26.

24. *And when he had given thanks;* see Note on Matt. xxvi. 26. Matthew reads it, "and blessed it." The words here used are, however, substantially the same as there; and this fact shows that since this was communicated to Paul *directly* by the Saviour, and in a manner distinct from that by which Matthew learned the mode of the institution, the Saviour designed that the exact form of the words should be used in its observance, and should thus be constantly borne in mind by his people. ¶ *Take eat,* &c.; see Note on Mat. xxvi. 26.

25. *After the same manner.* In like manner; likewise. With the same circumstances, and ceremonies, and designs. The purpose was the same. ¶ *When he had supped.* That is, all this occurred *after* the observance of the usual paschal supper. It could not, therefore, be a part of it, nor could it have been designed to be a festival or feast merely. The apostle introduces this evidently in order to show them that it could not be, as they seemed to have supposed, an occasion of feasting. It was *after* the supper, and was therefore to be observed in a distinct manner. ¶ *Saying, This cup,* &c.; see Note, Mat. xxvi. 27, 28. ¶ *Is the New Testament.* The new covenant which God is about to establish with men. The word "testament" with us properly denotes *a will*—an instrument by which a man disposes of his property after his death. This is also the proper classic meaning of the Greek word here used, διαθήκη (*diatheke*). But this is evidently not the sense in which the word is designed to be used in the New Testament. The idea of a *will* or *testament,* strictly so called, is not that which the sacred writers intend to convey by the word. The idea is evidently that of a compact, agreement, COVENANT, to which there is so frequent reference in the Old Testament, and which is expressed by the word ברית (*Berith*), a compact, a covenant, Of that word the proper translation in Greek would have been συνθηκη, a covenant, agreement. But it is remarkable that that word never is used by the LXX. to denote the covenant made between God and man. That translation uniformly employs for this purpose the word διαθήκη, *a will,* or *a testament,* as a translation of the Hebrew word, where there is a reference to the covenant which God is represented as making with men. The word συνθηκη is used by them but three times (Isa. xxviii. 15; xxx. 1; Dan. xi. 6), and in neither instance with any reference to the *covenant* which God is represented as making with man. The word διαθήκη, as the translation of ברית (*Berith*), occurs more than two hundred times. (See *Trommius' Concord.*) Now this must have evidently been of design. What the reason was which induced them to adopt this can only be conjectured. It may have been that as the translation was to be seen by the Gentiles as well as by the Jews (if it were not expressly made, as has been affirmed by Josephus and others, for the use of Ptolemy), they were unwilling to represent the eternal and infinite JEHOVAH as entering

ped, saying, This is the new testament in my blood: this do ye, as oft as ye drink *it*, in remembrance of me.

26 For as often as ye eat this bread, and drink this cup, [1] ye do shew the Lord's death till he come.[a]

27 Wherefore, whosoever shall

1 or *shew ye*.

a Rev.22.20.

into a *compact, an agreement* with his creature man. They, therefore, adopted a word which would represent him as expressing *his will* to them in a book of revelation. The version by the LXX. was evidently in use by the apostles, and by the Jews everywhere. The writers of the New Testament, therefore, adopted the word as they found it; and spoke of the new dispensation as a new *testament* which God made with man. The meaning is, that this was the new compact or covenant which God was to make with man in contradistinction from that made through Moses. ¶ *In my blood.* Through my blood; that is, this new compact is to be sealed with my blood, in illusion to the ancient custom of sealing an agreement by a sacrifice; see Note, Mat. xxvi. 28. ¶ *This do ye.* Partake of this bread and wine; that is, celebrate this ordinance. ¶ *As oft as ye drink it.* Not prescribing any time; and not even specifying the frequency with which it was to be done; but leaving it to themselves to determine how often they would partake of it. The time of the passover had been fixed by positive statute; the more mild and gentle system of Christianity left it to the followers of the Redeemer themselves to determine how often they would celebrate his death. It was commanded them to do it; it was presumed that their love to him would be so strong as to secure a frequent observance; it was permitted to them, as in prayer, to celebrate it on any occasion of affliction, trial, or deep interest when they would feel their need of it, and when they would suppose that its observance would be for the edification of the Church. ¶ *In remembrance of me.* This expresses the whole design of the ordinance. It is a simple memorial, or remembrancer; designed to recall in a striking and impressive manner the memory of the Redeemer. It does this by a tender appeal to the senses—by the exhibition of the broken bread, and by the wine. The Saviour knew how prone men would be to forget him; and he, therefore, appointed this ordinance as a means by which his memory should be kept up in the world. The ordinance is rightly observed when it recalls the memory of the Saviour; and when its observance is the means of producing a deep, and lively, and vivid impression on the mind, of his death for sin. This expression, at the institution of the supper, is used by Luke (chap. xxii. 19); though it does not occur in Matthew, Mark, or John.

26. *For as often.* Whenever you do this. ¶ *Ye eat this bread.* This is a direct and positive refutation of the doctrine of the papists that the *bread* is changed into the real body of the Lord Jesus. Here it is expressly called *bread*—bread still—bread after the consecration. Before the Saviour instituted the ordinance he took "bread"—it was bread then: it was "bread" which he "blessed" and "brake;" and it was bread when it was given to them; and it was bread when Paul here says they *ate*. How then can it be pretended that it is any thing else but bread? And what an amazing and astonishing absurdity it is to believe that that bread is changed into the flesh and blood of Jesus Christ! ¶ *Ye do show the Lord's death.* You set forth, or exhibit in an impressive manner, the fact that he was put to death; you exhibit the emblems of his broken body and shed blood, and your belief of the fact that he died. This shows that the ordinance was to be so far *public* as to be a proper showing forth of their belief in the death of the Saviour. It *should be* public. It is one mode of professing attachment to the Redeemer; and its public observance often has a most impressive effect on those who witness its observance. ¶ *Till he come.* Till he re-

eat this bread, and drink *this* cup of the Lord, unworthily,[a] shall be guilty of the body and blood of the Lord.

a John 6.63,64; chap.10.21.

turn to judge the world. This demonstrates, (1.) That it was the steady belief of the primitive church that the Lord Jesus would return to judge the world; and (2.) That it was designed that this ordinance should be perpetuated, and observed to the end of time. In every generation, therefore, and in every place where there are Christians, it is to be observed, until the Son of God shall return; and the necessity of its observance shall cease only when the whole body of the redeemed shall be permitted to see their Lord, and there shall be no need of those emblems to remind them of him, for all shall see him as he is.

27. *Wherefore* (ὥστε). So that, or it follows from what has been said. If this be the origin and intention of the Lord's supper, then it follows that whoever partakes of it in an improper manner is guilty of his body and blood. The design of Paul is to correct their improper mode of observing this ordinance; and having showed them the true nature and design of the institution, he now states the consequences of partaking of it in an improper manner. ¶ *Shall eat this bread;* see ver. 26. Paul still calls it *bread*, and shows thus that he was a stranger to the doctrine that the bread was changed into the very body of the Lord Jesus. Had the papal doctrine of transubstantiation been true, Paul could not have called it bread. The Romanists do not believe that it is bread, nor would they call it such; and this shows how needful it is for them to keep the Scriptures from the people, and how impossible to express their dogmas in the language of the Bible. Let Christians adhere to the simple language of the Bible, and there is no danger of their falling into the errors of the papists. ¶ *Unworthily.* Perhaps there is no expression in the Bible that has given more trouble to weak and feeble Christians than this. It is certain that there is no one that has operated to deter so many from the communion; or that is so often made use of as an excuse for not making a profession of religion. The excuse is, "I am unworthy to partake of this holy ordinance. I shall only expose myself to condemnation. I must therefore wait until I become more worthy, and better prepared to celebrate it." It is important, therefore, that there should be a correct understanding of this passage. Most persons interpret it as if it were *unworthy*, and not *unworthily*, and seem to suppose that it refers to their personal qualifications, to their *unfitness* to partake of it, rather than to the *manner* in which it is done. It is to be remembered, therefore, that the word here used is an *adverb*, and not an *adjective*, and has reference to the *manner* of observing the ordinance, and not to their personal qualifications or fitness. It is true that in ourselves we are all *unworthy* of an approach to the table of the Lord; *unworthy* to be regarded as his followers; *unworthy* of a title to everlasting life: but it does not follow that we may not partake of this ordinance in a worthy, *i. e.* a proper manner, with a deep sense of our sinfulness, our need of a Saviour, and with some just views of the Lord Jesus as our Redeemer. Whatever may be our consciousness of personal unworthiness and unfitness—and that consciousness cannot be too deep—yet we may have such love to Christ, and such a desire to be saved by him, and such a sense of *his* worthiness, as to make it proper for us to approach and partake of this ordinance. The term *unworthily* (ἀναξίως) means properly *in an unworthy or improper* MANNER, *in a manner unsuitable to the purposes for which it was designed or instituted;* and may include the following things, viz. (1.) Such an irregular and indecent observance as existed in the church of Corinth, where even gluttony and intemperance prevailed under the professed design of cele-

brating the supper. (2.) An observance of the ordinance where there should be no distinction between it and common meals (Note on ver. 29); where they did not regard it as designed to show forth the death of the Lord Jesus. It is evident that where *such* views prevailed, there could be no proper qualification for this observance; and it is equally clear that such ignorance can hardly be supposed to prevail now in those lands which are illuminated by Christian truth. (3.) When it is done for the sake of mockery, and when the purpose is to deride religion, and to show a marked contempt for the ordinances of the gospel. It is a remarkable fact that many infidels have been so full of malignity and bitterness against the Christian religion as to observe a mock celebration of the Lord's supper. There is no profounder depth of depravity than this; there is nothing that can more conclusively or painfully show the hostility of man to the gospel of God. It is a remarkable fact, also, that not a few such persons have died a most miserable death. Under the horrors of an accusing conscience, and the anticipated destiny of final damnation, they have left the world as frightful monuments of the justice of God. It is *also* a fact that not a few infidels who have been engaged in such unholy celebrations have been converted to that very gospel which they were thus turning into ridicule and scorn. Their consciences have been alarmed; they have shuddered at the remembrance of the crime; they have been overwhelmed with the consciousness of guilt, and have found no peace until they have found it in that blood whose shedding they were thus profanely celebrating. ¶ *Shall be guilty* (ἔνοχος). This word properly means obnoxious to punishment for personal crime. It always includes the idea of ill-desert, and of exposure to punishment on account of crime or ill-desert; Mat. v. 22; comp. Exod. xxii. 3; xxxiv. 7; Num. xiv. 18; xxxv. 27; Lev. xx. 9; see also Deut. xix. 10; Mat. xxvi. 66. ¶ *Of the body and blood of the Lord.* Commentators have not been agreed in regard to the meaning of this expression. Doddridge renders it, "Shall be counted guilty of profaning and affronting in some measure that which is intended to represent the body and blood of the Lord." Grotius renders it, "He does the same thing as if he should slay Christ." Bretschneider (Lex.) renders it, "Injuring by crime the body of the Lord." Locke renders it, "Shall be guilty of a misuse of the body and blood of the Lord;" and supposes it means that they should be liable to the punishment due to one who made a wrong use of the sacramental body and blood of Christ in the Lord's supper. Rosenmüller renders it, "He shall be punished for such a deed as if he had affected Christ himself with ignominy." Bloomfield renders it, "He shall be guilty respecting the body, *i. e.* guilty of profaning the symbols of the body and blood of Christ, and consequently shall be amenable to the punishment due to such an abuse of the highest means of grace." But it seems to me that this does not convey the fulness of the meaning of the passage. The obvious and literal sense is evidently that they should by such conduct be involved in the sin of putting the Lord Jesus to death. The phrase "the body and blood of the Lord," in this connection, obviously, I think, refers to his death,—to the fact that his body was broken, and his blood shed, of which the bread and wine were symbols; and to be *guilty* of that, means to be guilty of putting him to death; that is, to be involved in the crime, or to do a thing which should involve the same criminality as that. To see this, we are to remember, (1.) That the bread and wine were symbols or emblems of that event, and designed to set it forth. (2.) To treat with irreverence and profaneness the bread which was an emblem of his broken body, was to treat with irreverence and profaneness the body itself; and in like manner the wine, the symbol of his blood. (3.) Those, therefore who treated the symbols of his body and blood with profaneness and contempt were *united*

28 But let a man examine [a] himself, and so let him eat of *that* bread, and drink of *that* cup.

a 2 Cor.13.5; 1 John 3.20,21.

in spirit with those who put him to death. They evinced the same feelings towards the Lord Jesus that his murderers did. They treated him with scorn, profaneness, and derision; and showed that with the same spirit they would have joined in the act of murdering the Son of God. They would evince their hostility to the Saviour himself as far as they could do, by showing contempt for the memorials of his body and blood. The apostle does by no means, however, as I understand him, mean to say that any of the Corinthians *had* been thus guilty of his body and blood. He does not charge on them this murderous intention. But he states what is the fair and obvious construction which is to be put on a wanton disrespect for the Lord's supper. And the design is to guard them, and all others, against this sin. There can be no doubt that those who celebrate his death in mockery and derision *are* held guilty of his body and blood. They show that they have the spirit of his murderers; they evince it in the most awful way possible; and they who would thus join in a profane celebration of the Lord's supper would have joined in the cry, "Crucify him, crucify him," For it is a most fearful and solemn act to trifle with sacred things; and especially to hold up to derision and scorn, the bitter sorrows by which the Son of God accomplished the redemption of the world.

28. *But let a man examine himself.* Let him search and see if he have the proper qualifications—if he has knowledge to discern the Lord's body (Note, ver. 29); if he has true repentance for his sins; true faith in the Lord Jesus; and a sincere desire to live the life of a Christian, and to be like the Son of God, and be saved by the merits of his blood. Let him examine himself, and see whether he have the right feelings of a communicant, and can approach the table in a proper manner. In regard to this we may observe, (1.) That this examination should include the great question about his personal piety, and about his particular and special fitness for this observance. It should go back into the great inquiry whether he has ever been born again; and it should also have special reference to his immediate and direct preparation for the ordinance. He should not only be able to say *in general* that he is a Christian, but he should be able to say that he has *then* a particular preparation for it. He should be in a suitable frame of mind for it. He should have *personal* evidence that he is a penitent; that he has true faith in the Lord Jesus; that he is depending on him, and is desirous of being saved by him. (2.) This examination should be minute and particular. It should extend to the words, the thoughts, the feelings, the conduct. We should inquire whether in our family and in our business; whether among Christians, and with the world, we have lived the life of a Christian. We should examine our private thoughts; our habits of secret prayer and of searching the Scriptures. Our examination should be directed to the inquiry whether we are gaining the victory over our easily besetting sins and becoming more and more conformed to the Saviour. It should, in short, extend to all our Christian character; and every thing which goes to make up or to mar that character should be the subject of faithful and honest examination. (3.) It should be done because, (*a*) It is well to pause occasionally in life, and take an account of our standing in the sight of God. Men make advances in business and in property only when they often *examine* their accounts, and know just how they stand. (*b*) Because the observance of the Lord's supper is a solemn act, and there will be fearful results if it is celebrated in an improper manner. (*c*) Because self-examination supposes seriousness and calmness, and prevents precipitation and rashness—states of mind entirely unfavourable to a proper observance of the Lord's supper. (*d*)

29 For he that eateth and drinketh unworthily, eateth and drinketh [1] damnation to himself, not discerning the Lord's body.

[1] *judgment*, Rom.13.2.

Because by self-examination one may search out and remove those things that are offensive to God, and the sins which so easily beset us may be known and abandoned. (*e*) Because the approach to the table of the Lord is a solemn approach to the Lord himself; is a solemn profession of attachment to him; is an act of consecration to his service in the presence of angels and of men; and this should be done in a calm, deliberate and sincere manner; such a manner as may be the result of a prayerful and honest self-examination. ¶ *And so let him eat*, &c. And as the result of such examination, or *after* such an examination; that is, let the act of eating that bread be *always* preceded by a solemn self-examination. Bloomfield renders it, "and then," "then only." The sense is plain, that the communion should *always* be preceded by an honest and prayerful self-examination.

29. *For he that eateth*, &c. In order to excite them to a deeper reverence for this ordinance, and to a more solemn mode of observing it, Paul in this verse states another consequence of partaking of it in an improper and irreverent manner; comp. ver. 27. ¶ *Eateth and drinketh damnation.* This is evidently a figurative expression, meaning that by eating and drinking improperly he incurs condemnation; which is here expressed by eating and drinking condemnation itself. The word *damnation* we now apply, in common language, exclusively to the future and final punishment of the wicked in hell. But the word here used does not of necessity refer to that; and according to our use of the word now, there is a harshness and severity in our translation which the Greek does not require, and which probably was not conveyed by the word 'damnation" when the translation was made. In the margin it is correctly rendered "judgment." The word here used (κρῖμα) properly denotes *judgment;* the result of judging, that is, a sentence; then a sentence by which one is condemned, or condemnation; and then punishment; see Rom. iii. 8; xiii. 2. It has evidently the sense of judgment here; and means, that by their improper manner of observing this ordinance, they would expose themselves to the divine displeasure, and to punishment. And it refers, I think, to the punishment or judgment which the apostle immediately specifies, ver. 30, 32. It means a manifestation of the divine displeasure which might be evinced in this life; and which, in the case of the Corinthians, was manifested in the judgments which God had brought upon them. It cannot be denied, however, that a profane and intentionally irreverent manner of observing the Lord's supper will meet with the divine displeasure in the eternal world, and aggravate the doom of those who are guilty of it. But it is clear that this was not the punishment which the apostle had here in his eye. This is apparent, (1.) Because the Corinthians *did* eat unworthily, and yet the judgments inflicted on them were only temporal, that is, weakness, sickness, and temporal death (ver. 30); and, (2.) Because the reason assigned for these judgments is, that they might *not* be condemned with the wicked; *i. e.* as the wicked are in hell, ver. 32. *Whitby.* Comp. 1 Pet. iv. 17. ¶ *Not discerning the Lord's body.* Not *discriminating* (μὴ διακρίνων) between the bread which is used on this occasion and common and ordinary food. Not making the proper difference and distinction between this and common meals. It is evident that this was the leading offence of the Corinthians (see Notes, ver. 20, 21), and this is the proper idea which the original conveys. It does not refer to any intellectual or physical power to *perceive* that that bread represented the body of the Lord; not to any spiritual perception which it is often supposed that piety has to distinguish this; not to any view which faith may

30 For this cause many *are* weak and sickly among you, and many sleep.

31 For if [a] we would judge ourselves, we should not be judged.

a Ps.32.5; 1 John 1.9.

be supposed to have to discern the body of the Lord through the elements; but to the fact that they did not *distinguish* or *discriminate* between this and common meals. They did not regard it in a proper manner, but supposed it to be simply an historical commemoration of an event, such as they were in the habit of observing in honour of an idol or a hero by a public celebration. They, therefore, are able to "discern the Lord's body" in the sense intended here, who with a serious mind, *regard* it as an institution appointed by the Lord Jesus to commemorate his death; and who *distinguish* thus between this and ordinary meals and all festivals and feasts designed to commemorate other events. In other words, who deem it to be designed to show forth the fact that his body was broken for sin, and who desire to observe it as such. It is evident that all true Christians may have ability of this kind, and need not incur condemnation by any error in regard to this. The humblest and obscurest follower of the Saviour, with the feeblest faith and love, may regard it as designed to set forth the death of his Redeemer; and observing it thus, will meet with the divine approbation.

30. *For this cause.* On account of the improper manner of celebrating the Lord's supper; see ver. 21. ¶ *Many are weak* (ἀσθενεῖς). Evidently referring to prevailing bodily sickness and disease. This is the natural and obvious interpretation of this passage. The sense clearly is, that God had sent among them bodily distempers as an expression of the divine displeasure and judgment for their improper mode of celebrating the Lord's supper. That it was not uncommon in those times for God in an extraordinary manner to visit men with calamity, sickness, or death for their sins, is evident from the New Testament; see Note, chap. v. 5; Acts v. 1—10; xiii. 11; 1 Tim. i. 20; and perhaps 1 John v. 16; and James v. 14, 15. It may possibly have been the case that the intemperance and gluttony which prevailed on these occasions was the direct cause of no small part of the bodily disease which prevailed, and which in some cases terminated in death. ¶ *And many sleep.* Have died. The death of Christians in the Scriptures is commonly represented under the image of *sleep;* Dan. xii. 2; John xi. 11, 12; 1 Cor. xv. 51; 1 Thess. iv. 14; v. 10. *Perhaps* it may be implied by the use of this mild term here, instead of the harsher word *death,* that these were true Christians. This sentiment is in accordance with all that Paul states in regard to the church at Corinth. Notwithstanding all their irregularities, he does not deny that they were sincere Christians, and all his appeals and reasonings proceed on that supposition, though there was among them much ignorance and irregularity. God often visits his own people with trial; and though they are his children, yet this does not exempt them from affliction and discipline on account of their imperfections, errors, and sins. The *practical lesson* taught by this is, that Christians should serve God with purity; that they should avoid sin in every form; and that the commission of sin will expose them, as well as others, to the divine displeasure. The *reason* why this judgment was inflicted on the Corinthians was, that there might be a suitable impression made of the holy nature of that ordinance, and that Christians might be led to observe it in a proper manner. If it be asked whether God ever visits his people *now* with his displeasure for their improper manner of observing this ordinance, we may reply, (1.) That we have no reason to suppose that he inflicts *bodily* diseases and corporeal punishments on account of it. But, (2.) There is no reason to doubt that the improper observance of the Lord's supper, like the impro-

32 But when we are judged, we [a] are chastened of the Lord, that we should not be condemned with the world.

a Ps.94.12,13; Heb.12.5—11.

per observance of any other religious duty, will be followed with the expression of God's displeasure, and with a spiritual blighting on the soul. This may be evinced in the following modes. (*a*) In hardening the heart by an improper familiarity with the most sacred and solemn ordinances of religion. (*b*) Increased coldness and deadness in the service of God. If the ordinances of the gospel are not the means of making us better, they are the means of making us worse. (*c*) The loss of the favour of God, or of those pure, and spiritual, and elevated joys which we might have obtained by a proper observance of the ordinance. There is no reason to doubt that God may make it the occasion of *manifesting* his displeasure. It may be followed by a want of spiritual comfort and peace; by a loss of communion with God; and by a withholding of those comforts from the soul which *might* have been enjoyed, and which *are* imparted to those who observe it in a proper manner. The general principle is, that an improper discharge of any duty will expose us to his displeasure, and to the certain loss of all those favours which might have resulted from a proper discharge of the duty, and to the tokens of the divine displeasure. And this is as true of prayer, or of any other religious duty, as of an improper observance of the Lord's supper.

31. *For if we would judge ourselves.* If we would examine ourselves, (ver. 28); if we would exercise a strict scrutiny over our hearts and feelings, and conduct, and come to the Lord's table with a proper spirit, we should escape the condemnation to which they are exposed who observe it in an improper manner. If we would exercise proper *severity* and *honesty* in determining our own character and fitness for the ordinance, we should not expose ourselves to the divine displeasure. ¶ *We should not be judged.* We should not be exposed to the expression of God's disapprobation. He refers here to the punishment which had come upon the Corinthians for their improper manner of observing the ordinance; and he says that if they had properly examined themselves, and had understood the nature of the ordinance, that they would have escaped the judgments that had come upon them. This is as true now as it was then. If we wish to escape the divine displeasure; if we wish the communion *to be followed* with joy, and peace, and growth in grace, and not with blighting and spiritual barrenness, we should exercise a severe judgment on our character, and feelings, and motives; and should come to it with a sincere desire to honour Christ, and to advance in the divine life.

32. *But when we are judged.* This is added, evidently, to console those who had been afflicted on account of their improper manner of observing the Lord's supper. The sense is, that though they were thus afflicted by God; though he had manifested his displeasure at the manner in which they had observed the ordinance, yet the divine judgment in the case was not inexorable. They were not regarded by God as wholly strangers to piety, and would not be lost for ever. They should not be alarmed, therefore, as if there was no mercy for them; but they should rather regard their calamities as the chastening of the Lord on his own children, and as designed for their salvation. ¶ *We are chastened of the Lord.* It is *his* act; and it is not vengeance and wrath; but it is to be regarded as the chastisement of a father's hand, *in order* that we should not be condemned with the wicked. We are *under the discipline* (παιδευόμεθα) of the Lord; we are dealt with as children, and are corrected as by the hand of a father; comp. Heb. xii. 5—10, and 2 Cor. vi. 9. The *design* of God's correcting his children is, that they should

33 Wherefore, my brethren, when ye come together to eat, tarry one for another.

34 And if any man hunger, let him eat at home; that ye come not together unto condemnation.[1] And the rest will I set in order when I come.

CHAPTER XII.

NOW concerning spiritual *gifts*, brethren, I would not have you ignorant.

[1] *judgment.*

be *reclaimed*, and not *destroyed*. ¶ *That we should not be condemned with the world.* It is implied here, (1.) That the world—those who were not Christians, would be condemned; (2.) That Paul regarded the Corinthians, whom he addressed, and who had even been guilty of this improper manner of observing the Lord's supper, and who had been punished for it, as true Christians; and, (3.) That the purpose which God had in view in inflicting these judgments on them was, that they might be purified, and enlightened, and recovered from their errors, and saved. This is the design of God in the calamities and judgments which he brings on his own children.—And so now, if he afflicts us, or leaves us to darkness, or follows the communion with the tokens of his displeasure, it is, that we may be recovered to a deeper sense of our need of him; to juster views of the ordinance; and to a more earnest wish to obtain his favour.

33. *When ye come together to eat.* Professedly to eat the Lord's supper. ¶ *Tarry one for another.* Do not be guilty of disorder, intemperance, and gluttony; see Note, ver. 21. Doddridge understands this of the feast that he supposes to have preceded the Lord's supper. But the more obvious interpretation is, to refer it to the Lord's supper itself; and to enjoin perfect order, respect, and sobriety. The idea is, that the table was common for the rich and the poor; and that the rich should claim no priority or precedence over the poor.

34. *And if any man hunger,* &c. The Lord's supper is not a common feast; it is not designed as a place where a man may gratify his appetite. It is designed as a simple *commemoration*, and not as a *feast*. This remark was designed to correct their views of the supper, and to show them that it was to be distinguished from the ordinary idea of a feast or festival. ¶ *That ye come not together unto condemnation.* That the effect of your coming together for the observance of the Lord's supper be not to produce condemnation; see Note, ver. 29. ¶ *And the rest will I set in order,* &c. Probably he refers here to other matters on which he had been consulted; or other things which he knew required to be adjusted. The *other matters* pertaining to the order and discipline of the church I will defer until I can come among you, and personally arrange them. It is evident from this, that Paul at this time purposed soon to go to Corinth; see 2 Cor. i. 15, 16. It was doubtless true that there might be many things which it was desirable to adjust in the church there, which could not be so well done by letter. The main things, therefore, which it was needful to correct immediately, he had discussed in this letter; the other matters he reserved to be arranged by himself when he should go among them. Paul was disappointed in his expectations of returning among them as soon as he had intended (see 2 Cor. i. 17), and under this disappointment he forwarded to them another epistle. If all Christians would follow implicitly his directions here in regard to the Lord's supper, it would be an ordinance full of comfort. May all so understand its nature, and so partake of it, that they shall meet the approbation of their Lord, and so that it may be the means of saving grace to their souls.

CHAPTER XII.

THIS chapter commences a new subject, the discussion of which continues to the close of the fourteenth chapter. The general subject is that of spiritual endowments, or the right mode of exercising their spiritual gifts, and the degree of honour which was due to those who had been distinguished by God by the special influences of his Spirit. It is evident that many in the church at Corinth had been thus favoured; and it is evident that they had greatly abused these endowments, and that those who were thus favoured had claimed a precedency of honour above those who had been less distinguished. It is not improbable that they had in their letter to Paul (see Note, chap. vii. 1), requested his counsel on this subject, and asked him to teach them what measure of honour should be given to those who had been thus endowed. This subject, as it was of importance not only for them, but for the church at large in all future times, he proceeds to discuss in this, and the two following chapters; and this discussion closes the *second* part of the epistle; see the Introduction. The general scope of these chapters is this. (1.) He shows that all those endowments were conferred by the Holy Ghost, and were all for the use of the church; that the church was one, but that there was a necessity for diversified operations in that church; and that, therefore, no one should value himself on that gift above his brother, and no one should feel himself dishonoured because he had not been thus favoured. All filled important places in the church, just as the various members and parts of the human system were necessary for its symmetry, action and health; and all therefore, should be willing to occupy the place which God had assigned them, chap. xii. (2.) In chapter xiii. he recommends *love*, or charity, as of more value than all other spiritual gifts put together, and therefore recommends that *that* should be especially the object of their desire. (3.) In chapter xiv. he gives particular rules about the proper exercise of spiritual gifts in their public assemblies. This chapter, therefore, is occupied in stating and illustrating the position that all spiritual gifts are conferred by the Holy Ghost, and that no one should so value himself on this gift as to despise those who had not been thus endowed: and that no one who had not thus been favoured should be dejected, or regard himself as dishonoured. This statement is illustrated in the following manner.

(1.) Paul states the importance of the subject, ver. 1.

(2.) He reminds them that they were formerly in a state of ignorance, sin, and idolatry, ver. 2.

(3.) He states *one* mark of being under the influence of the Spirit of God—that is, that it would lead them to acknowledge and honour Jesus Christ. If the Spirit by which they were influenced led them to this, it was proof that it was the Holy Ghost, ver. 3. If any *pretenders* to inspiration were in the habit of speaking disrespectfully of Jesus Christ, or of calling him "*accursed,*" it proved that they were not under the influence of the Holy Ghost.

(4.) There were *diversities* in the operations of the Spirit, but however various were these operations, they all proceeded from the same agent, ver. 4—11. All were not, therefore, to expect precisely the same influences or operations; nor were they to suppose that because there were various operations, that therefore they were not influenced by the Spirit of God.

(5.) Paul states and illustrates the truth that the church is one, ver. 12—27. As the body is one, yet has many members, so is it with the church, ver. 12. The body has many members, and no members in the body are useless, but all perform important parts, however unimportant they may seem to be; and no one member can say that it has no need of the others. So it is in the church, ver. 13—27.

(6.) This beautiful allegory, drawn from the functions of the various parts of the human body, Paul applies now to the church, and shows (ver. 28—30) that the same thing should be expected in the church of Christ. It followed, therefore, that those who were not as highly favoured as others should not regard themselves as useless, and decline their station in the church. It followed also, that those who were in inferior stations should

2 Ye know that ye were Gentiles, carried away unto these dumb [a] idols, even as ye were led.

a 1 Thess.1.9.

not envy those who had been more highly favoured; and that those who were in more elevated stations, and who had been more signally favoured, should not look down on those beneath them with contempt. It followed also, that they should regard themselves as one body; and love and cherish each other with constant Christian affection.

(7.) Paul tells them that it was not improper to desire the highest endowments, but says that he will propose an object of desire to be preferred to these gifts—and that is LOVE, ver. 31.

1. *Now concerning*. It is now time that I should speak of spiritual endowments. He had no doubt been consulted in regard to them, and probably various questions had been proposed, which he now proceeded to answer. ¶ *Spiritual* gifts. The word "gifts" is not in the original. The Greek refers to "spiritual" things in general, or to any thing that is of a spiritual nature. The whole discussion, however, shows that he refers to the various endowments, gifts, or graces that had been bestowed in different degrees on the members of the church—including the distinctions in graces, and in degrees of office and rank, which had been made in the Christian church in general (chap. xii.), as well as the extraordinary endowments of the gift of tongues which had been bestowed upon many, chap. xiv. ¶ *I would not have you ignorant*. The subject is of so much importance that it demands particular attention and special care; comp. Note, chap. x. 1. I would not have you ignorant in regard to the nature of those endowments; the spirit with which they should be received; the rules to which they who are thus favoured should be subjected; and the feelings and views which should be cherished in all the members of the church in regard to them. Nothing is of more importance in the church than the doctrine respecting the influences and endowments of the Holy Spirit.

2. *Ye know*, &c. This verse is regarded by many as a parenthesis. But it is not necessary to suppose that it is so, or that it does not cohere with that which follows. The design seems to be to remind them of their former miserable condition as idolaters, in order to make them more sensible of their advantages as Christians, and that they might be led more highly to appreciate their present condition. Paul often refers Christians to their former condition, to excite in them gratitude for the mercies that God has conferred on them in the gospel; see Note, chap. vi. 11, comp. Rom. vi. 17; Eph. ii. 11, 12; Titus iii. 3. ¶ *That ye were Gentiles*. Heathen; worshippers of idols. The idea is, that they were pagans; that they had no knowledge of the true God, but were sunk in miserable superstition and idolatry. ¶ *Carried away*. Led along; that is, deluded by your passions, deluded by your priests, deluded by your vain and splendid rites of worship. The whole system made an appeal to the senses, and *bore along* its votaries as if by a foreign and irresistible impulse. The word which is used (ἀπαγόμενοι) conveys properly the idea of being carried into bondage, or being led to punishment, and refers here doubtless to the strong means which had been used by crafty politicians and priests in their former state to delude and deceive them. ¶ *Unto these dumb idols*. These idols which could not speak—an attribute which is often given to them, to show the folly of worshipping them; Ps. cxv. 5; cxxxv. 15; Hab. ii. 18, 19. The ancient priests and politicians deluded the people with the notion that oracles were uttered by the idols whom they worshipped, and thus they maintained the belief in their divinity. The idea of Paul here seems to be, (1.) That their idols never could have uttered the oracles which were ascribed to them, and consequently that they had been deluded. (2.) That these idols could never have endowed them with such

3 Wherefore I give you to understand, that no man [a] speaking by the Spirit of God calleth Jesus [1] accursed: and [b] *that* no man can

a Mark 9.39; 1 John 4,2,3.

1 or, *anathema*. b Mat.16.17.

spiritual privileges as they now had, and consequently that their present state was far preferable to their former condition. ¶ *Even as ye were led.* Were led by the priests in the temples of the idols. They were under strong delusions and the arts of cunning and unprincipled men. The idea is, that they had been under a strong infatuation, and were entirely at the control of their spiritual leaders—a description remarkably applicable now to all forms of imposture in the world. No system of paganism consults the freedom and independence of the mind of man; but it is everywhere characterized as a system of *power*, and not of *thought;* and all its arrangements are made to secure that power without an intelligent assent of the understanding and the heart.

3. *Wherefore I give you to understand.* I make known to you. The force of this expression is, *I give you this rule to distinguish,* or by which you may know what influences and operations are from God. The design of the passage is, to give them some simple general guide by which they could at once recognise the operations of the Spirit of God, and determine whether they who claimed to be under that operation were really so. That rule was, that all who were truly influenced by the Holy Ghost would be disposed to acknowledge and to know Jesus Christ; and where this disposition existed, it was of itself a clear demonstration that it was the operation of the Spirit of God. The same rule substantially is given by John (1 John iv. 2), by which to test the nature of the spirit by which men profess to be influenced. "Hereby know ye the Spirit of God: Every spirit that confesses that Jesus Christ is come in the flesh is of God," comp. also Note to Mat. xvi. 17. ¶ *That no man.* No one (οὐδεὶς). It may refer to a man, or to demons, or to those who pretended to be under inspiration of any kind. And it may refer to the Jews who may have pretended to be under the influence of God's Spirit, and who yet anathematized and cursed the name of Jesus. Or it may be intended simply as a general rule; meaning that *if any one,* whoever he might be, should blaspheme the name of Jesus, whatever were his pretensions, whether professing to be under the influence of the Holy Spirit among the Jews, or to be inspired among the Gentiles, it was full proof that he was an impostor. The argument is, *that the Holy Spirit in all instances would do honour to Jesus Christ, and would prompt all who were under his influence to love and reverence his name.* ¶ *Speaking by the Spirit of God.* Under the influence of inspiration. ¶ *Calleth.* Says, or would say; that is, no such one would use the language of anathema in regard to him. ¶ *Accursed.* Marg. *Anathema* (ἀνάθεμα); see Note, Acts xxiii. 14; Rom. ix. 3; comp. 1 Cor. xvi. 22; Gal. i. 8, 9. The word is one of execration, or cursing; and means, that no one under the influence of the Holy Spirit could curse the name of Jesus, or denounce him as execrable and as an impostor. The effect of the influences of the Spirit would be in all instances to inspire reverence for his name and work. It is probable that the *Jews* were here principally intended, since there is a bitterness and severity in the language which accords with all their expressions of feeling towards Jesus of Nazareth. It is possible, also, and indeed probable, that the priests and priestesses of the pagan gods who pretended to be under the influence of inspiration might denounce the name of Jesus, because they would all be opposed to the purity of his religion. ¶ *And that no man can say,*&c. That is, that it cannot occur, or even happen, that any one will acknowledge Jesus as the Messiah who is not influenced by the Holy Ghost. The meaning is, not that no one has physical ability *to say* that Jesus is

say that Jesus is the Lord, but by the Holy Ghost.

4 Now there are diversities [a] of gifts, but the same Spirit.

a Heb.2.4; 1 Pet.1.10.

Lord unless aided by the Holy Ghost, since all men can *say* this ; but that no one will be disposed heartily to say it; no one will acknowledge him as their Lord; it can never happen that any one will confess him as the true Messiah who has not been brought to this state by the agency of the Holy Ghost. ¶ *Is the Lord.* Is the Messiah ; or shall acknowledge him as their Lord. ¶ *But by the Holy Ghost.* Unless he is influenced by the Holy Spirit. This is a very important verse, not only in regard to the particular subject under consideration in the time of Paul, but also in its practical bearing at present. We may learn from it, (1.) That it is a proof that any man is under the influence of the Holy Spirit who is heartily disposed to honour the name and work of Jesus Christ. (2.) Those forms and modes of religion ; those religious opinions and practices, will be most in accordance with the designs of the Spirit of God, which do most to honour the name and work of Jesus Christ. (3.) It is true that no man will ever cherish a proper regard for Jesus Christ, nor love his name and work, unless he is influenced by the Holy Ghost. No man loves the name and work of the Redeemer by following simply the inclinations of his own corrupt heart. In all instances of those who have been brought to a willingness to honour him, it has been by the agency of the Holy Ghost. (4.) If any man, in any way, is disposed to disparage the work of Christ, to speak lightly of his person or his name ; or holds doctrines that infringe on the fulness of the truth respecting his divine nature, his purity, his atonement, it is proof that he is not under the influence of the Spirit of God. Just in proportion as he shall disparage that work or name, just in that proportion does he give evidence that he is not influenced by the Divine Spirit ; but by proud reason, or by imagination, or by a heart that is not reconciled to God. (5.) All true religion is the production of the Holy Spirit. For religion consists essentially in a willingness to honour, and love, and serve the Lord Jesus Christ ; and where *that* exists, it is produced by the Holy Spirit. (6.) The influence of the Holy Spirit should be cherished. To grieve away that Spirit is to drive all proper knowledge of the Redeemer from the soul ; to do this is to leave the heart to coldness, and darkness, and barrenness, and spiritual death.

4. *Now there are diversities of gifts.* There are different endowments conferred on Christians. For the meaning of the word *gifts,* see Note, Rom. i. 11 ; comp. Rom. v. 15, 16 ; vi. 23 ; xi. 29 ; xii. 6 ; 1 Cor. i. 7 ; vii. 7. ¶ *But the same Spirit.* Produced by the same Spirit—the Holy Ghost. What those diversities of gifts are, the apostle enumerates in ver. 8—11. The design for which he refers to these various endowments is evidently to show those whom he addressed, that since they are all produced by the same Holy Spirit, have all the same divine origin, and are all intended to answer some important purpose and end in the Christian church, that, therefore, none are to be despised ; nor is one man to regard himself as authorized to treat another with contempt. The Spirit has divided and conferred those gifts according to his sovereign will ; and his arrangements should be regarded with submission, and the favours which he confers should be received with thankfulness. That the Holy Spirit—the third person of the adorable Trinity—is here intended by the word "Spirit," seems to be manifest on the face of the passage, and has been the received interpretation of the church until it was called in question by some recent German commentators, at the head of whom was Eichhorn. It is not the design of these Notes to go into an examination of questions of criticism, such as an inquiry like this would involve.

5 And there are differences of administrations, but the same Lord.

1 or, *ministries.*

6 And there are diversities [a] of operations; but it is the same God which worketh all in all.

a Rom.12.6,&c.

Nor is it necessary. Some of the arguments by which the common interpretation is defended are the following. (1.) It is the obvious interpretation. It is that which occurs to the great mass of readers, as the true and correct exposition. (2.) It accords with the usual meaning of the word Spirit. No other intelligible sense can be given to the word here. To say, with Eichhorn, that it means "nature," that there are the same natural endowments, though cultivated in various measures by art and education, makes manifest nonsense, and is contrary to the whole structure and scope of the passage. (3.) It accords with all the other statements in the New Testament, where the endowments here referred to "wisdom," "knowledge," "faith," "working of miracles," &c., are traced to the Holy Spirit, and are regarded as his gift. (4.) The harmony, the concinnity of the passage is destroyed by supposing that it refers to any thing else than the Holy Spirit. In this verse the agency of the Spirit is recognised, and *his* operations on the mind referred to; in the next verse the agency of the Son of God (see Note on the verse) is referred to; and in the following verse, the agency of God—evidently the Father—is brought into view; and thus the entire passage (ver. 4—6) presents a connected view of the operations performed by the Father, Son, and Holy Ghost in the work of redemption. To deny that this verse refers to the Holy Spirit is to break up the harmony of the whole passage, and to render it in no small degree unmeaning. But if this refers to the Holy Spirit, then it is an unanswerable argument for his personality, and for his being on an equality with the Father and the Son.

5. *Of administrations.* Marg. *Ministries.* The word properly denotes *ministries;* so that there are different ranks and grades in the ministries which Christ has appointed, to wit, those specified in ver. 9, 10, 28. ¶ *But the same Lord.* This refers evidently to the Lord Jesus, by whom these various orders of ministers were appointed, and under whose control they are; see Note, Acts i. 24; comp. Eph. iv. 5. The term *Lord,* when it stands by itself in the New Testament, usually refers to the Lord Jesus, the name by which he was commonly known by the disciples; see John xx. 25. The fact also that this stands between the mention of the work of the Spirit (ver. 4) and the work of God (ver. 6), and the fact that to the Lord Jesus appertained the appointment of these various grades of officers in the church (comp. Mat. x. 1, seq., and Luke x. 1, seq.), is further proof that this refers to him. The design of the verse is, to show that all these offices had their appointment from him; and that since all were his appointment, and all were necessary, no one should be proud of an elevated station; no one should be depressed, or feel himself degraded, because he had been designated to a more humble office.

6. *Of operations.* Of works; to wit, of miracles, such as God produces in the church, in the establishment and defence of his religion. There are different operations on the mind and heart; and different powers given to man, or different qualifications in building up and defending his cause. Or it may be, possibly, that Paul here refers to the works of God mainly for mere *illustration,* and by the word "operations" means the works which God has performed in creation and providence. His works are various. They are not all alike, though they come from the same hand. The sun, the moon, the stars, the earth are different; the trees of the forest, the beasts of the field, the fowls of the air, the inhabitants of the

7 But the manifestation of the
Spirit is given to every man to
profit [a] withal.
8 For to one is given, by the
Spirit, [b] the word of wisdom; [c] to
another the word of knowledge, [d]
by the same Spirit;
9 To another faith [e] by the

a Eph.4.7. b Isa.11.2,3. c chap.2.6,7. d chap. 13.2. e Eph.2.8.

deep are different; the flowers, and shrubs, and herbs are different from each other; yet, however much they may vary, they are formed by the same hand, are the productions of the same God, are to be regarded as proofs of the same wisdom and power. The same thing should be expected in his church; and we should anticipate that the endowments of its members would be various. ¶ *But it is the same God.* The same Father; all these operations are produced by the same God. They should not, therefore, be undervalued or despised; nor should any one be unduly elated, or pride himself on what has been conferred by God alone. ¶ *All in all.* All these operations are to be traced to him. His agency is everywhere. It is as really seen in the insect's wing as in the limbs of the mammoth; as really in the humblest violet as in the loftiest oak of the forest. All, therefore, should regard themselves as under his direction, and should submit to his arrangements. If men regard their endowments as the gift of God, they will be thankful for them, and they will not be disposed to despise or undervalue others who have been placed in a more humble condition and rank in the church.

7. *But the manifestation of the Spirit.* The word "manifestation" (φανέρωσις) means properly that which makes manifest, conspicuous, or plain; that which illustrates, or makes any thing seen or known. Thus conduct manifests the state of the heart; and the actions are a manifestation, or *showing forth* of the real feelings. The idea here is, that there is given to those referred to, such gifts. endowments, or graces as shall *manifest* the work and nature of the Spirit's operations on the mind; such endowments as the Spirit makes himself known by to men. All that he produces in the mind is a manifestation of his character and work, in the same way as the works of God in the visible creation are a manifestation of his perfections ¶ *Is given to every man.* To every man whose case is here under consideration. The idea is not at all that the manifestation of the Spirit is given to *all* men indiscriminately, to pagans, and infidels, and scoffers as well as to Christians. The apostle is discoursing only of those who are Christians, and his declaration should be confined to them alone. Whatever may be true of other men, this statement should be confined wholly to Christians, and means simply that the Spirit of God gives to each Christian such graces and endowments as he pleases; that he distributes his gifts to all, not equally, but in a manner which he shall choose; and that the design of this is, that all Christians should use his endowments for the common good. This passage, therefore, is very improperly adduced to prove that the gifts and graces of the Holy Spirit are conferred alike on all men, and that pagans, and blasphemers, and sinners in general are under his enlightening influences. It has no reference to any such doctrine, but should be interpreted as referring solely to Christians, and the various endowments which are conferred on them. ¶ *To profit withal* (πρὸς τὸ συμφέρον). Unto profit; *i. e.* for utility, or use; or to be an advantage to the church; for the common good of all. This does not mean that each one must cultivate and improve his graces and gifts, however true that may be, but that they are to be used for the common good of the church; they are bestowed *for utility*, or *profit;* they are conferred in such measures and in such a manner as are best adapted to be useful, and to do good. They are bestowed not on all equally, but in such a manner as shall best subserve the interests of

piety and the church, and as shall tend harmoniously to carry on the great interests of religion, and further the welfare of the whole Christian body. The doctrine of this verse is, therefore, (1.) That the Holy Spirit bestows such endowments on all Christians as he pleases; and, (2.) That the design is, in the best manner to promote the common welfare—the peace and edification of the whole church. It follows from this, (1.) That no Christian should be unduly elated, as if he were more worthy than others, since *his* endowments are the simple gift of God; (2.) That no Christian should be depressed and disheartened, as if he occupied an inferior or unimportant station, since *his* place has also been assigned him by God; (3.) That all should be contented, and satisfied with their allotments in the church, and should strive only to make the best use of their talents and endowments; and, (4.) That all should employ their time and talents for the common utility; for the furtherance of the common welfare, and the advancement of the kingdom of Christ on earth.

8. *For to one is given.* In order to show what endowments he refers to, the apostle here particularizes the various gifts which the Holy Spirit imparts in the church. ¶ *By the Spirit.* By the Holy Ghost; by his agency on the mind and heart. ¶ *The word of wisdom.* One he has endowed with *wisdom,* or has made distinguished for wise, and prudent, and comprehensive views of the scheme of redemption, and with a faculty of clearly explaining it to the apprehension of men. It is not certain that the apostle meant to say that this was the most important or most elevated endowment because he places it first in order. His design does not seem to be to observe the order of importance and value, but to state, as it occurred to him, the fact that these various endowments *had* been conferred on different men in the church. The sense is, that one man would be prominent and distinguished as a *wise* man—a prudent counsellor, instructer, and adviser. ¶ *To another the word of knowledge.* Another would be distinguished for knowledge. He would be learned; would have a clear view of the plan of salvation, and of the doctrines and duties of religion. The same variety is observed in the ministry at all times. One man is eminent as a wise man; another as a man of intelligence and knowledge; and both may be equally useful in their place in the church. ¶ *By the same Spirit.* All is to be traced to the same Spirit; all, therefore, may be really useful and necessary; and the one should not pride himself in his endowments above the other.

9. *To another faith.* Another shall be distinguished for simple confidence in God; and *his* endowment is also given by the same Spirit. Many of the most useful men in the church are distinguished mainly for their simple confidence in the promises of God; and often accomplish more by prayer and by their faith in God than others do who are distinguished for their wisdom and learning. Humble piety and reliance in the divine promises, and that measure of ardour, fearlessness, and zeal which result from such confidence; that belief that all obstacles *must* be and *will* be overcome that oppose the gospel; and that God *will* secure the advancement of his cause, will often do infinitely more in the promotion of his kingdom than the most splendid endowments of learning and talent. Indeed, if a man were disposed to do good on the widest scale possible, to do the utmost that he possibly could in saving men, he would best accomplish it by seeking simple *faith* in God's aid and promises, and then under the influence of this, engage with ardour in doing what he could. Faith is one of the highest endowments of the Christian life; and yet, though all may obtain it, it is one of the rarest endowments. Perhaps by many it is despised, *because* it may be obtained by all; because it is a grace in which the poor and the humble may be as much distinguished as the man of splendid talents and profound learning. ¶ T

same Spirit; to another the gifts
of healing, [a] by the same Spirit;
10 To another the working of
miracles; to another prophecy;
to another discerning of spirits; [b]
to another *divers* kinds of tongues; [c]

a Mark 16.18; James 5.14. b 1 John 4.1. c Acts 2.4,7—11.

---

another the gifts of healing; see Mark xvi. 18. This was promised to the disciples of the Saviour; and in the early church was conferred on many; comp. Acts v. 12, 15, 16; xix. 12. It would seem from this passage that the gift of healing was conferred on some in a more eminent degree than on others.

10. *To another the working of miracles.* Commentators have felt some perplexity in distinguishing this from what is mentioned in ver. 9, of the gift of healing. It is evident that the apostle there refers to the power of working miracles in healing inveterate and violent diseases. The expression here used, "working of miracles" (ἐνεργήματα δυνάμεων,) refers probably to the more *extraordinary* and *unusual* kinds of miracles; to those which were regarded as in advance of the power of healing diseases. It is possible that it may denote what the Saviour had reference to in Mark xvi. 18, where he said they should take up serpents, and if they drank any deadly thing it should not hurt them; and possibly also to the power of raising up the dead. That this power was possessed by the apostles is well known; and it is possible that it was possessed by others also of the early Christians. It is clear from all this that there was a *difference* even among those who had the power of working miracles, and that this power was conferred in a more eminent degree on some than on others. Indeed, the *extraordinary* endowments conferred on the apostles and the early Christians, seem to have been regulated to a remarkable degree in accordance with the rule by which *ordinary* endowments are conferred on men. Though all men have understanding, memory, imagination, bodily strength, &c., yet one has these in a more eminent degree than others; and one is characterized for the possession of one of those qualities more than for another. Yet all are bestowed by the same God. So it was in regard to the extraordinary endowments conferred on the early Christians; comp. chap. xiv., especially ver. 32.

10. *To another prophecy;* see Note, Rom. xii. 6. ¶ *To another discerning of spirits;* comp. 1 John iv. 1. This must refer to some power of searching into the secrets of the heart; of knowing what were a man's purposes, views, and feelings. It may relate either to the power of determining by what spirit a man spoke who pretended to be inspired, whether he was truly inspired or whether he was an impostor; or it may refer to the power of seeing whether a man was sincere or not in his Christian profession. That the apostles had this power, is apparent from the case of Ananias and Sapphira, (Acts v. 1—10), and from the case of Elymas, Acts xiii. 9—11. It is evident that where the gift of prophecy and inspiration was possessed, and where it would confer such advantages on those who possessed it, there would be many pretenders to it; and that it would be of vast importance to the infant church, in order to prevent imposition, that there should be a power in the church of detecting the imposture. ¶ *To another* divers *kinds of tongues.* The power of speaking various languages; see Acts ii. 4, 7—11. This passage also seems to imply that the extraordinary endowments of the Holy Spirit were not conferred on all alike. ¶ *To another the interpretation of tongues.* The power of interpreting foreign languages; or of interpreting the language which might be used by the "prophets" in their communications; see Note, chap. xiv. 27. This was evidently a faculty different from the power of speaking a foreign language; and yet it might be equally useful. It would appear possible that some might have had the power of speaking foreign languages who were not themselves apprized of the meaning, and

to another the interpretation of tongues:

11 But all these worketh that one and the self-same Spirit, dividing [a] to every man severally as he will.

12 For as the body is one, and hath many members, and all the

a ver.6.

that interpreters were needful in order to express the sense to the hearers. Or it may have been that in a promiscuous assembly, or in an assembly made up of those who spoke different languages, a part might have understood what was uttered, and it was needful that an interpreter should explain it to the other portion; see Notes on chap. xiv. 28.

11. *But all these.* All these various endowments. ¶ *Worketh.* Produces. All these are to be traced to him. ¶ *That one and the self-same Spirit.* The Holy Spirit, Acts ii. They were all, though so different in themselves, to be traced to the Holy Ghost, just as all the natural endowments of men—their strength, memory, judgment, &c.—though so various in themselves, are to be traced to the same God. ¶ *Dividing to every man severally.* Conferring on each one as he pleases. He confers on each one that which he sees to be best, and most wise, and proper. ¶ *As he will.* As he chooses; or as in his view seems best. Dr. Doddridge remarks, that this word does "not so much express arbitrary pleasure, as a determination founded on *wise* counsel." It implies, however, that he does it as a sovereign; as he sees to be right and best. He distributes these favours as to him seems best adapted to promote the welfare of the whole church and to advance his cause. Some of the doctrines which are taught by this verse are the following: (1.) The Holy Ghost is *a person.* For, he acts as a person; distributes favours, confers endowments and special mercies "as he will." This proves that he is, in some respects, distinguished from the Father and the Son. It would be absurd to say of an *attribute* of God, that it confers favours, and distributes the various endowments of speaking with tongues, and raising the dead. And if so, then the Holy Ghost is *not* an attribute of God. (2.) He is a sovereign. He gives to all as he pleases. In regard to spiritual endowments of the highest order, he deals with men as he does in the common endowments bestowed on men, and as he does in temporal blessings. He does not bestow the same blessings on all, nor make all alike. He dispenses his favours by a rule which he has not made known, but which, we may be assured, is in accordance with wisdom and goodness. He wrongs no one; and he gives to all the favours which *might* be connected with eternal life. (3.) No man should be proud of his endowments. Whatever they may be, they are the gifts of God, bestowed by his sovereign will and mercy. But assuredly we should not be proud of that which is the mere *gift* of another; and which has been bestowed, not in consequence of any merit of ours, but according to his mere sovereign will. (4.) No man should be depressed, or should despise his own gifts, however humble they may be. In their own place, they may be as important as the higher endowments of others. That God has placed him where he is, or has given less splendid endowments than he has to others, is no fault of his. There is no crime in it; and he should, therefore, strive to improve his "one talent," and to make himself useful in the rank where he is placed. And, (5.) No man should despise another because he is in a more humble rank, or is less favoured than himself. God has made the difference, and we should *respect* and *honour* his arrangements, and should show that respect and honour by regarding with kindness, and treating as fellow labourers with us, all who occupy a more humble rank than we do.

12. *For as the body is one.* The general sentiment which the apostle had been illustrating and enforcing was, that all the endowments which

members of that one body: being many, are one body; so [a] also *is* Christ.

13 For by one Spirit are we all [b] baptized into one body, whether *we be* Jews or Gentiles, [1] whether *we be* bond or free; and have been all made to drink [c] into one Spirit.

a ver.27. b John 1.16; Eph.4.5. 1 *Greeks.* c John 7.37–39.

were possessed in the church were the work of the same Holy Spirit, and that they ought to be appropriately cherished and prized, as being all useful and valuable in their places. This sentiment he now illustrates (ver. 12—27) by a beautiful similitude taken from the mutual dependence of the various parts of the human body. The human body is one, and yet is composed of various members and parts that all unite harmoniously in one whole. ¶ *Being many.* Or, although they are many; or while they are in some respects separate, and perform distinct and different functions, yet they all unite in one harmonious whole. ¶ *So also is Christ.* The church is represented as the body of Christ (ver. 27), meaning that it is one, and that he sustains to it the relation of Head; comp. Eph. i. 22, 23. As the *head* is the most important part of the body, it may be put for the whole body; and the name *Christ* here, the head of the church, is put for the whole body of which he is the head; and means here the Christian society, or the church. This figure, of a part for the whole, is one that is common in all languages; see Note, Rom. xii. 4, 5.

13. *For by one Spirit.* That is, by the agency or operation of the same Spirit, the Holy Ghost, we have been united into one body. The idea here is the same as that presented above (ver. 7. 11), by which all the endowments of Christians are traced to the same Spirit. Paul here says, that that Spirit had *so* endowed them as to fit them to constitute one body, or to be united in one, and to perform the various duties which resulted from their union in the same Christian church. The idea of its having been done by one and the same Spirit is kept up and often presented, in order that the endowments conferred on them might be duly appreciated. ¶ *Are we all.* Every member of the church, whatever may be his rank or talents, has received his endowments from the same Spirit. ¶ *Baptized into one body.* Many suppose that there is reference here to the ordinance of baptism by water. But the connection seems rather to require us to understand it of the baptism of the Holy Ghost (Mat. iii. 11); and if so, it means, that by the agency of the Holy Spirit, they had all been fitted, each to his appropriate place, to constitute the body of Christ—the church. If, however, it refers to the ordinance of baptism, as Bloomfield, Calvin, Doddridge, &c. suppose, then it means, that by the very profession of religion as made at baptism, by there being but one baptism (Eph. iv. 5), they had all professedly become members of one and the same body. The former interpretation, however, seems to me best to suit the connection. ¶ *Whether we be Jews or Gentiles.* There is no difference. All are on a level. In regard to the grand point, no distinction is made, whatever may have been our former condition of life. ¶ *Bond or free.* It is evident that many who were slaves were converted to the Christian faith. Religion, however, regarded all as on a level; and conferred no favours on the free which it did not on the slave. It was one of the happy lessons of Christianity, that it taught men that in the great matters pertaining to their eternal interests they were on the same level. This doctrine would tend to secure, more than any thing else could, the proper treatment of those who were in bondage, and of those who were in humble ranks of life. At the same time it would not diminish, but would increase *their* real respect for their masters, and for those who were above them, if they regarded them as fellow Christians, and destined to the same heaven; see Note, chap. vii. 22. ¶ *And have been all made to drink,* &c, This probably

14 For the body is not one member, but many.
15 If the foot shall say, Because I am not the hand, I am not of the body; is it therefore not of the body?
16 And if the ear shall say, Because I am not the eye, I am not of the body; is it therefore not of the body?
17 If the whole body *were* an eye, where *were* the hearing? If the whole *were* hearing, where *were* the smelling?
18 But now hath God set [a] the members every one of them in the body as [b] it hath pleased him.
19 And if they were all one member, where *were* the body?
20 But now *are they* many members, yet but one body.

a ver.28.

b Rom.12.3;ver.11.

refers to their partaking together of the cup in the Lord's supper. The sense is, that by their drinking of the same cup commemorating the death of Christ, they had partaken of the same influences of the Holy Ghost, which descend alike on all who observe that ordinance in a proper manner. They had shown also, that they belonged to the same body, and were all united together; and that however various might be their graces and endowments, yet they all belonged to the same great family.

14. *For the body*, &c. The body is made up of many members, which have various offices. So it is in the church. We are to expect the same variety there; and we are not to presume either that all will be alike, or that any member that God has placed there will be useless.

15. *If the foot shall say*, &c. The same figure and illustration which Paul here uses occurs also in heathen writers. It occurs in the apologue which was used by Menenius Agrippa, as related by Livy (lib. ii. cap. 32), in which he attempted to repress a rebellion which had been excited against the nobles and senators, as useless and cumbersome to the state. Menenius, in order to show the folly of this, represents the different members of the body as conspiring against the stomach, as being inactive, and as refusing to labour, and consuming every thing. The consequence of the conspiracy which the feet, and hands, and mouth entered into, was a universal wasting away of the whole frame for want of the nutriment which would have been supplied from the stomach. Thus he argued it would be by the conspiracy against the nobles, as being inactive, and as consuming all things. The representation had the desired effect, and quelled the rebellion. The same figure is used also by Æsop. The idea here is, that as the foot and the ear could not pretend that they were not parts of the body, and even not important, because they were not the eye, &c.; that is, were not more honourable parts of the body; so no Christian, however humble his endowments, could pretend that he was useless because he was not more highly gifted, and did not occupy a more elevated rank.

17. *If the whole body*, &c. The idea in this verse is, that all the parts of the body are useful in their proper place, and that it would be as absurd to require or expect that all the members of the church should have the same endowments, as it would be to attempt to make the body *all eye*. If all were the same; if all had the same endowments, important offices which are now secured by the other members would be unknown. All, therefore, are to be satisfied with their allotment; all are to be honoured in their appropriate place.

18. *Hath God set the members*, &c. God has formed the body, with its various members, as he saw would best conduce to the harmony and usefulness of all.

19. *And if all were one member.* If there were nothing but an eye, an ear, or a limb, there would be no body The idea which this seems intended to illustrate is, that if there was not variety of talent and endowment in the church, the church could not itself exist. If, for example, there

21 And the eye cannot say unto the hand, I have no need of thee: nor again, the head to the feet, I have no need of you.

22 Nay much more, those [a] members of the body, which seem to be more feeble, are necessary:

23 And those *members* of the body which we think to be less honourable, upon these we [1] bestow more abundant honour; and our uncomely *parts* have more abundant comeliness.

24 For our comely *parts* have

a Eccl 4.9-12; 9.14,15.

1 or, *put on*.

were nothing *but* apostles, or prophets, or teachers; if there were none but those who spoke with tongues or could interpret them, the church could not exist. A variety of talents and attainments in their proper places is as useful as are the various members of the human body.

21. *And the eye cannot say to the hand*, &c. The hand in its place is as needful as the eye; and the feet as the head. Nay, the eye and the head could not perform their appropriate functions, or would be in a great measure useless but for the aid of the hands and feet. Each is useful in its proper place. So in the church. Those that are most talented, and most richly endowed with gifts, cannot say to those less so, that there is no need of their aid. All are useful in their place. Nay, those who are most richly endowed could very imperfectly perform their duties without the aid and co-operation of those of more humble attainments.

22. *Which seem to be more feeble*. Weaker than the rest; which seem less able to bear fatigue and to encounter difficulties; which are more easily injured, and which become more easily affected with disease. It is possible that Paul may here refer to the brain, the lungs, the heart, &c., as more feeble in their structure, and more liable to disease than the hands and the feet, &c., and in reference to which disease is more dangerous and fatal. ¶ *Are more necessary*. The sense seems to be this. A man can live though the parts and members of his body which are more strong were removed; but not if those parts which are more feeble. A man can live if his arm or his leg be amputated; but not if his brain, his lungs or his heart be removed. So that, although these parts are more feeble, and more easily injured, they are really more necessary to life, and therefore more useful than the more vigorous portions of the frame. Perhaps the idea is—and it is a beautiful thought—that those members of the church which are most retiring and feeble apparently; which are concealed from public view, unnoticed and unknown—the humble, the meek, the peaceful, and the prayerful—are often more necessary to the true welfare of the church than those who are eminent for their talent and learning. And it is so. The church can better spare many a man, even in the ministry, who is learned, and eloquent, and popular, than some obscure and humble Christian, that is to the church what the heart and the lungs are to the life. The one is strong, vigorous, active, like the hands or the feet, and the church often depends on them; the other is feeble, concealed, yet vital, like the heart or the lungs. The vitality of the church could be continued though the man of talent and learning should be removed; as the body may live when the arm or the leg is amputated;—but that vitality could *not* continue if the saint of humble and retiring piety, and of fervent prayerfulness, were removed, any more than the body can live when there is no heart and no lungs.

23. *We bestow more abundant honour*. Marg. "Put on." The words rendered "abundant honour" here, refer to clothing. We bestow upon them more attention and honour than we do on the face that is deemed comely, and that is not covered and adorned as the other parts of the body are. ¶ *More abundant comeliness*. We adorn and decorate the body with gay apparel. Those parts which decency requires us to conceal we not only cover, but we endeavour as

no need; but God hath tempered the body together, having given more abundant honour to that *part* which lacked:

25 That there should be no [1] schism in the body; but *that* the members should have the same care one for another.

26 And whether one member suffer, all the members suffer with

[1] or, *division*.

far as we can to adorn them. The face in the mean time we leave uncovered. The idea is, that, in like manner, we should not despise or disregard those members of the church who are of lower rank, or who are less favoured than others with spiritual endowments.

24. *For our comely parts.* The face, &c. ¶ *Have no need.* No need of clothing or ornament. ¶ *But God hath tempered the body together.* Literally *mingled* or mixed; that is, has made to coalesce, or strictly and closely joined. He has formed a strict union; he has made one part dependent on another, and necessary to the harmony and proper action of another. Every part is useful, and all are fitted to the harmonious action of the whole. God has so arranged it, in order to produce harmony and equality in the body, that those parts which are less comely by nature should be more adorned and guarded by apparel. ¶ *Having given more abundant honour,* &c. By making it necessary that we should labour in order to procure for it the needful clothing; thus making it more the object of our attention and care. We thus bestow more abundant honour upon those parts of the body which a suitable protection from cold, and heat, and storms, and the sense of comeliness, requires us to clothe and conceal. The "more abundant honour," therefore, refers to the greater attention, labour, and care which we bestow on those parts of the body.

25. *That there should be no schism.* Marg. *Division;* see Note on chap. xi. 18. The sense here is, that the body might be united, and be one harmonious whole; that there should be no separate interests; and that all the parts should be equally necessary, and truly dependent on each other; and that no member should be regarded as separated from the others, or as needless to the welfare of all. The sense to be illustrated by this is, that no member of the church, however feeble, or illiterate, or obscure, should be despised or regarded as unnecessary or valueless; that all are needful in their places; and that it should not be supposed that they belonged to different bodies, or that they could not associate together, any more than the less honourable and comely parts of the body should be regarded as unworthy or unfit to be united to the parts that were deemed to be more beautiful or honourable. ¶ *Should have the same care.* Should care for the same thing; should equally regard the interests of all, as we feel an equal interest in all the members and parts of the body, and desire the preservation, the healthy action, and the harmonious and regular movement of the whole. Whatever part of the body is affected with disease or pain, we feel a deep interest in its preservation and cure. The idea is, that no member of the church should be overlooked or despised; but that the whole church should feel a deep interest for, and exercise a constant solicitude over, all its members.

26. *And whether one member suffer.* One member, or part of the body. ¶ *All the members suffer with it.* This, we all know, is the case with the body. A pain in the foot, the hand, or the head excites deep solicitude. The interest is not confined to the part affected; but we feel that we ourselves are affected, and that our body, as a whole, demands our care. The word "suffer" here refers to disease, or sickness. It is true also that not only we feel an *interest* in the part that is affected, but that disease in any one part tends to diffuse itself through, and to affect the whole frame. If not arrested, it is conveyed by the blood through all the members until life itself is destroyed. It is not by

it; or one member be honoured, all the members rejoice with it.

27 Now ye are the body of Christ, and members[a] in particular.

28 And God hath set some in the church; first, apostles; [b] secondarily, prophets; [c] thirdly, teachers; after that, miracles; [d]

a Eph.5.30. b Luke 6.13. c Acts 13.1. d ver.10.

mere interest, then, or sympathy, but it is by the natural connection and the inevitable result that a diseased member tends to affect the whole frame. There is not, indeed, in the church the same *physical* connection and *physical* effect, but the union is really not less close and important, nor is it the less certain that the conduct of one member will affect all. It is implied here also, that we *should* feel a deep interest in the welfare of all the members of the body of Christ. If one is tempted or afflicted, the other members of the church should feel it, and "bear one another's burdens, and so fulfil his law." If one is poor, the others should aid him, and supply his wants; if one is persecuted and opposed for righteousness' sake, the others should sympathize with him, and make common cause with him. In all things pertaining to religion and to their mutual welfare, they should feel that they have a common cause, and regard it as a privilege to aid one another. Nor should a man regard it as any more a burden and hardship to aid a poor or afflicted brother in the church, than it should be deemed a hardship that the head, and the heart, and the hands should sympathize when any other member of the body is diseased. ¶ *Or one member be honoured.* If applied to the body, this means, if one member or part be regarded and treated with special care; be deemed honourable; or be in a sound, healthy, and vigorous condition. If applied to the church, it means, if one of its members should be favoured with extraordinary endowments; or be raised to a station of honour and influence above his brethren. ¶ *All the members rejoice with it.* That is, in the body, all the other members partake of the benefit and honour. If one member be sound and healthy, the benefit extends to all. If the hands, the feet, the heart, the lungs, the brain be in a healthy condition, the advantage is felt by all the members, and all derive advantage from it. So in the church. If one member is favoured with remarkable talent, or is raised to a station of influence, and exerts his influence in the cause of Christ, all the members of the church partake of the benefit. It is for the common good; and all should rejoice in it. This consideration should repress envy at the elevation of others, and should lead all the members of a church to rejoice when God, by his direct agency, or by the arrangements of his providence, confers extraordinary endowments, or gives opportunity for extended usefulness to others.

27. *Now ye.* Ye Christians of Corinth, as a part of the whole church that has been redeemed. ¶ *Are the body of Christ.* The allusion to the human body is here kept up. As all the members of the human body compose one body, having a common head, so it is with all the members and parts of the Christian church. The specific idea is, that Christ is the Head of the whole church; that he presides over all; and that all its members sustain to each other the relation of fellow-members in the same body, and are subject to the same head; comp. Note, chap. xi. 3. The church is often called the body of Christ; Eph. i. 23; Col. i. 18, 24. ¶ *And members in particular.* You are, as individuals, members of the body of Christ; or each individual is a member of that body.

28. *And God hath set.* That is, has appointed, constituted, ordained. He has established these various orders or ranks in the church. The apostle, having illustrated the main idea that God had conferred various endowments on the members of the church, proceeds here to specify particularly what he meant, and to refer more directly to the various ranks

then gifts of healing, [a] helps, [b] governments, [c] [1] diversities of tongues. [d]

29 *Are* all apostles? *are* all prophets? *are* all teachers? *are* all [1] workers of miracles?

a ver.9. *b* Num.11.17. *c* Heb.13.17,24. 1 or, *kinds.* *d* Acts 2.8-11. 1 or, *powers.*

which existed in the church. ¶ *Some in the church.* The word "some," in this place (οὓς), seems to mean rather *whom,* "and whom God hath placed in the church," or, they whom God hath constituted in the church in the manner above mentioned are, first, apostles, &c. ¶ *First, apostles.* In the first rank or order; or as superior in honour and in office. He has given them the highest authority in the church; he has more signally endowed them and qualified them than he has others. ¶ *Secondarily, prophets.* As second in regard to endowments and importance. For the meaning of the word "prophets," see Note on Rom. xii. 6. ¶ *Thirdly, teachers.* As occupying the third station in point of importance and valuable endowments. On the meaning of this word, and the nature of this office, see Note on Rom. xii. 7. ¶ *After that, miracles.* Power. (δυνάμεις). Those who had the power of working miracles; referred to in ver. 10. ¶ *Then gifts of healings.* The power of healing those who were sick; see Note on ver. 9; comp. James v. 14, 15. ¶ *Helps* (ἀντιλήψεις). This word occurs no where else in the New Testament. It is derived from ἀντιλαμβάνω, and denotes properly, *aid, assistance, help;* and then those who render aid, assistance, or help; helpers. *Who* they were is not known. They might have been those to whom was intrusted the care of the poor, and the sick, and strangers, widows, and orphans, &c.; *i. e.* those who performed the office of deacons. Or they may have been those who attended on the apostles to aid them in their work, such as Paul refers to in Rom. xvi. 3. "Greet Priscilla, and Aquilla, my *helpers* in Christ Jesus;" and in ver. 9, "Salute Urbane our *helper* in Christ;" see Note on Rom. xvi. 3. It is not possible, perhaps, to determine the precise meaning of the word, or the nature of the office which they discharged; but the word means, in general, those who in any way aided or rendered assistance in the church, and may refer to the temporal affairs of the church, to the care of the poor, the distribution of charity and alms, or to the instruction of the ignorant, or to aid rendered directly to the apostles. There is no evidence that it refers to a distinct and permanent *office* in the church; but may refer to aid rendered by any class in any way. Probably many persons were profitably and usefully employed in various ways as aids in promoting the temporal or spiritual welfare of the church. ¶ *Governments* (κυβερνήσεις). This word is derived from κυβερνάω, *to govern;* and is usually applied to the government or *steering* of a ship. The word occurs no where else in the New Testament, though the word κυβερνήτης (governor) occurs in Acts xxvii. 11, rendered "master," and in Rev. xviii. 17, rendered "shipmaster." It is not easy to determine what particular office or function is here intended. Doddridge, in accordance with Amyraut, supposes that distinct offices may not be here referred to, but that the same persons may be denoted in these expressions as being distinguished in various ways; that is, that the same persons were called helpers in reference to their skill in aiding those who were in distress, and governments in regard to their talent for doing business, and their ability in presiding in councils for deliberation, and in directing the affairs of the church. There is no reason to think that the terms here used referred to permanent and established ranks and orders in the ministry and in the church; or in permanent offices which were to continue to all times as an essential part of its organization. It is certain that the "order" of *apostles* has ceased, and also the "order" of *miracles,* and the order of *healings,* and of *diversity of tongues.* And it is certain that in the use of these terms of office, the apostle does not affirm that they *would* be permanent, and essential to the very existence of the church; and from the passage before us, therefore, it cannot be argued that there was to be an order of men in the church who were to be called *helps*, or *governments*. The truth probably was, that the circumstances of the primitive churches required the aid of many persons in various capacities which might not be needful or proper in other times and circumstances. Whether, therefore, this is to be regarded as a permanent arrangement that there should be "governments" in the church, or an order of men intrusted with the sole office of governing, is to be learned not from this passage, but from other parts of the New Testament. Lightfoot contends that the word which is here used and translated "governments" does not refer to the power of *ruling*, but to a person endued with a deep and comprehensive mind, one who is wise and prudent; and in this view Mosheim, Macknight, and bishop Horsley coincide. Calvin refers it to the elders to whom the exercise of discipline was intrusted. Grotius understands it of the pastors (Eph. iv. 1), or of the elders who presided over particular churches; Rom. xii. 8. Locke supposes that they were the same as those who had the power of discerning spirits. The simple idea, however, is that of *ruling*, or exercising government; but whether this refers to a permanent office, or to the fact that some were specially qualified by their wisdom and prudence, and in virtue of this usually regulated or directed the affairs of the church by giving counsel, &c., or whether they were *selected* and appointed for this purpose for a time; or whether it refers to the same persons who might also have exercised other functions, and this in addition, cannot be determined from the passage before us. All that is clear is, that there were those who administered government in the church. But the passage does not determine the form, or manner; nor does it *prove*—whatever may be true—that such an office was to be permanent in the church.

[There can be little doubt that the κυβερνήσεις, or governments, refer to offices of rule and authority in the church. Two things, therefore, are plain from this text: 1. That in the primitive church there were rulers distinct from the people or church members, to whom these were bound to yield obedience. 2. That these rulers were appointed of God. "God set them in the church." As to the question of *permanence*, on which our author thinks this passage affirms nothing: a distinction must be made between those offices which were obviously of an extraordinary kind, and which therefore must cease; and those of an ordinary kind, which are essential to the edification of the church in all ages. "The universal commission which the apostles received from their Master to make disciples of all nations, could not be permanent as to the extent of it, because it was their practice to ordain elders in every city, and because the course of human affairs required, that after Christianity was established, the teachers of it should officiate in particular places. The infallible guidance of the Spirit was not promised in the same measure to succeeding teachers. But being, in their case, vouched by the power of working miracles, it directed the Christians of their day, to submit implicitly to their injunctions and directions; and it warrants the Christian world, in all ages, to receive with entire confidence, that system of faith and morality which they were authorised to deliver in the name of Christ. But as all protestants hold that this system was completed when the canon of scripture was closed—it is admitted by them, that a great part of the apostolical powers ceased with those to whom Jesus first committed them. Amongst the *ordinary* functions belonging to their office as teachers, are to be ranked not only preaching the word, and dispensing the sacraments, but also that rule and government over Christians as such, which is implied in the idea of the church as a society."—*Hill's Lectures*, vol. ii. p. 479. Now, though these extraordinary offices and functions have ceased with the age of the apostles, and of miraculous influence; it by no means follows, that the ordinary offices of teaching and ruling have ceased also. What was plainly of a *peculiar* kind, and could not possibly be *imitated* after the withdrawment of miraculous power, is quite distinct from that which, not depending on such power, is suited to the condition of the church always. Proceeding on any other principle, we should find it impossible to argue at all on what ought to be the constitution of the church, from any hints we find in the New Testament. What is extraordinary cannot be permanent, but what is ordinary must be so. See the Supplementary Note on ch. v. 4.]

30 Have all the gifts of healing? do all speak with tongues? do all interpret?

31 But covet [a] earnestly the best [b] gifts: and yet shew I unto you a more excellent way.

a chap.14.39. b Mat.5.6; Luke 10.42.

¶ *Diversities of tongues.* Those endowed with the power of speaking various languages; see Note on ver. 10.

29, 30. Are *all apostles*? &c. These questions imply, with strong emphasis, that it could not be, and ought not to be, that there should be perfect equality of endowment. It was not a matter of fact that all were equal, or that all were qualified for the offices which others sustained. Whether the arrangement was approved of or not, it was a simple matter of fact that some were qualified to perform offices which others were not; that some were endowed with the abilities requisite to the apostolic office, and others not; that some were endowed with prophetic gifts, and others were not; that some had the gift of healing, or the talent of speaking different languages, or of interpreting and that others had not.

31. *But covet earnestly.* Gr. "Be zealous for" (Ζηλοῦτε). This word, however, may be either in the indicative mood (ye do covet earnestly), or in the imperative, as in our translation. Doddridge contends that it should be rendered in the indicative mood, for he says it seems to be a contradiction that after the apostle had been showing that these gifts were not at their own option, and that they ought not to emulate the gifts of another, or aspire to superiority, to undo all again, and give them such contrary advice. The same view is given by Locke, and so Macknight. The Syriac renders it, "Because you are zealous of the best gifts, I will show to you a more excellent way." But there is no valid objection to the common translation in the imperative, and indeed the connection seems to demand it. Grotius renders it, "Pray to God that you may receive from him the best, that is, the most useful endowments." The sense seems to be this, "I have proved that *all* endowments in the church are produced by the Holy Spirit; and that he confers them as he pleases. I have been showing that no one should be proud or elated on account of extraordinary endowments; and that, on the other hand, no one should be depressed, or sad, or discontented, because he has a more humble rank. I have been endeavouring to repress and subdue the spirit of discontent, jealousy, and ambition; and to produce a willingness in all to occupy the station where God has placed you. But, I do not intend to deny that it is *proper* to desire the most useful endowments; that a man should wish to be brought under the influence of the Spirit, and qualified for eminent usefulness. I do not mean to say that it is wrong for a man to regard the higher gifts of the Spirit as valuable and desirable, if they may be obtained; nor that the spirit which seeks to excel in spiritual endowments and in usefulness, is improper. Yet all cannot be apostles; all cannot be prophets. I would not have you, therefore, seek *such* offices, and manifest a spirit of ambition. I would seek to regulate the desire which I would not repress as improper; and in order to that, I would show you that, instead of aspiring to offices and extraordinary endowments which are beyond your grasp, there *is* a way, more truly valuable, that is open to you all, and where all may excel." Paul thus endeavours to give a practicable and feasible turn to the whole subject, and further to repress the longings of ambition and the contentions of strife, by exciting emulation to obtain that which was accessible to them all, and *which, just in the proportion in which it was obtained,* would repress discontent, and strife, and ambition, and produce order, and peace, and contentedness with their endowments and their lot,—the main thing which he was desirous of producing in this chapter. This, therefore, is one of the *happy turns* in

CHAPTER XIII.

THOUGH I speak with the tongues of men and of angels, and have not charity, [b] I am become *as* sounding brass, or a tinkling cymbal.

a 2 Cor.12.4. b 1Pet 4.8.

which the writings of Paul abounds. He did not denounce their zeal as wicked. He did not attempt at once to repress it. He did not say that it was wrong to desire high endowments. But he showed them an endowment which was more valuable than all the others; which was accessible to all; and which, if possessed, would make them contented, and produce the harmonious operation of all the parts of the church. That endowment was LOVE. ¶ *A more excellent way;* see the next chapter. "I will show you a more excellent way of evincing your *zeal* than by aspiring to the place of apostles, prophets, or rulers, and that is by cultivating universal charity or love."

CHAPTER XIII.

THIS chapter is a continuation of the subject commenced in chap. xii. In that chapter Paul had introduced the subject of the various endowments which the Holy Spirit confers on Christians, and had shown that these endowments, however various they were, were conferred in such a manner as best to promote the edification and welfare of the church. In the close of that chapter (ver. 31) he had said that it was lawful for them to desire the most eminent of the gifts conferred by the Spirit; and yet says that there was *one* endowment that was more valuable than all others, and that might be obtained by all, and that he proposed to recommend to them. That was LOVE; and to illustrate its nature, excellency, and power, is the design of this exquisitely beautiful and tender chapter. In doing this, he dwells particularly on three points or views of the excellency of love; and the chapter may be regarded as consisting of three portions.

I. The excellency of love above the power of speaking the languages of men and of angels; above the power of understanding all mysteries; above all faith, even of the highest kind; and above the virtue of giving all one's goods to feed the poor, or one's body to be burned. All these endowments would be valueless without love, ver. 1—3.

II. A statement of the characteristics of love; or its happy influences on the mind and heart, ver. 4—7.

III. A comparison of love with the gift of prophecy, and with the power of speaking foreign languages, and with knowledge, ver. 8—13. In this portion of the chapter, Paul shows that love is superior to them all. It will live in heaven; and will constitute the chief glory of that world of bliss.

1. *Though I speak with the tongues of men.* Though I should be able to speak all the languages which are spoken by men. To speak foreign languages was regarded then, as it is now, as a rare and valuable endowment; comp. Virg. Æn. vi. 625, seq. The word *I* here is used in a popular sense, and the apostle designs to illustrate, as he often does, his idea by a reference to himself, which, it is evident, he wishes to be understood as applying to those whom he addressed. It is evident that among the Corinthians the power of speaking a foreign language was regarded as a signally valuable endowment; and there can be no doubt that some of the leaders in that church valued themselves especially on it; see chap. xiv. To correct this, and to show them that all this would be vain without love, and to induce them, therefore, to seek for love as a more valuable endowment, was the design of the apostle in this passage. Of this verse Dr. Bloomfield, than whom, perhaps, there is no living man better qualified to give such an opinion, remarks, that "it would be difficult to find a finer passage than this in the writings of Demosthenes himself." ¶ *And of angels.* The language of angels; such as they speak. Were I endowed with the faculty of eloquence and persuasion which we attribute to them; and the

power of speaking to any of the human family with the power which they have. The language of angels here seems to be used to denote the highest power of using language, or of the most elevated faculty of eloquence and speech. It is evidently derived from the idea that the angels are *superior* in all respects to men; that they must have endowments in advance of all which man can have. It may possibly have reference to the idea that they must have some mode of communicating their ideas one to another, and that this dialect or mode must be far superior to that which is employed by man. Man is imperfect. All his modes of communication are defective. We attribute to the angels the idea of perfection; and the idea here is, that even though a man had a far higher faculty of speaking languages than would be included in the endowment of speaking all the languages of men as men speak them, and even had the higher and more perfect mode of utterance which the angels have, and yet were destitute of love, all would be nothing. It is possible that Paul may have some allusion here to what he refers to in 2 Cor. xii. 4, where he says that when he was caught up into paradise, he heard unspeakable words which it was not possible for a man to utter. To this higher, purer language of heaven he may refer here by the language of the angels. It was not with him mere *conjecture* of what that language might be; it was language which he had been permitted himself to hear. Of that scene he would retain a most deep and tender recollection; and to that language he now refers, by saying that even *that* elevated language would be valueless to a creature if there were not love. ¶ *And have not charity* (ἀγάπην δὲ μὴ ἔχω). And have not LOVE. This is the proper and usual meaning of the Greek word. The English word *charity* is used in a great variety of senses; and some of them cannot be included in the meaning of the word here. It means, (1.) In a general sense, love, benevolence, good-will; (2.) In theology, it includes supreme love to God and universal good-will to men; (3.) In a more particular sense, it denotes the love and kindness which springs from the natural relations, as the *charities* of father, son, brother; (4.) Liberality to the poor, to the needy, and to objects of beneficence, as we speak commonly of *charity*, meaning almsgiving, and of charitable societies; (5.) *Candour*, liberality in judging of men's actions; indulgence to their opinions; attributing to them good motives and intentions; a disposition to judge of them favourably, and to put on their words and actions the best construction. This is a very common signification of the word in our language now, and this is one modification of the word *love*, as all such charity is supposed to proceed from *love* to our neighbour, and a desire that he should have a right to *his* opinions as well as we to ours. The Greek word ἀγάπη means properly *love*, affection, regard, good-will, benevolence. It is applied, (*a*) To love in general; (*b*) To the love of God and of Christ; (*c*) The love which God or Christ exercises towards Christians, (Rom. v. 5; Eph. ii. 4; 2 Thess. iii. 5); (*d*) The effect, or proof of beneficence, favour conferred; Eph. i. 15; 2 Thess. ii. 10; 1 John iii. 1. *Robinson, Lex.* In the English word *charity*, therefore, there are now some ideas which are not found in the Greek word, and especially the idea of *almsgiving*, and the common use of the word among us in the sense of *candour*, or *liberality in judging*. Neither of these ideas, perhaps, are to be found in the use of the word in the chapter before us; and the more proper translation would have been, in accordance with the usual mode of translation in the New Testament, LOVE. Tindal in his translation, renders it by the word *love*. The *love* which is referred to in this chapter, and illustrated, is mainly *love to man* (ver. 4—7); though there is no reason to doubt that the apostle meant also to include in the general term love to God, or love in general. His *illustrations*, however, are chiefly drawn from the effects of love towards men. It properly means love to the whole church, love to the whole world: love

2 And though I have *the gift of* prophecy, [a] and understand all mysteries, and all knowledge; and though I have all faith, so

a chap.14.1.

to all creatures which arises from true piety, and which centres ultimately in God.—*Doddridge.* It is this love whose importance Paul, in this beautiful chapter, illustrates as being more valuable than the highest possible endowments without it. It is not necessary to suppose that any one *had* these endowments, or had the power of speaking with the tongues of men and angels; or had the gift of prophecy, or had the highest degree of faith, who had no love. The apostle *supposes* a case; and says that if it *were* so, if all these *were* possessed without love, they would be comparatively valueless; or that love was a more valuable endowment than all the others would be without it. ¶ *I am become.* I am. I shall be. ¶ *As sounding brass.* Probably a *trumpet.* The word properly means *brass;* then that which is made of brass; a trumpet, or wind instrument of any kind made of brass or copper. The sense is that of a sounding or resounding instrument, making a great noise, apparently of great importance, and yet without vitality; a mere instrument; a base metal that merely makes a sound. Thus noisy, valueless, empty, and without vitality would be the power of speaking all languages without love. ¶ *Or a tinkling cymbal.* A cymbal giving a clanging, clattering sound. The word rendered "tinkling" (ἀλαλάζον, from ἀλαλή or αλαλα, *a war-cry*) properly denotes a loud cry, or shout, such as is used in battle; and then also a loud cry or mourning, cries of lamentation or grief; the loud *shriek* of sorrow, Mark v. 38, "Them that wept and *wailed* greatly." It then means a clanging or clattering sound, such as was made on a cymbal. The cymbal is a well-known instrument, made of two pieces of brass or other metal, which, being struck together, gives a tinkling or clattering sound. Cymbals are commonly used in connection with other music. They make a tinkling, or clanging, with very little variety of sound. The music is little adapted to produce emotion, or to excite feeling. There is no melody and no harmony. They were, therefore, well adapted to express the idea which the apostle wished to convey. The sense is, "If I could speak all languages, yet if I had not love, the faculty would be like the clattering, clanging sound of the cymbal, that contributes nothing to the welfare of others. It would all be hollow, vain, useless. It could neither save me nor others, any more than the notes of the trumpet, or the jingling of the cymbal, would promote salvation. *Love* is the vital principle; it is that without which all other endowments are useless and vain."

2. *And though I have* the gift of *prophecy;* see Note, chap. xii. 10; xiv. 1. ¶ *And understand all mysteries.* On the meaning of the word *mystery,* see Note, chap. ii. 7. This passage proves that it was one part of the prophetic office, as referred to here, to be able to understand and explain the *mysteries* of religion; that is, the things that were before unknown, or unrevealed. It does not refer to the prediction of future events, but to the great and deep truths connected with religion; the things that were unexplained in the old economy, the meaning of types and emblems; and the obscure portions of the plan of redemption. All these might be *plain* enough if they were revealed; but there were many things connected with religion which God had not chosen to reveal to men. ¶ *And all knowledge;* Note, chap. xii. 8. Though I knew every thing. Though I were acquainted fully with all the doctrines of religion; and were with all sciences and arts. ¶ *And though I have all faith, so that I could remove mountains.* Thould I should have the highest kind of faith. This is referred to by the Saviour (Mat. xvii. 20,) as the highest kind of faith; and Paul here had this fact doubtless in his eye. ¶ *I am nothing.* All would be of no value. It would not save me.]

that I could remove [a] mountains, and have not charity, I am nothing. [b]

3 And though [c] I bestow all my goods to feed *the poor*, and though [d] I give my body to be

a Mat.17.20. b Mat.21.19. c Mat.6.1,2. d Mat.7.22,23; James 2.14.

should still be an unredeemed, unpardoned sinner. I should do good to no one; I should answer none of the great purposes which God has designed; I should not by all this secure my salvation. All would be in vain in regard to the great purpose of my existence. None of these things could be placed before God as a ground of acceptance in the day of judgment. Unless I should have *love*, I should still be lost. A somewhat similar idea is expressed by the Saviour, in regard to the day of judgment, in Mat. vii. 22, 23, "Many will say unto me in that day, Lord, Lord, have we not prophesied in thy name? and in thy name have cast out devils? and in thy name done many wonderful works? And then will I profess unto them, I never knew you: depart from me, ve that work iniquity."

3. *And though I bestow.* The Greek word here used (ψωμίσω, from ψάω, to break off) meant properly to break off, and distribute in small portions; to feed by morsels; and may be applicable here to distributing one's property in small portions. Charity or alms to the poor, was usually distributed at one's gate (Luke xvi. 20,) or in some public place. Of course, if property was distributed in this manner, many more would be benefitted than if all were given to one person. There would be many more to be thankful, and to celebrate one's praises. This was regarded as a great virtue; and was often performed in a most ostentatious manner. It was a gratification to wealthy men who desired the praise of being benevolent, that *many* of the poor flocked daily to their houses to be fed; and against this desire of distinction, the Saviour directed some of his severest reproofs; see Mat. vi. 1—4. To make the case as strong as possible, Paul says that if ALL that a man had were dealt out in this way, in small portions, so as to benefit as many as possible, and yet were not attended *with true love towards God and towards man*, it would be all false, hollow, hypocritical, and really of no value in regard to his own salvation. It would profit nothing. It would not be such an act as God would approve; it would be no evidence that the soul would be saved. Though good might be done to others. yet where the *motive* was wrong, it could not meet with the divine approbation, or be connected with his favour. ¶ *And though I give my body to be burned.* Evidently as a martyr, or a witness to the truth of religion. Though I should be willing to lay down my life in the most painful manner, and have not charity, it would profit me nothing. Many of the ancient prophets were called to suffer martyrdom, though there is no evidence that any of them were burned to death as martyrs. Shadrach, Mesheeh, and Abednego were indeed thrown into a fiery furnace, because they were worshippers of the true God; but they were not consumed in the flame, Dan. iii. 19—26; comp. Heb. xi. 34. Though Christians were early persecuted, yet there is no evidence that they were burned as martyrs as early as this epistle was written. Nero is the first who is believed to have committed this horrible act; and under his reign, and during the persecution which he excited, Christians were covered with pitch, and set on fire to illuminate his gardens. It is possible that some Christians had been put to death in this manner when Paul wrote this epistle; but it is more probable that he refers to this as *the most awful kind of death*, rather than as any thing which had really happened. Subsequently, however, as all know, this was often done, and thousands, and perhaps tens of thousands, of Christians have been called to evince their attachment to religion in the flames. ¶ *And have not charity.* Have no love to God, or to men; have no true piety. If I do it from any selfish or

burned, and have not charity, it profiteth me nothing.

4 Charity suffereth [a] long, *and* is kind; charity envieth [b] not;

a Prov.10.12.

b James 3.16.

sinister motive; if I do it from fanaticism, obstinacy, or vain-glory; if I am deceived in regard to my character, and have never been born again. It is not *necessary* to an explanation of this passage to suppose that this ever *had* been done, for the apostle only puts a supposable case. There is reason, however, to think that it *has* been done frequently; and that when the desire of martyrdom became the *popular passion,* and was believed to be connected infallibly with heaven, not a few have been willing to give themselves to the flames who never knew any thing of love to God or true piety. Grotius mentions the instance of Calanus, and of Peregrinus the philosopher, who did it. Although this was not the common mode of martyrdom in the time of Paul, and although it was then perhaps unknown, it is remarkable that he should have referred to that which in subsequent times became the common mode of death on account of religion. In his time, and before, the common mode was by stoning, by the sword, or by crucifixion. Subsequently, however, all these were laid aside, and *burning* became the common way in which martyrs suffered. So it was, extensively, under Nero; and so it was, exclusively, under the Inquisition; and so it was in the persecutions in England in the time of Mary. Paul seems to have been *directed* to specify this rather than stoning, the sword, or crucifixion, in order that, in subsequent times, martyrs might be led to examine themselves, and to see whether they were actuated by true love to God in being willing to be consumed in the flames. ¶ *It profiteth me nothing.* If there is no true piety, there can be no benefit in this to my soul. It will not save me. If I have no true love to God, I must perish, after all. *Love,* therefore, is more valuable and precious than all these endowments. Nothing can supply its place; nothing can be connected with salvation without it.

4. *Charity suffereth long.* Paul now proceeds to illustrate the *nature* of love, or to show how it is exemplified. His illustrations are all drawn from its effect in regulating our conduct towards others, or our intercourse with them. The *reason* why he made use of this illustration, rather than its nature as evinced towards *God,* was, probably, because it was especially necessary for them to understand in what way it should be manifested towards each other. There were contentions and strifes among them; there were of course suspicions, and jealousies, and heart-burnings; there would be unkind judging, the imputation of improper motives, and selfishness; there were envy, and pride, and boasting, all of which were inconsistent with love; and Paul therefore evidently designed to correct these evils, and to produce a different state of things by showing them what would be produced by the exercise of love. The word here used (μακροθυμεῖ) denotes *longanimity,* slowness to anger or passion; long-suffering, patient endurance, forbearance. It is opposed to *haste;* to passionate expressions and thoughts, and to irritability. It denotes the state of mind which can BEAR LONG when oppressed, provoked, calumniated, and when one seeks to injure us; comp. Rom. ii. 4; ix. 22; 2 Cor. vi. 6; Gal. v. 22; Eph. iv. 2; Col. iii. 12; 1 Tim. i. 16; 2 Tim. iii. 10; iv. 2; 1 Pet. iii. 20; 2 Pet. iii. 15. ¶ *And is kind.* The word here used denotes to be good-natured, gentle, tender, affectionate. Love is benignant. It wishes well. It is not harsh, sour, morose, ill-natured. Tindal renders it, "is courteous." The idea is, that under all provocations and ill-usage it is gentle and mild. *Hatred* prompts to harshness, severity, unkindness of expression, anger, and a desire of revenge. But love is the reverse of all these. A man who truly loves another will be *kind* to him, desirous of doing him good; will be *gentle,* not severe and harsh;

charity [1] vaunteth not itself, is not puffed [a] up.

5 Doth not behave itself unseemly, seeketh not [b] her own, is

1 or, *is not rash*. a Col.2.18.

b chap.10.24.

will be *courteous* because he desires his happiness, and would not pain his feelings. And as religion is love, and prompts to love, so it follows that it requires courtesy or true politeness, and will secure it; see 1 Pet. iii. 8. If all men were under the influence of true religion, they would always be *truly* polite and courteous; for true politeness is nothing more than an expression of benignity, or a desire to promote the happiness of all around us. ¶ *Envieth not* (οὐ ζηλοῖ). This word properly means to be *zealous* for or against any person or thing; *i. e.* to be eager for, or anxious for or against any one. It is used often in a good sense (1 Cor. xii. 31; Note, xiv. 1, 39; 2 Cor. xi. 2, &c.); but it may be used in a bad sense—to be zealous *against* a person; to be jealous of; to envy. Acts vii. 9; xvii. 5; James iv. 2, "Ye kill and *envy*." It is in this sense, evidently, that it is used here,—as denoting zeal, or ardent desire *against* any person. The sense is, love does not envy others the happiness which they enjoy; it delights in their welfare; and as their happiness is increased by their endowments, their rank, their reputation, their wealth, their health, their domestic comforts, their learning &c., those who are influenced by love *rejoice* in all this. They would not diminish it; they would not embarrass them in the possession; they would not detract from that happiness; they would not murmur or repine that they themselves are not so highly favoured.—To envy is to feel uneasiness, mortification, or discontent at the sight of superior happiness, excellence or reputation enjoyed by another; to repine at another's prosperity; and to fret oneself on account of his real or fancied superiority. Of course, it may be excited by *any thing* in which another excels, or in which he is more favoured than we are. It may be excited by superior wealth, beauty, learning, accomplishment, reputation, success. It may extend to any employment, or any rank in life. A man may be envied because he is happy while we are miserable; well, while we are sick; caressed, while we are neglected or overlooked; successful, while we meet with disappointment; handsome, while we are ill-formed; honoured with office, while we are overlooked. He may be envied because he has a better farm than we have, or is a more skilful mechanic, or a more successful physician, lawyer, or clergyman. *Envy commonly lies in the same line of business, occupation, or rank.* We do not usually envy a monarch, a conqueror, or a nobleman, unless we are *aspiring* to the same rank. The farmer does not usually envy the blacksmith, but another farmer; the blacksmith does not usually envy the schoolmaster, or the lawyer, but another man in the same line of business with himself. The physician envies another physician more learned or more successful; the lawyer, another lawyer; the clergyman, another clergyman. The fashionable female, who seeks admiration or flattery on account of accomplishment or beauty, envies another who is more distinguished and more successful in those things. And so the poet envies a rival poet; and the orator, a rival orator; and the statesman, a rival statesman. The correction of all these things is *love.* If we loved others; if we rejoiced in their happiness, we should not envy them. *They are not to blame* for these superior endowments; but if those endowments are the direct gift of God, *we* should be thankful that he has made others happy; if they are the fruit of their own industry, and virtue, and skill and application, we should esteem them the more, and value them the more highly. They have not injured *us;* and *we* should not be unhappy, or seek to injure them, because God has blessed them, or because they have been more industrious, virtuous, and successful than we have. Every man should have his own level in society, and we should rejoice in the happiness of all.—Love will produce another effect. We should not *envy* them, because he that is under the influence of Christian love is more happy than those in the world who are usually the objects of envy. There is often much wretchedness under a clothing "of purple and fine linen." There is not *always* happiness in a splendid mansion; in the caresses of the great; in a post of honour; in a palace, or on a throne. Alexander the Great wept on the throne of the world. Happiness is in the heart; and contentment, and the love of God, and the hope of heaven produce happiness which rank, and wealth, and fashion, and earthly honour cannot purchase. And could the sad and heavy hearts of those in elevated ranks of life be always seen; and especially could their end be seen, there would be no occasion or disposition to envy them.

> Lord, what a thoughtless wretch was I,
> To mourn, and murmur, and repine,
> To see the wicked placed on high,
> In pride and robes of honour shine!
>
> But oh! their end, their dreadful end!
> Thy sanctuary taught me so;
> On slipp'ry rocks I see them stand,
> And fiery billows roll below.
>
> Now let them boast how tall they rise,
> I'll never envy them again;
> There they may stand with haughty eyes,
> Till they plunge deep in endless pain.
>
> Their fancied joys how fast they flee,
> Like dreams as fleeting and as vain;
> Their songs of softest harmony
> Are but a prelude to their pain.
>
> Now I esteem their mirth and wine
> Too dear to purchase with my blood;
> Lord, 'tis enough that thou art mine,
> My life, my portion, and my God.

¶ *Vaunteth not itself* (περπερεύεται, from πέρπερος, a boaster, braggart. *Robinson.*) The idea is that of boasting, bragging, vaunting. The word occurs no where else in the New Testament. Bloomfield supposes that it has the idea of acting precipitously, inconsiderately, incautiously; and this idea our translators have placed in the margin, "*he is not rash.*" But most expositors suppose that it has the notion of boasting, or vaunting of one's own excellencies or endowments. This spirit proceeds from the idea of *superiority* over others; and is connected with a feeling of contempt or disregard for them. Love would correct this, because it would produce a desire that they should be happy—and to treat a man with contempt is not the way to make him happy; love would regard others with esteem—and to boast over them is not to treat them with esteem; it would teach us to treat them with affectionate regard—and no man who has affectionate regard for others is disposed to boast of his own qualities over them. Besides, love produces a state of mind just the opposite of a disposition to boast. It receives its endowments with gratitude; regards them as the gift of God; and is disposed to employ them not in vain boasting, but in purposes of utility, in doing good to all others on as wide a scale as possible. The boaster is not a man who does good. To *boast* of talents is not to employ them to advantage to others. It will be of no account in feeding the hungry, clothing the naked, comforting the sick and afflicted, or in saving the world. Accordingly, the man who does the most good is the least accustomed to boast; the man who boasts may be regarded as doing nothing else. ¶ *Is not puffed up* (φυσιοῦται). This word means to blow, to puff, to pant; then to inflate with pride, and vanity, and self-esteem. See the word explained in the Note on chap. viii. 1. It perhaps differs from the preceding word, inasmuch as that word denotes the *expression* of the feelings of pride, vanity, &c., and this word the feeling itself. A man may be very proud and vain, and not express it in the form of boasting. That state is indicated by this word. If he gives expression to this feeling, and boasts of his endowments, that is indicated by the previous word. Love would prevent this, as it would the former. It would destroy the *feeling*, as well as the *expression* of it. It would teach a man that others had good qualities as well as he; that they had high endowments as well as he; and would *dispose* him to concede to them full credit for all that they have, and not to be vain-glorious of his

not *a* easily provoked, thinketh no evil;

6 Rejoiceth *b* not in iniquity, but rejoiceth 1 in the truth;

a Prov.14.17. *b* Rom.1.32. 1 or, *with.*

own. Besides, it is not the *nature* of love to fill the mind in this manner. Pride, vanity, and even knowledge (chap. viii. 1), may swell the mind with the conviction of self-importance; but love is humble, meek, modest, unobtrusive. A brother that loves a sister is not filled with pride or vanity on account of it; a man that loves the whole world, and desires its salvation, is not filled with pride and vanity on account of it. Hence the Saviour, who had *most* love for the human race, was at the farthest possible remove from pride and vanity.

5. *Doth not behave itself unseemly* (οὐκ ἀσχημονεῖ). This word occurs in chap. vii. 36. See Note on that verse. It means to conduct improperly, or disgracefully, or in a manner to deserve reproach. Love seeks that which is proper or becoming in the circumstances and relations of life in which we are placed. It prompts to the due respect for superiors, producing veneration and respect for their opinions; and it prompts to a proper regard for inferiors, not despising their rank, their poverty, their dress, their dwellings, their pleasures, their views of happiness; it prompts to the due observance of all the *relations* of life, as those of a husband, wife, parent, child, brother, sister, son, daughter, and produces a proper conduct and deportment in all these relations. The proper idea of the phrase is, that it prompts to all that is fit and becoming in life; and would save from all that is unfit and unbecoming. There may be included in the word also the idea that it would prevent any thing that would be a violation of decency or delicacy. It is well known that the Cynics were in the habit of setting at defiance all the usual ideas of decency; and indeed this was, and is, commonly done in the temples of idolatry and pollution every where. Love would prevent this, because it teaches to promote the *happiness* of all, and of course to avoid every thing that would offend purity of taste and mar enjoyment. In the same way it prompts to the fit discharge of all the relative duties, because it leads to the desire to promote the happiness of all. And in the same manner it would lead a man to avoid profane and indecent language, improper allusions, double meanings and inuendoes, coarse and vulgar expressions, because such things pain the ear, and offend the heart of purity and delicacy. There is much that is indecent and unseemly still in society that would be corrected by Christian love. What a change would be produced if, under the influence of that love, nothing should be said or done in the various relations of life but what would be *seemly, fit, and decent!* And what a happy influence would the prevalence of this love have on the intercourse of mankind! ¶ *Seeketh not her own.* There is, perhaps, not a more striking or important expression in the New Testament than this; or one that more beautifully sets forth the nature and power of that love which is produced by true religion. Its evident meaning is, that it is not selfish; it does not seek its own happiness exclusively or mainly; it does not seek its own happiness to the injury of others. This expression is not, however, to be pressed as if Paul meant to teach that a man should not regard his own welfare at all; or have no respect to his health, his property, his happiness, or his salvation. Every man is bound to pursue such a course of life as will ultimately secure his own salvation. But it is not simply or mainly that he may be happy that he is to seek it. It is, that he may thus glorify God his Saviour; and accomplish the great design which his Maker has had in view in his creation and redemption. If his happiness is the main or leading thing, it proves that he is supremely selfish; and selfishness is not religion. The expres-

sion here used is *comparative*, and denotes that this is not the main, the chief, the only thing which one who is under the influence of love or true religion will seek. True religion, or love to others, will prompt us to seek their welfare with self-denial, and personal sacrifice and toil. Similar expressions, to denote comparison, occur frequently in the sacred Scriptures. Thus, where it is said (Hos. vii. 6; comp. Micah vi. 8; Mat. ix. 13), "I desired mercy, and not sacrifice;" it is meant, "I desired mercy *more* than I desired sacrifice; I did not wish that mercy should be forgotten or excluded in the attention to the mere ceremonies of religion." The sense here is, therefore, that a man under the influence of true love or religion does not make his own happiness or salvation the main or leading thing; he does not make all other things subservient to this; he seeks the welfare of others, and desires to promote their happiness and salvation, even at great personal sacrifice and self-denial. It is the *characteristic* of the man, not that he promotes his own worth, health, happiness, or salvation, but that he lives to do good to others. Love to others will prompt to that, and that alone. There is not a particle of selfishness in true love. It seeks the welfare of others, and of all others. That true religion will produce this, is evident every where in the New Testament; and especially in the life of the Lord Jesus, whose whole biography is comprehended in one expressive declaration, "who went about DOING GOOD;" Acts x. 38. It follows from this statement, (1.) That no man is a Christian who lives for himself alone; or who makes it his main business to promote his own happiness and salvation. (2.) No man is a Christian who does not deny himself; or no one who is not willing to sacrifice his own comfort, time, wealth, and ease, to advance the welfare of mankind. (3.) It is this principle which is yet to convert the world. Long since the whole world would have been converted, had all Christians been under its influence. And when ALL Christians make it their grand object *not* to seek their own, but the good of others; when true charity shall occupy its appropriate place in the heart of every professed child of God, then this world will be speedily converted to the Saviour. Then there will be no want of funds to spread Bibles and tracts; to sustain missionaries, or to establish colleges and schools; then there will be no want of men who shall be willing to go to any part of the earth to preach the gospel; and then there will be no want of prayer to implore the divine mercy on a ruined and perishing world. O may the time soon come when all the selfishness in the human heart shall be dissolved, and when the whole world shall be embraced in the benevolence of Christians, and the time, and talent, and wealth of the whole church shall be regarded as consecrated to God, and employed and expended under the influence of Christian love! Comp. Note, chap. x. 24. ¶ *Is not easily provoked* (παρ-οξύνεται). This word occurs in the New Testament only in one other place. Acts xvii. 16, "His spirit *was stirred* within him when he saw the city wholly given to idolatry." See Note on that place. The word properly means to sharpen by, or with, or on any thing (from ὀξύς, *sharp*), and may be applied to the act of sharpening a knife or sword; then it means to sharpen the mind, temper, courage of any one; to excite, impel, &c. Here it means evidently to rouse to anger; to excite to indignation or wrath. Tindal renders it, "is not provoked to anger." Our translation does not exactly convey the sense. The word "easily" is not expressed in the original. The translators have inserted it to convey the idea that he who is under the influence of love, though he may be provoked, that is, injured, or though there might be incitements to anger, yet that he would not be roused, or readily give way to it. The meaning of the phrase in the Greek is, that a man who is under the influence of love or religion is not *prone* to violent anger or exasperation; it is not his character to be hasty, excited, or passionate. He is calm, serious, patient. He looks soberly at things; and though he may be injured, yet he governs his passions, restrains his temper, subdues his feelings. This, Paul says, would be produced by love. And this is apparent. If we are under the influence of benevolence, or love to any one, we shall not give way to sudden bursts of feeling. We shall look kindly on his actions; put the best construction on his motives; deem it possible that we have mistaken the nature or the reasons of his conduct; seek or desire explanation (Mat. v. 23, 24); wait till we can look at the case in all its bearings; and suppose it possible that he may be influenced by good motives, and that his conduct will admit a satisfactory explanation. That true religion is designed to produce this, is apparent every where in the New Testament, and especially from the example of the Lord Jesus; that it actually does produce it, is apparent from all who come under its influence in any proper manner. The effect of religion is no where else more striking and apparent than in changing a temper naturally quick, excitable, and irritable, to one that is calm, and gentle, and subdued. A consciousness of the presence of God will do much to produce this state of mind; and if we truly loved all men, we should be soon angry with none. ¶ *Thinketh no evil.* That is, puts the best possible construction on the motives and the conduct of others. This expression also is *comparative.* It means that love, or that a person under the influence of love, is not malicious, censorious, disposed to find fault, or to impute improper motives to others. It is not only "not easily provoked," not soon excited, but it is not disposed to *think* that there was any evil intention even in cases which might tend to irritate or exasperate us. It is not disposed to think that there was any evil in the case; or that what was done was with any improper intention or design; that is, it puts the best possible construction on the conduct of others, and supposes, as far as can be done, that it was in consistency with honesty, truth, friendship, and love. The Greek word (λογίζεται) is that which is commonly rendered *impute,* and is correctly rendered here *thinketh.* It means, does not reckon, charge, or impute to a man any evil intention or design. We desire to think well of the man whom we love; nor will we think ill of his motives, opinions, or conduct until we are compelled to do so by the most irrefragable evidence. True religion, therefore, will prompt to charitable judging; nor is there a more striking evidence of the destitution of true religion than a disposition to impute the worst motives and opinions to a man.

6. *Rejoiceth not in iniquity.* Does not rejoice over the *vices* of other men; does not take delight when they are guilty of crime, or when, in any manner, they fall into sin. It does not find pleasure in hearing others accused of sin, and in having it proved that they committed it. It does not find a malicious pleasure in the *report* that they have done wrong; or in following up that report, and finding it established. Wicked men often find pleasure in this (Rom. i. 32), and rejoice when others have fallen into sin, and have disgraced and ruined themselves. Men of the world often find a malignant pleasure in the report, and in the evidence that a member of the Church has brought dishonour on his profession. A man often rejoices when an enemy, a persecutor, or a slanderer has committed some crime, and when he has shown an improper spirit, uttered a rash expression, or taken some step which shall involve him in ignominy. But love does none of these things. It does not desire that an enemy, a persecutor, or a slanderer should do evil, or should disgrace and ruin himself It does not rejoice, but grieves, when a professor of religion, or an enemy of religion—when a personal friend or foe has done any thing wrong. It neither loves the wrong, nor the fact that it has been done. And perhaps there is no greater triumph of the gospel than in its enabling a man to rejoice that even his enemy and persecutor in any respect does well; or to rejoice that he is in any way honoured and respected among men. Human nature, without the gospel, manifests a dif-

7 Beareth [a] all things, believeth
[b] all things, hopeth [c] all things,
endureth [d] all things.

8 Charity never faileth: but
whether *there be* prophecies, they
shall fail; but whether *there be*

a Rom.15.1. *b* Ps.119.66. *c* Rom.8.24. *d* Job 13.15.

ferent feeling; and it is only as the heart is subdued by the gospel, and filled with universal benevolence, that it is brought to rejoice when all men do well. ¶ *Rejoiceth in the truth.* The word *truth* here stands opposed to *iniquity*, and means virtue, piety, goodness. It does not rejoice in the *vices*, but in the *virtues* of others. It is pleased, it rejoices when they *do well.* It is pleased when those who differ from us conduct themselves in any manner in such a way as to please God, and to advance their own reputation and happiness. They who are under the influence of that love rejoice that good is done, and the truth defended and advanced, whoever may be the instrument; rejoice that others are successful in their plans of doing good, though they do not act with us; rejoice that other men have a reputation well earned for virtue and purity of life, though they may differ from us in opinion, and may be connected with a different denomination. They do not rejoice when other denominations of Christians fall into error; or when their plans are blasted; or when they are calumniated, and oppressed, and reviled. By whomsoever good is done, or wheresoever, it is to them a matter of rejoicing; and by whomsoever evil is done, or wheresoever, it is to them a matter of grief; see Phil. i. 14—18. The *reason* of this is that all sin, error, and vice will ultimately ruin the happiness of any one; and as *love* desires their happiness, it desires that they should walk in the ways of virtue, and is grieved when they do not. What a change would the prevalence of this feeling produce in the conduct and happiness of mankind! How much ill-natured joy would it repress at the faults of others? How much would it do to repress the pains which a man often takes to circulate reports disadvantageous to his adversary; to find out and establish some flaw in his character; to prove that he has said or done something disgraceful and evil! And how much would it do even among Christians, in restraining them from rejoicing at the errors, mistakes, and improprieties of the friends of revivals of religion, and in leading them to mourn over their errors in secret, instead of taking a malicious pleasure in promulgating them to the world! This would be a very different world if there were none to rejoice in iniquity; and the church would be a different church if there were none in its bosom but those who rejoiced in the truth, and in the efforts of humble and self-denying piety.

7. *Beareth all things.* Comp. Note, chap. ix. 12. Doddridge renders this, "covers all things." The word here used (στέγει) properly means *to cover* (from στέγη, a covering, roof; Mat. viii. 8; Luke vii. 6); and then to hide, conceal, not to make known. If this be the sense here, then it means that love is disposed to *hide* or *conceal* the faults and imperfections of others; not to promulgate or blazon them abroad, or to give any undue publicity to them. Benevolence to the individual or to the public would require that these faults and errors should be concealed. If this is the sense, then it accords nearly with what is said in the previous verse. The word may also mean, to forbear, bear with, endure. Thus it is used in 1 Thess. iii. 1, 5. And so our translators understand it here, as meaning that love is patient, long-suffering, not soon angry not disposed to revenge. And if this is the sense, it accords with the expression in ver. 4, "love suffers long." The more usual classic meaning is the former; the usage in the New Testament seems to demand the latter. Rosenmüller renders it, "*bears* all things;" Bloomfield prefers the other interpretation. Locke and Macknight render it "cover." The *real* sense of the passage is not materially varied, whichever interpretation is adopted. It means, that in regard to the errors and faults of others, there is a disposi-

tion *not* to notice or to revenge them. There is a willingness to conceal, or to bear with them patiently. ¶ *All things.* This is evidently to be taken in a popular sense, and to be interpreted in accordance with the connection. All universal expressions of this kind demand to be thus limited. The meaning must be, "as far as it can consistently or lawfully be done." There are offences which it is not proper or right for a man to conceal, or to suffer to pass unnoticed. Such are those where the laws of the land are violated, and a man is called on to testify, &c. But the phrase here refers to private matters; and indicates a disposition *not* to make public or to avenge the faults committed by others. ¶ *Believeth all things.* The whole scope of the connection and the argument here requires us to understand this of the conduct of others. It cannot mean, that the man who is under the influence of love is a man of *universal credulity;* that he makes no discrimination in regard to things to be believed; and is as prone to believe a falsehood as the truth; or that he is at no pains to inquire what is true and what is false, what is right and what is wrong. But it must mean, that in regard to the conduct of others, there is a disposition to put the best construction on it; to believe that they may be actuated by good motives, and that they intend no injury; and that there is a willingness to suppose, as far as can be, that what is done is done consistently with friendship, good feeling, and virtue. Love produces this, because it rejoices in the happiness and virtue of others, and will not believe the contrary except on irrefragable evidence. ¶ *Hopeth all things.* Hopes that all will turn out well. This must also refer to the conduct of others; and it means, that however dark may be appearances; how much soever there may be to produce the fear that others are actuated by improper motives or are bad men, yet that there is a *hope* that matters may be explained and made clear; that the difficulties may be made to vanish; and that the conduct of others may be made to *appear* to be fair and pure. Love will *hold on to this hope* until all possibility of such a result has vanished and it is compelled to believe that the conduct is not susceptible of a fair explanation. This hope will extend to *all things*—to words and actions, and plans; to public and to private intercourse; to what is said and done in our own presence, and to what is said and done in our absence. Love will do this, because it delights in the virtue and happiness of others, and will not credit any thing to the contrary unless compelled to do so. ¶ *Endureth all things.* Bears up under, sustains, and does not murmur. Bears up under all persecutions at the hand of man; all efforts to injure the person, property, or reputation; and bears all that may be laid upon us in the providence and by the direct agency of God; comp. Job xiii. 15. The connection requires us to understand it principally of our treatment at the hands of our fellow-men.

8. *Charity never faileth.* Paul here proceeds to illustrate the value of love, from its *permanency* as compared with other valued endowments. It is valuable, and is to be sought because it will always abide; may be always exercised; is adapted to all circumstances, and to all worlds in which we may be placed, or in which we may dwell. The word rendered *faileth* (ἐκπίπτει) denotes properly to fall out of, to fall from or off; and may be applied to the stars of heaven falling (Mark xiii. 25), or to flowers that fall or fade (James i. 11; 1 Pet. i. 24), or to chains falling from the hands, &c.; Acts xii. 7. Here it means to fall away, to fail; to be without effect, to cease to be in existence. The expression *may* mean that it will be adapted to all the situations of life, and is of a nature to be always exercised; or it may mean that it will continue to all eternity, and be exercised in heaven for ever. The connection demands that the latter should be regarded as the true interpretation; see ver. 13. The sense is, that while other endowments of the Holy Spirit must soon cease and be valueless, LOVE would abide, and would always exist. The *argu-*

ment is, that we ought to seek that which is of enduring value; and that, therefore, love should be preferred to those endowments of the Spirit on which so high a value had been set by the Corinthians. ¶ *But whether* there be *prophecies.* That is, the *gift* of prophecy, or the power of speaking as a prophet; that is, of delivering the truth of God in an intelligible manner under the influence of inspiration: the gift of being a public speaker, of instructing and edifying the church, and foretelling future events; see Note, chap. xiv. 1. ¶ *They shall fail.* The gift shall cease to be exercised; shall be abolished, come to naught. There shall be no further use for this gift in the light and glory of the world above, and it shall cease. God shall be the teacher there. And as there will be no need of confirming the truth of religion by the prediction of future events, and no need of warning against impending dangers there, the gift of foretelling future events will be of course unknown. In heaven, also, there will be no need that the faith of God's people shall be encouraged, or their devotions excited, by such exhortations and instructions as are needful now; and the endowment of prophecy will be, therefore, unknown. ¶ There be *tongues.* The power of speaking foreign languages. ¶ *They shall cease.* Macknight supposes this means that they shall cease in the church after the gospel shall have been preached to all nations. But the more natural interpretation is, to refer it to the future life; since the main idea which Paul is urging here is the value of love above all other endowments, from the fact that it would be *abiding,* or permanent—an idea which is more certainly and fully met by a reference to the future world than by a reference to the state of things in the church on earth. If it refers to heaven, it means that the power of communicating thoughts there will not be by the medium of learned and foreign tongues. What *will* be the mode is unknown. But as the diversity of tongues is one of the fruits of sin (Gen. xi.), it is evident that in those who are saved there will be deliverance from all the disadvantages which have resulted from the confusion of tongues. Yet LOVE will not cease to be necessary; and LOVE will live for ever. ¶ *Whether* there be *knowledge;* see Note, chap. xiv. 8. This refers, I think, to knowledge as *we now possess it.* It cannot mean that there will be no knowledge in heaven; for there must be a vast increase of knowledge in that world among all its inhabitants. The idea in the passage here, I think, is, "All the knowledge which we now possess, valuable as it is, will be obscured and lost, and rendered comparatively valueless, in the fuller splendours of the eternal world; as the feeble light of the stars, beautiful and valuable as it is, *vanishes,* or is lost in the splendours of the rising sun. The knowledge which we now have is valuable, as the gift of prophecy and the power of speaking foreign languages is valuable, but it will be lost in the brighter visions of the world above." That this is the sense is evident from what Paul says in illustration of the sentiment in ver. 9, 10. *Now* we know in part. What we deem ourselves acquainted with, we imperfectly understand. There are many obscurities and many difficulties. But in that future world we shall know distinctly and clearly (ver. 12); and then the knowledge which we now possess will appear so dim and obscure, that it will seem to have vanished away and disappeared,

"As a dim candle dies at noon."

Macknight and others understand this of the knowledge of the mysteries of the Old Testament, or "the inspired knowledge of the ancient revelations, which should be abolished when the church should have attained its mature state;" a most meagre, jejune, and frigid interpretation. It is true, also, that not only shall our imperfect knowledge seem to have vanished in the superior light and glory of the eternal world but that much of that which here *passes* for knowledge shall be then unknown. Much of that which is called *science*

tongues, they shall cease; whether *there be* knowledge, it shall vanish away.

9 For we know in part, [a] and we prophesy in part;

10 But [b] when that which is perfect is come, then that which is in part shall be done away.

11 When I was a child, I spake as a child, I understood as a child,

a chap.8.2.

b 1 John 3.2.

is "falsely so called;" and much that is connected with literature that has attracted so much attention, will be unknown in the eternal world. It is evident that much that is connected with criticism, and the knowledge of language, with the different systems of mental philosophy which are erroneous; perhaps much that is connected with anatomy, physiology, and geology; and much of the science which now is connected with the arts, and which is of use only as tributary to the arts, will be then unknown. Other subjects may rise into importance which are now unknown; and possibly things connected with science which are now regarded as of the least importance will then become objects of great moment, and ripen and expand into sciences that shall contribute much to the eternal happiness of heaven. The essential idea in this passage is, that all the knowledge which we now possess shall lose its effulgence, be dimmed and lost in the superior light of heaven. But LOVE shall live there; and we should, therefore, seek that which is permanent and eternal.

9. *For we know in part.* Comp. Note on chap. xii. 27. This expression means "*only* in part;" that is, *imperfectly.* Our knowledge here is imperfect and obscure. It may, therefore, all vanish in the eternal world amidst its superior brightness; and we should not regard that as of such vast value which is imperfect and obscure; comp. Note chap. viii. 2. This idea of the obscurity and imperfection of our knowledge, as compared with heaven, the apostle illustrates (ver. 11) by comparing it with the knowledge which a child has, compared with that in maturer years; and (ver. 12) by the knowledge which we have in looking through a glass—an imperfect medium—compared with that which we have in looking closely and directly at an object without any medium. ¶ *And we prophesy in part.* This does not mean that we partly *know* the truths of religion, and partly *conjecture* or *guess* at them; or that we know only a part of them, and *conjecture* the remainder. But the apostle is showing the imperfection of the prophetic gift; and he observes, that there is the same imperfection which attends knowledge. It is only in part; it is imperfect; it is indistinct, compared with the full view of truth in heaven; it is obscure, and all that is imparted by that gift will soon become dim and lost in the superior brightness and glory of the heavenly world. The *argument* is, that we ought not to seek so anxiously that which is so imperfect and obscure, and which must soon vanish away; but we should rather seek that love which is permanent, expanding, and eternal.

10. *But when that which is perfect is come.* Does come; or shall come. This proposition is couched in a general form. It means that when *any* thing which is perfect is seen or enjoyed, then that which is imperfect is forgotten, laid aside, or vanishes. Thus, in the full and perfect light of day, the imperfect and feeble light of the stars vanishes. The sense here is, that *in heaven*—a state of absolute perfection—that which is "in part," or which is imperfect, shall be lost in superior brightness. All imperfection will vanish. And all that we here possess that is obscure shall be lost in the superior and perfect glory of that eternal world. All our present unsatisfactory modes of obtaining knowledge shall be unknown. All shall be clear, bright, and eternal.

11. *When I was a child.* The idea here is, that the knowledge which we now have, compared with that which

I [1] thought as a child; but when I became a man, I put away childish things.

12 For now we see through a glass, [a] darkly; [1] but then face to face: now I know in part; but then shall I know even as also I am known.

1 or, *reasoned*.

a 2 Cor.3.18. 1 or, *in a riddle*.

---

we shall have in heaven, is like that which is possessed in infancy compared with that we have in manhood; and that as, when we advance in years, we lay aside, as unworthy of our attention, the views, feelings, and plans which we had in boyhood, and which we then esteemed to be of so great importance, so, when we reach heaven, we shall lay aside the views, feelings, and plans which we have in this life, and which we now esteem so wise and so valuable. The word *child* here (νήπιος) denotes properly a babe, an infant, though without any definable limitation of age. It refers to the first periods of existence; before the period which we denominate boyhood, or youth. Paul here refers to a period when he could *speak*, though evidently a period when his speech was scarcely intelligible—when he first began to articulate. ¶ *I spake as a child.* Just beginning to articulate, in a broken and most imperfect manner. The idea here is, that our knowledge at present, compared with the knowledge of heaven, is like the broken and scarcely intelligible efforts of a child to speak compared with the power of utterance in manhood. ¶ *I understood as a child.* My understanding was feeble and imperfect. I had narrow and imperfect views of things. I knew little. I fixed my attention on objects which I now see to be of litte value. I acquired knowledge which has vanished, or which has sunk in the superior intelligence of riper years. "I was affected as a child. I was thrown into a transport of joy or grief on the slightest occasions, which manly reason taught me to despise." —*Doddridge.* ¶ *I thought as a child.* Marg. *Reasoned.* The word may mean either. I thought, argued, reasoned in a weak and inconclusive manner. My thoughts, and plans, and argumentations were puerile, and such as I now see to be short-sighted and erroneous. Thus it will be with our thoughts compared to heaven. There will be, doubtless, *as much* difference between our present knowledge, and plans, and views, and those which we shall have in heaven, as there is between the plans and views of a child and those of a man. Just before his death, Sir Isaac Newton made this remark: "I do not know what I may appear to the world; but to myself I seem to have been only like a boy playing on the sea-shore, and diverting myself by now and then finding a smoother pebble or a prettier shell than ordinary, while the great ocean of truth lay all undiscovered before me."—*Brewster's Life of Newton*, pp. 300, 301. Ed. New York, 1832.

12. *For now we see through a glass.* Paul here makes use of another illustration to show the imperfection of our knowledge here. Compared with what it will be in the future world, it is like the imperfect view of an object which we have in looking through an obscure and opaque medium compared with the view which we have when we look at it "face to face." The word *glass* here (ἔσοπτρον) means properly a mirror, a looking-glass. The mirrors of the ancients were usually made of polished metal; Ex. xxxviii. 8; Job xxxvii. 18. Many have supposed (see Doddridge, in loc. and Robinson's Lexicon) that the idea here is that of seeing objects by reflection from a mirror, which reflects only their imperfect forms. But this interpretation does not well accord with the apostle's idea of seeing things obscurely. The most natural idea is that of seeing objects by an imperfect medium, by looking *through* something in contemplating them. It is, therefore, probable that he refers to those transparent substances which the ancients had, and which they used in their windows occasionally; such

as thin plates of horn, transparent stone, &c. Windows were often made of the *lapis specularis* described by Pliny (xxxvi. 22), which was pellucid, and which admitted of being split into thin *laminæ* or scales, probably the same as mica. Humboldt mentions such kinds of stone as being used in South America in church windows.—*Bloomfield.* It is not improbable, I think, that even in the time of Paul the ancients had the knowledge of glass, though it was probably at first very imperfect and obscure. There is some reason to believe that glass was known to the Phenicians, the Tyrians, and the Egyptians. Pliny says that it was first discovered by accident. A merchant vessel, laden with nitre or fossil alkali, having been driven on shore on the coast of Palestine near the river Belus, the crew went in search of provisions, and accidentally supported the kettles on which they dressed their food upon pieces of fossil alkali. The river sand above which this operation was performed was vitrified by its union with the alkali, and thus produced glass. —See Edin. Ency., art. *Glass.* It is known that glass was in quite common use about the commencement of the Christian era. In the reign of Tiberius an artist had his house demolished for making glass malleable. About this time drinking vessels were made commonly of glass; and glass bottles for holding wine and flowers were in common use. That glass was in quite common use has been proved by the remains that have been discovered in the ruins of Herculaneum and Pompeii. There is, therefore, no impropriety in supposing that Paul here may have alluded to the imperfect and discoloured glass which was then in extensive use; for we have no reason to suppose that it was then as transparent as that which is now made. It was, doubtless, an imperfect and obscure medium, and, therefore, well adapted to illustrate the nature of our knowledge here compared with what it will be in heaven. ¶ *Darkly.* Marg. *In a riddle* (ἐν αἰνίγματι). The word means a riddle; an enigma; then an obscure intimation. In a riddle a statement is made with some resemblance to the truth; a puzzling question is proposed, and the solution is left to conjecture. Hence it means, as here, obscurely, darkly, imperfectly. Little is known; much is left to conjecture;—a very accurate account of most of that which passes for knowledge. Compared with heaven, our knowledge here much resembles the obscure intimations in an enigma compared with clear statement and manifest truth. ¶ *But then.* In the fuller revelations in heaven. ¶ *Face to face.* As when one looks upon an object openly, and not through an obscure and dark medium. It here means, therefore, *clearly, without obscurity.* ¶ *I know in part;* ver. 9. ¶ *But then shall I know.* My knowledge shall be clear and distinct. I shall have a clear view of those objects which are now so indistinct and obscure. I shall be in the presence of those objects about which I now inquire; I shall *see* them; I shall have a clear acquaintance with the divine perfections, plans, and character. This does not mean that he would know *every thing,* or that he would be omniscient; but that in regard to those points of inquiry in which he was then interested, he would have a view that would be distinct and clear—a view that would be clear, arising from the fact that he would be present with them, and permitted to see them, instead of surveying them at a distance, and by imperfect mediums. ¶ *Even as also I am known. In the same manner* (καθὼς), not *to the same extent.* It does not mean that he would know God as clearly and as fully as God would know him; for his remark does not relate to the *extent,* but to the *manner* and the comparative *clearness* of his knowledge. He would see things as he was now seen and would be seen there. It would be face to face. He would be in their presence. It would not be where *he* would be seen clearly and distinctly, and himself compelled to look upon all objects confusedly and obscurely, and through an imperfect medium. But he would be with

13 And now abideth faith, [a] hope, charity, these three; but the greatest of these *is* charity.

[a] Heb.10.35, 39; 1 Pet.1.21.

them; would see them face to face; would see them without any medium; would see them *in the same manner* as they would see him. Disembodied spirits, and the inhabitants of the heavenly world, have this knowledge: and when we are there, we shall see the truths, not at a distance and obscurely, but plainly and openly.

13. *And now abideth. Remains* (μένει). The word means properly to remain, continue, abide; and is applied to persons remaining in a place, in a state or condition, in contradistinction from removing or changing their place, or passing away. Here it must be understood to be used to denote *permanency,* when the other things of which he had spoken had passed away; and the sense is, that faith, hope, and love would *remain* when the gift of tongues should cease, and the need of prophecy, &c.; that is, these should survive them all. And the connection certainly requires us to understand him as saying that faith, hope, and love would survive *all* those things of which he had been speaking, and must, therefore, include knowledge (ver. 8, 9,), as well as miracles and the other endowments of the Holy Spirit. They would survive them all; would be valuable when they should cease; and should, therefore, be mainly sought; and of these the greatest and most important is love. Most commentators have supposed that Paul is speaking here only of this life, and that he means to say that in this life these three exist; that "faith, hope, and charity exist in this scene *only,* but that in the future world faith and hope will be done away, and therefore the greatest of these is charity."—*Bloomfield.* See also Doddridge, Macknight, Rosenmüller, Clarke, &c. But to me it seems evident that Paul means to say that faith, hope, and love will survive *all* those other things of which he had been speaking; that *they* would vanish away, or be lost in superior attainments and endowments; that the time would come when they would be useless: but that faith, hope, and love would then remain; but of *these,* for important reasons, love was the most valuable. Not because it would *endure* the longest, for the apostle does not intimate that, but because it is more important to the welfare of others, and is a more eminent virtue than they are. As the strain of the argument requires us to look to another state, to a world where prophecy shall cease and knowledge shall vanish away, so the same strain of argumentation requires us to understand him as saying that faith, and hope, and love will subsist there; and that there, as here, LOVE will be of more importance than faith and hope. It cannot be objected to this view that there will be no occasion for faith and hope in heaven. That is assumed without evidence, and is not affirmed by Paul. He gives no such intimation. Faith is *confidence* in God and in Christ; and there will be as much necessity of *confidence* in heaven as on earth. Indeed, the great design of the plan of salvation is to restore *confidence* in God among alienated creatures; and heaven could not subsist a moment without *confidence;* and faith, therefore, must be eternal. No society—be it a family, a neighbourhood, a church, or a nation; be it mercantile, professional, or a mere association of friendship—can subsist a moment without mutual *confidence* or faith, and in heaven such confidence in God MUST subsist for ever. And so of hope. It is true that many of the objects of hope will then be realized, and will be succeeded by possession. But will the Christian have nothing to hope for in heaven? Will it be nothing to expect and desire greatly augmented knowledge, eternal enjoyment; perfect peace in all coming ages, and the happy society of the blessed for ever? All heaven cannot be enjoyed at once; and if there is any thing *future* that is an object of desire, there will be hope. *Hope* is a compound emotion, made up of a *desire* for an object and an *expectation* of obtaining it. But both these will exist in heaven. It is folly to say that a redeemed saint will

CHAPTER XIV.

FOLLOW after charity, and desire spiritual [a] *gifts;* but rather that ye may prophesy.

a Eph.1.3.

not *desire* there eternal happiness; it is equal folly to say that there will be no strong expectation of obtaining it. All that is said, therefore, about faith as about to cease, and hope as not having an existence in heaven, is said without the authority of the Bible, and in violation of what must be the truth, and is contrary to the whole scope of the reasoning of Paul here. ¶ *But the greatest of these* is *charity.* Not because it is to *endure* the longest, but because it is the more important virtue; it exerts a wider influence; it is more necessary to the happiness of society; it overcomes more evils. It is *the* great principle which is to bind the universe in harmony, which unites God to his creatures, and his creatures to himself, and which binds and confederates all holy beings with each other. It is therefore more important, because it pertains to *society* to the great kingdom of which God is the head, and because it enters into the very conception of a holy and happy organization. Faith and hope rather pertain to individuals; love pertains to society, and is that without which the kingdom of God cannot stand. Individuals may be saved by faith and hope; but the whole immense kingdom of God depends on LOVE. It is, therefore, of more importance than all other graces and endowments; more important than prophecy and miracles, and the gift of tongues and knowledge, because it will SURVIVE them all; more important than faith and hope, because, although it may co-exist with them, and though they all shall live for ever, yet LOVE enters into the very nature of the kingdom of God; binds society together; unites the Creator and the creature; and blends the interests of all the redeemed, and of the angels, and of God, INTO ONE.

CHAPTER XIV.

THIS chapter is a continuation of the subject commenced in chap. xii. and pursued through chap. xiii. In chap. xii. Paul had entered on the discussion of the various endowments which the Holy Spirit confers on Christians, and had shown that these endowments were bestowed in a different degree on different individuals, and yet so as to promote in the best way the edification of the church. It was proper, he said (chap. xii. 31), to desire the more eminent of these endowments, and yet there was one gift of the Spirit of more value than all others, which might be obtained by all, and which should be an object of desire to all. That was LOVE; and to show the nature, power, and value of this, was the design of the thirteenth chapter,—certainly one of the most tender and beautiful portions of the Bible. In this chapter the subject is continued with special reference to the subject of *prophecy,* as being the most valuable of the miraculous endowments, or the extraordinary gifts of the Spirit.

In doing this, it was necessary to correct an erroneons estimate which they had placed on the power of speaking foreign languages. They had prized this, perhaps, because it gave them importance in the eyes of the heathen. And in proportion as they valued this, they undervalued the gift of being able to edify the church by speaking in a known and intelligible language. To correct this misapprehension; to show the relative value of these endowments, and especially to recommend the gift of "prophecy" as the more useful and desirable of the gifts of the Spirit, was the leading design of this chapter. In doing this, Paul first directs them to seek for charity. He also recommends to them, as in chap. xii. 31, to desire spiritual endowments, and of these endowments especially to desire prophecy; ver. 1. He then proceeds to set forth the advantage of speaking in intelligible language, or of speaking so that the church may be edified, by the following considerations, which comprise the chapter:—

1. The advantage of being understood, and of speaking for the edification of the church; ver. 2—5.

2. No man could be useful to the

church except he delivered that which was understood, any more than the sound of a trumpet in times of war would be useful, unless it were so sounded as to be understood by the army; ver. 6—11.

3. It was the duty of all to seek to edify the church; and *if* a man could speak in an unknown tongue, it was his duty also to seek to be able to interpret what he said; ver. 12—15.

4. The use of tongues would produce embarrassment and confusion, since those who heard them speak would be ignorant of what was said, and be unable to join in the devotions; ver. 16, 17.

5. Though Paul himself was more signally endowed than any of them, yet he prized far more highly the power of promoting the edification of the church, though he uttered but five words, if they were understood, than all the power which he possessed of speaking foreign languages; ver. 18, 19.

6. This sentiment illustrated from the Old Testament; ver. 20, 21.

7. The real use of the power of speaking foreign languages was to be a sign to unbelievers,—an evidence that the religion was from God, and not to be used among those who were already Christians; ver. 22.

8. The effect of their all speaking with tongues would be to produce confusion and disorder, and disgust among observers, and the conviction that they were deranged; but the effect of order, and of speaking intelligibly, would be to convince and convert them; ver. 23—25.

9. The apostle then gives *rules* in regard to the proper conduct of those who were able to speak foreign languages; ver. 26—32.

10. The great rule was, that order was to be observed, and that God was the author of peace; ver. 33.

11. The apostle then gives a positive direction that on no pretence are women to be allowed to speak in the church, even though they should claim to be inspired; ver. 34, 35.

12. He then required all to submit to his authority, and to admit that what he had spoken was from the Lord; ver. 36, 37. And then,

13. Concludes with directing them to desire to prophesy, and not to forbid speaking with tongues on proper occasions, but to do all things in decency and order; ver. 38—40.

1. *Follow after charity.* Pursue love (chap. xiii. 1); that is, earnestly desire it; strive to possess it; make it the object of your anxious and constant solicitude to obtain it, and to be influenced by it always. Cultivate it in your own hearts, as the richest and best endowment of the Holy Spirit, and endeavour to diffuse its happy influence on all around you. ¶ *And desire spiritual* gifts. I do not forbid you, while you make the possession of love your great object, and while you do not make the desire of spiritual gifts the occasion of envy or strife, to desire the miraculous endowments of the Spirit and to seek to excel in those endowments which he imparts; see Note, chap. xii. 31. The main thing was to cultivate a spirit of love. Yet it was not improper also to desire to be so endowed as to promote their highest usefulness in the church. On the phrase "spiritual gifts," see Note, chap. xii. 1. ¶ *But rather that ye may prophesy.* But especially, or particularly desire to be qualified for the office of prophesying. The apostle does not mean to say that prophecy is to be preferred to love or charity; but that, of the spiritual gifts which it was proper for them to desire and seek, *prophecy* was the most valuable. That is, they were not most earnestly and especially to desire to be able to speak foreign languages or to work miracles; but they were to desire to be qualified to speak in a manner that would be edifying to the church. They would naturally, perhaps, most highly prize the power of working miracles and of speaking foreign languages. The object of this chapter is to show them that the ability to speak in a plain, clear, instructive manner, so as to edify the church and convince sinners, was a more valuable endowment than the power of working miracles, or the power of speaking foreign languages. On the meaning of the word *prophesy*, see Note, Rom. xi. 6. To what is said there on the nature of this office, it

2 For he that speaketh in an *unknown* tongue, [a] speaketh not unto men, but unto God: for [b] no man [1] understandeth *him;* how-

a Acts 10.46. b Acts 22.9. 1 heareth.

seems necessary only to add an idea suggested by Prof. Robinson (Gr. and Eng. Lexicon, Art. Προφήτης), that the prophets were distinguished from the teachers (διδάσκαλοι), "in that, while the latter spoke in a calm, connected, didactic discourse adapted to instruct and enlighten the hearers, the prophet spoke more from the impulse of sudden inspiration, from the light of a sudden revelation at the moment (1 Cor. xiv. 30, ἀποκάλυφθῃ), and his discourse was probably more adapted, by means of powerful exhortation, to awaken the feelings and conscience of the hearers." The idea of speaking from *revelation*, he adds, seems to be fundamental to the correct idea of the nature of the prophecy here referred to. Yet the communications of the prophets were always in the vernacular tongue, and were always in intelligible language, and in this respect different from the endowments of those who spoke foreign languages. The same truth might be spoken by both; the influence of the Spirit was equally neceesary in both; both were inspired; and both answered important ends in the establishment and edification of the church. The gift of tongues, however, as it was the most striking and remarkable, and probably the most rare, was most highly prized and coveted. The object of Paul here is, to show that it was really an endowment of less value, and should be less desired by Christians than the gift of prophetic instruction, or the ability to edify the church in language intelligible and understood by all, under the immediate influences of the Holy Spirit.

2. *For he that speaketh in an* unknown *tongue.* This verse is designed to show that the faculty of speaking intelligibly, and to the edification of the church, is of more value than the power of speaking a foreign language. The reason is, that however valuable may be the endowment in itself, and however important the truth which he may utter, yet it is as if he spoke to God only. No one could understand him. ¶ *Speaketh not unto men.* Does not speak so that men can understand him. His address is really not made to men, that is, to the church. He might have this faculty without being able to speak to the edification of the church. It is possible that the power of speaking foreign languages and of prophesying were sometimes united in the same person; but it is evident that the apostle speaks of them as different endowments, and they probably were found usually in different individuals. ¶ *But unto God.* It is as if he spoke to God. No one could understand him but God. This must evidently refer to the addresses *in the church*, when Christians only were present, or when those only were present who spoke the same language, and who were unacquainted with foreign tongues. Paul says that *there* that faculty would be valueless compared with the power of speaking in a manner that should edify the church. He did not undervalue the power of speaking foreign languages when foreigners were present, or when they went to preach to foreigners; see ver. 22. It was only when it was needless, when all present spoke one language, that he speaks of it as of comparatively little value. ¶ *For no man understandeth* him. That is, no man in the church, since they all spoke the same language, and that language was different from what was spoken by him who was endowed with the gift of tongues. As God only could know the import of what he said, it would be lost upon the church, and would be useless. ¶ *Howbeit in the Spirit.* Although, by the aid of the Spirit, he should, in fact, deliver the most important and sublime truths. This would doubtless be the case, that those who were thus endowed *would* deliver most important truths, but they would be *lost* upon those who heard them, because they could not understand them. The phrase "in the Spirit," evidently means "by the Holy Spirit," *i. e.*, by his aid and influence. Though

beit in the spirit he speaketh mysteries.

3 But he that prophesieth speaketh unto men *to* edification, and exhortation, and comfort.

4 He that speaketh in an *unknown* tongue edifieth himself; but he that prophesieth edifieth the church.

5 I would that ye all spake with tongues, but rather that ye prophesied: for greater *is* he that prophesieth than he that speaketh with tongues, except he interpret,

---

he should be *really* under the influence of the Holy Spirit, and though the important truth which he delivers should be imparted by his aid, yet all would be valueless unless it were understood by the church. ¶ *He speaketh mysteries.* For the meaning of the word *mystery*, see Note, chap. ii. 7. The word here seems to be synonymous with sublime and elevated truth; truth that was not before known, and that might be of the utmost importance.

3. *But he that prophesieth;* Note, ver. 1. He that speaks under the influence of inspiration in the common language of his hearers. This seems to be the difference between those who spoke in foreign languages and those who prophesied. Both were under the influence of the Holy Spirit; both might speak the same truths; both might occupy an equally important and necessary place in the church; but the language of the one was intelligible to the church, the other not; the one was designed to edify the church, the other to address those who spoke foreign tongues, or to give demonstration, by the power of speaking foreign languages, that the religion was from God. ¶ *Speaketh unto men.* So as to be understood by those who were present. ¶ To *edification;* Note, chap. x. 8, 23. Speaks so as to enlighten and strengthen the church. ¶ *And exhortation;* see Note, Rom. xii. 8. He applies and enforces the practical duties of religion, and urges motives for a holy life. ¶ *And comfort.* Encouragement. That is, he presents the *promises* and the *hopes* of the gospel; the various considerations adapted to administer comfort in the time of trial. The other might do this, but it would be in a foreign language, and would be useless to the church.

4. *Edifieth himself.* That is, the truths which are communicated to him by the Spirit, and which he utters in an unknown language, may be valuable, and may be the means of strengthening his faith, and building him up in the hopes of the gospel, but they can be of no use to others. His own holy affections might be excited by the truths which he would deliver, and the consciousness of possessing miraculous powers might excite his gratitude. And yet, as Doddridge has well remarked, there might be danger that a man might be injured by this gift when exercised in this ostentatious manner.

5. *I would that ye all spake with tongues.* "It is an important endowment, and is not, in its place, to be undervalued. It may be of great service in the cause of truth, and if properly regulated, and not abused, I would rejoice if these extraordinary endowments were conferred on all. I have no envy against any one who possesses it; no opposition to the endowment; but I wish that it should not be overvalued; and would wish to exalt into proper estimation the more useful but humble gift of speaking for the edification of the church." ¶ *Greater* is *he that prophesieth.* This gift is of more value, and he really occupies a more elevated rank in the church. He is more *useful.* The idea here is, that talents are not to be estimated by their *brilliancy*, but by their *usefulness.* The power of speaking in an unknown tongue was certainly a more striking endowment than that of speaking so as simply to be *useful*, and yet the apostle tells us that the latter is the more valuable. So it is always. A man who is useful, however humble and unknown he may be, really occupies a more elevated and venerable rank than the man of most splendid talents and dazzling eloquence, who

that the church may receive edifying.[a]

6 Now, brethren, if I come unto you speaking with tongues, what shall I profit you, except I shall speak to you either by revelation,[b] or by knowledge, or by prophesying, or by doctrine?

a ver.26.

b ver.26.

accomplishes nothing in saving the souls of men. ¶ *Except he interpret.* However important and valuable the truth might be which he uttered, it would be useless to the church, unless he should explain it in language which they could understand. In that case, the apostle does not deny that the power of speaking foreign languages was a higher endowment and more valuable than the gift of prophecy. That the man who spoke foreign languages had the power of interpreting, is evident from this verse. From ver. 27, it appears that the office of interpreting was sometimes performed by others.

6. *Now, brethren, if I come unto you, &c.* The truth which the apostle had been illustrating in an abstract manner, he proceeds to illustrate by applying it to himself. If he should come among them speaking foreign languages, it could be of no use unless it were interpreted to them. ¶ *Speaking with tongues.* Speaking foreign languages; that is, speaking them *only*, without any interpreter. Paul had the power of speaking foreign languages (ver. 18); but he did not use this power for ostentation or display, but merely to communicate the gospel to those who did not understand his native tongue. ¶ *Either by revelation.* Macknight renders this, "speak INTELLIGIBLY;" that is, as he explains it, "by the revelation peculiar to an apostle." Doddridge, "by the revelation of some gospel doctrine and mystery." Locke interprets it, that you might understand the revelation, or knowledge," &c.; but says in a note, that we cannot now certainly understand the difference between the meaning of the four words here used. "It is sufficient," says he, "to know that these terms stand for some intelligible discourse tending to the edification of the church." Rosenmüller supposes the word *revelation* stands for some "clear and open knowledge of any truth arising from meditation." It is probable that the word here does not refer to divine inspiration, as it usually does, but that it stands opposed to that which is unknown and unintelligible, as that which is *revealed* (ἀποκάλυψις) stands opposed to what is unknown, concealed, *hidden*, obscure. Here, therefore, it is synonymous, perhaps, with *explained.* "What shall it profit, unless that which I speak be brought out of the obscurity and darkness of a foreign language, and *uncovered* or explained!" The original sense of the word *revelation* here is, I suppose, intended (ἀποκάλυψις, from ἀποκαλύπτω, *to uncover*), and means that the sense should be uncovered, *i. e.* explained or what was spoken could not be of value. ¶ *Or by knowledge.* By making it intelligible. By so explaining it as to make it understood. Knowledge here stands opposed to the *ignorance* and *obscurity* which would attend a communication in a foreign language. ¶ *Or by prophesying;* Note, ver. 1. That is, unless it be communicated, through interpretation, in the manner in which the prophetic teachers spoke; that is, made intelligible, and explained, and actually brought down to the usual characteristics of communications made in their own language. ¶ *Or by doctrine.* By teaching (διδαχῇ). By instruction; in the usual mode of plain and familiar instruction. The sense of this passage, therefore, is clear. Though Paul should utter among them, as he had abundant ability to do, the most weighty and important truths, yet, unless he interpreted what he said in a manner clear from obscurity, like *revelation;* or intelligibly, and so as to constitute *knowledge;* or in the manner that the prophets spoke, in a plain and intelligible manner; or in the manner usual in simple and plain *instruction*, it would be useless to them. The perplexities of commentators may be seen stated in Locke, Bloomfield, and Doddridge.

7 And even things without life
giving sound, whether pipe or
harp, except they give a distinction in the [1] sounds, how shall it be
known what is piped or harped?

1 or, *tunes*.

8 For if the trumpet [a] give an
uncertain sound, who shall prepare
himself to the battle?
9 So likewise ye, except ye utter
by the tongue words [1] easy to be

a Num.10.9 1 *significant*.

7. *Things without life.* Instruments of music. ¶ *Whether pipe.* This instrument (αὐλὸς) was usually made of reeds, and probably had a resemblance to a flageolet. ¶ *Or harp.* This instrument (κιθάρα) was a stringed instrument, and was made in the same way as a modern harp. It usually had ten strings, and was struck with the plectrum, or with a key. It was commonly employed in praise. ¶ *Except they give a distinction in the sounds.* Unless they give a difference in the *tones*, such as are indicated in the gamut for music. ¶ *How shall it be known*, &c. That is, there would be no time, no music. Nothing would be indicated by it. It would not be fitted to excite the emotions of sorrow or of joy. All music is designed to excite emotions; but if there be no difference in the tones, no emotion would be produced. So it would be in words uttered. Unless there was something that was fitted to excite thought or emotion; unless what was spoken was made *intelligible*, no matter how important in itself it might be, yet it would be useless.

8. *For if the trumpet give an uncertain sound.* The trumpet was used commonly in war. It is a well-known wind instrument, and was made of brass, silver, &c. It was used for various purposes in war—to summon the soldiers; to animate them in their march; to call them forth to battle; to sound a retreat; and to signify to them what they were to do in battle, whether to charge, advance, or retreat, &c. It therefore employed a *language* which was intelligible to an army. An uncertain sound was one in which none of these things were indicated, or in which it could not be determined what was required. ¶ *Who shall prepare himself*, &c. The apostle selects a single instance of what was indicated by the trumpet, as an illustration of what he meant. The idea is, that foreign tongues spoken in their assembly would be just as useless in regard to their duty, their comfort, and edification, as would be the sound of a trumpet when it gave one of the usual and intelligible sounds by which it was known what the soldiers were required to do. Just as we would say, that the mere beating on a drum would be useless, unless some tune was played by which it was known that the soldiers were summoned to the parade, to advance, or to retreat.

9. *So likewise ye*, &c. To apply the case. If you use a foreign language, how shall it be known what is said, or of what use will it be, unless it is made intelligible by interpretation? ¶ *Utter by the tongue.* Unless you speak. ¶ *Words easy to be understood.* Significant words (margin), words to which your auditors are accustomed. ¶ *For ye shall speak into the air.* You will not speak so as to be understood; and it will be just the same as if no one was present, and you spoke to the air. We have a proverb that resembles this: "You may as well speak to the winds:" that is, you speak where it would not be understood, or where the words would have no effect. It may be observed here, that the practice of the papists accords with what the apostle here condemns, where worship is conducted in a language not understood by the people; and that there is much of this same kind of speaking now, where unintelligible terms are used, or words are employed that are above the comprehension of the people; or where doctrines are discussed which are unintelligible, and which are regarded by them without interest. All preaching should be plain, simple, perspicuous, and adapted to the capacity of the hearers.

10. *There are it may be*, &c. There has been considerable variety in the

understood, how shall it be known what is spoken? for ye shall speak into the air.

10 There are, it may be, so many kinds of voices in the world, and none of them *is* without signification.

11 Therefore if I know not the meaning of the voice, I shall be unto him that speaketh a barbarian; [a] and he that speaketh *shall be* a barbarian unto me.

12 Even so ye, forasmuch as ye are zealous of [1] spiritual *gifts*, seek that ye may excel to the edifying of the church.

13 Wherefore let him that speaketh in an *unknown* tongue, pray that he may interpret.

a Rom.1.1.

1 *spirits.*

interpretation of this expression. Rosenmüller renders it, "for the sake of example." Grotius supposes that Paul meant to indicate that there were, perhaps, or might be, as many languages as the Jews supposed, to wit, seventy. Beza and others suppose it means, that there may be as many languages as there are nations of men. Bloomfield renders it, "Let there be as many kinds of languages as you choose." Macknight, "There are, no doubt, as many kinds of languages in the world as ye speak." Robinson (Lex.) renders it, "If so happen, it may be; perchance, perhaps;" and says the phrase is equivalent to "for example." The sense is, "There are perhaps, or for example, very many kinds of voices in the world, and all are significant. None are used by those who speak them without meaning; none speak them without designing to convey some intelligible idea to their hearers." The *argument* is, that as *all* the languages that are in the world, however numerous they are, are for *utility*, and as none are used for the sake of mere display, so it should be with those who had the power of speaking them in the Christian church. They should speak them only when and where they would be understood. ¶ *Voices.* Languages.

11. *The meaning of the voice.* Of the language that is uttered, or the sounds that are made. ¶ *I shall be unto him,* &c. What I say will be unintelligible to him, and what he says will be unintelligible to me. We cannot understand one another any more than people can who speak different languages. ¶ *A barbarian;* see Note, Rom. i. 14. The word means one who speaks a different, or a foreign language.

12. *Even so ye.* Since you desire spiritual gifts, I may urge it upon you to seek to be able to speak in a clear and intelligible manner, that you may edify the church. This is one of the most valuable endowments of the Spirit; and this should be earnestly desired. ¶ *Forasmuch as ye are zealous.* Since you earnestly desire; Note, chap. xii. 31. ¶ *Spiritual* gifts. The endowments conferred by the Holy Spirit; Note, chap. xii. 1. ¶ *Seek that ye may excel,* &c. Seek that you may be able to convey truth in a clear and plain manner; seek to be distinguished for that. It is one of the most rare and valuable endowments of the Holy Spirit.

13. *Pray that he may interpret.* Let him ask of God ability that he may explain it clearly to the church. It would seem probable that the power of speaking foreign languages, and the power of conveying truth in a clear and distinct manner, were not always found in the same person, and that the one did not of necessity imply the other. The truth seems to have been, that these extraordinary endowments of the Holy Spirit were bestowed on men in some such way as *ordinary* talents and mental powers are now conferred; and that they became in a similar sense *the characteristic mental endowments of the individual,* and of course were subject to the same laws, and liable to the same kinds of abuse, as mental endowments are now. And as it *now* happens that one man may have a peculiar faculty for acquiring and expressing himself in a foreign language who may not be by any means

14 For if I pray in an *unknown* tongue, my spirit prayeth; but my understanding is unfruitful.

15 What is it then? I will pray with the spirit, [a] and I will pray with the understanding also:

a John 4,24.

distinguished for clear enunciation, or capable of conveying his ideas in an interesting manner to a congregation, so it was then. The apostle, therefore, directs such, if any there were, instead of priding themselves on their endowments, and instead of always speaking in an unknown tongue, which would be useless to the church, to *pray* for the more useful gift of being able to convey their thoughts in a clear and intelligible manner in their vernacular tongue. This would be useful. The truths, therefore, that they had the power of speaking with eminent ability in a foreign language, they ought to desire to be able to *interpret* so that they would be intelligible to the people whom they addressed in the church. This seems to me to be the plain meaning of this passage, which has given so much perplexity to commentators. Macknight renders it, however, "Let him who prayeth in a foreign language, pray so as SOME ONE may interpret;" meaning that he who prayed in a foreign language was to do it by two or three sentences at a time, so that he might be followed by an interpreter. But this is evidently forced. In order to this, it is needful to suppose that the phrase ὁ λαλῶν, "that speaketh," should be rendered, contrary to its obvious and usual meaning, "who prays," and to supply τις, *some one*, in the close of the verse. The obvious interpretation is that which is given above; and this proceeds only on the supposition that the power of speaking foreign languages and the power of interpreting were not always united in the same person—a supposition that is evidently true, as appears from chap. xii. 10.

14. *For if I pray*, &c. The reference to prayer here, and to singing in ver. 15, is designed to illustrate the propriety of the general sentiment which he is defending, that public worship should be conducted in a language that would be intelligible to the people. However well meant it might be, or however the *heart* might be engaged in it, yet unless it was intelligible, and the understanding could join in it, it would be vain and profitless. ¶ *My spirit prayeth.* The word *spirit* here (πνεῦμα) has been variously understood. Some have understood it of the Holy Spirit—the Spirit by which Paul says he was actuated. Others of the *spiritual gift*, or that spiritual influence by which he was endowed. Others of the mind itself. But it is probable that the word "spirit" refers to the *will;* or to the mind, as the seat of the affections and emotions; *i. e.* to the heart, desires, or intentions. The word *spirit* is often used in the Scriptures as the seat of the affections, and emotions, and passions of various kinds; see Mat. v. 3, "Blessed are the poor in spirit;" Luke x. 21, "Jesus rejoiced in spirit." So it is the seat of ardour or fervour (Luke i. 17; Acts xviii. 25; Rom. xii. 11); of grief or indignation; Mark iii. 12; John xi. 33; xiii. 21; Acts xvii. 16. It refers also to feelings, disposition, or temper of mind, in Luke ix. 55; Rom. viii. 15. Here it refers, it seems to me to the heart, the will, the disposition, the feelings, as contradistinguished from the understanding; and the sense is, "My feelings find utterance in prayer; my heart is engaged in devotion; my prayer will be acceptable to God, who looks upon the feelings of the heart, and I may have true enjoyment; but my understanding will be unfruitful, that is, will not profit others. What I say will not be understood by them; and of course, however much benefit *I* might derive from my devotions, yet they would be useless to others." ¶ *But my understanding* (ὁ δὲ νοῦς μου). My intellect, my mind; my mental efforts and operations. ¶ *Is unfruitful.* Produces nothing that will be of advantage to them. It is like a barren tree; a tree that bears nothing that can be of

I will sing [a] with the spirit, and I will sing with the understanding [b] also.

[a] Eph.5.19; Col.3.16.

16 Else, when thou shalt bless with the spirit, how shall he that occupieth the room of the unlearn-

[b] Ps. 47.7.

---

benefit to others. They cannot understand what I say, and of course, they cannot be profited by what I utter.

15. *What is it then?* What shall I do? What is the proper course for me to pursue? What is my practice and my desire; see the same form of expression in Rom. iii. 9, and vi. 15. It indicates the *conclusion* to which the reasoning had conducted him, or the course which he would pursue in view of all the circumstances of the case. ¶ *I will pray with the spirit,* &c. I will endeavour to *blend* all the advantages which can be derived from prayer; I will *unite* all the benefits which *can* result to myself and to others. I deem it of vast importance to pray with the spirit in such a way that the *heart* and the *affections* may be engaged, so that I may myself derive benefit from it; but I will also unite with that, utility to others; I will use such language that they may understand it, and be profited. ¶ *And I will pray with the understanding also.* So that others may understand me. I will make the appropriate use of the intellect, so that it may convey ideas, and make suitable impressions on the minds of others. ¶ *I will sing with the spirit.* It is evident that the same thing might take place in singing which occurred in prayer. It might be in a foreign language, and might be unintelligible to others. The affections of the man himself might be excited, and his heart engaged in the duty, but it would be profitless to others. Paul, therefore, says that he would so celebrate the praises of God as to excite the proper affections in his own mind, and so as to be intelligible and profitable to others. This passage proves, (1.) That the praises of God are to be celebrated among Christians, and that it is an important part of worship; (2.) That the *heart* should be engaged in it, and that it should be so performed as to excite proper affections in the hearts of those who are engaged in it; and, (3.) That it should be so done as to be *intelligible* and edifying to others. The *words* should be so uttered as to be distinct and understood. There should be clear enunciation as well as in prayer and preaching, since the design of sacred music in the worship of God is not only to utter praise, but it is to impress the sentiments which are sung on the heart by the aid of musical sounds and expression more deeply than could otherwise be done. If this is not done, the singing might as well be in a foreign language. Perhaps there is no part of public worship in which there is greater imperfection than in the mode of its psalmody. At the same time, there is scarcely any part of the devotions of the sanctuary that may be made more edifying or impressive. It has the *advantage*—an advantage which preaching and praying have not—of using the sweet tones of melody and harmony to *impress* sentiment on the heart: and it should be done.

16. *Else* (Ἐπεὶ). Since; if this is not done; if what is said is not intelligible, how shall the unlearned be able appropriately to express his assent, and join in your devotions? ¶ *When thou shalt bless.* When thou shalt bless God, or give thanks to him. If thou shalt lead the devotions of the people in expressing thanksgiving for mercies and favours. This may refer to a part of public worship, or to the thanks which should be expressed at table, and the invocation of the divine blessing to attend the bounties of his providence. Paul had illustrated his subject by prayer and by singing; he now does it by a reference to the important part of public worship expressed in giving thanks. ¶ *With the spirit.* In the manner referred to above; that is, in an unknown tongue, in such a way that your own *heart* may be engaged in it, but which would be unintelligible to

ed say Amen at thy giving [a] of
thanks? seeing he understandeth
not what thou sayest.
17 For thou verily givest thanks
well, but the other is not edified.
18 I thank my God, I speak with
tongues more than ye all.
19 Yet in the church I had
rather speak five words with my
understanding, that *by my voice* I
might teach others also, than ten
thousand words in an *unknown*
tongue.
20 Brethren, be not [b] children in

a chap.11.24.

b Eph.4.14,15; Heb.6.1—3; 2.Pet.3.18.

others. ¶ *He that occupieth the room.* Is in the place, or the seat of the unlearned; that is, he who *is* unlearned. On the meaning of the word *room,* see Note, Luke xiv. 8. To *fill a place* means to occupy a station, or to be found in a state or condition. ¶ *Of the unlearned* (τοῦ ἰδιώτου). On the meaning of this word, see Note, Acts iv. 13. Here it means one who was unacquainted with the foreign language spoken by him who gave thanks. It properly denotes a man in *private,* in contradistinction from a man in *public* life; and hence a man who is ignorant and unlettered, as such men generally were. ¶ *Say Amen.* This word means *truly, verily;* and is an expression of affirmation (John iii. 5) or of assent. Here it means *assent.* How can he pronounce *the* AMEN; how can he express his assent; how can he join in the act of devotion? This *might* have been, and probably *was,* expressed aloud; and there is no impropriety in it. It *may,* however, be *mental*—a silent assent to what is said, and a silent uniting in the act of thanksgiving. In one way or the other, or in both, the assent should always be expressed by those who join in acts of public worship.

17. *For thou verily givest thanks well.* That is, even if you use a foreign language. You do it with the heart; and it is accepted by God as *your* offering; but the other, who cannot understand it, cannot be benefited by it.

18. *I thank my God.* Paul here shows that he did not undervalue or despise the power of speaking foreign languages. It was with him a subject of thanksgiving that he could speak so many; but he felt that there were more valuable endowments than this; see the next verse. ¶ *With tongues more than ye all.* I am able to speak more foreign languages than all of you. *How many* languages Paul could speak, he has no where told us. It is reasonable, however, to presume that he was able to speak the language of any people to whom God in his providence, and by his Spirit, called him to preach. He had been commissioned to preach to the *Gentiles,* and it is probable that he was able to speak the languages of all the nations among whom he ever travelled. There is no account of his being under a necessity of employing an interpreter wherever he preached.

19. *Yet in the church.* In the Christian assembly. The word *church* does not refer to the *edifice* where Christians worshipped, but to the organized body of Christians. ¶ *I had rather,* &c. It is probable that in the Christian assembly, usually, there were few who understood foreign languages. Paul, therefore, would not speak in a foreign language when its only use would be mere display. ¶ *With my understanding.* So as to be intelligible to others; so that *I* might understand it, and so that at the same time others might be benefitted.

20. *Brethren, be not children in understanding.* Be not childish; do not behave like little children. They admire, and are astonished at what is striking, novel, and what may be of no real utility. They are pleased with any thing that will amuse them, and at little things that afford them play and pastime. So your admiration of a foreign language, and of the ability to speak it, is of as little solid value as the common sports and plays of boys. This, says Doddridge, is an admirable stroke of oratory, and adapted to bring down their pride by showing them that those things on which they were disposed to value

understanding: howbeit in malice be [a] ye children, but in understanding be [1] men. [b]

a Ps.131.2; Mat.18 3; Rom.16.19; 1Pet.2 2.
1 *perfect*, or *of a riper age*. *b* Ps.114.99.

21 In the law [c] it is written, [d] With *men of* other tongues and other lips will I speak unto this

c John 10.34. *d* Isa.28.11,12.

themselves were *childish*. It is sometimes well to appeal to Christians in this manner, and to show them that what they are engaged in is *unworthy* the dignity of the understanding—unfit to occupy the time and attention of an immortal mind. Much, alas! very much of that which engages the attention of Christians is just as unworthy of the dignity of the mind, and of their immortal nature, as were the aims and desires which the apostle rebuked among the Christians at Corinth. Much that pertains to dress, to accomplishment, to living, to employment, to amusement, to conversation, will appear, when we come to die, to have been like the playthings of *children;* and we shall feel that the immortal mind has been employed, and the time wasted, and the strength exhausted in that which was foolish and puerile. ¶ *Howbeit in malice be ye children.* This is one of Paul's most happy turns of expression and of sentiment. He had just told them that in one respect they ought not to be children. Yet, as if this would appear to be speaking lightly of children—and Paul would not speak lightly of any one, even of a child—he adds, that in *another* respect it would be well to be like them—nay, not only like children, but like infants. The phrase "be ye children," here, does not express the force of the original νηπιάζετε. It means, "be *infants*," and is emphatic, and was used, evidently, by the apostle of design. The meaning may be thus expressed. "Your admiration of foreign languages is like the sports and plays of *childhood*. In this respect be not children (παιδία); be men. Lay aside such childish things. Act worthy of the *understanding* which God has given you. I have mentioned children. Yet I would not speak unkindly or with contempt even of them. *In one respect* you may imitate them. Nay, you should not only be like *children*, that are somewhat advanced in years, but like *infants*. Be as free from malice, from any ill-will toward others, from envy, and every improper passion, as they are." This passage, therefore, accords with the repeated declaration of the Saviour, that in order to enter into heaven, it was needful that we should become as little children; Mat. xviii. 3. ¶ *Be men.* Margin, "*Perfect*, or *of a riper age*" (τέλειοι). The word means *full grown men*. Act like them whose understandings are mature and ripe.

21. *In the law it is written.* This passage is found in Isa. xxviii. 11, 12. The word *law* here seems to mean the same as revelation; or is used to denote the Old Testament in general. A similar use occurs in John x. 34, and John xv. 25. ¶ *With* men of *other tongues*, &c. This passage, where it occurs in Isaiah, means, that God would teach the rebellious and refractory Jews submission to himself, by punishing them amidst a people of another language, by removing them to a land—the land of Chaldea—where they would hear only a language that to them would be unintelligible and barbarous. Yet, notwithstanding this discipline, they would be still, to some extent, a rebellious people. The passage in Isaiah has no reference to the miraculous gift of tongues. and cannot have been used by the apostle as containing any intimation that such miraculous gifts would be imparted. It seems to have been used by Paul, because the *words* which occurred in Isaiah would *appropriately express* the idea which he wished to convey (see Note, Mat. i. 23), that God would make use of foreign languages for *some valuable purpose*. But he by no means intimates that Isaiah had any such reference; nor does he quote this as a fulfilment of the prophecy; nor does he mean to say, that God would accomplish *the same purpose* by the use

people; and yet for all that will they not hear me, saith the Lord.

22 Wherefore tongues are for a sign, [a] not to them [b] that believe, but to them that believe not: but prophesying *serveth* not for them that believe not, but for them which believe.

23 If therefore the whole church be come together into one place,

a Mark 16.17; Acts 2.6,&c. b 1Tim.1.9.

of foreign languages, which was contemplated in the passage in Isaiah. The sense is, as God accomplished an important purpose by the use of a foreign language in regard to his ancient people, as recorded in Isaiah, so he will make use of foreign languages to accomplish important purposes still. They shall be used in the Christian church to effect important objects, though not in the same manner, nor for the same end, as in the time of the captivity. What the design of making use of foreign languages was, in the Christian church, the apostle immediately states; ver. 22, 23. ¶ *Yet for all that,* &c. Notwithstanding all this chastisement that shall be inflicted on the Jews in a distant land, and among a people of a different language, they will still be a rebellious people. This is the sense of the passage, as it is used by Isaiah; see Isa. xxviii. 12. It is not quoted literally by the apostle, but the main idea is retained. He does not appear to design to apply this to the Corinthians, unless it may be to intimate that the power of speaking foreign languages did not of necessity secure obedience. It might be that this power might be possessed, and yet they be a sinful people; just as the Jews were admonished by the judgments of God, inflicted by means of a people speaking a foreign language, and yet were not reformed or made holy.

22. *Wherefore.* *Thus* ("Ωστε), or wherefore. The apostle does not mean to say that what he was about to state was a direct conclusion from the passage of Scripture which he had quoted, but that it followed from all that he had said, and from the whole view of the subject. "The true statement or doctrine is, that tongues are for a sign," &c. ¶ *Tongues.* The power of speaking foreign languages. ¶ *Are for a sign.* An *indication,* an evidence, or a proof that God has imparted this power, and that he attends the preaching of the gospel with his approbation. It is a *sign,* or a *miracle,* which, like all other miracles, may be designed to convince the unbelieving world that the religion is from God. ¶ *Not to them that believe.* Not to Christians. They are already convinced of the truth of religion, and they would not be benefited by that which was spoken in a language which they could not understand. ¶ *But to them that believe not.* It is a miracle designed to convince them of the truth of the Christian religion. God alone could confer the power of thus speaking; and as it was conferred expressly to aid in the propagation of the gospel, it proved that it was from God; see Note on Acts ii. 1—15. ¶ *But prophesying.* Speaking in a calm, connected, didactic manner, in language intelligible to all under the influence of inspiration; see Notes on ver. 1. ¶ *For them that believe not.* Is not particularly intended for them; but is intended mainly for the edifying of the church. It is not so striking, so replete with proofs of the divine presence and power as the gift of tongues. Though it may be really under the influence of the Holy Spirit, and may be really by inspiration, yet it is not so evidently such as is the power of speaking foreign languages. It was, therefore, better adapted to edify the church than to convince gainsayers. At the same time the *truths* conveyed by it, and the consolations administered by it, might be as clear evidence to the church of the attending power, and presence, and goodness of God, as the power of speaking foreign languages might be to infidels.

23. *Be come together into one place.* For public worship. ¶ *And all speak with tongues.* All speak with a variety

and all speak with tongues, and there come in *those that are* unlearned or unbelievers, will they not say that ye are mad? [a]

24 But if all prophesy, and there come in one that believeth not, or *one* unlearned, he is convinced of all, he is judged of all:

25 And thus are the secrets of his heart made manifest; and so, fall-

[a] Acts 2.13.

of unknown tongues; all speak foreign languages. The idea is, that the church would usually speak the same language with the people among whom they dwelt; and if they made use of foreign languages which were unintelligible to their visitors, it would leave the impression that the church was a bedlam. ¶ *And there come in* those that are *unlearned.* Those that are unacquainted with foreign languages, and to whom, therefore, what was said would be unintelligible. ¶ *Or unbelievers.* Heathen, or Jews, who did not believe in Christ. It is evident from this that such persons often attended on the worship of Christians. Curiosity might have led them to it; or the fact that they had relatives among Christians might have caused it. ¶ *That ye are mad.* They will not understand what is said; it will be a confused jargon; and they will infer that it is the effect of insanity. Even though it might not, therefore, be in itself improper, yet a regard to the honour of Christianity should have led them to abstain from the use of such languages in their worship when it was needless. The apostles were charged, from a similar cause, with being intoxicated; see Acts ii. 13.

24. *But if all prophesy.* Note, ver. 1. If all, in proper order and time, shall utter the truths of religion in a language intelligible to all. ¶ *Or* one *unlearned.* One unacquainted with the nature of Christianity, or the truths of the gospel. ¶ *He is convinced of all.* He will be convinced by all that speak. He will understand what is said; he will see its truth and force, and he will be satisfied of the truth of Christianity. The word here rendered *convinced* (ἐλέγχεται) is rendered *reprove* in John xvi. 8, "And when he is come, he will *reprove* the world of sin," &c. Its proper meaning is to *convict,* to show one to be wrong; and then to rebuke, reprove, admonish, &c. Here it means, evidently, that the man would be convicted, or convinced of his error and of his sin; he would see that his former opinions and practice had been wrong; he would see and acknowledge the force and truth of the Christian sentiments which should be uttered, and would acknowledge the error of his former opinions and life. The following verse shows that the apostle means something more than a mere convincing of the understanding, or a mere conviction that his opinions had been erroneous. He evidently refers to what is now known also as *conviction* for sin; that is, a deep sense of the depravity of the heart, of the errors and follies of the past life, accompanied with mental anxiety, distress, and alarm. The force of truth, and the appeals which should be made, and the observation of the happy effects of religion, would convince him that he was a sinner, and show him also his need of a Saviour. ¶ *He is judged by all.* By all that speak; by all that they say. The *effect* of what they say shall be, as it were, to pass a *judgment* on his former life; or to condemn him. What is said will be approved by his own conscience, and will have the effect to condemn him in his own view as a lost sinner. This is now the effect of faithful preaching, to produce deep self-condemnation in the minds of sinners.

25. *And thus are the secrets of his heart made manifest.* Made manifest to himself in a surprising and remarkable manner. He shall be led to see the *real* designs and motives of his heart. His conscience would be awakened; he would recall his former course of life; he would see that it was evil; and the present state of his heart would be made known to himself. It is possible that he would *sup-*

ing down on *his* face, he will worship God, and report that God is [a] in you of a truth.

a Isa.45.14; Zech.8.23.

26 How is it then, brethren? when ye come together, every one of you hath a psalm, hath a doc-

pose that the speaker was aiming directly at him, and *revealing* his feelings to others; for such an effect is often produced. The convicted sinner often supposes that the preacher particularly intends *him,* and wonders that he has such an acquaintance with his feelings and his life; and often supposes that he is designing to disclose his feelings to the congregation. It is *possible* that Paul here may mean that the prophets, by inspiration, would be able to reveal some secret facts in regard to the stranger; or to state the ill design which he might have had in coming into the assembly; or to state some things in regard to him which could be known only to himself; as was the case with Ananias and Sapphira (Acts v. 1, seq.); but perhaps it is better to understand this in a more general sense, as describing the proper and more common effect of truth, when it is applied by a man's own conscience. Such effects are often witnessed now; and such effects show the truth of religion; its adaptedness to men; the omniscience and the power of God; the design of the conscience, and its use in the conversion of sinners. ¶ *And so falling down on* his *face.* The usual posture of worship or reverence in eastern countries. It was performed by sinking on the knees and hands, and then placing the face on the ground. This might be done publicly; or the apostle may mean to say that it would lead him to do it in private. ¶ *He will worship God.* He will be converted, and become a Christian. ¶ *And report that God,* &c. Will become your friend, and an advocate for the Christian religion. An enemy will be turned to a friend. Doubtless this was often done. It is now often done. Paul's argument is, that they should so conduct their public devotions as that they should be adapted to produce this result.

26. *How is it then, brethren?* Note, ver. 15. What is the fact? What actually occurs among you? Does that state of things exist which I have described? Is there that order in your public worship which is demanded and proper? It is implied in his asking this question that there might be some things among them which were improper, and which deserved reproof. ¶ *When ye come together.* For worship. ¶ *Every one of you,* &c. That is, all the things which are specified would be found among them. It is, evidently, not meant that all these things would be found in the same person, but would all exist at the same time; and thus confusion and disorder would be inevitable. Instead of waiting for an intimation from the presiding officer in the assembly, or speaking in succession and in order, each one probably regarded himself as under the influence of the Holy Spirit; as having an important message to communicate, or as being called on to celebrate the praises of God; and thus confusion and disorder would prevail. Many would be speaking at the same time, and a most unfavourable impression would be made on the minds of the strangers who should be present, ver. 23. This implied reproof of the Corinthians is certainly a reproof of those public assemblies where many speak at the same time; or where a portion are engaged in praying, and others in exhortation. Nor can it be urged that in such cases those who engage in these exercises are under the influence of the Holy Spirit; for, however true that may be, yet it is no more true than it was in Corinth, and yet the apostle reproved the practice there. The Holy Spirit is the author of order, and not of confusion (ver. 33); and true religion prompts to peace and regularity, and not to discord and tumult. ¶ *Hath a psalm.* Is disposed to sing; is inclined to praise; and, however irregular or improper, expresses his thanks in a public manner, Note, ver. 15. ¶ *Hath a doc-*

trine, [a] hath a tongue, hath a revelation, hath an interpretation. Let [b] all things be done unto edifying.

27 If any man speak in an *unknown* tongue, *let it be* by two, or at the most *by* three, and *that* by course; and let one interpret.

28 But if there be no interpreter, let him keep silence in the church; and let him speak to himself and to God.

29 Let [c] the prophets speak two or three, and let the other judge.

30 If *any thing* be revealed to

a ver.6. b ver.40. c ver.39; 1 Thess.5.19,20.

trine. Has some religious truth on his mind which he deems it of special importance to inculcate, Note, ver. 6. ¶ *Hath a tongue.* Has something made known to him in a foreign language, or has a power of speaking a foreign language, and exercises it, though it produces great confusion. ¶ *Hath a revelation.* Some truth which has been particularly revealed to him; perhaps an explanation of some mystery (*Doddridge*); or a revelation of some future event (*Macknight*); or a prophecy (*Bloomfield*); or a power of explaining some of the truths couched in the types and figures of the Old Testament. *Grotius.* ¶ *Hath an interpretation.* An explanation of something that has been uttered by another in a foreign language; Note, chap. xii. 10. ¶ *Let all things,* &c. Let this be the great principle, to promote the edification of the church; Note, ver. 12. If this rule were followed, it would prevent confusion and disorder.

27. Let it be *by two, or at the most* by *three.* That is, two, or at most three in one day, or in one meeting. So Grotius, Rosenmüller, Doddridge, Bloomfield, and Locke, understand it. It is probable that many were endowed with the gift of tongues; and it is certain that they were disposed to exercise the gift even when it could be of no real advantage, and when it was done only for ostentation. Paul had shown to them (ver. 22), that the main design of the gift of tongues was to convince unbelievers; he here shows them that if that gift *was* exercised in the church, it should be in such a way as to promote edification. They should not speak at the same time; nor should they regard it as necessary that all should speak at the same meeting. It should not be so as to produce disorder and confusion; nor should it be so as to detain the people beyond a reasonable time. The speakers, therefore, in any one assembly should not exceed two or three. ¶ *And* that *by course.* Separately; one after another. They should not all speak at the same time. ¶ *And let one interpret.* One who has the gift of interpreting foreign languages, (Note, chap. xii. 10), so that they may be understood, and the church be edified.

28. *But if there be no interpreter.* If there be no one present who has the gift of interpretation. ¶ *And let him speak to himself and to God;* see Note, ver. 2, 4. Let him commune with himself, and with God; let him meditate on the truths which are revealed to him, and let him in secret express his desires to God.

29. *Let the prophets,* Note, ver. 1. ¶ *Speak two or three.* On the same days, or at the same meeting; Note, ver. 27. ¶ *And let the other judge.* The word "other" (οἱ ἄλλοι, *the others*), Bloomfield supposes refers to the other *prophets;* and that the meaning is, that they should decide whether what was said was dictated by the Holy Spirit, or not. But the more probable sense, I think, is that which refers it to the rest of the congregation, and which supposes that they were to compare one doctrine with another, and deliberate on what was spoken, and determine whether it had evidence of being in accordance with the truth. It may be that the apostle here refers to those who had the gift of discerning spirits, and that he meant to say that they were to determine by what spirit the prophets who spoke were actuated. It was possible that those who claimed to be prophets might err, and it was the duty of all to examine whether that which was uttered was

another that sitteth by, let the [a]
first hold his peace.
31 For ye may all prophecy one
by one, that all may learn, and all
may be comforted.
32 And the spirits [b] of the prophets are subject to the prophets.
33 For God is not *the author* of
[1] confusion, but of peace, as [c] in
all churches of the saints.

a Job 32.11. *b* 1 John 4.1. 1 *tumult*, or *unquietness*. *a* chap.11.16.

in accordance with truth. And if this was a duty then, it is a duty now; if it was proper even when the teachers claimed to be under divine inspiration, it is much more the duty of the people now. No minister of religion has a right to demand that all that he speaks shall be regarded as truth, unless he can give good reasons for it: no man is to be debarred from the right of canvassing freely, and comparing with the bible, and with sound reason, all that the minister of the gospel advances. No minister who has just views of his office, and a proper acquaintance with the truth, and confidence in it, would desire to prohibit the people from the most full and free examination of all that he utters. It may be added, that the Scripture everywhere encourages the most full and free examination of all doctrines that are advanced; and that true religion advances just in proportion as this spirit of candid, and earnest, and prayerful examination prevails among a people; see Note, Acts xvii. 11; comp. 1 Thess. v. 21.

30. *If* any thing *be revealed to another.* If, while one is speaking, an important truth is revealed to another, or is suggested to his mind by the Holy Spirit, which he feels it to be important to communicate. ¶ *Let the first hold his peace.* That is, let him that was speaking conclude his discourse, and let there not be the confusion arising from two persons speaking at the same time. Doddridge understands this as meaning, that he to whom the revelation was made should sit still, until the other was done speaking, and not rise and rudely interrupt him. But this is to do violence to the language. So Macknight understands it, that the one who was speaking was *first* to finish his discourse, and be silent, before the other began to speak. But this is evidently a forced construction. Locke understands it as meaning, that if, while one was speaking, the meaning of what he said was revealed to another, the first was to cease speaking until the other had interpreted or explained it. But the obvious meaning of the passage is, that the man that was speaking was to close his discourse and be silent. It does not follow, however, that he was to be rudely interrupted. He might close his discourse deliberately, or perhaps by an intimation from the person to whom the revelation was made. At any rate, two were not to speak at the same time, but the one who was speaking was to conclude before the other addressed the assembly.

31. *For ye may all prophecy*, &c. There is time enough for all; there is no need of speaking in confusion and disorder. Every person may have an opportunity of expressing his sentiments at the proper time. ¶ *That all may learn.* In such a manner that there may be edification. This might be done if they would speak one at a time in their proper order.

32. *And the spirits of the prophets.* See in ver. 1 for the meaning of the word prophets. The evident meaning of this is, that they were able to *control* their inclination to speak; they were not under a *necessity* of speaking, even though they might be inspired. There was no need of disorder. This verse gives confirmation to the supposition, that the extraordinary endowments of the Holy Spirit were subjected to substantially the same laws as a man's natural endowments. They were conferred by the Holy Ghost; but they were conferred on free agents, and did not interfere with their free agency. And as a man, though of the most splendid talents and commanding eloquence, has *control* over his own mind, and is not *com-*

34 Let [a] your women keep silence in the churches; for it is not permitted unto them to speak; but *they are commanded* to be [b] under obedience, as also saith [c] the law.

a 1Tim.2.11,12. b Eph.5.22; Tit.2.5; 1Pet.3.1. c Gen.3.16; Num.30.3—12; Esth.1.20.

pelled to speak, so it was with those who are here called prophets. The immediate reference of the passage is to those who are called *prophets* in the New Testament: and the interpretation should be confined to them. It is not improbable, however, that the same thing was true of the prophets of the Old Testament; and that it is really true as a general declaration of *all* the prophets whom God has inspired, that they *had* control over their own minds, and could speak or be silent at pleasure. In this the spirit of true inspiration differed essentially from the views of the heathen, who regarded themselves as driven on by a wild, controlling influence, that *compelled* them to speak even when they were unconscious of what they said. Universally, in the heathen world, the priests and priestesses supposed or feigned that they were under an influence which was incontrollable; which took away their powers of self-command, and which made them the mere organs or unconscious instruments of communicating the will of the gods. The Scripture account of inspiration is, however, a very different thing. In whatever way the mind was influenced, or whatever was the mode in which the truth was conveyed, yet it was not such as to destroy the conscious powers of free agency, nor such as to destroy the individuality of the inspired person, or to annihilate what was peculiar in his mode of thinking, his style, or his customary manner of expression.

33. *God is not* the author *of confusion.* Marg. *Tumult,* or *unquietness.* His religion cannot tend to produce disorder. He is the God of peace; and his religion will tend to promote order. It is calm, peaceful, thoughtful. It is not boisterous and disorderly. ¶ *As in all churches of the saints.* As was everywhere apparent in the churches. Paul here appeals to them, and says that this was the fact wherever the true religion was spread, that it tended to produce peace and order. This is as true now as it was then. And we may learn, therefore, (1.) That where there is disorder, there is little religion. Religion does not *produce* it; and the tendency of tumult and confusion is to drive religion away. (2.) True religion will not lead to tumult, to outcries, or to irregularity. It will not prompt many to speak or pray at once; nor will it justify tumultuous and noisy assemblages. (3.) Christians should regard God as the author of peace. They should always in the sanctuary demean themselves in a reverent manner, and with such decorum as becomes men when they are in the presence of a holy and pure God, and engaged in his worship. (4.) All those pretended conversions, however sudden and striking they may be, which are attended with disorder, and confusion, and public outcries, are to be suspected. Such excitement may be *connected with* genuine piety, but it is no part of pure religion. That is calm, serious, orderly, heavenly. No man who is under its influence is disposed to engage in scenes of confusion and disorder. Grateful he may be, and he may and will express his gratitude; prayerful he will be, and he will pray; anxious for others he will be, and he will express that anxiety; but it will be with seriousness, tenderness, love; with a desire for the order of God's house, and not with a desire to break in upon and disturb all the solemnities of public worship.

34. *Let your women keep silence,* &c. This rule is positive, explicit, and universal. There is no ambiguity in the expressions; and there can be no difference of opinion, one would suppose, in regard to their meaning. The sense evidently is, that in all those things which he had specified, the women were to keep silence; they were to take no part. He had dis-

35 And if they will learn any thing, let them ask their husbands at home: for it is a shame for women to speak in the church.

coursed of speaking foreign languages, and of prophecy; and the evident sense is, that in regard to all these they were to keep silence, or were not to engage in them. These pertained solely to the male portion of the congregation. These things constituted the business of the public teaching; and in this the female part of the congregation were to be silent. "They were not to teach the people, nor were they to interrupt those who were speaking."—*Rosenmüller*. It is probable that, on pretence of being inspired, the women had assumed the office of public teachers. In chap. xi. Paul had argued against their doing this in a certain manner—without their veils (chap. xi. 4), and he had shown, that *on that account*, and *in that manner*, it was improper for them to assume the office of public teachers, and to conduct the devotions of the church. The force of the argument in chap. xi. is, that what he there states would be a sufficient reason against the practice, even if there were no other. It was contrary to all decency and propriety that they should appear *in that manner* in public. He *here* argues against the practice ON EVERY GROUND; forbids it altogether; and shows that on every consideration it was to be regarded as improper for them even so much as *to ask a question* in time of public service. There is, therefore, no inconsistency between the argument in chap. xi. and the statement here; and the force of the whole is, that *on every consideration* it was improper, and to be expressly prohibited, for women to conduct the devotions of the church. It does not refer to those only who claimed to be inspired, but to all; it does not refer merely to acts of public preaching, but to all acts of speaking, or even asking questions, when the church is assembled for public worship. No rule in the New Testament is more positive than this; and however plausible may be the reasons which may be urged for disregarding it, and for suffering women to take part in conducting public worship, yet the authority of the apostle Paul is positive, and his meaning cannot be mistaken; comp. 1 Tim. ii. 11, 12. ¶ *To be under obedience.* To be subject to their husbands; to acknowledge the superior authority of the man; Note, chap. xi. 3. ¶ *As also saith the law;* Gen. iii. 16, "And thy desire shall be to thy husband, and he shall rule over thee."

35. *And if they will learn any thing.* If any thing has been spoken which they do not understand; or if on any particular subject they desire more full information, let them inquire of their husbands in their own dwelling. They may there converse freely; and their inquiries will not be attended with the irregularity and disorder which would occur should they interrupt the order and solemnity of public worship. ¶ *For it is a shame.* It is disreputable and shameful; it is a breach of propriety. Their station in life demands modesty, humility, and they should be free from the ostentation of appearing so much in public as to take part in the public services of teaching and praying. It does not become their rank in life; it is not fulfilling the object which God evidently intended them to fill. He has appointed *men* to rule; to hold offices; to instruct and govern the church; and it is improper that women should assume that office upon themselves. This evidently and obviously refers to the church assembled for public worship, in the ordinary and regular acts of devotion. There the assembly is made up of males and females, of old and young, and there it is improper for them to take part in conducting the exercises. But this cannot be interpreted as meaning that it is improper for females to speak or to pray in meetings of their own sex, assembled for prayer or for benevolence; nor that it is improper for a female to speak or to pray in a Sabbath-school. Neither of these come under the apostle's idea of a church. And in such meetings, no rule of propriety or of the Scrip-

36 What! came the word of God out from you? or [a] came it unto you only?
37 If [b] any man think himself to be a prophet, or spiritual, let him acknowledge that the things that I write unto you are the commandments of the Lord.

a chap.4.7. b 2Cor.10.7; 1John 4.6.

tures is violated in their speaking for the edification of each other, or in leading in social prayer. It may be added here, that on this subject the Jews were very strenuous, and their laws were very strict. The Rabbins taught that a woman should know nothing but the use of the distaff, and they were specially prohibited from asking questions in the synagogue, or even from reading. See *Lightfoot.* The same rule is still observed by the Jews in the synagogues.

36. *What! came the word of God out from you?* The meaning of this is, "Is the church at Corinth the *mother church?* Was it first established; or has it been alone in sending forth the word of God? You have adopted customs which are unusual. You have permitted women to speak in a manner unknown to other churches; see chap. xi. 16. You have admitted irregularity and confusion unknown in all the others. You have allowed many to speak at the same time, and have tolerated confusion and disorder. Have you any *right* thus to differ from others? Have you any authority, as it were, to dictate to them, to teach them, contrary to their uniform custom, to allow these disorders? Should you not rather be conformed to them, and observe the rules of the churches which are older than yours?" The *argument* here is, that the church at Corinth was *not* the first that was established; that it was one of the *last* that had been founded; and that it could, therefore, claim no right to differ from others, or to prescribe to them. The same argument is employed in chap. xi. 16; see Note. ¶ *Or came it unto you only?* As you are not the first of those who believed, neither are you the only ones. God has sent the same gospel to others, and it is travelling over the world. Others, therefore, have the same right as you to originate customs and peculiar habits; and as this would be attended with confusion and disorder, you should all follow the same rule, and the customs which do not prevail in other churches should not be allowed in yours.

37. *If any man think himself to be a prophet;* Note, ver. 1. If any man claim to be divinely endowed. Macknight renders it, "be really a prophet." But the more correct meaning here is, doubtless, "If any man *profess* to be a prophet; or is *reputed* to be a prophet." *Bloomfield.* The proper meaning of the word δοκέω is to seem to one's self; to be of opinion, to suppose, believe, &c.; and the reference here is to one who should *regard himself,* or who should believe and profess to be thus endowed. ¶ *Or spiritual.* Regarding himself as under the extraordinary influence of the Spirit. ¶ *Let him acknowledge,* &c He will show that he is truly under the influence of the Holy Spirit, by acknowledging my authority, and by yielding obedience to the commands which I utter in the name and by the authority of the Lord. All would probably be disposed to acknowledge the right of Paul to speak to them; all would regard him as an apostle; and all would show that God had influenced their hearts, if they listened to his commands, and obeyed his injunctions. I do not speak by my own authority, or in my own name, says Paul. I speak in the name of the Lord; and to obey the commands of the Lord is a proof of being influenced by his Spirit. True religion everywhere, and the most ardent and enthusiastic zeal that is prompted by true religion, will show their genuineness and purity by a sacred and constant regard for the commands of the Lord. And that zeal which disregards those commands, and which tramples down the authority of the Scriptures and the peace and order of the church, gives demonstration that it is not genuine. It is false zeal, and, however ardent, will not ultimately do good to the cause.

38 But if any be ignorant, let him be ignorant.
39 Wherefore, brethren, covet to prophesy, and forbid not to speak with tongues.
40 Let [a] all things be done decently and in order.

a ver.26,33.

38. *But if any be ignorant, &c.* If any one *affects* to be ignorant of my authority, or whether I have a right to command. If he affects to *doubt* whether I am inspired, and whether what I utter is in accordance with the will of God. ¶ *Let him be ignorant.* At his own peril, let him remain so, and abide the consequences. I shall not take any further trouble to debate with him. I have stated my authority. I have delivered the commands of God. And now, if he disregards them, and still doubts whether all this is said by divine authority, let him abide the consequences of rejecting the law of God. I have given full proof of my divine commission. I have nothing more to say on that head. And now, if he chooses to remain in ignorance or incredulity, the fault is his own, and he must answer for it to God.

39. *Covet to prophesy;* Note, ver. 1. This is the *summing up* of all that he had said. It was *desirable* that a man should wish to be able to speak, under the teaching of the Holy Spirit, in such a manner as to edify the church. ¶ *And forbid not, &c.* Do not suppose that the power of speaking foreign languages is useless, or is to be despised, or that it is to be prohibited. *In its own place* it is a valuable endowment; and on proper occasions the talent should be exercised; see in ver. 22.

40. *Let all things be done decently and in order.* Let all things be done in an *appropriate* and *becoming* manner; *decorously,* as becomes the worship of God. Let all be done *in order, regularly,* without confusion, discord, tumult. The word used here (κατὰ τάξιν) is properly a military term, and denotes the order and regularity with which an army is drawn up. This is a general rule, which was to guide them. It was simple, and easily applied. There might be a thousand questions started about the modes and forms of worship, and the customs in the churches, and much difficulty might occur in many of these questions; but here was a simple and plain rule, which might be easily applied. Their good sense would tell them what became the worship of God; and their pious feelings would restrain them from excesses and disorders. This rule is still applicable, and is safe in guiding us in many things in regard to the worship of God. There are many things which cannot be subjected to *rule,* or exactly prescribed; there are many things which may and must be left to pious feeling, to good sense, and to the views of Christians themselves, about what will promote their edification and the conversion of sinners. The rule in such questions is plain. Let all be done *decorously,* as becomes the worship of the great and holy God; let all be without confusion, noise, and disorder.

In view of this chapter, we may remark:—

(1.) That public worship should be in a language understood by the people; the language which they commonly employ. Nothing can be clearer than the sentiments of Paul on this. The whole strain of the chapter is to demonstrate this, in opposition to making use of a foreign and unintelligible language in any part of public worship. Paul specifies in the course of the discussion every part of public worship; *public preaching* (ver. 2, 3, 5, 13, 19); *prayer* (ver. 14, 15); *singing* (ver. 15); and insists that all should be in a language that should be understood by the people. It would almost seem that he had anticipated the sentiments and practice of the Roman Catholic denomination. It is remarkable that a practice should have grown up, and have been defended, in a church professedly Christian, so directly in opposition to the explicit meaning of the New Testament. Perhaps there is not even in the Roman Catholic denomination, a more striking instance of a custom or doctrine in direct contradiction to the Bible. If any thing is plain and obvious, it is that worship, in order to be edifying, should be in a language that is understood by the people. Nor can that service be acceptable to God which is not understood by those who offer it; which conveys no idea to their minds, and which cannot, therefore, be the homage of the heart. Assuredly, God does not require the offering of unmeaning words. Yet, this has been a grand device of the great enemy of man. It has contributed to keep the people in ignorance and superstition; it has prevented the mass of the people from seeing how utterly unlike the New Testament are the sentiments of the papists; and it has, in connection with the kindred doctrine that the Scripture should be withheld from the people, contributed to perpetuate that dark system, and to bind the human mind in chains. Well do the Roman Catholics know, that if the Bible were given to the people, and public worship conducted in a language which they could understand, the system would soon fall. It could not live in the midst of light. It is a system which lives and thrives only in darkness.

(2.) Preaching should be simple and intelligible. There is a great deal of preaching which might as well be in a foreign tongue as in the language which is actually employed. It is dry, abstruse, metaphysical, remote from the common manner of expression, and the common habits of thought among men. It may be suited to schools of philosophy, but it cannot be suited to the pulpit. The preaching of the Lord Jesus was simple, and intelligible even to a child. And nothing can be a greater error, than for the ministers of the gospel to adopt a dry and metaphysical manner of preaching. The most successful preachers have been those who have been most remarkable for their simplicity and clearness. Nor is simplicity and intelligibleness of manner inconsistent with bright thought and profound sentiments. A diamond is the most pure of all minerals; a river may be deep, and yet its water so pure that the bottom may be seen at a great depth; and glass in the window is most valuable the clearer and purer it is, when it is itself least seen, and when it gives no obstruction to the light. If the purpose is that the glass may be *itself* an ornament, it may be well to stain it; if to give light, it should be pure. A very shallow stream may be very muddy; and because the bottom cannot be seen, it is no evidence that it is deep. So it is with style. If the purpose is to convey thought, to enlighten and save the soul, the style should be plain, simple, pure. If it be to bewilder and confound, or to be admired as unintelligible, or perhaps as profound, then an abstruse and metaphysical, or a flowery manner may be adopted in the pulpit.

(3.) We should learn to value *useful* talent more than that which is splendid and showy; ver. 3. The whole scope of this chapter goes to demonstrate that we should more highly prize and desire that talent which may be *useful* to the church, or which may be useful in convincing unbelievers (ver. 24, 25), than that which merely dazzles, or excites admiration. Ministers of the gospel who preach as they should do, engage in their work to win souls to Christ, not to induce them to admire eloquence; they come to teach men to adore the great and dreadful God, not to be loud in their praises of a mortal man.

(4.) Ministers of the gospel should not aim to be admired. They should seek to be useful. Their aim should not be to excite admiration of their acute and profound talent for reasoning; of their clear and striking power of observation; of their graceful manner; of their glowing and fervid eloquence; of the beauty of their words, or the eloquence of their well-turned periods. They should seek to build up the people of God in holy faith, and so to present truth as that it shall make a deep impression on mankind. No work is so important, and so serious in its nature and results, as the ministry of the gospel; and in no

CHAPTER XV.

MOREOVER, brethern, I [a] declare unto you the gospel which I preached unto you, which [b] also ye have received, and wherein [c] ye stand:

a Gal.1.11. b chap. 1.4-8. c 1 Pet.5.12.

work on earth should there be more seriousness, simplicity, exactness, and correctness of statement, and invincible and unvarying adherence to simple and unvarnished truth. Of all places, the pulpit is the last, in which to seek to excite admiration, or where to display profound learning, or the powers of an abstract and subtle argumentation, *for the sake* of securing a reputation. Cowper has drawn the character of what a minister of the gospel should be, in the well-known and most beautiful passage in the "Task."

Would I describe a preacher, such as Paul
Were he on earth, would hear, approve, and
 own,
Paul should himself direct me. I would trace
His master-strokes, and draw from his design.
I would express him simple, grave, sincere;
In doctrine uncorrupt; in language plain;
And plain in manner; decent, solemn, chaste,
And natural in gesture; much impress'd
Himself, as conscious of his awful charge,
And anxious mainly that the flock he feeds
May feel it too; affectionate in look,
And tender in address, as well becomes
A messenger of grace to guilty men.

He stablishes the strong, restores the weak,
Reclaims the wanderer, binds the broken
 heart,
And, arm'd himself in panoply complete
Of heavenly temper, furnishes with arms,
Bright as his own, and trains, by every rule
Of holy discipline, to glorious war,
The sacramental host of God's elect.

CHAPTER XV.

THIS important and deeply interesting chapter, I have spoken of as the *third* part of the epistle. See the Introduction. It is more important than any other portion of the epistle, as it contains a connected, and laboured, and unanswerable argument for the main truth of Christianity, and, consequently, of Christianity itself; and it is more interesting to us as *mortal* beings, and as having an instinctive dread of death, than any other portion of the epistle. It has always, therefore, been regarded with deep interest by expositors, and it is worthy of the deepest attention of all. If the argument in this chapter is solid, then Christianity is true; and if true, then this chapter unfolds to us the most elevated and glorious prospect which can be exhibited to dying, yet immortal man.

There were, probably, two reasons why the apostle introduced here this discussion about the resurrection. *First*, it was desirable to introduce a condensed and connected statement of the main argument for the truth of Christianity. The Corinthians had been perplexed with subtle questions, and torn by sects and parties, and it was possible that in their zeal for sect and party, they would lose their hold on this great and vital argument for the truth of religion itself. It might be further apprehended, that the enemies of the gospel, from seeing the divisions and strifes which existed there, would take advantage of these contentions, and say that a religion which produced *such* fruits could not be from God. It was important, therefore, that they should have access to an argument plain, clear, and unanswerable, for the truth of Christianity; and that thus the evil effects of their divisions and strifes might be counteracted. *Secondly*. It is evident from ver. 12, that the important doctrine of the resurrection of the dead had been denied at Corinth, and that this error had obtained a footing in the church itself. On what grounds, or by what portion or party it was denied, is unknown. It may have been that the influence of some Sadducean teacher may have led to the rejection of the doctrine; or it may have been the effect of philosophy. From Acts xvii. 32, we know that among some of the Greeks, the doctrine of the resurrection was regarded as ridiculous; and from 2 Tim. ii. 18, we learn that it was held by some that the resurrection was passed already, and consequently that there was nothing but a spiritual resurrection. To counteract these errors, and to put the doctrine of the resurrection of the dead on a firm foundation, and thus to furnish a demonstration of the truth of Christianity, was the design of this chapter.

The chapter may be regarded as divided into four parts, and four questions in regard to the resurrection are solved. 1. Whether there is any resurrection of the dead? ver. 1—34. 2. With what body will the dead rise? ver. 35—51. 3. What will become of those who shall be alive when the Lord Jesus shall come to judge the world? ver. 51—54. 4. What are the practical bearings of this doctrine? ver. 55—58.

I. The dead will be raised; ver. 1—34. This Paul proves by the following arguments, and illustrates in the following manner.

(1.) By adducing *reasons* to show that Christ rose from the dead; ver. 1—11.

(*a*) From the Scripture; ver. 1—4.

(*b*) From the testimony of eyewitnesses; ver. 5—11.

(2.) By showing the absurdity of the contrary doctrine; ver. 12—34.

(*a*) If the dead do not rise, it would follow that Christ has not risen; ver. 13.

(*b*) If Christ is not risen, he is preached in vain, and faith is reposed in him for naught; ver. 14.

(*c*) It would follow that the apostles would be false witnesses and wicked men; whereas, the Corinthians had abundant reason to know the contrary; ver. 15.

(*d*) The faith of the Corinthians must be vain if he was not risen, and they must regard themselves as still unpardoned sinners, since all their hope of pardon must arise from the fact that his work was accepted, and that he was raised up; ver. 16, 17.

(*e*) If Christ was not risen, then all their pious friends who had believed in him must be regarded as lost; ver. 18.

(*f*) It would follow that believers in Christ would be in a more miserable condition than any others, if there was no resurrection; ver. 19.

(*g*) Baptism for the resurrection of the dead would be absurd and in vain, unless the dead arose; it would be vain to be baptized with the belief, and on the ground of the belief that Christ rose, and on the ground of the hope that they would rise; ver. 29.

(*h*) It would be in vain that the apostles and others had suffered so many toils and persecutions, unless the dead should rise; ver. 30—32.

In the course of this part of his argument (ver. 20—28) Paul introduces an *illustration* of the doctrine, or a statement of an important *fact* in regard to it, thus *separating* the argument in ver. 19 from the next, which occurs in ver. 29. Such interruptions of a train of thinking are not uncommon in the writings of Paul, and indicate the *fulness* and *richness* of his conceptions, when some striking thought occurs, or some plausible objection is to be met, and when he suspends his argument in order to state it. This interjected portion consists of the following items. (1.) A triumphant and joyful assurance that Christ *had in fact* risen; as if his mind was full, and he was impatient of the delay caused by the necessity of slow argumentation; ver. 19, 20. (2.) He *illustrates* the doctrine, or shows that it is *reasonable* that the certainty of the resurrection should be demonstrated by one in human nature, since death had been introduced by man; ver. 21, 22. This is an argument from *analogy*, drawn from the obvious propriety of the doctrine that man should be raised up in a manner somewhat similar to the mode in which he had been involved in ruin. (3.) He states the *order* in which all this should be done; ver. 23—28. It is possible that some may have held that the resurrection must have been already passed, since it depended so entirely and so closely on the resurrection of Christ; comp. 2 Tim. ii. 18. Paul, therefore, meets this objection; and shows that it must take place in a regular order; that Christ rose first, and that they who were his friends should rise at his coming. He then states what would take place at that time, when the work of redemption should have been consummated by the resurrection of the dead, and the entire recovery of all the redeemed to God, and the subjection of every foe.

II. What will be the nature of the bodies that shall be raised up? ver. 35—51.

This inquiry is illustrated,

(1.) By a reference to grain that is sown; ver. 36—38.

(2.) By a reference to the fact that there are different kinds of flesh; ver. 39.

(3.) By a reference to the fact that there *are* celestial bodies and earthly bodies; ver. 40.

(4.) By the fact that there is a difference between the sun, and moon, and stars; ver. 41.

(5.) By a *direct statement*, for which the mind is prepared by these illustrations, of the important changes which the body of man must undergo, and of the nature of that body which he will have in heaven; ver. 42—50. It is,

(*a*) Incorruptible; ver. 42.

(*b*) Glorious; ver. 43.

(*c*) Powerful; ver. 43.

(*d*) A spiritual body; ver. 44.

(*e*) It is like the body of the second man, the Lord from heaven; ver. 45—50.

III. What will become of those who shall be alive when the Lord Jesus shall return to raise the dead?

Ans. They shall be changed instantly, and fitted for heaven, and made like the glorified saints that shall be raised from the dead; ver. 51—54.

IV. The practical consequences or influences of this doctrine; ver. 55—58.

(1.) The doctrine is glorious and triumphant; it overcame all the evils of sin, and should fill the mind with joy; ver. 55—57.

(2.) It should lead Christians to diligence, and firmness of faith, and patience, since their labour was not to be in vain; ver. 58.

1. *Moreover.* But (δὲ). In addition to what I have said, or in that which I am now about to say, I make known the main and leading truth of the gospel. The particle δὲ is "strictly adversative, but more frequently denotes transition and conversion, and serves to introduce *something else*, whether opposite to what precedes, or simply continuative or explanatory."—*Robinson.* Here it serves to introduce another topic that was not properly a continuation of what he had said, but which pertained to the same general subject, and which was deemed of great importance. ¶ *I declare unto you* (Γνωρίζω). This word properly means to make known, to declare, to reveal (Luke ii. 15; Rom. ix. 22, 23); then to tell, narrate, inform (Eph. vi. 21; Col. iv. 7, 9); and also to put in mind of, to impress, to confirm; see Note, chap. xii. 3. Here it does not mean that he was communicating to them any new truth, but he wished to remind them of it; to state the arguments for it, and to impress it deeply on their memories. There is an *abruptness* in our translation which does not exist in the original. *Bloomfield.* ¶ *The gospel;* Note, Mark i. 1. The word here means the *glad announcement*, or the *good news* about the coming of the Messiah, his life, and sufferings, and death, and especially his resurrection. The main subject to which Paul refers in this chapter is the resurrection: but he includes in the word gospel here, the doctrine that he died for sins, and was buried, as well as the doctrine of his resurrection; see ver. 3, 4. ¶ *Which I preached unto you.* Paul founded the church at Corinth; Acts xviii. 1, seq. It was proper that he should remind them of what *he* had taught them at first; of the great elementary truths on which the church had been established, but from which their minds had been diverted by the other subjects that had been introduced as matters of debate and strife. It was fair to presume that they would regard with respect the doctrines which the founder of their church had first proclaimed, if they were reminded of them; and Paul, therefore, calls their attention to the great and vital truths

2 By which also ye are saved, if [a] ye keep [1] in memory [2] what I preached unto you, unless [b] ye have believed in vain.

3 For I delivered unto you first of all that which I also received, how that Christ died for our sins according [c] to the Scriptures;

a Heb.3.6. 1 or, *hold fast.* 2 *by what speech.* b Gal.3.4.

c Gen.3.15; Ps.xxii; Isa.liii; Dan.9.26; Zech. 13.7; Luke 24.26,46.

by which they had been converted, and by which the church had thus far prospered. It is well, often, to remind Christians of the truths which were preached to them *when* they were converted, and which were instrumental in their conversion. When they have gone off from these doctrines, when they had given their minds to speculation and philosophy, it has a good effect to *remind* them that they were converted by the simple truths, that Christ died, and was buried, and rose again from the dead. The argument of Paul here is, that they owed all the piety and comfort which they had to these doctrines; and that, therefore, they should still adhere to them as the foundation of all their hopes. ¶ *Which also ye have received.* Which you embraced; which you all admitted as true; which were the means of your conversion. I would remind you, that, however that truth may *now* be denied by you, it was once received by you, and you professed to believe in the fact that Christ rose from the dead, and that the saints would rise. ¶ *And wherein ye stand.* By which your church was founded, and by which all your piety and hope has been produced, and which is at the foundation of all your religion. You were built up *by* this, and by this only can you stand as a Christian church. This doctrine was vital and fundamental. This demonstrates that the doctrines that Christ died "for sins," and rose from the dead, are fundamental truths of Christianity. They enter into its very nature; and without them there can be no true religion.

2. *By which also ye are saved.* On which your salvation depends; the belief of which is indispensable to your salvation; see Note on Mark xvi. 16. The apostle thus shows the *importance* of the doctrine. In every respect it demanded their attention. It was that which was first preached among them; that which they had solemnly professed; that by which they had been built up; and that which was connected with their salvation. It does not mean simply that by this they were brought into a salvable state (Clarke, Macknight, Whitby, Bloomfield, &c.), but it means that their hopes of eternal life rested on this; and by this they were then *in fact* saved from the condemnation of sin, and were in the possession of the hope of eternal life. ¶ *If ye keep in memory.* Margin, as in the Greek, *if ye hold fast.* The idea is, that they were saved by this, or would be, if they faithfully retained or held the doctrine as he delivered it; if they observed it, and still believed it, notwithstanding all the efforts of their enemies, and all the arts of false teaching to wrest it from them. There is a doubt delicately suggested here, whether they did in fact still adhere to his doctrine, or whether they had not abandoned it in part for the opposite. ¶ *Unless ye have believed in vain.* You will be saved by it, if you adhere to it, unless it shall turn out that it was vain to believe, and that the doctrine was false. That it was *not* false, he proceeds to demonstrate. Unless all your trials, discouragements, and hopes were to no purpose, and all have been the result of imposture; and unless all your profession is false and hollow, you will be saved by this great doctrine which I first preached to you.

3. *For I delivered unto you;* Note, chap. xi. 23. ¶ *First of all.* Among the first doctrines which I preached. As the leading and primary doctrines of Christianity. ¶ *That which I also received.* Which had been communicated to me. Not doctrines of which I was the author, or which were to be

4 And that he was buried, and that he rose again the third day according [a] to the Scriptures;

5 And that he was seen of [b] Cephas, then of the twelve.

6 After that, he was seen of

a Ps.16.10; Hos.6.2.

b Luke 23.34,&c.

regarded as my own. Paul here refers to the fact that he had received these doctrines from the Lord Jesus by inspiration; comp. Note, chap. x. 23; Gal. i. 2. This is one instance in which he claims to be under the divine guidance, and to have received his doctrines from God. ¶ *How that Christ died for our sins.* The Messiah, The Lord Jesus, died as an expiatory offering on account of our sins. They caused his death; for them he shed his blood; to make expiation for them, and to wipe them away, he expired on the cross. This passage is full proof that Christ did not die merely as a martyr, but that his death was to make atonement for sin. That he died as an atoning sacrifice, or as a vicarious offering, is here declared by Paul to be among the *first* things that he taught; and the grand fundamental truth on which the church at Corinth had been founded, and by which it had been established, and by which they would be saved. It follows that there can be no true church, and no well-founded hope of salvation, where the doctrine is not held that Christ died for sin. ¶ *According to the Scriptures.* The writings of the Old Testament; Note, John v. 39. It is, of course, not certain to what parts of the Old Testament Paul here refers. He teaches simply that the doctrine is contained there that the Messiah would die for sin; and, in his preaching, he doubtless adduced and dwelt upon the particular places. *Some* of the places where this is taught are the following: Psa. xxii; Isa. liii; Dan. ix. 26; Zech. xii. 10; comp. Luke xxiv. 26, 46. See also Hengstenberg's Christology of the O. T. vol. i. pp. 187, 216, translated by Keith.

4. *And that he was buried.* That is, evidently according to the Scriptures; see Isa. liii. 9. ¶ *And that he rose again the third day,* &c. That is, that he should rise from the dead was foretold in the Scriptures. It is not of necessity implied that it was predicted that he should rise *on the third day,* but that he should rise from the dead. See the argument for this stated in the discourse of Peter, in Acts ii. 24—32. The particular passage which is there urged in proof of his resurrection is derived from Ps. xvi.

5. *And that he was seen of Cephas.* Peter; Note, John i. 42. The resurrection of Christ was *a fact* to be proved, like all other facts, by competent and credible witnesses. Paul, therefore, appeals to the witnesses who had attested, or who yet lived to attest, the truth of the resurrection of the Lord Jesus; and shows that it was not possible that so many witnesses should have been deceived. As this was not the first time in which the evidence had been stated to them, and as his purpose was merely to *remind* them of what they had heard and believed, he does not adduce *all* the witnesses to the event, but refers only to the more important ones. He does not, therefore, mention the woman to whom the Saviour first appeared, nor does he refer to *all* the times when the Lord Jesus manifested himself to his disciples. But he does not refer to them in *general* merely, but mentions *names,* and refers to persons who *were then alive,* who could attest the truth of the resurrection. It may be observed, also, that Paul observes probably the exact *order* in which the Lord Jesus appeared to the disciples, though he does not mention *all* the instances. For an account of the persons to whom the Lord Jesus appeared after his resurrection, and the order in which it was done, see Notes on the Gospels, vol. i. pp. 333—336. ¶ *Then of the twelve.* The apostles; still called "the twelve," though Judas was not one of them. It was common to call the apostles "the twelve." Jesus appeared to the apostles at one time in the absence of Thomas (John xx. 19, 24); and also to them when Thomas was present, John xx. 24—29.

above five hundred brethren at once; of whom the greater part remain unto this present, but some are fallen asleep.

Probably Paul here refers to the latter occasion, when all the surviving apostles were present.

6. *Above five hundred brethren at once.* More than five hundred Christians or followers of Jesus at one time. This was *probably* in Galilee, where the Lord Jesus had spent the greater part of his public ministry, and where he had made most disciples. The place, however, is not designated, and, of course, cannot be known. It is remarkable that this fact is omitted by all the evangelists; but why they should have omitted so remarkable a proof of the resurrection of the Lord Jesus, is unknown. There is a slight circumstance hinted at in Mat. xxviii. 10, which may throw some light on this passage. After his resurrection, Jesus said to the women who were at the sepulchre, "Go tell my brethren that they go into Galilee, and there shall they see me." And in ver. 16 it is said, "The eleven disciples went away into Galilee, into a mountain where Jesus had appointed them." Jesus had spent most of his public life in Galilee. He had made most of his disciples there. It was proper, therefore, that those disciples, who would, of course, hear of his death, should have some public confirmation of the fact that he had risen. It is very probable, also, that the eleven who went down into Galilee after he rose would apprize the brethren there of what had been said to them, that Jesus would meet them on a certain mountain; and it is morally certain that they who had followed him in so great numbers in Galilee would be drawn together by the report that the Lord Jesus, who had been put to death, was about to be seen there again alive. Such is human nature, and such was the attachment of these disciples to the Lord Jesus, that it is morally certain a large concourse would assemble on the slightest rumour that such an occurrence was to happen. Nothing more would be necessary anywhere to draw a concourse of people than a rumour that one who was dead would appear again; and in this instance, where they ardently loved him, and when, perhaps, many believed that he would rise, they would naturally assemble in great numbers to see him once more. One thing is proved by this, that the Lord Jesus had many more disciples than is generally supposed. If there were five hundred who could be assembled at once in a single part of the land where he had preached, there is every reason to suppose that there were many more in other parts of Judea. ¶ *The greater part remain unto this present.* Are now alive, and can be appealed to, in proof that they saw him. What more conclusive argument for the truth of his resurrection *could* there be than that five hundred persons had seen him, who had been intimately acquainted with him in his life, and who had become his followers? If the testimony of five hundred could not avail to prove his resurrection, no number of witnesses could. And if five hundred men could thus be deceived, any number could; and it would be impossible to substantiate *any* simple matter of fact by the testimony of eye-witnesses. ¶ *But some are fallen asleep.* Have died. This is the usual expression employed in the Scripture to describe the death of saints. It denotes, (1.) The calmness and peace with which they die, like sinking into a gentle sleep; (2.) The hope of a resurrection, as we sink to sleep with the expectation of again awaking: see Note, John xi. 11; 1 Cor. 11. 30.

7. *After that, he was seen of James.* This appearance is not recorded by the evangelists. It is mentioned in the fragment of the apocryphal gospel according to the Hebrews, which is, however, of no authority. It is probable that the Lord Jesus appeared often to the disciples, as he was forty days on earth after his resurrection, and the evangelists have only mentioned the more prominent instances, and enough to substantiate the fact of his resurrection. This

7 After that, he was seen of
James; then of all the apostles.
8 And last [a] of all, he was seen
of me also, as of [1] one born out of
due time.
9 For I am the least [b] of the

a Acts 9.17.

1 or, *an abortive*. b Eph.3.7,8.

James, the fathers say, was James the Less, the brother or cousin-german of the Lord Jesus. The other James was dead (see Acts xii. 1) when this epistle was written. This James, the author of the epistle that bears his name, was stationed in Jerusalem. When Paul went there, after his return from Arabia, he had an interview with James (see Gal. i. 19, "But other of the apostles saw I none, save James the Lord's brother"), and it is highly probable that Paul would state to him the vision which he had of the Lord Jesus on his way to Damascus, and that James also would state to Paul the fact that *he* had seen him after he rose. This may be the reason why Paul here mentions the fact, because he had it from the lips of James himself. ¶ *Then of all the apostles.* By all the apostles. Perhaps the occasion at the sea of Galilee, recorded in John xxi. 14. Or it is possible that he frequently met the apostles assembled together, and that Paul means to say, that during the forty days after his resurrection he was often seen by them.

8. *And last of all.* After all the other times in which he appeared to men; after he had ascended to heaven. This passage proves that the apostle Paul saw the same Lord Jesus, the same *body* which had been seen by the others, or else his assertion would be no proof that he was risen from the dead. It was not a fancy, therefore, that he had seen him; it was not the work of imagination; it was not even a *revelation* that he had risen; it was a real *vision* of the ascended Redeemer. ¶ *He was seen of me also.* On the way to Damascus, see Acts ix. 3—6, 17. ¶ *As of one born out of due time.* Marg. Or, *an abortive.* Our translation, to most readers, probably, would not convey the real meaning of this place. The expression, "as of one born out of due time," would seem to imply that Paul meant to say that there was some unfitness *as to the time* when he saw the Lord Jesus; or that it was *too late* to have as clear and satisfactory a view of him as those had who saw him before his ascension. But this is by no means the idea in the passage. The word here used (ἔκτρωμα) properly means an abortion, one born prematurely. It is found no where else in the New Testament; and here it means, as the following verse shows, one that was *exceedingly unworthy;* that was not worth regard; that was unfit to be employed in the service of the Lord Jesus; that had the same relation to that which was worthy of the apostolic office which an abortion has to a living child. The word occurs (in the Septuagint) in Job iii. 16; Eccl. vi. 3, as the translation of נֵפֶל, *nephel*, an abortion, or untimely birth. The expression seems to be proverbial, and to denote any thing that is vile, offensive, loathsome, unworthy; see Num. xii. 11. The word, I think, has no reference to the mode of *training* of the apostle, as if he had not had the same opportunity as the others had, and was therefore, compared with their advantages, like an untimely child compared with one that had come to maturity before its birth, as Bloomfield supposes; nor does it refer to his diminutive stature, as Wetstein supposes; but it means that he felt himself *vile*, guilty, unworthy, abominable as a persecutor, and as unworthy to be an apostle. The verse following shows that this is the sense in which the word is used.

9. *For.* A reason for the appellation which he had given to himself in ver. 8. ¶ *I am the least of the apostles.* Not on account of any defect in his commission, or any want of qualification to bear witness in what he saw, but on account of *the* great crime of his life, the fact that he had been a persecutor. Paul could never forget that; as a man who has been profane

apostles, that am not meet to be called an apostle, because I persecuted the church of God.

10 But by the grace of God I am what I am: and his grace which *was bestowed* upon me was not in vain; but I laboured more abundantly than they all: yet not I, [a] but the grace of God which was with me.

a Matt.10.20.

and a scoffer, when he becomes converted, can never forget the deep guilt of his former life. The effect will be to produce humility, and a deep sense of unworthiness, ever onward. ¶ *Am not meet to be called an apostle.* Am not fit to be regarded as a follower of the Lord Jesus, and as appointed to defend his cause, and to bear his name among the Gentiles. Paul had a deep sense of his unworthiness; and the memory of his former life tended ever to keep him humble. Such should be, and such will be, the effect of the remembrance of a life of sin on those who become converted to the gospel, and especially if they are intrusted with the high office of the ministry, and occupy a station of importance in the church of God. ¶ *Because I persecuted the church of God;* see Acts ix. It is evident, however, that deeply as Paul might feel his unworthiness, and his unfitness to be called an apostle, yet that this did not render him an incompetent *witness* of what he had seen. He was unworthy; but he had no doubt that he had seen the Lord Jesus; and amidst all the expressions of his deep sense of his unfitness for his office, he never once intimates the slightest doubt that he had seen the Saviour. He felt himself fully qualified to testify to that; and with unwavering firmness he *did* testify to it to the end of life. A man may be deeply sensible that he is unworthy of an elevated station or office, and yet not the *less* qualified to be a witness. Humility does not disqualify a man to give testimony, but rather furnishes an additional qualification. There is no man to whom we listen more attentively, or whose words we more readily believe, than the modest and humble man,—the man who has had abundant opportunities to observe that of which he testifies, and yet who is deeply humble. Such a man was the apostle Paul; and he evidently felt that, much as he felt his unworthiness, and ready as he was to confess it, yet his testimony on the subject of the resurrection of the Lord Jesus ought to have, and would have, great weight in the church at Corinth; comp. Note on Acts ix. 19.

10. *But by the grace of God I am what I am.* By the *favour* or mercy of God. What I have is to be traced to him, and not to any native tendency to goodness, or any native inclination to his service, or to any merit of my own. All my hopes of heaven; all my zeal; all my success; all my piety; all my apostolic endowments, are to be traced to him. Nothing is more common in the writings of Paul, than a disposition to trace all that he had to the *mere* mercy and grace of God. And nothing is a more certain indication of true piety than such a disposition. The reason why Paul *here* introduces the subject seems to be this. He had incidentally, and undesignedly, introduced a comparison *in one respect* between himself and the other apostles. He had not had the advantages which they had. Most of all, he was overwhelmed with the recollection that he had been a persecutor. He felt, therefore, that there was a peculiar obligation resting on him to make up by diligence for the want of their advantages of an early personal conversation with the Lord Jesus, and to express his gratitude that so great a sinner had been made an apostle. He, therefore, says, that he had not been idle. He had been enabled by the grace of God, to labour more than all the rest, and he had thus shown that he had not been insensible of his obligations. ¶ *But I laboured more abundantly,* &c. I was more diligent in preaching; I encountered more perils: I have exerted myself more. The records of his life, compared with the records of the other apostles, fully show this. ¶ *Yet*

11 Therefore whether *it were* I or they, so we preach, and so ye believed.

12 Now if Christ be preached that he rose from the dead, how [a] say some among you that there is no resurrection of the dead?

13 But if [b] there be no resurrec-

a Acts 26.8. *b* 1 Thess.4.14.

not I. I do not attribute it to myself. I would not boast of it. The *fact* is plain, and undeniable, that I *have* so laboured. But I would not attribute it to myself. I would not be proud or vain. I would remember my former state; would remember that I was a persecutor; would remember that all my disposition to labour, and all my ability, and all my success, are to be traced to the mere favour and mercy of God. So every man who has just views feels who has been favoured with success in the ministry. If a man has been successful as a preacher; if he has been self-denying, laborious, and the instrument of good, he cannot be insensible to the fact, and it would be foolish affectation to pretend ignorance of it. But he may feel that it is all owing to the mere mercy of God; and the effect will be to produce humility and gratitude, not pride and self-complacency.

11. *Therefore, whether* it were *I or they.* I or the other apostles. It is comparatively immaterial by whom it was done. The establishment of the truth is the great matter; and the question by whom it is done is one of secondary importance. ¶ *So we preach.* So we all preach. We all defend the same great doctrines; we all insist on the fact that the Lord Jesus died and rose; and this doctrine you all have believed. This doctrine is confirmed by *all* who preach; and this enters into the faith of *all* who believe. The design of Paul is to affirm that the doctrines which he here refers to were great, undeniable, and fundamental doctrines of Christianity; that they were proclaimed by *all* the ministers of the gospel, and believed by *all* Christians. They were, therefore, immensely important to all; and they must enter essentially into the hopes of all.

12. *Now if Christ,* &c. Paul, having (ver. 1—11) stated the *direct* evidence for the resurrection of the Lord Jesus, proceeds here to demonstrate that the dead would rise, by showing how it followed from the fact that the Lord Jesus had risen, and by showing what consequences would follow from denying it. The whole argument is based on the fact that the Lord Jesus had risen. If *that* was admitted, he shows that it *must* follow that his people would also rise. ¶ *Be preached.* The word *preached* here seems to include the idea of *so* preaching as to be believed; or so as to *demonstrate* that he did rise. If this was the doctrine on which the church was based, that the Lord Jesus rose from the dead, how could the resurrection of the dead be denied? ¶ *How say.* How can any say; how can it be maintained? ¶ *Some among you.* See the introduction to the chapter. Who these were is unknown. They may have been some of the philosophic Greeks, who spurned the doctrine of the resurrection (see Acts xvii. 32); or they may have been some followers of Sadducean teachers; or it may be that the Gnostic philosophy had corrupted them. It is most probable, I think, that the denial of the resurrection was the result of reasoning after the manner of the Greeks, and the effect of the introduction of philosophy into the church. This has been the fruitful source of most of the errors which have been introduced into the church. ¶ *That there is no resurrection of the dead.* That the dead cannot rise. How can it be held that there *can* be no resurrection, while yet it is admitted that Christ rose? The argument here is twofold. (1.) That Christ rose was one *instance* of a fact which demonstrated that there *had been* a resurrection, and of course that it was possible. (2.) That such was the connection between Christ and his people that the admission of this fact involved also the doc-

tion of the dead, then is Christ not risen.

14 And if [a] Christ be not risen, then *is* our preaching vain, and your faith *is* also vain.

15 Yea, and we are found false

a Acts 17.31.

trine that all his people would also rise. This argument Paul states at length in the following verses. It was probably held by them that the resurrection was *impossible.* To all this, Paul answers in accordance with the principles of inductive philosophy as now understood, by demonstrating *a fact,* and showing that such an event *had* occurred, and that consequently all the difficulties were met. Facts are unanswerable demonstrations; and when a fact is established, all the obstacles and difficulties in the way must be admitted to be overcome. So philosophers now reason; and Paul, in accordance with these just principles, laboured simply to establish *the fact* that one had been raised, and thus met at once all the objections which could be urged against the doctrine. It would have been most in accordance with the philosophy of the Greeks to have gone into a metaphysical discussion to show that it was not impossible or absurd, and this might have been done. It was most in accordance with the principles of true philosophy, however, to establish *the fact* at once, and to argue *from* that, and thus to meet all the difficulties at once. The doctrine of the resurrection, therefore, does not rest on a metaphysical subtilty; it does not depend on human reasoning; it does not depend on analogy; it rests just as the sciences of astronomy, chemistry, anatomy, botany, and natural philosophy do, *on well ascertained facts;* and it is now a well understood principle of all true science that no difficulty, no obstacle, no metaphysical subtilty; no embarrassment about being able to see HOW it is, is to be allowed to destroy the conviction in the mind which the facts are fitted to produce.

13. *But if there be no resurrection of the dead.* If the whole subject is held to be impossible and absurd, then it must follow that Christ is not risen, since there were the same difficulties in the way of raising him up which will exist in any case. He was dead and was buried. He had lain in the grave three days. His human soul had left the body. His frame had become cold and stiff. The blood had ceased to circulate, and the lungs to heave. In his case there was the same difficulty in raising him up to life that there is in any other; and if it is held to be impossible and absurd that the dead should rise, then it must follow that Christ has not been raised. This is the first consequence which Paul states as resulting from the denial of this doctrine, and this is inevitable. Paul thus shows them that the denial of the doctrine, or the maintaining the general proposition "that the dead would not rise," led also to the denial of the *fact* that the Lord Jesus had risen, and consequently to the denial of Christianity altogether, and the annihilation of all their hopes. There was, moreover, such a close connection between Christ and his people, that the resurrection of the Lord Jesus made their resurrection certain. See 1 Thess. iv. 14; see Note, John xiv. 19.

14. *And if Christ is not risen, then is our preaching vain.* Another consequence which must follow if it be held that there was no resurrection, and consequently that Christ was not risen. It would be vain and useless to preach. The substance of their preaching was that Christ was raised up; and all their preaching was based on that. If that were not true, the whole system was false, and Christianity was an imposition. The word *vain* here seems to include the idea of useless, idle, false. It would be *false* to affirm that the Christian system was from heaven; it would be useless to proclaim such a system, as it could save no one. ¶ *And your faith is also vain.* It is useless to believe. It can be of no advantage. If Christ was not raised, he was an impostor, since he repeatedly declared that he would rise (Mat. xvi. 21;

witnesses of God; because we have testified of God that he raised up Christ: whom he raised not up, if so be that the dead rise not.

16 For if the dead rise not, then is not Christ raised:

17 And if Christ be not raised, your faith [a] *is* vain; ye are yet in your sins.

18 Then they also which are fallen asleep in Christ are perished.

a Rom.4.25.

xviii. 22, 23; Luke ix. 22), and since the whole of his religion depended on that. The system could not be true unless Christ had been raised, as he said he would be; and to believe a false system could be of no use to any man. The argument here is one addressed to all their feelings, their hopes, and their belief. It is drawn from all their convictions that the system was true. Were they, could they be prepared to admit a doctrine which involved the consequence that all the evidences which they had that the apostles preached the truth were delusive, and that all the evidences of the truth of Christianity which had affected their minds and won their hearts were false and deceptive? If they were not prepared for this, then it followed that they should not abandon or doubt the doctrine of the resurrection of the dead.

15. *Yea, and we are found.* We are; or we shall be proved to be. It will follow, if the Lord Jesus was not raised up, that we have been false witnesses. ¶ *Of God.* Respecting God. It will be found that we have affirmed that which is not true of God; or have said that he has done that which he has not done. Nothing could be regarded as a greater crime than this, whatever might be the immediate subject under consideration. To bear false witness of a man, or to say that a man has done what he has not done, is regarded as a grievous crime. How much more so to bear false testimony of God! ¶ *Because we have testified of God.* Or rather *against* God (κάτὰ τοῦ ϑεοῦ). Our evidence has been *against* him. We have affirmed that which is not true; and tnis is *against* God. It is implied here that it would be a *crime* to testify that God had raised up the Lord Jesus if he had not done it; or that it would be affirming that of God which would be *against* his character, or which it would be improper for him to do. This would be so, (1.) Because it would be wrong to bear *any* false witness of God, or to affirm that he had done what he had not done; (2.) Because *if* the Lord Jesus had not been raised up, it would prove that he was an *impostor,* since he had declared that he would be raised up; and to affirm of God that he had raised up an impostor would be *against* him, and would be highly dishonourable to him. ¶ *If the dead rise not.* If there is, and can be no resurrection. If this general proposition is true that there can be no resurrection, then it will apply to Christ as well as any others, and must prove that he did not rise. The *argument* in this verse is this. (1.) If it was denied that Christ was raised, it would prove that all the apostles were false witnesses of the worst character; false witnesses against God. (2.) This the apostle seems to have presumed they *could not* believe. They had had too many evidences that they spoke the truth; they had seen their uniform respect *for* God, and desire to bear witness of him and in his favour; they had had too conclusive evidence that they were inspired by him, and had the power of working miracles; they were too fully convinced of their honesty, truth, and piety, ever to believe that they could be false witnesses against God. They had had ample opportunity to know whether God did raise up the Lord Jesus; and they were witnesses who had no inducement to bear a false witness in the case.

16. *For if the dead rise not,* &c. This is a repetition of what is said in ver. 13. It is repeated here, evidently, because of its importance. It was a

great and momentous truth which would *bear* repetition, that if there was no resurrection, as some held, then it would follow that the Lord Jesus was not raised up.

17. *Your faith is vain*, ver. 14. The meaning of this passage here is, that their faith was vain, *because*, if Christ was not raised up, they were yet unpardoned sinners. The pardon of sin was connected with the belief of the resurrection of the Lord Jesus, and, if he was not raised, they were still in a state of sin. ¶ *Ye are yet in your sins.* Your sins are yet unpardoned. They can be forgiven only by faith in him, and by the efficacy of his blood. But if he was not raised, he was an impostor; and, of course, all your hopes of pardon by him, and through him, must be vain. The argument in this verse consists in an appeal to their Christian experience and their hopes. It may be thus expressed: (1.) You have reason to believe that your sins are forgiven. You cherish that belief on evidence that is satisfactory to you. But if Christ is not raised, that cannot be true. He was an impostor, and sins cannot be forgiven by him. As you are not, and cannot be prepared to admit that your sins are not forgiven, you cannot admit a doctrine which involves that. (2.) You have evidence that you are not under the dominion of sin. You have repented of it; have forsaken it; and are leading a holy life. You know that, and cannot be induced to doubt this fact. But all that is to be traced to the doctrine that the Lord Jesus rose from the dead. It is only by believing that, and the doctrines which are connected with it, that the power of sin in the heart has been destroyed. And as you *cannot* doubt that under the influence of *that truth* you have been enabled to break off from your sins, so you cannot admit a doctrine which would involve it as a consequence that you are yet under the condemnation and the dominion of sin. You *must* believe, therefore, that the Lord Jesus rose; and that, if he rose, others will also. This argument is good also now, just so far as there is evidence that, through the belief of a risen Saviour, the dominion of sin has been broken; and every Christian is, therefore, in an important sense, a witness of the resurrection of the Lord Jesus,—a living proof that a system which can work so great changes, and produce such evidence that sins are forgiven as are furnished in the conversion of sinners, must be from God; and, of course, that the work of the Lord Jesus was accepted, and that he was raised up from the dead.

18. *Then they also*, &c. This verse contains a statement of another consequence which must follow from the denial of the resurrection—that all Christians who had died had failed of salvation, and were destroyed. ¶ *Which are fallen asleep in Christ.* Which have died as Christians; Note, ver. 6; 1 Thess. iv. 15. ¶ *Are perished.* Are destroyed; are not saved. They hoped to have been saved by the merits of the Lord Jesus; they trusted to a risen Saviour, and fixed all their hopes of heaven there; but if he did not rise, of course the whole system was delusion, and they have failed of heaven, and been destroyed. Their bodies lie in the grave, and return to their native dust without the prospect of a resurrection, and their souls are destroyed. The *argument* here is mainly an appeal to their feelings: "Can you believe it possible that the good men who have believed in the Lord Jesus are destroyed? Can you believe that your best friends, your kindred, and your fellow Christians who have died, have gone down to perdition? Can you believe that they will sink to woe with the impenitent, and the polluted, and abandoned? If you *cannot*, then it must follow that they are saved. And then it will follow that you *cannot* embrace a doctrine which involves this consequence." And this argument is a sound one still. There are multitudes who are made good men by the gospel. They are holy, humble, self-denying, and prayerful friends of God. *They have become such by the belief of the death and resurrection of the Lord Jesus.* Can it be believed that they

19 If in this life only we have hope in Christ, we [a] are of all men most miserable.

20 But now is [b] Christ risen from the dead, *and* become the first-fruits [c] of them that slept.

a John 16.2; chap.4.13; 2 Tim.3.12.

b 1 Pet.1.3. c Acts 26.23; Col.1.18; Rev.1.5

will be destroyed? That they will perish with the profane, and licentious, and unprincipled? That they will go down to dwell with the polluted and the wicked? "Shall not the Judge of all the earth do right?" Gen. viii. 25. If it *cannot* be so believed, then they will be saved; and *if* saved it follows that the system is true which saves them, and, of course, that the Lord Jesus rose from the dead. We may remark here, that a denial of the truth of Christianity involves the belief that its friends will perish with others; that all their hopes are vain; and that their expectations are delusive. He, therefore, who becomes an infidel *believes* that his pious friends —his sainted father, his holy mother, his lovely Christian sister or child, is deluded and deceived; that they will sink down to the grave to rise no more; that their hopes of heaven will all vanish, and that they will be destroyed with the profane, the impure, and the sensual. And if infidelity demands *this* faith of its votaries, it is a system which strikes at the very happiness of social life, and at all our convictions of what is true and right. It is a system that is withering and blighting to the best hopes of men. *Can* it be believed that God will destroy those who are living to his honour; who are pure in heart, and lovely in life, *and who have been made such by the Christian religion?* If it cannot, then every man knows that Christianity *is not false*, and that infidelity IS NOT TRUE.

19. *If in this life only we have hope in Christ.* If our hope in Christ shall not be followed by the resurrection of the dead and future glory, and if all our hopes shall be disappointed. ¶ *We are*, &c. Doddridge, Macknight, Grotius, and some others, suppose that this refers to the apostles only, and that the sense is, that if there was no resurrection, they, of all men, would be most to be pitied, since they had exposed themselves to such a variety of dangers and trials, in which nothing could sustain them but the hope of immortality. If they failed in that they failed in every thing. They were regarded as the most vile of the human family; they suffered more from persecution, poverty, and perils than other men; and if, after all, they were to be deprived of all their hopes, and disappointed in their expectation of the resurrection, their condition would be more deplorable than that of any other men. But there is no good reason for supposing that the word "we," here, is to be limited to the apostles. For, (1.) Paul had not mentioned the apostles particularly in the previous verses; and, (2.) The argument demands that it should be understood of all Christians, and the declaration is as true, substantially, of all Christians as it was of the apostles. ¶ *Of all men most miserable.* More to be pitied or commiserated than any other class of men. The word here used (ἐλεεινότεροι) means, properly, more deserving of pity, more pitiable. It *may* mean sometimes, more wretched or unhappy; but this is not necessarily its meaning, nor is it its meaning here. It refers rather to their condition and hopes than to their personal feeling; and does not mean that Christians are unhappy, or that their religion does not produce comfort, but that their condition would be most deplorable; they would be more deserving of pity than any other class of men. This would be, (1.) Because no other men had so elevated hopes, and, of course, no others could experience so great disappointment. (2.) They were subjected to more trials than any other class of men. They were persecuted and reviled, and subjected to toil, and privation, and want, on account of their religion; and if, after all, they were to be disappointed, their condition was truly deplorable. (3.) They do not indulge in the pleasures of this life; they do not give themselves, as others do, to the enjoyments of this world. They volun-

tarily subject themselves to trial and self-denial; and if they are not admitted to eternal life, they are not only disappointed in this but they are cut off from the sources of happiness which their fellow-men enjoy in this world.—*Calvin.* (4.) On the whole, therefore, there would be disappointed hopes, and trials, and poverty, and want, and all for naught; and no condition could be conceived to be more deplorable than where a man was looking for eternal life, and for it subjecting himself to a life of want, and poverty, persecution, and tears, and should be finally disappointed. This passage, therefore, does not mean that virtue and piety are not attended with happiness; it does not mean that, even if there were no future state, a man would not be more happy if he walked in the paths of virtue than if he lived a life of sin; it does not mean that the Christian has no happiness in *religion itself*—in the love of God, and in prayer, and praise, and in purity of life. In all this he has enjoyment; and even if there were *no* heaven, a life of virtue and piety would be more happy than a life of sin. But it means that the condition of the Christian would be more *deplorable* than that of other men; he would be more to be pitied. All his high hopes would be disappointed. Other men have no such hopes to be dashed to the ground; and, of course, no other men would be such objects of pity and compassion. The *argument* in this verse is derived from the high hopes of the Christian. "Could they believe that all their hopes were to be frustrated? Could they subject themselves to all these trials and privations, without believing that they would rise from the dead? Were they prepared, by the denial of the doctrine of the resurrection, to put themselves in the condition of the most miserable and wretched of the human family—to *admit* that they were in a condition most to be deplored?

20. *But now is Christ risen,* &c. This language is the bursting forth of a full heart and of overpowering conviction. It would seem as if Paul were *impatient* of the slow process of argument; weary of meeting objections, and of stating the consequences of a denial of the doctrine; and longing to give utterance *to what he knew,* that Christ was risen from the dead. That was a point on which he was certain. He had seen him after he was risen; and he could no more doubt this fact than he could any other which he had witnessed with his own eyes. He makes, therefore, this strong affirmation; and in doing it, he at the same time affirms that the dead will also rise, since he had shown (ver. 12—18) that all the objection to the doctrine of the resurrection was removed by the *fact* that Christ had risen, and had shown that *his* resurrection involved the certainty that his people also would rise. There is peculiar force in the word "*now*" in this verse. The meaning may be thus expressed: "I have showed the consequences which would follow from the supposition that Christ was not raised up. I have shown how it would destroy all our hopes, plunge us into grief, annihilate our faith, make our preaching vain, and involve us in the belief that our pious friends have perished, and that we are yet in our sins. I have shown how it would produce the deepest disappointment and misery. *But* all this was mere supposition. There is no reason to apprehend any such consequences, or to be thus alarmed. *Christ* is *risen.* Of that there is no doubt. That is not to be called in question. It is established by irrefragable testimony; and *consequently* our hopes are not vain, our faith is not useless, our pious friends have not perished, and we shall not be disappointed." ¶ *And become the first-fruits.* The word rendered *first-fruits* (ἀπαρχὴ) occurs in the New Testament in the following places; Rom. viii. 23. (see Note on this place); xi. 16; xvi. 5; 1 Cor. xv. 20, 23; xvi. 15; James i. 18; Rev. xiv. 4. It occurs often in the LXX. as the translation of חלב, *ehlab, fat,* or fatness (Num. xviii. 12, 29, 30, 32); as the translation of מעשר, *moshar,* the tenth or tithe (Deut. xii. 6); of עון, *shoon,* iniquity (Num. xviii. 1); of ראשית, *rashith,* the beginning, the commencement, the first (Ex. xxiii. 19; Lev. xxiii. 10; Num. xv. 18, 19, &c.):

21 For [a] since by man *came* death, [b] by man *came* also the resurrection of the dead.

22 For as in Adam all die, even so in Christ shall all be made alive.

a Rom.5.12,17. *b* John 11.25.

of תרומה, *tharoomeh,* oblation, offering; lifting up; of that which is lifted up or waved as the first sheaf of the harvest, &c. Ex. xxv. 2, 3; xxxv. 5; Num. v. 9; xviii. 8, &c. The first-fruits, or the first sheaf of ripe grain, was required to be offered to the Lord, and was waved before him by the priest, as expressing the sense of gratitude by the husbandman, and his recognition of the fact that God had a right to all that he had; Lev. xxiii. 10—14. The word, therefore, comes to have two senses, or to involve two ideas: (1.) That which is *first,* the beginning, or that which has the priority of time; and, (2.) That which is a part and portion of the whole which is to follow, and which is the earnest or pledge of that; as the first sheaf of ripe grain was not only the *first* in order of time, but was the earnest or pledge of the entire harvest which was soon to succeed. In allusion to this, Paul uses the word here. It was not merely or mainly that Christ was the first in order of time that rose from the dead, for Lazarus and the widow's son had been raised before him; but it was that he was chief in regard to the dignity, value, and importance of his rising; he was connected with all that should rise, as the first sheaf of the harvest was with the crop; he was *a part* of the mighty harvest of the resurrection, and his rising was *a portion* of that great rising, as the sheaf was a portion of the harvest itself; and he was so connected with them all, and their rising so depended on his, that his resurrection was a demonstration that they would rise. It may also be implied here, as Grotius and Schoettgen have remarked, that he is the first of those who were raised *so* as not to die again; and that, therefore, those raised by Elisha and by the Saviour himself do not come into the account. They all died again; but the Saviour will not die, nor will those whom he will raise up in the resurrection die any more. He is, therefore, the first of those that thus rise, and a portion of that great host which shall be raised to die no more. *May* there not be another idea? The first sheaf of the harvest was consecrated to God, and *then* all the harvest was regarded as consecrated to him. May it not be implied that, by the resurrection of the Lord Jesus, *all* those of whom he speaks are regarded as sacred to God, and as consecrated and accepted by the resurrection and acceptance of him who was the first-fruits? ¶ *Of them that slept.* Of the pious dead; Note, ver. 6.

21. *For since by man came death.* By Adam, or by means of his transgression; see ver. 22. The sense is, evidently, that in consequence of the sin of Adam all men die, or are subjected to temporal death. Or, in other words, man would not have died had it not been for the crime of the first man; see Note on Rom. v. 12. This passage may be regarded as proof that death would not have entered the world had it not been for transgression; or, in other words, if man had not sinned, he would have remained immortal on the earth, or would have been translated to heaven, as Enoch and Elijah were, without seeing death. The apostle here, by "man," undoubtedly refers to Adam; but the particular and specific idea which he intends to insist on is, that, as death came by human nature, or by a human being, by a man, so it was important and proper that immortality, or freedom from death, should come in the same way, by one who was a man. Man introduced death; man also would recover from death. The evil was introduced by one man; the recovery would be by another. ¶ *By man* came *also.* By the Lord Jesus, the Son of God in human nature. The resurrection came by him, because he first rose—first of those who should not again die; because he proclaimed the doctrine, and placed it on a firm foundation; and because by his power the

dead will be raised up. Thus he came to counteract the evils of the fall, and to restore man to more than his primeval dignity and honour. The resurrection through Christ will be with the assurance that all who are raised up by him shall never die again.

22. *For as in Adam* (ἐν τῷ Ἀδὰμ). By Adam; by the act, or by means of Adam; as a consequence of his act. His deed was the procuring cause, or the reason, why all are subjected to temporal death; see Gen. iii. 19. It does not mean that all men became actually dead when he sinned, for they had not then an existence; but it must mean that the death of all can be traced to him as the procuring cause, and that his act made it certain that all that came into the world would be mortal. The sentence which went forth against him (Gen. iii. 19) went forth against all; affected all; involved all in the certainty of death; as the sentence that was passed on the serpent (Gen. iii. 14) made it certain that all serpents would be "cursed above all cattle," and be prone upon the earth; the sentence that was passed upon the woman (Gen. iii. 16) made it certain that all women would be subjected to the same condition of suffering to which Eve was subjected; and the sentence that was passed on man (Gen. iii. 17) that he should cultivate the ground in sorrow all the days of his life, that it should bring forth thistles and thorns to him (ver. 18), that he should eat bread in the sweat of his brow (ver. 19), made it certain that this would be the condition of all men as well as of Adam. It was a blow at the head of the human family, and they were subjected to the same train of evils as he was himself. In like manner they were subjected to death. It was done in Adam, or *by* Adam, in the same way as it was in him, or by him, that they were subjected to toil, and to the necessity of procuring food by the sweat of the brow; see Notes, Rom. v. 12—19; see ver. 47, 48. ¶ *All die.* All mankind are subjected to temporal death; or are mortal. This passage has been often adduced to prove that all mankind became sinful in Adam, or in virtue of a covenant transaction with him; and that they are subjected to spiritual death as a punishment for his sins. But, whatever may be the truth on that subject, it is clear that *this* passage does not relate to it, and should not be adduced as a proof text For, (1.) The words *die* and *dieth* obviously and usually refer to temporal death; and they should be so understood, unless there is something in the connection which requires us to understand them in a figurative and metaphorical sense. But there is, evidently, no such necessity here. (2.) The context requires us to understand this as relating to temporal death. There is not here, as there is in Rom. v., any intimation that men became sinners in consequence of the transgression of Adam, nor does the course of the apostle's argument require him to make any statement on that subject. His argument has reference to the subject of temporal death, and the resurrection of the dead; and not to the question in what way men became sinners. (3.) The whole of this argument relates to the *resurrection of the dead.* That is the main, the leading, the exclusive point. He is demonstrating that the dead would rise. He is showing how this would be done. It became, therefore, important for him to show in what way men were subjected to temporal death. His argument, therefore, requires him to make a statement *on that point,* and that only; and to show that the resurrection by Christ was adapted to meet and overcome the evils of the death to which men were subjected by the sin of the first man. In Rom. v. the design of Paul is to prove that the effects of the work of Christ were more than sufficient to meet ALL the evils introduced by the sin of Adam. This leads him to an examination *there* of the question in what way men became sinners. *Here* the design is to show that the work of Christ is adapted to overcome the evils of the sin of Adam *in one specific matter—the matter under discussion, i. e.* on the point of the resurrection; and his argument therefore requires him to show *only* that temporal death, or mortality, was

introduced by the first man, and that this has been counteracted by the second; and to this specific point the interpretation of this passage should be confined. Nothing is more important in interpreting the Bible than to ascertain the specific point in the argument of a writer to be defended or illustrated, and *then* to confine the interpretation to that. The argument of the apostle here is ample to prove that all men are subjected to temporal death by the sin of Adam; and that this evil is counteracted fully by the resurrection of Christ, and the resurrection through him. And to this point the passage should be limited. (4.) If this passage means, that in Adam, or by him, all men became sinners, then the correspondent declaration "all shall be made alive" must mean that all men shall become righteous, or that all shall be saved. This would be the natural and obvious interpretation; since the words "be made alive" must have reference to the words "all die," and must affirm the co-relative and opposite fact. If the phrase "all die" there means all become sinners, then the phrase "all be made alive" must mean all shall be made holy, or be recovered from their spiritual death; and thus an *obvious* argument is furnished for the doctrine of universal salvation, which it is difficult, if not impossible, to meet. It is not a sufficient answer to this to say, that the word "all," in the latter part of the sentence, means all the elect, or all the righteous; for its most natural and obvious meaning is, that it is co-extensive with the word "all" in the former part of the verse. And although it has been held by many who suppose that the passage refers only to the resurrection of the dead, that it means that all the righteous shall be raised up, or all who are given to Christ, yet that interpretation is not the obvious one, nor is it yet sufficiently clear to make it the basis of an argument, or to meet the strong argument which the advocate of universal salvation will derive from the former interpretation of the passage. It *is* true *literally* that ALL the dead will rise; it is *not* true literally that all who became mortal, or became sinners by means of Adam, will be saved. And it must be held as a great principle, that this passage is *not* to be so interpreted as to teach the doctrine of the salvation of all men. At least, this may be adopted as a principle in the argument with those who adduce it to prove that all men became sinners by the transgression of Adam. This passage, therefore, should not be adduced in proof of the doctrine of imputation, or as relating to the question how men became sinners, but should be limited to the subject that was immediately under discussion in the argument of the apostle. *That object was, to show that the doctrine of the resurrection by Christ was such as to meet the obvious doctrine that men became mortal by Adam; or that the one was adapted to counteract the other.* ¶ *Even so* (οὕτω.) In this manner; referring not merely to the certainty of the event, but to the mode or manner. As the death of all was occasioned by the sin of one, even so, in like manner, the resurrection of all shall be produced by one. His resurrection shall meet and counteract the evils introduced by the other, so far as the subject under discussion is concerned; that is, so far as relates to temporal death. ¶ *In Christ.* By Christ; in virtue of him; or as the result of his death and resurrection. Many commentators have supposed that the word "all" here refers only to believers, meaning all who were united to Christ, or all who were his friends; all included in a covenant with him; as the word "all" in the former member of the sentence means all who were included in the covenant with Adam; that is, all mankind. But to this view there are manifest objections. (1.) It is not the *obvious* sense; it is not that which will occur to the great mass of men who interpret the Scriptures on the principles of common sense; it is an interpretation which is to be *made out* by reasoning and by theology—always a suspicious circumstance in interpreting the Bible. (2.) It is not necessary. All the wicked will be raised up from the dead as well as all the righteous, Dan. xii.

23 But [a] every man in his own order; Christ the first-fruits; afterward they that are Christ's at his coming.

a 1 Thess.4.15—17.

2; John v. 28, 29. (3.) The form of the passage requires us to understand the word "all" in the same sense in both members, unless there be some indispensable necessity for limiting the one or the other. (4.) The argument of the apostle requires this. For his object is to show that the effect of the sin of Adam, by introducing *temporal* death, will be counteracted by Christ in raising up all who die; which would not be shown if the apostle meant to say that only *a part* of those who had died in consequence of the sin of Adam would be raised up. The argument would then be inconclusive. But now it is complete if it be shown that *all* shall be raised up, whatever may become of them afterwards. The sceptre of death shall be broken, and his dominion destroyed, by the fact that ALL shall be raised up from the dead. ¶ *Be made alive.* Be raised from the dead; be made alive, in a sense contradistinguished from that in which he here says they were subjected to death, by Adam. If it should be held that *that* means that all were made sinners by him, then this means, as has been observed, that all shall be made righteous, and the doctrine of universal salvation has an unanswerable argument; if it means, as it obviously does, that all were subjected to temporal death by him, then it means that all shall be raised from the dead by Christ.

[That the whole human family, in consequence of the sin of Adam, are subjected not only to temporal but to spiritual and eternal death, is without doubt a doctrine of scripture. As much is comprehended in the original sentence, Gen. ii. 17, which involved not Adam only but his posterity also. See the Supplementary Notes on Rom. v. 12. In this place, however, the apostle certainly *does* speak *especially*, if not *exclusively*, of temporal death. The scope of the passage demands this admission. Yet it by no means follows, that the text "ought not to be adduced in proof of the doctrine of imputation." Of that doctrine it is strong proof; "In Adam all die," or are subjected to natural death. Now, if all are visited with penal evil—with death through Adam, does not this involve the imputation of his guilt? It will not do to say that each sins *personally*, and therefore dies; for infants die, and all men come into the world under the necessity of dying. The infliction of the punishment *prior* to all personal guilt, proves, that the cause of it must be sought higher, viz. in the imputation of Adam's guilt. See the Supplementary Notes on Rom. v.

As to the question, whether the "all" in the latter clause of the verse be co-extensive with the "all" in the former: although the author has very ingeniously argued that it must be so regarded, there is this insuperable objection to his whole theory, that the apostle *does not once speak of the resurrection of the wicked* in this chapter. In the very next verse he speaks of "them *that are Christ's* at his coming," and then goes on to show the glory of the *saints'* resurrection body, and concludes in such a strain of triumph as plainly confines the whole discourse to the case of the righteous. *Their* resurrection is the specific point of which the apostle is treating, and the author should have remembered his own excellent canon, that *to this* the interpretation of a passage should be confined. Besides it will occur to any one on reading the passage, that the resurrection here referred to is throughout spoken of as a *vast benefit*, secured by the mediation of Christ. "The design," says the commentator, "is to show that the work of Christ is adapted to overcome the evils of the sin of Adam in one specific matter, *i. e.* on the point of the resurrection. His argument, therefore, requires the apostle to show *only* that temporal death introduced by the first man has been counteracted by the second." But where is the *benefit* to them who rise "to shame and everlasting contempt?" And what kind of counteraction of evil is this? The *evils of the sin of Adam* would be *mitigated* to the wicked, if rather they were allowed to slumber in the grave for ever. To them annihilation would comparatively be a benefit. Their resurrection on the other hand *would counteract no evil* but inconceivably increase, and eternally perpetuate whatever comes under that name. The "all" in the last clause, therefore, must be taken in a restricted sense, embracing the righteous only. The verse is to be explained on the principle of representation. Adam and Christ are the heads of their respective covenants. All represented by the one die in him, and all represented by the other live in him. It is on the same principle that Rom. v. 15, is to be interpreted. See the Supplementary Note there. Finally, it is obvious, that the text thus explained can give no encouragement to the doctrine of universal salvation whatever.

24 Then *cometh* the end, when he shall have delivered up the kingdom [a] to God, even the Father; when he shall have put down all rule and all authority and power.

a Dan.7.14,27.

Bloomfield has this excellent Note on the verse: "The previous comparison ὥσπερ ἐν τῷ Αδαμ παντες ἀποθνησκουσιν forbids the supposition. (*i. e.* that the παντες includes also unbelievers). In Adam all die, ἐφ ῳ παντες ἡμαρτον. Rom. v. 12; but in Christ only those can live and rise who are justified through him, and this none are without faith in him. That Paul taught also a resurrection of the ἄδικοι to judgment, is clear from other parts of scripture, Acts xxiv. 15, but it is not to that he is referring here."

23. *But every man.* Every one, including Christ as well as others. ¶ *In his own order.* In his proper order, rank, place, time. The word τάγμα usually relates to military order or array; to the arrangement of a cohort, or band of troops; to their being properly marshalled with the officers at the head, and every man in his proper place in the ranks. Here it means that there was a proper *order* to be observed in the resurrection of the dead. And the design of the apostle is, probably, to counteract the idea that the resurrection was passed already, or that there was no future resurrection to be expected. The *order* which is here referred to is, doubtless, mainly that of *time;* meaning that Christ would be first, and then that the others would follow. But it also means that Christ would be first, because it was *proper* that he should be first. He was first in rank, in dignity, and in honour; he was the leader of all others, and their resurrection depended on his. And as it was proper that a leader or commander should have the first place in a march, or in an enterprise involving peril or glory, so it was proper that Christ should be first in the resurrection, and that the others should follow on in due order and time. ¶ *Christ the first-fruits.* Christ first in time, and the pledge that they should rise; see Note on ver. 20. ¶ *Afterward.* After he has risen. Not before, because their resurrection depended on him. ¶ *They that are Christ's.* They who are Christians. The apostle, though in ver. 22 he had stated the truth that *all* the dead would rise, yet here only mentions Christians, because to them only would the doctrine be of any consolation, and because it was to them particularly that this whole argument was directed. ¶ *At his coming.* When he shall come to judge the world, and to receive his people to himself. This proves that the dead will not be raised until Christ shall re-appear. He shall come for that purpose; and he shall assemble all the dead, and shall take his people to himself; see Matt. xxv. And this declaration fully met the opinion of those who held that the resurrection was past already; see 2 Tim. ii. 18.

24. *Then* cometh *the end.* Then *is* the end; or then *is* the consummation. It does not mean that the end, or consummation is to *follow* that event; but that this *will be* the ending, the winding up, the consummation of the affairs under the mediatorial reign of Christ. The word *end* (τέλος) denotes properly a limit, termination, completion of any thing. The proper and obvious meaning of the word here is, that then shall be the end or completion of the work of redemption. That shall have been done which was intended to be done by the incarnation and the work of the atonement; the race shall be redeemed; the friends of God shall be completely recovered; and the administration of the affairs of the universe shall be conducted as they were before the incarnation of the Redeemer. Some understand the word "end" here, however, as a metaphor, meaning "the *last*, or the rest of the dead;" but this is a forced and improbable interpretation. The word *end* here may refer to the end of human affairs, or the end of the kingdoms of this world, or it may refer to the ends of the mediatorial kingdom of the Redeemer; the consummation of his peculiar reign and work result-

ing in the surrender of the kingdom to the Father. The connection demands the *last* interpretation, though this involves also the former. ¶ *When he shall have delivered up* (παραδῷ). This word means properly to give *near, with,* or *to* any one; to give over, to deliver up.—*Robinson.* It is applied to the act of delivering up *persons* to the power or authority of others, as *e. g.* to magistrates for trial, and condemnation, (Mat. v. 25; Mark xv. 1; Luke xx. 20); to lictors, or soldiers, for punishment (Mat. xviii. 24); or to one's enemies, Mat. xxvi. 15. It is applied also to persons or things delivered over or surrendered to do or suffer any thing, Acts xv. 26; 1 Cor. xiii. 3; Eph. iv. 19. It is also applied to persons or things delivered over to the care, charge, or supervision of any one, in the sense of giving up, intrusting, committing, Mat. xi. 27; xxv. 14; Luke iv. 6, 10, 22. Here the obvious sense is that of surrendering, giving back, delivering up, rendering up that which had been received, implying that an important trust had been received, which was now to be rendered back. And according to this interpretation, it means, (1.) That the Lord Jesus had received or been intrusted with an important power or office as mediator; comp. Note, Mat. xviii. 18. (2.) That he had executed the purpose implied in that trust or commission; and, (3.) That he was now rendering back to God that office or authority which he had received at his hands. As the work had been accomplished which had been contemplated in his design; as there would be no further necessity for mediation when redemption should have been made, and his church recovered from sin and brought to glory; there would be no further need of that *peculiar* arrangement which had been implied in the work of redemption, and, of course, all the intrustment of power involved in that would be again restored to the hands of God. The idea, says Grotius, is, that he would deliver up the kingdom as the governors of provinces render again or deliver up their commission and authority to the Cæsars who appointed them. There is no absurdity in this view. For *if* the world was to be redeemed, it was necessary that the Redeemer should be intrusted with power sufficient for his work. When that work was done, and there was no further need of that peculiar exercise of power, then it would be proper that it should be restored, or that the government of God should be administered as it was before the work of redemption was undertaken; that the Divinity, or the Godhead, as *such,* should preside over the destinies of the universe. Of course, it will not follow that the Second Person of the Trinity will surrender *all* power, or *cease* to exercise government. It will be that power only which he had *as* Mediator; and whatever part in the administration of the government of the universe he shared as Divine before the incarnation, he will *still* share, with the additional *glory* and *honour* of having redeemed a world by his death. ¶ *The kingdom.* This word means properly dominion, reign, the exercise of kingly power. In the New Testament it means commonly the reign of the Messiah, or the dominion which God would exercise through the Messiah; the reign of God over men by the laws and institutions of the Messiah; see Note, Mat. iii. 2. Here it means, I think, evidently, dominion in general. It cannot denote the peculiar administration over the world involved in the work of mediation, for that will be ended; but it means that the empire, the sovereignty, shall have been delivered up to God. His enemies shall have been subdued. His power shall have been asserted. The authority of God shall have been established, and the kingdom, or the dominion, shall be in the hands of God himself; and he shall reign, not in the peculiar form which existed in the work of mediation, but absolutely, and as he did over obedient minds before the incarnation. ¶ *To God.* To God *as* God; to the Divinity. The Mediator shall have given up the peculiar power and rule as Mediator, and it shall be exercised by God as God. ¶ *Even the Father.* And (καὶ) the Father. The word *Father,* as applied to God in the Scriptures, is used in two senses—to designate *the* Father, the first person of the Trinity as distinguished from the Son; and in a broader, wider sense, to denote God as sustaining the relation of a Father to his creatures; as the Father of all. Instances of this use are too numerous to be here particularly referred to. It is in this latter sense, perhaps, that the word is used here—not to denote that the second person of the Trinity is to surrender all power into the hands of the first, or that he is to cease to exercise dominion and control; but that the power is to be yielded into the hands of God *as* God, *i. e.* as the universal Father, as the Divinity, without being exercised in any peculiar and special manner by the different persons of the Godhead, as had been done in the work of redemption. At the close of the work of redemption this *peculiar* arrangement would cease; and God, *as* the universal Father and Ruler of all, would exercise the government of the world; see, however, Note on ver. 28. ¶ *When he shall have put down.* When he shall have *abolished,* or brought to naught, all that opposed the reign of God. ¶ *All rule,* &c. All those mighty powers that opposed God and resisted his reign. The words here used do not seem intended to denote the several departments or forms of opposition, but to be general terms, meaning that whatever opposed God should be subdued. They include, of course, the kingdoms of this world; the sins, pride, and corruption of the human heart; the powers of darkness—the spiritual dominions that oppose God on earth, and in hell; and death and the grave. All shall be completely subdued, and cease to interpose any obstacles to the advancement of his kingdom and to his universal reign. A monarch reigns when all his enemies are subdued or destroyed; or when they are prevented from opposing his will, even though all should not voluntarily submit to his will. The following remarks of Prof. Bush present a plausible and ingenious view of this difficult passage, and they are, therefore, subjoined here. "If the opinion of the eminent critic, Storr, may be admitted, that the kingdom here said to be delivered up to the Father is *not* the kingdom of Christ, but the rule and dominion of all adverse powers—an opinion rendered very probable by the following words: "when he shall have *put down* (Gr. done away, abolished) all rule, and all authority and power,"—and ver. 25, "till he hath put all *enemies* under his feet"—then is the passage of identical import with Rev. xi. 15, referring to precisely the same period: "And the seventh angel sounded; and there were great voices in heaven, saying, The kingdoms of the world are become the kingdoms of our Lord and of his Christ; and he shall reign for ever and ever. It is, therefore, we conceive, but a peculiar mode of denoting the *transfer*, the *making over* of the kingdoms of this world from their former despotic and antichristian rulers to the sovereignty of Jesus Christ, the appointed heir and head of all things, whose kingdom is to be everlasting. If this interpretation be correct, we are prepared to advance a step farther, and suggest that the phrase, *he shall have delivered up* (Greek, παραδῷ), be understood as an instance of the idiom in which the verb is used without any personal nominative, but has reference to the *purpose of God as expressed in the Scriptures;* so that the passage may be read, "Then cometh the end (*i. e.* not the close, the final winding up, but the perfect developement, expansion, completion, consummation of the divine plans in regard to this world), when the prophetic announcements of the Scriptures require the delivering up (*i. e.* the making over) of all adverse dominion into the hands of the Messiah, to whose supremacy we are taught to expect that every thing will finally be made subject."—*Illustrations of Scripture.* A more extended examination of this difficult passage may be seen in Storr's Opuscula, vol. i. pp. 274—282. See also Biblical Repository, vol. iii. pp. 748—755.

25 For he [a] must reign, till he hath put all enemies under his feet.
26 The last enemy *that* shall be destroyed [b] *is* death.
27 For he [c] hath put all things

a Ps.2.6-10; 45.3-6; 110.1; Eph.1.22; Heb.1.13. b Hos.13.14; 2 Tim.1.10; Rev.20.14. c Ps.8.6.

25. *For he must reign.* It is fit, or proper (δεῖ), that he should reign till this is accomplished. It is proper that the mediatorial kingdom should continue till this great work is effected. The word "must" here refers to the propriety of this continuance of his reign, and to the fact that this was contemplated and predicted as the work which he would accomplish. He came to subdue all his enemies; see Ps. ii. 6—10; or Ps. cx. 1, "The Lord said unto my Lord, Sit thou at my right hand until I make thine enemies thy footstool." Paul, doubtless, had this passage in his eye as affirming the necessity that he should reign until all his foes should be subdued. That this refers to the Messiah is abundantly clear from Mat. xxii. 44, 45.

26. *The last enemy* that *shall be destroyed* is *death.* The other foes of God should be subdued *before* the final resurrection. The enmity of the human heart should be subdued by the triumphs of the gospel. The sceptre of Satan should be broken and wrested from him. The false systems of religion that had tyrannized over men should be destroyed. The gospel should have spread everywhere, and the world be converted to God. And nothing should remain but to *subdue* or destroy death, and that would be by the resurrection. It would be, (1.) Because the resurrection would be a *triumph* over death, showing that there was one of greater power, and that the sceptre would be wrested from the hands of death. (2.) Because death would cease to reign. No more would ever die. All that should be raised up would live for ever; and the effects of sin and rebellion in this world would be thus for ever ended, and the kingdom of God restored. Death is here personified as a tyrant, exercising despotic power over the human race; and *he* is to be subdued.

27. *For he hath put.* God has put by promise, purpose, or decree. ¶ *All things under his feet.* He has made all things subject to him; or has appointed him to be head over all things; comp. Mat. xxviii. 18; John xvii. 2; Eph. i. 20—22. It is evident that Paul here refers to some promise or prediction respecting the Messiah, though he does not expressly quote any passage, or make it certain to what he refers. The *words* "hath put all things under his feet" are found in Ps. viii. 6, as applicable to *man*, and as designed to show the dignity and dominion of man. Whether the psalm has any reference to the Messiah, has been made a question. Those who are disposed to see an examination of this question, may find it in Stuart on the Hebrews, on chap. ii. 6—8; and in Excurses ix. of the same work, pp. 568—570. Ed. 1833. In the passage before us, it is not *necessary* to suppose that Paul meant to say that the psalm had a particular reference to the Messiah. All that is implied is, that it was the intention of God to subdue all things to him; this was the general strain of the prophecies in regard to him; this was the purpose of God; and this idea is accurately expressed in the words of the psalm; or these words will convey the *general sense* of the prophetic writings in regard to the Messiah. It may be true, also, that although the passage in Ps. viii. has no immediate and direct reference to the Messiah, yet it *includes* him as one who possessed human nature. The psalm may be understood as affirming that all things were subjected to *human nature; i. e.* human nature had dominion and control over all. But this was more particularly and eminently true of the Messiah than of any other man. In all other cases, great as was the dignity of man, yet his control over "all things" was limited and partial. In the Messiah

under his feet. But when he saith, All things are put under *him*; *it is* manifest that he is excepted which did put all things under him.

28 And when all things shall be

it was to be complete and entire. His dominion, therefore, was a complete *fulfilment*, *i. e. filling up* (πλήρωμα) of the words in the psalm. Under him alone was there to be an entire accomplishment of what is there said; and as that psalm was to be fulfilled, as it was to be true that it might be said of man that all things were subject to him, it was to be fulfilled mainly in the person of the Messiah, whose human nature was to be exalted above all things; comp. Heb. ii. 6—9 ¶ *But when he saith.* When God says, or when it is said; when that promise is made respecting the Messiah. ¶ It is *manifest.* It must be so; it must be so understood and interpreted. ¶ *That he is excepted,* &c. That God is excepted; that it cannot mean that the appointing power is to be subject to him. Paul may have made this remark for several reasons. Perhaps, (1.) To avoid the possibility of cavil, or misconstruction of the phrase, "all things," as if it meant that God would be included, and would be subdued to him; as among the heathen, Jupiter is fabled to have expelled his father Saturn from his throne and from heaven. (2.) It might be to prevent the supposition, from what Paul had said of the extent of the Son's dominion, that he was in any respect superior to the Father. It is implied by this exception here, that when the necessity for the peculiar mediatorial kingdom of the Son should cease, there would be a resuming of the authority and dominion of the Father, in the manner in which it subsisted before the incarnation. (3.) The expression may also be regarded as intensive or emphatic; as denoting, in the most absolute sense, that there was *nothing* in the universe, but God, which was not subject to him. God was the *only* exception; and his dominion, therefore, was absolute over all other beings and things.

28. *And when*, &c. In this future time, when this shall be accomplished. This implies that the time has not yet arrived, and that his dominion is now exercised, and that he is carrying forward his plans for the subjugation of all things to God. ¶ *Shall be subdued unto him.* Shall be brought under subjection. When all his enemies shall be overcome and destroyed; or when the hearts of the redeemed shall be entirely subject to God. When God's kingdom shall be fully established over the universe. It shall then be seen that he is Lord of all. In the previous verses he had spoken of the promise that all things should be subjected to God; in this, he speaks of its being actually done. ¶ *Then shall the Son also himself be subject*, &c. It has been proposed to render this, "*even then* shall the Son," &c.; implying that he *had* been all along subject to God; had acted under his authority; and that this subjection would continue *even then* in a sense similar to that in which it had existed; and that Christ would *then* continue to exercise a delegated authority over his people and kingdom. See an article "on the duration of Christ's kingdom," by Prof. Mills, in Bib. Rep. vol. iii. p. 748, seq. But to this interpretation there are objections. (1.) It is not the obvious interpretation. (2.) It does not seem to comport with the design and scope of the passage, which most evidently refers to some change, or rendering back of the authority of the Messiah; or to some resumption of authority by the Divinity, or by God as God, in a different sense from what existed under the Messiah. (3.) Such a statement would be unnecessary and vain. Who could reasonably doubt that the Son would be as much subject to God when all things had been subdued to him as he was before? (4.) It is not necessary to suppose this in order to reconcile the passage with what is said of the perpetuity of

subdued [a] unto him, then shall the Son also himself be subject unto him [b] that put all things under him, that God may be all in all.

a Phil.3.21. *b* chap.11.3.

Christ's kingdom and his eternal reign. That he would reign; that his kingdom would be perpetual, and that it would be unending, was indeed clearly predicted; see 2 Sam. vii. 16; Ps. xlv. 6; Isa. ix. 6, 7; Dan. ii. 44; vii. 14; Luke i. 22, 23; Heb. i. 8. But these predictions may be all accomplished on the supposition that the peculiar mediatorial kingdom of the Messiah shall be given up to God, and that he shall be subject to him. For, (*a*) His kingdom will be perpetual, in contradistinction from the kingdoms of this world. They are fluctuating, changing, short in their duration. His shall not cease, and shall continue to the end of time. (*b*) His kingdom shall be perpetual, because those who are brought under the laws of God by him shall remain subject to those laws for ever. The sceptre never shall be broken, and the kingdom shall abide to all eternity. (*c*) Christ, the Son of God, in his divine nature, *as God*, shall never cease to reign. As Mediator, he may resign his commission and his *peculiar* office, having made an atonement, having recovered his people, having protected and guided them to heaven. Yet as one with the Father; as the "Father of the everlasting age" (Isa. ix. 6), he shall not cease to reign. The functions of a peculiar office may have been discharged, and delegated power laid down, and that which appropriately belongs to him in virtue of his own nature and relations may be resumed and executed for ever; and it shall still be true that the reign of the Son of God, in union, or in *oneness* with the Father, shall continue for ever. (5.) The interpretation which affirms that the Son shall then be subject to the Father in the sense of laying down his delegated authority, and ceasing to exercise his mediatorial reign, has been the common interpretation of all times. This remark is of value only, because, in the interpretation of plain words, it is not probable that men of all classes and ranks in different ages would err. ¶ *The Son also himself.* The term "Son of God" is applied to the Lord Jesus with reference to his human nature, his incarnation by the Holy Ghost, and his resurrection from the dead; see Note on Rom. i. 4. [For the evidence of the eternal sonship, see the supplementary Note on the same passage.] It refers, I apprehend, to that in this place. It does not mean that the second person in the Trinity, as such, should be subject to the first; but it means the Incarnate Son, the Mediator,—the man that was born and that was raised from the dead, and to whom this wide dominion had been given,—should resign that dominion, and that the government should be re-assumed by the Divinity *as* God. As man, he shall cease to exercise any distinct dominion. This does not mean, evidently, that the union of the divine and human nature will be dissolved; nor that important purposes may not be answered by that continued union for ever; nor that the divine perfections may not shine forth in some glorious way through the man Christ Jesus; but that *the purpose of government* shall no longer be exercised in that way; the mediatorial kingdom, as such, shall no longer be continued, and power shall be exercised by God as God. The redeemed will still adore their Redeemer as their incarnate God, and dwell upon the remembrance of his work and upon his perfections (Rev. i. 5, 6; v. 12; xi. 15); but not as exercising the peculiar power which he now has, and which was needful to effect their redemption. ¶ *That God may be all in all.* That God may be SUPREME; that the Divinity, the Godhead, may rule; and that it may be seen that he is the Sovereign over all the universe. By the word "God" (ὁ Θεὸς), Whitby and Hammond, I think correctly, understand the Godhead, the Divine Na-

29 Else what shall they do which [a] are baptized for the dead, if the

a Rom.6.3,4.

ture, the Divinity, consisting of the three persons, without respect to any peculiar office or kingdom.

29. *Else what shall they do*, &c. The apostle here resumes the argument for the resurrection which was interrupted at ver. 19. He goes on to state further consequences which must follow from the denial of this doctrine, and thence infers that the doctrine must be true. There is, perhaps, no passage of the New Testament in respect to which there has been a greater variety of interpretation than this; and the views of expositors now by no means harmonize in regard to its meaning. It is possible that Paul may here refer to some practice or custom which existed in his time respecting baptism, the knowledge of which is now lost. The various opinions which have been entertained in regard to this passage, together with an examination of them, may be seen in Pool's Synopsis, Rosenmüller, and Bloomfield. It may be not useless just to refer to some of them, that the perplexity of commentators may be seen. (1.) It has been held by some that by "the dead" here is meant the Messiah who was put to death, the plural being used for the singular, meaning "the dead one." (2.) By others, that the word baptized here is taken in the sense of washing, cleansing, purifying, as in Mat. viii. 4; Heb. ix. 10; and that the sense is, that the dead were carefully washed and purified when buried, with the hope of the resurrection, and, as it were, preparatory to that. (3.) By others, that to be baptized for the dead means to be baptised *as* dead, being baptized into Christ, and buried with him in baptism, and that by their immersion they were regarded *as* dead. (4.) By others, that the apostle refers to a custom of vicarious baptism, or being baptized for those who were dead, referring to the practice of having some person baptized in the place of one who had died without baptism. This was the opinion of Grotius, Michaelis, Tertullian, and Ambrose. Such was the estimate which was formed, it is supposed, of the importance of baptism, that when one had died without being baptized, some other person was baptized over his dead body in his place. That this custom prevailed in the church *after* the time of Paul, has been abundantly proved by Grotius, and is generally admitted. But the objections to this interpretation are obvious. (*a*) There is *no* evidence that such a custom prevailed in the time of Paul. (*b*) It cannot be believed that Paul would give countenance to a custom so senseless and so contrary to the Scripture, or that he would make it the foundation of a solemn argument. (*c*) It does not accord with the strain and purpose of his argument. If *this* custom had been referred to, his design would have led him to say, "What will become of them *for whom* others have been baptized? Are we to believe that they have perished?" (*d*) It is far more probable that the custom referred to in this opinion arose from an erroneous interpretation of this passage of Scripture, than that it existed in the time of Paul. (5.) There remain two other opinions, both of which are plausible, and one of which is probably the true one. One is, that the word *baptized* is used here as it is in Mat. xx. 22, 23; Mark x. 39; Luke xii. 50, in the sense of being overwhelmed with calamities, trials, and sufferings; and as meaning that the apostles and others were subjected to great trials on account of the dead, *i. e.* in the hope of the resurrection; or with the expectation that the dead would rise. This is the opinion of Lightfoot, Rosenmüller, Pearce, Homberg, Krause, and of Prof. Robinson (Lex. art. Βαπτίζω), and has much that is plausible. That the word is thus used to denote a deep sinking into calamities, there can be no doubt. And that the apostles and early Christians subjected themselves, or were subjected to great and overwhelming

dead rise not at all? why are they then baptized for the dead?

30 And why stand we in [a] jeopardy every hour?

[a] 2Cor.11.26.

calamities on account of the hope of the resurrection, is equally clear. This interpretation, also, agrees with the general tenor of the argument; and *is* an argument for the resurrection. And it implies that this was the full and constant belief of all who endured these trials, that there would be a resurrection of the dead. The *argument* would be, that they should be slow to adopt an opinion which would imply that all their sufferings were endured for naught, and that God had supported them in this in vain; that God had plunged them into all these sorrows, and had sustained them in them only to disappoint them. That this view is plausible, and that it suits the strain of remark in the *following* verses, is evident. But there are objections to it. (*a*) It is not the usual and natural meaning of the word baptize. (*b*) A metaphorical use of a word should not be resorted to unless necessary. (*c*) The literal meaning of the word here will as well meet the design of the apostle as the metaphorical. (*d*) This interpretation does not relieve us from any of the difficulties in regard to the phrase "for the dead;" and, (*e*) It is altogether more natural to suppose that the apostle would derive his argument from the baptism of *all* who were Christians, than from the figurative baptism of a few who went into the perils of martyrdom.—The other opinion, therefore, is, that the apostle here refers to *baptism* as administered to all believers. This is the most correct opinion; is the most simple, and best meets the design of the argument. According to this, it means that they had been baptized with the hope and expectation of a resurrection of the dead. They had received this as one of the leading doctrines of the gospel when they were baptized. It was a part of their full and firm belief that the dead would rise. The *argument* according to this interpretation is, that this was an essential article of the faith of a Christian; that it was embraced by all; that it constituted a part of their very profession; and that for any one to deny it was to deny that which entered into the very foundation of the Christian faith. If they embraced a different doctrine, if they denied the doctrine of the resurrection, they struck a blow at the very nature of Christianity, and dashed all the hopes which had been cherished and expressed at their baptism. And what could they do? What would become of them! What would be the destiny of all who were thus baptized? Was it to be believed that all their hopes at baptism were vain- and that they would all perish? As such a belief could not be entertained, the apostle infers that, if they held to Christianity at all, they must hold to *this* doctrine as a part of their very profession. According to this view, the phrase "for the dead" means, with reference to the dead; with direct allusion to the condition of the dead, and their hopes; with a belief that the dead will rise. It is evident that the passage is elliptical, and this seems to be as probable as any interpretation which has been suggested. Mr. Locke says, frankly, "What this baptizing for the dead was, I know not; but it seems, by the following verses, to be something wherein they exposed themselves to the danger of death." Tindal translates it, "*over* the dead." Doddridge renders it, "*in the room of the dead*, who are just fallen in the cause of Christ, but are yet supported by a succession of new converts, who immediately offer themselves to fill up their places, as ranks of soldiers that advance to the combat in the room of their companions who have just been slain in their sight."

30. *And why stand we in jeopardy.* Why do we constantly risk our lives, and encounter danger of every kind? This refers particularly to Paul himself and the other apostles, who were constantly exposed to peril by land or by sea in the arduous work of making known the gospel. The argument

31 I protest by [1]your rejoicing [a]
which I have in Christ Jesus our
Lord, I [b] die daily.
32 If [2] after the manner of men

1 some read, *our*. a Phil. 3.3. b Rom.8.36.

I have fought with beasts at Ephesus, what advantageth it me, if the
dead rise not? Let us [c] eat and
drink, for to-morrow we die.

2 or, *to speak after*. c Eccl.2.24; Isa.22.13.

here is plain. It is, that such efforts would be vain, useless, foolish, unless there was to be a glorious resurrection. They had no other object in encountering these dangers than to make known the truths connected with that glorious future state; and if there were no such future state, it would be wise for them to avoid these dangers. "It would not be supposed that we would encounter these perils constantly, unless we were sustained with the hope of the resurrection, and unless we had evidence which convinced our own minds that there would be such a resurrection." ¶ *Every hour.* Constantly; comp. 2 Cor. xv. 26. So numerous were their dangers, that they might be said to occur every hour. This was particularly the case in the instance to which he refers in Ephesus, ver. 32.

31. *I protest* (νὴ). This is a particle of swearing, and denotes a strong asseveration. The subject was important; it deeply interested his feelings; and he makes in regard to it a strong protestation; comp. John iii. 5. "I solemnly affirm, or declare." ¶ *By your rejoicing.* Many MSS. here read "by *our* rejoicing," but the correct reading is doubtless that which is in the present Greek text, by your rejoicing. The meaning of the phrase, which is admitted by all to be obscure, is probably, "I protest, or solemnly declare by the glorying or exultation which I have on your account; by all my ground of glorying in you; by all the confident boasting and expectation which I have of your salvation." He hoped for their salvation. He had laboured for that. He had boasted of it, and confidently believed that they would be saved. Regarding that as safe and certain, he says it was *just as certain* that he died daily on account of the hope and belief of the resurrection. "By our hopes and joys as Christians; by our dearest expectations and grounds of confidence, I swear, or solemnly declare, that I die daily." Men swear or affirm by their objects of dearest affection and desire; and the meaning here is, "So certainly as I confidently expect your salvation, and so certainly as we look to eternal life, so certain is it that I am constantly exposed to die, and suffer that which may be called a daily death." ¶ *Which I have in Christ Jesus.* The rejoicing, boasting, glorying in regard to you which I am permitted to cherish through the grace and favour of the Saviour. His boasting, or confident expectation in regard to the Corinthians, he enjoyed only by the mercy of the Lord Jesus, and he delighted to trace it to him ¶ *I die daily;* comp. Rom. viii. 36. I endure so many sufferings and persecutions, that it may be said to be a daily dying. I am constantly in danger of my life; and my sufferings each day are equal to the pains of death. Probably Paul here referred particularly to the perils and trials which he then endured at Ephesus; and his object was to impress their minds with the firmness of *his* belief in the certainty of the resurrection, on account of which he suffered so much, and to show them that all their hopes rested also on this doctrine.

32. *If after the manner of men.* Marg. *To speak after the manner of men* (κατὰ ἄνθρωπον). There has been a great difference of opinion in regard to the meaning of these words. The following are some of the interpretations proposed. (1.) If I have fought after the manner of men, who act only with reference to this life, and on the ordinary principles of human conduct, as men fought with wild beasts in the amphitheatre. (2.) Or if, humanly speaking, or speaking after the manner of men, I have fought, referring to the fact that he had contended with *men* who should be regarded as wild beasts. (3.) Or, that I may speak of myself as men

speak, that I may freely record the events of my life, and speak of what has occurred. (4.) Or, I have fought with wild beasts as far as it was possible for man to do it while life survived. (5.) Or, as much as was in the power of man, who had destined me to this; if, so far as depended on man's will, I fought, supposing that the infuriated multitude demanded that I should be thus punished. So Chrysostom understands it. (6.) Or, that Paul actually fought with wild beasts at Ephesus. (7.) Others regard this as a *supposable* case; on the supposition that I *had* fought with wild beasts at Ephesus. Amidst this variety of interpretation, it is not easy to determine the true sense of this difficult passage. The following thoughts, however, may perhaps make it clear.

(1.) Paul refers to some *real* occurrence at Ephesus. This is manifest from the whole passage. It is not a supposable case.

(2.) It was some *one* case when his life was endangered, and when it was regarded as remarkable that he escaped and survived; comp. 2 Cor. i. 8—10.

(3.) It was *common* among the Romans, and the ancients generally, to expose criminals to fight with wild beasts in the amphitheatre for the amusement of the populace. In such cases it was but another form of dooming them to certain death, since there was no human possibility of escape; see Adam's Rom. Ant., p. 344. That this custom prevailed at the East, is apparent from the following extract from Rosenmüller; and there is no improbability in the supposition that Paul was exposed to this:—"The barbarous custom of making men combat with wild beasts has prevailed in the East down to the most modern times. Jurgen Andersen, who visited the states of the Great Mogul in 1646, gives an account in his Travels of such a combat with animals, which he witnessed at Agra, the residence of the Great Mogul. His description affords a lively image of those bloody spectacles in which ancient Rome took so much pleasure, and to which the above words of the apostle refer. Alamardan-chan, the governor of Cashmire, who sat among the chans, stood up, and exclaimed, 'It is the will and desire of the great mogul, Schah Choram, that if there are any valiant heroes who will show their bravery by combating with wild beasts, armed with shield and sword, let them come forward; if they conquer, the mogul will load them with great favour, and clothe their countenance with gladness.' Upon this three persons advanced, and offered to undertake the combat. Alamardan-chan again cried aloud, 'None should have any other weapon than a shield and a sword; and whosoever has any breastplate under his clothes should lay it aside, and fight honourably.' Hereupon a powerful lion was let into the garden, and one of the three men above mentioned advanced against him; the lion, on seeing his enemy, ran violently up to him; the man, however, defended himself bravely, and kept off the lion for a good while, till his arms grew tired; the lion then seized the shield with one paw, and with the other his antagonist's right arm, so that he was not able to use his weapon; the latter, seeing his life in danger, took with his left hand his Indian dagger, which he had sticking in his girdle, and thrust it as far as possible into the lion's mouth: the lion then let him go; the man, however, was not idle, but cut the lion almost through with one stroke, and after that entirely to pieces. Upon this victory the common people began to shout, and call out, 'Thank God, he has conquered.' But the mogul said, smiling, to this conqueror, 'Thou art a brave warrior, and hast fought admirably! But did I not command to fight honourably only with shield and sword? But, like a thief, thou hast stolen the life of the lion with thy dagger.' And immediately he ordered two men to rip up his belly, and to place him upon an elephant, and, as an example to others, to lead him about, which was done on the spot. Soon after a tiger was set loose; against which a tall, powerful man advanced with an air of defiance, as if he would cut the tiger up. The tiger, however, was far too sagacious and active, for, in the first attack, he seized the combatant by the neck, tore his throat, and then his whole body in pieces. This enraged another good fellow, but little, and of mean appearance, from whom one would not have expected it: he rushed forward like one mad, and the tiger on his part undauntedly flew at his enemy; but the man at the first attack cut off his two fore paws, so that he fell, and the man cut his body to pieces. Upon this the king cried, 'What is your name?' He answered, 'My name is Geyby.' Soon after one of the king's servants came and brought him a piece of gold brocade, and said, 'Geyby, receive the robe of honour with which the mogul presents you.' He took the garment with great reverence, kissed it three times, pressing it each time to his eyes and breast, then held it up, and in silence put up a prayer for the health of the mogul; and when he concluded it, he cried, 'May God let him become as great as Tamerlane, from whom he is descended. May he live seven hundred years, and his house continue to eternity!' Upon this he was summoned by a chamberlain to go from the garden up to the king; and when he came to the entrance, he was received by two chans, who conducted him between them to kiss the mogul's feet. And when he was going to retire, the king said to him, 'Praised be thou, Geyby-chan, for thy valiant deeds, and this name shalt thou keep to eternity. I am your gracious master, and thou art my slave.' "—*Bush's Illustrations.*

(4.) It is the most *natural* interpretation to suppose that Paul, on some occasion, had such a contest with a wild beast at Ephesus. It is that which would occur to the great mass of the readers of the New Testament as the obvious meaning of the passage.

(5.) The state of things in Ephesus when Paul was there (Acts xix.) was such as to make it nowise improbable that he would be subjected to such a trial.

(6.) It is no objection to this supposition that Luke has not recorded this occurrence in the Acts of the Apostles. No conclusion adverse to this supposition can be drawn from the mere *silence* of the historian. Mere silence is not a contradiction. There is no reason to suppose that Luke designed to record *all* the perils which Paul endured. Indeed, we know from 2 Cor. xi. 24—27, that there must have been *many* dangers which Paul encountered which are not referred to by Luke. It must have happened, also, that many important events must have taken place during Paul's abode at Ephesus which are not recorded by Luke; Acts xix. Nor is it any objection to this supposition that Paul does not, in 2 Cor. xi. 24—27, mention particularly this contest with a wild beast at Ephesus. His statement there is *general.* He does not descend into particulars. Yet, in 2 Cor. xi. 23, he says that he was "in deaths oft,"—a statement which is in accordance with the supposition that in Ephesus he may have been exposed to death in some cruel manner.

(7.) The phrase κατὰ ἄνθρωπον, *as a man,* may mean, that, *to human appearance,* or so far as man was concerned, had it not been for some divine interposition, he would have been a prey to the wild beasts. Had not God interposed and kept him from harm, as in the case of the viper at Melita (Acts xxviii. 5), he would have been put to death. He was sentenced to this; was thrown to the wild beast; had every *human* prospect of dying; it was done on account of his religion; and but for the interposition of God, he would have died. This I take to be the fair and obvious meaning of this passage, demanded alike by the language which is used and by the tenor of the argument in which it is found. ¶ *What advantageth it me?* What benefit shall I have? Why should I risk my life in this manner? see Note on ver. 19. ¶ *Let us eat and drink.* These words are taken from Isa. xxii. 13. In their original application they refer to the Jews when besieged by Sennacherib and the army of the Assyrians. The prophet says, that instead of weeping, and fasting, and humiliation, as became them in such circumstances, they had given themselves up to feasting and revelry, and that their language was, "Let us eat and drink, for to-morrow

33 Be not deceived: evil [a] communications corrupt good manners.

a chap. 5.6.

we shall die;" that is, there is no use in offering resistance, or in calling upon God. We must die; and we may as well enjoy life as long as it lasts, and give ourselves up to unrestrained indulgence. Paul does not quote these words as having any original reference to the subject of the resurrection, but as language appropriately expressing the idea, that if there is no future state; if no resurrection of the dead: if no happy result of toils and sufferings in the future world, it is vain and foolish to subject ourselves to trials and privations here. We should rather make the most of this life; enjoy all the comfort we can; and make pleasure our chief good, rather than look for happiness in a future state. This *seems* to be the language of the great mass of the world. They look to no future state. They have no prospect, no desire of heaven; and they, therefore, seek for happiness here, and give themselves up to unrestrained enjoyment in this life. ¶ *To-morrow.* Very soon. We have no security of life; and death is so near that it may be said we must die to-morrow. ¶ *We die.* We *must* die. The idea here is, "We must die, without the prospect of living again, unless the doctrine of the resurrection be true."

33. *Be not deceived.* By your false teachers, and by their smooth and plausible arguments. This is an *exhortation.* He had thus far been engaged in an *argument* on the subject. He now entreats them to beware lest they be deceived—a danger to which they were very liable from their circumstances. There was, doubtless, much that was plausible in the objections to the doctrine of the resurrection; there was much subtilty and art in their teachers, who denied this doctrine; perhaps, there was something in the character of their own minds, accustomed to subtle and abstruse inquiry rather than to an examination of simple facts, that exposed them to this danger. ¶ *Evil communications.* The word rendered "communications" means, properly, a being together; companionship; close intercourse; converse. It refers not to *discourse* only, but to intercourse, or companionship. Paul quotes these words from Menander (in Sentent. Comicor. Gr. p. 248, ed. Steph.), a Greek poet. He thus shows that he was, in some degree at least, familiar with the Greek writers; comp. Note, Acts xvii. 28. Menander was a celebrated comic poet of Athens, educated under Theophrastus. His writings were replete with elegance, refined wit, and judicious observations. Of one hundred and eight comedies which he wrote, nothing remains but a few fragments. He is said to have drowned himself, in the 52d year of his age, B. C. 293, because the compositions of his rival Philemon obtained more applause than his own. Paul quoted this sentiment from a Greek poet, perhaps, because it might be supposed to have weight with the Greeks. It was a sentiment of one of their own writers, and here was an occasion in which it was exactly applicable. It is implied in this, that there were some persons who were endeavouring to corrupt their minds from the simplicity of the gospel. The sentiment of the passage is, that the intercourse of evil-minded men, or that the close friendship and conversation of those who hold erroneous opinions, or who are impure in their lives, tends to corrupt the morals, the heart, the sentiments of others. The particular thing to which Paul here applies it is the subject of the resurrection. Such intercourse would tend to corrupt the simplicity of their faith, and pervert their views of the truth of the gospel, and *thus* corrupt their lives. It is *always* true that such intercourse has a pernicious effect on the mind and the heart. It is done, (1.) By their direct effort to corrupt the opinions, and to lead others into sin. (2.) By the secret, silent influence of their words, and conversation, and example. We have less horror at vice by becoming familiar with it; we look with less alarm on error when we hear it often expressed; we become less watchful

34 Awake [a] to righteousness, and sin not; for some have not the knowledge of God: I [b] speak *this* to your shame.

35 But some *man* will say, How [c] are the dead raised up? and with what body do they come?

a Rom.13.11; Eph.5.14. b chap.6.5. c Ezek.37.3.

and cautious when we are constantly with the gay, the worldly, the unprincipled, and the vicious. Hence Christ sought that there should be a pure society, and that his people should principally seek the friendship and conversation of each other, and withdraw from the world. It is in the way that Paul here refers to, that Christians embrace false doctrines; that they lose their spirituality, love of prayer, fervour of piety, and devotion to God. It is in this way that the simple are beguiled, the young corrupted, and that vice, and crime, and infidelity spread over the world.

34. *Awake to righteousness;* see Note, Rom. xiii. 11. The word here translated "awake" denotes, properly, to awake up from a deep sleep or torpor; and is usually applied to those who awake, or become sober after drunkenness. The phrase "to righteousness" (δικαίως) may mean either "rouse to the ways of righteousness; to a holy life; to sound doctrine," &c.; or it may mean "as it is right and just that you should do." Probably the latter is the correct idea, and then the sense will be, "Arouse from stupidity on this subject; awake from your conscious security; be alarmed, as it is *right* and *proper* that you should do, for you are surrounded by dangers, and by those who would lead you into error and vice; rouse from such wild and delusive opinions as these persons have, and exercise a constant vigilance as becomes those who are the friends of God and the expectants of a blessed resurrection." ¶ *And sin not.* Do not err; do not depart from the truth and from holiness; do not embrace a doctrine which is not only erroneous, but the tendency of which is to lead into sin. It is implied here, that if they suffered themselves to embrace a doctrine which was a denial of the resurrection, the effect would be that they would fall into sin; or that a denial of that doctrine led to a life of self-indulgence and transgression. This truth is everywhere seen: and against this effect Paul sought to guard them. He did not regard the denial of the doctrine of the resurrection as a harmless speculation, but as leading to most dangerous consequences in regard to their manner of life or their conduct. ¶ *For some have not.* Some among you. You are surrounded by strangers to God; you have those among you who would lead you into error and sin. ¶ *I speak this to your shame.* To your shame as a church; because you have had abundant opportunities to know the truth, and because it is a subject of deep disgrace that there are any in your bosom who deny the doctrine of the resurrection of the dead, and who are strangers to the grace of God.

35. *But some* man *will say.* An objection will be made to the statement that the dead will be raised. This verse commences the *second* part of the chapter, in which the apostle meets the objections to the argument, and shows in what manner the dead will be raised. See the Analysis. That objections were made to the doctrine is apparent from ver. 12. ¶ *How are the dead raised up?* (Πῶς.) In what way or manner; by what means. This I regard as the *first* objection which would be made, or the first inquiry on the subject which the apostle answers. The question is one which would be likely to be made by the subtle and doubting Greeks. The apostle, indeed, does not draw it out at length, or state it fully, but it may be regarded probably as substantially the same as that which has been made in all ages. "How is it possible that the dead should be raised? They return to their native dust. They become entirely disorganized. Their dust may be scattered; how shall it be re-collected? Or they may be burned at the stake, and how shall the particles

36 *Thou* fool! that [a] which thou sowest is not quickened, except it die.

37 And that which thou sowest, thou sowest not that body that shall be, but bare grain, it may

a John 12.24.

which composed their bodies be re-collected and re-organized? Or they may be devoured by the beasts of the field, the fowls of heaven, or the fishes of the sea, and their flesh may have served to constitute the food of other animals, and to form *their* bodies; how can it be re-collected and re-organized? Or it may have been the food of plants, and like other dust have been used to constitute the leaves or the flowers of plants, and the trunks of trees; and *how* can it be remoulded into a human frame?" This objection the apostle answers in ver. 36—38. ¶ *And with what body do they come?* This is the *second* objection or inquiry which he answers. It may be understood as meaning, "What will be the form, the shape, the size, the organization of the new body? Are we to suppose that *all* the matter which at any time entered into its composition here is to be re-collected, and to constitute a colossal frame? Are we to suppose that it will be the same as it is here, with the same organization, the same necessities, the same wants? Are we to suppose that the aged will be raised *as* aged, and the young *as* young, and that infancy will be raised in the same state, and remain such for ever? Are we to suppose that the bodies will be gross, material, and needing support and nourishment, or, that there will be a new organization?" All these and numerous other questions have been asked, in regard to the bodies at the resurrection; and it is by no means improbable that they were asked by the subtle and philosophizing Greeks, and that they constituted a part of the reasoning of those who denied the doctrine of the resurrection. This question, or objection, the apostle answers ver. 39—50. It has been doubted, indeed, whether he refers in this verse to *two* inquiries—to the *possibility* of the resurrection, and to the *kind* of bodies that should be raised; but it is the most obvious interpretation of the verse, and it is certain that in his argument he discusses both these points.

36. Thou *fool.* Foolish, inconsiderate man! The meaning is, that it was foolish to make this objection, when the same difficulty existed in an undeniable *fact* which fell under daily observation. A man was a fool to urge that as an objection to religion which *must* exist in the undeniable and every-day facts which they witnessed. The idea is, "The same difficulty may be started about the growth of grain. Suppose a man who had never seen it, were to be told that it was to be put into the earth; that it was to die; to be decomposed; and that from the decayed kernel there should be seen to start up first a slender, green, and tender spire of grass, and that this was to send up a strong stalk, and was to produce hundreds of similar kernels at some distant period. These facts would be as *improbable* to him as the doctrine of the resurrection of the dead. When he saw the kernel laid in the ground; when he saw it decay; when apparently it was returning to dust, he would ask, HOW CAN these be connected with the production of similar grain? Are not all the indications that it will be totally corrupted and destroyed?" Yet, says Paul, this is connected with the hope of the harvest, and this fact should remove all the objection which is derived from the fact that the body returns to its native dust. The idea is, that there is an analogy, and that the *main* objection in the one case would lie equally well against the acknowledged and indisputable fact in the other. It is evident, however, that this argument is of a popular character, and is not to be pressed to the quick; nor are we to suppose that the resemblance will be in all respects the same. It is to be used as Paul used it. The objection was, that the body died, and returned to dust, and could not, therefore, rise again. The reply

chance of wheat, or of some other *grain:*
38 But God [a] giveth it a body
as it hath pleased him, and to every seed his own body.
39 All flesh *is* not the same flesh:

a Gen.1.11,12.

of Paul is, "You may make the same objection to grain that is sown. That dies also. The main body of the kernel decays. *In itself* there is no prospect that it will spring up. Should *it stop here,* and had you *never seen* a grain of wheat grow; had you only seen it in the earth, as you have seen the body in the grave, there would be the same difficulty as to how it would produce other grains, which there is about the resurrection of the body." ¶ *Is not quickened.* Does not become alive; does not grow. ¶ *Except it die;* see Note, John xii. 24. The main body of the grain decays that it may become food and nourishment to the tender germ. *Perhaps* it is implied here also that there was a *fitness* that men should die in order to obtain the glorious body of the resurrection, in the same way as it is *fit* that the kernel should die, in order that there may be a new and beautiful harvest.

37. *And that which thou sowest.* The seed which is sown. ¶ *Not that body that shall be.* You sow one kernel which is to produce many others. They shall not be the same that is sown. They will be *new* kernels raised from that; of the same kind, indeed, and showing their intimate and necessary connection with that which is sown. It is implied here that the body which will be raised will not be the same in the sense that the same particles of matter shall compose it, but the same only in the sense that it will have sprung up from that; will constitute the same order, rank, species of being, and be subject to the same laws, and deserve the same course of treatment as that which died; as the grain *produced* is subject to the same laws, and belongs to the same rank, order, and species as that which is sown. And as the same particles of matter which are sown do not enter into that which shall be in the harvest, so it is taught that the same particles of matter which constitute the body when it dies, do not constitute the new body at the resurrection. ¶ *But bare grain.* Mere grain; a mere kernel, without any husk, leaf, blade, or covering of any kind. Those are added in the process of reproduction. The design of this is to make it appear more remarkable, and to destroy the force of the objection. It was not only *not* the grain that should be produced, but it was without the appendages and ornaments of blade, and flower, and beard of the new grain. How could any one tell but what it would be so in the resurrection? How could any know but what there might be appendages and ornaments there, which were not connected with the body that died? ¶ *It may chance of wheat,* &c. For example; or suppose it be wheat or any other grain. The apostle adduces this merely for an *example;* not to intimate that there is any *chance* about it.

38. *But God giveth it a body,* &c. God gives to the seed sown its own proper body, formation, and growth. The word *body* here, as applied to grain, seems to mean the whole *system,* or arrangement of roots, stalks, leaves, flowers, and kernels that start out of the seed that is sown The meaning is, that such a form is produced from the seed sown as God pleases. Paul here traces the result to God, to show that there is no chance, and that it did not depend on the nature of things, but was dependent on the wise arrangement of God. There was nothing in the decaying kernel itself that would produce this result; but God chose that it should be so. There is nothing in the decaying body of the dead which in itself should lead to the resurrection, but God chose it should be so. ¶ *As it hath pleased him.* As he chose. It is by his arrangement and agency. Though it is by regular laws, yet it is as God pleases. He acts according to his own pleasure, in the formation of each root, and stalk, and kernel of

but *there is* one *kind of* flesh of men, another flesh of beasts, another of fishes, *and* another of birds.

grain. It is, probably, here intimated that God would give to each one of the dead at the resurrection such a body as he should choose, though it will be, doubtless, in accordance with general laws. ¶ *And to every seed his own body.* That which appropriately belongs to it; which it is fitted to produce; which is of the same kind. He does not cause a stalk of rye to grow from a kernel of wheat; nor of maize from barley; nor of hemp from lentiles. He has fixed proper laws, and he takes care that they shall be observed. So it will be in the resurrection. Every one shall have his own, *i. e.* his proper body—a body which shall belong to him, and be fitted to him. The wicked shall not rise with the body of the just, or with a body adapted to heaven; nor shall the saint rise with a body adapted to perdition. There shall be a fitness or appropriateness in the new body to the character of him who is raised. The *argument* here is designed to meet the inquiry HOW should the body be raised, and it is that there is nothing more remarkable and impossible in the doctrine of the resurrection, than in the fact constantly before us, that grain that seems to rot sends up a shoot or stalk, and is reproduced in a wonderful and beautiful manner. In a manner similar to this, the body will be raised; and the illustration of Paul meets all the difficulties about the *fact* of the resurrection. It cannot be shown that one is more difficult than the other; and as the facts of vegetation are constantly passing before our eyes, we ought not to deem it strange if *similar* facts shall take place hereafter in regard to the resurrection of the dead.

39. *All flesh is not the same flesh.* This verse and the following are designed to answer the question (ver. 35), "with what bodies do they come?" And the argument here is, that there are *many kinds* of bodies; that all are not alike; that while they are *bodies*, yet they partake of different qualities, forms, and properties; and that, *therefore*, it is not absurd to suppose that God may transform the human body into a different form, and cause it to be raised up with somewhat different properties in the future world. Why, the argument is, why should it be regarded as impossible? Why is it to be held that the human body may not undergo a transformation, or that it will be absurd to suppose that it may be different in some respects from what it is now? Is it not a matter of fact that there is a great variety of bodies even on the earth? The word *flesh* here is used to denote *body*, as it often is. 1 Cor. v. 5; 2 Cor. iv. 11; vii. 1; Phil. i. 22, 24; Col. ii. 5; 1 Pet. iv. 6. The idea here is, that although all the bodies of animals may be composed essentially of the same elements, yet God has produced a wonderful variety in their organization, strength, beauty, colour, and places of abode, as the air, earth, and water. It is not *necessary*, therefore, to suppose that the body that shall be raised shall be precisely like that which we have here. It is certainly *possible* that there may be *as great* a difference between that and our present body, as between the most perfect form of the human frame here and the lowest reptile. It would still be *a body*, and there would be no absurdity in the transformation. The body of the worm, the chrysalis, and the butterfly is the same. It is the same animal still. Yet how different the gaudy and gay butterfly from the creeping and offensive caterpillar! So there *may* be a similar change in the body of the believer, and yet be still the same. Of a sceptic on this subject we would ask, whether, if there had been a *revelation* of the changes which a caterpillar might undergo before it became a butterfly—a new species of existence adapted to a new element, requiring new food, and associated with new and other beings—if he had never *seen* such a transformation, would it not be attended with all the difficulty which now encompasses the doctrine of the

40 *There* [a] *are* also celestial bodies, and bodies terrestrial: but the glory of the celestial *is* one, and the *glory* of the terrestrial *is* another.

41 *There is* one glory of the sun, [b] and another glory of the moon, and another glory of the stars: for *one* star differeth from *another* star in glory.

42 So also *is* the resurrection of the dead. It is sown in corruption; it is raised in incorruption.

a Gen.1.16. b Ps. 19.4,5

resurrection? The sceptic would no more have believed it *on the authority of revelation* than he will believe the doctrine of the resurrection of the dead. And no infidel can prove that the one is attended with any more difficulty or absurdity than the other.

40. There are *also celestial bodies.* The planets; the stars; the host of heaven; see ver. 41. ¶ *And bodies terrestrial.* On earth; earthly. He refers here to the bodies of men, beasts, birds, &c.; perhaps, also, of trees and vegetables. The sense is, "There is a great variety of bodies. Look upon the heavens, and see the splendour of the sun, the moon, and the stars. And then look upon the earth, and see the bodies there—the bodies of men, and brutes, and insects. You see here two entire *classes* of bodies. You see how they differ. Can it be deemed strange if there should be a difference between our bodies when on earth and when in heaven? Do we not, *in fact,* see a vast difference between what strikes our eye here on earth and in the sky? And why should we deem it strange that between bodies adapted to live *here* and bodies adapted to live *in heaven,* there should be a difference, *like* that which is seen between the objects which appear on earth and those which appear in the sky?" The argument is a popular one; but it is striking, and meets the object which he has in view. ¶ *The glory of the celestial* is *one.* The splendour, beauty, dignity, magnificence of the heavenly bodies differs much from those on earth. That is *one thing;* the beauty of earthly objects is *another* and *a different thing.* Beautiful as may be the human frame; beautiful as may be the plumage of birds; beautiful as may be the flower, the fossil, the mineral, the topaz, or the diamond; yet they *differ* from the heavenly bodies, and are not to be compared with them. Why should we deem it strange that there may be a similar difference between the body as adapted to its residence here and as adapted to its residence in heaven?

41. There is *one glory of the sun,* &c. The sun has one degree of splendour, and the moon another, and so also the stars. They differ from each other in magnitude, in brightness, in beauty. The idea in this verse differs from that in the former. In that (ver. 40) Paul says, that there was a difference between the different *classes* of bodies; between those in heaven and those on earth. He here says, that in the former *class,* in the heavenly bodies themselves, there was a difference. They not only differed from those on earth, but they differed from each other. The sun was more splendid than the moon, and one star more beautiful than another. The idea here is, therefore, not only that the bodies of the saints in heaven shall differ from those on earth, but that they shall differ among themselves, in a sense somewhat like the difference of the splendour of the sun, the moon, and the different stars. Though *all* shall be unlike what they were on earth, and all shall be glorious, yet there may be a difference in that splendour and glory. The *argument* is, since we see so great differences *in fact* in the works of God, why should we doubt that he is able to make the human body different from what it is now, and to endow it with immortal and eternal perfection?

42. *So also* is *the resurrection.* In a manner similar to the grain that is sown, and to the different degrees of splendour and magnificence in the bodies in the sky and on the earth. The

43 It [a] is sown in dishonour; it is raised in glory: it is sown in weakness; it is raised in power:

a Dan.12.3; Mat.13.43; Phil.3.21.

dead shall be raised in a manner analogous to the springing up of grain; and there shall be a difference between the body here and the body in the resurrection. ¶ *It is sown.* In death. As we sow or plant the kernel in the earth. ¶ *In corruption.* In the grave; in a place where it shall be corrupt; in a form tending to putrefaction, disorganization, and dust. ¶ *It is raised in incorruption.* It will be so raised. In the previous verses (36—41) he had reasoned from analogy, and had demonstrated that it was *possible* that the dead should rise, or that there was no greater difficulty attending it than actually occurred in the events which were in fact constantly taking place. He here states positively what would be, and affirms that it was not only possible, but that such a resurrection would actually occur. They body would be raised "in incorruption," "uncorruptible" (ver. 52); that is, no more liable to decay, sickness, disorganization, and putrefaction. This is *one* characteristic of the body that shall be raised, that it shall be no more liable, as here, to wasting sickness, to disease, and to the loathsome corruption of the grave. That God *can* form a body of that kind, no one can doubt; that he actually will, the apostle positively affirms. That such *will* be the bodies of the saints is one of the most cheering prospects that can be presented to those who are here wasted away by sickness, and who look with dread and horror on the loathsome putrefaction of the tomb.

43. *It is sown in dishonour.* In the grave, where it is shut out from human view; hurried away from the sight of friends; loathsome and offensive as a mass turning to decay. There is, moreover, a kind of disgrace and ignominy attending it here, as under the curse of God, and, on account of sin, sentenced to the offensiveness of the grave. ¶ *It is raised in glory.* In honour; in beauty; honoured by God by the removal of the curse, and in a form and manner that shall be glorious. This refers to the fact that every thing like dishonour, vileness, ignominy, which attends it here shall be removed there, and that the body shall bear a resemblance to the glorified body of Jesus Christ, Eph. iii. 21. It shall be adapted to a world of glory; and every thing which here rendered it vile, valueless, cumbersome, offensive, or degraded, shall be there removed. Of course, every idea which we can get from this is chiefly negative, and consists in denying that the body will have there the qualities which here render it vile or loathsome. The word glory (δόξα) means dignity, splendour, honour, excellence, perfection; and is here used as denoting the *combination* of all those things which shall rescue it from ignominy and disgrace. ¶ *It is sown in weakness.* Weak, feeble, liable to decay. Here disease prostrates the strength, takes away its power, consigns it to the dust. It denotes the many weaknesses, frailties, and liabilities to sickness, to which we are here exposed. Its feeble powers are soon prostrate; its vital functions soon cease in death. ¶ *It is raised in power.* This does not denote power like that of God, nor like the angels. It does not affirm that it shall be endued with remarkable and enormous physical strength, or that it shall have the power of performing what would now be regarded as miraculous. It is to be regarded as the opposite of the word "weakness," and means that it shall be no longer liable to disease; no more overcome by the attacks of sickness; no more subject to the infirmities and weaknesses which it here experiences. It shall not be prostrate by sickness, nor overcome by fatigue. It shall be capable of the service of God without weariness and languor; it shall need no rest as it does here (see Rev. vii. 15; comp. xxii. 5); but it shall be in a world where there shall be no fatigue, lassitude, disease; but where there shall be ample power to engage in the service of God for ever.

44 It is sown a natural body; it is raised a spiritual body. There is a natural body, and **there is** a spiritual [a] body.

a Luke 24.31; John 20.19,26.

There is, however, no improbability in supposing that the physical powers of man, as well as his intellectual, *may be* greatly augmented in heaven. But on this point there is no revelation.

44. *It is sown a natural body* (σῶμα ψυχικόν). This word, "natural," denotes properly that which is endowed with *animal* life, having breath, or vitality. The word from which it is derived (ψυχή) denotes properly the breath; vital breath; the soul, as the vital principle; the animal soul, or the vital spirit; the soul, as the seat of the sentient desires, passions, and propensities; and then a living thing, an animal. It may be applied to *any* animal, or any living thing, whether brutes or men. It is distinguished from the soul or spirit (πνεῦμα), inasmuch as that more commonly denotes the *rational* spirit, the immortal soul, that which thinks, reasons, reflects, &c. The word "natural" here, therefore, means that which has *animal* life; which breathes and acts by the laws of the animal economy; that which draws in the breath of life; which is endowed with senses, and which has need of the *supports* of animal life, and of the refreshments derived from food, exercise, sleep, &c. The apostle here, by affirming that the body will be spiritual, intends to deny that it will need that which is now necessary to the support of the animal functions; it will not be sustained in that way; it will lay aside these peculiar animal organizations, and will cease to convey the idea which we now attach to the word *animal*, or to possess that which we now include under the name of *vital functions*. Here the body of man is endowed simply with *animal* functions. It is the dwelling-place indeed of an immortal mind; but *as* a body it has the properties of *animal* life, and is subject to the same laws and inconveniences as the bodies of other animals. It is sustained by breath, and food, and sleep; it is endowed with the organs of sense, the eye, the ear, the smell, the touch, by which alone the soul can hold communication with the external world; it is liable to disease, languor, decay, death. These *animal* or *vital* functions will cease in heaven, and the body be raised in a different mode of being, and where all the inconveniences of this mere animal life shall be laid aside. ¶ *It is raised a spiritual body.* Not a mere spirit, for then it would not be a body. The word *spiritual* (πνευματικόν) here stands opposed to the word *natural*, or *animal*. It will *not* be a body that is subject to the laws of the vital functions, or organized or sustained in that way. It will still be a "body" (σῶμα), but it will have *so far* the nature of spirit as to be *without* the vital functions which here control the body. This is all that the word here means. It does not mean refined, sublimated, or transcendental; it does not mean that it will be without shape or form; it does not mean that it will not be properly *a body*. The idea of Paul seems to be this: "We conceive of soul or spirit as not subject to the laws of vital or animal agency. It is independent of them. It is not sustained or nourished by the functions of the animal organization. It has an economy of its own; living without nourishment; not subject to decay; not liable to sickness, pain, or death. So will be the body in the resurrection. It will not be subject to the laws of the vital organization. It will be so much LIKE a spirit as to be continued without food or nutriment; to be destitute of the peculiar physical organization of flesh, and blood, and bones; of veins, and arteries, and nerves, as here (ver. 50.); and it will live in the manner in which we conceive spirits to live; sustained, and exercising its powers, without waste, weariness, decay, or the necessity of having its powers recruited by food and sleep." All, therefore, that has been said about a refined body, a body that shall be spirit, a body that shall be pure, &c., whatever may be its truth, is not

45 And so it is written, [a] The first man Adam was made a living soul; the [b] last Adam *was made* a quickening spirit.

a Gen.2.7.

b John 5.21; 6.33,40.

sustained by this passage. It will be a body without the vital functions of the animal economy; a body sustained in the manner in which we conceive the spirit to be. ¶ *There is a natural body.* This seems to be added by Paul in the way of strong affirmation arising from earnestness, and from a desire to prevent misconception. The affirmation is, that there *is* a natural body; that is apparent: it is everywhere seen. No one can doubt it. So, with equal certainty, says Paul, there *is* a spiritual body. It is just as certain and indisputable. This assertion is made, not because the evidence of both is the same, but is made on his apostolic authority, and is to be received on that authority. That there was an animal body was apparent to all; that there was a spiritual body was a position which he affirmed to be as certain as the other. The only proof which he alleges is in ver. 45, which is the proof, arising from revelation.

45. *And so it is written*, Gen. ii. 7. It is only the first part of the verse which is quoted. ¶ *The first man Adam was made a living soul.* This is quoted exactly from the translation by the LXX, except that the apostle has added the words "first" and "Adam." This is done to designate whom he meant. The meaning of the phrase "was made a living soul" (ἐγένετο εἰς ψυχὴν ζῶσαν—in Hebrew, לנפש חיה) is, became a living, animated being; a being endowed with life. The use of the word "soul" in our translation, for ψυχὴ and נפש (*nephesh*), does not quite convey the idea. We apply the word *soul*, usually, to the intelligent and the immortal part of man; that which reasons, thinks, remembers, is conscious, is responsible, &c. The Greek and Hebrew words, however, more properly denote that which is alive, which is animated, which breathes, which has an animal nature, Note on ver. 44. And this is precisely the idea which Paul uses here, that the first man was made an animated being by having breathed into him the breath of life (Gen. ii. 7), and that it is the image of this animated or vital being which we bear, ver. 48. Neither Moses nor Paul deny that in addition to this, man was endowed with a rational soul, an immortal nature; but that is not the idea which they present in the passage in Genesis which Paul quotes. ¶ *The last Adam.* The second Adam, or the "second man," ver. 47. That Christ is here intended is apparent, and has been usually admitted by commentators. Christ here seems to be called *Adam* because he stands in contradistinction from the first Adam; or because, as we derive our animal and dying nature from the one, so we derive our immortal and undying bodies from the other. From the one we derive an animal or vital existence; from the other we derive our immortal existence, and resurrection from the grave. The one stands at the head of all those who have an existence represented by the words, "a living soul;" the other of all those who shall have a spiritual body in heaven. He is called "the *last* Adam;" meaning that there shall be no other after him who shall affect the destiny of man in the same way, or who shall stand at the head of the race in a manner similar to what had been done by him and the first father of the human family. They sustain peculiar relations to the race; and in this respect they were "the first" and "the last" in the peculiar economy. The name "Adam" is not elsewhere given to the Messiah, though a comparison is several times instituted between him and Adam. [See the supplementary Note on ver. 22; also on Rom. v. 12.] ¶ *A quickening spirit* (εἰς πνεῦμα ζωοποιοῦν). A vivifying spirit; a spirit giving or imparting life. Not a being having mere vital functions, or an animated nature, but a being who has the power of imparting life. This is not a quotation from any part of the Scriptures, but seems to be used by Paul

46 Howbeit that *was* not first which is spiritual, but that which is natural; and afterward that which is spiritual.

47 The [a] first man *is* of the earth, earthy: the second man *is* the Lord from heaven.

48 As *is* the earthy, such *are*

a John 3.13,31.

either as affirming what was true on his own apostolic authority, or as conveying the *substance* of what was revealed respecting the Messiah in the Old Testament. There may be also reference to what the Saviour himself taught, that he was the source of life; that he had the power of imparting life, and that he gave life to all whom he pleased; see Note, John i. 4; v. 26, "For as the Father hath life in himself, so hath he given to the Son to have life in himself." ver. 21, "For as the Father raiseth up the dead, and quickeneth them, even so the Son quickeneth whom he will." The word "spirit," here applied to Christ, is in contradistinction from "a living being," as applied to Adam, and seems to be used in the sense of spirit of life, as raising the bodies of his people from the dead, and imparting life to them. He was constituted not as having life merely, but as endowed with the power of imparting life; as endowed with that spiritual or vital energy which was needful to impart life. All life is the creation or production of *spirit* (Πνεῦμα); as applied to God the Father, or the Son, or the Holy Spirit. *Spirit* is the source of all vitality. God is a spirit, and God is the source of all life. And the idea here is, that Christ had such a spiritual existence, such power as a spirit; that he was the source of all life to his people. The word spirit is applied to his exalted spiritual nature, in distinction from his human nature, in Rom. i. 4; 1 Tim. iii. 16; 1 Pet. iii. 18. The apostle does not here affirm that he had not a human nature, or a vital existence as a man; but that his *main* characteristic in contradistinction from Adam was, that he was endowed with an elevated spiritual nature, which was capable of imparting vital existence to the dead.

46. *Howbeit.* There is a due order observed, ver. 23. The decaying, the dying, the weak, the corruptible, in the proper order of events, was first. This order was necessary, and this is observed everywhere. It is seen in the grain that dies in the ground, and in the resurrection of man. The imperfect is succeeded by the perfect; the impure by the pure; the vile and degraded by the precious and the glorious. The idea is, that there is a tendency towards perfection, and that God observes the proper order by which that which is most glorious shall be secured. It was not his plan that all things in the beginning should be perfect; but that perfection should be the work of time, and should be secured in an appropriate *order* of events. The design of Paul in this verse seems to be to vindicate the statement which he had made, by showing that it was in accordance with what was everywhere observed, that the proper *order* should be maintained. This idea is carried through the following verses.

47. *The first man.* Adam. ¶ Is *of the earth.* Was made of the dust; see Gen. ii. 7. ¶ *Earthy.* Partaking of the earth: he was a mass of animated clay, and could be appropriately called "DUST;" Gen. iii. 19. Of course, he must partake of a nature that was low, mean, mortal, and corruptible. ¶ *The second man.* Christ; see Note on ver. 45. He is called the *second* man, as being the second who sustained a relation to men that was materially to affect their conduct and destiny; the second and the last (ver. 45), who should sustain a peculiar headship to the race. ¶ *The Lord from heaven.* Called in chap. ii. 8, the "Lord of glory;" see Note on that place. This expression refers to the fact that the Lord Jesus had a heavenly origin, in contradistinction from Adam, who was formed from the earth. The Latin Vulgate renders this, "the second man from heaven is heavenly;" and this idea seems to accord with the meaning in the former member of the

they also that are earthy: and as *is* the heavenly, such *are* they also that are heavenly.

49 And as we have borne the image of the earthy, we shall also [a] bear the image of the heavenly.

50 Now this I say, brethren,

a Rom.8.29.

verse. The sense is, evidently, that as the first man had an earthly origin, and was, therefore, earthy, so the second man being from heaven, as his proper home, would have a body adapted to that abode; unlike that which was earthy, and which would be fitted to his exalted nature, and to the world where he would dwell. And while, therefore, the phrase "from heaven" refers to his heavenly origin, the essential idea is, that he would have a body that was adapted to such an origin and such a world—a body unlike that which was earthy. That is, Christ had a glorified body to which the bodies of the saints must yet be made like.

48. *As* is *the earthy.* Such as Adam was. ¶ *Such* are *they also,* &c. Such are all his descendants; all who derive their nature from him. That is, they are frail, corruptible, mortal; they live in an animal body as he did, and like him, they are subject to corruption and decay. ¶ *And as* is *the heavenly.* As is he who was from heaven; as is the Lord Jesus now in his glorified body. ¶ *Such* are *they also,* &c. Such will they be also. They will be like him; they will have a body like his. This idea is more fully expressed in Phil. iii. 21, "Who shall change our vile body, that it may be fashioned like unto his glorious body."

49. *And as we have borne the image of the earthy.* As like our first father, we are frail, decaying, dying; as we are so closely connected with him as to be like him. This does not refer, mainly, to one bearing his moral character, but to the fact that we are, like him, subject to sickness, frailty, sorrow, and death. ¶ *We shall also bear the image of the heavenly.* The Lord Jesus Christ, who was from heaven, and who is in heaven. As we are so closely connected with Adam as to resemble him, so by the divine arrangement, and by faith in the Lord Jesus, we are so closely connected with him that we shall resemble him in heaven. And as he is now free from frailty, sickness, pain, sorrow, and death, and as he has a pure and spiritual body, adapted to a residence in heaven, so shall we be in that future world. The *argument* here is, that the connection which is formed between the believer and the Saviour is as close as that which subsisted between him and Adam; and as that connection with Adam involved the certainty that he would be subjected to pain, sin, sickness, and death, so the connection with Christ involves the certainty that he will like him be free from sin, sickness, pain, and death, and like him will have a body that is pure, incorruptible, and immortal.

50. *Now this I say, brethren.* "I make this affirmation in regard to this whole subject. I do it as containing the substance of all that I have said. I do it in order to prevent all mistake in regard to the nature of the bodies which shall be raised up." This affirmation is made respecting all the dead and all the living, that there must be a material and important change in regard to them before they can be prepared for heaven. Paul had proved in the previous verses that it was *possible* for God to give us bodies different from those which we now possess; he here affirms, in the most positive manner, that it was indispensable that we should have bodies different from what we now have. ¶ *Flesh and blood.* Bodies organized as ours now are. "Flesh and blood" denotes such bodies as we have here,—bodies that are fragile, weak, liable to disease, subject to pain and death. They are composed of changing particles; to be repaired and strengthened daily; they are subject to decay, and are wasted away by sickness, and of course they cannot be fitted to a world where there shall

that [a] flesh and blood cannot inherit the kingdom of God; neither doth corruption inherit incorruption.

51 Behold, I show you a mystery: We [b] shall not all sleep, but we shall all be changed.

a John 3.3,5.

b 1 Thess.4.15-17.

be no decay and and no death. ¶ *Cannot inherit.* Cannot be admitted as heir to the kingdom of God. The future world of glory is often represented as an heirship; see Note on Rom. viii. 17. ¶ *The kingdom of God.* Heaven; appropriately called his kingdom, because he shall reign there in undivided and perfect glory for ever. ¶ *Neither doth corruption,* &c. Neither can that which is in its nature corruptible, and liable to decay, be adapted to a world where all is incorruptible. The apostle here simply states the fact. He does not tell us *why* it is impossible. It *may be* because the mode of communication there is not by the bodily senses; it may be because such bodies as ours would not be fitted to relish the pure and exalted pleasures of an incorruptible world; it may be because they would interfere with the exalted worship, the active service, and the sleepless employments of the heavenly world; it may be because *such* a body is constituted to derive pleasure from objects which shall not be found in heaven. It is adapted to enjoyment in eating and drinking, and the pleasures of the eye, the ear, the taste, the touch; in heaven the soul shall be awake to more elevated and pure enjoyments than these, and, of course, such bodies as we here have would impede our progress and destroy our comforts, and be ill adapted to all the employments and enjoyments of that heavenly world.

51. *Behold I show you.* This commences the *third* subject of inquiry in the chapter,—the question, what will become of those who are alive when the Lord Jesus shall return to raise the dead? This was an *obvious* inquiry, and the answer was, perhaps, supposed to be difficult. Paul answers it directly, and says that they will undergo an instantaneous change, which will make them like the dead that shall be raised. ¶ *A mystery.* On the meaning of this word, see Note, chap. ii. 7. The word here does not mean any thing which was in its nature unintelligible, but that which to them had been hitherto unknown. "I now communicate to you a truth which has not been brought into the discussion, and in regard to which no communication has been made to you." On this subject there had been no revelation. Though the Pharisees held that the dead would rise, yet they do not seem to have made any statement in regard to the living who should remain when the dead should rise. Nor, perhaps, had the subject occupied the attention of the apostles; nor had there been any direct communication on it from the Lord Jesus himself. Paul then here says, that he was about to communicate a great truth which till then had been unknown, and to resolve a great inquiry on which there had as yet been no revelation. ¶ *We shall not all sleep. We Christians;* grouping all together who then lived and should live afterwards, for his discussion has relation to them all. The following remarks may, perhaps, remove some of the difficulty which attends the interpretation of this passage. The *objection* which is made to it is, that Paul expected to live until the Lord Jesus should return; that he, therefore, expected that the world would soon end, and that in this he was mistaken, and could not be inspired. To this, we may reply, (1.) He is speaking of Christians as such—of the whole church that had been redeemed—of the entire mass that should enter heaven; and he groups them all together, and connects himself with them, and says, "*We* shall not die; we Christians, including the whole church, shall not *all* die," &c. That he did not refer only to those whom he was then

addressing, is apparent from the whole discussion. The argument relates to Christians—to the church at large; and the affirmation here has reference to that church considered as one church that was to be raised up on the last day. (2.) That Paul did not expect that the Lord Jesus would *soon* come, and that the world would *soon* come to an end, is apparent from a similar place in the epistle to the Thessalonians. In 1 Thess. iv. 15, he uses language remarkably similar to that which is here used: "*We* which are alive, and remain unto the coming of the Lord," &c. This language was interpreted by the Thessalonians as teaching that the world would soon come to an end, and the effect had been to produce a state of alarm. Paul was, therefore, at special pains to show in his second epistle to them, that he did not mean any such thing. He showed them (2 Thess. ii.) that the end of the world was *not* near; that very important events were to occur before the world would come to an end; and that his language did not imply any expectation on his part that the world would soon terminate, or that the Lord Jesus would soon come. (3.) Parallel expressions occur in the other writers of the New Testament, and with a similar signification. Thus, John (1 Epis. ii. 18) says, "It is the last time;" comp. Heb. i. 2. But the meaning of this is not that the world would soon come to an end. The prophets spoke of a period which they called "the last days" (Isa. ii. 2; Micah iv. 1; in Hebrew, "the after days"), as the period in which the Messiah would live and reign. By it they meant the dispensation which should be *the last;* that under which the world would close; the reign of the Messiah, which would be the *last* economy of human things. But it did not follow that this was to be a *short* period; or that it might not be longer than any one of the former, or than *all* the former put together. This was that which John spoke of as the last time. (4.) I do not know that the proper doctrine of inspiration suffers, if we admit that the apostles *were* ignorant of the exact time when the world would close; or even that in regard to the precise period when that would take place, they might be in error. The following considerations may be suggested on this subject, showing that the claim to inspiration did not extend to the knowledge of this fact. (*a*) That they were not omniscient, and there is no more absurdity in supposing that they were ignorant on *this* subject than in regard to any other. (*b*) Inspiration extended to the *order* of future events, and not to the *times.* There is in the Scriptures *no* statement of the *time* when the world would close. Future events were made to pass before the minds of the prophets, as *in a landscape.* The *order* of the images may be distinctly marked, but the *times* may not be designated. And even events which may occur in fact at distant periods, may in vision appear to be near each other; as in a landscape, objects which are in fact separated by distant intervals, like the ridges of a mountain, may appear to lie close to each other. (*c*) The Saviour expressly said, that it was not designed that they should *know* when future events would occur. Thus, after his ascension, in answer to an inquiry whether he then would restore the kingdom to Israel, he said (Acts i. 7), "It is not *for you* to know the times or the seasons which the Father hath put in his own power." See Note on that verse. (*d*) The Saviour said that even he himself, as man, was ignorant in regard to the exact time in which future events would occur. "But of that day, and that hour, knoweth no man, no, not the angels which are in heaven, neither the Son, but the Father;" Mark xiii. 32. (*e*) The apostles *were in fact* ignorant, and mistaken in regard to, at least, the time of the occurrence of *one* future event, the death of John; xxi. 23. There is, therefore, no departure from the proper doctrine of inspiration, in supposing that the apostles were not inspired on these subjects, and that they might be ignorant like others. The proper *order* of events they state truly and exactly; the

52 In a moment, [a] in the twinkling of an eye, at the last trump: for the [b] trumpet shall sound, and the dead [c] shall be raised incorruptible, and we shall be changed.

53 For this corruptible must put on incorruption, and this mortal [d] *must* put on immortality.

54 So when this corruptible shall have put on incorruption,

a 2Pet.3.10. b Zech.9.14; Mat.24.31. c John 5.25. d 2Cor.5.4; 1John 3.2.

exact *time* God did not, for wise reasons, intend to make known. ¶ *Shall not all sleep.* Shall not all die; see Note, chap. xi. 30. ¶ *But we shall all be changed.* There is considerable variety in the reading of this passage. The Vulgate reads it, "We shall all indeed rise, but we shall not all be changed." Some Greek MSS. read it, "We shall all sleep, but we shall not all be changed." Others, as the Vulgate, "We shall all rise, but we shall not all be changed." But the present Greek text contains, doubtless, the true reading; and the sense is, that all who are alive at the coming of the Lord Jesus shall undergo such a change as to fit them for their new abode in heaven; or such as shall make them like those who shall be raised from the dead. This change will be instantaneous (ver. 52), for it is evident that God can as easily change the living as he can raise the dead; and as the affairs of the world will then have come to an end, there will be no necessity that those who are then alive should be removed by death; nor would it be proper that they should go down to lie any time in the grave. The ordinary laws, therefore, by which men are removed to eternity, will not operate in regard to them, and they will be removed at once to their new abode.

52. *In a moment* (ἐν ἀτόμῳ). In an *atom*, scil. of time; a point of time which cannot be cut or divided (α priv. and τομη, from τέμνω, to cut). A single instant; immediately. It will be done instantaneously. ¶ *In the twinkling of an eye.* This is an expression also denoting the least conceivable duration of time. The *suddenness* of the coming of the Lord Jesus is elsewhere compared to the coming of a thief in the night; 2 Pet. iii. 10. The word rendered "twinkling" (ῥιπῇ, from ῥίπτω, to throw, cast) means a throw, cast, jerk, as of a stone; and then a *jerk* of the eye, *i. e.* a wink.—*Robinson.* ¶ *At the last trump.* When the trumpet shall sound to raise the dead. The word "last" here does not imply that any trumpet shall have been *before* sounded at the resurrection, but is a word denoting that this is the consummation or close of things; it will end the economy of this world; it will be connected with the *last* state of things. ¶ *For the trumpet shall sound;* see Note, Mat. xxiv. 31. ¶ *And the dead shall be raised;* Note, John v. 25.

53. *For this corruptible,* &c. It is necessary that a change should take place, either by dying and then being raised, or by being changed without seeing death; for we cannot enter heaven as we are now. ¶ Must *put on.* The word here used (ἐνδύνω) properly means to go in, to envelope, to put on as a garment; and then to put on any thing; as the soul is, as it were, clothed with, or invested with a body; and here it means, must be endued with, or furnished with. It is equivalent to saying that this corruptible must become incorruptible, and this mortal must become immortal. We must cease to be corruptible and mortal, and must become incorruptible and immortal. The righteous who remain till the coming of Christ shall be at once changed, and invested, as Enoch and Elijah were, with incorruption and immortality.

54. *So when,* &c. In that future glorious world, when all this shall have been accomplished. ¶ *Then shall be brought to pass.* Then shall be fully accomplished; these words shall then receive their entire fulfilment; or this event shall meet all that is implied in these words. ¶ *The*

and this mortal shall have put
on immortality, then shall be
brought to pass the saying that
is written, Death [a] is swallowed
up in victory.
55 O [b] death, where *is* thy

[a] Isa.25.8. [b] Hos.13.14.

saying that is written. What is written, or the record which is made. These words are quoted from Isa. xxv. 8; and the fact that Paul thus quotes them, and the connection in which they stand, prove that they had reference to the times of the gospel, and to the resurrection of the dead. Paul does not quote directly from the Hebrew, or from the LXX., but gives the substance of the passage. ¶ *Death.* Referring here, undoubtedly, to death in the proper sense; death as prostrating the living, and consigning them to the grave. ¶ *Is swallowed up.* Κατεπόθη (from καταπίνω, to drink down, to swallow down) means to absorb (Rev. xii. 16, , to overwhelm, to drown (Heb. [illegible]. 29); and then to destroy or remove. The idea may be taken from a whiripool, or Maelstrom, that absorbs all that comes near it; and the sense is, that he will abolish or remove death; that is, cause it to cease from its ravages and triumphs. ¶ *In victory* (εἰς νῖκος). Unto victory; so as to ɔbtain a complete victory. The Hebrew (Isa. xxv. 8) is לנצח, The LXX. often render the word נצח, which properly means splendour, purity, trust, perpetuity, eternity, perfection, by νῖκος, victory; 2 Kings ii. 26; Job xxxvi. 7; Lam. iii. 18; v. 20; Amos i.; ii.; viii. 7. The Hebrew word here may be rendered either *unto the end, i. e.* to completeness or perfection, or unto victory, with triumph. It matters little which is the meaning, for they both come to the same thing. The idea is, that the power and dominion of death shall be entirely destroyed, or brought to an end.

55. *O death.* This triumphant exclamation is the commencement of the *fourth* division of the chapter,—the practical consequences of the doctrine. It is such an exclamation as every man with right feelings will be disposed to make, who contemplates the ravages of death; who looks upon a world where in all forms he has reigned, and who then contemplates the glorious truth, that a complete and final triumph has been obtained over this great enemy of the happiness of man, and that man would die no more. It is a triumphant view which bursts upon the soul as it contemplates the fact that the work of the second Adam has repaired the ruins of the first, and that man is redeemed; his body will be raised; not another human being should die, and the work of death should be ended. Nay, it is more. Death is not only at an end; it shall not only cease, but its evils shall be repaired; and a glory and honour shall encompass the body of man, such as would have been unknown had there been no death. No commentary can add to the beauty and force of the language in this verse; and the best way to see its beauty, and to enjoy it, is to sit down and think of DEATH; of what death has been, and has done; of the millions and millions that have died; of the earth strewed with the dead, and "arched with graves;" *of our own death;* the certainty that *we* must die, and our parents, and brothers, and sisters, and children, and friends; that all, *all* must die;—and *then* to suffer the truth, in its full-orbed splendour, to rise upon us, that the time will come when DEATH SHALL BE AT AN END. Who, in such contemplation, can refrain from the language of triumph, and from hymns of praise? ¶ *Where* is *thy sting?* The word which is here rendered *sting* (κέντρον) denotes properly a prick, a point, hence a goad or stimulus; *i. e.* a rod or staff with an iron point, for goading oxen; (see Note, Acts ix. 5); and then a *sting* properly, as of scorpions, bees, &c. It denotes here a venomous thing, or weapon, applied to death personified, as if death employed it to destroy life, as the sting of a bee or a scorpion is used. The idea is derived from the venomous sting of serpents, or other reptiles, as being destructive

sting? O grave, [1] where *is* thy victory?

1 or, *hell*.

56 The [a] sting of death *is* sin; and [b] the strength of sin *is* the law.

a Rom.6.23. b Rom.4.15

and painful. The language here is the language of exultation, as if that was taken away or destroyed. ¶ *O grave* (ᾅδη). Hades, the place of the dead. It is not improperly rendered, however, *grave*. The word properly denotes a place of darkness; then the world, or abodes of the dead. According to the Hebrews, Hades, or Sheol, was a vast subterranean receptacle, or abode, where the souls of the dead existed. It was dark, deep, still, awful. The descent to it was through the grave; and the spirits of all the dead were supposed to be assembled there; the righteous occupying the *upper* regions, and the wicked the lower; see Note on Isa. xiv. 9; comp. Lowth, Lect. on Heb. Poet. vii. Campbell, Prel. Diss. vi. part 2, § 2. It refers here to the dead; and means that the grave, or Hades, should no longer have a victory. ¶ *Thy victory*. Since the dead are to rise; since all the graves are to give up all that dwell in them; since no man will die after that, where is its victory? It is taken away. It is despoiled. The power of death and the grave is vanquished, and Christ is triumphant over all. It has been well remarked here, that the words in this verse rise above the plain and simple language of prose, and resemble a hymn, into which the apostle breaks out in view of the glorious truth which is here presented to the mind. The whole verse is indeed a somewhat loose quotation from Hos. xiii. 14, which we translate,

"O death, I will be thy plagues;
O grave, I will be thy destruction."

But which the LXX. render,

"O death, where is thy punishment?
O grave, where is thy sting?"

Probably Paul did not intend this as a direct quotation; but he spoke as a man naturally does who is familiar with the language of the Scriptures, and used it to express the sense which he intended, without meaning to make a direct and literal quotation. The form which Paul uses is so poetic in its structure that Pope has adopted it, with only a change in the location of the members, in the "Dying Christian:"

"O grave, where is thy victory?
O death, where is thy sting?"

56. *The sting of death*. The sting which death bears; that with which he effects his purpose; that which is made use of to inflict death; or that which is the cause of death. There would be no death without sin. The apostle here *personifies* death, as if it were a living being, and as making use of sin to inflict death, or as being the sting, or envenomed instrument, with which he inflicts the mortal agony. The idea is, that sin is the cause of death. It introduced it; it makes it certain; it is the cause of the pain, distress, agony, and horror which attends it. Had there been no sin, men would not have died. If there were no sin, death would not be attended with horror or alarm. For why should innocence be afraid to die? What has innocence to fear anywhere in the universe of a just God? The fact, therefore, that men die, is proof that they are sinners; the fact that they feel horror and alarm, is proof that they feel themselves to be guilty, and that they are afraid to go into the presence of a holy God. If *this* be taken away, if sin be removed, of course the horror, and remorse, and alarm which it is fitted to produce will be removed also. ¶ Is *sin*. Sin is the cause of it; see Note, Rom. v. 12. ¶ *The strength of sin*. Its power over the mind; its terrific and dreadful energy; and *especially* its power to produce alarm in the hour of death. ¶ Is *the law*. The pure and holy law of God. This idea Paul has illustrated at length in Rom. vii. 9—13: see Notes on that passage. He probably made the statement here in order to meet the Jews, and to show that the law of God had no power to take away the fear of death; and that,

57 But thanks [a] *be* to God, which giveth us the victory [b] through our Lord Jesus Christ.

a Rom.7.25. *b* Rom.8.37; 1John 5.4,5.

58 Therefore, my beloved brethren, [a] be ye steadfast, unmovable, always abounding in the work of the Lord,

a 2Pet.3.14.

therefore, there was need of the gospel, and that this alone could do it. The Jews maintained that a man might be justified and saved by obedience to the law. Paul here shows that it is the law which gives its chief vigour to sin, and that it does not tend to subdue or destroy it; and that power is seen most strikingly in the pangs and horrors of a guilty conscience on the bed of death. There was need, therefore, of the gospel, which alone could remove the *cause* of these horrors, by taking away sin, and thus leaving the pardoned man to die in peace; comp. Note, Rom. iv. 15.

57. *But thanks* be *to God;* see Note, Rom. vii. 25. ¶ *Which giveth us the victory.* Us who are Christians; all Christians. The victory over sin, death, and the grave. *God* alone is the author of this victory. He formed the plan; he executed it in the gift of his Son; and he gives it to us *personally* when we come to die. ¶ *Through our Lord Jesus Christ.* By his death, thus destroying the power of death; by his resurrection and triumph over the grave; and by his grace imparted to us to enable us to sustain the pains of death, and giving to us the hope of a glorious resurrection; comp. Note, Rom. vii. 25; viii. 37.

58. *Therefore, my beloved brethren.* In view of the great and glorious truths which have been revealed to us respecting the resurrection, Paul closes the whole of this important discussion with an exhortation to that firmness in the faith which ought to result from truths so glorious, and from hopes so elevated as these truths are fitted to impart. The exhortation is so plain, that it needs little explanation; it so obviously follows from the argument which Paul had pursued, that there is little need to attempt to enforce it. ¶ *Be ye steadfast* (ἑδραῖοι, from ἕδρα). Seated, sedentary (Robinson); perhaps with an allusion to a *statue* (Bloomfield); or perhaps to wrestling, and to standing one's ground (Wolf). Whatever may be the allusion, the sense is clear. Be firm, strong, confident in the faith, in view of the truth that you will be raised up. Be not shaken or agitated with the strifes, the temptations, and the cares of life. Be fixed in the faith, and let not the power of sin, or the sophistry of pretended philosophy, or the arts of the enemy of the soul seduce you from the faith of the gospel. ¶ *Unmovable.* Firm, fixed, stable, unmoved. This is probably a stronger expression than the former, though meaning substantially the same thing—that we are to be firm and unshaken in our Christian hopes, and in our faith in the gospel. ¶ *Always abounding in the work of the Lord.* Always engaged in doing the will of God; in promoting his glory, and advancing his kingdom. The phrase means not only to be engaged in this, but to be engaged diligently, laboriously; excelling in this. The "work of the Lord" here means that which the Lord requires; all the appropriate duties of Christians. Paul exhorts them to practise every Christian virtue, and to do all that they could do to further the gospel among men. ¶ *Forasmuch as ye know.* Gr. *Knowing.* You know it by the arguments which have been urged for the truth of the gospel; by your deep conviction that that gospel is true. ¶ *Your labour is not in vain.* It will be rewarded. It is not as if you were to die and never live again. There will be a resurrection, and you will be suitably recompensed then What you do for the honour of God will not only be attended with an approving conscience, and with happiness here, but will be met with the glorious and eternal rewards of heaven. ¶ *In the Lord.* This probably means, "Your labour or work in the Lord, *i. e.* in the cause of the Lord, will not be in vain." And the senti-

forasmuch as ye know that your labour is not in vain in the Lord.

ment of the whole verse is, that the hope of the resurrection and of future glory should stimulate us to great and self-denying efforts in honour of Him who has revealed that doctrine, and who purposes graciously to reward us there. Other men are influenced and excited to great efforts by the hope of honour, pleasure, or wealth. Christians should be excited to toil and self-denial by the prospect of immortal glory; and by the assurance that their hopes are not in vain, and will not deceive them.

Thus closes this chapter of inimitable beauty, and of unequalled power of argumentation. Such is the prospect which is before the Christian. He shall indeed die like other men. But his death is *a sleep*—a calm, gentle, undisturbed sleep, in the expectation of being again awaked to a brighter day, ver. 6. He has the assurance that his Saviour rose, and that his people shall *therefore* also rise, ver. 12—20. He encounters peril, and privation, and persecution; he may be ridiculed and despised; he may be subjected to danger, or doomed to fight with wild beasts, or to contend with men who resemble wild beasts; he may be doomed to the pains and terrors of a martyrdom at the stake, but he has the assurance that all these are of short continuance, and that before him there is a world of eternal glory; ver. 29—32. He may be poor, unhonoured, and apparently without an earthly friend or protector; but his Saviour and Redeemer reigns; ver. 25. He may be opposed by wicked men, and his name slandered, and body tortured, and his peace marred, but his enemies shall all be subdued; ver. 26, 27. He will himself die, and sleep in his grave, but he shall live again; ver. 22, 23. He has painful proof that his body is corruptible, but it will be incorruptible; that it is now vile, but it will be glorious; that it is weak, frail, feeble, but it will yet be strong, and no more subject to disease or decay; ver. 42, 43. And he will be brought under the power of death, but death shall be robbed of its honours, and despoiled of its triumph. Its sting from the saint is taken away, and it is changed to a blessing. It is now not the dreaded monster, the king of terrors it is a friend that comes to remove him from a world of toil to a world of rest; from a life of sin to a life of glory. The grave is not to him the gloomy *abode*, the permanent resting-place of his body; it is a place of rest for a little time; grateful like the bed of down to a wearied frame, where he may lie down and repose after the fatigues of the day, and gently wait for the morning. He has nothing to fear in death; nothing to fear in the dying pang, the gloom, the chill, the sweat, the paleness, the fixedness of death; nothing to fear in the chilliness, the darkness, the silence, the corruption of the grave. All this is in the way to immortality, and is closely and indissolubly connected *with* immortality; ver. 55—57. And in view of all this, we should be patient, faithful, laborious, self-denying; we should engage with zeal in the work of the Lord; we should calmly wait till our change come; ver. 58. No other system of religion has any such hopes as this; no other system does *any* thing to dispel the gloom, or drive away the horrors of the grave. How foolish is the man who rejects the gospel—the only system which brings life and immortality to light! How foolish to reject the doctrine of the resurrection, and to lie down in the grave without peace, without hope, without any belief that there will be a world of glory; living without God, and dying like the brute. And yet infidelity seeks and claims its chief triumphs in the attempt to convince poor dying man that he has no solid ground of hope; that the universe is "without a Father and without a God;" that the grave terminates the career of man for ever; and that in the grave he sinks away to eternal annihilation. Strange that man should seek such degradation! Strange that *all* men, conscious that they must die, do not at once greet

CHAPTER XVI.

NOW concerning the collection for the saints, as [a] I have given order to the churches of Galatia, even so do ye.

a Gal.2.10.

Christianity as their best friend, and hail the doctrine of the future state, and of the resurrection, as that which is adapted to meet the deeply-felt evils of this world; to fill the desponding mind with peace; and to sustain the soul in the temptations and trials of life, and in the gloom and agony of death!

CHAPTER XVI.

THE *doctrinal* part of this epistle was closed at the end of the fifteenth chapter; see the Introduction. Before closing the epistle, Paul adverts to some subjects of a miscellaneous nature, and particularly to the subject of a collection for the poor and persecuted Christians in Judea, on which his heart was much set, and to which he several times adverts in his epistles; see Note on ver. 1. This subject he had suggested to them when he was with them, and they had expressed, some time before, the utmost readiness to make the collection, and Paul had commended their readiness when he was urging the same subject in Macedonia; see 2 Cor. ix. It is evident, however, that for some cause, perhaps owing to the divisions and contentions in the church, this collection had not yet been made. Paul, therefore, calls their attention to it, and urges them to make it, and to forward it either by him alone, or with others, whom they might designate, to Judea; ver. 1—4. In connection with this, he expresses his intention of coming to Corinth, and perhaps of passing the winter with them. He was then in Ephesus. He was expecting to go to Macedonia, probably on the business of the collection. He purposed *not* to visit them on his way *to* Macedonia, but on his return. He had formerly intended to pass through Corinth on his way to Macedonia, and had perhaps given them such an intimation of his purpose; 2 Cor. i. 16, 17. But from some cause (see Notes on 2 Cor. i. 15—23), he tells the Corinthians that he had abandoned the purpose of seeing them on the way to Macedonia, though he still intended to go to Macedonia, and would see them on his return; ver. 5—7. At that time there was a state of things in Ephesus which required his presence. His labours were greatly blessed; and, as a consequence which often attends the successful preaching of the gospel, there was much opposition. He had resolved, therefore, to remain in Ephesus until Pentecost; ver. 8, 9. In the mean time, to show them his deep interest in them, he informed them that Timothy was coming among them, for whom he asked a kind and cordial reception, and assured them that he had endeavoured to persuade Apollos to visit them, but was not able; ver. 10—12. Paul then urges them to watch, and be firm, and live in love (ver. 13, 14); and then besought them to show particular attention to the family of Stephanas, the first-fruits of Achaia (ver. 15, 16); and expresses his gratitude that Stephanas, and Fortunatus, and Achaicus had come to him at Ephesus; ver. 17, 18. They were probably the persons by whom the Corinthians had sent their letter (chap. viii. 1), and by whom Paul sent this epistle. He then closes the whole epistle with Christian salutations; with an expression of regard in his own handwriting; with a solemn charge to love the Lord Jesus Christ, as the great thing to be done, and with the assurance that, if not done, it would expose the soul to a dreadful curse when the Lord should come; with an invocation of the grace of the Lord Jesus to be with them; and with a tender expression of his own love to them all; ver. 19—24.

1. *Now concerning the collection for the saints.* The use of the article here shows that he had mentioned it to them before, and that it was a subject which they would readily understand. It was not new to them, but it was needful only to give some instructions in regard to the *manner* in which it should be done, and not in regard to the occasion for the collection, or the duty of making it. Accordingly, all his instructions relate simply to the *manner* in which

2 Upon the first [a] *day* of the week let every one of you lay by him in store, as *God* hath prospered him, that there be no gatherings when I come.

a Acts 20.7; Rev.1.10.

the collection should be made. The word rendered *collection* (λογία) does not occur anywhere else in the New Testament, and is not found in the classic writers. It is from λέγω, to collect, and, undoubtedly, here refers to a contribution, or collection of money for a charitable purpose. The word *saints* (ἁγίους) here refers, doubtless, to *Christians;* to the persecuted Christians in Judea. There were many there; and they were generally poor, and exposed to various trials. In regard to the meaning of this word, and the circumstances and occasion of this collection; see Notes on Rom. xv. 25, 26. ¶ *As I have given order* (διέταξα). As I have directed, enjoined, commanded, arranged. It does not mean that he had assumed the authority to *tax* them, or that he had *commanded* them to make a collection, but that he had left directions as to the best *manner* and *time* in which it should be done. The collection was voluntary and cheerful in all the churches (Rom. xv. 26, 27; 2 Cor. ix. 2); and Paul did not assume authority to impose it on them as a tax. Nor was it necessary. Self-denial and liberality were among the distinguishing virtues of the early Christians; and to be a Christian *then* implied that a man would freely impart of his property to aid the poor and the needy. The order related solely to the manner of making the collection; and as Paul had suggested one mode to the churches in Galatia, he recommended the same now to the Corinthians. ¶ *To the churches of Galatia.* Galatia was a province in Asia Minor. On its situation, see Note, Acts xvi. 6. There were evidently several churches planted in that region; see Gal. i. 2. At what time he gave this order to the churches there is not mentioned; though it was doubtless on occasion of a visit to the churches there; see Acts xvi. 6.

2. *Upon the first* day *of the week.* Greek, "On one of the Sabbaths." The Jews, however, used the word *Sabbath* to denote the week; the period of seven days; Mat. xxviii. 1; Mark xvi. 9; Luke xviii. 12; xxiv. 1; John xx. 1, 19; comp. Lev. xxiii. 15; Deut. xvi. 9. It is universally agreed that this here denotes the first day of the week, or the Lord's day. ¶ *Let every one of you.* Let the collection be universal. Let each one esteem it his duty and his privilege to give to this object. It was not to be confined to the rich only, but was the common duty of all. The poor, as well as the rich, were expected to contribute according to their ability. ¶ *Lay by him in store* (παρ' ἑαυτῷ τιθέτω θησαυρίζων). Let him lay up at home, treasuring up as he has been prospered. The Greek phrase, "by himself," means, probably, the same as at home. Let him set it apart; let him designate a certain portion; let him do this *by himself*, when he is at home, when he can calmly look at the evidence of his prosperity. Let him do it not under the influence of pathetic appeals, or for the sake of display when he is with others; but let him do it as a matter of principle, and when he is by himself. The phrase in Greek, "treasuring up," may mean that each one was to put the part which he had designated into the common *treasury.* This interpretation seems to be demanded by the latter part of the verse. They were to lay it by, and to put it into the common treasury, that there might be no trouble of collecting when he should come. Or it may, perhaps, mean that they were individually to *treasure it up*, having designated in their own mind the sum which they could give, and have it in readiness when he should come. This was evidently to be done not on one Sabbath only, but was to be done on each Lord's-day until he should come. ¶ *As God hath prospered him.* The word "God" is not in the original, but it is evidently understood, and necessary to the sense. The word rendered "hath prospered" (εὐοδῶται) means, properly, to set forward on one's way; to prosper one's

3 And when I come, whomsoever *a* ye shall approve by *your* letters, them will I send to bring your [1] liberality unto Jerusalem.

a 2 Cor.8.19.

1 *gift.*

journey; and then to prosper, or be prospered. This is the rule which Paul lays down here to guide the Christians at Corinth in giving alms,—a rule that is as applicable now, and as valuable now, as it was then. ¶ *That there be no gatherings when I come.* No collections (λογίαι, ver. 1). The apostle means that there should be no trouble in collecting the small sums; that it should all be prepared; that each one might have laid by what he could give; and that all might be ready to be handed over to him, or to whomsoever they might choose to send with it to Jerusalem; ver. 3.—In view of this important verse, we may remark, (1.) That there is here clear proof that the first day of the week was observed by the church at Corinth as holy time. If it was not, there can have been no propriety in selecting that day in preference to any other in which to make the collection. It was the day which was set apart to the duties of religion, and therefore an appropriate day for the exercise of charity and the bestowment of alms. There can have been no reason why this day should have been designated except that it was a day set apart to religion, and therefore deemed a proper day for the exercise of benevolence towards others. (2.) This order extended also to the churches in Galatia, proving also that the first day of the week was observed by them, and was regarded as a day proper for the exercise of charity towards the poor and the afflicted. And if the first day of the week was observed, by apostolic authority, in those churches, it is morally certain that it was observed by others. This consideration, therefore, demonstrates that it was the custom to observe this day, and that it was observed by the authority of the early founders of Christianity. (3.) Paul intended that they should be *systematic* in their giving, and that they should give from *principle,* and not merely under the impulse of feeling. (4.) Paul designed that the habit of doing good with their money should be *constant.* He, therefore, directed that it should be on the return of each Lord's-day, and that the subject should be constantly before their minds. (5.) It was evident that Paul in this way would obtain *more* for his object than he would if he waited that they should give all at once. He therefore directed them honestly to lay by each week what they could *then* give, and to regard it as a sacred *treasure.* How much would the amount of charities in the Christian churches be swelled if this were the practice now, and if *all* Christians would lay by *in store* each week what they could then devote to sacred purposes. (6.) The true rule of giving is, "as the Lord hath prospered us." If he has prospered us, we owe it to him as a debt of gratitude. And according to our prosperity and success, we should honestly devote our property to God. (7.) It is right and proper to lay by of our wealth for the purposes of benevolence on the Sabbath-day. It is right to do good then (Mat. xii. 12); and one of the appropriate exercises of religion is to look at the evidence of our prosperity with a view to know what we may be permitted to give to advance the kingdom of the Lord Jesus. (8.) If every Christian would honestly do this every week, it would do much to keep down the spirit of worldliness that now prevails everywhere in the Christian church; and if every Christian would conscientiously follow the direction of Paul here, there would be no want of funds for any well-directed plan for the conversion of the world.

3. *Whomsoever ye shall approve by* your *letters.* There has been great variety of opinion in regard to the proper construction of this verse. Macknight supposes that the "letters" here referred to were not letters either to or from the apostle, but letters signed and sent by the church at Corinth, designating their appointment and their authority. With this interpretation Doddridge coincides; and this is required by the usual point-

4 And if it be meet that I go
also, they shall go with me.
5 Now I will come unto you,
[a] when I shall pass through Macedonia:
for I do pass through Macedonia.
6 And it may be that I will
abide, yea, and winter with you,
that ye may bring me on my journey
whithersoever I go.
7 For I will not see you now by
the way; but I trust to tarry a
while with you, if the Lord permit.

a 2 Cor.1.15.

---

ing of the Greek text, where the comma is inserted after the word letters, as in our translation. But a different interpretation has been proposed by inserting the comma after the word "approve," so that it shall read, "Whom you approve, or designate, them I will send *with letters* to convey your charity to Jerusalem." This is followed by Griesbach, Locke, Rosenmüller, Bloomfield, Beza, Hammond, Grotius, Whitby, &c. Certainly this accords better with the design of the passage. For it is evident (see ver. 4) that, though Paul was willing to go, yet he was not expecting to go. If he did not go, what was more natural than that he should offer to give them letters of commendation to his brethren in Judea? Mill has doubted whether this construction is in accordance with Greek usage, but the names above cited are sufficient authority on that subject. The proper construction, therefore, is, that Paul would give them letters to his friends in Jerusalem, and certify their appointment to dispense the charity, and commend the persons sent to the favour and hospitality of the church there. ¶ *Your liberality.* Marg. *Gift.* Your donation; your alms. The Greek word χάριν usually signifies grace, or favour. Here it means an act of grace or favour; kindness; a favour conferred; benefaction: comp. 2 Cor. viii. 4, 6, 7, 19.

4. *And if it be meet*, &c. If it be judged desirable and best. If my presence can further the object; or will satisfy you better; or will be deemed necessary to guide and aid those who may be sent, I will be willing to go also. For some appropriate and valuable remarks in regard to the apostle Paul's management of pecuniary matters, so a[illegible]t to excite suspicion, and to pr[illegible]serve a blameless reputation, see Paley's Horæ Paulinæ, chap. iv. No. 1, 3. Note.

5. *Now I will come unto you.* I purpose to come unto you. He had expected to see them on his way to Macedonia, but, on some account, had been induced to abandon that design. See Notes, 2 Cor. i. 15—17. ¶ *When I shall pass through Macedonia.* When I shall have passed through Macedonia. He proposed to go to Macedonia first, and, having passed through that country, visiting the churches, to go to Corinth. For the situation of Macedonia, see Note, Acts xvi. 9. ¶ *For I do pass through Macedonia.* I design to do it. It is my present intention. Though he had abandoned, from some cause, the design of passing through Corinth on his way to Macedonia, yet he had not given up the design itself. It was still his intention to go there.

6. *That ye may bring me on my journey.* That you may accompany me, or aid me, and furnish me the means of going on my journey. It was customary for the apostles to be attended by some members of the churches and friends in their travels. See Note, Acts x. 23. ¶ *On my journey*, &c. Probably to Judea. This was evidently his intention. But wherever he should go, it would be gratifying to him to have their aid and companionship.

7. *For I will not see you now by the way.* On the way to Macedonia. Something had occurred to change his mind, and to induce him to go to Macedonia by another way. ¶ *But I trust to tarry a while with you.* That is, on my return from Macedonia, ver. 5. Greek, "I *hope* to remain with you a little while. ¶ *If the Lord permit.* The apostle did not use the language of certainty and of confidence. He felt his dependence on

8 But I will tarry at Ephesus
until Pentecost.
9 For a great door [a] and effec-
tual is opened unto me, and *there are* many adversaries.[b]
10 Now if Timotheus [c] come,

a 2 Cor.2.12; Rev.3.8. b Phil.3.18. c Acts 19.22.

God, and regarded all as under his direction; see the same form of expression in 1 Cor. iv. 19, and the Note on that place.

8. *But I will tarry at Ephesus.* This passage proves that this letter was written from Ephesus. It is by such indications as this usually that we are able to determine the place where the epistles were written. In regard to the situation of Ephesus, see Note on Acts xviii. 19. ¶ *Until Pentecost.* This was a Jewish festival occurring fifty days after the Passover, and hence called the *Pentecost.* See Note, Acts ii. 1. As there were Jews at Corinth, and doubtless in the church, they would understand the time which Paul referred to; and as he was a Jew, he naturally used their mode of reckoning time where it would be understood. Doubtless the great festivals of the Jews were well known among most of the cities of Greece, as there were Jews in them all who were scrupulous in their observances. It is no improbable supposition, also, that *Christians* every where regarded this day with deep interest, as being the day on which the Holy Spirit descended on the apostles and on the people of Jerusalem, Acts ii.

9. *For a great door.* There is abundant opportunity for usefulness. The word *door* is used evidently to denote an occasion or an opportunity for doing any thing. It is the means by which we have entrance or access; and hence denotes facility in doing any thing when there is no obstruction; see Acts xiv. 27; 2 Cor. ii. 12; Col. iv. 3. ¶ *And effectual.* That is, *effective*, or adapted to success; presenting opportunity for great effects. There is abundant opportunity to preach the gospel; there is attention to what is spoken, and great interest in it; there is great encouragement to labour. It is possible that this was one of the reasons why Paul had changed his mind about passing through Corinth on his way to Macedonia. It would require *time* to visit Corinth, as he would wish to remain there; and an unexpected opportunity having arisen for doing good, he judged it best to remain at Ephesus as long as practicable, and then to go at once to Macedonia. ¶ *And* there are *many adversaries.* Many opposers; many who resist the gospel. These were doubtless in part Jews who excited opposition to him, and in part the friends of Demetrius; see Acts xix. That Paul had great success in Ephesus, and that his labours were attended with a great revival of religion there, is manifest from that chapter. We may remark here, (1.) That such a work of grace, such a setting open a great and effectual door, is often the occasion of increased opposition to the gospel. It is no uncommon thing that the adversaries of Christ should be excited at such times; and we are not to be surprised if the same thing should occur now which occured in the time of Paul. (2.) This was regarded by Paul as no reason why he should leave Ephesus, but rather as a reason why he should remain there. It was regarded by him as an evidence that the Holy Spirit was there. It was proof that the enemies of God were alarmed, and that the kingdom of Christ was advancing. His presence, also, would be needed there, to encourage and strengthen the young converts who would be attacked and opposed; and he deemed it his duty to remain. A minister should never wish to make enemies to the gospel, nor seek to excite them to make opposition; but such opposition is often evidence that the Spirit of God is among a people; that the consciences of sinners are aroused and alarmed; and that the great enemy of God and man is making, as he was at Ephesus, a desperate effort to preserve his kingdom from being destroyed. (3.) A minister should regard it as his duty in a

see that he may be with you
without fear: for he worketh [a]
the work of the Lord, as I also *do*.
11 Let no man therefore despise
[b] him: but conduct [c] him forth
in peace, that he may come unto
me: for I look for him with the
brethren.
12 As touching *our* brother
Apollos, [d] I greatly desired him to
come unto you with the brethren:
but his will was not at all to come

a Phil.2.19-22. *b* 1 Tim.4.12. *c* 3 John 6. *d* chap.1.12.

special manner to be among his people when there is such opposition excited. His presence is needed to comfort and encourage the church; and when the minds of men are excited, it is often the best time to present truth, and to defend successfully the great doctrines of the Bible. (4.) Ministers should not be *discouraged* because there is opposition to the gospel. It is one ground of encouragement. It is an indication of the presence of God in awakening the conscience. And it is far more favourable as a season to do good than a dead calm, and when there is universal stagnation and unconcern.

10. *Now if Timotheus come.* Paul had sent Timothy to them (see Note, chap. iv. 17, 18), but as he had many churches to visit, it was not absolutely certain that he would go to Corinth. ¶ *May be with you without fear.* Let him be received kindly and affectionately. Timothy was then a young man; Acts xvi. 1—3; 1 Tim. iv. 12. There might be some danger that he might feel himself embarrassed among the rich, the gay, and the great. Paul, therefore, asks them to encourage him, to receive him kindly, and not to embarrass him. Perhaps, also, there may be some reference to the false teachers whom Timothy might be called on to oppose. They were powerful, and they might endeavour to intimidate and alarm him. Paul, therefore, asks the church to sustain him in his efforts to defend the truth. ¶ *For he worketh the work of the Lord.* He is engaged in the service of the Lord; and he is worthy of your confidence, and worthy to be sustained by you.

11. *Let no man, therefore, despise him.* Let no one despise him on account of his youth and inexperience. It is probable that some of the more wealthy and proud, some who valued themselves on their wisdom and experience, would be disposed to look upon him with contempt. On another occasion, he directed Timothy so to live as that no one should have occasion to despise him on account of his youth (1 Tim. iv. 12); and he here urges on the Corinthians, that they should not despise him because he was a young man, and comparatively inexperienced. A minister of the gospel, though young, should receive the respect that is due to his office; and if he conducts himself in accordance with his high calling, his youth should be no barrier to the confidence and affection of even aged and experienced Christians. It should be rather a reason why they should treat him with affection, and encourage him in his work. ¶ *But conduct him forth in peace.* That is, when he leaves you. Attend him on his way, and help him forward on his journey to me; see Note on ver. 6. ¶ *For I look for him with the brethren.* Erastus accompanied Timothy in this journey (Acts xix. 22), and probably there were others with him. Titus also had been sent to Corinth (2 Cor. xii. 17, 18), and it is not improbable that Paul had desired Titus to bring with him to Ephesus some of the Corinthian brethren, as he might need their assistance there.—*Grotius.*

12. *As touching* our *brother Apollos.* Tindal renders this, "To speak of brother Apollo." In regard to Apollos, see Note, chap. i. 12. ¶ *His will was not at all to come at this time.* It is probable that there were matters which detained him, or which required his presence in Ephesus. It is not known why Apollos had left Corinth, but it has been supposed that it was on account of the dissensions which existed there. For the same

at this time; but he will come
when he shall have convenient
time.
13 Watch [a] ye, stand [b] fast in
the faith, quit you like men, [c] be
strong. [d]
14 Let [e] all your things be done
with charity.

a 1 Pet.5.8. *b* 2 Thess.2.15. *c* chap.14.20. *d* Eph.6.10. *e* 1 Pet.4.8.

reason he might not be induced to return there while those dissensions lasted and there might be employment which he had where he then was which rendered his presence there important. The Latin fathers say that Apollos did after this return to Corinth, when the religious differences had been settled.—*Bloomfield.* It is probable that the Corinthians had requested, by the messengers who carried their letter to Paul, that either he or Apollos would come and visit them. Paul states, in reply, that he had endeavoured to prevail on Apollos to go, but had not succeeded. ¶ *He will come when he shall have convenient time.* The Greek word means, when he should have leisure, or a good opportunity. He might then be engaged; or he might be unwilling to go while their contentions lasted. They had probably (chap. i. 12) endeavoured to make him the head of a party, and on that account he might have been unwilling to return at present among them. But Paul assures them that he designed to come among them at some future time. This was said probably to show them that he still retained his affection for them, and had a tender solicitude for their peace and prosperity. Had this not been said, they might, perhaps, have inferred that he was offended, and had no desire to come among them.

13. *Watch ye.* The exhortation in this and the following verse is given evidently in view of the peculiar dangers and temptations which surrounded them. The word here used (Γρηγορεῖτε) means, to keep awake, to be vigilant, &c.; and this may, perhaps, be a military metaphor derived from the duty of those who are stationed as sentinels to guard a camp, or to observe the motions of an enemy. The term is frequently used in the New Testament, and the duty frequently enjoined; Mat. xxiv. 41, 42; xxv. 13; Mark xiii. 35; Luke xxi. 36; Acts xx. 31; 1 Thess. v. 6; 2 Tim. iv. 5. The sense here is, that they were to watch, or be vigilant, against all the evils of which he had admonished them,—the evils of dissension, or erroneous doctrines, of disorder, of false teachers, &c. They were to watch lest their souls should be ruined, and their salvation endangered; lest the enemies of the truth and of holiness should steal silently upon them, and surprise them. They were to watch with the same vigilance that is required of a sentinel who guards a camp, lest an enemy should come suddenly upon them, and surprise the camp when the army was locked in sleep. ¶ *Stand fast in the faith.* Be firm in holding and defending the truths of the gospel. Do not yield to any foe, but maintain the truth, and adhere to your confidence in God and to the doctrines of the gospel with unwavering constancy; see Note, chap. xv. 1. Be firm in maintaining what you believe to be true, and in holding on to your personal confidence in God, notwithstanding all the arts, insinuations, and teachings of seducers and the friends of false doctrine. ¶ *Quit you like men* (ἀνδρίζεσθε, from ἀνήρ, a man). The word occurs no where else in the New Testament. In the LXX. it occurs in Josh. i. 6, 7, 9, 18; 1 Chron. xxviii. 20; 2 Chron. xxxii. 7; Neh. ii. 1; and in eighteen other places. See Trommius' Concordance. It occurs also in the classic authors; see Xen. Oec. v. 4. It means, to render one manly or brave; to show one's-self a man; that is, not to be a coward, or timid, or alarmed at enemies, but to be bold and brave. We have a similar phrase in common use: "Be a man," or "Show yourself a man;" that is, be not mean, or be not cowardly. ¶ *Be strong.* Be firm,

15 I beseech you, brethren, (ye know the house of Stephanas, that it is the [a] first-fruits of Achaia, and *that* they have addicted themselves to the ministry of the saints,)
16 That ye submit [b] yourselves unto such, and to every one that helpeth with *us*, and laboureth.
17 I am glad of the coming of Stephanas and Fortunatus and Achaicus: for that which was lacking [c] on your part they have supplied.

a Rom.16.5. b Heb.13.17. c Phil 2.30.

fixed, steadfast; comp. Eph. vi. 10, "Be strong in the Lord, and in the power of his might."

14. *Let all your things*, &c. All that you do. This direction is repeated on account of its great importance, and because it is a *summing up* of all that he had said in this epistle; see chap. xiii; xiv. 1. Here he says, that charity, or love, was to regulate all that they did. This was a simple rule; and if this was observed, every thing would be done well.

15. *I beseech you, brethren*. The construction here is somewhat involved, but the sense is plain. The words, "I beseech you," in this verse, are evidently to be taken in connection with ver. 16, "I beseech you that ye submit yourselves unto such," &c. The design is to exhort them to pay proper deference to Stephanas, and to all who sustained the same rank and character: and the remainder of ver. 15 is designed to state the reason why they should show respect and kindness to the household of Stephanas. ¶ *Ye know the house*. You are acquainted with the household, or family. Probably a considerable portion, or all, of the family of Stephanas had been converted to the Christian faith. ¶ *Of Stephanas;* see Note, chap. i. 16. Paul there says that he had baptized his family. ¶ *That it is the first-fruits of Achaia*. They were the first converted to the Christian religion in Achaia; see Note, Rom. xvi. 5. Respecting Achaia, see Note, Acts xviii. 12. ¶ *That they have addicted themselves*, &c. That they have devoted themselves to the service of Christians. That is, by aiding the ministry; by showing hospitality; by providing for their wants; by attending and aiding the apostles in their journeys, &c.

16. *That ye submit yourselves*, &c. The word used here means evidently that you would show them proper deference and regard; that you would treat them with distinguished respect and honour for what they have done. ¶ *And to every one that helpeth with us*, &c. Every one that aids us in the ministry, or provides for our wants, &c. It is possible that Stephanas lived among them at this time (Note, chap. i. 16), though he had been converted in Achaia; and it is probable that, as Corinth was a central place and a thoroughfare, others might come among them who were the personal friends of Paul, and who had aided him in the ministry. Towards all such he bespeaks their kind, and tender, and respectful regards.

17. *I am glad of the coming*. That is, I am glad that they have come to me at Ephesus. I rejoice that he who was converted by my ministry in Achaia, and who has so long shown himself to be a personal friend to me, and an aid in my work, came where I am. ¶ *Stephanas*. The same person evidently mentioned in the previous verses. Probably he, as one of the oldest and most respected members of the church, had been selected to carry the letter of the Corinthians (chap. vii. 1) to Paul, and to consult with him respecting the affairs of the church there. ¶ *Fortunatus and Achaicus*. These persons are not referred to anywhere else in the New Testament. It appears that Fortunatus survived Paul, for he was subsequently the messenger of the church at Corinth to that at Rome, and bore back to the Corinthians the epistle which Clement of Rome sent to them. See that epistle, § 59. ¶ *For that which was lacking*, &c. The word which is here used, and rendered

18 For they have refreshed
my spirit and yours: therefore
acknowledge [a] ye them that are
such.
19 The churches of Asia salute you. Aquila [b] and Priscilla
salute you much in the Lord,
with the church [c] that is in their
house.
20 All the brethren greet you.
Greet ye one another with a holy
kiss.

a 1 Thess.5.12. b Acts 18.26. c Rom.16.5.15.

"that which was lacking" (ὑστέρημα), does not occur in the classic writers. It means properly that which is wanting, want, lack.—*Robinson.* It may be used to denote a want or lack of any kind, whether of support, sustenance, aid, consolation, information, or counsel; see Luke xxi. 4; Phil. ii. 30; 1 Thess. iii. 10. What this was which the Corinthians had neglected or failed to furnish Paul, and which had been supplied by the presence of these persons, can be only a matter of conjecture; and different commentators have supposed different things. It might be a neglect to provide for his wants, or a defect of informing him about their affairs in the letter which they had sent him; or it might be that these persons had furnished, by their presence and conversation, those consolations and friendly offices which the church at Corinth would have rendered had they been all present; and Paul may mean to say, that he had enjoyed with them that friendly intercourse and Christian communion which he had desired with them, but which was lacking, *i. e.* which he had not been permitted to enjoy by reason of his absence. This is the view which is given by Rosenmüller, Doddridge, Bloomfield; and as Paul does not seem here inclined to blame them, this view is most in accordance with the general strain of the passage.

18. *For they have refreshed my spirit.* By their presence and conversation. They have given me information respecting the state of things in the church; and their society has been with me of the most gratifying and cheering kind. ¶ *And yours.* "By removing," says Locke, "those suspicions and fears that were on both sides." "By thus supplying your absence, they have benefited us both. For Paul gained information of those absent, and they gained in the counsel afforded to them by the apostle."—*Bloomfield.* "For they refreshed my spirit by their obliging behaviour and edifying conversation, as, I doubt not, they have often refreshed yours by their ministrations among you."—*Doddridge.* The sense seems to be, that their visit to him would be a benefit to both; would result in imparting comfort, a good understanding, an increase of their mutual attachment, and ultimately a large accession to their mutual joy when they should again meet. ¶ *Therefore acknowledge ye them that are such.* Receive affectionately; recognise as brethren; cherish, treat kindly all that evince such a spirit; see Notes on ver. 15, 16. The apostle here designs, evidently, that the Corinthians should receive them kindly on their return, and regard with deference and respect the counsel which they might offer, and the message which they might bear from him.

19. *The churches of Asia.* The word "Asia" in the New Testament usually denotes Asia Minor in general; see Note on Acts ii. 9. It was sometimes used in a more limited sense, to denote the region around Ephesus, and of which Ephesus was the centre and capital; see Note, Acts xvi. 6. This is the region undoubtedly which is intended here. ¶ *Salute you.* Greet you; send respectful and affectionate Christian regards; see Note, Rom. xvi. 3. ¶ *Aquila and Priscilla;* see Note on Acts xviii. 26. ¶ *Much in the Lord.* With affectionate Christian salutations; or as Christians. Wishing the blessing and favour of the Lord. ¶ *With the church that is in their house;* Note, Rom. xvi. 5.

20. *All the brethren,* &c. All the Christians with whom Paul was con-

21 The salutation of *me* Paul with mine own hand.
22 If any man love [a] not the Lord Jesus Christ, let him be anathema [b] maran-atha.[c]

a Eph.6.24. b Gal.1.8,9. c Jude 14,15.

nected in Ephesus. They felt a deep interest in the church at Corinth, and sent to them Christian salutations. ¶ *With a holy kiss;* see the Note on Rom. xvi. 16.

21. *The salutation of me, Paul, with mine own hand.* It is evident that Paul was accustomed to employ an amanuensis in penning his epistles (see Note on Rom. xvi. 22), though he signed his own name, and expressed his Christian salutation in every epistle, 2 Thess. iii. 17; comp. Col. iv. 18. This gave a sanction to what was written; was a proof that it was his own, and was a valuable token of affectionate regard. It was a proof that there was no fraud or imposition. *Why* he employed an amanuensis is not known.

22. *If any man love not the Lord Jesus Christ.* This is a most solemn and affecting close of the whole epistle. It was designed to direct them to the great and essential matter of religion, the love of the Lord Jesus; and was intended, doubtless, to turn away their minds from the subjects which had agitated them, the disputes and dissensions which had rent the church into factions, to the great inquiry whether they truly loved the Saviour. It is implied that there was danger, in their disputes and strifes about minor matters, of neglecting the love of the Lord Jesus, or of substituting attachment to a party in the place of that love to the Saviour which alone could be connected with eternal life. ¶ *Let him be anathema.* On the meaning of the word *anathema,* see Note, chap. xii. 3. The word properly means accursed, or devoted to destruction; and the idea here is, that he who did not believe in the Lord Jesus, and love him, would be, and ought to be. devoted to destruction, or accursed of God. It expresses what *ought* to be done; it expresses *a truth* in regard to God's dealings, not the *desire* of the apostle. No matter what any man's endowments might be; no matter what might be his wealth, his standing, or his talent; no matter if he were regarded as a ruler in the church, or at the head of a party; yet if he had not true love to the Lord Jesus, he could not be saved. This sentiment is in accordance with the declaration of the Scripture everywhere. See particularly, John iii. 31; Micah xvi. 16, and the Note on the latter place. ¶ *Maran-atha.* These are Syriac words, *Moran Etho* — "the Lord comes;" *i. e.* will come. The reason why this expression is added may be. (1.) To give the greater *solemnity* to the declaration of the apostle; *i. e.* to give it an emphatic form. (2.) To intimate that, though there were no earthly power to punish a want of love to the Saviour; though the state could not, and ought not to punish it; and though the church could not exclude all who did not love the Lord Jesus from its bosom, yet they could not escape. For, the Lord would himself come to take vengeance on his enemies; and no one could escape. Though, therefore, those who did not love the Lord Jesus could not be punished by men, yet they could not escape divine condemnation. The Lord would come to execute vengeance himself, and they could not escape. It is probable (see Lightfoot in loco) that the Jews were accustomed to use such a form in their greater excommunication, and that they meant by it, that the person who was thus devoted to destruction, and excommunicated, *must* be destroyed; for the Lord would come to take vengeance on all his enemies. "It certainly was not now, for the first time, used as a new kind of cursing by the apostle; but was the application of a current mode of speech to the purpose he had in contemplation. Perhaps, therefore, by inspecting the manners of the East, we may illustrate the import of this singular passage. The nearest approach to it that I have

23 The grace [a] of our Lord Jesus Christ *be* with you.

24 My love *be* with you all in Christ Jesus. Amen.

a Rom.16.20.

been able to discover is in the following extract from Mr. Bruce; and though, perhaps, this does not come up to the full power of the apostle's meaning, yet, probably, it gives the idea which was commonly attached to the phrase among the public. Mr. Bruce had been forced by a pretended saint, in Egypt, to take him on board his vessel, as if to carry him to a certain place—whereas, Mr. Bruce meant no such thing; but, having set him on shore at some little distance from whence he came, 'we slacked our vessel down the stream a few yards, filling our sails, and stretching away. On seeing this, our saint fell into a desperate passion, cursing, blaspheming, and stamping with his feet; at every word crying "*Shar Ullah!*" *i. e.* "*May God send and do justice!*" This appears to be the strongest execration this passionate Arab could use, *i. e.* 'To punish you adequately is out of my power: I remit you to the vengeance of God.' Is not this the import of *anathema maranatha?*"—*Taylor* in Calmet. This solemn declaration, or denunciation, the apostle wrote with his own hand, as the summary of all that he had said, in order that it might be attentively regarded. There is not a more solemn declaration in the Bible; there is not a more fearful denunciation; there is no one that will be more certainly executed. No matter *what* we may have—be it wealth, or beauty, or vigour, or accomplishment, or adorning, or the praise and flattery of the world; no matter if we are elevated high in office and in rank; no matter if we are honoured by the present age, or gain a reputation to be transmitted to future times; yet if we have not love to the Saviour, we cannot be saved. We must be devoted to the curse; and the Lord Jesus will soon return to execute the tremendous sentence on a guilty world. How important then to ask whether we have that love? Whether we are attached to the Lord Jesus in such a manner as to secure his approbation? Whether we so love him as to be prepared to hail his coming with joy, and to be received into his everlasting kingdom.—In the close of the Notes on this epistle, I may ask any one who shall read these pages whether he has this love? And I may press it upon the attention of each one, though I may never see their faces in the flesh, as *the* great inquiry which is to determine their everlasting destiny. The solemn declaration stands here, that if they do *not* love the Lord Jesus, they will be, and they ought to be, devoted to destruction. The Lord Jesus will soon return to make investigation, and to judge the world. There will be no escape; and no tongue can express the awful horrors of an ETERNAL CURSE PRONOUNCED BY THE LIPS OF THE SON OF GOD.

23. *The grace,* &c. Note, Rom. xvi. 20.

24. *In Christ Jesus.* Through Christ Jesus; or in connection with your love to him; *i. e.* as Christians. This is an expression of tender regard to them as Christian brethren; of his love for the church; and his earnest desire for their welfare. It is in accordance with the usual manner in which he closes his epistles; and it is peculiarly tender, affectionate, and beautiful here, when we consider the manner in which he had been treated by many of the Corinthians; and as following the solemn declaration in ver. 22. Paul loved them; loved them intensely, and was ever ready to express his affectionate regard for them *all,* and his earnest desire for their salvation.

The subscription to the epistle, "The first epistle to the Corinthians," &c., was evidently written by some other hand than that of Paul, and has no claim to be regarded as inspired. Probably these subscriptions were added a considerable time after the epistles were first written; and in some instances evidently by some person who was not well informed on the subject; see the Note at the end of the Epistle to the Romans. In this instance, the subscription is evidently in its main statement false. The epistle bears internal marks that it was written from Ephesus, though there is every probability that it was sent by three of the persons who are here mentioned. It is absurd, however, to suppose that *Timothy* was concerned in bearing the epistle to them, since it is evident that when it was written he was already on a visit to the churches, and on his way to Corinth; see Notes on chap. xvi. 10, 11; iv. 17. There is not the slightest internal evidence that it was written from Philippi: but every thing in the epistle concurs in the supposition that it was sent from Ephesus. See the Introduction to the epistle. There is, however, a considerable variety among the MSS. in regard to the subscription; and they are evidently none of them of any authority, and as these subscriptions generally mislead the reader of the Bible, it would have been better had they been omitted.